Managing Organizational Change

A Multiple Perspectives Approach

Third Edition

Ian Palmer

Richard Dunford

David A. Buchanan

Mc
Graw
Hill
Education

MANAGING ORGANIZATIONAL CHANGE: A MULTIPLE PERSPECTIVES APPROACH, THIRD EDITION

Published by McGraw-Hill Education, 2 Penn Plaza, New York, NY 10121. Copyright © 2017 by McGraw-Hill Education. All rights reserved. Printed in the United States of America. Previous editions © 2009 and 2006. No part of this publication may be reproduced or distributed in any form or by any means, or stored in a database or retrieval system, without the prior written consent of McGraw-Hill Education, including, but not limited to, in any network or other electronic storage or transmission, or broadcast for distance learning.

Some ancillaries, including electronic and print components, may not be available to customers outside the United States.

This book is printed on acid-free paper.

1 2 3 4 5 6 7 8 9 0 DOC/DOC 1 0 9 8 7 6

ISBN 978-0-07-353053-6
MHID 0-07-353053-0

Senior Vice President, Products & Markets: *Kurt L. Strand*
Vice President, General Manager, Products & Markets: *Michael Ryan*
Vice President, Content Design & Delivery: *Kimberly Meriwether David*
Managing Director: *Susan Gouijnstook*
Director: *Michael Ablassmeir*
Brand Manager: *Laura Hurst Spell*
Director, Product Development: *Meghan Campbell*
Marketing Manager: *Casey Keske*
Digital Product Analyst: *Sankha Basu*
Director, Content Design & Delivery: *Terri Schiesl*
Program Manager: *Faye M. Herrig*
Content Project Managers: *Jeni McAtee, Evan Roberts, Karen Jozefowicz*
Buyer: *Laura M. Fuller*
Design: *Studio Montage, St. Louis MO*
Content Licensing Specialists: *Deanna Dausener*
Cover Image: © *Charles Taylor/123RF*
Compositor: *Lumina Datamatics, Inc.*
Printer: *R. R. Donnelley*

All credits appearing on page or at the end of the book are considered to be an extension of the copyright page.

Cartoon page 101: Toothpaste For Dinner et al. (hereafter TFD/ND/MTTS) are copyright 2002–2013 Drew & Natalie Dee. TFD/ND/MTTS may not be reproduced in print or broadcast media without explicit written permission from Drew & Natalie Dee. We do not permit any entity to run a "feed" or online syndication of TFD/ND/MTTS, or to "scrape" the content. TFD/ND/MTTS or any derivatives of such, including text from the comics or redrawn/altered versions of the comics themselves, may not be imprinted on any merchandise available for sale, including but not limited to t-shirts, buttons, stickers, coffee mugs, guns/ammunition, motorized vehicles, food/food products, or living animals without the explicit written permission of Drew & Natalie Dee. Any text, images, or other media/communication sent to Drew & Natalie Dee shall be considered the property of Drew & Natalie Dee and may be reproduced in full or part on TFD/ND/MTTS or another website operated by Drew & Natalie Dee.

Library of Congress Cataloging-in-Publication Data
Palmer, Ian, 1957-
Managing organizational change : a multiple perspectives approach / Ian Palmer, Richard Dunford,
    David A. Buchanan. -- Third Edition.
        p. cm.
    Revised edition of Managing organizational change, 2009.
    Includes bibliographical references and index.
    ISBN 978-0-07-353053-6 (alk. paper)
    1. Organizational change. 2. Organizational change--Management. I. Dunford, Richard.
        II. Buchanan, David A. III. Title.
    HD58.8.P347 2016
    658.4'06--dc23

                                                                                            2015033668

The Internet addresses listed in the text were accurate at the time of publication. The inclusion of a website does not indicate an endorsement by the authors or McGraw-Hill Education, and McGraw-Hill Education does not guarantee the accuracy of the information presented at these sites.

mheducation.com/highered

DEDICATIONS

From Ian   To Dianne, Matthew, and Michelle

From Richard   To Jill, Nick, and Ally

From David   To Lesley with love—and thanks

This book is also dedicated to the memory of Gib Akin, our co-author from 2005 to 2014.

Acknowledgements

A number of people have contributed to this edition, and we owe them all a debt of gratitude, including Jonathan Bamber, Lesley Buchanan, Daloni Carlile, Mimi Clarke, and Alastair McLellan. In addition, we would like to thank our McGraw-Hill Education team, including Michael Ablassmeir, Director, Laura Hurst Spell, Senior Product Developer; Jeni McAtee, Evan Roberts, Karen Jozefowicz, Content Project Managers; Gunjan Chandola (Lumina), Full-Service Content Project Manager; and DeAnna Dausener, Content Licensing Specialist. We would also like to thank the second edition reviewers for their helpful feedback: Diane Bandow, Troy University; Cynthia Bean, University of South Florida–St. Petersburg; Bradford R. Frazier, Pfeiffer University; Dominie Garcia, San Jose State University; Selina Griswold, University of Toledo; Mark Hannan, George Washington University; Christopher S. Howard, Pfeiffer University; Jim Kerner, Athens State University; Catherine Marsh, North Park University; Patricia A. Matuszek, Troy University; Ranjna Patel, Bethune Cookman University; Mary Sass, Western Washington University; Dennis Self, Troy University; Patricia Scescke, National Louis University.

Brief contents

Contents

Preface

Since the previous edition of this book published in 2009, the organizational world has changed dramatically—the global financial crisis, fresh geopolitical tensions, environmental concerns, greater focus on corporate social responsibility, economic uncertainties, emerging new markets, dramatic technological developments, demographic shifts, changing consumer tastes and expectations. Add to that mix the growing significance of social media, where positive and critical views of organizations and their products and services can be shared instantly and globally with large numbers of people.

From a management perspective, it feels as though the drivers for organizational change are now more numerous, and that the pace of change has also increased; more pressure, more change, faster change. While the pace of change may only appear to have quickened, failure to respond to those pressures, and in some cases failure to respond quickly enough, can have significant individual and corporate consequences. The personal and organizational stakes appear to have increased.

The management of organizational change thus remains a topic of strategic importance for most sectors, public and private. Current conditions have, if anything, increased the importance of this area of management responsibility. This new edition, therefore, is timely with regard to updating previous content, while introducing new and emerging trends, developments, themes, debates, and practices.

In the light of this assessment, we believe that the multiple perspectives approach is particularly valuable, recognizing the variety of ways in which change can be progressed, and reinforcing the need for a tailored and creative approach to fit different contexts. Our images of how organizational change should be managed affect the approaches that we take to understanding and managing change. Adopting different images and perspectives helps to open up new and more innovative ways of approaching the change management process. We hope that this approach will help to guide and to inspire others in pursuit of their own responsibilities for managing organizational change.

This text is aimed at two main readers. The first is an experienced practicing manager enrolled in an MBA or a similar master's degree program, or taking part in a management development course that includes a module on organizational change management. The second is a senior undergraduate, who may have less practical experience, but who will probably have encountered organizational change through temporary work assignments, or indirectly through family and friends. Our senior undergraduate is also likely to be planning a management career, or to be heading for a professional role that will inevitably involve management—and change management—responsibilities. Given the needs and interests of both types of readers, we have sought to present an appropriate blend of research and theory on the one hand, and practical management application on the other.

Instructors who have used our previous edition will find many familiar features in this update. The chapter structure and sequence of the book remain much the same, with some minor adjustments to accommodate new material. The overall argument is again underpinned by the observation that the management of organizational change is in part a rational or technical task, and is also a creative activity, with the need to design novel strategies and processes that are consistent with the needs of unique local conditions. We hope that readers will find the writing style and presentation clear and engaging. We have also maintained the breadth of coverage of the different traditions and perspectives that contribute to the theory and practice of managing organizational change, with international examples where appropriate.

The development of this new edition has introduced new content and new pedagogical features. The new content for this edition includes the following:

Depth of change: Change can be categorized and understood with regard to how deeply it penetrates an organization. A "depth of change" model is explained, using a "shallow to transformational" scale, forming the basis for discussion and analysis at various points in the text (chapters 1, 4, and 12).

New tensions and debates: A new section explores contemporary dilemmas in organizational change management. One of these concerns striking the balance between large-scale transformational change (which can be disruptive) and "sweating the small stuff" (which can create a platform for further changes). A second concerns pace, with some commentators advising how to speed up change, while others warn of the dangers of "the acceleration trap" (chapter 1).

Change managers or change leaders: Some commentators claim this is an important distinction, while others argue that this is a words game. Can we resolve this debate (chapter 2)?

Post-crisis change: Recommendations for change from investigations into accidents, misconduct, and catastrophes are often not implemented. We explore why this should be the case—in conditions where it might be presumed that change would be welcome and straightforward (chapter 3). We also consider briefly the problems and practice of communication during and after crises (chapter 7).

Change in a recession: Is change more challenging when economic conditions are difficult? A new section argues that change may be more straightforward during a recession (chapter 3).

Innovation: We explore how change is driven by the proactive development, adoption, and diffusion of product and operational innovations, along with the distinction between sustaining and disruptive innovations, and the nature and development of innovative organization cultures (chapter 4).

Built to change: We explore the organizational capabilities that contribute to change, adaptation, responsiveness, and agility, considering mechanistic and organic management systems, segmentalist and integrative cultures, and the concept of the "built-to-change" organization (chapter 4).

Change communication strategies: This chapter has been thoroughly updated, with the emphasis on change communication, exploring the characteristics of effective change communication strategies, the potential impact and applications of social media as corporate communications tools, and the "communication escalator" (chapter 7).

Middle management blockers: The traditional stereotype has middle managers subverting top team initiatives. Recent research suggests that this image is wrong, and that middle management are often the source of creative strategic ideas as well as the "engine room" for delivery (chapters 8 and 12).

Organization development and sense-making approaches: As in the previous edition, recent developments in organization development, appreciative inquiry, positive organizational scholarship, and dialogic organization development are explored (chapter 9).

Contingency and processual approaches: Covered in the last edition, recent developments have been incorporated to update these sections, reflecting their influence on theory and practice (chapter 10).

Praiseworthy and blameworthy failures: The section on "recognizing productive failures" has been updated with recent commentary suggesting that some failures should be rewarded (chapter 11).

The effective change manager: What does it take? This new chapter explores the capabilities of change managers, considering competency frameworks, interpersonal communication processes and skills, issue-selling tactics, and the need for the change manager to be politically skilled (chapter 12).

The pedagogical features in the text include:

- learning outcomes identified at the beginning of each chapter;
- fewer, and shorter, "high-impact" case studies of organizational change and other diagnostic and self-assessment exercises for classroom use;
- movie recommendations, identifying clips that illustrate theoretical and practical dimensions of organizational change management;
- a short "roundup" section at the end of each chapter, with reflections for the practicing change manager, and summarizing the key learning points (linked to the learning outcomes);
- a small number of suggestions for further reading at the end of each chapter.

Since this book was first published, we have continued our conversations with managers who have been using it as part of their teaching, consulting, and other organizational change activities. In so many of these conversations, it was reassuring to hear how the multiple perspectives framework that underpins this book struck the right chord with them, opening up new, innovative, and different ways of seeing, thinking, conceptualizing, and practicing organizational change. We hope that this new and updated third edition will continue to inspire various change journeys, and we look forward to more conversations along the way.

Online Resources

Instructors: If you are looking for teaching materials in this subject area, such as case studies, discussion guides, organizational diagnostics, self-assessments, company websites, or audio-visual materials (feature films, YouTube clips) to use in lectures and tutorials, then go to McGraw-Hill Connect: connect.mheducation.com

Continually evolving, McGraw-Hill Connect has been redesigned to provide the only true adaptive learning experience delivered within a simple and easy-to-navigate environment, placing students at the very center.

- Performance Analytics – Now available for both instructors and students, easy-to-decipher data illuminates course performance. Students always know how they are doing in class, while instructors can view student and section performance at a glance.

- Personalized Learning – Squeezing the most out of study time, the adaptive engine within Connect creates a highly personalized learning path for each student by identifying areas of weakness and providing learning resources to assist in the moment of need.

This seamless integration of reading, practice, and assessment ensures that the focus is on the most important content for that individual.

The Connect Management Instructor Library is your repository for additional resources to improve student engagement in and out of class. You can select and use any asset that enhances your lecture.

The Connect Instructor Library includes:

- Instructor Manual
- PowerPoint files
- Test Bank

Students: If you are looking for additional materials to improve your understanding of this subject and improve your grades, go to McGraw-Hill Connect: connect.mheducation.com

Manager's Hot Seat: Now instructors can put students in the hot seat with access to an interactive program. Students watch real managers apply their years of experience when confronting unscripted issues. As the scenario unfolds, questions about how the manager is handling the situation pop up, forcing the student to make decisions along with the manager. At the end of the scenario, students watch a post-interview with the manager and view how their responses matched up to the manager's decisions. The Manager's Hot Seat videos are now available as assignments in Connect.

LearnSmart: LearnSmart, the most widely used adaptive learning resource, is proven to improve grades. By focusing students on the most important information each student needs to learn, LearnSmart personalizes the learning experience so they can study as efficiently as possible.

SmartBook: An extension of LearnSmart, SmartBook is an adaptive ebook that helps students focus their study time more effectively. As students read, SmartBook assesses comprehension and dynamically highlights where they need to study more.

Groundwork: Understanding and Diagnosing Change

The central theme of the four chapters in Part 1 is *groundwork*. How are we to approach an understanding of organizational change? With what approaches, perspectives, or images of change management should we be working? What drivers and pressures produce organizational change? What diagnostic tools can we use in order to decide what aspects of the organization and its operations will need to change or will benefit from change?

Chapter 1

Managing Change: Stories and Paradoxes

Learning objectives

By the end of this chapter you should be able to:

LO 1.1   Understand how stories of change can contribute to our knowledge of theory and practice.

LO 1.2   Explain why managing organizational change is both a creative and a rational process.

LO 1.3   Identify the main tensions and paradoxes in managing organizational change.

LO 1.4   Evaluate the strengths and limitations of our current understanding of this field.

CHANGE MANAGEMENT

LO 1.1 LO 1.2 Stories About Change: What Can We Learn?

Changing organizations is as messy as it is exhilarating, as frustrating as it is satisfying, as muddling-through and creative a process as it is a rational one. This book recognizes these tensions and how they affect those who are involved in managing organizational change. Rather than pretend that these tensions do not exist, or that they are unimportant, we confront them head on, considering how they can be addressed and managed, recognizing the constraints that they can impose. We also want to demonstrate how the images that we hold about the way in which change should be managed, and of the role of change agents, affect how we approach change and the outcomes we think are possible.

To begin this exploration, we present three stories of recent changes. The first concerns the turnaround of the Beth Israel Deaconess Medical Center in Boston. The second concerns the new organizational model introduced at Sears Holdings in an attempt to restore falling sales and profits. The third concerns innovative efforts to restore falling sales and a fading brand at J. C. Penney, a retailer. These stories address different problems, but they display many common issues concerning the management of change. Each of these accounts comes with a set of assessment questions. We would like to ask you to think through the answers to those questions for yourself, or in a class discussion.

Our aim is to demonstrate that stories about change can be one valuable source of practical lessons, as well as helping to contribute to our general understanding of change. These stories are of course distinctive, one-off. How can they contribute to knowledge and practice in general, in other sectors and organizations? Stories are one of the main ways of knowing, communicating, and making sense of the world (Czarniawska, 1998; Pentland, 1999; Dawson and Andriopoulos, 2014). Our stories have actors: change leaders, other managers, staff, customers. They take decisions that lead to actions that trigger responses: acceptance, resistance, departure. There is a plot: a serious problem that could be solved by organizational change. There are consequences: to what extent did the change solve the problem, and were other problems created along the way? The sequence of events unfolds in a typical manner: … and then … and then. This tells us *why* the outcomes were reached.

Our narratives are not just descriptions of a change process, of what happened. They also provide us with *explanations*. These are *process narratives*. Process narratives have several advantages over more traditional (quantitative, statistical) research methods (Mohr, 1982; Poole et al., 2000; Van de Ven and Poole, 2005):

- they tell us about the context, give us a sense of the whole, a broader frame of reference;
- complexity can be expressed within a coherent sequence of events;
- the nature and significance of the causal factors acting on events are exposed;
- the narrative patterns transcend individual cases.

This approach is based on what is called *narrative knowing* (Langley, 2009). Because stories can reveal the mechanisms or logics behind a sequence of events, they are *process theories*. (We will explore process perspectives on change in chapter 10.) What combinations of factors drive, slow down, accelerate, block the change process? The three stories that follow explain the relative success of the organizational changes at Beth Israel, Sears, and J. C. Penney. We will ask you to consider the extent to which those explanations, each based on a single unique case narrative, can be applied to managing organizational change in general, in other settings.

Although our three stories are quite different from each other, they have common features, with regard to the issues and processes that shape the outcomes of organizational change. Despite the differences, they demonstrate common tensions and the choices that are involved in the change process. When you have made your own assessments, in response to the questions that precede each story, you will find our suggested answers in the Roundup section at the end of the chapter.

LO 1.1 The Story of Beth Israel Deaconess Medical Center

Issues to Consider as You Read This Story

1. Identify five factors that explain the success of this corporate turnaround.
2. How would you describe Paul Levy's role and contributions to this turnaround?
3. What insights does this story have to offer concerning the role of the change leader?
4. What lessons about managing organizational change can we take from this experience and apply to other organizations, in healthcare and in other sectors? Or, are the lessons unique to Beth Israel Deaconess Medical Center?

The Setting

This is the story of a corporate turnaround, rescuing the organization from financial disaster and restoring its reputation, competitiveness, and profitability. Based in Boston, Massachusetts, the Beth Israel Deaconess Medical Center (BID) was created in 1996 by the merger of two hospitals. The business case for the merger was that the larger organization (over 600 beds) would be better able to compete with, for example, the Massachusetts General Hospital and the Brigham Women's Hospital. The two merged hospitals had different cultures. Beth Israel had a casual management style that encouraged professional autonomy and creativity. Deaconess Hospital was known for its rules-based, top-down management. Staff were loyal to their own organization. After the merger, the Beth Israel culture dominated, and many Deaconess staff, especially nurses, left to join the competition.

The Problems

By 2002, BID was losing $100 million a year and faced "financial meltdown." There were problems with the quality and safety of care, with low staff morale, and with poor relationships between clinical staff and management. The media attention was damaging BID's reputation.

The Solutions

External management consultants recommended drastic measures to turn around the hospital's finances, and Paul Levy was appointed chief executive officer of BID in 2002. Levy had no healthcare background and little knowledge of hospitals. He felt that gave him an advantage, as he was a "straight talker" and could act as an "honest broker." But staff were skeptical at first.

Levy's turnaround strategy was based on two themes: transparency and commitment to quality. His first action was to share with all staff the full scale of the financial difficulties, to create "a burning platform," from which escape would only be possible by making radical changes. His second approach was to signal absolute commitment to the continuous improvement of quality, in order to build trust and to establish a sense of common purpose. Levy described his management style:

> Perhaps I had an overly developed sense of confidence, but my management approach is that people want to do well and want to do good and I create an appropriate environment. I trust people. When people make mistakes it isn't incompetence, it's insufficient training or the wrong environment. What I've learned is that my management style can work.

Phase 1: With the hospital "bleeding money," urgent action was necessary. Levy accepted some of the management consultants' recommendations, and several hundred jobs were lost, in an attempt to restore financial balance. He refused to reduce nursing levels, but the financial crisis was resolved.

Phase 2: Medical staff were tired of poor relationships with management. In 2003, Levy hired Michael Epstein, a doctor, as chief operating officer. Epstein met with each clinical department to win their support for the hospital's nonclinical objectives and to break down silo working. Kathleen Murray, who had joined BID in 2002, was director of performance assessment and regulatory compliance. The hospital had no annual operating plans, and she set out to correct this, starting with two departments that had volunteered to take part in phase 1, orthopaedics and pancreatic surgery. Other departments soon joined in. Operating plans had four goals, addressing quality and safety, patient satisfaction, finance, and staff and referrer satisfaction. One aim was to make staff proud of the outcomes and create a sense of achievement. Although the performance of doctors would now be closely monitored, the introduction of operating plans was seen as a major turning point.

Phase 3: To help address the view that medical errors were inevitable, Levy appointed Mark Zeidel as chief of medicine. Zeidel introduced an initiative that cut "central line infection" rates, reducing costs as well as harm to patients and providing the motivation for more improvements. The board of directors were not at first convinced that performance data should be published, but Levy was persuasive, and he put the information on his public blog, which he started in 2006, and which became popular with staff, the public, and the media, with over 10,000 visitors a day. Levy explained:

> The transparency website is the engine of our work. People like to see how they compare with others, they like to see improvements. Transparency is also important for clinical leaders and our external audience of patients and insurers. We receive encouraging feedback from patients. We've also managed to avoid a major controversy with the media despite our openness. Transparency's major societal and strategic imperative is to provide creative tension within hospitals so that they hold themselves accountable. This accountability is what will drive doctors, nurses and administrators to seek constant improvements in the quality and safety of patient care.

Other performance data were published, for the hospital and for individual departments. This included measures to assess whether care was evidence-based, effective, safe, patient-centered, timely, efficient, and equitable. Progress in meeting priorities for quality and safety could be tracked on the hospital's website, and the data were used by staff to drive quality improvements. The board also set tough goals to eliminate preventable harm and increase patient satisfaction. Every year, staff were invited to summarize their improvement work in poster sessions, featuring the work of 95 process improvement teams from across the hospital.

Levy hired staff with expertise in lean methods. Previously an option, training in quality and safety became mandatory for trainee doctors, who had to take part in improvement projects. The culture was collaborative, and nurses had the respect of doctors. Patients often chose BID for the quality of nursing care. The departmental quality improvement directors met twice a month to share experiences. Department meetings routinely discussed adverse events. A patient care committee fulfilled a statutory requirement for board oversight of quality and safety. The office of decision support collected data on complication rates, infection rates, department-specific quality measures, and financial goals. A senior nurse said: "We felt a sense of ownership with issues of quality. We have dashboards up in the units to see how we are doing. Staff know what the annual operating goals are, as they are actively involved in setting them and integrating them into their work."

The Outcomes

By 2010, BID was one of the leading academic health centers in the United States, with 6,000 employees and state-of-the-art clinical care, research, and teaching. Competing effectively with other major healthcare organizations, BID was generating annual revenues of over $1.2 billion.

Postscript

Paul Levy resigned in January 2011. He explained his decision in a letter to the board of directors, making this available to staff and the public on his blog. The letter included the following remarks:

> I have been coming to a conclusion over the last several months, perhaps prompted by reaching my 60th birthday, which is often a time for checking in and deciding on the next stage of life. I realized that my own place here at BID had run its course. While I remain strongly committed to the fight for patient quality and safety, worker-led process improvement, and transparency, our organization needs a fresh perspective to reach new heights in these arenas. Likewise, for me personally, while it has been nine great years working with outstanding people, that is longer than I have spent in any one job, and I need some new challenges.

Story Sources

Abbasi, K. (2010) *Improvement in Practice: Beth Israel Deaconess Case Study.* London: The Health Foundation.
http://www.bidmc.org/
http://runningahospital.blogspot.co.uk/2011/01/transitions.html

LO 1.1 The Story of Sears Holdings

Issues to Consider as You Read This Story

1. How would you describe Eddie Lampert's leadership style?
2. How would you assess his approach to implementing major organizational change—in this case, restructuring the whole company with a new organizational model?
3. On balance, would you assess his organizational model as having been a success, or not?
4. What lessons about managing organizational change can we take from this experience and apply to other organizations, in this or other sectors?

The Setting

Sears Holdings Corporation was a specialty retailer, formed in 2005 by the merger of Kmart and Sears Roebuck. The merger was the idea of Eddie Lampert, a billionaire hedge fund manager who owned 55 percent of the new company and who became chairman. Based in Illinois, the company operated in the United States and Canada, with 274,000 employees, 4,000 retail stores, and annual revenues (2013) of $40 billion. Sears and Kmart stores sold home merchandise, clothing, and automotive products and services. The merged company was successful at first, due to aggressive cost cutting.

The Problem

By 2007, two years after the merger, profits were down by 45 percent.

The Chairman's Solution

Lampert decided to restructure the company. Sears was organized like a classic retailer. Department heads ran their own product lines, but they all worked for the same merchandising and marketing leaders, with the same financial goals. The new model ran Sears like a hedge fund portfolio with autonomous businesses competing for resources. This "internal market" would promote efficiency and improve corporate performance. At first, the new structure had around 30 business units, including product divisions, support functions, and brands, along with units focusing on e-commerce and real estate. By 2009, there were over 40 divisions. Each division had its own president, chief marketing officer, board of directors, profit and loss statement, and strategy that had to be approved by Lampert's executive committee. With all those positions to fill at the head of each unit, executives jostled for the roles, each eager to run his or her own multibillion-dollar business. The new model was called SOAR: Sears Holdings Organization, Actions, and Responsibilities.

When the reorganization was announced in January 2008, the company's share price rose 12 percent. Most retail companies prefer integrated structures, in which different divisions can be compelled to make sacrifices, such as discounting goods, to attract more shoppers. Lampert's colleagues argued that his new approach would create rival factions. Lampert disagreed. He believed that decentralized structures, although they might appear "messy," were more effective, and that they produced better information. This would give him access to better data, enabling him to assess more effectively the individual components of the company and its assets. Lampert also argued that SOAR made it easier to divest businesses and open new ones, such as the online "Shop Your Way" division.

Sears was an "early adopter" of online shopping. Lampert (who allegedly did all his own shopping online) wanted to grow this side of the business, and investment in the stores was cut back. He had innovative ideas: smartphone apps, netbooks in stores, a multiplayer game for employees. He set up a company social network, "Pebble," which he joined under the pseudonym "Eli Wexler," so that he could engage with employees. However, he criticized other people's posts and argued with store associates. When staff worked out that Wexler was Lampert, unit managers began tracking how often their employees were "Pebbling." One group organized Pebble conversations about random topics so that they would appear to be active users.

The Chairman

At the time of the merger, investors were confident that Lampert could turn the two companies around. One analyst described him as "lightning fast, razor-sharp smart, very direct." Many of those who worked for him described him as brilliant (although he could overestimate his abilities). The son of a lawyer, it was rumored that he read corporate reports and finance textbooks in high school, before going to Yale University. He hated focus groups and was sensitive to jargon such as "vendor." His brands chief once used the word "consumer" in a presentation. Lampert interrupted, with a lecture on why he should have used the word "customer" instead. He often argued with experienced retailers, but he had good relationships with managers who had finance and technology backgrounds.

From 2008, Sears' business unit heads had an annual personal videoconference with the chairman. They went to a conference room at the headquarters in Illinois, with some of Lampert's senior aides, and waited while an assistant turned on the screen on the wall opposite the U-shaped table and Lampert appeared. Lampert ran these meetings from his homes in Greenwich, Connecticut; Aspen, Colorado; and subsequently Florida, earning him the nickname "The Wizard of Oz." He visited the headquarters in person only twice a year, because he hated flying. While the unit head worked through the PowerPoint presentation, Lampert didn't look up, but dealt with his emails, or studied a spreadsheet, until he heard something that he didn't like—which would then lead to lengthy questioning.

In 2012, he bought a family home in Miami Beach for $38 million and moved his hedge fund to Florida. Some industry analysts felt that Sears' problems were exacerbated by Lampert's "penny pinching" cost savings, which stifled investment in its stores. Instead of store improvements, Sears bought back stock and increased its online presence. In 2013, Lampert became chairman and chief executive, the company having gone through four other chief executives since the merger.

The Outcomes

Instead of improving performance, the new model encouraged the divisions to turn against each other. Lampert evaluated the divisions, and calculated executives' bonuses, using a measure called "business operating profit" (BOP). The result was that individual business units focused exclusively on their own profitability, rather than on the welfare of the company. For example, the clothing division cut labor to save money, knowing that floor salesmen in other units would have to pick up the slack. Nobody wanted to sacrifice business operating profits to increase shopping traffic. The business was ravaged by infighting as the divisions—behaving in the words of one executive like "warring tribes"—battled for resources. Executives brought laptops with screen protectors to meetings so that their colleagues couldn't see what they were doing. There was no collaboration, no cooperation. The Sears and Kmart brands suffered. Employees gave the new organization model a new name: SORE.

The reorganization also meant that Sears had to hire and promote dozens of expensive chief financial officers and chief marketing officers. Many unit heads underpaid middle managers to compensate. As each division had its own board of directors, some presidents sat on five or six boards, which each met monthly. Top executives were constantly in meetings.

The company posted a net loss of $170 million for the first quarter in 2011. In November, Sears discovered that rivals planned to open on Thanksgiving at midnight, and Sears executives knew that they should also open early. However, it wasn't possible to get all the business unit heads to agree, and the stores opened as usual, the following morning. One vice president drove to the mall that evening and watched families flocking into rival stores. When Sears opened the next day, cars were already leaving the parking lot. That December, Sears announced the closure of over 100 stores. In February 2012, Sears announced the closure of its nine "The Great Indoors" stores.

From 2005 to 2013, Sears' sales fell from $49.1 billion to $39.9 billion, the stock value fell by 64 percent, and cash holdings hit a 10-year low. In May 2013, at the annual shareholders' meeting, Lampert pointed to the growth in online sales and described a new app, "Member Assist," that customers could use to send messages to store associates. The aim was "to bring online capabilities into the stores." Three weeks later, Sears reported a first quarter loss of $279 million, and the share price fell sharply. The online business contributed 3 percent of total sales. Online sales were growing, however, through the "Shop Your Way" website. Lampert argued that this was the future of Sears, and he wanted to develop "Shop Your Way" into a hybrid of Amazon and Facebook.

Story Sources

Kimes, M. 2013. At Sears, Eddie Lampert's warring divisions model adds to the troubles.
    Bloomberg Businessweek, July 11.
http://www.businessweek.com/articles/2013-07-11/
    at-sears-eddie-lamperts-warring-divisions-model-adds-to-the-troubles.
http://en.wikipedia.org/wiki/Sears_Holdings
http://www.forbes.com/profile/edward-lampert
http://www.searsholdings.com
http://www.shopyourway.com

LO 1.1 The Story of J. C. Penney

Issues to Consider as You Read This Story

1. What aspects of Ron Johnson's turnaround strategy were appropriate, praiseworthy?
2. What mistakes did Ron Johnson make?
3. What would you suggest he could have done differently?

The Setting

J. C. Penney Company, Inc. (known as JCPenney, or JCP for short) was one of America's largest clothing and home furnishing retailers. An iconic brand, founded by James Cash Penney and William Henry McManus in 1913, the headquarters were in Plano, Texas. By 2014, with annual revenues of around $13 billion, and 159,000 employees, JCP operated 1,100 retail stores and a shopping website at jcp.com. JCP once had over 2,000 stores, back in 1973, but the 1974 recession led to closures. The company's main customers were middle-income families, and female. JCP had a "promotional department store" pricing strategy with a confusing system of product discounts. There were around 600 promotions and coupon offers a year. Mike Ullman, chief executive since 2004, had grown sales with a strong private label program, with brands such as Sephora, St. John's Bay clothing, MNG by Mango, and Liz Claiborne. Another 14 stores were opened in 2004, and the e-commerce business exceeded the $1 billion revenue mark in 2005.

The Problems

When the stock reached an all-time high of $86 in 2007, JCP was performing well. However, the recession in 2008 affected sales badly; core customers had mortgage and job security problems. Between 2006 and 2011, sales fell from $19.9 billion to $17 billion. JCP had one of the lowest annual sales per square foot for department stores (around $150). Macy's and Kohl's, the main competition, had sales per square foot of around $230. In 2011, the catalogue business, with nineteen outlet stores, was closed, along with seven other stores and two call centers. *The New York Times* accused JCP of "gaming" Google search results to increase the company's ranking in searches, a practice called "spamdexing." Google's retaliation dramatically reduced JCP's search visibility.

In 2008, JCP struck a deal with Ralph Lauren to launch a new brand, American Living, sold only in their stores. But JCP was not allowed to use Ralph Lauren's name or the Polo logo. The idea failed. Sales continued to fall. In 2011, 50 to 70 percent of all sales were discounted, based on a "high-low" pricing strategy. An item would be priced initially at, say, $100. Customers would see the product and like it, but not like the price. After six weeks, the price was marked down, say, to $50, and the goods started to sell. But those items had been sitting on a shelf doing nothing for over a month.

The Solutions

In 2010, two billionaire investors, Bill Ackman and Steven Roth, approached Ullman with an offer to buy large amounts of JCP stock. They felt that the company had potential. Ackman and Roth were invited to join the board, attending their first meeting in February 2011. Leaving that meeting, Ullman was involved in a serious car accident, suffered multiple injuries, and spent three months in a neck brace, making his existing health problems worse. The board wanted a replacement, and there were no internal candidates. Ullman suggested Ron Johnson, who was working for Steve Jobs at Apple. Johnson then met with Ackman and Roth to explore possibilities. Johnson said that he was concerned about the lack of innovation in department stores, and he brought a positive, "can do" approach more typical of Silicon Valley than retailing.

In November 2011, Ron Johnson was appointed chief executive officer. JCP stock rose 17 percent on the announcement. Johnson had been responsible for setting up Apple's highly profitable retail stores, and he had also been successful at another retailer, Target. In December, after one month in post, he presented to the board his plans to revive the company with a fundamentally new way of doing business. The board agreed. Johnson told a journalist, "I came in because they wanted to transform; it wasn't just to compete or improve." In a board update before leaving, Ullman noted that Johnson had not asked him any questions about how the business was currently running.

Johnson moved quickly. First, he wanted to transform the culture. In February 2012, he installed a large transparent acrylic cube in the company headquarters. The cube was a version of the new company logo. Johnson told staff that he did not want to see the old logo anywhere in the building. For a week, staff threw "old Penney" items into the cube: T-shirts, mugs, stationery, pens, tote bags.

Second, no more promotions. Why wait six weeks to mark an item down to the price at which it would sell? Why not sell at that price from the start? Johnson simplified the pricing structure with "everyday" prices, which were what used to be sale values; "monthly value," for selected items; and "best price," linked to paydays—the first and third Fridays of each month. The stores were tidier, with no messy clearance racks, and the customer relationship became "fair and square" (another slogan).

Third, Johnson developed a "store within a store" strategy, with each store becoming a collection of dozens of separate "boutiques." He wanted a higher percentage of younger and higher-priced brands such as Joe Fresh clothes, Martha Stewart home furnishings, Michael Graves Designs, Happy Chic, and furniture from the British designer Sir Terence Conran. These new boutiques, of course, were not interested in having their brands diluted by discount pricing. Traditionally, JCP got 50 percent of sales from its own brands, which were displayed by product (bath mats) rather than brand (Martha Stewart). When a director asked him when he was going to test his new approach, Johnson replied that he had made his decision relying, like Steve Jobs, on instinct. Hundreds of stores were to be redesigned by the end of 2012. JCP already sold Levi's jeans, but Johnson wanted 700 Levi's boutiques in the stores; building these boutiques cost JCP $120 million. Southpole, a clothing brand that appealed to black and Hispanic customers, was dropped. St. John's Bay, a less fashionable women's clothing brand generating $1 billion annual revenues, was dropped.

The speed of these changes would be motivating and unifying, Johnson thought. He wanted to rebrand an old, stale company with a modern name and logo. Johnson was a charismatic and passionate presenter. He said that the changes would be painful and would take four years to complete. The board were awed by the scale of the transformation, but they did not challenge him. Johnson talked about the "six Ps": product, place, presentation, price, promotion, personality. One analyst noted, "One 'P' that seems to be missing is people." Employees were also excited about the developments, especially when Johnson threw them a lavish party, costing $3 million.

Johnson wanted to make checkout simpler, with roving clerks taking payment on iPads. Millions were spent on equipping stores with Wi-Fi. He also wanted all items to have an RFID tag, but that proved to be too expensive. He also decided to separate the store buying group from the JCP.com buying group, an approach used by Apple. However, this meant that there was no coordination between what was available online and what customers could find in the stores. Johnson was more concerned with "the look and feel" of the physical stores, and less support went to the website.

Johnson hired his own new team of top executives, who distanced themselves from the existing staff; most of them refused to move to Dallas, flying there weekly instead. If you were not part of this new team, you were out of the loop. One director called the "old" staff DOPES: dumb old Penney's employees. Veterans called the new team the Bad Apples. The new human resources director cancelled performance reviews as being too bureaucratic. This made it easier to fire people; managers did not have to consult performance data before making that decision. The new team recruited Ellen DeGeneres—a television celebrity and lesbian—to appear in JCP advertising. A conservative group, One Million Moms, threatened a boycott, claiming that, "DeGeneres is not a true representation of the type of families that shop at their store. The majority of J.C. Penney customers will be offended and chose to no longer shop there." The relationship with DeGeneres was discontinued. Johnson introduced a new exchange policy; customers could return an item, without a receipt, and receive cash. This policy was immediately abused, and one popular item was returned so often that its sales turned negative. The plan to put Martha Stewart stores into JCP stalled when Macy's sued, claiming breach of its own agreement with the home furnishings brand.

The Outcomes

The results published in February 2012 were poor. Revenues had fallen by $4.3 billion, making a $1 billion loss. The stock fell to $18, and Standard & Poor's cut JCP's debt rating to CCC+ (a long way from "triple A"). In April 2012, JCP laid off 13 percent of its office staff in Texas, closed one of its call centers, and also "retired" many managers, supervisors, and long-serving employees on the grounds that new working practices required less oversight. In May 2012, store sales were down 20 percent compared with the previous year. Johnson had projected a short-term drop in sales, but not by that much. He commented that, "I'm completely convinced that our transformation is on track," leading to a 5.9 percent rise in the stock. In July 2012, a further 350 headquarters staff were laid off. By October 2012, online sales were almost 40 percent down over the year. It was estimated that the decision to separate the two buying groups had cost JCP around $500 million.

During Johnson's two-year tenure, the price of the JCP stock fell by almost 70 percent, and sales fell in 2012 by 25 percent, resulting in a net loss of $985 million. JCP had alienated its traditional customers, who were used to shopping for discounts, but had not attracted new ones, and 20,000 employees had lost their jobs. In March 2013, Steven Roth, who had backed Johnson's appointment but who had now lost faith, sold over 40 percent of his JCP shares at a loss of $100 million. Bill Ackman resigned from the board in August, selling his shares at a loss of $470 million.

In April 2013, the company chairman told Johnson that the board would be accepting his resignation; within a few weeks, all but one of the other senior staff hired by Johnson had also left. Mike Ullman was reinstated. He immediately restored the old promotional pricing model. In May, JCP ran an "apology ad," with an earnest female voice admitting, "We learned a very simple thing, to listen to you." A coincidence of timing, in June, Johnson's renovated home departments opened in stores, selling Jonathan Adler lamps, Conran tables, and Pantone sheets. Too expensive for core customers, these departments failed and were withdrawn. However, traditional sales in stores started to grow slowly, and by November, Internet sales had increased by 25 percent on the previous year (Ullman had reintegrated the stores and online buyers). Sales of the private brand merchandise lines that had been restored also began to return to previous levels.

The JCP brand had been damaged. Sales per square foot of shopping space had fallen steadily since 2010 as shoppers turned to Macy's and Kohl's. Macy's sales per square foot had risen. With sales and profitability falling, in January 2014, JCP closed 33 underperforming stores (3 percent of the total), with 2,000 layoffs. This would reduce annual operating costs by $65 million, but the company had made a loss of $1.4 billion in 2013. After 100 years in business, with Mike Ullman back in charge, JCP stock continued to fall in the first half of 2014. Commenting on Johnson's legacy at JCP, one analyst said, "Nobody will be attempting something similar for a very long time."

Story Sources

Reingold, J., Jones, M., and Kramer, S. 2014. How to fail in business while really, really trying. *Fortune*, July 4, 169(5):80–92.

http://ir.jcpenney.com/phoenix.zhtml?c=70528&p=irol-homeprofile

http://www.jcpenney.com/

http://en.wikipedia.org/wiki/J._C._Penney

http://www.forbes.com/sites/hbsworkingknowledge/2013/08/21/what-went-wrong-at-j-c-penney/

LO 1.3 LO 1.4 Tension and Paradox: The State of the Art

tension   when two or more ideas are in opposition to each other
paradox   when two or more apparently correct ideas contradict each other

From a management perspective, organizational change is seen as problematic. How do we persuade people to accept new technologies that will make their skills, knowledge, and working practices obsolete? How quickly can people who find themselves with new roles, and new relationships, learn how to operate effectively after a major reorganization? How about this new system for capturing and processing customer information? We prefer the old system because it works just fine. Change can be difficult. Change that is not well managed, however, can generate frustration and anger.

Most estimates put the failure rate of planned changes at around 60 to 70 percent (Keller and Aiken, 2008; Burnes, 2011; Rafferty et al., 2013). In a global survey of 2,000 executives by the consulting company McKinsey, only 26 percent of respondents said that their transformational changes had successfully improved performance and enabled the organization to sustain further improvements (Jacquemont et al., 2015). There is, therefore, no shortage of advice. However, that advice is both extensive and fragmented. The literature—research and other commentary—can be difficult to access, and to absorb, for the following reasons (Iles and Sutherland, 2001):

multiple perspectives	there are contributions from several different schools, academic disciplines, and theoretical perspectives—there are several *literatures*
conceptual spread	the concepts that are used range in scale, from whole schools of thought or perspectives, through methodologies, to single tools
fluid boundaries	depending on the definitions of change and change management in use, the boundaries of the topic vary between commentators

| *rich history* | interesting and useful contributions date from the 1940s, and recent work has not necessarily made previous commentary irrelevant |
| *varied settings* | as with our stories, evidence and examples come from a range of organizational types and contexts, using different methodologies |

LO 1.2   *Multiple perspectives* is the most significant of these properties of the literature. That is usually seen as a problem—"the experts can't agree." We disagree, and we prefer instead to emphasize the advantages in adopting a multiple perspectives approach to the management of organizational change. First, a perspective that works in one context may not work well in a different setting: we will explore contingency frameworks in chapter 10. Second, this is a way of opening up debate: "Should we define our problem in these terms, or in some other way?" Third, multiple perspectives encourage the search for creative solutions: "Can we combine ideas from two or more approaches and adapt them to fit our context?" We will meet all of these characteristics again in later chapters.

The practicing manager, less interested in theoretical perspectives, wants to know "what works?" There are difficulties in providing a clear answer to that question, too, for the following reasons:

many variables	even with simple changes, the impact is multidimensional, and measuring "effectiveness" has to capture all of the factors to produce a complete picture
slippery causality	it is difficult to establish cause and effect clearly across complex processes that unfold over time, usually at the same time as lots of other changes
many stakeholders	different stakeholders have different views of the nature of the problem, the appropriate solution, and the desirable outcomes— whose measures to use?

What works well in one setting may not work well in another. The broad outlines of a good change strategy are widely known and accepted. What matters is the detail, concerning how a strategy or intervention is designed for a particular organization. For example, most practical guidelines begin by suggesting that change will be more readily accepted if there is a "sense of urgency" that underpins the business case for change. That sense of urgency can be seen in the financial meltdown at Beth Israel and the falling profitability at both Sears and J. C. Penney. Note, however, that there are many different ways in which a sense of urgency can be established and communicated. Some methods may emphasize the "burning platform" in a way that heightens anxiety and encourages escape. Other approaches might encourage instead a "burning ambition" to confront and solve the problem.

 What works depends on the context. It is rarely possible to just do what someone else has done. Change is in part a rational process; we know what kinds of issues need to be taken into account. Change is also a creative process; it is always necessary to design—to create—an approach that is consistent with local circumstances. Accounts of how other organizations have handled change can be a rich source of ideas that can be adapted creatively to address similar problems in other settings.

LO 1.3   The field of change management is also rich in tensions and paradoxes. We will explore six of these briefly, in the form of key questions. These issues will also appear in later

chapters. You will probably encounter further tensions, in your reading across the subject and in practice. How these tensions and paradoxes are managed has implications for the process and outcomes of change.

Transformational Change, or Sweat the Small Stuff?

Where to start—with sweeping radical changes, or a gradual process of incremental initiatives? We will explore a simple model for "locating" the scale of change in the next section. However, faced with geopolitical, economic, demographic, sociocultural, and technological developments, most organizations seem to think in terms of deep transformational change. The Beth Israel, Sears, and J. C. Penney stories reflect this view, implementing whole-organizational changes to deal with survival threats. This may mean that minor changes are seen as less valuable and important and are overlooked in favor of the "high impact" initiatives. This could be a mistake. Moore and Buchanan (2013), for example, demonstrate how an initiative designed to fix small problems rapidly in an acute hospital generated major performance improvements for almost no cost. In this case, "sweating the small stuff" was an enabling strategy, getting people involved (the small problems were identified by staff), establishing a reputation for getting things done, and creating the platform for further developments. Shallower changes can facilitate and complement the deeper initiatives, and evidence suggests that these should not be underestimated.

Systematic Tools, or Messy Political Process?

If one looks below the surface of cases of managed change, one can always discern the ever-present effect of the "other side" of organizational life. The ambiguities, uncertainties, ambivalences, tensions, politics and intrigues are always involved, and are influential and addressed in some manner—however half-cocked, fudged, guessed at, messed up or little understood.

(Badham, 2013, p. 24)

Most of the practical guidance on change implementation (chapters 9 and 10) suggests a straightforward sequence of steps, with advance support from diagnostic tools and assessments (chapters 4 and 5). This is a systematic process, with helpful tools. We have already suggested that change is a creative process as well as a rational one. It is also a political process. Organizations are political systems, and because there are often "winners and losers," change is a political process. The systematic tools-based approach, the creativity, and the politics work hand in hand. We will explore the political skills that change managers require later (chapter 12). It is important to recognize that, despite what the textbook or the change management consultant says, those systematic tools are only part of the answer to "how to do it, and how to get it right."

Organizational Capabilities, or Personal Skills?

Beth Israel, you may remember, was formed by the merger of two organizations with different cultures. One had a casual management style that encouraged professional autonomy and creativity. The other was known for its rules-based, top-down management. The research evidence suggests that the "casual" style is likely to be more open to change, and that this will be a more "agile" and responsive organization. Top-down management and rules suggest that change will be slow, if it happens at all, dependent on due process and committee cycles. In other words, we need to pay attention to organizational capabilities to understand the change drivers and barriers (chapter 5). The skills of change leaders are of course also important. However, skilled change agents struggle in rules-based organizations, and agile and responsive organizations still need capable change agents. We will explore the capabilities of effective change managers in chapter 12.

Rapid Change, or the Acceleration Trap?

The pace of change—social, political, economic, technological—appears to have accelerated. Can organizations keep up? There is now a considerable amount of advice on how to speed up change, to accelerate the pace. Rapid change, however, can cause problems. Can people keep up? Change too fast, and you run the danger of destabilizing the organization and creating staff burnout. There is also, therefore, advice on how to manage "painless change" and how to avoid "the acceleration trap." We will explore the dilemma of pace further in chapter 3.

Change Leader, or Distributed Leadership?

It is widely assumed that change needs a champion, a senior figure, who sets the direction, inspires others, and drives the project. A lot of work has gone into identifying the competencies of the "ideas champion," the effective change leader. This parallels work on the capabilities of effective leaders in general (although most researchers argue that leadership success is highly contingent). However, in most organizations, change is not a solo performance but a team effort. There is usually a "guiding coalition" of more or less senior managers, who guarantee permission for change, oversee progress, and unblock problems that arise. Research has also shown how change is driven by large numbers of organizational members, in an approach that is also called "distributed leadership," "leadership constellations," or "leadership in the plural."

Learning Lessons, or Implementing Lessons?

Change following crises, accidents, misconduct, failures, and other extreme events often does not happen. There is always an investigation, which produces recommendations for preventing such an event from happening again (or at least reducing the probability). The evidence shows that those recommendations are often ignored. One might assume that, in such circumstances, change would be rapid, straightforward, and welcome. The distinction between passive learning (identifying lessons) and active learning (implementing changes) is important here. The latter does not automatically follow. Why is that not the case? In exploring "why organizations change" in chapter 3, we will also consider why organizations do not change, when they perhaps should.

Change Has Never Been So Fast

That this is an age of change is an expression heard frequently today. Never before in the history of mankind have so many and so frequent changes occurred. These changes that we see taking place all about us are in that great cultural accumulation which is man's social heritage. It has already been shown that these cultural changes were in earlier times rather infrequent, but that in modern times they have been occurring faster and faster until today mankind is almost bewildered in his effort to keep adjusted to these ever increasing social changes. This rapidity of social change may be due to the increase in inventions which in turn is made possible by the accumulative nature of material culture (i.e., technology).

Source: Ogburn (1922), pp. 199–200.

The perceptive reader will have noticed that the answer to each of these six paradoxes, these six questions, is in each case "both." We need big change and small change. Change is at the same time a systematic process and a political one. We need both organizational and individual capabilities. The pace of change must, if possible, vary with circumstances. Change is almost always driven by "a cast of characters" that includes one or more champions and many supporters. There is no point in learning lessons if we do not then implement them. As noted earlier, the way in which these tensions are confronted and managed both drives and constrains the change process, and influences the outcomes.

LO 1.4 Assessing Depth of Change

We have noted the tension between "transformational change and the small stuff." Depth is one metaphor that can be used to categorize change. Figure 1.1 presents a framework for that assessment.

FIGURE 1.1
Assessing Depth of Change

Off the scale	Disruptive innovation Frame-breaking, mold-breaking Redraw dramatically organization and sector boundaries
Deeper	Paradigm shift, strategic change New ways of thinking and solving problems, whole system change New ways of doing business
Deep change	Change the mission, vision, values, the organization's philosophy, in order to symbolize a radical shift in thinking and behavior
	Change the organization's definition of success Create new goals, objectives, targets
Sustaining innovation	Improve business planning to symbolize a shift in thinking Tighten up on documentation, reporting, controls
	Reallocate resources Grow some departments, cut others, create new units
Shallow change	Fine tuning: cut costs, improve efficiencies Constantly "nibble away" making minor improvements
Not on the scale	"Sweat the small stuff"—quickly solve the minor annoying problems that nobody has bothered to fix; "grease the wheels"

At the bottom of this figure sits the "small stuff" that may not even be regarded as "change." In the middle of the scale we have "sustaining innovation," which involves improving on current practices. At the top of the scale is "disruptive innovation," which involves radically new business models and working methods (Christensen, 2000). One obvious point to make is that, in considering change in an organization, the proposed solution should be consistent with the diagnosis of the problem. Using shallow changes to address strategic challenges may not be appropriate, and attempting to solve minor difficulties with disruptive innovation could consume disproportionate amounts of time and resources.

Shallow changes are usually easier to implement than frame-breaking changes. Transformational "off the scale" changes are more challenging because they are costly and time-consuming, and they affect larger numbers of people in more significant ways, potentially generating greater resistance. In most cases, many changes are likely to be under way at the same time, at different depths. Recognizing this, many organizations have established corporate project or program management offices (PMOs) to support and coordinate their initiatives (Ward and Daniel, 2013). The U.S. Project Management Institute's white paper (2012) gives examples of the aims and benefits of PMOs at the State Auto insurance company in Ohio and the National Cancer Institute in Maryland.

One of the tensions in this framework concerns the ambitions of the individual manager. When interviewed for the next promotion, stories about the impact of the deep transformations for which one has been responsible are typically more impressive than stories about minor stuff.

LO 1.4 What's Coming Up: A Road Map

This text is divided into three parts. Part 1, including this chapter, sets out the *groundwork*, and is concerned with understanding and diagnosing change, and with different images of change management. Part 2 focuses on *implementation*, exploring the substance of change, the role of vision, managing resistance, developing communication strategies, and several approaches to the implementation process. Part 3 examines two *running threads* that relate to all of the previous chapters. The first concerns managing the sustainability of change, which we argue has to be considered from the beginning and not managed as an afterthought. The second running thread is an assessment of what it takes to be an effective change manager—which is, of course, the theme of the book as a whole. Figure 1.2 sets out a road map, an overview of the content.

One of the main assumptions underpinning this road map is that our images of the roles of change leaders affect how we approach the other issues on the map. Remember, for example, how the different change leadership styles adopted by Paul Levy at Beth Israel, Eddy Lampert at Sears, and Ron Johnson at J. C. Penney colored their approaches to communicating the changes that they wanted to implement. This explains why "images," chapter 2, is at the center of the figure. However, by necessity, a book such as this follows a linear sequence for presentational reasons. This is not necessarily the sequence in which change leaders will need to consider these issues, or in which instructors will wish to introduce and explore these themes. What will work best depends on context. In some cases, the question of "vision" may be fundamental to the change process, and it would be unwise to proceed until that issue has been resolved. In many change models

FIGURE 1.2
To Be an Effective Change Manager, This Is What You Need …

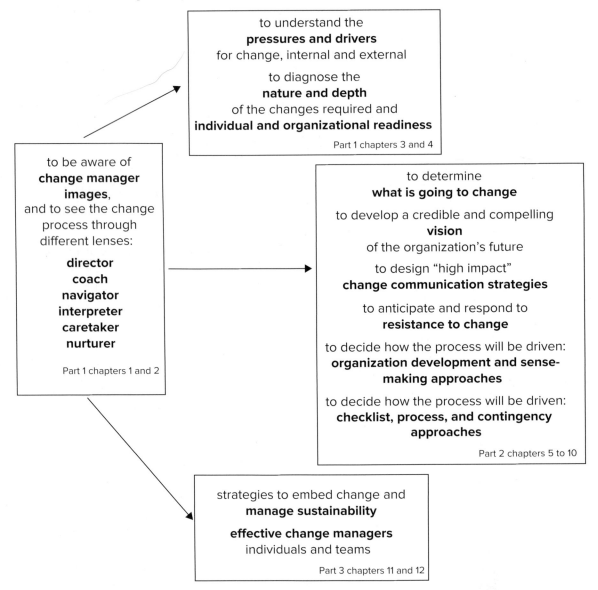

and textbooks, the question of sustainability is presented at the end, as it is here. However, if sustainability is not built into change implementation from the beginning, then this may become an unnecessary problem. Communication is another issue that is typically involved throughout the change process.

This road map comes with an added caution. If you follow the recipe correctly, that cake should be perfect; enjoy. However, success is not guaranteed by following a set of change implementation guidelines. There are two main reasons for this. First, designing a change process is a task with both technical and creative components; blending these components can in many circumstances be a challenging business involving much trial and error. Second, what works depends on organizational context, which is not stable but which can change suddenly and in unpredictable ways. External conditions can change, intensifying or removing the pressures for change. Budget considerations may mean that resources are diverted elsewhere. Key stakeholders change their minds and shift from supporting to resisting. There are numerous factors that are not under the control of change leaders, and things go wrong despite careful planning and preparation. This is one reason why, as chapter 12 explains, resilience or "bouncebackability" is a core attribute for effective change leaders.

[LO 1.1] Change Diagnostic: The Beth Israel Story

Here are the four questions that you were asked to consider while reading the Beth Israel story, followed by our suggested answers:

1. Identify five factors that explain the success of this corporate turnaround.
2. How would you describe Paul Levy's role and contributions to this turnaround?
3. What insights does this story have to offer concerning the role of the change leader?
4. What lessons about managing organizational change can we take from this experience and apply to other organizations, in healthcare and in other sectors? Or, are the lessons unique to Beth Israel Deaconess Medical Center?

The story of this turnaround has been cited as one from which other healthcare organizations can learn, in other countries. The account on which this case is based was commissioned by the Health Foundation in the United Kingdom. As we will see, many of the change management issues raised here are common and can be found in other sectors and cultures. While it is always possible to argue that healthcare is "special" in some respects, many of the change management concerns are generic.

1. **Identify five factors that explain the success of this corporate turnaround.**
   - The sense of urgency, the "burning platform," created deliberately by the new chief executive, who was open with all staff about the true position concerning the hospital's finances.
   - The focus that was consistently maintained on improving the quality and safety of patient care, which appealed (perhaps more than budget layouts) to the professional values of clinical staff.
   - The phased approach that involved, first and quickly, fixing the finances; second, repairing medical-managerial relationships and getting staff involved in operational plans; and third, focusing on safety issues and eliminating harm. Frontline staff involvement was key.
   - Making hospital and department performance data available to staff, the public, and the media, to inspire pride in achievement and to stimulate further improvements.
   - The creation of a "leadership constellation" through the appointment of other senior staff who understood and who supported the chief executive's goals and strategy (Denis et al., 2001).

2. **How would you describe Paul Levy's role and contributions to this turnaround?**
   - Did Paul Levy actually change anything directly? He described his style as "creating the environment" that enabled other people to do good work.
   - One of his main contributions was to insist on transparency, about the hospital's financial problems and with performance data. That transparency may have been uncomfortable for some, but it created pride in achievement and the motivation for continuous improvement.
   - A second key contribution concerned his consistency of purpose, the relentless focus on the quality and safety of patient care, which were issues that engaged and motivated clinical staff.
   - His innovative use of the Internet and his personal blog about "running a hospital" made sure that everyone—staff, patients, the wider community, the media—knew what he was thinking and doing and why, building respect and trust.
   - He stayed with BID for nine years. Not many chief executives stick around for this long. But tenure helps to build influence and reinforces the consistency of purpose.

3. **What insights does this story have to offer concerning the role of the change leader?**
   - Levy had no healthcare background. Maybe this means that one does not need specialist sector knowledge and experience to drive a corporate turnaround. But he made sure that he had access to those specialist resources though his other senior appointments.
   - He had confidence in his management approach. That confidence may be as important as the style—maybe a different style, applied consistently, could be just as effective, especially when it involved laying off a number of staff soon after taking up his new post, and standing up to the board of directors and defending a view different from theirs.
   - The role of a change leader is a demanding one, and it can be difficult to maintain for long periods. It is necessary to recognize when it is time to leave—and also to know when leaving would damage the project. Levy departed only after BID's financial, clinical, and operational performance goals had been achieved and the future of the hospital was secure.

4. **What lessons about managing organizational change can we take from this experience and apply to other organizations, in healthcare and in other sectors? Or, are the lessons unique to Beth Israel Deaconess Medical Center?**

   This is controversial. A lot of the research evidence concerning organizational change management—what works and what doesn't—relies on case study accounts such as this. Could an approach to rapid and radical organizational change that worked in a large hospital in Boston be applied to a small software design company in Sacramento? Looking at the details, the answer is probably "no"; the software company doesn't have to worry about medical engagement and patient safety metrics. Looking at the approach in general, however, the answer is probably "yes." If our software company was losing money and reputation, a new "straight talking" chief executive with clear and consistent goals, an inclusive management style, a strong management team, and a transparent approach to the use of performance data to motivate improvement could be a highly effective combination.

In other words, if we look beyond the details, we can see a number of actions that could well be applied in other settings. Also, when one gathers a number of such stories, of successes and failures, similar patterns emerge, especially with regard to establishing a sense of urgency and purpose, creating a strong and stable senior team, using "leadership constellations" to drive change, a participative management style, staff engagement, open communications, and transparency of performance information that is used for feedback, performance management, motivation, and reward purposes. The Beth Israel story is a compelling one, but it is neither idiosyncratic nor unique.

LO 1.1 Change Diagnostic: The Sears Holdings Story

Here are the four questions that you were asked to consider while reading the Sears Holdings story, followed by our suggested answers:

1. How would you describe Eddie Lampert's leadership style?
2. How would you assess his approach to implementing major organizational change—in this case, restructuring the whole company with a new organizational model?
3. On balance, would you assess his organizational model as having been a success, or not?
4. What lessons about managing organizational change can we take from this experience and apply to other organizations, in this or other sectors?

Is this the Sears story, or the Eddie Lampert story? One commentator concluded that, in addition to the other difficulties facing retailers, Sears had a unique problem—Lampert himself.

1. **How would you describe Eddie Lampert's leadership style?**

   Lampert could be described as a transformational leader. He was highly intelligent and decisive. He was innovative, concerning both the company structure and its service delivery. He had a clear and interesting vision for the online future of the business. Check out "Shop Your Way" for yourself.

   However, he also appears to have been an autocratic leader. There is little evidence to suggest that he either sought or considered the views of others, including his senior colleagues, before making business-critical decisions. He was something of a recluse, preferring to meet with his division heads infrequently, and through a video link (and he rarely allowed media interviews). His "engagement" with staff through the company's social network was more confrontational than consultative.

2. **How would you assess his approach to implementing major organizational change—in this case, restructuring the whole company with a new organizational model?**

   If rapid action is necessary to rescue an organization that is experiencing extreme difficulties, then an autocratic approach may be appropriate. It takes time to pause, to ask everyone else what they think should be done, to process that feedback, to develop a more widely informed decision, to check that with those involved, and then to implement the approach. By that time, the company could be bust. Lampert's "crisis management" style may thus have been appropriate immediately after the merger. Although profitability was declining, it is debatable whether that approach was appropriate in 2008.

A more prudent approach in this case would probably have been to listen to the views of colleagues, at all levels of the company, and to take those into account before imposing that reorganization. There could have been many other ways in which to achieve the required end results, including improved divisional and corporate performance, and data transparency. Whatever restructuring was implemented, it was probably going to be more successful if those who were affected understood the decision, had contributed significantly to it, and had agreed with it. "Behavioral flexibility" is one of the core capabilities of managers and leaders at all levels in an organization. This means adapting one's overall approach and personal style to fit the circumstances. Lampert did not do that.

3. **On balance, would you assess his organizational model as having been a success, or not?**

    From 2005 to 2013, the company's sales, profits, and share value fell. Although not mentioned in the case account, many experienced executives left the company, frustrated by the impact of the restructuring. Divisional collaboration was stifled, and it appears that the competition stimulated by the new organizational model was not healthy competition. The model, therefore, appears to have been damaging to the company's performance and to its reputation. The new model, however, made it easier for Lampert to set up the online business as a division run independently of the other units. It may thus be too early to assess the longer-term overall success of that organization restructuring.

4. **What lessons about managing organizational change can we take from this experience and apply to other organizations, in this or other sectors?**

    Change leaders need to adapt their style to fit the context. An autocratic style can rapidly resolve a crisis. In other circumstances, "decisive action" may leave others feeling that they have been excluded, and they may decide to undermine decisions that they feel were ill-advised (especially where the approach was considered to be idiosyncratic) as well as imposed on them.

LO 1.1 Change Diagnostic: The J. C. Penney Story

Here are the three questions that you were asked to consider while reading the J. C. Penney story, followed by our suggested answers:

1. What aspects of Ron Johnson's turnaround strategy were appropriate, praiseworthy?
2. What mistakes did Ron Johnson make?
3. What would you suggest he could have done differently?

1. **What aspects of Ron Johnson's turnaround strategy were appropriate, praiseworthy?**

    First, he was charismatic, passionate, energetic, and persuasive, using theatrics (the acrylic cube) to draw attention and generate excitement. These are useful characteristics for change leaders to possess, although in this case they contributed to the problems. It is possible to be too charismatic, too passionate, too energetic, too persuasive, too theatrical. Second, he was highly innovative, bringing lots of fresh ideas to a long-established and stale organization. Organizations that have been trading for a century will often benefit by importing new thinking and practices from other sectors. Third, he was action-oriented and wanted to move quickly, to bring about radical change rapidly.

2. **What mistakes did Ron Johnson make?**

Ignoring the company's traditional core customers was probably his first and most serious mistake. There was no market research, either directly with customer groups or indirectly through store staff and managers, to develop a better understanding of the buying habits and preferences of JCP customers. How would customers interpret the changes that he wanted to implement? It would have been helpful to know the answer to that question before proceeding. This lack of customer knowledge led to some disastrous marketing, and to pricing and merchandising strategies that alienated core customers without attracting new shoppers. Selling more expensive products seems like a good way to increase sales per square foot, but only if your customers want those items and can afford to buy them. Second, he allowed his new top team of "outsiders" to distance themselves from the existing JCP managers and staff. This meant that the top team had restricted access to the business knowledge stored in the corporate memory, and it also created unnecessary tensions between the DOPES and the Bad Apples. Third, he made critical decisions based on his own judgement, dismissing the views of other senior executives. Fourth, he acted rapidly. While speed may be necessary, especially in a crisis, introducing so many changes at a quick pace was destabilizing. Finally, and linked to the fourth point, he did not pilot test his big ideas before committing the investment and implementing them.

Johnson's approach to change at JCP had two other adverse consequences. First, he damaged the brand image, and that would take time—perhaps years—to repair. Second, he closed the door to any future JCP chief executive who might be tempted to play the part of charismatic innovator.

3. **What would you suggest he could have done differently?**

There is no correct answer to this question, but there is a wide range of possibilities. The first obvious suggestion concerns better customer intelligence. Did sales fall because middle-income families were hit by recession and customers became confused by pricing practices? Or would customers have welcomed an expansion of the range of JCP exclusive private brands and a modified promotions program instead? A second suggestion concerns testing new ideas in a small number of representative outlets to see how those would work before committing the whole organization. Third, review the decision to fill senior management roles with friends and "outsiders"; did the organization have internal candidates who could have filled at least some of those roles equally well? Find ways to integrate new with existing staff: teambuilding, corporate events, job rotations and partnerships, insisting that senior staff move to Dallas. In summary, these suggestions concern market research, pilot testing, recruitment, and promotions policy. However, this does not suggest that changes should have been made slowly, just a little less rapidly. That would have allowed mistakes and wrong turns to become apparent, so that they could be withdrawn, lessons learned, and revised plans put in place. Johnson's charisma, passion, and energy could have driven this alternative approach effectively.

A final suggestion for Ron Johnson would be: ask your board to probe and to challenge your decisions, and listen carefully to what they say. The why and how of change in this case would probably have been more successful if these had been the result of board decisions, and not Ron Johnson's decisions. The board themselves, in this case, seem to have made the mistake of not challenging their new, charismatic, persuasive, passionate chief executive.

EXERCISE 1.1

Writing Your Own Story of Change

LO 1.1

Think of a change that you have experienced, in either your work or personal life. We would like to ask you to write a story about that experience. Here is a definition of a story to help you:

A story expresses how and why life changes. It begins with a situation in which life is relatively in balance: You come to work day after day, week after week, and everything's fine. You expect it will go on that way. But then there's an event—in screenwriting, we call it the "inciting incident"—that throws life out of balance. You get a new job, or the boss dies of a heart attack, or a big customer threatens to leave. The story goes on to describe how, in an effort to restore balance, the protagonist's subjective expectations crash into an uncooperative objective reality. A good storyteller describes what it's like to deal with these opposing forces, calling on the protagonist to dig deeper, work with scarce resources, make difficult decisions, take action despite risks, and ultimately discover the truth. (McKee, 2003, p. 52)

Plan A

Write down your experience of change in about one page, and then answer these questions:

- What made this experience a "story"?
- What lessons for managing change can you take from your story?
- Compare these with the lessons from the Beth Israel, Sears, and J. C. Penney stories. Which are the same?
- From your experience, what new lessons have you added, particularly for future changes in which you might be involved?
- In small groups, share your lessons with colleagues. Which lessons are similar, and what are the differences among you?
- What three main conclusions can you take from these stories about managing change?

Plan B

In small groups of around four to six people, ask each of the group members to tell their story of change, taking only three or four minutes each. Record key elements of each story on flip-chart paper. When everyone has told their story, answer the following questions:

- What are the common themes and issues across these stories?
- What are the differences between these stories?
- Of the change lessons from Beth Israel, Sears, and J. C. Penney, which are revealed in the groups' stories, and which are absent? What are the implications of this?
- Are there any further lessons embedded in these stories that could apply to future changes in which group members may be involved?
- What three main conclusions can you take from these stories about managing change?

Additional Reading

Christensen, C. M., and Carlile, P. R. 2009. Course research: Using the case method to build and teach management theory. *Academy of Management Learning and Education* 8(2):240–51. Explains how to use stories and case studies in management teaching, to develop, test, and improve theory.

Denning, S. 2004. Telling tales. *Harvard Business Review* 82(5):122–29. Explains the power of organizational storytelling and demonstrates how leaders can use stories to tell people about themselves, trigger action, transmit values, encourage collaboration, "tame the grapevine," share knowledge, and "lead people into the future."

Hughes, M. 2011. Do 70 per cent of all organizational change initiatives really fail? *Journal of Change Management* 11(4):451–64. The author challenges the evidence behind the argument that so many change initiatives fail.

Metz, I., and Culik, C. T. 2008. Making public organizations more inclusive: A case study of the Victoria Police Force. *Human Resource Management* 47(2):369–87. A case study of rapid and successful culture change, led by a woman, Christine Nixon, recruited from outside the male-dominated police force. Note the lessons that the authors draw from this case.

Reisner, R. A. F. 2002. When a turnaround stalls. *Harvard Business Review* 80(2):45–52. This case study concerns the U.S. Postal Service and is written by Robert Reisner, vice president for strategic planning. Note the lessons that he draws from his experience.

Roundup

Successful change is not guaranteed, despite the care and attention given to implementation planning. If there is one firm prediction that we can make about change, it is that it will go wrong, however meticulously designed. Why? By definition, we are always doing it for the first time—in this organization, facing these problems, with these resources, given the past history—and so on. One cannot confidently predict what will happen. The change leader is always building the plane as it flies. This is not an argument against planning; it is an argument for recognizing when things are going wrong, learning from that, and adapting accordingly. So this text does not set out to tell change leaders "what to do." Such perspectives perpetuate the problem by creating the illusion that the outcomes can be kept under control if carefully planned steps are followed. Most people's experience of organizations suggests that they are complex and untidy—and political—arenas. Acknowledging these characteristics is the first step to taking a more realistic view of what change leaders can expect to achieve. As discussed in the next chapter, it is more appropriate to think in terms of *shaping* the change process rather than *controlling* it. We hope that reflective change leaders will accept that choices must be made for change to proceed, and that these are informed choices, not adopted on the grounds that there is "one best way" to approach the process.

Here is a short summary of the key points that we would like you to take from this chapter, in relation to each of the learning outcomes:

LO 1.1

* *Recognize how stories of change can contribute to our knowledge of theory and practice.*
   Stories can be read as process narratives, which explain what happened in a given context. These explanations are therefore theories of change, pointing to the combination

of factors interacting over time, leading to more or less successful change. While those theories cannot be copied simply to other organizations and contexts, they are still a rich source of general lessons, and aspects of one organization's approach can be adapted to fit other organizational contexts, if appropriate.

LO 1.2 * *Understand why managing organizational change is both a creative and a rational process.*

As with management practice in many other areas, what is going to work well when it comes to implementing change depends on the organizational context. While general guidelines help to identify the factors to take into consideration, the details have to be determined by local, informed management and staff judgement. That is a creative process.

LO 1.3 * *Identify the main tensions and paradoxes in managing organizational change.*

Should we focus on transformational changes, or do we need to "sweat the small stuff" as well? Should change be a rational, systematic process, or do we need to recognize the political dimension? What is more important, organizational capabilities or individual skills in implementing change? Should we accelerate the changes or adopt a more measured pace? Do we rely on one change champion or recognize the distributed contributions of many change agents? Once we have "learned the lessons" from a crisis or other extreme event, how do we ensure that these are put into practice?

LO 1.4 * *Assess the strengths and limitations of our current understanding of this field.*

There is a significant amount of commentary, but little consensus. Most of the advice says much the same thing, but the failure rate of change is still high. The commentary is highly fragmented and includes multiple perspectives and conceptualizations. Evidence comes from a range of different settings and approaches, and contributions from last century are still relevant today. Establishing cause and effect with regard to change and outcomes is made difficult by the many variables, and the many stakeholders typically involved.

References

Abbasi, K. 2010. *Improvement in practice: Beth Israel Deaconess case study*. London: The Health Foundation.

Badham, R. 2013. *Short change: An introduction to managing change*. Sumy, Ukraine: Business Perspectives.

Burnes, B. 2011. Why does change fail, and what can we do about it? *Journal of Change Management* 11(4):445–50.

Christensen, C. M. 2000. *The innovator's dilemma: When new technologies cause great firms to fail*. New York: HarperCollins.

Christensen, C. M., and Carlile, P. R. 2009. Course research: Using the case method to build and teach management theory. *Academy of Management Learning and Education* 8(2):240–51.

Czarniawska, B. 1998. *A narrative approach to organization studies*. Thousand Oaks, CA: Sage Publications.

Dawson, P., and Andriopoulos, C. 2014. *Managing change, creativity and innovation.* London: Sage Publications.

Denis, J.-L., Lamothe, L., and Langley, A. 2001. The dynamics of collective leadership and strategic change in pluralistic organizations. *Academy of Management Journal* 44(4):809–37.

Denning, S. 2004. Telling tales. *Harvard Business Review* 82(5):122–29.

Fernandez, S., and Rainey, H. G. 2006. Managing successful organizational change in the public sector. *Public Administration Review* 66(2):168–76.

Hughes, M. 2011. Do 70 per cent of all organizational change initiatives really fail? *Journal of Change Management* 11(4):451–64.

Iles, V., and Sutherland, K. 2001. *Organizational change: A review for health care managers, professionals and researchers.* London: National Co-ordinating Centre for NHS Service Delivery and Organization Research and Development.

Jacquemont, D., Maor, D., and Reich, A. 2015. *How to beat the transformation odds.* New York: McKinsey & Company.

Keller, S., and Aiken, C. 2008. *The inconvenient truth about change management: Why it isn't working and what to do about it.* Chicago and Toronto: McKinsey & Company.

Kimes, M. 2013. At Sears, Eddie Lampert's warring divisions model adds to the troubles. *Bloomberg Businessweek*, July 11. http://www.businessweek.com/articles/2013-07-11/at -sears-eddie-lamperts-warring-divisions-model-adds-to-the-troubles.

Langley, A. 2009. Studying processes in and around organizations. In *The Sage handbook of organizational research methods*, ed. D. A. Buchanan and A. Bryman (409–29). London: Sage Publications.

McKee, R. 2003. Storytelling that moves people. *Harvard Business Review* 81(6):51–55.

Metz, I., and Culik, C. T. 2008. Making public organizations more inclusive: A case study of the Victoria Police Force. *Human Resource Management* 47(2):369–87.

Mohr, L. B. 1982. *Explaining organizational behaviour: The limits and possibilities of theory and research.* San Francisco: Jossey-Bass Publishers.

Moore, C., and Buchanan, D. A. 2013. Sweat the small stuff: A case study of small scale change processes and consequences in acute care. *Health Services Management Research* 26(1):9–17.

Ogburn, W. F. 1922. *Social change: With respect to culture and original nature.* New York: B. W. Huebsch.

Pentland, B. T. 1999. Building process theory with narrative: From description to explanation. *Academy of Management Review* 24(4):711–24.

Poole, M. S., Van de Ven, A. H., Dooley, K., and Holmes, M. E. 2000. *Organizational change and innovation processes: Theory and methods for research.* Oxford and New York: Oxford University Press.

Project Management Institute. 2012. *The project management office: In sync with strategy*. Philadelphia: PMI Inc.

Rafferty, A. E., Jimmieson, N. L., and Armenakis, A. A. 2013. Change readiness: A multilevel review. *Journal of Management* 39(1):110–35.

Reingold, J., Jones, M., and Kramer, S. 2014. How to fail in business while really, really trying. *Fortune*, July 4, 169(5):80–92.

Reisner, R. A. F. 2002. When a turnaround stalls. *Harvard Business Review* 80(2):45–52.

Van de Ven, A. H., and Poole, M. S. 2005. Alternative approaches for studying organizational change. *Organization Studies* 26(9):1377–404.

Ward, J., and Daniel, E. 2013. The role of project management offices (PMOs) in IS project success and management satisfaction. *Journal of Enterprise Information Management* 26(3):316–36.

Chapter 2

Images of Change Management

Learning objectives

By the end of this chapter you should be able to:

LO 2.1 Evaluate the use that different authors make of the terms *change agent, change manager,* and *change leader*

LO 2.2 Understand the importance of organizational images and mental models

LO 2.3 Compare and contrast six different images of managing change and change managers

LO 2.4 Explain the theoretical underpinning of different change management images

LO 2.5 Apply these six images of managing change to your personal preferences and approach, and to different organizational contexts

LO 2.1   What's in a Name: Change Agents, Managers, or Leaders?

This chapter focuses on those who drive and implement change. We first consider how those individuals are described, and then explore different ways in which their roles can be understood. This is not just a theoretical discussion. An understanding of organizational change roles has profound practical implications for the way in which those roles are conducted. And if you are in a change management role, now or in future, the way in which you understand your position will affect how you fulfill those responsibilities and whether you are more or less successful.

The use of terms in this field has become confused, and we first need to address this problem. Do the terms *change agent*, *change manager*, and *change leader* refer to different roles in relation to organizational change? Or are these labels interchangeable?

For most of the twentieth century, the term *change agent* typically referred to an external expert management consultant who was paid to work out what was going wrong in an organization and to implement change to put things right. This model is still in use. In the United Kingdom, if your hospital is in financial difficulties, the national regulator, Monitor, will appoint a "turnaround director" (external expert change agent with a fancy job title) to sit on your board of directors and tell you how to cut costs and restore financial balance. External change agents do not all work like that. Many adopt the "process consultation" approach popularized by Edgar Schein (1999). Here, the role of the "expert" is to help members of the organization to understand and solve their own problems.

Today, a change agent is just as likely to be a member of the organization as an external consultant. The term is now often used more loosely, to refer to anyone who has a role in change implementation, regardless of job title or seniority. Given the scale and scope of changes that many organizations face, a significant number of internal change agents may be a valuable—perhaps necessary—resource. Internal change agents usually have a better understanding than outsiders of the changes that would lead to improvements. In short, when you see the term "change agent," it is important to check the meaning that is intended, unless that is obvious from the context. When we use the term *change agent* in this book, we will always indicate clearly to whom this applies.

Conventional wisdom says that, with regard to the other terms in our section heading, management and leadership are different roles, and that this is an important distinction. One of the main advocates of this distinction is John Kotter (2012). For him, change management refers to the basic tools and structures with which smaller-scale changes are controlled. Change leadership, in contrast, marshals the driving forces and visions that produce large-scale transformations. His main point, of course, is that we need more change leadership.

This argument has two flaws. The first concerns the assumption that large-scale transformations are more meaningful and potent, and are therefore more valuable than small-scale change. They are not, as the discussion of "depth of change" (figure 1.1) in chapter 1 suggested.

For example, Cíara Moore and David Buchanan (2013) report a change initiative called "Sweat the Small Stuff." Staff in one clinical service in an acute hospital were asked to identify small, annoying problems that had not been fixed for some time. These included broken equipment and faulty administrative processes. The five problems were addressed by a three-person team including an "animateur" who set up and coordinated the project, a clinical champion who engaged medical colleagues, and a "who knows who knows what" person whose administrative background and networks helped the team to identify short-cuts, "workarounds," and "the right people" to solve these problems quickly. All five problems were solved within five days. The total costs came to £89 for a piece of equipment, and the 40 minutes that the animateur spent in conversations. The benefits were "financial (US$35,000 income generation), processual (safer patient allocation), temporal (tasks performed more quickly, less waiting time), emotional (less annoyance, boredom, frustration), and relational (improved inter-professional relations)" (Moore and Buchanan, 2013, p. 13).

One of the overarching benefits of "sweating the small stuff" was better management-medical relationships, laying the foundation for further improvements, in this area and in others. Fixing the small stuff was beneficial in its own right and was the precursor for future major changes. The animateur's job title was "operations manager"; was she a change manager, or a change leader?

The second flaw in the argument concerns the belief that the contrasting definitions of these management and leadership concepts will survive contact with practice. They do not. While it may be possible to define clear categories in theory, in practice these roles are overlapping and indistinguishable. The general distinction between management and leadership is challenged by Henry Mintzberg (2009, pp. 8–9), who argues, "I don't understand what this distinction means in the everyday life of organizations. Sure, we can separate leading and managing conceptually. But can we separate them in practice? Or, more to the point, should we even try?" He asks, how would you like to be managed by someone who doesn't lead, or led by someone who doesn't manage? "We should be seeing managers *as* leaders, and leadership as management practiced well."

In short, management versus leadership is not a distinction worth arguing over, and may be more simply resolved by a combination of personal and contextual preference. In this book, we will use the terms *change management* (or *manager*) and *change leadership* (or *leader*) synonymously—unless there is a reason for making a distinction, which will then be explained.

LO 2.2 Images, Mental Models, Frames, Perspectives

More important than the terminology, the internal mental *images* that we have of our organizations influence our expectations and our interpretations of what is happening, and of what we think needs to change, and how (Morgan, 2006; Hatch and Cunliffe, 2012; Bolman and Deal, 2013). We typically hold these images, metaphors, frames of reference, or perspectives without being conscious of how they color our thinking, perceptions, and actions. These images, which can also be described as mental models, help us to make sense of the world around us, by focusing our attention in particular directions. The key point is that, while an image or mental model is a way of seeing things, a standpoint drawing our attention to particular issues and features, it is also a way of *not* seeing things, shifting our attention away from other factors, which may or may not be significant.

For example, if we have a mental image of organizations as machines, then we will be more aware of potential component "breakdowns" and see our role in terms of maintenance and repair. In contrast, if we think of organizations as political arenas, we are more likely to be aware of the hidden agendas behind decisions and try to identify the winners and losers. We are also likely to see our role, not as maintaining parts of a smooth-running machine, but as building coalitions, gathering support for our causes, and stimulating conflict to generate innovation. Shifting the lens again, we may see our organizations as small societies or "microcultures." With this image, we are more likely to focus on "the way things get done around here," and on how to encourage the values that are best aligned to the type of work that we do. A microculture image highlights the importance of providing vision and meaning so that staff identity becomes more closely associated with the work of the organization. Each frame thus orients us to a different set of issues.

There are no "right" and "wrong" images here. These are just different lenses through which the world in general, and organizations in particular, can be seen and understood. The images or lenses that we each use reflect our backgrounds, education, life experiences, and personal preferences. There are some problems for which a "machine" image may be more appropriate, and other problems where a "microculture" image is relevant. Some problems may best be understood if they are approached using two or three images or lenses at a time.

Those who are responsible for driving and implementing change also have their own images of organizations—and more importantly, *images of their role as change manager*. Those images clearly influence the ways in which change managers approach the change process, the issues that they believe are important, and the change management style that they will adopt. Like the child with a hammer who treats every problem as if it were a nail, the change manager is handicapped in drawing on only one particular image of that role. It is therefore important, first, to understand one's personal preferences—perhaps biases—in this regard. It is also important, second, to be able to switch from one image of the role to another, according to circumstances. This ability to work with *multiple perspectives, images, or frames concerning the change management role* is, we will argue, central to the personal effectiveness of the change manager and also to the effectiveness of the change process.

We will outline six different "ideal type" images of managing change, describing the assumptions that underpin each image and the theoretical views that support them. We will then explore how change managers can draw from and use these multiple perspectives and images of managing change.

LO 2.3 The Six-Images Framework

How are our images or mental models of organization and change formed? To answer this question, Ian Palmer and Richard Dunford (2002) first identify two broad images of the task of managing, which can be seen as either a *controlling* or as a *shaping* activity. They then identify three broad images of change outcomes, which can be seen as *intended*, *partially intended*, or *unintended*. Why focus on change outcomes and not on the change process in this approach? The outcomes of change do not always depend entirely on the decisions and actions of those who are implementing change. Change outcomes are often affected by events and developments outside the organization, and which are beyond the direct control of individual change managers, whose intentions may be swamped by those external factors. How change managers see those outcomes

TABLE 2.1
Images of
Change
Management

Images of Change Outcomes	Images of Managing	
	Controlling (Roles and Activities)	**Shaping (Enhancing Capabilities)**
Intended	director	coach
Partially intended	navigator	interpreter
Unintended	caretaker	nurturer

is therefore a significant component of their image of the change management role. Combining these images of managing and of change outcomes leads to the six images of managing organizational change summarized in table 2.1: *director, coach, navigator, interpreter, caretaker, nurturer.*

Management as Controlling

The image of management as a controlling function has deep historical roots, based on the work of Henri Fayol (1916, 1949) and his contemporaries (Gulick and Urwick, 1937) who described what managers do, captured by the clumsy acronym POSDCoRB. This stands for planning, organizing supervising, directing, coordinating, reporting, and budgeting—activities that the change manager, as well as the general manager, may be expected to carry out. This reflects a "top-down," hierarchical view of managing, associated with the image of organization as machine. The manager's job is to drive the machine in a particular direction. Staff are given defined roles. Resources (inputs) are allocated to departments to produce efficiently the required products and/or services (outputs). This image is today reflected in the work of Henry Mintzberg (2009), who describes contemporary management roles in terms of deciding, focusing, scheduling, communicating, controlling, leading, networking, building coalitions, and getting things done. Harold Sirkin et al. (2005) argue that "soft" factors such as culture, leadership, and motivation do not significantly affect the success of organizational change, and that change managers should concentrate on the "hard" factors instead—controlling, communicating, scheduling, monitoring. The hard factors have three properties:

> First, companies are able to measure them in direct or indirect ways. Second, companies can easily communicate their importance, both within and outside organizations. Third, and perhaps most important, businesses are capable of influencing those elements quickly. Some of the hard factors that affect a transformation initiative are the time necessary to complete it, the number of people required to execute it, and the financial results that intended actions are expected to achieve. Our research shows that change projects fail to get off the ground when companies neglect the hard factors. (Sirkin et al., 2005, p. 109)

Management as Shaping

This image of management as a shaping function, enhancing both individual and organizational capabilities, also has deep roots, based on the "human relations" school of management from the 1930s (Roethlisberger and Dickson, 1939; Mayo, 1945). It has also been influenced by the organization development movement (Bennis, 1969; Burke, 1987). This image is associated with a participative management style that encourages involvement in decision making in general, and in deciding the content and process of change in particular. Employee involvement in change is based on two assumptions. First, that those who are closest to the action will have a better understanding of how things can be improved. Second, that staff are more likely to be committed to making changes work if they have contributed to the design of those changes. Managing people is thus concerned with shaping (and not directly controlling) behavior in ways that benefit the organization. The contemporary concern with "employee engagement" is another manifestation of this image. From a global survey of over 2,500 executives carried out by McKinsey, a management consultancy, Keller et al. (2010, p. 1) argue that the success of transformational change depends on "engaging employees collaboratively throughout the company and throughout the transformation journey," and on "building capabilities—particularly leadership capabilities." They also found that:

> [W]hen leaders ensure that frontline staff members feel a sense of ownership, the results show a 70 per cent success rate for transformation. When frontline employees take the initiative to drive change, transformations have a 71 per cent success rate. When both principles are used, the success rate rises to 79 per cent. . . . Given the importance of collaboration across the whole organization, leaders at companies starting a transformation should put a priority on finding efficient and scalable ways to engage employees. (Keller et al., 2010, pp. 3 and 5)

There is no argument concerning which of these images—controlling or shaping—is "correct" and which is "wrong." It is possible to marshal argument and evidence in support of both frames. We may have to ask, however, which would be more appropriate or effective in given circumstances.

Table 2.1 also identifies three dominant images of change outcomes, based on the extent to which it is assumed that change outcomes can be wholly planned and achieved.

Intended Change Outcomes

The dominant assumption of this image is that intended change outcomes can be achieved as planned. This assumption is at the core of much of the commentary on organizational change and has dominated management practice for over half a century (Burnes, 2014). Change is the realization of prior intent through the actions of change managers. Chin and Benne (1976), whose work has been influential in this area, identify three broad strategies for producing intentional change:

> *Empirical-rational strategies* assume that people pursue their own self-interest. Effective change occurs when a change can be demonstrated as desirable and is aligned with the interests of the group who are affected. Where change has those properties, then intended outcomes will be achieved.
>
> *Normative–re-educative strategies* assume that changes occur when people abandon their traditional, normative orientations and commit to new ways of thinking. Producing intentional outcomes in this way involves changes in information and knowledge, but also in attitudes and values.
>
> *Power-coercive strategies* rely on achieving the intended outcomes through the compliant behavior of those who have less power. Power may of course be exercised by legitimate authority or through other, less legitimate, coercive means.

These three strategies share the view that the intended or desired outcomes of a change program can be achieved through using different change strategies.

Partially Intended Change Outcomes

In this image, it is assumed that some, but not all, planned change outcomes are achievable. Power, processes, interests, and the different skill levels of managers affect their ability to produce intended outcomes. As Mintzberg and Waters (1985) note, the link between initial intent and final outcome is not necessarily a direct one. This is due to the fact that both intended and unintended consequences may emerge from the actions of change managers; intended outcomes may be adapted along the way, or externally imposed forces may modify what was originally intended. For these reasons, change initiatives do not always deliver the outcomes that were planned.

Unintended Change Outcomes

Less attention has been paid to this image in commentary on change management, but this is a common theme in mainstream organization theory. This image recognizes that managers often have great difficulty in achieving the change outcomes that were intended. This difficulty stems from the variety of internal and external forces that can push change in unplanned directions. Internal forces can include interdepartmental politics, long-established working practices that are difficult to dislodge, and deep-seated perceptions and values that are inconsistent with desired changes. External forces can include confrontational industrial relations (which can bring management-inspired changes to a standstill), legislative requirements (tax demands, regulatory procedures), or industry-wide trends affecting an entire sector (trade sanctions, run on the stock market). These internal and external forces typically override the influence of individual change managers, whose intentions can be easily swamped. On occasion, of course, intentions and outcomes may coincide, but this is often the result of chance rather than the outcome of planned, intentional change management actions.

LO 2.3 LO 2.4 Six Images of Change Management

Table 2.1 identifies six different images of change management, each dependent in turn on contrasting images of the function of managing, on the one hand, and of the delivery of change outcomes, on the other. We can now outline each of these images and their theoretical underpinnings.

Change Manager as Director (Controlling Intended Outcomes)

The *director* image views management as controlling and change outcomes as being achievable as planned. The change manager's role here, as the title indicates, is to steer the organization toward the desired outcomes. This assumes that change involves a strategic management choice upon which the well-being and survival of the organization depends. Let us assume that an organization is "out of alignment" with its external environment, say, with regard to the information demands of a changing regulatory system and the more effective responses of competitors. The change management response could involve a new corporate IT system, to capture more efficiently and to analyze larger volumes of data. The director image assumes that this can be mandated, that the new system can be implemented following that command and that it will work well, leading to a high-performing organization that is more closely aligned to its external environment.

© Helder Almeida/Shutterstock

What theoretical support does this image have? As chapter 10 will explain, there are a number of "*n*-step" models, guidelines, or "recipes" for change implementation that are based on the image of the change manager as *director*. The change manager is advised to follow the steps indicated (the number of steps varies from model to model), more or less in the correct sequence, and regardless of the nature of the change, in order to ensure successful outcomes. These models are united by the optimistic view that the intended outcomes of change can be achieved, as long as change managers follow the model. One of the best known "*n*-step" models was developed by John Kotter (1995), who advocates a careful planning process, working through the eight steps in his approach more or less in sequence, and not missing or rushing any of them. Even Kotter acknowledges that change is usually a messy, iterative process. Nevertheless, he remains confident that, if followed correctly, his "recipe" will increase the probability of a successful outcome.

As chapter 10 will also explain, *contingency theories* of change argue that there is no "one best model" for change managers to follow. These perspectives argue that the most appropriate approach is contingent; that is, it depends on the context and on the circumstances (Stace and Dunphy, 2001; Huy, 2001). Contingency theorists thus part company with *n*-step "best practice" guides, suggesting that a range of factors such as the scale and urgency of the change, and the receptivity of those who will be affected, need to be considered when framing an implementation strategy. In other words, the "best way" will depend on a combination of factors—but as long as the change manager takes those factors into account, and follows the contingent model, then the intended outcomes should be delivered.

Change Manager as Navigator (Controlling Some Intended Outcomes)

In the *navigator* image, control is still at the heart of management action, although a variety of external factors mean that, although change managers may achieve some intended change outcomes, they may have little control over other results. Outcomes are at least partly emergent rather than completely planned, and result from a variety of influences, competing interests, and processes. For example, a change manager may wish to restructure a business unit by introducing cross-functional teams to assist product development. While a change manager may be able to establish teams (an intentional outcome), getting them to work effectively may be challenging if there is a history of distrust, information hoarding, and boundary protection by the business units. In this situation, functional managers may appoint to the cross-functional teams people who they know will keep the interests of their department uppermost and block any decisions that might decrease their organizational power (an unintended outcome of putting the teams in place).

© Nova Development

Exploring why change initiatives stall, Eric Beaudan (2006, p. 6) notes, "No amount of advance thinking, planning and communication guarantees success. That's because change is by nature unpredictable and unwieldy. The military have a great way to put this: 'no plan survives contact with the enemy.'" He also argues that "leaders need to recognize that the initial change platform they create is only valid for a short time. They need to conserve their energy to confront the problematic issues that will stem from passive resistance and from the unpredictable side effects that change itself creates" (Beaudan, 2006, p. 6). Change may be only partially controllable, with change managers navigating the process toward a set of outcomes, not all of which may have been intended.

What theoretical support does this image have? Processual theories (see chapter 10) argue that organizational changes unfold over time in a messy and iterative manner, and thus rely on the image of change manager as navigator (Langley et al., 2013; Dawson and Andriopoulos, 2014). In this perspective, the outcomes of change are shaped by a combination of factors including the past, present, and future *context* in which the organization functions, including external and internal factors; the substance of the change, which could be new technology, process redesign, a new payment system, or changes to organization structure and culture; the implementation *process* (tasks, decisions, timing); *political behavior*, inside and outside the organization; and the interactions between these factors. The role of the change manager is not to direct, but to identify options, accumulate resources, monitor progress, and navigate a way through the complexity.

Change managers must accept that there will be unanticipated disruptions, and that options and resources need to be reviewed. Change navigators are also advised to encourage staff involvement. For senior management, rather than directing and controlling the process, the priority is to ensure receptivity to change and that those involved have the skills and motivation to contribute. However, given the untidy, nonlinear nature of change processes, navigators—consistent with the metaphor—have room to maneuver; the course of change may need to be plotted and replotted in response to new information and developments. There is no guarantee that the final destination will be that which was initially intended. In some instances, change may be ongoing, with no clear end point.

Change Manager as Caretaker (Controlling Unintended Outcomes)

In the *caretaker* image, the (ideal) management role is still one of control, although the ability to exercise that control is severely constrained by a range of internal and external forces that propel change relatively independent of management intentions. For example, despite the change manager's desire to encourage entrepreneurial and innovative behavior, this may become a failing exercise as the organization grows, becomes more bureaucratic,

© Jeff DeWeerd/Getty Images

and enacts strategic planning cycles, rules, regulations, and centralized practices. In this situation, the issues linked to inexorable growth are outside the control of an individual change manager. In this rather pessimistic image, at best managers are caretakers, shepherding their organizations along to the best of their ability.

Theoretical support for the caretaker image can be drawn from three organizational theories: life-cycle, population ecology, and institutional theory.

Life-cycle theory views organizations passing through well-defined stages from birth to growth, maturity, and then decline or death. These stages are part of a natural developmental cycle. There is an underlying logic or trajectory, and the stages are sequential (Van de Ven and Poole, 1995). There is little that managers can

TABLE 2.2
Life-Cycle Stages and Caretaker Activities

Developmental Stage	Caretaker Activities
Entrepreneurial Stage Founder initiates an idea	• Make sure that resources are available • Establish market niche • Design processes to aid innovation and creativity • Ensure founder generates commitment to vision
Collectivity Stage Coordination through informal means as group identity develops	• Coordinate communication and decision making • Build cohesion and morale with goals and culture • Develop skills through appropriate reward systems
Formalization Stage Formalization of operations, emphasizing rules and procedures, efficiency and stability	• Facilitate shift to professional management • Monitor internal operations and external environment • Focus procedures on efficiency and quality • Strike balance between autonomy, coordination, and control
Elaboration Stage Change and renewal as structure becomes more complex and environment changes	• Adapt current products and develop new ones • Ensure structure facilitates divisional coordination • Plan for turnaround, cutbacks, and renewal

Source: Adapted from Harrison and Shirom, 1999, pp. 307–14.

do to prevent this natural development; at best they are caretakers of the organization as it passes through the various stages. Harrison and Shirom (1999) identify the caretaker activities associated with the main stages in the organizational life cycle, and these are summarized in table 2.2. Change managers thus have a limited role, smoothing the various transitions rather than controlling whether or not they occur.

Population ecology theory focuses on how the environment selects organizations for survival or extinction, drawing on biology and neo-Darwinism (White et al., 1997). Whole populations of organizations can in this perspective change as a result of ongoing cycles of *variation*, *selection*, and *retention*:

• Organizational *variation* occurs as the result of random chance.
• Organizational *selection* occurs when an environment selects organizations that best fit the conditions.
• Organizational *retention* involves forces (e.g., inertia and persistence) that sustain organizational forms, thus counteracting variation and selection (Van de Ven and Poole, 1995).

Some population ecology theorists suggest that there are limited actions that change managers can take to influence these forces, such as:

• interacting, perhaps through key stakeholders, with other organizations to lessen the impact of environmental factors;
• repositioning the organization in a new market or other environment.

In general, however, the implication of this perspective is that managers have little sway over change where whole populations of organizations are affected by external forces.

For example, managers of many financial institutions struggled to deal with the widespread global crisis triggered by the collapse of Lehman Brothers, an investment bank, in September 2008. That event affected adversely the global population of finance organizations (and the governments that had to recapitalize them).

Institutional theory argues that change managers take broadly similar decisions and actions across whole populations of organizations. The central concern of this perspective is not to explain change, but to understand "the startling homogeneity of organizational forms and practices" (DiMaggio and Powell, 1983, p. 148). These similarities can be explained by the pressures associated with the interconnectedness of organizations that operate in the same sector or environment. DiMaggio and Powell (1983) distinguish three such pressures, which in practice interact:

- *coercive*, including social and cultural expectations and government-mandated changes;
- *mimetic*, as organizations imitate or model themselves on the structures and practices of other organizations in their field, often those that they consider more successful and legitimate;
- *normative*, through the professionalization of work such that managers in different organizations adopt similar values and working methods that are similar to each other.

Not all organizations succumb to these pressures; there are what DiMaggio and Powell call "deviant peers." However, the assumption is that these external forces are inexorable and individual managers have only limited ability to implement change outcomes that are not consistent with these forces. At best, change managers are caretakers with little influence over the long-term direction of change.

Change Manager as Coach (Shaping Intended Outcomes)

In the *coach* image, the assumption is that change managers (or change consultants) can intentionally shape the organization's capabilities in particular ways. Like a sports coach, the change manager shapes the organization's or the team's capabilities to ensure that, in a competitive situation, it will be more likely to succeed. Rather than dictating the state of each play as the director might do, the coach relies on establishing the right values, skills, and "drills" so that the organization's members can achieve the desired outcomes.

What theoretical support does this image have? Organization development (OD) theory reinforces the image of the change manager as coach, by stressing the importance of values such as humanism, democracy, and individual development (see chapter 9). OD "interventions" are designed to develop appropriate skills, reduce interpersonal and interdivisional conflict, and to structure activities in ways that help the organization's members better understand, define, and solve their own problems. As the OD movement evolved, the emphasis shifted from team-based and other small-scale interventions to organization-wide programs, designed to "get the whole system in the room" (Weisbord, 1987, p. 19; Burnes and Cook, 2012). As a movement underpinned by values, OD advocates can be evangelical about the advantages of helping organization members develop their own skills in problem solving to achieve their intended outcomes, claiming not only that the approach works but that it produces results with less resistance, greater speed, and higher commitment (Axelrod, 1992).

© Jorg Greuel/Getty Images

Change Manager as Interpreter (Shaping Some Intended Outcomes)

The change manager as *interpreter* has the task of creating meaning for others, helping them to make sense of events and developments that, in themselves, constitute a changed organization. It is up to change managers to represent to others just what these changes mean. However, there are often competing interpretations of the same issues, especially where there are different groups who do not necessarily share common interests and perceptions (Buchanan and Dawson, 2007). This suggests that only some meanings—and therefore some change intentions—are likely to be realized.

In this contested climate, managers as interpreters "need to be able to provide legitimate arguments and reasons for why their actions fit within the situation and should be viewed as legitimate" (Barge and Oliver, 2003, p. 138). Downsizing, for example, is one situation where competing interpretations are inevitable. Change managers may portray this action as a way of strengthening the organization in the face of environmental pressures and thus protecting more effectively the jobs of those who remain. Others, however, may tell different stories, of management incompetence and of underhand ways of "outplacing" politically troublesome individuals or even whole departments under the cover of "efficiency." Stephen Denning (2004), mentioned in chapter 1, emphasizes the power of storytelling, observing, "I've seen stories help galvanize an organization around a defined business goal" (p. 122), and that a "well told story" can be more inspiring and motivating than a detailed analytical approach. In other words, when it comes to interpreting the meaning of change for others, the effective interpreter tells better stories than the competition.

What theoretical support does this image have? Architect of the influential processual perspective on organizational change, Andrew Pettigrew (1985, p. 442) sees the "management of meaning" as central. He argues, "The management of meaning refers to a process of symbol construction and value use designed to create legitimacy for one's own ideas, actions, and demands, and to delegitimize the demands of one's opponents." The change manager seeking to introduce significant, strategic change may thus be faced with the prospect of trying to create a story that will dislodge a well-established ideology, culture, and system of meaning. Change managers, of course, do not have a monopoly on storytelling skills; sometimes the stories of others are better, and they "win."

The interpreter image is central to Karl Weick's (1995; 2000) sense-making theory of organizational change. Sense-making, Weick explains, is what we do when we face a problem—a surprise or a crisis, for example—and have to work out how we are going to respond. For sense-making to work in these situations, however, four factors have to be present. First, it has to be possible to take some action to address the problem; almost any action will do, as long as experiment and exploration are allowed. Second, that action must be directed toward a purpose or goal. Third, the context must allow people to be attentive to what is happening and to update their understanding accordingly. Fourth, people need to be allowed to share their views openly, in a climate of mutual trust and respect. Weick calls these four components of sense-making *animation*, *direction*, *attention*, and *respectful interaction*.

Interpreters at Work *Four Conditions for Changing Mindsets*

Emily Lawson and Colin Price (2010) argue that the success of change relies on persuading individuals to change their "mindsets"—to think differently about their jobs and the way in which they work. They identify three levels of organizational change. First, desired outcomes (increased revenue) can often be achieved without changing working practices (selling noncore assets, for example). Second, employees can be asked to change working practices in line with current thinking (finding ways to reduce waste, for example). The third level involves fundamental changes in organization culture, in collective thinking and behavior—from reactive to proactive, hierarchical to collegial, inward-looking to externally focused. There are four conditions for changing mindsets at level three:

Employees will alter their mindsets only if they see the point of the change and agree with it—at least enough to give it a try. The surrounding structures (reward and recognition systems, for example) must be in tune with the new behaviour. Employees must have the skills to do what it requires. Finally, they must see people they respect modelling it actively. Each of these conditions is realized independently; together they add up to a way of changing the behaviour of people in organizations by changing attitudes about what can and should happen at work.

(Lawson and Price, 2010, p. 32)

Weick (2000, p. 225) also observes that emergent, continuous, cumulative change is the norm in most organizations. The textbook focus on planned, transformational, revolutionary, disruptive change is partial and misleading. Emergent change involves the development of new ways of working that were not previously planned:

> The recurring story is one of autonomous initiatives that bubble up internally; continuous emergent change; steady learning from both failure and success; strategy implementation that is replaced by strategy making; the appearance of innovations that are unplanned, unforeseen, and unexpected; and small actions that have surprisingly large consequences.

Emergent changes are thus driven by continuous sense-making, often by frontline staff, and not by senior management. Indeed, top team intervention may inhibit change. Weick (2000, p. 234) argues that, while the four sense-making activities of animation, direction, attention, and respectful interaction are necessary for learning, adaptation, and change, "they are also the four activities most likely to be curbed severely in a hierarchical command-and-control system." For successful change, Weick concludes, management must become interpreters, recognizing that "organizational change is emergent change laid down by choices made on the front line. *The job of management is to author interpretations and labels that capture the patterns in those adaptive choices. . . . Management doesn't create change. It certifies change*" (Weick, 2000, p. 238; emphasis added).

Change Manager as Nurturer (Shaping Unintended Outcomes)

The image of change manager as *nurturer* assumes that even small changes can have a large impact on organizations, and that managers may be unable to control the outcomes of these changes (Thietart and Forgues, 1995). However, they may nurture the organization, developing qualities that enable positive self-organizing. Like a parent's relationship with a child, future outcomes are nurtured or shaped, but the ability to produce intended

© pagadesign/Getty Images

outcomes is limited because of the impact of much wider, sometimes chaotic forces and influences. Specific directions and outcomes of change cannot be intentionally produced but rather emerge and are shaped through the qualities and capabilities of the organization.

Perspectives supporting the nurturer image include chaos theory and Confucian/Taoist theory.

Chaos theory argues that organizational change is nonlinear, is fundamental rather than incremental, and does not necessarily entail growth (table 2.3). Chaos theorists, drawing also on complexity theory, explore how organizations "continuously regenerate themselves through adaptive learning and interactive structural change. These efforts periodically result in the spontaneous emergence of a whole new dynamic order, through a process called self-organization" (Lichtenstein, 2000, p. 131). The phenomenon of self-organization is driven by the chaotic nature of organizations, which in turn is a consequence of having to grapple simultaneously with both change and stability. In this context, the change manager has to nurture the capacity for self-organization, with limited ability to influence the direction and nature of the spontaneous new orders that may emerge. This may sound abstract and puzzling, but this describes the emergent strategy—nurturing capabilities—that the successful Brazilian entrepreneur Ricardo Semler (2000) adopted in his manufacturing company, Semco. This explains how Semco successfully diversified into electronics.

Semco *A Chaotic Business?*

Semco is a well-known South American manufacturing business. The company has a flat hierarchy and emphasizes staff empowerment to engage in decisions about virtually all company issues, from strategy to setting their own salaries. Ricardo Semler, the Brazilian majority owner of Semco, discussed how the company moved away from manufacturing, making industrial pumps and white goods, and into e-business and other services that now account for 75 percent of its business. Many of the company practices and philosophies illustrate principles of chaos theory. For example, Semler maintains that the company successfully "went digital without a strategy." He attributes this to what some might term a chaotic management style whereby, in his words:

[R]ather than dictate Semco's identity from on high, I've let our employees shape it through their individual efforts, interests, and initiatives.

That rather unusual management philosophy has drawn a good deal of attention over the years. . . . The way we work—letting our employees choose what they do, where and when they do it, and even how they get paid—has seemed a little too radical for mainstream companies.

. . . [S]ome of the principles that underlie the way we work will become increasingly common and even necessary in the new economy. In particular, I believe we have an organization that is able to transform itself continuously and organically—without formulating complicated mission statements and strategies, announcing a bunch of top-down directives, or bringing in an army of change-management consultants. (Semler, 2000, pp. 51–52)

TABLE 2.3
Chaos Theory and Change Management

Change Management Actions	Core Elements
Managing transitions	Destabilize people Get them involved in decision making and problem solving
Building resilience	Develop ability to absorb change
Destabilizing the system	Create a state of tension, act as devil's advocate Seek disconfirmation of organizational beliefs Nurture creativity to cope with a chaotic environment
Managing order and disorder, the present and the future	Balance the needs for order and change
Creating and maintaining a learning organization	Make continuous learning available to everyone

Source: Adapted from Tetenbaum (1998).

Confucian/Taoist theory—perhaps better regarded as a philosophy—adopts assumptions with regard to organizational change that are fundamentally different from Western views (Marshak, 1993). Change is regarded as:

- cyclical, involving constant ebb and flow;
- processional, involving harmonious movement from one state to another;
- journey-oriented, involving cyclical change with no end state;
- based on maintaining equilibrium, or achieving natural harmony;
- observed and followed by those who are involved, who seek harmony with their universe; and
- normal rather than exceptional.

Taoist Approach to Change Leadership

Richard Pascale and Jerry Sternin (2005) discuss the role of change leaders in circumstances where there are no "off the shelf" remedies or coping strategies for dealing with the organization's problems. The role of the leader, they argue, is to be a facilitator rather than a "path breaker." This means identifying and encouraging the "positive deviants" in the organization, who are already doing things differently—and better. The key "is to engage the members of the community you want to change in the process of discovery, making them the evangelists of their own conversion experience" (p. 74). To illustrate what is involved, they quote the well-known Taoist poem written by Lao-tzu:

Learn from the people

Plan with the people

Begin with what they have

Build on what they know

Of the best leaders

When the task is accomplished

The people all remark

We have done it ourselves

Organizational change outcomes from this standpoint are not intended so much as produced through the nurturing of a harmonious Yin-Yang philosophy in which each new order contains its own negation. Embedded in this philosophy, therefore, is an image of the change manager as nurturer.

LO 2.5 Using the Six-Images Framework

Each of these images of managing change represents a Weberian "ideal type." They are "ideal" in the sense that a "pure" version of the concept may not exist, but they give us a set of benchmarks, or templates, against which practice can be compared. (Note: "ideal" does not in this case mean "desirable.") These images are not separate categories; they form two continua, from controlling to shaping management roles, and from planned to unintended outcomes. The boundaries of these six images are blurred, and their elements may overlap in practice. The case study at the end of this chapter, "The Turnaround Story at Leonard Cheshire," illustrates how this happens in practice.

These six images are enduring, each having, as we have seen, differing theoretical underpinnings that serve to legitimate them. Nevertheless, as already noted, the *caretaker* and *nurturer* images are less frequently discussed in relation to change management—although they are more widely accepted in other domains of organization theory, particularly where there is less practice orientation. In contrast, the *director*, *navigator*, *coach*, and *interpreter* images involve more active, intentional, and directional views of the ability of change managers to produce organizational change, whether through control or shaping actions. In this sense, they are more positive images than caretaking and nurturing, which reflect a more reactive view of managerial effectiveness—in terms of both why changes occur and the extent to which these changes are driven by management intentions. Managers obviously do not like to feel that they are insignificant players in their organizational worlds. Rather, the assumption that they are able to produce positive and intentional change is an important component of the Western change management lexicon.

The need to be seen to be producing positive intentional change was demonstrated to us in the following example. A well-known change consultant based in Washington, DC, told us how he intended to use the six-images framework in a major international organization to help their staff to understand the impact of the culture of the organization and its many competing discourses of change. The company agreed to use the framework and even requested copyright permission. However, some senior executives argued against using it, "because it might legitimate managers not assuming responsibility for initiating and managing change; it might give them an out." This was for two reasons. First, there was the possibility of seeing change having unintended outcomes. Second, there was the possibility that change managers would have minimal impact where the organization was dominated by enforced change from the outside. The six-images framework was not used.

This example is instructive for the following reasons. Some commentators distinguish between topics that are "sacred" and those that are "profane." Some topics are not to be questioned, and to do so is not legitimate. The experience of our Washington consultant indicates that the idea that change can be controlled to produce intentional outcomes is sacred. It is profane to suggest otherwise—that managers may be overwhelmed by forces beyond their control. The view that we would like to promote in this text is that it is time to end this divide. It is necessary to recognize that, in the long run, such a distinction is unhelpful. This stance hinders change managers by discouraging a reflective, self-critical view of their actions and of what is achievable in any given context.

So, how should the six-images framework be used in practice? There are three inter-related issues where reflection on the part of the change manager is valuable: surfacing assumptions about change, assessing dominant images of change, and using multiple images and perspectives of change.

Surfacing Assumptions about Change

The six-images framework guides us in reflecting on the images and assumptions we hold about managing change. As we noted at the start of this chapter, we all have mental models and these help us to simplify and to make sense of the complex organizational worlds in which we operate. At the same time as they simplify and illuminate, they turn our attention toward some things and away from others. Being aware of the mental models with which we work helps us think more carefully about their relevance—and the extent to which the assumptions they entail are really ones that are going to be of assistance to us in approaching organizational change.

Being aware of these images enables change managers to assess the assumptions that are being made by others with whom they are working or interacting or from whom they are taking advice. Resulting from this assessment may be actions to reorient the images others have of the particular change in which they are involved by providing new images through which the change can be seen.

For example, a change manager working with a navigator image may get others, who may view change through a director image, to acknowledge that unanticipated outcomes may occur as change unfolds. The navigator may persuade others to accept that one possibility of engaging in a change is that their current view of what is desired at the end may shift as the process unfolds and new possibilities emerge. In this sense, awareness of differing change management images can lead to an educational process within a change team. It requires encouragement of conversations around images and assumptions about the anticipated change, testing these with the group, and ensuring that all members of the team share common change image(s). This ensures that individual change managers are not talking past one another and making assumptions that are not shared by others.

Assessing Dominant Images of Change

The six-images framework encourages change managers to reflect on whether they are dominated by one particular image, and on the limitations of that perspective. For example, the director image turns our attention to the outcomes we want to achieve and the steps needed to get there; at the same time, it turns our attention away from whether the outcomes are really achievable (or even desirable) and whether unintentional outcomes also might occur should we pursue a particular change course.

The framework also directs attention to whether the organization in which the change is to occur is dominated by a particular view of what is achievable and how change should unfold. Indeed, Hamel and Prahalad (1994) point out that some organizations are dominated by a particular view of how things should get done—almost to the point where the view is part of the "genetic coding" of the organization and is therefore seen as natural and not open for negotiation. In this case, change managers whose images are not consistent with the dominant organizational image may experience frustration and stress as they work with a change that may be seen as less legitimate or irrelevant.

Using Multiple Images and Perspectives of Change

It is possible that a change manager's "image-in-use" may depend on their personal preferences, or it may be an unconscious decision based simply on the use of a familiar approach. One of the advantages of exposure to the range of images is to reduce the likelihood of a change manager using a single image because of a lack of understanding of the range of options. The six-images framework directs attention to the range of available options and to how their use may vary between contexts. A conscious choice of image-in-use can be based on at least the following four sets of considerations.

Image-in-use depends on the type of change. Change managers may assess some types of change as being more amenable to one image or approach rather than another. An interpreter approach might be seen as possible for one but not another type of change. Change managers are thus advised to adjust their image of change, and the perception of what is possible, depending on the situation. Anderson and Anderson (2001), for example, adopt a coaching image, arguing that developmental and transitional change can be managed from this perspective, but not transformational change. They draw on a navigator image in relation to transformational change, arguing that there are too many intangibles that can inhibit the achievement of predetermined outcomes; what is required is a mindset that accepts that organizations can be led into the unknown without the end point being predictable in advance.

Image-in-use depends on the context of the change. As chapter 10 explains, management approach should ideally be consistent with the context. In some settings, organizational members may be unhappy with the status quo and ready for change. The appropriate image-in-use in this context could be coach or interpreter, involving people in order to identify desired change outcomes and how those should be achieved. Where change faces hostility and resistance, and intended outcomes are thus in jeopardy, a caretaker or navigator image may be more appropriate. However, if change is necessary for the organization's survival, then a director image may necessary.

Image-in-use depends on the phase of change. Change processes pass through different phases (see chapter 10). Change managers may thus choose to use different images at different stages of the process, or depending on perceptions of the phase that change has reached. For example, in initiating an externally imposed or encouraged change (such as the Malcolm Baldrige Quality Awards) in order to continue as an accredited supplier, change managers may feel that the caretaker image is appropriate, as change was not generated internally. However, as change progresses, an interpreter image may become relevant, conveying to staff new meanings associated with the implementation such as enhanced professionalism and the possibility of diversifying into new areas.

Image-in-use depends on simultaneous involvement in multiple changes. At any given time, in any one organization, there are often many changes unfolding, in different business units or across the organization as a whole. Some of those changes could be externally driven, and a caretaker image may apply. Where externally generated change is not negotiable—a change in legislation, for example, demanding compliance—then a director image may be necessary. Other initiatives, however, may be internally generated, and a director image may again be appropriate to achieving desired outcomes in a controlled way. This implies that skilled and reflective change managers are able to adapt, to move between images depending on how conditions are developing. It may also be appropriate to manage simultaneously with multiple images where these are related to different but concurrent initiatives. As noted earlier, the Leonard Cheshire case below illustrates this possibility.

SELF-ASSESSMENT

What Is Your Image of Managing Change?

LO 2.5

What is your personal image of how to manage organizational change? This assessment is based on the six-images framework, and it sets out a series of beliefs, some of which are contradictory. This has been designed to profile your own beliefs and to encourage reflection concerning your approach to change. This is an assessment, not a test; there are no right or wrong answers. It should take you only 10 to 15 minutes to complete and score the assessment.

Rate each statement (tick the appropriate box) with regard to how closely it reflects your views, using this scale:

1	2	3	4	5
Strongly Disagree	Disagree	Neither Agree nor Disagree	Agree	Strongly Agree

		1	2	3	4	5
1	Communications should emphasize the inevitability of change and how best to cope with or survive it.	❑	❑	❑	❑	❑
2	Managers don't have to do anything about resistance to change because in the long run it won't have any impact.	❑	❑	❑	❑	❑
3	Managers' ability to control change is limited because other forces propel change regardless of managers' actions.	❑	❑	❑	❑	❑
4	The aim of communication about change is to send clear, unambiguous messages, so organization members understand what is going to happen and what is required of them.	❑	❑	❑	❑	❑
5	Articulating a vision is essential to successful change; top management should do this early in the process.	❑	❑	❑	❑	❑
6	Communication about change needs to foster supportive conditions and to convey the need for members to be ready to engage in change as it unfolds, often in unpredictable ways.	❑	❑	❑	❑	❑
7	Although managers can exert some control over how change unfolds, external factors also affect the process.	❑	❑	❑	❑	❑
8	A search for the deepest values of the organization is required, to find a vision that resonates with the organization's members; a vision cannot be provided by a CEO.	❑	❑	❑	❑	❑
9	Organizational change is unpredictable, and resistance may or may not affect the outcomes, but managers should respond to resistance anyway, as this could address the arguments.	❑	❑	❑	❑	❑
10	An appropriate vision for change is most likely to emerge through consultation with the organization's members.	❑	❑	❑	❑	❑

(Continued)

11	Probably the best way for managers to implement change is to shape staff abilities to succeed in the new circumstances.	❑	❑	❑	❑	❑
12	Communicating about change involves attending to the varied interests of stakeholders and persuading them of the benefits of change or, if necessary, modifying changes to produce the best outcome in a given situation.	❑	❑	❑	❑	❑
13	It is generally possible for managers to have significant control over how change happens in their organization.	❑	❑	❑	❑	❑
14	Managers should help resisters develop the capacity to cope with particular organizational changes.	❑	❑	❑	❑	❑
15	Communication about change should ensure that organization members are "on the same page" about the values linked to the change and the actions appropriate to those values.	❑	❑	❑	❑	❑
16	A vision for organizational change emerges from the clash of chaotic and unpredictable change forces; a vision cannot be articulated early in a change process.	❑	❑	❑	❑	❑
17	While managers cannot directly control how change happens in an organization, they can nurture staff capabilities, and thus encourage positive self-organizing.	❑	❑	❑	❑	❑
18	Managers should redirect change to go around resistance, when that occurs, rather than try to overcome it.	❑	❑	❑	❑	❑
19	To implement change successfully, managers must interpret the change for organizational members and help them to make sense of what is going on.	❑	❑	❑	❑	❑
20	Visions for organizational change are likely to have a limited impact unless they are consistent with events unfolding outside the organization; change comes less from a vision and more from the influence of external forces.	❑	❑	❑	❑	❑
21	Communication about change is best done with a persuasive account, to ensure that as many people as possible, inside and outside the organization, share a common understanding.	❑	❑	❑	❑	❑
22	Managers should deal with resistance to change by helping the organization's members understand the changes and what these imply for their own roles.	❑	❑	❑	❑	❑
23	Leaders cannot impose a vision for change, as competing stakeholders have different views; effective change management involves navigating these tensions.	❑	❑	❑	❑	❑
24	Managers can and should overcome resistance to change.	❑	❑	❑	❑	❑

Source: This assessment was designed by, and is reproduced here with the permission of Jean Bartunek, Professor of Management and Organization, Boston College, MA.

SELF-ASSESSMENT

Scoring

Transfer your ratings to this table. Add the ratings for each image, and calculate your average.

Director		**Coach**	
4	_____	10	_____
5	_____	11	_____
13	_____	14	_____
24	_____	15	_____
total:	_____	total:	_____
÷ 4 = average:	_____	÷ 4 = average:	_____

Navigator		**Interpreter**	
7	_____	8	_____
12	_____	19	_____
18	_____	21	_____
23	_____	22	_____
total:	_____	total:	_____
÷ 4 = average:	_____	÷ 4 = average:	_____

Caretaker		**Nurturer**	
1	_____	6	_____
2	_____	9	_____
3	_____	16	_____
20	_____	17	_____
total:	_____	total:	_____
÷ 4 = average:	_____	÷ 4 = average:	_____

You will have an average score of between 1 and 5 for each image. Consider the following questions, and where possible compare your answers with colleagues:

1. What are your two highest scores? These are your "dominant" images. Check your understanding of those images with the descriptions in table 2.4.

2. Do any of these images of change management involve actions that you would be uncomfortable taking? Why?

3. If you have one or two dominant images, how do you feel about being advised to use the other, low-scoring images, if conditions indicate that would be more appropriate?

4 If your six scores are similar, does this mean that you are able to act differently in different change settings?

TABLE 2.4
Six Images of Change Management

Image	Sound Bite	Approach to Change	When to Use
Director	"This is what is going to happen"	Management choice, command and control	When urgent change is required for survival, and change manager has better knowledge of solutions
Navigator	"I will tell you what I would like to happen"	Plan with care, but expect the unexpected	When the organization's history, culture, context, and politics will affect change plans
Caretaker	"Let us explore what might be possible"	Accept the force of external context factors and adapt as necessary	When environmental forces are overwhelming, affecting the entire sector
Coach	"How can we develop our capability to deal with change?"	Shape systemic capabilities—values, skills, drills—to respond effectively to change	When the organization's members need to resolve interpersonal conflicts and build understanding to solve their own problems
Interpreter	"We need to think differently about this"	Managing meaning through interpretations that explain and convey understanding to others	When different stakeholders have competing views of the same issues and they do not share common interests
Nurturer	"This is everybody's problem—how will we fix it?"	Develop resilience, encourage involvement, continuous learning, and self-organizing	When faced with competing and changing external pressures requiring constant regeneration and adaptive learning

We will refer to these images of change management throughout the book. We would therefore like you to reflect on the following additional questions:

1 Is it likely that most people will have one dominant image of change management?

2 Are change leaders more likely to be successful if they remain faithful to their dominant style(s)?

3 Are change leaders who have the capacity to apply a range of different images more likely to be successful?

4 In your judgement, do most managers have the behavioral flexibility to move between different styles, or do they tend to apply just one or a limited range of approaches?

EXERCISE 2.1

Assessing Change Managers' Images

LO 2.2

Your task, individually or in a small group, is to find and interview two people who have managed organizational change, or who have been directly involved in change implementation. Design a "topic guide" for your interviews. This should cover, for example, the organizational context; your interviewees' roles in relation to change; the nature of the changes in which they were involved; why those changes were significant; how the changes were implemented, covering key decisions, actions, turning points, crises; how your interviewees would describe their personal management styles; the outcomes of those changes—successful, or not. If possible, choose to interview managers from different organizations and sectors, to provide contrast. Once you have collected this interview evidence, consider the following questions:

- Which images of change did those two managers illustrate?
- How did those images affect their change management decisions and actions?
- Where they drew on more than one image, to what extent were those related to

  type of change?

  context of change?

  phase of change?

  their involvement in more than one change at the same time?

- What other factors did you identify?
- What conclusions can you draw from your analysis about the effects of images and mental models on the way that your interviewees approached their change management roles?

EXERCISE 2.2

The Turn-around Story at Leonard Cheshire

LO 2.5

Issues to Consider as You Read This Story   D, N, Coal

1. What image, or images, of change management does Clare Pelham illustrate?
2. What insights does this story have to offer concerning the role of the change leader?
3. What lessons about managing organizational change can we take from this experience and apply to other organizations, in healthcare and in other sectors?

The Context

Leonard Cheshire was the largest charity in the United Kingdom, supporting thousands of people with physical and learning disabilities and acquired brain injuries. The charity's support included care in a range of residential settings, respite services, and skills development to build confidence and to improve employability. The charity employed 7,500 staff in over 300 different services, in the United Kingdom and internationally. The charity also had the support of 3,500 volunteers.

The Problem

Clare Pelham was appointed chief executive in November 2010. The charity's income was £155 million, and it had a deficit of £5.4 million. The tenures of four previous chief executives had been short. Her immediate predecessor lasted 18 months, implementing a reorganization with the loss of 100 managerial and administrative jobs. Japan Tobacco International had been chosen, with much controversy, as a commercial partner. The Care Quality Commission, a national healthcare regulator, was about to restrict activities at some of the charity's care homes. The charity was founded in 1948 by Group Captain Geoffrey Leonard, who died in 1992. Pelham had worked as a volunteer at a Leonard Cheshire home as a teenager, but her ambitions had taken her into a management career in other public- and private-sector organizations. Now, how to solve the charity's problems?

The Solution

Phase 1: Pelham said, "I always start with the people." On her first day in her new role, she met with each of her senior managers individually. She then visited the charity's homes. Action was swift:

(Continued)

I started in November and by the first week in December we had a new strategy. You need to do things quickly. You also need to be clear as a group of people about why are we here? What do we believe in and how are we going to achieve it?

One of her other first actions was to hold a management board meeting with no agenda:

We talked about how we were going to work together. I suggested they all share with each other the things they had said to me personally. We came up with some ways of working. It was guidelines like, if you write anything down, it can be shown to anyone, copied or forwarded to anyone and you should be prepared to stand by what you have written.

The aim was to develop openness and trust. The guidelines also applied to conversations; "We agreed you should never say something about someone you would not say to their face." Pelham also banned the "b" and "f" words: blame, fault, failure. In order to build pride in the work of the charity, Pelham encouraged a culture of "you don't walk past":

If I am late or if anybody is late for anything and the reason is that it is because they saw something that was not OK and they stopped to address it, then that's fantastic. If you are doing something to make life easier or better for any individual person, what else could you be doing that is more important than that?

Phase 2: How did the focus on people and culture address the charity's financial problems? Pelham was also concerned with procedures, measurement, and information:

I think leadership is a caring profession. You cannot do it well if you do not care about the people. You need the heart, but you need to enable the people day to day and engage your head so I am quite big on having procedures because that's how you measure. Let's have ways of doing things, to protect the confidentiality of whistle-blowers, for example, or ensure safeguarding. Sometimes you want to depart from them but let's do that knowing you are doing it. You need information gathering so that you can see where you are and see a trend. It is no good saying that this is a good idea and not measuring. That's not going to do disabled people any good at all.

Fundraising was to become everyone's business, not a specialist function, and Pelham held regular meetings to gather ideas and prompt action. Significant savings came from making procurement more efficient and by reducing spending on expensive agency staff by more than a third while improving continuity of care. Pelham received personal weekly reports on these efficiencies. Speaking about her leadership role and style, she said:

It is my responsibility when things go wrong and if anyone is to blame it is me and if anyone is to go and answer for it or resign because of it, it is me. If you accept that people share your commitment and passion and values and they are not doing things as well as they can, you have to look in the mirror first and ask: what is it that you could have done to help them do the job they came in to do?

One indicator of Pelham's passion and values concerned her attitude to the traditional practice of making short support visits to older people. These visits, provided by local councils and care services, were funded to last only 15 minutes. She decided to start a campaign to stop this practice:

Our 15 minute campaign came out of a conversation where one of my colleagues talked me through what a 15 minute visit meant. I asked, "Are we OK with this?" We decided we would no longer bid for them and we would actively campaign against them. Our staff hate these visits and every day see people suffering. They love that we are prominent in trying to make this stop.

The charity's condemnation of these visits triggered outrage at the practice and was headline news. The government's Care Bill was amended accordingly—a triumph for Pelham.

The Outcomes

In 2013, the charity's income was £160 million, with a surplus of £3 million. Voluntary donations had increased by 20 percent over the previous two years, to £13.4 million. In 2014, Leonard Cheshire Disability had a surplus, and it started to expand and refurbish its supported living accommodation.

Story Sources

Carlisle, D. 2014. The woman who banned the f-word. *Health Service Journal* (February 28): 24–28.

http://www.leonardcheshire.org/

Additional Reading

Battilana, J., and Casciaro, T. 2013. The network secrets of great change agents. *Harvard Business Review* 91(7/8):62–68. Research concluding that it is the networks of change agents that can make them more successful, especially where the nature of their networks ("bridging" or "cohesive") matches the type of change that they are pursuing.

Chatman, J. 2014. Culture change at Genentech: Accelerating strategic and financial accomplishments. *California Management Review* 56(2):113–29. This is a case study of successful culture change in a pharmaceuticals company. The senior vice president, Jennifer Cook, said: "My leadership philosophy is that individuals are people first and employees second. Our best employees make a choice to come to work every day and we have to earn the right to have them want to come back. The way I look at it is that I'm bringing a framework and infrastructure as a way to harness the group's thinking, but it's their thinking" (p. 113). Contrast this philosophy with that of Ron Johnson at J. C. Penney (chapter 1).

McCreary, L. 2010. Kaiser Permanente's innovation on the front lines. *Harvard Business Review* 88(9):92–97. This famous healthcare organization has an internal "innovation consultancy" that employs change agents to watch, note, sketch, and identify better ways of working, asking staff how they feel about their work, holding "deep dive" events with staff to generate ideas. The aim is to introduce service-oriented innovation quickly and economically. This is a *caretaker* image of change managers—controlling, but looking for unpredictable outcomes.

Pascale, R. T., and Sternin, J. 2005. Your company's secret change agents. *Harvard Business Review* 83(5):72–81. Argues that the leader's role is not to direct change but to identify and encourage the organization's "positive deviants" who are creating new solutions and ways of working on their own initiative. This supports the *nurturer* image of the change manager, shaping conditions that again will lead to unpredicted outcomes.

Roundup

Reflections for the Practicing Change Manager

- To what extent are you more comfortable with one or another of the six images described in this chapter in terms of your own (current or anticipated) approach to managing change?
- Why is this the case?
- What are the strengths and limitations of the images that you have identified as most relevant to you?
- What skills do you think are associated with each image in order to use it well?
- Are there areas of personal skill development that are needed in order for you to feel more comfortable in using other change management images?

- Have you worked in an organization that was dominated by particular images or approaches to change?
- What barriers would you face in trying to bring consideration of alternative images in these organizations? What strategies could you use to assist you in overcoming these barriers?
- **As a small group exercise:** Compare your responses to the above questions. Where do you differ from colleagues? Why do those differences arise?

Here is a short summary of the key points that we would like you to take from this chapter, in relation to each of the learning outcomes:

LO 2.1 *Evaluate the use that different authors make of the terms* change agent, change manager, *and* change leader.
Some commentators argue that the distinction between change managers and change leaders is clear and significant. We have argued, in contrast, that in practice these two roles are closely intertwined. This is a semantic squabble that is not worth arguing about. The term *change agent* traditionally refers to an external consultant or adviser, and while that role is still common, the term today is used more loosely, to refer to internal as well as external change agents.

LO 2.2 *Understand the importance of organizational images and mental models.*
The images or mental models that we all have provide us with ways of understanding the world around us. While these images are useful, we have to appreciate that "ways of seeing" are also "ways of not seeing." Focusing on specific attributes of a situation of necessity means overlooking other attributes—which may sometimes be important. Change managers approach their task with an image of the organization, an image of the change process, and an image of their role in change. These mental models—our "images-in-use"—have profound implications for change management practice.

LO 2.3 *Compare and contrast six different images of managing change and change managers.*
We explored six images of the change manager: director, navigator, caretaker, coach, interpreter, and nurturer. Each is based on different assumptions about the role of management (controlling versus shaping) and about the change outcomes being sought (intended, partly intended, unintended).

LO 2.4   *Explain the theoretical underpinning of different change management images.*
Each image finds support in organization theory and change management theory, which was explored briefly. Nevertheless, it is important to recognize that these images, which have strikingly different implications for practice, are based on research evidence and theory.

LO 2.5   *Apply these six images of managing change to your personal preferences and approach, and to different organizational contexts.*
We identified three uses of the six-images framework: surfacing assumptions, assessing dominant images, and using multiple perspectives and images. There are no "right" and "wrong" images of change management. It is valuable to be able to interpret problems and solutions in general, and change processes in particular, from different standpoints. This "multiple perspectives" approach can help generate fresh thinking and creative solutions.

This framework has other uses, explored in later chapters. One concerns the assessment of change as successful or not. That judgement is often related to one image rather than another. We often ask: Was it managed well? What went right? What went wrong? Did we achieve what we wanted? However, judging success is open to interpretation. As Pettigrew et al. (2001, p. 701) argue, "Judgements about success are also likely to be conditional on who is doing the assessment and when the judgments are made." The six-images framework highlights the need to raise conversations early about judging the success of change, and to ensure a broadly common view of that judgement across the organization.

References   Anderson, L. A., and Anderson, D. 2001. Awake at the wheel: Moving beyond change management to conscious change leadership. *OD Practitioner* 33(3):4–10.

Axelrod, D. 1992. Getting everyone involved: How one organization involved its employees, supervisors, and managers in redesigning the organization. *Journal of Applied Behavioral Science* 28(4):499–509.

Barge, J. K., and Oliver, C. 2003. Working with appreciation in managerial practice. *Academy of Management Review* 28(1):124–42.

Battilana, J., and Casciaro, T. 2013. The network secrets of great change agents. *Harvard Business Review* 91(7/8):62–68.

Beaudan, E. 2006. Making change last: How to get beyond change fatigue. *Ivey Business Journal* (January/February):1–7.

Bennis, W. G. 1969. *Organization development: Its nature, origins, and prospects.* Reading, MA: Addison-Wesley.

Bolman, L., and Deal, T. 2013. *Reframing organizations: Artistry, choice, and leadership.* 5th ed. San Francisco: Jossey-Bass.

Buchanan, D. A., and Dawson, P. 2007. Discourse and audience: Organizational change as multi-story process. *Journal of Management Studies* 44(5):669–86.

Burke, W. W. 1987. *Organization development: A normative view*. Reading, MA: Addison-Wesley.

Burnes, B. 2014. *Managing change: A strategic approach to organizational dynamics*. 6th ed. Harlow, Essex: Pearson.

Burnes, B., and Cook, B. 2012. The past, present and future of organization development: Taking the long view. *Human Relations* 65(11):1395–429.

Carlisle, D. 2014. The woman who banned the f-word. *Health Service Journal* (February 28):24–28.

Chatman, J. 2014. Culture change at Genentech: Accelerating strategic and financial accomplishments. *California Management Review* 56(2):113–29.

Chin, R., and Benne, K. D. 1976. General strategies for effecting changes in human systems. In *The planning of change*, ed. W. G. Bennis, K. D. Benne, and K. E. Corey (22–45). New York: Holt, Rinehart & Winston.

Dawson, P., and Andriopoulos, C. 2014. *Managing change, creativity and innovation*. London: Sage Publications.

DiMaggio, P. J., and Powell, W. W. 1983. The iron cage revisited: Institutional isomorphism and collective rationality in organizational fields. *American Sociological Review* 48:147–60.

Fayol, H. 1916. Administration industrielle et générale. *Bulletin de la Societe de l'Industrie Minérale* 10:5–164.

Fayol, H. 1949. *General and industrial management*. Translated by C. Storrs. London: Sir Isaac Pitman & Sons.

Gulick, L., and Urwick, L. 1937. *Papers on the science of administration*. New York: Institute of Public Administration.

Hamel, G., and Prahalad, C. K. 1994. *Competing for the future*. Boston: Harvard Business School Press.

Harrison, M. I., and Shirom, A. 1999. *Organizational diagnosis and assessment*. Thousand Oaks, CA: Sage Publications.

Hatch, M. J., and Cunliffe, A. L. 2012. *Organization theory: Modern, symbolic and postmodern perspectives*. 3rd ed. Oxford: Oxford University Press.

Huy, Q. N. 2001. Time, temporal capability, and planned change. *Academy of Management Review* 26(4):601–23.

Keller, S., Meaney, M., and Pung, C. 2010. *What successful transformations share*. Chicago and London: McKinsey & Company.

Kotter, J. P. 1995. Leading change: Why transformation efforts fail. *Harvard Business Review* 73(2):59–67.

Kotter, J. P. 2012. *Leading change*. 2nd ed. Boston: Harvard University Press.

Langley, A., Smallman, C., Tsoukas, H., and Van de Ven, A. H. 2013. Process studies of change in organization and management: Unveiling temporality, activity, and flow. *Academy of Management Journal* 56(1):1–13.

Lawson, E., and Price, C. 2010. The psychology of change management. *The McKinsey Quarterly* (special edition: the value in organization):31–41.

Lichtenstein, B. B. 2000. Self-organized transitions: A pattern amidst the chaos of transformative change. *Academy of Management Executive* 14(4):128–41.

Marshak, R. J. 1993. Lewin meets Confucius: A re-view of the OD model of change. *Journal of Applied Behavioral Science* 29(4):393–415.

Mayo, E. 1945. *The social problems of an industrial civilization.* Cambridge, MA: Harvard University Press.

McCreary, L. 2010. Kaiser Permanente's innovation on the front lines. *Harvard Business Review* 88(9):92–97.

Mintzberg, H. 2009. *Managing.* Harlow, Essex: Financial Times Prentice Hall.

Mintzberg, H., and Waters, J. A. 1985. Of strategies deliberate and emergent. *Strategic Management Journal* 6(3):257–72.

Moore, C., and Buchanan, D. A. 2013. Sweat the small stuff: A case study of small scale change processes and consequences in acute care. *Health Services Management Research* 26(1):9–17.

Morgan, G. 2006. *Images of organization.* 3rd ed. London: Sage Publications.

Palmer, I., and Dunford, R. 2002. Who says change can be managed? Positions, perspectives and problematics. *Strategic Change* 11(5):243–51.

Pascale, R. T., and Sternin, J. 2005. Your company's secret change agents. *Harvard Business Review* 83(5):72–81.

Pettigrew, A. M. 1985. *The awakening giant: Continuity and change in ICI.* Oxford: Basil Blackwell.

Pettigrew, A. M., Woodman, R. W., and Cameron, K. S. 2001. Studying organizational change and development: Challenges for future research. *Academy of Management Journal* 44(4):697–713.

Roethlisberger, F. J., and Dickson, W. J. 1939. *Management and the worker.* Cambridge, MA: Harvard University Press.

Schein, E. 1999. *Process consultation revisited: Building the helping relationship.* Reading, MA: Addison-Wesley.

Semler, R. 2000. How we went digital without a strategy. *Harvard Business Review* 78(4):51–58.

Sirkin, H. J., Keenan, P., and Jackson, A. 2005. The hard side of change management. *Harvard Business Review* 83(10):108–18.

Stace, D. A., and Dunphy, D. 2001. *Beyond the boundaries: Leading and re-creating the successful enterprise.* 2nd ed. Sydney: McGraw-Hill.

Tetenbaum, T. J. 1998. Shifting paradigms: From Newton to chaos. *Organizational Dynamics*, Spring:21–32.

Thietart, R. A., and Forgues, B. 1995. Chaos theory and organizations. *Organization Science* 6(1):19–31.

Van de Ven, A. H., and Poole, M. S. 1995. Explaining development and change in organizations. *Academy of Management Review* 20(3):510–40.

Weick, K. E. 1995. *Sensemaking in organizations.* Thousand Oaks, CA/London: Sage Publications.

Weick, K. E. 2000. Emergent change as a universal in organizations. In *Breaking the code of change*, ed. M. Beer and N. Nohria (223–41). Boston: Harvard Business School Press.

Weisbord, M. 1987. Toward third-wave managing consulting. *Organizational Dynamics* 15(3):19–20.

White, M. C., Marin, D. B., Brazeal, D. V., and Friedman, W. H. 1997. The evolution of organizations: Suggestions from complexity theory about the interplay between natural selection and adaptation. *Human Relations* 50(11):1383–401.

Chapter 3

Why Change? Contemporary Pressures and Drivers

Learning objectives

By the end of this chapter you should be able to:

LO 3.1   Understand the environmental pressures that can trigger organizational change.

LO 3.2   Explain why not all organizations are affected equally by external pressures.

LO 3.3   Explain why organizations often fail to change following crises.

LO 3.4   Identify internal organizational factors that trigger change.

LO 3.5   Relate differing images of managing change to pressures for change.

"All I'm saying is now is the time to develop the technology to deflect an asteroid."

Frank Cotham The New Yorker Collection/The Cartoon Bank

LO 3.1   Environmental Pressures for Change

Managers are faced with a paradox. On the one hand, organizations are advised to change rapidly, or perish (Kotter, 2012). On the other, management is advised to avoid the risks of implementing too much change too quickly (Bruch and Menges, 2010). As noted in chapter 1, evidence suggests that the failure rate of planned change programs is high. One survey of senior executives found a success rate of only 30 percent (Keller and Aiken, 2008). Another, more optimistic study found that less than 60 percent of reorganizations are successful (CIPD, 2014).

As failures of organizational change appear to be widespread, and widely acknowledged, what drives managers to embark on such risky ventures? One answer is based on an economic perspective, and is aligned to "management as control" images and assumptions:

- In competitive economies, firm survival depends on satisfying shareholders. Failure to do this will lead investors either to move their capital to other companies, or to use their influence to replace senior management. Managers thus introduce change to improve organizational performance in terms of profitability and higher company share prices.

An alternative view, aligned with "management as shaping" images and assumptions, is the organizational learning perspective:

- Organizations and human systems are complex and evolving and cannot be reduced to a single objective of maximizing shareholder value. Change is also related to the need to increase an organization's adaptive capacity—because how to increase shareholder value, and the knowledge underpinning that goal, are likely to change over time. Change is explained by the desire to build capacity to respond to, and to shape, external pressures and demands.

Whatever the explanation, organizations are clearly faced with a variety of pressures to change, from many directions. *External* pressures for organizational change include, for example:

- economic and trading conditions, domestic and global;
- new technologies and materials;
- changes in customers' requirements and tastes;
- activities and innovations of competitors, mergers and acquisitions;
- legislation, regulation, and government policies;
- shifts in local, national, and international politics;
- changes in social and cultural values.

Internal pressures for organizational change can include, for example:

- new product and service design innovations;
- low performance and morale, high stress and staff turnover;
- new senior managers or top management team, who want to "make their mark";
- inadequate skills and knowledge base, triggering training programs;
- head office and factory relocation, closer to suppliers and markets;
- recognition of problems triggering reallocation of responsibilities;
- innovations in the manufacturing process;
- new ideas about how to deliver services to customers.

In what follows, we will explore a selection of these external and internal pressures. But change is not simply a matter of reacting to events. Organizations and individuals can anticipate trends and opportunities and be proactive as well. Susan Mohrman and Edward Lawler (2012, p. 42) argue that we need to focus on "next practice" as well as "best practice" because:

> The major challenge for organizations today is navigating high levels of turbulence. They operate in dynamic environments, in societies where the aspirations and purposes of various stakeholders change over time. They have access to ever-increasing technological capabilities and information. A key organizational capability is the ability to adapt as context, opportunities, and challenges change.

LO 3.5   Paradoxically, one outcome of change is often supposed to be equilibrium. Managers are expected to stabilize the unstable and destabilize the rigid; adapt to the present and anticipate the future; improve what is and invent what is to be; lead a renaissance while preserving tradition, the possibilities for which are grounded in the belief that progress is possible and that management can make a difference. As table 3.1 points out, the ways in

TABLE 3.1

Images of Change and Understanding the Pressures

Image	Understanding the Pressures for Change
Director	Change is a result of strategic pressure, entering new markets, or correcting an internal problem to improve efficiencies. These pressures are controllable, and the management task is to direct the organizational response.
Navigator	Change results from strategic threats and opportunities, and from the need to deal with internal problems. However, the best response may not be obvious, given the many and often conflicting priorities that management faces, and the range of influences and competing interests that need to be considered.
Caretaker	The pressures for organizational change are many and inexorable, and managers cannot control this agenda. External pressures arise from new regulations or market conditions, for example. Internal pressures can be triggered by growth or operational innovations. However, these pressures can be overwhelming, and they are difficult to resist. The role of management, as caretakers, is to look after the organization as it is buffeted by these pressures, having limited choice in the actions that need to be taken in response.
Coach	The pressures for change are constant. They arise from the need to coordinate teamwork, values, and mindsets, and to generate the collaboration that leads to improved organizational outcomes. Change pressures are therefore continuous and developmental, and they help to shape the organization's capabilities to respond to further change and to further improve performance.
Interpreter	Given the many internal and external pressures for change, staff need management to provide meaning, to help understand "what is going on." Those who will be affected need to understand the significance of their roles, what needs to happen and why, and where the organization is heading. Managers must help to make sense of changes. This is a sense-making role, providing clarity and contributing to individual identity and to organizational commitment.
Nurturer	Organizations change as a result of a variety of forces, some weak, some strong. The weaker pressures, however, can have a disproportionate impact on the organization. These pressures may not all be rational, but may instead be chaotic and difficult to coordinate. The management role, therefore, is to nurture or to develop the organization's adaptive capacity to respond to those challenges.

which managers experience those triggers of change, and those to which they attend, will be influenced by their images of managing change.

To understand why managers embark on apparently risky change ventures, this chapter begins by exploring the environmental pressures—some will argue imperatives—for organizational change. We then consider why some managers do not respond to such pressures. We take that discussion into an exploration of why "remedial" change often does not happen where it would be expected, following accidents, disasters, and other crises. Finally, we explore the numerous internal organizational pressures for change. It is important to recognize that there are many triggers of organizational change, and that those that are discussed here do not represent a comprehensive list.

Environmental pressures are explanations for change. These pressures take many forms, and include opportunities (e.g., new technologies, products, and markets) as well as threats (e.g., falling market share, tighter regulation, bad investments). At the extreme, change may be necessary to avoid going out of business altogether. Here, we will explore six sets of external environmental pressures that can lead to change. Change may come about as a response to fashion; demographic trends; external mandate; globalization and related geopolitical developments; "hypercompetition"; and threats to corporate credibility and reputation (figure 3.1).

An organization and its management rarely have the luxury of facing only one of these external environmental pressures at any given time. For many organizations in developed economies, most, if not all, of these pressures are constantly active, and all may be considered to be high priority.

Fashion

In 2001 Boeing, the well-known aircraft manufacturing company, initiated a series of changes under the direction of its chief executive, Philip M. Condit (Holmes et al., 2001). Condit was frustrated by the slow pace of change in the company, and concerned about slow growth in sales of commercial jet aircraft. His changes were similar to those introduced by Jack Welch at General Electric (GE), a multinational conglomerate that was widely recognized for its successful transformational changes. Following GE, the changes at Boeing included:

- a new corporate learning and training unit in St. Louis, to create a "unified company culture";
- changing the organization culture;

The Hype Cycle

You can often gain valuable insight from radical management innovations, even if they fizzle out. And they do fizzle out. Nine-tenths of the approximately 100 branded management ideas I've studied lost their popularity within a decade or so. These include GE's Work-Out, W.L. Gore's lattice structure, Xerox's communities of practice, Thermo Electron's Spinout model, and Google's 20% innovation time policy.

Source: Birkinshaw (2014), p. 55.

FIGURE 3.1

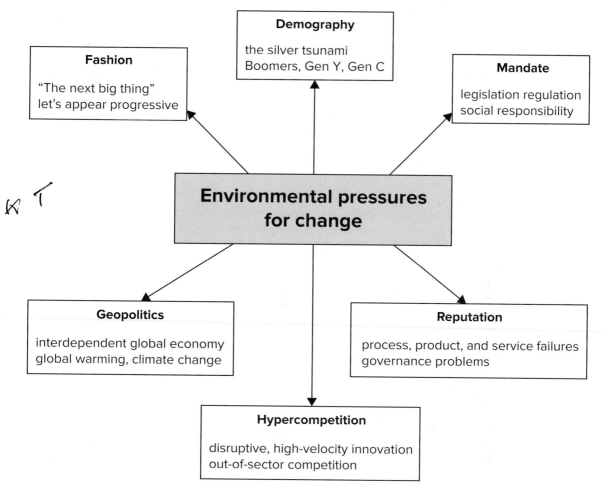

- restructuring the business into three key divisions—commercial, military, and space;
- giving the chief executives of those divisions greater freedom;
- making the divisions compete for access to corporate funding;
- setting high performance standards.

This is an example of what neo-institutional theorists refer to as *mimetic isomorphism* (DiMaggio and Powell, 1983). This occurs when organizations imitate (mimic) the structures and practices of others, but not necessarily in the same sector, and usually those that they consider to be legitimate and successful.

Organizational change can thus be a response to the latest management fad or fashion, as individual managers wish to be considered professional, progressive, and up to

Decade	Fashions
1950s	Management by objectives (MBO) Program evaluation and review technique (PERT) Employee assistance programs (EAPs)
1960s	Organization development Sensitivity training and T-groups The managerial grid (concern for staff, concern for results)
1970s	Quality of working life movement (QWL) Job enrichment Quality circles
1980s	Organization culture Total quality management (TQM) International Standards Organization 9000 (ISO 9000)
1990s	Business process reengineering (BPR) Autonomous, self-directed work groups High-performance organizations Lean and 5S: sort, systematize, shine, standardize, sustain
2000s	The learning organization Employee engagement Disruptive innovation
2010s	High reliability organizations (HROs) Built-to-change organizations The networked enterprise Big data, data analytics, artificial intelligence

date. As table 3.2 illustrates (selectively), management has been subjected to a constant stream of fads. Eric Abrahamson (1996) points out that, while appearing to be novel and valuable, many fads lack the systemic research that would legitimate their claims to enhance performance. The "fashion setters," including consulting firms, management gurus, business publications, and business school academics, do not necessarily profit from the critical assessment of these ideas. Some fads do benefit some organizations, but Abrahamson also argues that some fads—downsizing, for example—can have devastating implications for organizations and their employees. One reason for the failure of fads to deliver their promise is that most new methods, approaches, and techniques have to be tailored to the circumstances of each new setting. It is rarely possible to copy exactly what another organization has done and expect to achieve the same benefits over the same period of time.

It is unlikely that managers will succumb continually to pressures to implement fashionable changes that have limited benefits. Market forces and customer preferences propel organizations in some directions, and not in others. Fads go through cycles. An innovative idea first attracts the attention of journalists, academics, and consultants, and this is valuable in terms of codifying and publicizing new working practices. However, one result of this attention is to heighten expectations, which can then be dashed as further applications fail to deliver as promised. Enthusiasm can then be replaced by skepticism, and organizations start hunting for "the next big thing." Julian Birkinshaw (2014, p. 57) suggests that management should follow these steps before adopting another management fad:

1. *Wait*: Do not rush to adopt, but do not dismiss the approach either. Give the new idea time to succeed or fail.
2. *Identify the essence of the idea*: What is the underlying logic, what are the underpinning assumptions, what fresh insights led to this development?
3. *Look for results*: Did the new approach make the improvements that were expected? Were there any side effects? Would this work in your organization, or would your culture, systems, and structures be barriers?
4. *Experiment*: Set up a trial, gather the evidence, review, and continue if successful.

Birkinshaw (2014, p. 57) concludes: "It's easy to get so swept up in the glamour of a new idea that the prospect of implementing it seems straightforward. But remember that successful management innovators typically had to work very hard, over many years, to put their new ideas into place. Applying those ideas inside your own company is likely to take even longer."

Demography: From the Silver Tsunami to Generation C

Veterans, born 1925 to 1942; also known as the silent generation, matures, traditionalists

Baby Boomers, born 1943 to 1960; also just called Boomers

Generation X, born 1961 to 1981, also known as baby busters, the thirteenth, the lost generation

Generation Y, born since 1981 onward; also known as millennials, nexters, echo boomers

Generation C, born since 1990; connected, communicating, always clicking

These dates are approximate—different commentators disagree

(Parry and Urwin, 2011)

Demographic changes, affecting workforce composition and motivation, pose some of the greatest challenges for organizational change management in the twenty-first century. In all industrialized economies, the workforce is ageing, as we live longer and have fewer children. In 2010, the average (median) age of Americans rose to 37.2. In 2000, it was 35.3. The proportion of the population who have retired from employment is growing relative to the proportion still in work. This is an accelerating global phenomenon. In the United States, the percentage of the population aged 65 or over is expected to double, from only 10 percent in 1970 to 20 percent in 2050.

Baby Boomers have been described as a *silver tsunami* sweeping across affected countries (*The Economist*, 2010). This ageing population has social consequences. Boomers who were born after the Second World War (which ended in 1945) started celebrating their 60th birthdays from around 2006. In 2014, the global population of those aged 65 or more was 600 million; it was predicted that, by 2034, that population would almost double, to 1.1 billion (*The Economist*, 2014, p. 11). *Boomsday*, by Christopher Buckley (2007), is a fictional account of the anger of younger generations whose taxes pay for the pensions, health, and welfare of those Boomers in their old age. Governments have tried to raise retirement ages to reduce the drain on welfare, healthcare, and pension budgets.

The silver tsunami has change management consequences. Organizations will need to fill the gaps as Boomers retire, taking their knowledge and experience with them, while the proportion of skilled youngsters in the workforce is shrinking. Some older workers—"nevertirees"—have decided to carry on working, and organizations will have to learn how to manage them. Will older workers adapt to new technologies and working practices, and take management orders from youngsters? These are new problems, and there is little research or experience on which to draw. Some approaches to managing older workers include:

- exit interviews to capture their wisdom;
- mentoring systems in which Boomers coach their replacements;
- phased retirement rather than a sudden stop;
- shorter working weeks with flexible hours;
- pools of retired staff who can be called upon for special projects;
- working during busy periods punctuated by "Benidorm leave."

A recent survey of over 1,000 managers found that most organizations had not yet developed their age management policies (Pickard, 2010). Younger managers find it difficult to manage older workers, who have different drives and need flexibility (to care for elderly parents and grandchildren, for example). Management styles have to be consultative, drawing on the experience of older workers for whom money is probably not the main or only motivator.

Nevertirement and Nevertirees

Barclays Wealth is a bank for "high net worth" people (http://www.barclayswealth.com). To find out more about their customers' future plans, they surveyed 2,000 wealthy individuals, who had at least £1 million of assets to invest. They found that, rather than planning a conventional retirement, many planned to go on working (Leppard and Chittenden, 2010):

Country	% Planning to Work beyond Retirement Age
Saudi Arabia	92
United Arab Emirates	91
Qatar	91
South Africa	88
Latin America	78
UK	60
Ireland	59
USA	54
Japan	46
Spain	44
Switzerland	34

In other words, "nevertirement" could become more popular, and this may not apply just to the wealthy. Organizations will need to change their human resource policies and working practices to deal effectively with this trend.

Generation Y are the children of the Boomers. Do Boomers and Gen Ys want different things from work? Sylvia Ann Hewlett and colleagues (2009) suggest that these groups actually share a number of attitudes, behaviors, and preferences. Their findings are based on surveys of around 4,000 college graduates, followed by focus groups and interviews. The rewards from work that Boomers regard as important are:

1. High-quality colleagues
2. An intellectually stimulating workplace
3. Autonomy regarding work tasks
4. Flexible work arrangements
5. Access to new experiences and challenges
6. Giving back to the world through work
7. Recognition from the company or the boss

The rewards from work that Gen Ys regard as important are:

1. High-quality colleagues
2. Flexible work arrangements
3. Prospects for advancement
4. Recognition from the company or the boss
5. Steady rate of advancement and promotion
6. Access to new experiences and challenges

Both groups want to serve a wider purpose, want opportunities to explore their interests and passions, and say that flexible working and work-life balance are important to them. They also share a sense of obligation to the wider society and the environment. (Gen Xs are less likely to find those obligations important.) When choosing an employer, money is less important, as they are interested in other forms of reward: teamwork, challenge, new experiences, recognition.

In the context of managing organizational change, and given these demographic trends, the contributions of vision (chapter 6) and communications (chapter 7) are likely to be central to engaging the commitment and motivation of those who are going to be involved. Human resource management policy and practice will need to emphasize teamwork, collaboration, flexible working, flexible retirement, project work, short-term assignments, opportunities to support external causes, and eco-friendly work environments. Another valuable practice may involve intergenerational mentoring; Boomers often welcome the chance to mentor and support Gen Ys, who can share their potentially better understanding of social networking technologies.

Generation C is the label given to those born after 1990. "C" stands for "connected, communicating, content-centric, computerized, community oriented, always clicking" (Friedrich et al., 2011, p. 3). This is the first generation to have grown up with the Internet, social media, and mobile handheld computing, for whom 24/7 mobile and Internet connectivity are taken for granted and freedom of expression is the norm. These technologies encourage more flexible forms of working, and less hierarchical organizations, and they are blurring the boundaries between work and personal life.

By 2020, Gen C will make up over 40 percent of the population in America, Europe, and the BRIC countries (Friedrich et al., 2011). Gen C will be "on the grid 24/7": being connected around the clock is normal. The number of mobile phone users in the world is expected to grow from 4.6 billion in 2012 to 6 billion in 2020. Over the same period, the number of Internet users will increase from 1.7 billion to 4.7 billion. Gen C will thus have a wide range of personal relationships driven by social networks, voice channels, online groups, blogs, and electronic messaging. These facilities will create fast-moving business and political pressures as information and ideas spread more widely, more quickly. Most Gen C employees will bring their own computers to work rather than use corporate resources. There will probably be more work done by virtual project groups, with fewer face-to-face meetings, and less frequent travel. Organizations will probably have to change working conditions and practices to accommodate those preferences, and to exploit the opportunities.

External Mandate

In 1996, ChevronTexaco (then Texaco) settled a racial discrimination lawsuit for $176 million. The suit was filed by the company's African-American staff, who alleged that managers and employees were involved in racist acts. They claimed that racism was institutionalized in the company's culture and practices to such an extent that it "caused Texaco to be branded the worst of corporate rogues" (Labich, 1999). The settlement followed other companies such as Shoney's, which in 1992 paid $133 million to settle a discrimination suit on behalf of 20,000 people, and Denny's, which in 1994 paid $54 million to settle two cases in which customers claimed the restaurant had not served or seated them (Faircloth, 1998). In 2000 Coca-Cola settled a case for $192 million (Salter, 2003).

The settlement agreements for ChevronTexaco and Coca-Cola included organizational changes, to establish external diversity task forces and to monitor company practices and ensure fair treatment for minorities (Salter, 2003). Both companies were under court orders to improve their record on diversity management. This led to other changes in corporate policies and cultural practices. For example, at ChevronTexaco, staff had to attend diversity training, managers attended communication courses, minorities were targeted for new hires, and key executive appointments were made to symbolize the shift in culture. New change programs were implemented to eliminate racism from hiring, retention, and promotion decisions (Labich, 1999). In September 2002, the fifth report of ChevronTexaco's *Equity and Fairness Task Force* outlined the changes made in the 1996 settlement; there were still some problems to be solved, but the company culture had changed for the better.

It is now widely accepted that organizations should support a range of environmental as well as social causes. The economist Milton Friedman (1970) once argued, "The business of business is business." His view is now unfashionable. The *corporate social responsibility* (CSR) movement expects companies to promote environmental or "green" issues as well as social policies. This has become a major source of pressure for change. Many organizations are addressing these issues, to strengthen their reputations as "responsible corporate citizens." The importance of this viewpoint has been highlighted in the twenty-first century by the corporate scandals at Enron, WorldCom, and the Japanese company livedoor, where executives were accused of fraudulent transactions that benefitted them personally. These cases led to new regulations affecting corporate governance in America—the infamous *Sarbanes-Oxley Act* of 2002. Expensive and cumbersome to implement, that legislation was designed to restore public confidence by improving corporate accounting controls. Table 3.3 lists typical CSR policies (Huczynski and Buchanan, 2013, p. 68).

TABLE 3.3
CSR Policies and Practices

Environment
1. Pollution control
2. Product improvement
3. Repair of environment
4. Recycling waste materials
5. Energy saving

Equal Opportunities
1. Minority employment
2. Advancement of minorities
3. Advancement of women
4. Support for minority businesses
5. Support for other disadvantaged groups

Personnel
1. Employee health and safety
2. Training
3. Personal counselling
4. Subcontractor code of behavior
5. Providing medical care or insurance

Community Involvement
1. Charitable donations
2. Promoting and supporting public health initiatives
3. Support for education and the arts
4. Community involvement projects

Products
1. Safety
2. Quality
3. Sustainability, percentage of materials that can be recycled

Suppliers
1. Fair terms of trade
2. Blacklisting unethical, irresponsible suppliers
3. Subcontractor code

Change is often forced on organizations through formally mandated legislation and regulation. Neo-institutional theorists call this *coercive isomorphism* (DiMaggio and Powell, 1983), which may be formal or informal:

- *Formal coercive pressures* include government mandates such as new laws and policies. Organizations are thus forced to change to meet new requirements relating to, for example, pollution, taxation, or affirmative action. Subsidiary organizations may be forced to adopt accounting standards, performance criteria, and other practices to suit the parent organization.

Coca-Cola   *Thirsty for Sustainability*

Sensitive to accusations that it runs a wasteful, unethical, and polluting business that does not make a social contribution, Coca-Cola in Europe responded with a series of corporate responsibility initiatives (Wiggins, 2007):

- Restricting the marketing of its products to children

- Working with the World Wildlife Fund to find ways to cut back and to replenish the 290 billion liters of water that the company uses annually

- Working with Greenpeace to develop environmentally friendly beverage coolers and vending machines to reduce the emission of hydrocarbon greenhouse gasses

- Monitoring the agricultural impact of the company's tea, coffee, and juice drinks products, which require it to purchase ingredients from around the globe

Websites accuse the company of exaggerating the benefits of an unhealthy product, of management complicity in the deaths of union organizers in bottling plants in South America, and of reducing and polluting local water supplies in India:

www.killercoke.org

www.indiaresource.org/campaigns/coke/2004/risingstruggles.html

- *Informal coercive pressures* arise when interdependent organizations persuade (perhaps force) each other to behave in particular ways, and to collude with each other in certain actions. Although not formally or legally required, resisting these pressures means breaching strong cultural norms; conformity may not be mandatory, but is expected.

These pressures for change, therefore, can be overwhelming, and irresistible.

Globalization and Geopolitical Developments

In the twenty-first century, developed Western economies see both threats and opportunities in the economic growth of countries such as Brazil, Russia, India, and China—the so-called BRIC economies. Those economies have lower labor costs and have become attractive locations for manufacturing operations and for customer service call centers. There is a widespread perception that "outsourcing" manufacturing and service operations in this way is happening at the expense of jobs in North America and Europe. Collectively, these trends and developments have been captured by the label *globalization*—the intensification of worldwide social and business relationships that link localities in such a way that local conditions are shaped by distant events.

Natural disasters in one part of the world can have global consequences. In March 2011, one of the strongest earthquakes ever recorded occurred off the northeast coast of Japan. The earthquake triggered a cascading event sequence that included a tsunami followed by containment failures at the Fukushima nuclear power plant. These events led to considerable loss of life, damage to property, disruption to business, damage to the Japanese economy, and censure for government ministers and power company managers for regulatory failures contributing to the power plant problems (Kingston, 2012). The quake and tsunami closed key ports and airports and disrupted the global supply chain for semiconductor products (of which Japan produces 20 percent). Honda, Mitsubishi, Nissan, Suzuki, and Toyota suspended their car manufacturing operations, and Nissan considered moving a production line to the United States. Component supplies to Boeing and Sony were also disrupted. The terrorist attacks on New York on September 11, 2001, and the outbreak of severe acute respiratory syndrome (SARS) were radically different crises that also had global implications for a range of organizations, and not just airlines and related businesses.

In the face of such events, companies may need to review supply chains, joint ventures, the locations of their facilities, and other investment decisions. Many types of geopolitical event can have consequences for organizations that trade with and/or have investments in affected regions. Examples include civil war (e.g., Syria, since 2011), political instability (e.g., Egypt, since 2011), and other international geopolitical tensions (e.g., Russia and Ukraine, since 2014). Organizations may simply withdraw facilities and discontinue relationships with regions and organizations perceived to represent physical or financial risks. In 2001, faced with escalating violence from separatist Aceh rebels, Exxon suspended gas production at its Arun facility in Indonesia and evacuated its staff.

John Kotter (1995) argued that four sets of forces were translating global trends and developments into organizational adaptations and changes: new technologies, the expansion of international trade, maturing markets, and the end of the "cold war." While the latter set of factors may have been stalled, if not reversed, by the Russian annexation of the

Cloud Control

External pressures for organizational change can have "knock on" effects on internal support functions not directly involved in shifts in strategy. Adobe is a global software company, known for products such as Acrobat, Flash Player, and Photoshop. Based in San Jose, California, Adobe has 11,000 employees in 43 countries, with annual revenues of $4.5 billion, half of which are generated outside the United States. New technologies, however, are opening up opportunities for small competitors.

In 2011, Adobe decided to stop selling its licensed products in shrink-wrapped packages and became a cloud-based provider of digital services. Instead of receiving a CD in a box, customers either download the software they require or pay a monthly subscription. For employees, this meant new ways of working, and a new role for the human resource (HR) function.

Adobe had a traditional office-bound administrative HR function. That worked well when Adobe was selling software products, but it was less appropriate to the cloud-based approach. HR had to work as "business partners" located in employee resource centers. HR consulting teams worked on problems directly with senior managers and with staff on the ground. HR roles became more varied and, being

less office-bound, more people-oriented. Rather than wait for calls, HR staff conducted "walk-ins," visiting on their own initiative parts of the company to explore what support they could provide. Adobe employs large numbers of "millennials" (Gen Ys) who are motivated by innovation, change, and personal development. Keeping them engaged meant designing varied, challenging jobs.

Adobe also stopped conducting annual performance reviews, as they consumed a lot of management time, demotivated staff, and contributed to high staff turnover. With the new "check in" system, staff review and set their own development goals when they think this is appropriate, with immediate and ongoing feedback rather than an annual conversation. HR runs workshops for managers on providing effective, positive feedback. Staff turnover has fallen to its lowest level ever.

Why did HR at Adobe change the way in which it operated? Because the company strategy and culture had changed, and HR had to find new ways of working to support those developments.

Sources:
http://www.adobe.com/company/fast-facts.html
Smedley, T. 2014. Send in the cloud. *People Management*, May: 43–44.

FIGURE 3.2
Globalization and Organizational Change

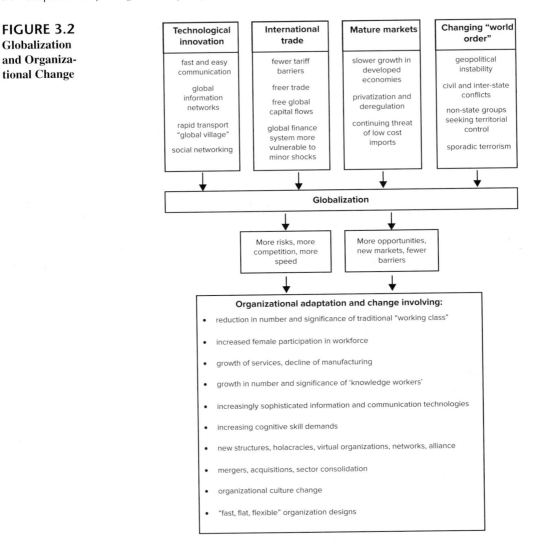

Ukrainian province of Crimea in 2014, Kotter's general argument remains valid, particularly with regard to the series of organizational adaptations and changes that he identifies. Figure 3.2 presents an updated version of his argument.

Another significant geopolitical pressure affecting all organizations, regardless of size, sector, or location, is climate change due to global warming—an issue that has risen to prominence since Kotter developed his argument. Climate change has the potential to reshape dramatically the organizational landscape, in many ways. Traditionally seen as another corporate social responsibility issue, Michael Porter and Forest Reinhardt (2007, p. 22) argue that climate change has now become a business problem, with operational and strategic dimensions:

A firm that has more employees than it needs in its shipping department is operationally ineffective; its managers are wasting resources and creating a drag on performance. In the same way, a firm that produces excess emissions in its shipping operations is also operationally ineffective—it is wasting resources and incurring unnecessary costs that are certain to rise. Implementing best practices in managing climate-related costs is the minimum required to remain competitive.

In addition to understanding its emission costs, every firm needs to evaluate its vulnerability to climate-related effects such as regional shifts in the availability of energy and water, the reliability of infrastructures and supply chains, and the prevalence of infectious diseases. The firm's leaders should systematically assess these risks and then decide which to reduce through redesigning operations, which to transfer to others through insurance or hedging contracts, and which to bear.

To assess the strategic implications, Porter and Reinhardt (2007) argue that organizations need to adopt an "inside out, outside in" perspective. "Inside out" means understanding the impact that the organization has on its environment. "Outside in" means assessing how climate change will affect how the organization operates. Regulations concerning greenhouse gas emissions and emissions costs are likely to make some business models expensive, particularly those that rely on transport-intensive supply chains. E-commerce, with high numbers of small shipments, may be affected.

Eric Lowitt (2014) argues that, although a warmer planet is threatening to many organizations, there are also opportunities. Lowitt suggests how to reduce operational, regulatory, and reputational risks, and provides ideas for cutting costs, improving performance, improving customer relationships, and increasing competitiveness and organizational resilience. He explores a range of organizational responses to four climate change issues concerning: threats to raw material supplies; rising costs of energy and materials; threats to distribution from extreme weather events; and alienating customers by ignoring environmental impacts (table 3.4 summarizes).

Table 3.4
Climate Change Impacts and Organizational Responses

Impacts	Responses
Unpredictable availability of raw materials, volatile prices	**ExxonMobil** includes a carbon emissions price in pro forma financial calculations **Walmart** suppliers must certify that all sourcing of materials is legal and environmentally sound
Wasted energy and materials drive up manufacturing costs and threaten regulatory action	**Apple** has a manufacturing plant in Arizona that runs entirely on renewable energy **Nike** has a facility that eliminates the use of water and process chemicals in fabric dyeing
Extreme weather events disrupt transport and distribution	**HP** and **Dell** have increased their use of ocean freight shipments, rather than air, due to climate change concerns **BT** (British Telecommunications) plans infrastructure investment on the basis of flooding scenarios, 50 to 100 years ahead
Alienate customers by ignoring environmental impacts	**Patagonia** has a "buy less" campaign that encourages customers to resale used Patagonia items **Ford** improved the fuel economy of its top-selling truck by making the body from aluminum to reduce the vehicle weight

Hypercompetition

In 1998 Gateway, the personal computer company, faced fierce competition, overshadowed by Dell, its direct-sales rival. Gateway founder and chief executive Ted Waitt took the company through a major restructuring, hiring 10 new top managers and changing the way the company went about doing business, including its name, products, alliances, and business strategy (Kirkpatrick, 1999). In 2008, the California-based battery and electric powertrain maker Tesla launched its first all-electric sports car, the Roadster. Tesla was not previously considered to be in the automotive manufacturing sector. Rejecting the traditional automotive dealership model, Tesla sold its cars directly to customers through "galleries" located in shopping malls. The first driverless cars are likely to have been developed by Google, an Internet services company. The Internet and smartphones have also generated innovative business models, such as the "freemium," where customers get the basic product free and pay a premium, usually a subscription, for more powerful functions. Examples include LinkedIn, Dropbox, Spotify, and NYTimes.com (Kumar, 2014). In 2013, the U.S. Central Intelligence Agency awarded a $600 million contract for a data center, not to IBM or another computer company, but to Amazon, an online retailer.

These developments represent the *hypercompetitive* environment that many organizations now face (D'Aveni, 1994). Terms such as "disruptive innovation," "high velocity," "postbureaucratic," and "chaotic" have been used to describe this environment, which some commentators associate with a "postmodern organizational paradigm." When organizations from other sectors start selling products and services that compete with yours, you are facing hypercompetition.

Aligned with the rise of e-commerce and the Internet, organizations are faced with global changes in consumer preferences, industry boundaries, social values, and, as mentioned earlier, demographics. Organizations are forced to deliver goods and services more quickly, more customized, and more flexibly. But hypercompetition means that market leaders cannot be complacent. By 2007, Dell was facing challenging times, as profits and share price declined. After 20 years of outstanding performance, with sales rising from $500 million in 1991 to $32 billion in 2001, Dell was facing the combined

Pressure to Change at YouTube

It is not only established, pre-digital age organizations that are subject to pressure to change. The "new kids on the block" are not exempt, as Nicole LaPorte (2014) explains.

One of the key reasons that Susan Wojcicki was appointed in 2014 as Google's senior vice president in charge of YouTube was that, despite YouTube being one of Google's most important brands, there was a perception that the brand was "punching below its weight" (Ynon Kreiz, CEO of Maker Studios: La Porte, 2014, p. 61). There was a widespread view that YouTube had yet to develop a business model that produced the volume of revenue that its popularity should deliver. While Facebook's market capitalization was $170 billion, that of YouTube was only $15–$20 billion, reflecting the fact that Facebook had been more successful in migrating its audience and business to phones.

What Worries Dropbox?

Dropbox CEO Drew Houston is concerned that Dropbox needs to keep evolving and not rest on its laurels. He's worried that his business will be attacked, not by Google, Microsoft, or Apple, but by "the next twenty-something who wedges her way into his user base and peels off Dropbox's features before he can build more of them" (McCorvey, 2015, p. 104). He doesn't want to join the list of innovative companies who, within a short space of time, go from being "the disruptor" to "the disrupted."

His awareness of this danger is manifest in that one of the first things that he shows new recruits to Dropbox is a slideshow featuring the logos of Myspace, Netscape, Lotus, RIM, and Friendster as cautionary tales.

"What do these companies have in common?" Houston asks his new colleagues. "No one wears their T-shirts anymore, except maybe as a Halloween costume" (McCorvey, 2015, p. 104).

effects of the decline in the quality of after-sales service, highly efficient competitors such as Lenovo who had substantially eroded Dell's cost advantage, and growing consumer sentiment that Dell was "well off the pace" (Kirkpatrick, 2006). Michael Dell commented, "This has been a wake-up call for us. We're using this whole period as a time to re-examine every part of the company. If you ask, 'Is Dell in the penalty box?' Yeah, Dell's in the penalty box. Then we'll use this opportunity to fix everything" (Kirkpatrick, 2006, p. 36).

Such pressures have required a variety of organizational changes, as in the case of Delphi Corporation (previously Delphi Automotive Systems Corporation). The Delphi plant in Oak Creek, Wisconsin, is an automotive supplier of catalytic converters. Its history dates back some 100 years, although it was spun off as a former division of General Motors in 1999. A number of dramatic changes were made to the plant in the subsequent two years, moving it from an old-style assembly line to one based on small cells of workers. Each cell of around four people was organized in the form of a U or a circle, and plastic conveyor systems that could be dismantled quickly and reformed to meet new orders were used to deliver the necessary parts. The workers in each cell were involved in decision making, with responsibility for work scheduling, quality, and productivity. The modular and portable nature of the workstations enabled greater flexibility, speed, and customization in manufacturing converters. This was necessary to meet the demands of automakers who wanted converters customized to meet their specific needs, and who also were reducing the numbers of their suppliers.

These business environment pressures meant that the former delivery time of 21 days was no longer adequate, and neither was the inflexible assembly line, which was unable to deliver product variety. The end result of the changes was a system that could complete customized orders in five days and productivity that was 25 percent higher. However, even changes such as these in its Oak Creek plant could not fend off the hypercompetitive pressures facing the Delphi Corporation across its operations. In October 2006, the Delphi Corporation filed for bankruptcy, having shed some 1,200 people from its Oak Creek plant over the previous year. Their chief executive Robert Miller indicated in February 2007 that, in relation to all its U.S. plants, the company was discussing with stakeholders a comprehensive restructuring to restore competitiveness (Dressang and Barrett, 2006). The pressures of hypercompetition are not always easy to anticipate.

Maintaining Corporate Credibility and Reputation

Reputational pressures can arise suddenly. In August 2007, Mattel, the world's largest toy manufacturer, recalled more than 10 million toys as a result of quality-control problems in the Chinese factories where they were made. Business journalists were asking two key questions: "What is going to be the reputational damage?" and "What is Mattel going to do to try to minimize it?"

During the 1990s, Walt Disney Company was cited by *BusinessWeek* as having one of the worst corporate boards in the United States. Issues included close ties between the chief executive and directors, lack of management experience, and minimal oversight of the company (Lavelle, 2002). However, it was not until the corporate crises that confronted Enron, Tyco, and WorldCom that Disney and other companies started to change their governance structures and practices. At Disney:

- only independent directors were allowed on audit and compensation committees;
- limits were placed on the number of other boards of which directors can be members;
- directors had to own a minimum of $100,000 in stock of the company;
- board meetings were held separate to management;
- ties between the company and directors were severed;
- consulting firms were not used for financial auditing purposes.

Change is thus often associated with maintaining proper corporate governance mechanisms to ensure a positive reputation. Some companies (such as Walmart) have a board-level director responsible for reputation management. Corporate reputation, defined as "a collective representation of a firm's past actions and results that describes the firm's ability to deliver valued outcomes to multiple stakeholders," is an intangible but important corporate asset, being positively correlated with organizational performance (Fombrun and van Riel, 1997, p. 10). Maintaining and enhancing corporate reputation is therefore important to an organization's survival, although the pressure to change to maintain reputation may vary from company to company.

Sometimes strategic changes can signal that an organization is taking steps to "put its house in order." One common sign of "a new era" is the symbolic exit of a high-profile appointment, such as the chief executive; examples include the departures of Gerald Levin from AOL Time Warner, Jean-Marie Messier from Vivendi Universal, and Thomas Middelhoff from Bertelsmann. Gunther and Wheat (2002, p. 130) note, "These executives, as it happened, had all bet too heavily on the Internet; their companies performed poorly, and they were held accountable. That's the way shareholder capitalism is supposed to work." These symbolic actions attempt to influence shareholders' sense-making processes with respect to the credibility and reputation of the organization. Of course, some changes that are intended to create a positive image may be disrupted by other events. One iconic example was the Macondo Well blowout in the Gulf of Mexico in April 2010 that killed 11 workers and seriously damaged the reputation for risk management and safety that BP had been trying to rebuild following previous disastrous or damaging workplace incidents (National Commission, 2011).

LO 3.2 Why Do Organizations Not Change in Response to Environmental Pressures?

Organizations and their managers do not all respond to external pressures for change in the same way. Some resist, some delay their response, and some may not even recognize the issues as important. To explain why external pressures do not always lead to change, we will outline four debates. The first concerns the tension between organizational learning and "threat-rigidity." The second concerns objective versus cognitive constructions of the environment. The third involves the balance between forces for change and forces for stability. Finally, we consider bridging and buffering strategies.

Organizational Learning versus Threat-Rigidity

Not all organizations adapt when faced with external pressures. In the 1990s, Walt Disney did not rectify its corporate governance until prompted by other similar scandals. Nike was slow to respond to criticism for having products made offshore in exploitative working conditions. It is not clear, therefore, whether environmental pressures facilitate or inhibit adaptation and innovative organizational change. Organizational learning theorists argue that environmental pressures do lead to change, as managers learn from problems and try to close the gap between performance and aspirations. Threat-rigidity theory, however, argues that pressures inhibit change, as management decisions become constrained when faced with threatening problems (Mone et al., 1998).

Clark Gilbert (2005, 2006) considers the case of an organization facing discontinuous change, triggered by fundamental shifts in its operating environment. One example is the development of digital media, which have affected traditional "hard copy" newspaper (and textbook) print products. Gilbert argues that change results from performance gaps. These gaps may be threat-based, such as a decline in sales and profit. Gaps may also be opportunity-based, such as developing new products. Threats, however, can trigger rigid behavioral responses, restricting information flow, constraining decisions, and emphasizing control over existing resources. Opportunity-based responses, on the other hand, may suggest new, flexible ways of working, but because current capabilities and practices remain successful, commitment to change may be lacking.

Gilbert argues that this paradox occurs because "it is not that one set of capabilities suddenly becomes obsolete, to be replaced with another. Rather, it stems from the fact that the path from one capability to the other is not continuous. In such settings, the previous position may continue to evidence residual fit, even while the new position expands and develops" (Gilbert, 2006, p. 151). IBM continued to develop its mainframe products for 20 years, despite the emergence of the minicomputer market that fundamentally changed the industry. The paradox suggests that companies in this situation need to be able to have coexisting frames that focus on both threats and opportunities, one frame protecting current business and the other helping to move the company into new arenas. This can be achieved, for example, through structural differentiation, with separate organizational units dominated by different cognitive frames. Senior management must be able to integrate these competing frames, ensuring that the company takes appropriate, timely actions across its operations.

"Trapped by success" is another reason why organizations can fail to respond to pressures for change. Sull (1999) argues that successful companies may be trapped by their "winning formula" when conditions change. Arrogance founded on success can lead to the assumption that market dominance will continue unchallenged. Cognitive frames thus become blinkered by success; operating routines become embedded as correct; relationships with stakeholders inhibit the exploration of new ventures; shared beliefs become company dogma. Organizations can thus become "learning disabled" and not respond appropriately to pressures for change. Some commentators argue that Nestlé was slow to respond to the impact of the Internet because of the long-term market success of its brands. That success linked a risk-averse culture to a bureaucratic structure. Similarly, one interpretation of Dell's declining fortunes in 2006 is that it "succumbed to complacency in the belief that its business model would always keep it far ahead of the pack" (Byrnes et al., 2007).

Environment: Objective Entity versus Cognitive Construction

It is tempting to think of the environment, "the world out there," as a physical presence generating pressures to which management then has to respond. That notion has been challenged by the strategic choice perspective, which argues that organizations make or "enact" their own environments by deciding the sectors and markets in which they will operate. Those decisions are typically based on the personal preferences of powerful senior managers (Child, 1972, 1997). The strategic choice perspective challenged the view that an organization's internal structure and processes were largely determined by external contingencies and that managers were therefore limited to ensuring that the organization was appropriately adapted to its context.

Treating the environment as an objective reality, the question of the accuracy of management perceptions of the key contingences and pressures arises. Boyd et al. (1993) identify two kinds of perceptual errors:

- A Type 1 error occurs when the environment is (objectively) stable, but managers perceive it as turbulent and take (unnecessary) actions.
- A Type 2 error occurs when managers threaten the survival of their firms by failing to act because they perceive the environment as stable when it is (objectively) turbulent.

Advocating the "enacted environment" perspective, Linda Smircich and Charles Stubbart (1985) also argue that "the outside world" is a construction based on individual perceptions. Even within a single organization, managers are likely to interpret differently what is happening in the external environment and to reach different conclusions with regard to changes that may or may not be desirable. William Bogner and Pamela Barr (2000) take this position further, arguing that managers' sense-making contributes to the perpetuation of hypercompetitive environments. They suggest that managers' cognitive frameworks influence what they notice, how they interpret events, and the resultant actions. The shared beliefs that develop over time in an industry then become taken for granted. In hypercompetitive environments, Bogner and Barr (2000, p. 221) argue:

> A common cognitive framework emerges that suggests to managers that success is based on a series of rapid and anticipatory actions that move industry to the next round of competition. Institutional forces pressure firms to adopt the behaviors of those that are more successful, and process-dominated recipes emerge as the new industry recipe when it becomes apparent that the better-performing firms are those that utilize the adaptive sense-making processes.

In other words, hypercompetitive environments and the organizational changes associated with them are perpetuated by the cognitive interpretations of managers. In this perspective, managers are trapped by their cognitive sense-making frames.

Forces for Change versus Forces for Stability

Mark Mone et al. (1998) argue that four sets of factors affect whether or not environmental pressures will lead to innovation and change when an organization is faced with decline:

Institutionalized mission: Where stakeholders have clear expectations of how an organization will pursue its goals, the organization's capacity to innovate will be constrained. In contrast, relaxed or ill-defined stakeholder expectations can act as a catalyst for innovation by giving the organization more flexibility to respond to the problems it faces.

Power structures: The capacity for innovation is constrained when power is diffuse in an organization, but power that is concentrated acts as a catalyst by increasing the capacity for making decisions and allocating resources to implement change.

Resource commitment: Where resources are already committed, innovation is stifled, but where there are high levels of uncommitted resources, innovation is encouraged.

Explanations of the problem: Where organizational decline is perceived to be beyond management control, attempts to innovate are unlikely; where decline is attributed to controllable factors, the necessity for and incentive to innovate are clearer.

These arguments alert us to the need to consider both the forces for stability and for change, and how those forces compete and interact. For example, a hypercompetitive environment could be seen as an "obvious" driver of innovation and change. But as Carrie Leana and Bruce Barry (2000) argue, this view overlooks the forces for stability that may also be in play along with those forces for change: "both are a necessary part of organizations' effective functioning in the long-term." Table 3.5 summarizes these forces.

TABLE 3.5
Forces for Change, Forces for Stability

Forces for Change	Forces for Stability
Adaptability of the organization to its environment	*Institutionalism* of current practices due to solidity of past practices and power structures
Cost containment, e.g., making human resources a variable rather than a fixed cost	*Transaction costs*, e.g., stable employment allows investment in staff development
Impatient capital markets demanding more immediate returns on investments	*Sustained advantage* gained through stable organizational relationships difficult to imitate
Control through managerially imposed performance targets	*Organizational social capital*, established trust among coworkers becomes a valued asset
Competitive advantage, being responsive to changing market conditions	*Predictability and uncertainty reduction*, the need for which inhibits change

Source: Based on Leana and Barry (2000).

Bridging (Adapting) versus Buffering (Shielding)

Responding to pressures for change arising from environmental uncertainty is a classic theme in organization theory. James Thompson (1967, p. 159) argued, "Uncertainty appears as the fundamental problem for complex organizations, and coping with uncertainty, as the essence of the administrative process." There are two broad strategies for managing uncertainty: bridging and buffering.

Bridging strategies are designed to maintain organizational effectiveness by adapting to external changes. For example, in a school, bridging strategies may be used to lift student educational performance in deprived socioeconomic areas. Strategies might include inviting parents and other family members to assist classroom teachers.

Buffering strategies are designed to maintain organizational efficiency by avoiding change, by shielding the organization from external pressures. Thompson (1967) describes a number of techniques for smoothing the effects of external shocks through forecasting, planning, and stockpiling: "By the time environmental shock waves reach the stability-sensitive technical core, they are diffused into manageable adjustments and innovations" (Lynn, 2005, p. 39). Returning to the school example, a principal may shield teaching staff by insisting on following formal rules that state that external groups such as parents, community agencies, and businesses must make any initial contact through the principal rather than directly to a teacher. Martin Meznar et al. (2006) found that when organizations were "in the public eye," getting a lot of press coverage, buffering strategies were more likely to increase. This involved using public relations techniques to promote their position and to change public perceptions and expectations.

In practice, the avoidance of organizational change by buffering may also depend on organizational networks, which are able to "share" buffering strategies across a number of organizations. Most organizations may have to engage both buffering and bridging strategies simultaneously, depending on the circumstances that they face. However, buffering may make an organization less competitive, by insulating it against necessary innovation and change.

LO 3.3 Why Do Organizations Not Change after Crises?

Why would organizations not implement change following accidents, crises, and disasters, in order to prevent further similar events? This is a situation in which it might be assumed that change would be welcome, automatic, straightforward. Expectations and receptiveness should be high, resistance low. The evidence shows, however, that these assumptions are often incorrect.

Victoria Climbié, an eight-year-old girl, was killed by her guardians in the London borough of Haringey in 2000. The public inquiry into her death, chaired by Lord Laming (2003), blamed systemic failures among the agencies responsible for monitoring vulnerable children: local authority, social services, National Health Service, police. The inquiry made 108 recommendations. In 2007, also in Haringey, 17-month-old Peter Connelly was killed by his mother and her boyfriend, while under the supervision of the same agencies that had failed Victoria (Care Quality Commission, 2009; Laming, 2009). These cases attracted significant press and media coverage in the United Kingdom. Interviewed in January 2008, Laming observed that many child protection agencies had ignored his recommendations (BBC, 2008). Asked how he felt about similar cases of child abuse since his report in 2003, Laming replied, "I despair about the organizations that have not put in place the recommendations which I judged to be little more than good basic practice. I reject the notion that any of this is rocket science. I believe this is about day by day good practice, and I am disappointed if there are organizations that took several years to put in place recommendations that I judged could be put in place within a matter of months." Victoria and Peter suffered appalling abuse. Press coverage included graphic images of their injuries. How could a similar tragedy occur in the same setting? Why were Laming's (2003) recommendations not all implemented if they were "good practice"?

This is a recurring narrative that applies to many different kinds of event. Another iconic example concerns the losses of the NASA space shuttles *Challenger* (1986) and *Columbia* (2003), the causes of which displayed striking similarities (Vaughan, 1996; Columbia Accident Investigation Board, 2003; Mahler and Casamayou, 2009). The NASA shuttle losses were complex incidents, and they have been subjected to exhaustive analysis, but two conclusions are significant. First, although the immediate causes of these disasters were technical (O-ring failure; foam insulation damaged a wing), the main contributory causes were organizational: budget pressures, launch program expectations, management style, subcontractor relationships. Second, there were failures in organizational learning (see chapter exercise 11.3). Mahler and Casamayou (2009) offer an interesting analysis of what NASA learned from the *Challenger* disaster, what was not learned from that event, and what was learned but subsequently forgotten—leading ultimately to the *Columbia* disaster.

One of the main reasons for failures to change after extreme events thus concerns organizational learning difficulties. Brian Toft and Simon Reynolds (2005) distinguish between passive learning (identifying lessons) and active learning (implementing changes). Many organizations, it appears, focus on passive learning but overlook active learning, or find that difficult to achieve.

In explaining why organizations do not change following crises, Amy Edmondson (2011, p. 49) notes the effort that goes into after-action reviews, postmortems, and investigations: "Time after time I saw that these painstaking efforts led to no real change." The problem, Edmondson argues, is that most managers think that failures are bad (some are), and that learning from these events is straightforward (ask people what went wrong and tell them to avoid similar mistakes in future). Both of those views, she argues, are incorrect. Failure is not always bad, and learning from organizational failures is complex; it is almost always necessary to look further than "procedures weren't followed." That involves what she calls "first-order reasoning," looking at immediate causal factors such as the failed O-ring. She argues that it is also necessary to understand the second- and third-order reasons. That is challenging because complex failures typically involve combinations of many events across different parts of an organization over time. Edmondson (2011, p. 54) advocates the use of multidisciplinary team-based analysis to explore those kinds of issues, and offers the following example:

> A team of leading physicists, engineers, aviation experts, naval leaders, and even astronauts devoted months to an analysis of the *Columbia* disaster. They conclusively established not only the first-order cause—a piece of foam had hit the shuttle's leading edge during launch—but also second-order causes: a rigid hierarchy and schedule-obsessed culture at NASA made it especially difficult for engineers to speak up about anything but the most rock-solid concerns.

Edmondson also argues that organizational failures lie on a continuum, from praiseworthy (innovative experiments that just didn't work) to blameworthy (deliberate sabotage). However, speaking of this continuum (which we will consider again in chapter 11), she notes that:

> When I ask executives to consider how many of the failures in their organizations are truly blameworthy, their answers are usually in single digits—perhaps 2% to 5%. But when I ask how many are treated as blameworthy, they say (after a pause or a laugh) 70% to 90%. The unfortunate consequence is that many failures go unreported and their lessons are lost.

(Edmondson, 2011, p. 50)

For effective post-incident change, Edmondson argues, the organization needs a "psychologically safe environment" in which failures can be discussed openly. This involves five steps:

1. There must be a shared understanding of the kinds of failures that can occur in a particular context, and why openness is important for learning.
2. Those who report failures—the "messengers"—should be praised, rather than shot.
3. Known problems must be acknowledged, and mistakes admitted openly and honestly.
4. To defuse resistance and defensiveness, management must invite participation, seeking ideas and creating opportunities for staff to analyze failures and explore remedies.
5. There must be clarity concerning actions that are blameworthy, so boundaries are clear, and people are accountable.

Adopting a different perspective, David Buchanan (2011) argues that explanations for failures in post-incident change may lie in the altered nature of the organizational context. Mainstream commentary on change management focuses on change with *progressive*, developmental agendas—restructuring, quality, process redesign, innovation, new technology and working practices—aimed at cost reduction, quality, time to market, "agility," customer service, growth, market share, and profitability. Changes following extreme events, in contrast, have *defensive* agendas, which aim to prevent things from happening. The contrasts between "routine" and "post-incident" contexts are summarized in table 3.6.

TABLE 3.6
Routine and Extreme Contexts

Routine Contexts	Post-Incident Contexts
Business development	Control of risk
Progressive agenda: make things happen	Defensive agenda: stop things from happening
Take risks	Minimize risks
Participation of those involved	Participation as witnesses
Our own communications strategy	Overtaken by media commentary
Local ownership of the agenda	Externally imposed agenda
Local implementation	All comparable sites affected
Local control of implementation timing	Implementation when directed
Exciting for change agents	Unappealing for change agents

The context following an extreme event may itself be nonroutine, rendering conventional change guidance (participation, communication) difficult to apply. Receptiveness may be low if the incident is seen as atypical, and recommended changes may be seen as a costly overreaction. In cases of mistake or misconduct, controls imposed to deter "the guilty" also apply to "the innocent," fostering resentment. The membership of an investigating team influences both the nature and credibility of recommendations. Different stakeholders and advocacy groups may disagree with each other's opinions and may use the incident to pursue other agendas (Smith and Elliott, 2007). Externally imposed change, by an inquiry or regulatory body, may not be seen as legitimate. Introducing changes while emotions are running high may increase anxiety and resistance (Bowers et al., 2006); change under "normal" conditions is often stressful, without the complication of an extreme event.

Buchanan (2011) also argues that implementing a defensive change agenda may be less appealing for the change manager. The main indicator of the success of that agenda is the nonoccurrence of the next event. That may be less exciting than the development of something new (products, systems, business models), which in career terms is also likely to be more rewarding. It may be helpful therefore, in a post-incident context, to design a change agenda that marries progressive and developmental components with defensive, preventive elements.

LO 3.4 Internal Organizational Change Drivers

In this section, we discuss five potential drivers from within the organization (figure 3.3), related to:

- growth;
- integration and collaboration;
- corporate identity;
- a new chief executive;
- power and politics.

Growth

Organizations often grow as they age, especially if they are successful. In 1992, Kevin Sharer joined Amgen Inc., now a leading Fortune 500 biotechnology company, as its president and chief operating officer. His aim was to turn it into a major pharmaceutical company. To grow the business, Amgen had to move beyond its start-up days when decisions were based on hallway conversations, scientists had little consideration for the company's market, and salespeople were only loosely accountable for sales. When Sharer became chief executive in 2000, he introduced a series of organizational changes. These included individual rather than regional-based performance targets for sales representatives; monitoring the number of sales calls made each week; and hand-held computers to record details of sales conversations so that poor tactics could be identified and rectified (Hemp, 2004).

Robert Herbold faced similar issues when he left Procter & Gamble to join Microsoft. He was astounded at the lack of discipline in Microsoft in terms of how decisions were

FIGURE 3.3
Internal Organizational Change Drivers

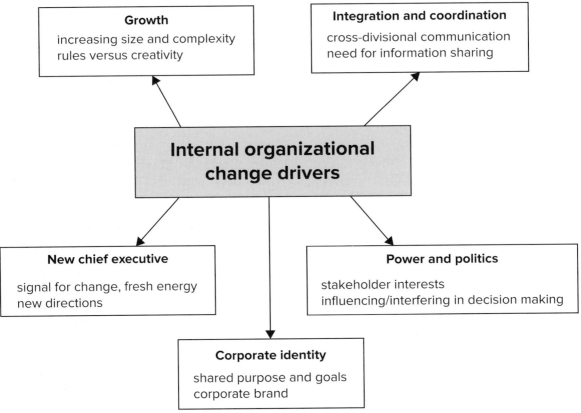

made and priorities were established. The hallmark corridor decision making of start-up companies was not appropriate for managing an organization as large and as complex as Microsoft. Herbold established formalized decision-making processes and other protocols, to balance entrepreneurial creativity with the need for greater discipline. The changes at Amgen and Microsoft both involved the routinization of work practices. Such changes are often the result of growth, implemented to handle the complexity of a growing business, to bring rigor to their operations (Herbold, 2002).

Of course, not all organizations continue to grow. One study of small business owners in Britain found that many of these managers actively resisted the growth of their businesses beyond the point at which they lost personal control of day-to-day operations. Beyond this point, they lost job satisfaction, which, at least for some, was why they had moved from large organizations in the first place and set up their own company (Scase and Goffee, 1987). Other writers have observed that growth is not necessarily a linear, sequential movement from one stage to the next. As discussed in chapter 2, chaos theory argues that change may be nonlinear and fundamental rather than incremental and may not involve growth. In addition, younger organizations may fail to grow because of the inexperience of their managers and through lack of organizational slack or the resources to absorb bad business decisions. For other new organizations, the growth challenge is to maintain the "entrepreneurial feel":

> *Google has been phenomenally successful. But it has a challenge ahead if it is to retain the culture and feel associated with its success. It's easy to feel like an outlaw band that's changing the world when you have 100 employees. It's incredibly difficult when you have 10,000 or 100,000.*

(Lachinsky, 2007, p. 57)

Integration and Coordination

Some changes are made in order to better integrate the organization or create economies of scale across different business units. SunAmerica, a financial network of brokers, was acquired by the giant insurance company American International Group (AIG). The resultant broker-dealer network consisted of six businesses: Advantage Capital, FSC Securities, Royal Alliance, Sentra Securities, Spelman, and SunAmerica Securities. Signalling greater integration of these businesses, the name was changed from the SunAmerica Financial Network to the AIG Advisory Group. At the same time, changes entailing consolidation across the different businesses included centralization in New York, San Diego, and Phoenix of recruitment, legal compliance, and advisory services. Other changes included the creation of uniform standards across the businesses, better profiling of the AIG brand, and leveraging buying power across the network (Cooper and Kulkowski, 2002).

When Dick Brown became chief executive of EDS in 1999, he became head of a company that had pioneered IT services, but whose market share was being eroded by faster, newer IT companies. Brown saw that coordination and information sharing in EDS were weak. He found that he could not even send an email to all 140,000 people who worked for the company, as there were 16 separate email systems. In addition, the company had 48 different business units, which involved a lot of duplication and which often did not communicate well with each other or have a consistent customer orientation. This meant that some parts of the organization were involved in activities that other parts had tried and rejected, but this information was not transmitted. This also meant that there was a lack of coordination between business units in collaborating to solve customers' problems. For example, EDS was in danger of losing Continental, a major client for whom it handled reservation, accounting, and payroll systems. Unfortunately, these systems kept crashing, and projects were delivered late and with poor-quality results. Brown launched a series of cultural and structural changes to provide a more overt customer orientation. The impetus for these changes was better coordination and collaboration across the multiple business units of the company. In 2003, EDS replaced Brown after a period of earnings warnings, an SEC probe, and a contract problem. Nevertheless, Brown claimed that as a result of changes during his four-year tenure, there were four business lines rather than 48 business units, costs had been reduced by $5 billion, and productivity had increased (Breen, 2001).

Corporate Identity

When Antoine Cau became chief executive of the Forte Hotel Group, which included London Hotels, UK Hotels, and International Hotels, he found that they were often in competition with each other, and that hotel employees lacked cultural identity with Forte and its brand. Service excellence was key to achieving customer satisfaction, which was linked to employee satisfaction. In order to address these issues, Cau created four distinct market segments: Le Meridien, Posthouse, Heritage, and Travelodge. He then introduced a cultural change program across the four hotel groups. His aim was to enhance the commitment of staff, strengthening the identity of the Forte brand, and to improve customer service. These aims were achieved by promoting staff development and employee recognition schemes to increase job satisfaction (Erstad, 2001).

When Philip N. Diehl became head of the U.S. Mint, it was seen as slow, inefficient, and lacking in commercial performance standards. Its main goal was to produce coins, but the Mint had no idea of the magnitude of its coin inventory. It also manufactured collectible and commemorative coins. However, the timing of commemorative issues was dictated by Congress, sometimes five or six times a year. This meant that commemorative coins were no longer rare and were of decreasing interest to collectors. The Mint faced an identity crisis: Was it a passive organization making coins, including commemoratives, simply following the dictates of the Federal Reserve and Congress? Or should it act more like a market-based organization, launching its own products and promotional campaigns? Establishing a new identity for the Mint through organizational changes such as making commemorative coins more collectable (by issuing fewer of them), using online marketing, portraying its role as a purveyor of history, and marketing innovations such as the 50 State Quarters Program helped move it toward a new, more modern, customer-focused identity (Muoio, 1999).

A New Chief Executive

The new broom phenomenon, when a new chief executive arrives, can act as a signal that old ways are about to change. Arthur Martinez became head of the merchandising group at Sears at a time when the company produced one of its worst sales records, reporting a net loss of $3.9 billion, most of which came from the merchandising group. In "new broom" tradition, in his first 100 days, Martinez started a turnaround plan, reorienting marketing away from being a "man's store," to appeal to women as well. At the same time as moving into cosmetics and other specialty store products, he closed 113 stores, eliminated the 100-year-old Sears catalogue, reengineered store operations, and, through training, incentives, and new staffing procedures, moved the company toward a service culture to appeal to both male and female customers (Rucci et al., 1998).

When Kenneth D. Lewis took over as CEO of Bank of America, he instituted what has since been called "a quiet revolution," moving the business "from empire-building to value creation." Rather than follow the growth strategy of his predecessor, he sought to grow profits by downscaling the bank's operations, getting rid of underperforming businesses such as auto leasing, and divesting unprofitable customer segments. He also brought in new managers to infuse the organization with new ideas and sought to improve customer service through enhanced training programs for tellers, moving away from organizing around product lines in favor of customers, and encouraging cross-selling of products by tying executive salaries to performance targets. These moves apparently had their desired effect: by March 2007, Bank of America claimed, under Lewis's leadership, to be "one of the world's largest financial institutions and the fifth most profitable company in the world" (Faust, 2002).

When 35-year-old Kate Betts took over as editor-in-chief at *Harper's Bazaar*, she was charged with changing the 130-year-old company. The company had stagnated compared to other magazines such as *Vogue* and *Elle* and was seen as stodgy and tedious—descriptions not best associated with fashion magazines. In "new broom" form, in her first six months, she changed the magazine's logos, typeface, and staff in order to create a new mindset and a better profile for the magazine. This included replacing over half of the senior staff with her own "dream team" in order to regain market share related to younger readers (Brooker, 2000).

However, unlike Lewis at Bank of America, not all new broom changes are necessarily the right ones. Bercovici (2003) claims that Betts "threw *Bazaar* into a newsstand nosedive." In 2001 Glenda Bailey replaced Betts as editor-in-chief. Bercovici also argues that "much of Bailey's revamp has amounted to undoing Betts' misbegotten innovations, returning the magazine to its roots as a haven for the fashion elite," which included "restoring the old *Harper's Bazaar* logo, which Betts had replaced with a blocky modernist design."

In Rosabeth Moss Kanter's (2003, pp. 64–65) analysis of organizational turnarounds at Gillette, the BBC, and Invensys, she notes that they were all led by a new chief executive. She asks: "Does this mean that only a new broom can sweep clean?" Her answer is that this is probably the case. New CEOs have advantages over their predecessors:

- They are likely to be able to create energy for change.
- They are not constrained by past practice.
- They can focus on the organization's known but unresolved "sacred cows."
- Having no association with previous customer relationship issues, they are able to handle customer-related problems with credibility.

Power and Politics

Power and political pressures come in many forms. Some are associated with board-level changes. The tussle between Philip Purcell and John Mack for the chief executive's position at Morgan Stanley after the company had been bought by Dean Witter and Discover Financial Services Inc. in 1997 is one example; Purcell became CEO (Thornton and Reed, 2001). As noted above, another example concerned the ousting of Jean-Marie Messier, CEO of Vivendi, in mid-2002. *The Economist* (2002) claimed that it was the Bronfman family, a major shareholder in the company, which had lost nearly $2 billion due to poor share performance over the previous year, who were behind the push to get rid of Messier. Removing Messier was also aligned with the interests of the French political right, who were concerned about ownership issues related to television and telephone companies.

Some changes are made to alter traditional internal power relationships, to speed up decision making, and to allow wider involvement. One example was at IBM when Sam Palmisano took over as CEO from Lou Gerstner. In January 2003, he abolished the 92-year-old, 12-person executive management team. Described as the "inner bastion of power and privilege" at IBM, this committee was the "inner sanctum" that made decisions about IBM's strategy and direction. In disbanding the committee, Palmisano sent a message that power relationships were being restructured to avoid decisions being slowed down by waiting for the monthly meetings of this committee (Ante, 2003).

Other power pressures leading to change relate to internal conflicts. For example, at Roche, the pharmaceutical company, a range of organizational changes were made, including teamwork, in order to assist the fast-developing field of genomics. In 1999 Lee Babiss,

Using Power and Politics to Secure the City

Interorganizational politics can sometimes block change. Christopher Dickey (2009) describes how, following the terrorist attacks on the World Trade Center on September 11, 2001, the New York Police Department (NYPD) created a Counter-Terrorism Bureau (CTB). To be successful, the CTB had to be invisible to the public, who were paying for this service through taxation, and the Bureau's intelligence gathering took place elsewhere on the planet, which meant taking New York cops off the city streets. The new Real Time Crime Center at One Police Plaza in Manhattan cost $11 million. But three years after the attacks, people had started to forget. To counteract the apathy, the Bureau organized impressive shows of force, deliberately turning up without warning at high-profile targets like the Empire State Building, to remind the public that the bad guys were still out there.

The CTB also had to work with other agencies, particularly "the three-letter guys": FBI, CIA, ATF, DEA. Relations between the FBI and the CTB were managed through a Joint Terrorism Task Force. The head of the NYPD Intelligence Division was David Cohen:

> Cohen's years at Langley and in the New York office of the CIA had taught him "there's no such

thing as information sharing, there is only information trading," as he told his colleagues at the NYPD. You go to the FBI and say, "Tell me what you're doing," they're going to say, "Go f*** yourself," is the way another senior official with the NYPD put it.

> Back channels to the CIA or other parts of the intelligence community could only take you so far. To get the stuff you needed, you had to be able to pull your weight. You had to be giving as well as getting. Otherwise you were going to be like the puny kid having sand kicked in his face by bullies. (Dickey, 2009, p. 140)

This led to an "overseas program," with NYPD operatives working abroad in liaison positions with forces that had their own counter-terrorist units, to exchange and gather intelligence. This meant that Cohen was able to establish a power base through his own intelligence operation, and the three-letter guys had to come and ask him for information. Information sharing then became possible. The ability to understand and to use power and organization politics effectively was fundamental to the success of the NYPD CTB in its efforts to detect and prevent future attacks.

head of preclinical research at Roche's headquarters at Nutley, noticed that there were an increasing number of corridor conversations between researchers working on genomics and those working in other areas such as oncology and cancer research. He sought to harness these interactions by creating interdisciplinary research teams that cut across traditional power and scientific departmental boundaries. For example, the Genomics Oncology (or GO) team brought together a diverse group of researchers united by the aim of using genomic innovations to assist the development of anticancer drugs. However, not all teams at Roche worked well. Previously, from the mid-1990s onward, teams of scientists were set up to compete with each other for access to scarce resources. Over time, these interactions became internal warfare, leading to the hoarding of technical expertise and knowledge within teams. It also led to a reluctance to abandon team projects, especially where the careers of research scientists were linked to their success. In 1998 this was abandoned in favor of a collaborative approach that recognized the importance of establishing team structures that shared knowledge and information.

EXERCISE 3.1

Top Team Role Play

LO 3.5

1. In groups of three, choose an organizational change with which you are familiar, perhaps in your current employment, or in an organization about which you have recently been reading. If neither of those options works, then, for the purposes of this exercise, invent an organization and a change initiative.

2. Now revisit table 3.1, "Images of Change and Understanding the Pressures." Each person in your group must choose one of those images of managing change and will play that role.

3. Your group is now in a senior management board meeting. You are discussing an agenda item at the request of the chairman of your board, who wants to know why the organization is going through the change that you have identified.

4. Debate how you will respond to the chairman's request, with each member of your group (board) playing their role based on the change management image that they have selected.

5. When you have decided how you are going to respond to the chair's request, consider the following questions:

   Did one of your images better explain the rationale for change than the others, and why?

   On reflection, what criteria did you use for making this judgement with regard to the comparative advantage of a particular image?

   Is there an image with which you personally have a particular affinity or preference? Why? What would it take for you to change that preference?

EXERCISE 3.2

Case Analysis: The Sunderland City Story

LO 3.1

Is change more difficult in a recession? As you read the following account of change in a local government agency in England (based on MacLachlan, 2011), consider the following questions:

1. What features of a downturn can make managing organizational change more difficult?

2. What features of a downturn can make managing organizational change more straightforward?

3. Sunderland City Council introduced several changes to deal with the twin goals of maintaining services and reducing spending. What factors explain the success of their program?

With the recession that began in 2009, local government in England had to cut spending while maintaining the same levels of services to the local population. Could costs be cut with a radical redesign of services and new ways of working? Sunderland City Council employed 8,000 people in the northeast of England, receiving two-thirds of their budget from central government. In 2010–11, funding fell 10 percent, by £58 million, and more cuts were expected over the next three years. Management wondered whether, given the sharp downturn in the economy, staff would be demotivated and concerned about layoffs. At the start of 2010, the Council launched a transformation program; could things be done differently, but without losing jobs?

Unwilling to force staff to retire early or accept redeployment, the Council created an internal jobs market. This encouraged staff in areas that were shrinking to apply for jobs in expanding services, using a web-enabled assessment and employee-job matching system.

(Continued)

This was linked to a retraining program designed to transform the skills profile of the work-force, focusing on personality, values, and potential, as well as on knowledge and past experience. An employee portal was established to allow staff to create their own CVs.

Resistance to these moves came not from staff but from managers who felt that their recruitment decisions were being constrained. For staff who were unable to find new roles, a unit was established called "Switch": Staff Working In Transition and CHange. Over 200 people between roles, including managers, worked in this unit, reducing the Council's use of temporary staff on fixed-term contracts, for maternity cover, for exam-ple. The Switch team was also used to drive change, with efficiency savings projects, designing future job roles, and providing careers advice to other staff in transition.

The flexible working scheme was popular, allowing staff voluntarily to reduce their paid hours (with the option to increase them again), and to "purchase" up to two weeks' additional annual leave by spreading the salary sacrifice over the year. A "be your own boss" scheme offered support to employees who wanted to start their own businesses, giving them 20 days' paid leave and access to a small business adviser. The 50 staff who wanted to proceed continued working part time for the Council to give them some income security while they established their businesses. Local employers were invited to "borrow" and to pay Council staff on secondments.

EXERCISE 3.3

The Reputa-tion Trap: Can You Escape?

`LO 3.1`

What happens if a company cannot change how it is viewed by consumers? As you read this case, consider the following questions:

1. What does this case reveal about the challenges faced by successful businesses? Is it possible to be too successful?

2. How does a successful organization determine whether an environmental change is a brief fad or fashion to be ignored, or a development that requires a fundamental rethinking of the way in which it does business?

3. What change issues does this case raise with regard to the significance of reputation?

4. What actions would you recommend be taken by Big Food and the fast-food compa-nies that have been caught in the reputation trap?

Try this simple test. Say the following out loud: Artificial colors and flavors. Pesticides. Preser-vatives. High-fructose corn syrup. Growth hormones. Antibiotics. Gluten. Genetically modified organisms. If any one of these terms raised a hair on the back of your neck, left a sour taste in your mouth, or made your lips purse with disdain, you are part of Big Food's multibillion-dollar problem. In fact, you may even belong to a growing consumer class that has some of the world's biggest and best-known companies scrambling to change their businesses. (Kowitt, 2015, p. 61)

Fortune magazine prides itself on being able to feel and report "the pulse" of U.S. busi-ness. In 2014 and 2015, two articles by Beth Kowitt, "Fallen Arches" and "The War on Big Food," explored the impact that consumer preference for healthy foods was having on Big Food organizations such as General Mills and Kraft, and also on some fast-food outlets like McDonald's and Subway. A growing number of consumers are suspicious of processed foods. Ironically, although processing (e.g., salting and curing) has traditionally been associ-ated with reducing the risk of illness from the food we eat, food processing is now seen as the antithesis of healthy eating.

The annual sales of processed food are declining, but these are the core products of mul-tibillion-dollar Big Food companies. Since 2009, the top 25 food and beverage companies in the United States have lost market share equivalent to $18 billion. Some fast-food companies are also facing a similar shift in consumer preferences. For example, in 2014, in their U.S. operations, McDonald's reported four consecutive quarters of falling sales, and an overall 30 percent drop in profit, while Subway's sales dropped 3 percent, or $400 million.

Big Food has reacted by increasingly marketing their products as "natural," reviewing their product recipes, and acquiring many small health and natural food companies. However, this has not resolved their reputational problem. According to Gary Hirshberg, founder and chairman of Stonyfield Farm, "There's enormous doubt and scepticism about whether large companies can deliver naturality and authenticity" (Kowitt, 2015, p. 64). According to Don Thompson, CEO of McDonald's, "People today are questioning the integrity and quality of the food at a much higher level" (Kowitt, 2014, p. 116). Some fast-food brands, such as Chipotle Mexican Grill (annual growth rate 20 percent) and Firehouse Subs, are thriving in this environment, but not McDonald's or Subway. McDonald's seems to be suffering from its past success, which built its reputation as the quintessential fast-food brand. Today, however, it is operating in an environment where a growing number of customers are choosing "fresh and healthy" rather than "fast and convenient" (Kowitt, 2014, p. 109). The challenge for McDonald's is to convince customers that it can be both.

Subway might seem to be a strange brand to have suffered from the "move to health," given that its growth has in the past been due to its positioning as a healthy alternative to "traditional" fast food. As one indicator of Subway's success, it is "the world's most ubiquitous restaurant chain," with almost 44,000 outlets in 110 countries (Harwell, 2015). However, according to Darren Tristan, executive vice president of the industry research firm Technomic, Subway's problem is that "fresh" no longer means what Subway offers. For example, people want meat that has been freshly cut, not a precut slice peeled off wax paper. Subway has also been criticized for using the food additive azodicarbonamide (E927, a flour bleaching and dough conditioning agent) in its bread.

Summarizing the situation, IBIS World food analyst Andrew Alvarez observes, "We're in a new environment—the Chipotle environment—with a new type of rhetoric, quality and marketability. Subway's platform, its presentation, almost looks primordial" (Harwell, 2015, p. 5).

Case Sources:

Harwell, D. 2015. The rise and fall of Subway, the world's biggest food chain. *The Washington Post*, May 30:
http://www.washingtonpost.com/business/economy/the-rise-and-fall-of-subway-the-worlds-biggest-food-chain/2015/05/29/0ca0a84a-fa7a-11e4-a13c-193b1241d51a_story.html, accessed June 20, 2015.
Kowitt, B. 2014. Fallen arches: Can McDonald's get its mojo back? *Fortune*, December 1:106–16.
Kowitt, B. 2015. The war on big food. *Fortune*, May 21:61–70.

Additional Reading

Abrahamson, E. 2004. *Change without pain: How managers can overcome initiative overload, organizational chaos, and employee burnout*. Boston: Harvard Business School Press. Argues the need to manage carefully the pace of change, rather than have ongoing dramatic transformations that destabilize the organization and burn out staff.

Beard, A., and Hornik, R. 2011. It's hard to be good. *Harvard Business Review* 89(11):88–96. Profiles five organizations with exemplary approaches to responsible business practices: Royal DSM (Netherlands), Southwest Airlines (United States), Broad Group (China), Potash Corporation (Canada), and Unilever (United Kingdom).

Benn, S., Dunphy, D., and Griffiths, A. 2014. *Organizational change for corporate sustainability*. 3rd ed. London: Routledge. Develops a unified view combining ecological and human sustainability, with case studies and practical advice for change agents.

Buchanan, D. A. 2011. Good practice, not rocket science: Understanding failures to change after extreme events. *Journal of Change Management* 11(3):273–88. Distinguishes post-incident organization contexts from "routine" contexts in order to identify the potential barriers to change following accidents, failures, and other crises.

Bughin, J., Chui, M., and Manyika, J. 2010. Clouds, big data, and smart assets: Ten tech-enabled business trends to watch. *McKinsey Quarterly* (August):1–14. Explores how organizations are developing new business models to exploit rapidly developing technologies, such as "distributed cocreation," "networks as organizations," "the Internet of things," and "big data."

Gratton, L. 2011. *The shift: The future of work is already here*. London: Collins. Explores how the forces of globalization, society change, demography, technology, and use of natural resources are reshaping work and organizations; offers advice on how to "future-proof" your career.

Roundup

Here is a short summary of the key points that we would like you to take from this chapter, in relation to each of the learning outcomes:

LO 3.1

Understand the environmental pressures that can trigger organizational change.
We explored external pressures that encourage organizations to change. *Fashion*: managers want to appear to be "progressive," looking out for "the next big thing." *Demography*: organizations need to consider how to address the changing motives of each new generation and the approaching "silver tsunami" of an ageing workforce. *Mandate*: many changes are nonnegotiable, driven by legislation and regulation, and others are difficult to avoid, such as expectations of corporate responsibility. *Geopolitics*: in

Reflections for the Practicing Change Manager

- To what extent can you identify the external environmental pressures for change in your organization?

- To what extent can you influence whether and how to change?

- Do you relate better to one or more of the change management images outlined in table 3.1, with regard to the organizational changes in which you are involved? Why is this the case?

- Which of the possible reasons for avoiding change that have been discussed in this chapter have you experienced? On reflection, how might you have contributed to overcoming those avoidance tactics? And how would you judge your likely success in that attempt?

- How easy is it to raise issues in your organization about the rationale for specific changes? Is there a dominant rationale? And if so, why?

- What personal criteria might you adopt to ensure that you are initiating change "for the right reasons"? Set out some key questions that might help to guide you in future, to ensure that your rationale for change is clear to you and clear to those who will be affected.

a highly interdependent global economy, events in distant locations can have "ripple effects" around the planet, and all organizations need to address the implications of climate change and global warming. *Reputation*: an organization's sales and credibility can be badly affected by process, product, service, and internal governance failures, and rapid changes to restore and build reputation may often be necessary. *Hypercompetition*: change is being driven by disruptive, high-velocity innovation, which is partly technology-driven, and can be seen most vividly in "out-of-sector" competition, where organizations which are not in your business sector start to steal your customers.

It is important to note two further points. First, these six sets of pressures are interrelated, and most or all of them may be active at any one time. Second, this list of pressures is not comprehensive but is constantly shifting with local, national, and international trends and developments.

LO 3.2
Explain why not all organizations are affected equally by external pressures.
We explored four sets of explanations for the absence of change in the face of external pressures. First, external threat can lead to rigidity rather than innovation, as decision making becomes constrained and focused. Second, a pressure for change has to be perceived and interpreted as such before action is triggered, and if those external events are not understood as significant, change is unlikely to happen. Third, even in the face of a clear need for change, forces for stability may interfere. These include stakeholder expectations, which limit innovation; dispersed power, which impedes decision making; and a lack of resources to support innovation. Fourth, management may decide to use buffering strategies to shield the organization from adaptive change.

LO 3.3
Explain why organizations often fail to change following crises.
Although it might be expected that change following accidents, failures, and other crises would be straightforward, this is not always the case. The causes of these incidents are usually complex and systemic, requiring systemic solutions that can be difficult and costly to implement. Many organizations are good at passive learning (identifying lessons) but not so good at active learning (implementing those changes). Not all failures are blameworthy; some are praiseworthy. Most failures, however, are treated as blameworthy, and this is a further barrier to active learning, as it maintains a psychologically unsafe environment. The post-incident change agenda is often a defensive one, designed to stop such incidents from happening again. This is less appealing to change managers, who can experience more challenge and career rewards from implementing progressive change. It may be helpful to combine defensive agendas with progressive agendas to progress the former.

LO 3.4
Identify internal organizational factors that trigger change.
We explored five sets of internal triggers of organizational change. *Growth* generates problems of increased size and complexity, and at some point the need for formal rules interferes with the need for creativity and innovation. *Integration and coordination* are common problems in larger organizations, often requiring cultural, structural, and process solutions to improve cross-divisional communication and information sharing. *A new chief executive* is often expected to bring fresh ideas and energy and to move the organization in new directions. *Corporate identity* may be an abstract concept, but shared purpose and goals, and a strong corporate brand, can be valuable competitive

assets requiring appropriate changes to protect and build them. *Power and politics* both drive and interfere with organizational change, depending on the interests of stakeholders and their ability to influence management decision making.

LO 3.5   *Relate differing images of managing change to pressures for change.*
Chapter 2 discussed three uses of the six-images framework: surfacing assumptions, assessing dominant images, and using multiple perspectives. We argued that there are no "right" and "wrong" images of change management and that it is valuable to be able to interpret problems and solutions in general, and change processes in particular, from different standpoints. This "multiple perspectives" approach can help to generate fresh thinking and creative solutions. In this chapter, we have seen how external and internal pressures or drivers do not necessarily lead to change; those pressures are filtered through the perceptions of the need for change, and those perceptions are in turn colored by the images that managers have of the change process. One manager's reaction to a particular external or internal pressure, therefore, may not be shared by others. The issues discussed in this chapter suggest that more successful change managers are likely to be those who have a clear, personal understanding about the pressures on them to change their organizations, a well-developed rationale for what they are attempting to achieve, and a clear view of the likely effects of their actions.

References   Abrahamson, E. 1996. Management fashion. *Academy of Management Review* 21(1):254–85.

Abrahamson, E. 2004. *Change without pain: How managers can overcome initiative overload, organizational chaos, and employee burnout.* Boston: Harvard Business School Press.

Anonymous. 2002. Maître dethroned. *The Economist* 364(8280):58–59.

Anonymous. 2010. The silver tsunami. *The Economist*, February 6:72.

Anonymous. 2014. A billion shades of grey. *The Economist*, April 26:11.

Ante, S. A. 2003. The new blue. *BusinessWeek Online*, March 17.

BBC. 2008. File on 4: Child protection policies, programme number 08VQ3930LHO. http://news.bbc.co.uk/1/shared/bsp/hi/pdfs/22_01_08_fo4_abuse.pdf, accessed March 2008.

Beard, A., and Hornik, R. 2011. It's hard to be good. *Harvard Business Review* 89(11):88–96.

Benn, S., Dunphy, D., and Griffiths, A. 2014. *Organizational change for corporate sustainability.* 3rd ed. London: Routledge.

Bercovici, J. 2003. From Harper's Bazaar to Bailey's Bazaar. *Media Life Magazine.com*, February 12.

Birkinshaw, J. 2014. Beware the next big thing. *Harvard Business Review* 92(5):50–57.

Bogner, W. C., and Barr, P. S. 2000. Making sense in hypercompetitive environments: A cognitive explanation for the persistence of high velocity competition. *Organization Science* 11(2):212–26.

Bowers, L., Simpson, A., Eyres, S., Nijman, H., Hall, C., Grange, A., and Phillips, L. 2006. Serious untoward incidents and their aftermath in acute inpatient psychiatry: The Tomkins Acute Ward study. *International Journal of Mental Health Nursing* 15(4):226–34.

Boyd, B. K., Dess, G. G., and Rasheed, A. M. A. 1993. Divergence between archival and perceptual measures of the environment: Causes and consequences. *Academy of Management Review* 210(2):204–26.

Breen, B. 2001. How EDS got its groove back. *Fast Company* 51(October):106–16.

Brooker, K. 2000. New blood for an old brand. *Fortune* 141(4):289–90.

Bruch, H., and Menges, J. I. 2010. The acceleration trap. *Harvard Business Review* 88(4):80–86.

Buchanan, D. A. 2011. Good practice, not rocket science: Understanding failures to change after extreme events. *Journal of Change Management* 11(3):273–88.

Buckley, C. 2007. *Boomsday*. London: Allison & Busby.

Bughin, J., Chui, M., and Manyika, J. 2010. Clouds, big data, and smart assets: Ten tech-enabled business trends to watch. *McKinsey Quarterly* (August):1–14.

Byrnes, N., Burrows, P., and Lee, L. 2007. Where Dell went wrong. *BusinessWeek*, February 19:62–63.

Care Quality Commission. 2009. *Review of the involvement and action taken by health bodies in relation to the case of Baby P*. London: CQC.

Child, J. 1972. Organization structure, environment, and performance: The role of strategic choice. *Sociology* 6(1):1–22.

Child, J. 1997. Strategic choice in the analysis of action, structure, organizations and environment: Retrospect and prospect. *Organization Studies* 18(1):43–76.

CIPD. 2014. *Change management factsheet*. London: Chartered Institute for Personnel and Development.

Columbia Accident Investigation Board. 2003. *Columbia Accident Investigation Board report, volumes I to VI*. Washington, DC: National Aeronautics and Space Administration and the Government Printing Office.

Cooper, E., and Kulkowski, L. 2002. AIG changes name of broker group; consolidation next? *On Wall Street* 12(10):15–18.

D'Aveni, R. 1994. *Hypercompetition: Managing the dynamics of strategic maneuvering*. New York: Free Press.

Dickey, C. 2009. *Securing the city: Inside America's best counterterror force—the NYPD*. New York: Simon and Schuster.

DiMaggio, P. J., and Powell, W. W. 1983. The iron cage revisited: Institutional isomorphism and collective rationality in organizational fields. *American Sociological Review* 48:147–60.

Dressang, J., and Barrett, R. 2006. Oak Creek could lose Delphi jobs: Unions say only four plants likely to survive bankruptcy. *Milwaukee Journal Sentinel*, March 31.

Edmondson, A. 2011. Strategies for learning from failure. *Harvard Business Review* 89(4):48–55.

Erstad, M. 2001. Commitment to excellence at the Forte Hotel Group. *International Journal of Contemporary Hospitality Management* 13(7):347–51.

Faircloth, A. 1998. Guess who's coming to Denny's. *Fortune* 138(3):108–10.

Faust, D. 2002. Whipping a behemoth into shape. *Business Week Online*, January 21.

Fombrun, C., and van Riel, C. 1997. The reputational landscape. *Corporate Reputation Review* 1(1 & 2):5–12.

Friedman, M. 1970. The social responsibility of business is to increase its profits. *New York Times Magazine*, September 13.

Friedrich, R., Peterson, M., and Koster, A. 2011. The rise of Generation C. *Strategy+Business Magazine*, no. 62 (Spring):1–6.

Gilbert, C. G. 2005. Unbundling the structure of inertia: Resource versus routine rigidity. *Academy of Management Journal* 48(5):741–63.

Gilbert, C. G. 2006. Change in the presence of residual fit: Can competing frames coexist? *Organization Science* 17(1):150–67.

Gratton, L. 2011. *The shift: The future of work is already here*. London: Collins.

Gunther, M., and Wheat, A. 2002. The directors. *Fortune* 146(7) (October 14):130.

Harwell, D. 2015. The rise and fall of Subway, the world's biggest food chain. *The Washington Post*, May 30:5.

Hemp, P. 2004. A time for growth: An interview with Amgen CEO Kevin Sharer. *Harvard Business Review* 82(7/8):66–74.

Herbold, R. J. 2002. Inside Microsoft: Balancing creativity and discipline. *Harvard Business Review* 80(1):72–79.

Hewlett, S. A., Sherbin, L., and Sumberg, K. 2009. How Gen Y and Boomers will reshape your agenda. *Harvard Business Review* 87(7/8), pp. 71–76.

Holmes, S., Matlack, C., Arndt, M., and Zellner, W. 2001. Boeing attempts a U-turn at high speed. *BusinessWeek*, no. 3728 (16 April):126–28.

Huczynski, A. A., and Buchanan, D. A. 2013. *Organizational behaviour*. 8th ed. Harlow, Essex: Financial Times Prentice Hall.

Kanter, R. M. 2003. Leadership and the psychology of turnarounds. *Harvard Business Review* 81(6):58–67.

Keller, S., and Aiken, C. 2008. *The inconvenient truth about change management: Why it isn't working and what to do about it*. Chicago and Toronto: McKinsey & Company.

Kingston, J. (ed.). 2012. *Natural disaster and nuclear crisis in Japan: Response and recovery after Japan's 3/11*. London: Routledge.

Kirkpatrick, D. 1999. New home, new CEO: Gateway is moo and improved. *Fortune* 140(12):B10.

Kirkpatrick, D. 2006. In the penalty box. *Fortune*, September(18):28–36.

Kotter, J. P. 1995. *The new rules: How to succeed in today's post-corporate world*. New York: Free Press.

Kotter, J. P. 2012. Accelerate! *Harvard Business Review* 90(11):44–52.

Kowitt, B. 2014. Fallen arches: Can McDonald's get its mojo back? *Fortune*, December 1:106–16.

Kowitt, B. 2015. The war on big food. *Fortune*, May 21:61–70.

Kumar, V. 2014. Making "freemium" work. *Harvard Business Review* 92(5):27–29.

Labich, K. 1999. No more at Texaco. *Fortune* 140(5):205–12.

Lachinsky, A. 2007. Search and enjoy. *Fortune*, January 22:48–57.

Laming, W. 2003. *The Victoria Climbié inquiry*. Norwich: Her Majesty's Stationery Office.

Laming, W. 2009. *The protection of children in England: A progress report*. London: The Stationery Office.

LaPorte, N. 2014. Rebooting YouTube. *Fast Company*, September:58–64

Lavelle, L. 2002. The best and worst boards. *BusinessWeek*, no. 3669:120–28.

Leana, C. R., and Barry, B. 2000. Stability and change as simultaneous experiences in organizational life. *Academy of Management Review* 25(4):753–59.

Leppard, D., and Chittenden, M. 2010. Britain's "nevertirees" lead way in refusing to quit work. *The Sunday Times*, September 26:15.

Lowitt, E. 2014. How to survive climate change and still run a thriving business. *Harvard Business Review* 92(4):87–92.

Lynn, M. L. 2005. Organizational buffering: Managing boundaries and cores. *Organization Studies* 26(1):37–61.

MacLachlan, R. 2011. A switch in time. *People Management*, July:36–39.

Mahler, J. G., and Casamayou, M. H. 2009. *Organizational learning at NASA: The Challenger and Columbia accidents*. Washington, DC: Georgetown University Press.

McCorvey, J. J. 2015. Dropbox versus the world. *Fast Company*, April:96–104.

Meznar, M. B., Johnson, J. H., and Mizzi, P. J. 2006. No news is good news? Press coverage and corporate public affairs management. *Journal of Public Affairs* 6(1):58–68.

Mohrman, S. A., and Lawler, E. E. 2012. Generating knowledge that drives change. *Academy of Management Perspectives* 26(1):41–51.

Mone, M. A., McKinley, W., and Barker, V. L. 1998. Organizational decline and innovation: A contingency framework. *Academy of Management Review* 23(1):115–32.

Muoio, A. 1999. Mint condition. *Fast Company*, no. 30 (December):330–48.

National Commission on the BP Deepwater Horizon Oil Spill and Offshore Drilling. 2011. *Deep Water: The Gulf oil disaster and the future of offshore drilling.* Washington, DC: National Commission.

Parry, E., and Urwin, P. 2011. Generational differences in work values: A review of theory and evidence. *International Journal of Management Reviews* 13(1):79–96.

Pickard, J. 2010. Retirement age: Grey matters. *People Management*, September 16:28.

Porter, M. E., and Reinhardt, F. L. 2007. A strategic approach to climate. *Harvard Business Review* 85(10):22–26.

Rucci, A. J., Kirn, S. P., and Quinn, R. T. 1998. The employee-customer profit chain at Sears. *Harvard Business Review* 76(1):82–97.

Salter, C. 2003. A reformer who means business. *Fast Company*, no. 69 (April):102.

Scase, R., and Goffee, R. 1987. *The real world of the small business owner.* London: Croom Helm.

Smedley, T. 2014. Send in the cloud. *People Management*, May:43–44.

Smircich, L., and Stubbart, C. 1985. Strategic management in an enacted world. *Academy of Management Review* 10(4):724–36.

Smith, D., and Elliott, D. 2007. Exploring the barriers to learning from crisis: Organizational learning and crisis. *Management Learning* 38(5):519–38.

Sull, D. N. 1999. Why good companies go bad. *Harvard Business Review* 77(4):42–52.

Thompson, J. D. 1967. *Organizations in action.* New York: McGraw-Hill.

Thornton, E., and Reed, S. 2001. Morgan Stanley's midlife crisis. *BusinessWeek*, no. 3738 (June 25):90–94.

Toft, B., and Reynolds, S. 2005. *Learning from disasters: A management approach.* 3rd ed. Houndmills, Basingstoke: Palgrave Macmillan.

Vaughan, D. 1996. *The Challenger launch decision: Risky technology, culture, and deviance at NASA.* Chicago: University of Chicago Press.

Wiggins, J. 2007. Coke develops thirst for sustainability. *Financial Times*, July 2:26.

Chapter 4

What to Change? A Diagnostic Approach

Learning objectives

By the end of this chapter, you should be able to:

LO 4.1   Understand the use of diagnostic models in planning organizational change

LO 4.2   Use strategic analysis tools to assess the need for organizational change

LO 4.3   Diagnose organizational receptiveness to and individual readiness for change, and use those assessments as the basis for action to increase receptiveness and readiness

LO 4.4   Explain the characteristics of the "built-to-change" organizational model, and assess the applicability, strengths, and limitations of this approach

When asked "would you rather work for change, or just complain?" 81% of the respondents replied, "Do i have to pick? This is hard."

LO 4.1 Organizational Models

The theme of this chapter is *diagnosis*. With regard to organizational change, what is the problem? Can we improve our understanding of the context and nature of the problem? And can this diagnostic approach help us to solve the problem, or problems, that we find? In short—what has to change? This chapter introduces a number of diagnostic frameworks and tools. Some diagnostic models consider the operation of the organization as a whole, such as the "7-S Model." Others, such as "scenario planning," start with strategy. Some are designed to explore specific aspects of the change process, such as organizational and individual readiness for change. The "built-to-change" model argues that organizations can be designed in a way that makes "change management" diagnostic tools redundant.

The way in which these diagnostic models, frameworks, and tools are deployed depends on the image of change management in use (chapter 2).

Director   You can use these diagnostics to strengthen your knowledge base and confidence with regard to what needs to change, identifying key relationships and focusing on where change is needed and the results that you want.

Navigator   You will also find these diagnostics useful to "map" the organization's environment and help you to assess appropriate responses.

Caretaker   You will be less impressed by the capability of these diagnostics to support change, but those which focus on the external environment (PESTLE and scenario planning) help to identify trends and developments to which the organization should respond.

Coach   You will probably be more interested in diagnostics that focus on goals and on the capabilities required to achieve them.

Interpreter   You will find particularly useful the diagnostics that emphasize images, framing, and cognitive maps.

Nurturer   With your interest in emergent strategy, you may not be convinced about the value of this diagnostic approach.

Who does the diagnosing? This is an important question, and answers vary. Some perspectives see this as a senior management prerogative, perhaps also involving external consultants and advisers. Those consultants may use their diagnostic expertise to help their clients to manage the change process, rather than to determine the content of the changes. However, other perspectives emphasize the need to involve at the diagnostic stage those who will be affected by change; involvement can strengthen commitment to the change process, and thus increase the probability of success. Some organization development (OD) consultants explicitly reject the role of "diagnostician," arguing that their role is to help the organization's members to do this for themselves.

Our treatment of models relies on the following assumptions:

- The members of an organization, managers and staff, have their own views of "how things work," and "what causes what." In other words, "diagnosis" with regard to organizational change is going to happen whether or not explicit diagnostic tools are used.

- Implicit causal models have the power to influence how we think about organizational issues and problems, and what we believe are the appropriate courses of action.

- The option of not using a diagnostic model, therefore, is not available. We either use an implicit model, or choose an explicit one, such as those described in this chapter.
- Implicit models based on accumulated experience can provide valuable insights. However, implicit models have limitations. First, they may be based on the limited experience of a small number of people. Second, because they are implicit, it is difficult for others to understand the assumptions underlying decisions based on those models.

Warner Burke (2013) identifies five ways in which explicit models are useful:

1. *Simplify complexity*: They use a manageable number of categories to help simplify complex, multivariate situations
2. *Highlight priorities*: They help to prioritize the issues that need most attention.
3. *Identify interdependencies*: They identify key organizational interdependencies (e.g., strategy and structure).
4. *Provide a common language*: They provide a common language with which different stakeholder groups can discuss organizational properties.
5. *Offer a process guide*: They can offer guidance with respect to the appropriate sequence of actions in a change process.

This chapter describes several organizational models. Each adopts a different focus on aspects of organizational functioning, and no one model, or small collection of models, can be described as "best." It is always important to choose, or to adapt, a model that fits the organization's problem by triggering discussion and analysis among those involved, leading ultimately to action. In many cases, in terms of problem solving, the debate that a model prompts can be more important than the model itself. Our aims here are to illustrate the variety of models that are available, in order to give you a basis from which to choose those that most closely fit your interests and purposes.

The Six-Box Organizational Model

Marvin Weisbord (1976, p. 431) developed one of the first organizational diagnostics, which he described as "my efforts to combine bits of data, theories, research, and hunches into a working tool that anyone can use." In the context of our discussion of implicit and explicit models, it is interesting to note that Weisbord subtitled his article, "Six Places to Look for Trouble With or Without a Theory." It is not surprising that his model is based on sets of factors or "boxes":

1. *Purposes*: What business are we in?
2. *Structure*: How do we divide up the work?
3. *Rewards*: Do all tasks have incentives?
4. *Helpful mechanisms*: Have we adequate coordinating technologies?
5. *Relationships*: How do we manage conflict among people?
6. *Leadership*: Does someone keep the other five boxes in balance?

Weisbord (1976, p. 431) uses a radar screen analogy: "Just as air controllers use radar to chart the course of an aircraft—height, speed, distance apart and weather—those seeking to improve an organization must observe relationships among the boxes and not focus on any particular blip."

As a change diagnostic, therefore, this model has two main applications. First, in providing a small set of categories that simplify (perhaps oversimplify) the complexity of an organization, this facilitates the process of deciding which factors or sets of factors are generating problems, and which therefore require attention. Second, it reminds the change manager to consider the wider systemic implications of actions that address only one or two of those categories or boxes.

The 7-S Framework

The 7-S framework was developed by Robert Waterman, Tom Peters, and Julien Phillips (1980) while they were working as management consultants with McKinsey & Company. They argue that organizational effectiveness is influenced by many factors, and that successful change depends on the relationships between those factors. In an approach similar to that of Weisbord (1976), they identify seven sets of factors (figure 4.1):

Structure in this framework refers to the formal organization design.

Strategy concerns how the organization plans to anticipate or respond to changes in its external environment in order to strengthen its competitive position.

Systems are the formal and informal procedures that determine how things get done—budgeting, cost accounting, IT, and training systems, for example. Waterman et al. (1980, p. 21) note that one way to change an organization without disruptive reorganization is to change the systems.

Style refers to patterns of management actions, how managers spend their time, what they pay attention to, the signals that they send about priorities, and attitude to change.

Staff can refer to appraisal, training, and development processes, and also to attitude, motivation, and morale—but more importantly in this framework, this refers to how managers are developed.

FIGURE 4.1
The 7-S
Framework

Source: Based on
Waterman et al.,
(1980, p.18).

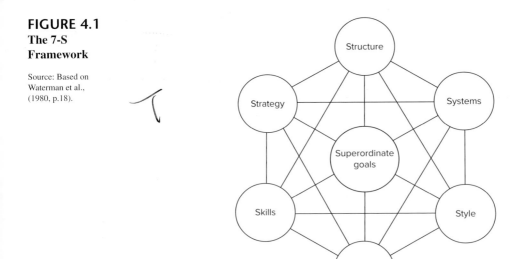

Skills concern what an organization does best, expressed in the dominant attributes and capabilities that distinguish it from competitors.

Superordinate goals refer to the organization's guiding concepts, values, aspirations, and future direction—which are sometimes captured by the term "vision," discussed here in chapter 6. In later versions of the 7-S framework, these goals are also referred to as "shared values."

As a change diagnostic, this framework emphasizes the interconnectedness of the seven sets of factors, and also argues that the "soft" issues (style, staff, skills, shared values) are just as important as structure, strategy, and systems. Waterman et al. (1980, p. 17) explain:

> Our assertion is that productive organization change is not simply a matter of structure, although structure is important. It is not so simple as the interaction between strategy and structure, although strategy is critical too. Our claim is that effective organizational change is really the relationship between structure, strategy, systems, style, skills, staff, and something we call superordinate goals. (The alliteration is intentional: it serves as an aid to memory.)

The framework thus identifies the areas on which to focus, the questions to ask, and the relationships and alignments to consider when planning organizational change. A full 7-S analysis, exploring each of the elements of the framework in depth, can be rich and valuable, but is time-consuming.

Applying 7-S to Intuit

In 2000, Steve Bennett, vice president of GE Capital, became chief executive of Intuit, a financial software and services company with three products, Quicken, TurboTax, and QuickBooks, which respectively had 73 percent, 81 percent, and 84 percent of their markets. However, given this market dominance, many analysts felt that Intuit was less profitable than it should be. The company also had a reputation for slow decision making, allowing competitors to steal a number of market opportunities. Bennett wanted to change all that. In his first few weeks, he visited most of Intuit's locations, addressed most of its 5,000 employees, and spoke personally to each of the top 200 executives. He concluded that staff were passionate about the firm's products, but that not much attention was being paid to internal processes (this account is based on Higgins, 2005).

In terms of the 7-S framework, this is what he did:

Strategy: To expand Intuit's portfolio, he expanded the product range by acquisition.

Structure: He created a flatter structure and decentralized decision making, giving business units greater control and responsibility for the product process from development to delivery.

Systems: The rewards system was more closely aligned to achieving strategic objectives.

Style: He emphasized the need for a performance-oriented focus, and he provided a vision for change, putting effort into "selling" that vision.

Staff: He built on the commitment of staff to Intuit's products by emphasizing the critical role of quality and efficiency in maintaining and building the company's reputation.

Skills: To enhance staff capabilities with regard to quality and efficiency, resources were allocated to training and development, and some select managers were hired from GE in specific skill areas.

Superordinate goals: Bennett's approach was "vision-driven," with his paper, "Steve's Dream for Intuit," outlining strategic objectives and how they would be achieved; to "sell" this vision, he communicated constantly with staff.

As a result of Bennett's changes, operating profits increased in 2002 and 2003 by 40 to 50 percent. By 2014, Intuit had global revenues of over $5 billion, with 8,000 employees in the United States, Canada, United Kingdom, India, and other countries (http://www.intuit.com).

The Star Model

The star model of organizational design, developed by Jay Galbraith et al. (2002), argues that, for an organization to be effective, its strategy, structure, processes, rewards, and people practices have to be in alignment (figure 4.2). This model thus overlaps with the McKinsey 7-S framework.

Strategy in this model plays a dominant role, because if the strategy is not clear, then there is no basis for making other design decisions.

Structure is defined as the formal authority relationships and grouping of activities, as shown on an organization chart.

Processes and lateral capability concern the formal and informal systems that coordinate the organization's activities.

Reward systems relate to how performance is measured and compensated, in ways that align individual actions to organizational objectives.

People practices concern the organization's human resource policies and practices: selection, training and development, performance management.

As a change diagnostic, this model emphasizes how these five elements are interconnected. Changes in one area are almost certain to affect others, and not always in predictable ways. Despite the significance of strategy, organizational performance will suffer if one or more of the five sets of factors is out of alignment with the others. For example, while changing the structure may be relatively straightforward and visible, this can have little or no impact on performance without complementary changes elsewhere in the organization. Galbraith et al. (2002) explain the implications of misalignment of each of the five "points of the star," as summarized in table 4.1.

FIGURE 4.2
The Star Model

Source: Based on Galbraith et al. (2002).

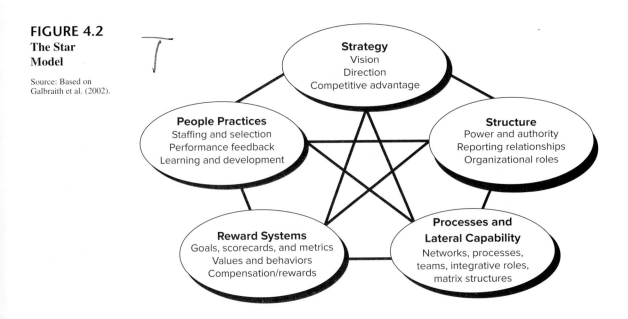

TABLE 4.1
The Impli-cations of Misalignment

Source: Based on Galbraith et al. (2002).

Design component	Leads to	Implications for practice
Strategy If strategy is missing, unclear, or not agreed	*Confusion*	No common purpose People pulling in different directions No criteria for decision making
Structure If the structure is not aligned to strategy	*Friction*	Inability to mobilize resources Ineffective execution Lost competitive advantage
Processes If coordinating mechanisms are left to chance	*Gridlock*	Lack of collaboration across boundaries Long decision and innovation cycle times No sharing of information and best practice
Rewards If metrics and rewards do not support the goals	*Internal competition*	Diffused energy, wrong results Low standards Frustration and staff turnover
People If staff are not enabled and empowered	*Low performance*	Effort without results Low job satisfaction

The Four-Frame Model

Lee Bolman and Terry Deal (2013) explain four different frames or lenses, each providing a different perspective on how an organization functions. Their aim is to promote the value of "multiframe thinking," which means seeing the same situation in different ways. Problems arise, they argue, when we become locked into our one favored way of seeing the world—and our organization—and then fail to see other critical aspects or issues. We met frames before, in chapter 2, in our discussion of mental models; same thing. The *structural* frame in this model concerns the organization of groups and teams. The *human resource* frame concerns how the organization is tailored to satisfy human needs and build effective interpersonal relationships and teamwork. The *political* frame concerns how power and conflict are dealt with, and how coalitions are formed. The *symbolic* frame relates to how the organization builds a culture that gives purpose and meaning to work and builds team cohesion. The four-frame model is illustrated in figure 4.3 (Bolman and Deal, 2013, p. 19).

Each frame is associated with a metaphor. The structural frame sees the organization as a machine, and the problem concerns efficient design. The human resource frame treats the organization as a family, and the task is to meet the needs of both the organization and its members. The political frame sees organizations as sites of collaboration and conflict, as the interests of internal and external stakeholders sometimes overlap, and sometimes differ. For the symbolic frame, the essence of the organization lies with its culture—symbols, beliefs, values, norms, rituals, and meanings.

As a change diagnostic, the four-frame model invites the change manager to see the organization through several different lenses at the same time. This can deepen understanding of problems and helps to generate creative solutions by highlighting previously unseen or unconsidered possibilities.

FIGURE 4.3
The Four-Frame Model

	Frame			
	Structural	**Human Resource**	**Political**	**Symbolic**
Organizational Metaphor	Factory or machine	Family	Jungle	Theatre, carnival, temple
Central Concepts	Roles, goals, policies, technology, environment	Needs, skills, relationships	Power, conflict, competition, politics	Culture, meaning, metaphor, ritual, ceremony, stories, heroes
Image of Leadership	Social architecture	Empowerment	Advocacy and political savvy	Inspiration
Basic Leadership Challenge	Attune structure to task, technology, environment	Align organizational and human needs	Develop agenda and power base	Create faith, beauty, meaning

Metaphorical Diagnostics

In many situations, diagnosis of the need for and substance of change can be enhanced by capturing the perspectives of a wide range of the staff who are involved—at all levels. However, getting people to talk about the "as is" situation, and what needs to change, can sometimes be awkward. A useful technique for overcoming this potential blockage builds on the concept of "frames," asking people to describe their organization (or part of the organization) and how it works using a metaphor (an image, or a simile): "My organization is like a well-oiled machine"; "My division is a shark-infested pond."

In our experience, most people quickly generate such an image when asked: "My organization is like a dinosaur—large, slow-moving, unresponsive to change, and headed for extinction." These images differ from one individual to another, and become the basis of discussion, as their originators provide further detail about what they intended to convey with their metaphor.

LO 4.2 Organization Strategy and Change

In this section, we shift the focus from organizational models to strategic analysis tools. Strategy is a major driver of change, but it is not the only factor. Here, we explain six tools that are in common use for exploring and shaping an organization's strategy. These are gap analysis, the PESTLE framework, scenario planning, elements of strategy, the strategic inventory, and the cultural web.

Gap Analysis

Gap analysis is a simple, flexible, and widely used tool for reviewing the current "as is" state of an organization, and what has to change. This involves asking three questions:

1. Where are we now?
2. Where do we want to get to?
3. What do we need to do in order to get there?

These are general questions that almost always elicit a response—from staff at all levels in an organization—and they are therefore a good basis for discussion. A key issue concerns the degree of consensus in the responses of those who are asked. If everyone agrees, then action may be rapid. However, if rapid action is not necessary in the circumstances, it can be useful to deliberately orchestrate a challenge to the consensus. That challenge could reinforce the consensus view, or it could prompt a reconsideration of "taken for granted" assumptions. A low degree of consensus prompts further attention to the organization's goals, on the grounds that commitment to action should have a reasonably broad base of agreement, at least concerning the first two questions. Agreement on the third question may be desirable but is not necessary as long as there is commitment to support the formal decision on the course of action to be taken.

Gap analysis is flexible with regard to focus and timescale. The first question can relate to the organization as a whole, or to one or more divisions. If appropriate, it can address a range of other specific issues: where are we now with regard to staff engagement, updating our information systems, developing new product lines, streamlining our procurement processes, and so on. The second question may ask, where do we want to get to in six months, or two years, or five years, and so on. The simplicity and flexibility of this tool make it both easy to use and powerful.

As a change diagnostic, this can be a helpful way of establishing a change agenda (what do we need to do in order to get there?) that has been explored in depth and that is understood by those involved. Through open discussion, the resultant agenda can gain a high degree of consensus, but the disagreements that have been aired will also be known and understood. One problem with gap analysis is that it often suggests a felt need for deep, transformational change (see figure 1.1, p. 18), which immediately generates an overwhelming and potentially resource-intensive agenda.

PESTLE Framework

PESTLE is an environmental scanning tool, which provides a structured method for organizing and understanding complex trends and developments across the political, economic, social, technological, legal, and ecological factors that can affect an organization. Figure 4.4 shows a typical PESTLE analysis. This is an illustration, and is not comprehensive. The tidy categories in the figure can overlap in practice; legislative changes may be politically motivated, and ecological concerns reflect changing social values and preferences. The point of the analysis, however, is to identify the environmental factors that may affect the organization now and in the future.

Environmental complexity makes prediction hazardous. We can predict demographic trends with some accuracy, with respect to mortality, and gender and age profiles. We can normally predict economic trends with some confidence in the short to medium term—say two to three years. Trends in social values and lifestyles, politics, technological innovation, or the impact of new technology cannot be predicted with much confidence—although that does not stop journalists and others from making the attempt. Predicting geopolitical events, such as terrorist attacks and wars, is even more difficult. PESTLE analysis thus relies heavily on informed guesswork and judgement.

As a change diagnostic, the environmental audit that PESTLE produces can be used to guide strategic decision making and contingency planning, to exploit opportunities, and to address potential threats and risks (Morrison and Daniels, 2010). The resultant agenda may involve immediate change initiatives and can also include longer-term change planning.

FIGURE 4.4
PESTLE Analysis

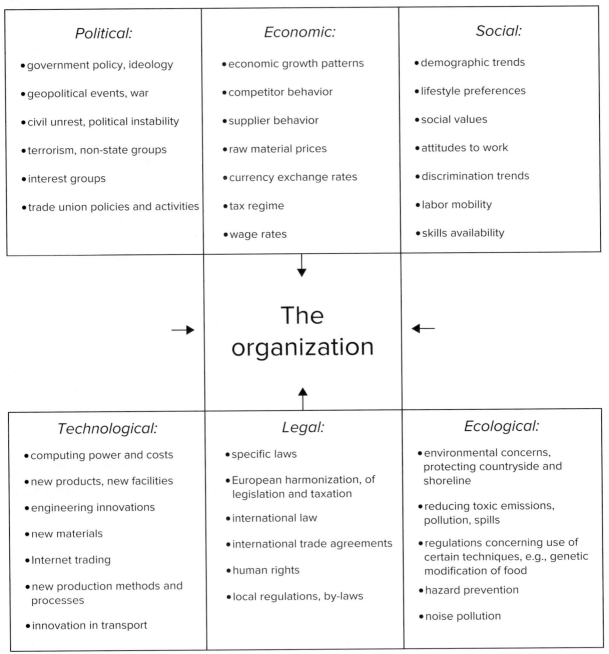

Political:

- government policy, ideology
- geopolitical events, war
- civil unrest, political instability
- terrorism, non-state groups
- interest groups
- trade union policies and activities

Economic:

- economic growth patterns
- competitor behavior
- supplier behavior
- raw material prices
- currency exchange rates
- tax regime
- wage rates

Social:

- demographic trends
- lifestyle preferences
- social values
- attitudes to work
- discrimination trends
- labor mobility
- skills availability

The organization

Technological:

- computing power and costs
- new products, new facilities
- engineering innovations
- new materials
- Internet trading
- new production methods and processes
- innovation in transport

Legal:

- specific laws
- European harmonization, of legislation and taxation
- international law
- international trade agreements
- human rights
- local regulations, by-laws

Ecological:

- environmental concerns, protecting countryside and shoreline
- reducing toxic emissions, pollution, spills
- regulations concerning use of certain techniques, e.g., genetic modification of food
- hazard prevention
- noise pollution

Scenario Planning

Scenario planning involves the imaginative development of one or more likely pictures of the characteristics of the possible futures for an organization sometimes, but not necessarily, considering "best-case/worst-case" possibilities. The organization can then plan an appropriate response to those futures (Verity, 2003). Recent concerns with regard to geopolitical risks have made scenario planning more popular (see "Scenario Planning in a High-Risk World, to 2018"). The results of a PESTLE analysis can of course contribute to scenario development. The Royal Dutch/Shell Company was responsible for developing scenario planning in the 1970s, and this tool is thus also known as the "Shell method."

For example, the consultancy company PricewaterhouseCoopers used scenario planning to explore the future of work (Arkin, 2007). They developed three possible scenarios for 2020:

Orange world   Big companies have been replaced by networks of small, specialized enterprises. People work on short-term contracts, exploring job opportunities online through portals developed by craft guilds.

Green world   Demographic change, climate, and sustainability are key business drivers. Employment law, employee relations, and corporate responsibility are vital in this heavily regulated environment.

Blue world   Huge corporations are like mini-states, providing staff with housing, health, education, and other welfare benefits. Human capital metrics are sophisticated, and people management is as powerful as finance.

As a change diagnostic, scenario planning encourages creative "blue skies" decision making, to identify the most probable futures for the organization. This analysis then forms the basis for prioritizing, planning, and acting to implement appropriate changes. Chapter exercise 4.2 invites you to carry out a scenario planning exercise for an organization with which you are familiar.

Scenario Planning in a High-Risk World, to 2018

The Economist Intelligence Unit (Mitchell, 2008) surveyed 600 global executives in 2008 and asked them which risks were the most threatening to their business over the next decade, to 2018. The top 12 risks that concerned these executives were:

- Increase in protectionism
- Major oil price shock
- Collapse in asset prices
- Emergence of a disruptive business model
- International terrorism
- Unexpected regulatory change
- Global recession
- Instability in the Middle East
- Increased competition from emerging-market companies
- Talent shortages
- Climate change
- Increased industrial pollution

Only 26 percent said that they used scenario planning regularly, 41 percent used it on an ad hoc basis, and 29 percent said that they would be using it in future.

Elements of Strategy

Strategy is often considered to be at the heart of change because it addresses the basic issues with which an organization has to deal: what are we seeking to achieve, and how? Strategy and change intersect because strategies can change ("change of strategy") and change may be necessary in order to realize a set strategy ("change for strategy"). Donald Hambrick and James Fredrickson (2001) developed a framework that characterizes organization strategy in terms of five mutually reinforcing elements: arenas, vehicles, differentiators, staging, and economic logic (table 4.2). Misalignment of these elements indicates a potential need for change.

From this perspective, only when all five strategic elements have been determined is it possible to assess the structures and systems that will be appropriate to pursuing the strategy. However, before moving to this stage, it is important to test the quality of the proposed strategy. Hambrick and Fredrickson (2001) suggest the six "key evaluation criteria" explained in table 4.3.

As a change diagnostic, therefore, this analysis identifies the organizational changes that are necessary in order to pursue a desired strategy. If for any reason (cost, time, expertise) those changes are difficult or impossible to implement, then the strategy may have to be reconsidered. This approach can also help to generate an integrated package of change initiatives that are mutually self-reinforcing, and which are aligned with organization

TABLE 4.2
The Elements of Strategy

1. **Arenas: What business will we be in?**
   - Which product categories?
   - Which market segments?
   - Which geographic areas?
   - Which core technologies?
   - Which value-creation stages?

2. **Vehicles: How will we get there?**
   - Internal development?
   - Joint ventures?
   - Licensing/franchising?
   - Acquisitions?

3. **Differentiators: How will we win in the marketplace?**
   - Image?
   - Customization?
   - Price?
   - Styling?
   - Product reliability?

4. **Staging**
   - Speed of expansion?
   - Sequence of initiatives?

5. **Economic Logic**
   - Lowest costs through scale advantage?
   - Lowest costs through scope and replication advantage?
   - Premium prices due to unmatchable service?
   - Premium prices due to proprietary product features?

Source: *Academy of Management Executive*, Hambrick and Fredrickson © 2001 by the Academy of Management (NY). Reproduced with permission of Academy of Management (NY) in the format Textbook via Copyright Clearance Center.

TABLE 4.3
Testing the
Quality of Your
Strategy: Key
Evaluation
Criteria

Key Evaluation Criteria

1. *Does your strategy fit with what's going on in the environment?*
   - Is there a healthy profit potential where you're headed?
   - Does strategy align with the key success factors of your chosen environment?

2. *Does your strategy exploit your key resources?*
   - With your particular mix of resources, does this strategy give you a good head start on your competitors?
   - Can you pursue this strategy more economically than competitors?

3. *Will your envisaged differentiators be sustainable?*
   - Will competitors have difficulty matching you?
   - If not, does your strategy explicitly include a ceaseless regimen of innovation and opportunity creation?

4. *Are the elements of your strategy internally consistent?*
   - Have you made choices of arenas, vehicles, differentiators, staging, and economic logic?
   - Do they all fit and mutually reinforce each other?

5. *Do you have enough resources to pursue this strategy?*
   - Do you have the money, managerial time and talent, and other capabilities to do all that you envision?
   - Are you sure you're not spreading your resources too thinly, only to be left with a collection of weak positions?

6. *Is your strategy implementable?*
   - Will your key constituencies allow you to pursue this strategy?
   - Can your organization make it through the transition?
   - Are you and your management team able and willing to lead the required changes?

Source: *Academy of Management Executive*, Hambrick and Fredrickson © 2001 by the Academy of Management (NY). Reproduced with permission of Academy of Management (NY) in the format Textbook via Copyright Clearance Center.

strategy. While integration and alignment may sound like straightforward advice, this can often be difficult to achieve in practice. For example, problems can arise when changes that are optimal for one division of the organization undermine activities and changes in other divisions (see point 5 in table 4.3 about spreading resources too thinly).

The Strategic Inventory

Strategy is about the future, committing resources to activities based on "assumptions, premises and beliefs about an organization's environment (society and its structure, the market, the customer, and the competition), its mission, and the core competencies needed to accomplish that mission" (Picken and Dess, 1998, p. 35). These assumptions, premises, and beliefs, often formed over time through experience, become a "mental grid" through which new information is sifted and interpreted. To the extent that this grid comprises assumptions and beliefs that accurately reflect the environment, the quality of strategic decision making is enhanced. However, when assumptions fail to reflect key elements of the business environment, they can lead to the adoption of inappropriate strategies, a phenomenon known as "strategic drift."

As a change diagnostic, identifying and validating management's strategic assumptions can be useful in assessing whether or not strategy is consistent with key elements of the

Assumptions and Strategy *Strategic Drift and the Beech Starship*

In the early 1980s, Raytheon Co. acquired Beech, a light-aircraft company that had fallen on hard times. The managers appointed by Raytheon proposed to reinvigorate Beech by producing an advanced turboprop aircraft based on the latest carbon-fiber technology. It was expected that this technology would enable Beech to compete at the lower end of the business jet market, with a product that was 60 percent the price of competitors as well as being more fuel efficient. An 85 percent scale model "Starship" was built and, on the basis of good reviews, Beech announced that it would invest in a new factory to make the plane, which would be ready for sale in two years (Picken and Dess, 1998).

This initiative was based on several assumptions:

1. That Beech could complete the design of the new aircraft and get Federal Aviation Administration (FAA) certification within two years.

2. That the new carbon-fiber technology would not be a significant problem, even though it was not covered by the existing regulations.

3. That sufficient aircraft would be built to justify the expenditure on a new factory.

However, the FAA had never certified an all-composite aircraft and insisted on compliance with the standards for metal aircraft. This led to a redesign, which increased the weight, which required a bigger engine, which needed more fuel, which meant more weight, which meant further redesign, and so on. Eventually, the Starship made it to market, but it was four years late, carried only 6 passengers rather than 10, and cruised at 335 knots instead of 400. The price advantage over jets had also disappeared. The expected demand failed to materialize, and the production line was closed.

business environment. This assessment can then identify whether an organization's strategy should be a focal point for change. To establish the degree of consensus on dominant strategic assumptions, Joseph Picken and Gregory Dess (1998) developed a "strategic inventory" (table 4.4).

TABLE 4.4
The Strategic Inventory

Defining the boundaries of the competitive environment
- What are the boundaries of our industry? What is our served market? What products or services do we provide?
- Who are the customers? Who are the noncustomers? What is the difference between them?
- Who are our competitors? Who are the noncompetitors? What makes one firm a competitor and the other not?
- What key competencies are required to compete in this industry? Where is the value added?

Defining the key assumptions
- Who is our customer? What kinds of things are important to that customer? How does he or she perceive us? What kind of relationships do we have?
- Who is the ultimate end user? What kinds of things are important to this end user? How does he or she perceive us? What kind of relationship do we have?
- Who are our competitors? What are their strengths and weaknesses? How do they perceive us? What can we learn from them?
- Who are the potential competitors? New entrants? What changes in the environment or their behavior would make them competitors?

- What is the industry's value chain? Where is value added? What is the cost structure? How does our firm compare? How about our competitors?
- What technologies are important in our industry? Product technologies? Production technologies? Delivery and service technologies? How does our firm compare? How about our competitors?
- What are the key factors of production? Who are the suppliers? Are we dependent on a limited number of sources? How critical are these relationships? How solid?
- What are the bases for competition in our industry? What are the key success factors? How do we measure up? How about our competitors?
- What trends and factors in the external environment are important to our industry? How are they likely to change? Over what time horizon?
- Are we able, in assessing our knowledge and assumptions, to separate fact from assumption?

Is our assumption set internally consistent?
- For each pair of assumptions, can we answer "yes" to the question: "If assumption A is true, does assumption B logically follow?"

Do we understand the relative importance of each of our assumptions?
- In terms of its potential impact on performance?
- In terms of our level of confidence in its validity?
- In terms of the likelihood and expectation of near-term change?
- In terms of its strategic impact?

Are our key assumptions broadly understood?
- Have we documented and communicated our key assumptions? To our key managers? To the boundary-spanners? To other key employees?

Do we have a process for reviewing and validating our key assumptions and premises?
- Is there a process in place? Are responsibilities assigned? Are periodic reviews planned and scheduled?

Picken and Dess (1998) suggest that, where there is consensus on strategic assumptions, the organization should seek an independent validation, to check for biases. Where significant divergence exists, attention should focus on which (and whose) assumptions are currently embedded in strategy, and which (and whose) can again be independently validated. The strategic inventory involves a more sophisticated analysis than that provided by the widely used SWOT approach to understanding an organization's strengths, weaknesses, opportunities, and threats. The danger with SWOT analysis is that it becomes a listing not of strengths but "perceived strengths," not weaknesses but "perceived weaknesses," and so on. It may simply capture existing beliefs, the current dominant logic, which may need to be challenged in order to improve organizational performance.

The Cultural Web

Organization culture is often seen as a response to performance problems and is a component of many change diagnostics. Gerry Johnson (1998; Johnson et al., 2013)

FIGURE 4.5
The Cultural Web

Source: Based on
Johnson (1998).

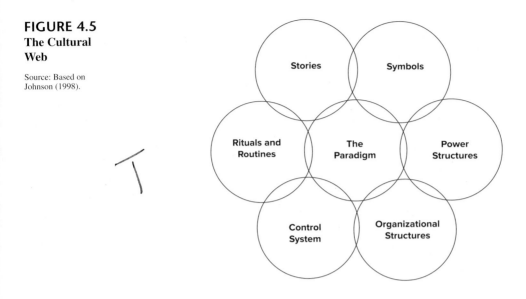

describes organization culture in terms of a "cultural web" that has seven elements (figure 4.5):

1. *The paradigm*: The set of assumptions commonly held throughout the organization with respect to basic elements of the business such as what business we're in, how we compete, who our competitors are.

2. *Rituals and routines*: These concern how organizational members treat each other and, perhaps more importantly, associated beliefs as to what is right and proper and valued in this regard.

3. *Stories*: As told by organization members, stories are a form of oral history and communicate and reinforce core elements of the culture.

4. *Symbols*: Logos, office design, dress style, language use, and other symbols convey aspects of the culture.

5. *Control systems*: What is valued in the organization is communicated through what is measured and rewarded.

6. *Power structures*: These concern the most influential management groups in the organization.

7. *Organizational structure*: The formal and informal differentiation and integration of tasks.

As a change diagnostic, Johnson (1998; Johnson et al., 2013) describes the value of "mapping" the organization's cultural web. First, exposing issues that are rarely discussed is a useful way of questioning traditional norms and habits. If what is taken for granted is never questioned, then change will be difficult. Second, cultural mapping can highlight potential barriers to change. Third, it may also be possible through this approach to identify aspects of the culture that are especially resistant to change. Fourth, a culture map can be the basis for considering the changes that will be necessary to pursue a new strategy. Finally, practical ideas for managing those changes can then be developed.

The unit of analysis for the cultural web is the organization as a whole. The change manager with a specific initiative in a particular division, therefore, may not find this approach helpful in identifying ways to increase the probability of success of that change project.

LO 4.3   Diagnosing Readiness for Change

The diagnostics that we have discussed so far have been designed to help decide whether or not an organization has to change, and if so, to determine what has to change. It is often appropriate to ask two other sets of questions before pressing ahead with implementation. First, is the organization as a whole receptive to change? We will explore this question through the concepts of *the receptive organizational context, absorptive capacity,* and *the innovative organization.* We will also discuss the technique of *force-field analysis* to assess how receptive an organization is to a particular change. Chapter exercise 4.3 offers another readiness diagnostic. Second, are those who will be affected ready for these changes? In this section, therefore, we will explore both organizational receptiveness (or readiness) and individual readiness (or receptiveness) to change. The aim, of course, is not simply to establish levels of organizational and individual readiness. Understanding why readiness may be low is a platform for remedial action, to strengthen receptiveness and readiness where appropriate.

The Receptive Organizational Context

Organizations vary in their receptiveness to change. This variation depends on a number of conditions (Eccles, 1984):

1. Is there pressure for change?
2. Is there a shared vision of the goals, benefits, and direction?
3. Do we have effective liaison and trust between those concerned?
4. Is there the will and power to act?
5. Do we have enough capable people with sufficient resources?
6. Do we have suitable rewards and defined accountability for actions?
7. Have we identified actionable first steps?
8. Does the organization have a capacity to learn and to adapt?

Where the answers to these questions are "yes," organizational receptiveness is high, and resistance to change is likely to be limited. However, without pressure, clear goals, trust, power to act, resources, and so on, receptiveness is likely to be low, and the changes will be more difficult to implement. It is important to note that an organization as a whole may be more or less receptive to change, regardless of the attitudes of individual members.

This simple receptiveness diagnostic highlights two practical issues. The first is timing. Some conditions (growing pressure, for example) may improve simply by waiting. The second concerns action, to strengthen the conditions when receptiveness is low. Remedial actions could involve:

- Ensuring that the rationale for change is strong and understood.
- Articulating a clear vision of goals and benefits.
- Confidence-building measures to develop interpersonal and interdivisional trust.
- Ensuring that key positions are held by dynamic, high-performing individuals.
- Developing change management capabilities across the organization.
- Providing adequate resources (people, technology, training) to support the proposed changes.
- Aligning performance management and reward systems with change goals.
- Clearly establishing the initial action plan.
- Developing learning organization capabilities.

The key point is that organizational receptiveness to change can be managed, by taking steps to change the conditions that lower receptiveness. Most of those steps are cost-neutral.

Absorptive Capacity

Wesley Cohen and Daniel Levinthal (1990) developed the related concept of "absorptive capacity," which they defined as the ability of an organization to value, to assimilate, and to apply new knowledge. Absorptive capacity depends on an organization's existing stock of knowledge and skills, and a "learning organization culture" with leadership and norms that support the acquisition, sharing, and application of new ideas. From their comprehensive review of work on this abstract and complex concept, Shaker Zahra and Gerard George (2002, p. 185) redefine absorptive capacity as "a dynamic capability pertaining to knowledge creation and utilization that enhances a firm's ability to gain and sustain a competitive advantage." They argue that absorptive capacity has four dimensions:

1. *Acquisition*: The ability to find and to prioritize new knowledge and ideas quickly and efficiently.
2. *Assimilation*: The ability to understand new knowledge and to link it to existing knowledge.
3. *Transformation*: The ability to combine, convert, and recodify new knowledge.
4. *Exploitation*: The ability to use new ideas productively.

Acquisition depends on the organization's external links and networks, which are often available only to a small number of professional staff and senior management. Assimilation, transformation, and exploitation rely more on internal capabilities, relationships, and systems. These four dimensions can also be managed. Actions to increase an organization's absorptive capacity include widening the exposure of staff to external networks; the use of job rotation and cross-functional teams to encourage the sharing of knowledge and ideas across organizational boundaries; wider employee participation in management decision making; and relaxing rules, procedures, and routines that stifle exploration and experimentation (Jansen et al., 2005). Once again, many of these actions are cost-neutral.

The Innovative Organization

A related perspective on receptiveness to change has focused on innovative organizations. Rosabeth Moss Kanter (1983; 1989) makes a distinction between *integrative* and *segmentalist* organization structures and cultures. Integrative structures and cultures display the following features:

- Holistic problem-solving
- Team orientation
- Cooperative environment
- Mechanisms for ideas generation and exchange
- Sense of purpose and direction
- Ability to overthrow history and precedent
- Use of internal and external networks
- Person- and creation-centered
- Results-oriented

Segmentalist organizations, in contrast, are characterized by the compartmentalization of problem-solving and a preoccupation with hierarchy, efficiency, and rules. Segmentalist organizations, Kanter argues, are "innovation smothering," and integrative organizations are "innovation stimulating." It is usually not difficult to identify innovation smothering and stimulating cultures by observing both the physical features of the organization (layouts, color schemes) and staff behavior; see "Charlie's Angels and the Red Star Corporation."

If we understand the features of an organization that respectively stimulate and smother creativity and innovation, then we can start to change or remove those that smother and strengthen those that stimulate. Table 4.5 illustrates the features to look for. These are not comprehensive lists, and you will be able to identify other stimulating and smothering features yourself, by observation.

Charlie's Angels and the Red Star Corporation

We are going to ask you to watch part of the movie *Charlie's Angels* (Columbia Pictures, directed by Joseph McGinty Nichol ["McG"], 2000). Charlie's Angels are three private investigators on a mission to rescue a billionaire who has been kidnapped for his sophisticated software skills. Go to DVD track 14, where Alex (played by Lucy Liu), masquerading as an "efficiency expert," leads the Angels into the Red Star Corporation headquarters, in an attempt to penetrate their security systems. Watch this sequence until the end of Alex's presentation, when she says, "Better yet, can anyone show me?" As you watch this short clip, consider the following questions:

- Is this an organization that stimulates or smothers creativity and innovation?
- How do you know? Identify the clues, visual and spoken, that support your assessment of the Red Star organization culture.
- What general characteristics of innovative organizations are illustrated here?

TABLE 4.5
Organizational Features That Stimulate and Smother Innovation

Stimulating Innovation	Smothering Innovation
No boundaries	Large organization
Flat organization structure	Many layers of management
Small unit size	Risk aversion, negativity
Fast approval processes	Closed-door policy
Empowerment of staff	Bureaucracy
Cross-functional teams	Controlled environment
Job rotation	Cumbersome approval processes
Flexible career paths	Too many procedure manuals
Supportive rewards and recognition	Segregation—keeping groups apart
Management backing for innovation	Avoid competition
Allocation of resources, including time	Encourage mediocrity, "good enough" is OK
Sharing information	Perfectionism, "not good enough" is punished
Positive culture that celebrates successes	"We've tried that before, we know best"
Encourage creative processes, brainstorming	Inadequate resources
Allowed to take risks and make mistakes	Overload, stress, burnout, people leaving
Focus on results and not methods	Emphasize the urgent, not the important
Exploit problems to create opportunities	Culture of blame, recriminations for failure
Links to external organizations and events	Inward looking
Weekend retreats, informal, out of office	No resources for training and development

Rules for Stifling Innovation

Rosabeth Moss Kanter (2002) instructs management on how to stifle innovation:

Regard a new idea from below with suspicion, because it's new, and because it's from below.

Insist that people who need your approval to act first go through several other levels of management to get their signatures.

Ask departments or individuals to challenge and criticize each others' proposals. That saves you the job of deciding; you just pick the survivor.

Express criticism freely, and withhold praise. That keeps people on their toes. Let them know that they can be fired at any time.

Treat identification of problems as signs of failure, to discourage people from letting you know when something in their area isn't working.

Control everything carefully. Make sure people count anything that can be counted, frequently.

And above all, never forget that you, the higher-ups, already know everything important about this business.

Force-Field Analysis

Force-field analysis is a popular diagnostic, developed in the mid-twentieth century by Kurt Lewin (1943; 1951). As a change diagnostic, this tool has two main purposes. First, it can be used to assess whether or not an organization is ready for a particular change initiative. Second, if readiness or receptiveness is low, force-field analysis can help to identify and prioritize the preparation or "groundwork" that may be required before implementation can begin. The analysis involves identifying the forces that are respectively driving and restraining movement toward a given set of outcomes, called the "target situation." The "field" is usually drawn like this:

Target Situation: Develop Customer-Orientation

Driving Forces ⟶	⟵ Restraining Forces
Static sales	Difficult to recruit capable sales staff
Increasingly aggressive competition	High turnover among part-time staff
Rising number of customer complaints	Trained and capable staff are "poached"
Brand being criticized on social media	Our competitors face similar problems
New chief executive supports this move	Cost of customer relationships training

This example is artificial, to illustrate the approach. It is unusual, for example, to have the same number of forces on the driving side as on the restraining side. Having constructed the field, the forces that have been identified can each be weighted or scored, say from 1 (weak) to 10 (strong), to produce a rough calculus to the balance of forces. This scoring procedure can give the analysis a false image of quantified rigor. More important than the forces and their scores is the discussion that produces the analysis. Who conducts this analysis is thus also important, often a project team or steering group. The underpinning discussion can expose wide differences in perception, both of the forces in play, and of their strength. The debate helps either to resolve those differences, or at least to allow those involved to know how their opinions vary, and how those differences have arisen.

If the driving forces are overwhelming, then the change can go ahead without significant problems. If the restraining forces are overwhelming, then the change may have to be abandoned, or delayed until conditions have improved. However, if the driving and restraining forces are more or less in balance, then the analysis can be used to plan appropriate action. The extent to which the force field is balanced is a matter of judgement. Used in a group setting, this method helps to structure what can often be an untidy discussion covering a wide range of factors and differing perceptions.

Managing a balanced force field to promote movement toward the target situation involves the following considerations:

1. Increasing the driving forces can often result in an increase in the resisting forces. This means that the current equilibrium does not change, but instead is maintained with increased tension.

2. Reducing the resisting forces is preferable, as this allows movement toward the desired outcomes or target situation without increasing tension.

3. Group norms are an important force in resisting and shaping organizational change.

Individual Readiness for Change

Individual readiness for change is a predisposition, perhaps even impatience, to welcome and embrace change. Where individual readiness is high, change may be straightforward. But when readiness is low, as with organizational receptiveness, some "groundwork" may be required to increase levels of change readiness among those who are going to be affected.

Rafferty et al. (2013) view change readiness as an individual attitude that has both cognitive and emotional (or "affective") dimensions. "Collective readiness" for change, of a group or organization, is based on the shared beliefs that develop through social interaction and shared experiences. Underpinning an individual's change readiness, therefore, are five beliefs:

1. *Discrepancy*: The belief that change is needed.
2. *Appropriate*: The belief that the proposed change is an appropriate response.
3. *Efficacy*: The individual's perceived capability to implement the change.
4. *Principal support*: The belief that the organization (management, peers) will provide resources and information.
5. *Valence*: The individual's evaluation of the personal costs and benefits; no benefits, no overall positive evaluation of readiness.

Individual change readiness is demonstrated through support for, openness toward, and commitment to change. These attitudes and behaviors can be influenced by three sets of factors. The first concerns external pressures, including industry and technology changes, new regulations, and professional group memberships. The second set of factors concerns what Rafferty et al. (2013) call "internal context enablers," including change participation and communication processes, and leadership. The third set of factors concern personal characteristics and include needs, values, and traits such as self-confidence, risk tolerance, dispositional resistance to change, and self-efficacy.

From a change management perspective, therefore, individuals' readiness for change can be assessed and can also be influenced. With regard to increasing readiness, research evidence points in particular to the power of the internal enablers. Individual readiness for change can be influenced by processes that are designed to enhance participation in decisions, by high-quality change communications, and by perceptions of the organization's history of change (previous experience, support for change, congruence of values). Again, there are practical steps that change managers can take in order to increase the probability that a change initiative will be welcome and successful—and most of those steps involve little or no expenditure.

Stakeholder Analysis

Another approach to assessing individual readiness for change involves stakeholder analysis, which focuses on the positions of key stakeholders. A stakeholder is anyone who is likely to be affected by an organizational change or program of changes, and who can influence the outcomes, directly or indirectly. Those stakeholders may be members of the organization, or of external groups and agencies, including other organizations. Stakeholder analysis usually involves the following steps:

1. Identify the stakeholders for the change initiative under consideration. Stakeholders may have a formal connection to the organization: owners, managers, suppliers, customers, employees. However, other individuals and groups are often able to exert influence: regulatory bodies, financial institutions, local government officials.

2. Establish what each of those stakeholders expects to gain or lose if the changes go ahead, and their respective power to support or block the initiative.

3. Check each stakeholder's "track record" with regard to comparable issues. Were they supportive, or not? If possible, identify what position your stakeholders are taking with regard to the current change. Behaviors are more significant than attitudes. Those who say that they are supporters may quickly switch their views in the face of difficulties. Equally, however, those who are initially hostile to the change may become supportive if they believe that the change will happen and be of benefit to them.

4. Use the planned benefits of the change to strengthen support for the proposals. It is often possible to find ways to address the concerns of those who feel they will lose out, by altering the nature of the changes proposed, perhaps, or by offering to reduce their losses in other ways.

The levels of stakeholders' power can be plotted against their interests, as shown in the "power-interest matrix" in figure 4.6. Action to manage the stakeholders for a given change initiative can then be based on this matrix (Grundy, 1997):

- Can new stakeholders be added to change the balance?
- Can oppositional stakeholders be encouraged to leave?
- Can the influence of pro-change stakeholders be increased?
- Can the influence of antagonistic stakeholders be decreased?
- Can the change be modified in a way that meets concerns without undermining the change?
- If stakeholder resistance is strong, should the proposal be revisited?

Stakeholder analysis informs change managers about the likely responses of key stakeholders, and steps can then be taken to manage those stakeholders, to weaken opposition and strengthen support.

It seems to be clear that, with regard to both organizational receptiveness to change and individual readiness to change, the change manager does not have to accept the diagnosis. There are practical—and often inexpensive—actions that can be taken to increase receptiveness and readiness. The diagnostic approaches described in this section help to identify what those actions could involve.

FIGURE 4.6
Power-Interest Matrix

Source: Based on Grundy (1997).

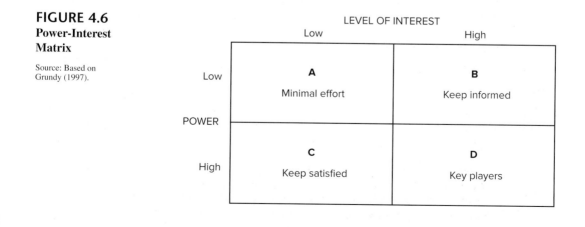

LO 4.4 Built-to-Change

The observation that some organizations are simply better able to manage and implement change than others has a long history. This notion of ability to change is different from assessing whether an organization is ready to change or can absorb further change. For example, from their study of the electronics sector in Scotland in the 1950s, Tom Burns and George Stalker (1961) distinguished between mechanistic and organic management systems (what we now call organization cultures). By mechanistic, they meant rigid and bureaucratic. Organic systems, in contrast, are flexible and adaptable (or "agile"). Their main argument still holds: mechanistic organizations perform well in stable environments, but in turbulent environments, organic organizations perform better. As we discussed earlier, Kanter (1983) subsequently "rediscovered" this argument in her distinction between "segmentalist" (mechanistic, bureaucratic) and "integrative" (organic, agile) cultures.

Echoing those previous arguments, Christopher Worley and Edward Lawler (2006) note that many businesses are organized in ways that discourage change, and that this is not consistent with the contemporary need for agility and adaptation. The competing organizational need for stability and predictability leads to structures and management practices that are designed to *minimize* variability and instability. The problem, they argue, is that organizations are usually built to last. The answer is to design organizations that are *built-to-change*, that are efficient in terms of today's performance and also flexible in responding to environmental trends and developments. The contrasts between traditional and built-to-change organization designs are summarized in table 4.6.

TABLE 4.6
Traditional and "Built-to-Change" Organization Design Principles

Traditional	Built-to-Change
Job descriptions that detail specific responsibilities	Goal-setting reviews to identify what individuals and teams should achieve in the near future
Hire people with the capabilities for the job for which they have applied	Hire people with initiative, who like change, who are quick learners and want development
Employment contract based on expectations set out in job description	Employment contract stating that support for change is an expected condition of employment
Job-related skills training	Ongoing training in skills to support change
Pay and rewards based on seniority and focused on individual job performance	Variety of rewards—bonuses, stock—for all staff, and group and unit bonuses linked to change
Pay for the job, and what it involves	Pay for the person, and what they contribute
Specialist market research and environmental scanning staff/departments; most staff thus have an internal focus	Maximize the "surface area" of staff in touch with customers and environment; most staff thus have an external as well as an internal focus
Hierarchical structures	Process-based, cross-functional network structures
Inflexible annual budgeting	Costs controlled by profit centers
Quarterly/annual performance updates	Transparent real-time performance information
Senior leaders set direction, give orders	Shared leadership, all levels in the organization
Leadership development for the "stars"	Leadership development for most staff

Source: Based on Worley and Lawler (2006).

The built-to-change organization uses design principles concerning talent management, reward systems, organization structure, information and decision processes, and leadership. This approach assumes that "continuous change is simply business as usual" (Worley and Lawler, 2006, p. 23). This presents a challenge to conventional approaches to change management, which assume the need for a planned organizational transition from one state to another. However, if an organization can be inherently built-to-change, then the processes and techniques of managing organizational change described in texts like this one may only be required rarely and in extreme circumstances.

From a survey of 40 service and manufacturing sector organizations, Worley and Lawler (2010, p. 2) conclude that any organization can develop agility, defined as "an evolving change and design capability, a leadership challenge that is never finished, only approached over time, but which yields consistently high levels of sustainable effectiveness." The organizations with consistently high performance had higher agility scores, measured using the design principles in table 4.6.

Chapter exercise 4.1 describes one organization that has developed "built-to-change" capabilities. Is this model effective, and is it more widely applicable?

Designed Not to Change

The reality is that today's organizations were simply never designed to change proactively and deeply—they were built for discipline and efficiency, enforced through hierarchy and routinization. As a result, there's a mismatch between the pace of change in the external environment and the fastest possible pace of change at most organizations. If it were otherwise, we wouldn't see so many incumbents struggling to intercept the future.

Source: Hamel and Zanini (2014).

EXERCISE 4.1

The Capital One Financial Story

As you read the following account, consider the following questions:

1. The "built-to-change" model has been promoted as desirable for most if not all organizations. However, from a corporate management perspective, what are potential *disadvantages* of developing a built-to-change organization?

2. From the perspective of an individual employee, what are the *benefits* of working in a built-to-change organization?

3. For the individual employee, what are the potential *disadvantages* of working in a built-to-change organization?

4. Capital One Financial operates in a fast-moving sector. To what extent will built-to-change design principles apply to organizations in other industries, with different environments?

Capital One Financial was one of America's largest financial services companies, with annual revenues of more than $20 billion, 45 million customer accounts, and around 40,000 employees. Worley and Lawler (2009) tell the story of how Capital One became a "built-to-change" organization by developing an "enterprise-wide change capability." Like all financial services organizations, Capital One had to respond, frequently and

(Continued)

rapidly, to regulatory changes and shifting market and economic conditions. To remain competitive, change had to be routine.

> In an era when environments are changing faster and faster, the rhetoric on organizational effectiveness is clear: successful organizations must be more agile and adaptable. Redesigning work processes, integrating acquired businesses, implementing large-scale information technology systems, and entering foreign markets are a few of the challenging changes companies are implementing. Any one of them can prove very difficult to accomplish—most estimates put the success rate for a large-scale organizational change at about 25–30 percent. Successfully implementing several of them in a short time period is virtually impossible. (Worley and Lawler, 2009, p. 245)

How did the company develop its change capability? Worley and Lawler (2009) identify four elements in Capital One's approach, summarized in table 4.7.

TABLE 4.7
Capital One: Built-to-Change Elements

Element	In Practice at Capital One
Focus on the future	Analysts' time spent on exploring future trends and implications
Momentary advantages	"Test and learn" approach to developing new income streams
Organizational flexibility	Hire people who like change, flat structures, vague job descriptions, decentralized decision making, pay for results, flexible performance management process, frequent reorganizations
Change capability	Competencies related to change, and ability to change routinely

Recognizing the need for constant change, a small number of "high potential" staff were given training in leadership and change management. This was successful in generating valuable change initiatives. However, this approach could not provide the enterprise-wide change capability that the company believed was necessary. Management did not want to set up either a central corporate resource or a group whose members could be assigned to help business units implement change as needed. The solution was the "Building a Change Capability" (BCC) project, which had three components.

First, create "versatilist" line managers with the knowledge and skills to lead change; neither generalists nor specialists, these versatilists were able to accelerate the change process on their own initiative, without asking for help.

Second, to achieve simplicity and speed, Capital One decided to use a standard change methodology across the organization, replacing the 17 different models that were previously in use, along with 160 different tools. The chosen approach was the ADKAR model, which stands for creating **A**wareness, having the **D**esire, the **K**nowledge, and the **A**bility, and **R**einforcement (Hiatt, 2006). This was easy for staff to understand and use, and was consistent with the previous change management training.

Third, two change courses were offered by the company's corporate university, to explain the ADKAR model and identify change management behaviors. The model and other relevant materials were also disseminated through a change management portal on the company intranet, with case studies, diagnostic tools, and templates with which to develop change and communication plans. The BCC project also meant that there would be no staff in the human resource management function with full-time jobs dedicated to change management, as the aim was to distribute those capabilities throughout the company.

BCC implemented several initiatives, including a large-scale systems conversion project, a human resources reengineering project, a system to measure and reward change management competencies, and a workplace redesign project called "Future of Work." The outcome for Capital One was:

> It does not "manage change" as if it were some unwanted intruder; it does not view change management as an afterthought to improve the chances of getting some key resistors to "buy into" a new initiative. Change is integrated into the way Capital One formulates strategy, structures itself, and measures and rewards performance. (Worley and Lawler, 2009, p. 245)

Success with this approach to change gave Capital One staff the confidence and desire to take on even more initiatives. Worley and Lawler (2009) argue that Capital One had effectively integrated change capabilities with business knowledge, creating a climate of continuous change. They offer three key learning points for other organizations. First, signal the commitment to developing change capability by providing training opportunities, and by rewarding the acquisition of change-related skills. Second, develop supportive organization structures and systems (table 4.6). Third, be prepared to learn from experience in the process of developing the organization's capacity for change. Change capability, they conclude, is the "missing ingredient" in organizational effectiveness.

EXERCISE 4.2

Scenario Planning

LO 4.3

Here is one structured methodology for scenario planning, for your own organization or for one with which you are familiar:

1. "Brainstorm" the range of environmental factors that have the potential to impact on the performance of your organization. In the spirit of brainstorming, accept all suggestions at this point, and suspend judgement as to the significance of any suggested factor.

2. Ask individuals to identify which factors from this list they believe to be the "key drivers" of the organization's performance over a specified time period—say, five years.

3. Aggregating these individual responses, identify the five most commonly cited key drivers; these could be, for example, exchange rates, new technologies, entry by new competitors, mergers, competition for key staff, costs and/or shortages of raw materials.

4. Using these key drivers as the core elements, construct three future scenarios for the organization: the most likely, an optimistic scenario, and a pessimistic one. The "most likely" scenario is constructed on the basis of the "best guess" as to what will happen to each of the five key drivers over the specified time frame. Note that "best guess" does not imply a casual approach; best guess can be based on sophisticated market intelligence and forecasting. The "optimistic" and "pessimistic" scenarios focus attention on how the organization might respond to each of those outcomes. The construction of the scenarios requires skill, and it is not uncommon for organizations to employ external consultants who are experienced in scenario development. Scenarios need to be compelling and plausible narratives, even if they are unlikely to happen. This is necessary if they are to form the basis of discussion concerning the organization's response to those three possible futures.

5. Finally, outline the different organizational change agendas that will be required to deal with each of those three possible futures.

**EXERCISE
4.3**

*Readiness
for Change
Analysis*

LO 4.3

The purpose of this diagnostic is to assess whether a *specific* organizational change initiative, project, or program has been well planned. Before you begin this assessment process, therefore, you must agree on a description of the proposed change or changes:

> The change proposal being considered is:

You can carry out this assessment on your own, or with colleagues in the organization—your steering group or project team, for example. Study the following items and circle the appropriate number on the scale. The number that you circle should reflect your view of the quality of the work carried out on that item, with respect to this change, so far. Keep the agreed definition of the proposed change in mind throughout this analysis.

This is a generic assessment tool, and the wording may not apply directly to your organization. If you feel that an item is not relevant to your circumstances, either ignore it, or think of a way in which that item should be reworded to make it more appropriate.

If you are working on this assessment with other members of your program, project, or change management team, complete this analysis individually before sharing and discussing your scores. You may find that different team members see things differently. Exploration of those differences can be extremely valuable in developing a shared understanding of the proposals, and in determining where the action priorities lie.

1. The change proposal has been financially justified as giving an adequate return on investment.

| no financial justification | 1 | 2 | 3 | 4 | 5 | 6 | 7 | full financial justification |

2. The assumptions on which the financial justification is based have been fully defined.

| assumptions not defined | 1 | 2 | 3 | 4 | 5 | 6 | 7 | assumptions clearly defined |

3. The costs of the proposed change have been realistically predicted—that is, all possible costs have been identified.

| costs not identified | 1 | 2 | 3 | 4 | 5 | 6 | 7 | all costs identified |

4. The costs of disruption to the present systems have been specifically identified.

| disruption costs not identified | 1 | 2 | 3 | 4 | 5 | 6 | 7 | disruption costs identified |

5. The leadership of the proposed change has been identified.

| change leaders not identified | 1 | 2 | 3 | 4 | 5 | 6 | 7 | change leaders identified |

6. The leaders of the proposed change are willing volunteers.

| change leaders are not willing volunteers | 1 | 2 | 3 | 4 | 5 | 6 | 7 | change leaders are willing volunteers |

7. A comprehensive implementation plan for the proposed change has been prepared.

| no comprehensive plan | 1 | 2 | 3 | 4 | 5 | 6 | 7 | comprehensive plan prepared |

Source: This analysis is based on Woodcock and Francis (1992).

8. All of those who could comment on the plan have had adequate time to study it.

no adequate comment	1	2	3	4	5	6	7	full comments available

9. Care has been taken to ensure that the risks inherent in the proposed change have been identified and assessed.

risks not identified or assessed	1	2	3	4	5	6	7	risks identified and assessed

10. Outside comment from impartial specialists has been invited on the wisdom of the proposed change.

no external comment invited	1	2	3	4	5	6	7	comprehensive external comment invited

11. Consideration has been given to the new skills that will be required for the effective implementation of the proposed change.

no consideration of skills requirement	1	2	3	4	5	6	7	full consideration of skills requirement

12. All those who could inhibit or stop the proposed change have been identified.

potential blockers not identified	1	2	3	4	5	6	7	potential blockers identified

13. A strategy has been devised for winning over all those who could inhibit or stop the proposed change.

no "winning over" strategy identified	1	2	3	4	5	6	7	comprehensive "winning over" strategy identified

14. The proposed change can be linked directly with the strategic plans of the organization.

no clear links with strategic plans	1	2	3	4	5	6	7	clear links with strategic plans

15. Those responsible for the proposed change have studied the nature and outcomes of similar initiatives in other organizations.

no other organizations visited or reviewed	1	2	3	4	5	6	7	several other organizations visited and reviewed

16. Although based on similar initiatives elsewhere, the need to tailor the proposed changes to the local context is recognized.

no allowances made for customization	1	2	3	4	5	6	7	realistic allowances made for customization

17. Clear success criteria and success measures have been identified.

no success criteria or measures identified	1	2	3	4	5	6	7	comprehensive success criteria and measures identified

18. Procedures have been established to help the organization learn from the experience of implementing these changes.

no learning procedures in place	1	2	3	4	5	6	7	comprehensive learning procedures in place

19. Top management is deeply committed to the success of the proposed changes.

no top management commitment	1	2	3	4	5	6	7	full top management commitment

20. The overall leadership of the proposed change is able and willing to exercise decisive leadership.

uncertain overall leadership	1	2	3	4	5	6	7	superior overall leadership

Scoring

Simply add the numbers that you have circled to produce a score between 20 and 140. If several members of your group or team have completed this analysis, then add all of their individual scores and calculate the average. What does the resultant score suggest?

20–40	Considerable anxiety should be experienced about the proposed changes.
41–80	Much work needs to be done to develop an effective change program.
81–100	The proposal is well developed, but change management can be improved.
101–140	This is a well-planned change proposal.

Action

Where are the main problems and blockages, and what can we do to address those? Identify those items that you scored with five points or less, or use the average item scores for the group or team as a whole. Select the five lowest-scoring items. Prioritize these, then brainstorm appropriate actions to address each of them in turn to improve readiness:

Problem Item	Appropriate Actions
1.	
2.	
3.	
4.	
5.	

Additional Reading

Blenko, M. W., Mankins, M. C., and Rogers, P. 2010. The decision-driven organization. *Harvard Business Review* 88(6):54–62. Argues that links between organization structure and performance are weak and that decision-making processes and decision quality are more important. Offers a diagnostic based on links between structure, roles, culture, and decisions.

Gardini, M., Giuliani, G., and Marricchi, M. 2011. *Finding the right place to start change*. Rome and Milan: McKinsey & Company. Argues the benefits of focusing initially on those staff groups who will have the most influence over the work that is going to change; starting in this way can accelerate the change process and contribute to long-term engagement.

Kanter, R. M. 2006. Innovation: The classic traps. *Harvard Business Review* 84(11): 73–83. Describes the steps that organizations need to take to become more flexible and innovative; identifies the strategy, process, structural, leadership, and communications mistakes that organizations typically make, and how to remedy these.

Miller, P., and Wedell-Wedellsborg, T. 2013. The case for stealth innovation. *Harvard Business Review* 91(3):90–97. Argues that, if you have a great new idea, the advice that you "get a mandate from the top" may be misguided. Better to innovate by stealth, "under the radar," until you have hard evidence and "proof of concept."

Wilkinson, A., and Kupers, R. 2013. Living in the futures: How scenario planning changed corporate strategy. *Harvard Business Review* 94(5):118–27. Describes how Shell developed scenario planning in the 1960s and assesses the company's use of the method. Finds that "a sustained scenario practice can make leaders comfortable with the ambiguity of an open future. It can counter hubris, expose assumptions that would otherwise remain implicit, contribute to shared and systemic sensemaking, and foster quick adaptation in times of crisis" (p. 127).

Roundup   This chapter has introduced a range of diagnostic tools that can contribute to the management of change by providing a perspective on a range of organizational situations. Models of "how organizations work" complement the implicit models that managers and others have in their heads. No one model is "correct" or "best," but each offers the opportunity to view the organization from a particular perspective. Choice of approach is therefore likely to be influenced by the image or images of change of those managers who are responsible for making the decisions. The models, frameworks, and tools from this chapter are summarized in table 4.8, which suggests when each may be useful.

Here is a short summary of the key points that we would like you to take from this chapter, in relation to each of the learning outcomes:

LO 4.1

Understand the use of diagnostic models in planning organizational change.
We explained a number of organizational models: the six-box model, the 7-S framework, the star model, and the four-frame model. Not difficult to apply in practice,

Reflections for the Practicing Change Manager

- Do you feel that you now have knowledge of a number of diagnostic tools/models?

- Do you believe that you could apply those tools and models when necessary?

- If you were to select two or three favorite tools/models, which would they be and why?

- Is there a key area of organizational activity where you would like a diagnostic tool that is not provided in this chapter? Where might you go to find such a tool?

- To what extent do your image(s) of change influence which diagnostic tools you are most comfortable using or see as most relevant?

TABLE 4.8
Change Diagnostics and Their Uses: A Summary

Diagnostic	Use When You Want To ...
Six-box model	Simplify the complexity, focus on key problems Be reminded of the systemic implications of actions in one area
7-S model	Recognize interconnectedness Pay attention to the "soft" factors as well as structure and strategy
Star model	Recognize interconnectedness and "knock on" effects Align your strategy, structure, people, processes, and rewards
Four-frame model	See the organization through different lenses at the same time Generate deeper understanding to develop creative solutions
Gap analysis	Develop a change agenda that addresses future conditions Generate understanding and consensus around the agenda
PESTLE framework	Understand the impact of multiple environmental pressures Exploit future opportunities and deal with risks and threats
Scenario planning	Encourage creative thinking and acceptance of uncertainty Prioritize, plan, and implement future-oriented changes
Elements of strategy	Identify changes necessary to pursue a given strategy Develop an integrated package of self-reinforcing changes
Strategic inventory	Clarify and validate strategic assumptions Decide what changes are necessary to drive strategy
Cultural web	Map and understand the components of the organization culture Challenge the taken for granted and identify barriers to change
Receptive context	Determine how receptive the organization is to change Decide action to increase receptiveness if necessary
Absorptive capacity	Assess the organization's ability to assimilate and apply new ideas Increase absorptive capacity with appropriate actions
Innovative organization	Assess if the organization stifles or stimulates innovation Develop or strengthen innovative organization characteristics
Force-field analysis	Assess the driving and restraining forces for a given change Manage the balance of forces to encourage the change
Readiness for change analysis	Assess organizational and individual readiness for a given change Identify the "groundwork" needed before the change goes ahead
Individual readiness	Assess individual readiness for a given change Take appropriate steps to increase individual readiness
Stakeholder analysis	Identify how those affected could influence the change process Manage stakeholders given their power and their interest
Built-to-change model	Ensure that change happens more quickly and smoothly Design an organization in which continuous change is routine

these models serve a number of purposes. They simplify complexity, highlight priorities, identify interdependencies, provide a common language, and offer a guide to the change implementation process.

LO 4.2

Use strategic analysis tools to assess the need for organizational change.
We explained several strategic analysis tools: gap analysis, the PESTLE framework, scenario planning, the elements of strategy framework, the strategic inventory, and the cultural web. Gap analysis is a simple but powerful tool for assessing the need for change. The other tools in this section generate more detailed assessments on need for and nature of change, based on more in-depth questioning of current strategy and future goals.

LO 4.4

Diagnose organizational receptiveness to and individual readiness for change, and use those assessments as the basis for action to increase receptiveness and readiness.
We explored the features of the receptive organizational context, the concept of "absorptive capacity," and properties of the innovative organization. We identified the steps that can be taken to strengthen receptiveness, to increase absorptive capacity, and to introduce organization features that stimulate (rather than smother) creativity and innovation. Force-field analysis can often be a useful technique in this respect. Organizational receptiveness may be necessary but is not sufficient, and we also explored the factors that influence individual readiness for change and how those can be influenced to strengthen readiness. Stakeholder analysis can often be a useful framework in this context.

LO 4.5

Explain the characteristics of the "built-to-change" organizational model, and assess the applicability, strengths, and limitations of this approach.
We contrasted "traditional" principles of organization design with "built-to-change" principles, concerning talent management, reward systems, organization structure, information and decision processes, and leadership. In an organization that is "built-to-change," continuous change is "business as usual" and does not have to involve a planned transition from one state to another. In short, the built-to-change model of the organization challenges the conventional change management models and principles described in this chapter. Given the design principles involved, any organization could potentially develop the agility that "built-to-change" implies.

Debrief: Charlie's Angels and the Red Star Corporation

Does the Red Star Corporation culture stimulate or smother innovation? Here is the evidence:

Clues	Implications
Straight rows of equally spaced desks facing in the same direction with identical tidy desktop layouts	Order, discipline, routine, standardization, regimentation, don't "step out of line"
Absence of color, everything white, flat bright lighting	No distractions, no colors, no stimulations, focus on the task in hand
All-male workforce	No diversity; these are software engineers, forgive them, it's not their fault

(Continued)

(Continued)

A ditzy female administrator	Even less diversity, women limited to subordinate "backroom" positions
Identical male office wear	No freedom of expression, suppression of personal identity by "uniform"
Tiered formal lecture theatre	One-way, top-down communication is the norm using this layout
Procedures reward mediocrity	Radical thinking is discouraged
Managers reject ideas from below	Don't challenge your boss, keep those great ideas to yourself, you'll only get into trouble

The general characteristics of organizational innovation illustrated here are:

1. We are all capable of generating creative, innovative ideas.
2. Organization culture and management style can smother creativity and innovation.
3. It sometimes takes an "external shock" (or person) to recognize the need to change the organization culture, to become more innovative.
4. If you come up with a great idea, don't tell me, show me.

References

Arkin, A. 2007. The generation game. *People Management* 13(24):24–27.

Blenko, M. W., Mankins, M. C., and Rogers, P. 2010. The decision-driven organization. *Harvard Business Review* 88(6):54–62.

Bolman, L., and Deal, T. 2013. *Reframing organizations: Artistry, choice, and leadership.* 5th ed. San Francisco: Jossey-Bass.

Burke, W. W. 2013. *Organizational change: Theory and practice.* 4th ed. Thousand Oaks, CA: Sage Publications.

Burns, T., and Stalker, G. M. 1961. *The management of innovation.* London: Tavistock Publications.

Cohen, W. M., and Levinthal, D. A. 1990. Absorptive capacity: A new perspective on learning and innovation. *Administrative Science Quarterly* 30:560–85.

Eccles, T. 1984. *Succeeding with change: Implementing action-driven strategies.* London: McGraw-Hill.

Galbraith, J., Downey, D., and Kates, A. 2002. *Designing dynamic organizations.* New York: AMACOM.

Gardini, M., Giuliani, G., and Marricchi, M. 2011. *Finding the right place to start change.* Rome and Milan: McKinsey & Company.

Grundy, T. 1997. Accelerating strategic change: The internal stakeholder dimension. *Strategic Change* 6(1):49–56.

Hambrick, D. C., and Fredrickson, J. W. 2001. Are you sure you have a strategy? *Academy of Management Executive* 15(4):48–59.

Hamel, G., and Zanini, M. 2014. *Build a change platform, not a change program.* London: McKinsey & Company.

Hiatt, J. 2006. *ADKAR: A model for change in business, government, and our community.* Loveland, CO: Prosci.

Higgins, J. M. (2005) The eight "s's" of successful strategy execution. *Journal of Change Management* 5(1):3–13.

Jansen, J. J. P., Ven Den Bosch, F. A. J., and Volberda, H. W. 2005. Managing potential and realized absorptive capacity: How do organizational antecedents matter? *Academy of Management Journal* 48(6):999–1015.

Johnson, G. 1998. Mapping and re-mapping organizational culture. In *Exploring techniques of analysis and evaluation in strategic management*, ed. V. Ambrosini, G. Johnson, and K. Scholes (137–51). New York and London: Financial Times Prentice Hall.

Johnson, G., Whittington, R., Scholes, K., Angwin, D., and Regnér, P. 2013. *Exploring strategy: Text and cases.* Harlow, Essex: Pearson Education.

Kanter, R. M. 1983. *The change masters: Corporate entrepreneurs at work.* London: George Allen & Unwin.

Kanter, R. M. 1989. *When giants learn to dance: Mastering the challenges of strategy, management, and careers in the 1990s.* London: Unwin.

Kanter, R. M. 2002. Creating the culture for innovation. In *Leading for innovation and organizing for results*, ed. F. Hesselbein, M. Goldsmith, and I. Somerville (73–85). San Francisco: Jossey-Bass.

Kanter, R. M. 2006. Innovation: The classic traps. *Harvard Business Review* 84(11):73–83.

Lewin, K. 1943. Defining the field at a given time. *Psychological Review* 50(3):292–310.

Lewin, K. (ed.). 1951. *Field theory in social science: Selected theoretical papers by Kurt Lewin.* London: Tavistock Publications. (UK edition published 1952, edited by Dorwin Cartwright.)

Miller, P., and Wedell-Wedellsborg, T. 2013. The case for stealth innovation. *Harvard Business Review* 91(3):90–97.

Mitchell, R. 2008. *Risk 2018: Planning for an unpredictable decade.* London: The Economist Intelligence Unit Ltd.

Morrison, M., and Daniels, K. 2010. *PESTLE Analysis Factsheet.* London: Chartered Institute of Personnel and Development.

Pettigrew, A. M., Ferlie, E., and McKee, L. 1992. *Shaping strategic change: Making change in large organizations—the case of the National Health Service.* London: Sage Publications.

Picken, J. C., and Dess, G. G. 1998. Right strategy—wrong problem. *Organizational Dynamics* 27(1):35–48.

Rafferty, A. E., Jimmieson, N. L., and Armenakis, A. A. 2013. Change readiness: A multi-level review. *Journal of Management* 39(1):110–35.

Verity, J. 2003. Scenario planning as a strategy technique. *European Business Journal* 15(4):185–95.

Waterman, R. H., Peters, T. J., and Phillips, J. R. 1980. Structure is not organization. *Business Horizons* (June):14–26.

Weisbord, M. R. 1976. Organizational diagnosis: Six places to look for trouble with or without a theory. *Group & Organization Studies* 1(4):430–47.

Wilkinson, A., and Kupers, R. 2013. Living in the futures: How scenario planning changed corporate strategy. *Harvard Business Review* 94(5):118–27.

Woodcock, M., and Francis, D. 1992. *Change*. Aldershot: Gower Publications.

Worley, C. G., and Lawler, E. E. 2006. Designing organizations that are built-to-change. *Sloan Management Review* 48(1):19–23.

Worley, C. G., and Lawler, E. E. 2009. Building a change capability at Capital One Financial. *Organizational Dynamics* 38(4):245–51.

Worley, C. G., and Lawler, E. E. 2010. Built-to-change organizations: Industry influences and performance implications. *Center for Effective Organizations Working Paper*, T 10-03 (571):1–13.

Zahra, S. A., and George, G. 2002. Absorptive capacity: A review, reconceptualization and extension. *Academy of Management Review* 27(2):185–203.

PART 2

Implementation: The Substance and Process of Change

The central theme of the six chapters in Part 2 is *implementation*. What is the substance of the changes that are to be introduced? What is the vision for the organization's future, given the external environment, technology developments, regulatory changes, and other trends? Is that vision interesting, exciting, compelling, motivating? Through what strategies should the vision and substance of change proposals be communicated to the organization's stakeholders? What is the nature of resistance and, if necessary, how should that be managed to capture the potential benefits of competing ideas as well as to address the concerns of the resisters? There are several approaches to change implementation, each drawing on different theoretical perspectives, with different implications for practice. What are these approaches, what are their benefits and drawbacks, and how can the change manager choose between them?

Chapter 5

What Changes— and What Doesn't?

Learning objectives

On completion of this chapter you should be able to:

LO 5.1 Explain several different ways of categorizing different types of change

LO 5.2 Identify practical implications of different types of change for the change manager

LO 5.3 Understand the difference between sustaining and disruptive innovation, and explain the practical implications of this distinction for change management

LO 5.4 Assess the significance of organizational culture with regard to organizational performance and reputation, and the role of leaders as culture architects

LO 5.5 Assess the potential impact of new digital technologies in general, and the potential organizational benefits of applications of social media in particular

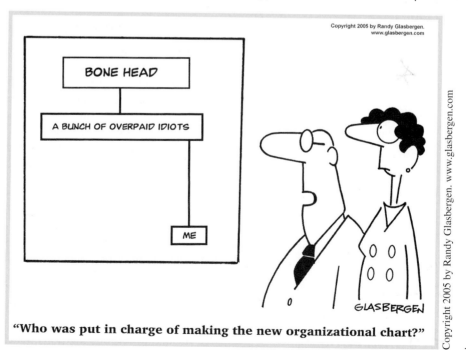

Copyright 2005 by Randy Glasbergen.
www.glasbergen.com

BONE HEAD

A BUNCH OF OVERPAID IDIOTS

ME

GLASBERGEN

"Who was put in charge of making the new organizational chart?"

What Changes?

What changes? Well, anything and everything, from an individual's job description, to a whole organizational system, which could involve other organizations as well. Here are some examples:

> aspirations, attitudes to risk and innovation, budgeting procedures, business model, collaboration and conflict, culture of the organization, downsizing, external relationships such as partnerships and joint ventures, information systems, leadership and management style, location and layout of facilities, manufacturing processes, materials used in products and service delivery, merger or acquisition, pay and reward systems, performance appraisal and management systems, performance targets, power bases, product design, role of customers/clients, role of middle management, service delivery models, skill mix, staff engagement, structure of the organization, success criteria, support services in-house or outsourced, teamwork, technology, workforce composition, working practices

The short version of this list might say that what changes can include strategy, structure, technology, systems and procedures, human resource management practices, internal and external relationships, leadership style, and culture. These issues are not independent. In practice, they are closely coupled and should be mutually reinforcing. They can, however, be contradictory, which is also potentially damaging. Common contradictions include:

- expecting high-performance teamwork while basing rewards on individual performance;
- encouraging middle management autonomy while withholding vital performance information;
- demanding cross-functional information exchange in a strong "organizational silo" structure;
- combining a staff engagement policy with an autocratic top-down leadership style.

It is also apparent that changes in one domain may have "knock-on" or "ripple" effects, creating or requiring changes in other areas. New technology, for example, is likely to change skill mix requirements, working practices, rewards, and performance appraisal and management systems, and may also require supportive changes in leadership and management behavior. These examples of knock-on effects are obvious, but they emphasize that "what doesn't change?" is also a relevant issue. In practice, the ripples from even simple changes in an organization can be difficult to predict, and thus difficult to manage. One example concerns the redesign of working practices in one area, which leads to performance improvements, which lead to pay increases for those involved, which trigger jealousy and anger in the areas which were not involved in the initiative. Extending the changes to those other areas should reduce the tension, but the anger and perceived sense of betrayal (why were we not chosen?) can be stored in the corporate memory for some time.

In sum, "what changes?" is a deceptively simple question, with a potentially complex series of answers. There are several ways in which the content or the substance of change can be categorized. For example, some changes are *planned*, while others are *emergent*. *Planned changes*, as the term suggests, are those that are implemented in anticipation of, or in response to, known trends and developments. Changes in motor vehicle engine design and manufacturing methods (technology, materials, and working practices) are likely to be prompted by changes in legislation regulating carbon emissions. *Emergent changes* are

What Changed at Barclays Bank?

The subprime mortgage crisis in 2008 had a major impact on the financial services sector. In addition to big losses, the sector faced tighter regulation of their investment activities, which were seen as aggressive and risky. Under its previous chief executive, Bob Diamond, Barclays Capital aspired to be the largest investment bank in the world, and additional staff were hired to grow that part of the business. But in 2012, it was revealed that staff were manipulating the London Inter-Bank Offered Rate (LIBOR), and Barclays was fined £290 million. The chairman, chief executive, and chief operating officer left the bank in July. An internal review criticized the investment business for its "win at all costs" culture that was arrogant and selfish and put financial gain before customers (Salz, 2013).

The reputational damage from the LIBOR scandal, and new regulatory requirements, meant a different approach. Antony Jenkins was appointed chief executive in 2012. In 2014, he announced the following changes, triggering an immediate 8 percent rise in the bank's share price:

Aspirations	"Capital" was dropped from the company name, which became just Barclays The "world leader" aim was abandoned, allowing Barclays to focus on the U.S. and UK markets, on Africa, and on a small number of Asian clients
Business model	Barclays would no longer trade in physical commodities, or in esoteric "derivative" products such as swaps and options, leveraged loans, and mortgage-backed securities The company would invest its own funds rather than those of its customers Investment banking would only account for 30 percent of the bank's profits Focus on a narrower range of customers, rather than on high-risk lending
Culture	"Customer first," clarity, and openness became priority, with a focus on customer relationships replacing an aggressive short-term approach to growth, which rewarded commercial drive and winning, and created a culture of fear of not meeting targets; pay for investment bankers was cut
Downsizing	Over three years, starting in 2014, branches were closed, and 19,000 jobs were cut, including many at the New York and London headquarters, staff in high street businesses (cashiers, branch managers), and 7,000 investment banking staff (some of whom were very high earners) Costs were cut by £1.7 billion in 2014
Technology	More automation of transactions to reduce costs, with more customers banking online or on mobile devices; 30 completely automated branches were opened by 2014, with the loss of 6,500 cashiers—retrained as "digital eagles" with iPads, to help customers use the new computer systems

These changes were designed to create a leaner, stronger, better balanced, and more focused business, generating increased return on equity and better rewards for shareholders. This was also designed to restore customer confidence and trust, and the bank's reputation. Addressing the previous cultural failings, an internal document, *The Barclay's Way:* *How We Do Business*, was published in 2013. This emphasized ethics, fairness, and customer/client relationships, and set out a values-driven code of conduct based on respect, integrity, service, excellence, and stewardship. (This account is based on Aldrick, 2013; Arnold and Sharman, 2014; Costello and Leroux, 2014; Goff, 2014; Treanor, 2014.)

those that just happen, or have to happen, in response to unforeseen events, such as the sudden opening of new market opportunities, or accidents and failures, or major geopolitical developments. It is difficult to plan ahead for those events in other than very general terms. As we discussed in chapter 2, it is possible to argue that emergent change is now more common, given the complex, fluid, and unpredictable nature of the environment in which most if not all of our organizations are operating (Weick, 2000). In contrast, much of the practical advice on change implementation assumes a carefully considered and planned approach.

We also need to distinguish between *incremental change*, which is gradual and small scale, and *transformational change*, which is radical and groundbreaking, and can often be rapid. There is a widespread perception today that organizational change up to the mid-twentieth century was typically incremental and infrequent, and that from the late twentieth century to the present, change has become more common and traumatic. However, as noted in chapter 1, some commentators argue that radical, transformational change is not new, but was also a feature of the first half of the twentieth century—if not before. But, there is a more important question here: is too much attention now lavished on large-scale transformational change, while the role of small-scale changes is overlooked?

Some commentators use the terms *first-order change* and *second-order change* to describe the difference between incremental and transformational change (e.g., Coghlan and Rashford, 2006).

First-order change involves a specific initiative that solves a problem, and/or makes improvements, in ways that do not present a challenge to current methods and thinking. First-order change is adaptive and implies a degree of continuity and order. This is captured in the expression, "change to stay the same" (Bate, 1994). The incorporation of a growing range of safety features in motor vehicles—from seat belts to electronic proximity sensors—is a series of first-order changes that improve the product without making any major changes to it.

Second-order change leads to organizational transformation, by introducing new products, services, and ways of doing business, based on creative lateral thinking that alters current core assumptions. Second-order change is disruptive and discontinuous, and is captured in the expression, "move to get to a new position" (Bate, 1994). The development of electric-powered self-driving motorcars, made by companies that are not considered to be in the automotive sector, is an example of second-order change.

David Coghlan and Nicholas Rashford (2006) also identify *third-order change*, based on the habitual questioning of assumptions and points of view, contributing to what can be a chaotic process of continual adaptation, self-renewal, and self-organization. What will come after electric and driverless cars, and "phone app taxi services"? Walmart and other retail supermarkets sell motorcars thus threatening established dealer networks. Given current global trends in house prices, will property developers and real estate agents offer discounted or free motorcars with house and apartment purchases as an inducement to customers? Will dealers in congested cities (Beijing, London, Mumbai, New York) provide free motorcycles with the cars that they sell, so that customers can make their own "park and ride" arrangements to get to work? Will we continue to own cars anyway, or hire them when we need them, ordering them by iPhone? These developments, and others more difficult to predict, are examples of third-order change that, in some sectors, could become the norm.

The categories of change that we have discussed so far have involved simple dichotomies ("either this or that type"), with third-order change offering another option. These are helpful categories, but they may be too simplified to deal with the complex patterns of contemporary organizational change. Depth is another metaphor that can be used to categorize different types of change, as shown in figure 5.1. At the bottom of this figure sits the "small stuff" that may not even be regarded as "change." Mid-scale includes "sustaining innovation," which involves improving on current practices. At the top of the scale is "disruptive innovation," which involves radically new business models and working methods (Christensen, 2000). It is not difficult to locate incremental and first-order change (shallow, sustaining), second-order or transformational change (deep, strategic), or third-order change (off the scale, disruptive) on this scale. The depth metaphor simply provides a richer picture of the patterns of change that we are likely to see in most organizations.

LO 5.2 What are the practical change management implications of these categories of change? The first, and most obvious, implication concerns matching solutions with problems.

FIGURE 5.1
Assessing Depth of Change

↑ **Off the scale**	Disruptive innovation Frame-breaking, mould-breaking Redraw dramatically organization and sector boundaries
Deeper	Paradigm shift, strategic change, *third-order change* New ways of thinking and solving problems, whole system change New ways of doing business
Deep change	Change the mission, vision, values, the organization's philosophy, to symbolize a radical shift in thinking and behaviour, *second-order change*
	Change the organization's definition of success Create new goals, objectives, targets
Sustaining innovation	Improve business planning to symbolize a shift in thinking Tighten up on documentation, reporting, controls
	Reallocate resources Grow some departments, cut others, create new units
Shallow change	Incremental, fine tuning: cut costs, find efficiencies, *first-order change* Constantly 'nibble away' making minor improvements
↓ **Not on the scale**	"Sweat the small stuff"-quickly solve the minor annoying problems that nobody has bothered to fix; "grease the wheels"

Despite the current fashion for deep transformational change, simple problems that are well understood can usually be resolved with simple, shallow, incremental changes. Addressing fundamental strategic opportunities and threats with fine-tuning, however, will typically lead to disappointment.

A second implication concerns the nature of the change management task. The management of shallow change typically requires less management capability and fewer resources than implementing frame-breaking initiatives. The former are likely to involve few departures from the familiar, may be relatively low in both cost and perceived risk, and pose little threat to the status quo with which people are comfortable. In contrast, deep, disruptive, or "off the scale" change is often abrupt, painful, risky, and expensive and can stimulate stronger and more widespread resistance, potentially creating a major management challenge.

A third practical issue concerns management reputation. Change management experience and capability have become "core selection factors" for candidates seeking promoted positions in many organizations (Beeson, 2009). Candidates who can answer those interview questions with accounts of the deep changes in which they have played a role are more likely to be preferred to those whose previous roles have involved them in only shallow, incremental initiatives. We have only anecdotal evidence to suggest that deeper changes can often be driven as much by personal career motives as by corporate need. Figure 5.1 can therefore be read not just as a change typology, but also as a personal positioning tool for ambitious change managers. Assess the profile of changes in which you are currently engaged. If this involves shallow initiatives, explore how you can become involved with, or personally generate, deep changes that you can then discuss at the next job or promotion interview.

As discussed earlier, a lot of attention has been paid to deep, disruptive, transformational change. However, in most organizations, at any given time, changes are likely to be taking place across the range covered in figure 5.1. Small changes can contribute to and support deeper initiatives. Some changes may start small but develop with experience into larger-scale initiatives. Deep changes demand time and resources, diverting attention from those necessary smaller-scale projects.

How to Choose Your Thrust and Limit Your Agenda

Most organizations come under pressure to change from many directions: creative new ideas, internal issues and inefficiencies, external trends and developments. These pressures can generate a long and complex change agenda. Paying attention to all of those issues, however, means spreading resources thinly and a potential loss of focus. Tom Peters (2014, pp. 8–9) argues that top management must limit the agenda by choosing one or two "plausible important thrusts." He identifies six criteria on which the choice of these thrusts should be based:

1. *Internal achievability*: Can a "cost-oriented" company begin to turn itself into a "product innovation" leader in three to five years?

2. *Political feasibility*: Can the top team be persuaded to support the thrust?

3. *Soundness in competitive or regulatory terms*: Is a marketing thrust a good choice for a high-cost producer in a shrinking market?

4. *Freshness*: Will it be perceived as a new direction?

5. *Early wins*: Will it be possible to show some results in the first few months, even though full-scale implementation may take years?

6. *Excitement*: Can most people from middle management on up eventually become enthusiastic about it?

This pattern of shallow to deep change raises a fourth challenge, to coordinate those initiatives to avoid duplication, overlap, and unnecessary cost. Research once suggested that most organizations experienced periods of stability that were interrupted on occasion by more profound changes. This was known as the theory of "punctuated equilibrium" (Romanelli and Tushman, 1994). That theory was based, however, on evidence from computer companies in the 1960s. That may not be the case today, as the pattern of change has become more programmatic. In response, many organizations have set up corporate program management offices (PMOs) to support and coordinate their initiatives (Ward and Daniel, 2013). A study by the Philadelphia-based Project Management Institute (2012) found that 84 percent of organizations had set up PMOs, which have the following benefits:

- reduce the number of projects that fail;
- deliver projects under budget and ahead of schedule;
- improve productivity;
- increase cost savings.

There is no standard PMO model, and this varies between organizations in terms of structure, location, and roles. The Project Management Institute study identified four factors contributing to the effectiveness of PMOs: First, they need a senior executive champion. Second, their role must be clearly understood. Third, the change professionals who staff the PMO must have the respect of functional departments. Finally, PMOs need to collaborate with functional departments in the development of initiatives, and not act as "change police."

For example, at State Auto Insurance Company in Ohio, change projects would appear at random, and the company had no mechanism to ensure that projects stayed within budget and met their objectives. A PMO was made responsible for methodology, governance, change management, delivery, and portfolio management. Units that want to launch change projects have to construct a business case showing their alignment with corporate strategy. At the National Cancer Institute in Bethesda, Maryland, the PMO head found that teams working on early-phase drug development projects started every project plan from scratch. But there was a lot of overlap, with 80 percent of the work activities being either identical or similar from one project to another. The PMO designed a system to avoid this duplication. Previously, the teams held 16 four-hour meetings to develop their project plan. This was cut to only four meetings (Project Management Institute, 2012).

We have identified different types of change, reaching beyond a simple categorization (first-order, second-order). We have described other ways to conceptualize change (using a depth metaphor) and to assess the profile of change in an organization at any one time. These categories and concepts have implications for change management practice: matching solutions to problems, assessing the complexity of the change management task, linking involvement in change to personal reputations and careers, and coordinating a wide portfolio of change through a program management office.

Through the rest of this chapter, we will develop these themes, first exploring different kinds of innovation and the distinction between sustaining and disruptive innovation. We then turn attention to two changes that are likely to confront many organizations: culture change and technology-driven change. These are often seen as second-order changes, but this depends on the perspective from which they are interpreted. The kinds of changes that can take place with regard to organizational culture and to how new technologies are used can be profound and transformational. Throughout, the challenges for change managers posed by innovation, culture change, and technology developments will be considered. The most obvious challenges, perhaps, involve maintaining the pace of change while ensuring effective implementation and sustained gains.

Innovation

LO 5.3   One of the key drivers of change is *innovation*. This term is not confined to new products. Other important innovations concern ways to organize, better working practices, and new ways to provide services. The word thus tends to be used in a broad sense, to mean the adoption of any product, system, process, program, service, or business model *new to this organization*. An idea may have developed elsewhere, but it can be seen as an innovation *here*.

It is helpful to identify different kinds of innovation. For example, we can distinguish between product innovations (new gadgets) and operational innovations. Michael Hammer (2004) describes operational innovation as finding new ways to lead, organize, work, motivate, and manage. He describes a vehicle insurance company that introduced "immediate response claims handling," operating 24 hours a day. This involved scheduling visits to claimants by claims adjusters who worked from mobile vans, and who turned up within nine hours. Previously, with office-based adjusters, it took a week to inspect a damaged vehicle. Handling 10,000 claims a day, adjusters were empowered to estimate damage and write a check on the spot. These operational innovations led to major cost savings, with fewer staff involved in claims handling, lower vehicle storage costs, better fraud detection, and reduction in payout costs. Customer satisfaction and loyalty also improved.

Toyota's Lean production system is another example of an operational innovation that improves product quality and reduces costs by redesigning the manufacturing process without directly affecting product design. Walmart has an innovative approach to purchasing and distribution, using "cross-docking," where goods are switched from one truck to the next at distribution centers without going into storage. Dell Computers' "build to order" business model was also a disruptive innovation.

Clayton Christensen and Michael Overdorf (2000) make a distinction between sustaining innovations and disruptive innovations, identified in figure 5.1. Sustaining innovations improve existing products and processes: a more fuel-efficient motorcar, streamlining an administrative process. Disruptive innovations introduce wholly new processes and services, such as an all-electric motorcar or social networking. Disruptive innovations imply deep transformational change.

Innovations that are disruptive do not necessarily involve chaos and upheaval. What is disrupted is often traditional ways of thinking and acting. Digital photography, for example, has not just replaced traditional "wet film" formats and the cameras that required them. This development has changed the ways in which we capture, manipulate, display, share, and think about images. The extra cost of taking more photographs is close to zero, and we are more likely to share our shots on a website, or display them on a digital photo frame or on television, than to print them for the family album. How many manufacturers

Disruptive Innovation in the Nineteenth Century *The Stethoscope*

That it [the stethoscope] will ever come into general use, not withstanding its value, I am extremely doubtful; because its beneficial application requires much time, and it gives a good deal of trouble both to the patient and practitioner, and because its whole hue and character is foreign, and opposed to all our habits and associations. It must be confessed that there is something ludicrous in the picture of a grave physician formally listening through a long tube applied to a patient's thorax, as if the disease within were a living being that could communicate its condition to the sense without. (John Forbes, in the preface to his translation of *De L'Auscultation Mediate ou Traite du Diagnostic des Maladies des Poumons et du Coeur* [A Treatise on Diseases of the Chest and on Mediate Auscultation], by R. T. H. Laennec, T&G Underwood, London, 1821.)

of cameras predicted that one day versions of their product would be given away free by mobile telephone companies? Digital photography has been a truly disruptive innovation.

The business model developed by the online retailer Amazon has disrupted the traditional retailing sector while changing our shopping habits. Although Amazon began by selling books, the company has diversified into selling everything, also allowing third parties to sell their goods through its website, and even selling its own consumer electronics products such as Fire Phone and Kindle. Amazon is also a major provider of cloud computer services. U.S. customers can find around 230 million different products on Amazon's website.

Challenges for the Change Manager (1)

Operational innovations can be more difficult to implement than product innovations. Potential users can see and touch a new product—a smartphone, for example—and they can try it out for themselves. An operational innovation, however, has to be implemented before anyone can really see how it is going to work—a streamlined process that will reduce time to market. This means that the benefits can take time to appear, particularly when the initial specification has to be adjusted with experience. Convincing others of the value of an operational innovation, therefore, is not always straightforward. Hammer (2004) argues that business culture undervalues operations, which are seen as boring and low status. Operations are not as glamorous, or as easily understood, as deal-making or new technology and are therefore not regarded as a source of competitive advantage. A further problem is that the "ownership" of an operational innovation may be vague, because it crosses functional boundaries.

Hammer (2004) argues that operational innovations are often driven by "catalysts" who are committed to finding and exploiting such opportunities, and who are relentless in their attempts to convince senior management. Everett Rogers (1995) observed that adoption of innovations follows a pattern. First, small numbers adopt, followed by "takeoff," achieving a critical mass of adopters. Finally, the pace slackens as saturation is reached, typically short of 100 percent (you never convince everyone). Rogers argues that this pattern is influenced by the five groups in table 5.1.

Hammer's catalysts are Rogers' innovators. Change is thus often dependent on innovators and early adopters in particular. Hammer offers four suggestions for accelerating the

TABLE 5.1
From Innovators to Laggards

Innovators	Usually the first in their social grouping to adopt new approaches and behaviors, a small category of individuals who enjoy the excitement and risks of experimentation
Early adopters	Opinion leaders who evaluate ideas carefully, and are more skeptical and take more convincing, but take risks, help to adapt new ideas to local settings, and have effective networking skills
Early majority	Those who take longer to reach a decision to change, but who are still ahead of the average
Late majority	Even more skeptical and risk averse, wait for most of their colleagues to adopt new ideas first
Laggards	Viewed negatively by others, the last to adopt new ideas, even for reasons that they believe to be rational

incidence of operational innovation. First, look for role models in other sectors. Second, challenge constraining assumptions ("this will never work because"). Third, turn the "special case" into the norm. And finally, rethink the core dimensions of the work—who does it, where, when, how thoroughly, with what results; how can these dimensions be redesigned to make the process more effective?

Challenges for the Change Manager (2)

Disruptive innovations can be more difficult to implement than sustaining innovations, as they are often viewed as risky. Christensen and Overdorf (2000) note that drastic change involving disruptive innovation can jeopardize an organization's business model and core capabilities (see "Not a Good Kodak Moment"). A further challenge is that disruptive products and services are often not as good as those in current use. The service provided by the low-cost business model of Southwest Airlines may not be as good as that of conventional carriers, but is simpler, more accessible, and cheaper. The quality of images produced by the first digital cameras was much poorer than that from film cameras. In addition, most organizations have no routine processes for dealing with disruptive innovations. Disruptive innovations are thus often introduced by smaller new entrants or start-ups in a sector, rather than by the older, larger, and dominant incumbents (Hwang and Christensen, 2008).

In contrast with disruptive innovations, it is easier to convince others of the value of sustaining innovations, which make existing processes, products, and services work better. Rogers (1995) argued that the probability of an innovation being accepted is increased when it has these properties:

1. Advantageous when compared with existing practice
2. Compatible with existing practices
3. Easy to understand
4. Observable in demonstration sites
5. Testable
6. Adaptable to fit local needs

Not a Good Kodak Moment

Kodak invented the first digital camera in 1975 and the first megapixel camera in 1986. So why did the development of digital photography drive Kodak to bankruptcy in 2012? In 1975, the costs of this new technology were high and the image quality was poor. Kodak believed that it could take at least another ten years before digital technology began to threaten their established camera, film, chemical, and photo printing paper businesses. That forecast proved to be accurate, but rather than prepare, Kodak decided to improve the quality of film, with sustaining innovations. With hindsight, it is easy to spot that mistake. But the market information available to management from the 1970s through the 1990s, combined with the company's financial performance, made the switch to digital appear risky. In 1976, Kodak accounted for 90 percent of film and 85 percent of camera sales in America. Kodak's annual revenues peaked in 1996, at $16 billion; profits in 1999 were $2.5 billion. However, success encouraged complacency and reinforced confidence in the brand. Analysts noted that it might be unwise to switch from making 70 cents on the dollar with film, to 5 cents with digital. But by 2011, Kodak's revenues had fallen to $6.2 billion, and the company was reporting losses.

Kodak's competitor, Fuji, recognized the same threat and decided to switch to digital while generating as much return as possible from film and developing new lines of business, including cosmetics based on chemicals used for film processing. Both companies had the same information, but they came to different assessments, and Kodak was too slow to respond. By the time Kodak began to develop digital cameras, mobile phones with built-in digital cameras had become popular.

Kodak invented the technology but did not recognize just how disruptive an innovation digital would prove to be, making their traditional business obsolete (Barabba, 2011; *The Economist*, 2012).

It is difficult to demonstrate these properties with disruptive innovations—which can be difficult to understand, cannot be observed and tested, and cannot be compared with current practice until after they have been implemented. For the organization seeking to develop the capabilities for handling disruptive innovation, Christensen and Overdorf (2000, p. 73) make the following suggestions: consider acquiring an organization that already has these capabilities; create an independent organization to deal with the problem; or create new structures, such as dedicated, cross-functional teams.

Change Manager as Disruptive Innovator

What advice is there for the change manager seeking to develop and implement disruptive innovations to their organization? Jeff Dyer, Hal Gregersen, and Clayton Christensen (2011) argue that anyone can be innovative by using the right approach. Innovators use the five habits shown in table 5.2.

These habits are not confined to a small number of special people; they can be developed. The change manager can thus become more innovative by following this advice, and by collaborating with "delivery-driven" colleagues. Dyer and colleagues argue that organizations also need to encourage these habits, stimulating employees to connect ideas, to challenge accepted practices, to watch what others are doing, to take risks and try things out, and to get out of the company to meet others.

In Defense of Sustaining Innovation

As argued in chapter 1, it would be a mistake to think that transformational, disruptive innovation is the solution to most current organizational problems, for at least

TABLE 5.2 The Five Habits of Disruptive Innovators		
Associating	Innovators are good at seeing connections between things that do not appear to be related, drawing ideas together from unrelated fields	
Questioning	Innovators are always challenging what others take for granted, asking, "Why is this done this way—why don't we do it differently?"	
Observing	Innovators watch the behavior of customers, suppliers, competitors—looking for new ways of doing things	
Experimenting	Innovators tinker with products and business models, sometimes accidentally, to see what happens, what insights emerge	
Networking	Innovators attend conferences and other social events to pick up ideas from people with different ideas, who may face similar problems, in other fields	

two reasons. First, considerable business benefit can be achieved through small-scale initiatives and sustaining innovations. Many healthcare organizations have imported "lean" techniques from manufacturing and made significant performance improvements that benefit patients, staff, and the organization as a whole (Graban, 2009). Second, many organizations have highly profitable businesses based on traditional products, such as Harris Tweed, Swiss watches, Samuel Adams Boston lager. Some traditional technologies, having once been overtaken by innovative replacements, have reemerged. In the United States, by 2014, 30 cities had reintroduced green "environment-friendly" trams or were planning to do so; sales of vinyl LPs increased from zero in 1993 to 6 million in 2013. New technology does not simply displace old technology. The appeal of some old technologies is enduring (sailing boats, paper books), and some items are bought for their aesthetic value, regardless of price (*The Economist*, 2014).

These considerations further complicate our answer to this chapter's question: what changes? There are different kinds and degrees of innovation. The challenge for the change manager is to determine which (or which combination) is appropriate to a particular organization at a given time. As Kodak's experience suggests, reaching that assessment involves judgement and intuition as well as data.

LO 5.4 Organizational Culture

Are people enthusiastic about working for this organization? Do they feel valued? Are there development and career opportunities? Are customers and clients valued and given good quality service? Are leaders and managers respected and trusted? Is information shared openly? Is teamwork and collaboration between divisions the norm? Do staff agree with the purpose of the organization? These are just some of the indicators of an organization's culture. When the answers to those questions turn to "no," then organizational effectiveness suffers.

One definition of organizational culture, therefore, is "the way we do things around here." A more technical definition regards organizational culture as the shared values, beliefs, and norms that influence the way employees think, feel, and act toward others,

Yang Yuanqing, Chief Executive of Lenovo

Lenovo [Chinese multinational computer manufacturer] *is often cited for sustaining a healthy corporate culture. What's the secret to that?*

"We focus on three elements. The first is an ownership culture: we try to empower people to think for themselves, to make decisions for themselves. Everyone is an engine. The second is a commitment culture: if you commit to something, you must deliver. The third is a pioneer culture: we encourage our people to be more innovative."

How do you actually promote innovative behavior?

"There are a lot of ways to do it. For example, I hold monthly brainstorming sessions with our R&D team. At each session we focus on one topic—it might be a product, a service, or a technology. Another approach is through the budget. For our R&D people, we allow 20% of the budget to be flexible, so they can decide which areas they want to focus on and what they want to develop"

Source: Yuanqing (2014), pp. 107–8: interviewed by *Harvard Business Review*.

both inside and outside the organization. It is also argued that organizations each have their own distinct "personality," or style, or ideology, or climate, which gives them their unique identity. For example, walk into a McDonald's restaurant and note the atmosphere, décor, lighting, attitude of staff to customers, style and variety of food and drinks, speed of service, cost, and any other details that catch your attention. Next, walk into one of McCormick & Schmick's restaurants and pay attention to those same factors; you will see a different culture. Ann Cunliffe (2008) argues that organizational culture is important because it:

- shapes the public image of an organization;
- influences organizational effectiveness;
- provides direction for the company;
- helps to attract, retain, and motivate staff.

This issue can be the cause of many problems. Falling sales, customer complaints, staff absenteeism and turnover, or poor public reputation, for example, can often be attributed to organizational culture. It is therefore not surprising that culture change programs have become popular. Some theorists argue that organizations cannot have distinct cultures in the way that human societies do. But we can accept that criticism and still find practical value in the concept if organizational culture is simply taken to cover the values, beliefs, and norms that shape employee—and management—behavior. If those behaviors are inappropriate or dysfunctional in some way, then "culture" offers a useful lens through which we can understand why, and what action we can take to change those behaviors.

We can also make a distinction between strong and weak organizational cultures (Gordon and DiTomaso, 1992). A strong culture is one in which the organization's values are widely shared and intensely held, and which thus guide behavior. A weak culture, in contrast, displays little agreement about core values or about expected behaviors. Strong cultures thus suggest emotional attachment and commitment to an organization, unity in approach, and "walking the talk." Much of the commentary on this topic thus assumes that companies with strong cultures perform better. The quotes that opened this section, from Lenovo's chief executive, support this view.

We also know that organizational culture can cause serious problems. NASA and the oil exploration company BP provide iconic examples of what can happen when culture goes wrong.

Organizational Culture at NASA, and the Columbia Space Shuttle Disaster

In February 2003, while the space shuttle *Columbia* was reentering the earth's atmosphere, a piece of insulating foam broke off and damaged the left wing. This caused the shuttle to disintegrate, killing the seven crew members. Why did this happen, particularly after the loss of the shuttle *Challenger* and its crew in 1986, when an O-ring failed at liftoff? In answering that question, the Columbia Accident Investigation Board (CAIB, 2003) considered a combination of physical and organizational causes, arguing that both had contributed to the disaster. Here is what the Board's report had to say about the organizational culture at NASA (emphasis added):

> *The organizational causes of this accident are rooted in the Space Shuttle Program's history and culture*, including the original compromises that were required to gain approval for the Shuttle, subsequent years of resource constraints, fluctuating priorities, schedule pressures, mischaracterization of the Shuttle as operational rather than developmental, and lack of an agreed national vision for human space flight. . . . *Cultural traits and organizational practices detrimental to safety were allowed to develop*, including: reliance on past success as a substitute for sound engineering practices; organizational barriers that prevented effective communication of critical safety information and stifled professional differences of opinion; lack of integrated management across program elements; and the evolution of an informal chain of command and decision-making processes that operated outside the organization's rules. (CAIB, 2003, pp. 9 and 177)
>
> *In the Board's view, NASA's organizational culture and structure had as much to do with this accident as the External Tank foam.* Organizational culture refers to the values, norms, beliefs, and practices that govern how an institution functions. At the most basic level, organizational culture defines the assumptions that employees make as they carry out their work. It is a powerful force that can persist through reorganizations and the reassignment of key personnel. (p. 177)
>
> Perhaps the most perplexing question the Board faced during its seven-month investigation into the *Columbia* accident was "How could NASA have missed the signals the foam was sending?" Answering this question was a challenge. The investigation revealed that in most cases, the Human Space Flight Program is extremely aggressive in reducing threats to safety. But we also know—in hindsight—that *detection of the dangers posed by foam was impeded by blind spots in NASA's safety culture.* (p. 184)
>
> *NASA's culture of bureaucratic accountability emphasized chain of command, procedure, following the rules, and going by the book.* While rules and procedures were essential for coordination, they had an unintended but negative effect. Allegiance to hierarchy and procedure had replaced deference to NASA engineers' technical expertise. (p. 200)

It was therefore not surprising that the CAIB report's first recommendation following this investigation was:

> *It is the Board's opinion that good leadership can direct a culture to adapt to new realities. NASA's culture must change, and the Board intends the following recommendations to be steps toward effecting this change.* (p. 225)

A comparison of the *Challenger* and *Columbia* disasters concluded that the causal factors were similar: structures for processing information, contractor relations, political and budgetary pressures—and organizational culture. This analysis argued that organizational learning and change were difficult for NASA—and for other public agencies—due to a combination of external political and economic pressures, and an organizational culture that was defensive, and characterized by a climate of fear of raising alarms (Mahler and Casamayou, 2009). (We revisit the *Challenger* and *Columbia* disasters in the case study exercise at the end of chapter 11.)

Organizational Culture at BP, and the Deepwater Horizon Disaster

On April 20, 2010, when the blowout preventer failed, a mile under water, the explosion and fire on the 33,000-ton Deepwater Horizon drilling rig in the Gulf of Mexico killed 11 of the 126 crew members and seriously injured 17 others. Oil poured from the Macondo wellhead on the seabed, drifting toward the Louisiana coast 50 miles away, threatening wildlife and the local fishing and tourism industries. Around 5 million barrels of crude oil spilled into the Gulf before the flow stopped on July 15. This was the biggest environmental disaster in the United States since the *Exxon Valdez* spilled 750,000 barrels of crude oil in Prince William Sound in 1989. The investigation blamed leadership and management for creating the conditions in which this accident was allowed to happen. Here is what the accident investigation said about BP's culture (National Commission, 2011; emphasis added):

> The immediate causes of the Macondo well blowout can be traced to a series of identifiable mistakes made by BP, Halliburton, and Transocean that reveal such systematic failures in risk management that *they place in doubt the safety culture of the entire industry.* (p. vii)
>
> Investments in safety, containment, and response equipment and practices failed to keep pace with the rapid move into deepwater drilling. Absent major crises, and given the remarkable financial returns available from deepwater reserves, *the business culture succumbed to a false sense of security. The Deepwater Horizon disaster exhibits the costs of a culture of complacency.* (p. ix)
>
> In the wake of the BP Deepwater Horizon disaster—a crisis that was unanticipated, on a scale for which companies had not prepared to respond—*changes in safety and environmental practices, safety training, drilling technology, containment and clean-up technology, preparedness, corporate culture, and management behavior will be required* if deepwater energy operations are to be pursued in the Gulf—or elsewhere. (p. 215)

If an organizational culture is dysfunctional, the potential outcomes, from these examples, include:

- loss of life and serious injury;
- widespread economic and environmental damage;
- damage to the reputations and careers of senior management;
- loss of public trust and confidence in the organization, if not the whole sector;
- massive fines for misconduct.

In other words, failure to manage organizational culture costs lives, reputations, careers—and money, affecting the wider community and the economy as well as causing internal organizational damage. The other likely outcome, as in these cases (and Barclays, discussed earlier), is that the organization is faced with a transformational change agenda. The investigation into the *Columbia* disaster concluded that the organizational culture at NASA had to change. The Deepwater investigation advised that BP's culture of complacency had to change to prevent further incidents and to regain public trust. (The crisis management aspects of the BP incident are explored in chapter 7.)

The Salz (2013) review *criticized* strong subcultures at Barclays, rather than praise them. An organization may have a strong culture and shared values, but it is important to know what those values are. Organizational cultures at Barclays, NASA, and BP appear to have been strong, but they were also wrong. Strong cultures can lead to inappropriate behaviors, encourage conformity, complacency, and inertia, and take time to develop and change. A survey in 2013 of over 1,000 financial services sector staff in the United Kingdom found that culture change was indeed slow. Only half the respondents agreed that there had been a culture change initiative led by senior management, and less than a fifth of those agreed that there had been any real change. A fifth of all respondents said that culture change initiatives had been superficial and ineffective. This survey concluded that:

> [W]hile some senior leaders in parts of the banking sector are having at least partial success in changing culture to become more customer focused, some parts of the industry are largely operating as before. This is reinforced by the survey findings that a third of respondents still identify shareholders as their organization's most important stakeholder, with only about 50% identifying customers as their most important stakeholder. (CIPD, 2013, p. 26)

Changing an organizational culture is in many respects similar to managing any other form of change. However, culture is usually defined in terms of shared values, beliefs, and norms. Those are attributes of individuals and groups that are difficult to change directly. Most approaches to culture change thus advocate action to change behavior, through new working practices, systems, and human resource policies. This approach assumes that, once the benefits of those new behaviors become clear, the values, beliefs, and norms that reinforce those behaviors will adjust naturally.

For example, Emily Lawson and Colin Price (2010) argue that the success of change relies on persuading individuals to change their "mindsets"—to think differently about their jobs and how they work. This first involves changing behavior. They identify three levels of change. First, some outcomes (increasing revenue) can be achieved without

Risky Culture

Inside Job (2010, director Charles Ferguson, narrated by Matt Damon) examines the global financial crisis of 2008. Over the previous decade, deregulation allowed the finance sector to take risks that older rules would have discouraged. As you watch this film, identify the various stakeholders (including academics), their competing interests, their relationships, and their efforts to conceal sensitive information. How did those competing interests, relationships, and "information games" contribute to the crisis? The film concludes that, despite this crisis, the underlying culture has remained much the same. How has the sector been able to avoid fundamental changes to financial regulation? What does this account reveal about the nature of organizational culture?

changing working practices (selling noncore assets). Second, staff can be asked to change working practices in line with current thinking (finding ways to reduce waste). The third level involves fundamental changes in organizational culture, in collective thinking and behavior—from reactive to proactive, hierarchical to collegial, inward-looking to externally focused. They identify three conditions for changing mindsets at level three:

> The surrounding structures (reward and recognition systems) must be in tune with the new behaviour. Employees must have the skills to do what it requires. Finally, they must see people they respect modelling it actively. Each of these conditions is realized independently; together they add up to a way of changing the behaviour of people in organizations by changing attitudes about what can and should happen at work. (Lawson and Price, 2010, p. 32)

In other words, "mindsets" may not be altered directly, but they can be changed by a careful rethinking of structures, skills, and role models. The effectiveness of Barclays' "truthfulness training" may thus depend not just on the training content but on the extent to which wider organizational conditions encourage the desired "mindset" or not.

Many organizations today, therefore, are concerned that their culture is appropriate, in the context of corporate strategy, performance, external scrutiny and regulation, and reputation. Culture change programs often target staff engagement, teamwork and collaboration, and information sharing and creativity, as well as costs, revenues, and customer service. For the change manager, it is important to remember that the role of the board, and of senior leadership in general, is key in this context.

Culture Change Starts with You

Yum Brands, the parent company of KFC, Pizza Hut, and Taco Bell, has returned 16.5 percent annually since 1997 (the year it was spun off from PepsiCo), compared with the 3.9 percent average achieved by the Standard & Poor's 500 large companies during this time. According to business journalist Geoff Colvin (2013, p. 62), "No one who follows Yum doubts that [CEO David] Novak's team building framework is at the heart of the company's success."

Novak inherited an organization where performance and morale were low, where headquarters blamed the franchisees and the franchisees blamed headquarters. He decided that the organizational culture had to change. Novak introduced a leadership development program, "Taking People With You," which focused on managers developing self-awareness with regard to their own truthfulness, reliability, openness, and self-centeredness, as well as how they treated other team members and responded to others' mistakes. "In Novak's program you're not fit to build a team until you've worked hard on yourself [and] only then does the program get into forming strategy, communicating it, and gaining alignment, plus the nuts and bolts of organization and process" (Colvin, 2013, p. 63).

LO 5.5 Technology

Developments in technology in general, and in information and computing technology in particular, have long-running and ongoing implications for organizational change management. Some developments have created disruptive innovation (online business models), while others have improved the productivity of individuals (word processing).

Early social science studies of technology in the 1950s focused on textile manufacturing (in India) and coal mining (in the United Kingdom). The Tavistock Institute of Human Relations, whose researchers conducted those studies, developed the sociotechnical systems perspective. This argues that the social organization of work is not wholly determined by technology, but can be—and therefore should be—designed taking into consideration the individual and social needs of employees. The aim of sociotechnical system design is thus to find the best fit between the social and technical dimensions. A system designed to meet social needs ignoring the technical system will run into difficulties. On the other hand, a system designed only to meet the demands of technology will raise social and organizational problems. Sociotechnical design thus aims for "joint optimization" of social and technical needs. The resultant sociotechnical system design is thus a matter of creative management choice (Emery and Trist, 1960).

These arguments are perhaps even more important today. Technological change appears to be rapid and relentless. In the rush to implement new technology and to gain benefits ahead of competitors, there may be little time to consider the social system design before the next development appears. This presents a challenge for the change manager. On the one hand, it may be necessary to maintain the pace of technology change. On the other hand, it will be helpful to ensure that the organization of the work of those who will operate new systems strengthens the staff capabilities, motives, and commitment that contribute to effective operation. Good sociotechnical design is still at a premium.

We will explore in this section the implication of two technology trends. The first concerns the impact of digitization. The second relates to corporate applications of social media. Most organizations, in most sectors, are likely to be affected by these developments, whether they wish to be or not. We do not have space to explore the extraordinary range of specialized new technologies that will affect specific sectors, such as 3-D printing (depositional manufacturing), or nanotechnology applications in medicine, for example. However, regardless of sector, new technologies tend to generate broadly similar organizational and change management issues, so the implications of our discussion will be widely applicable.

The Impact of Digitization

In a report from McKinsey, the consulting company, Martin Hirt and Paul Willmott (2014, p. 1) argue that digital technologies are "profoundly changing the strategic context: altering the structure of competition, the conduct of business, and, ultimately, performance across industries." Emphasizing that digitization is a "moving target," they identify three strategic opportunities:

- *enhancing interaction*, between customers, suppliers, employees, and other stakeholders, as consumers come to prefer tailored, mixed-media, digital online communication channels;
- *improving management decisions*, by processing "big data" and information from "the Internet of Things," and thus being able to refine (personalize) marketing allocations and reduce operational risks by sensing equipment breakdowns;
- *creating new business models*, such as crowdsourcing product development and peer-to-peer customer service.

These developments can drive down prices, as customers can instantly compare prices and rapidly switch to other sellers and brands. As we noted earlier, digitization lowers the entry barriers to start-ups in many areas, and established organizations will face competition from unexpected areas (such as food retailers offering financial services that compete with banks). Those employees who are displaced by digitization, as more processes (administrative and manufacturing) become automated, may not have the capabilities that will enable them to find employment in the more highly skilled jobs that remain. Hirt and Willmott (2014, p. 8) also point to the "relentlessly evolving business models—at higher velocity," which digitization is encouraging. Banks, taxi drivers, travel companies, camera makers, and universities—among others—are seeing traditional business models undermined by faster-moving and cheaper competitors whose offerings are more appealing to Internet-savvy consumers. The crowdsourcing website WhoCanFixMyCar.com may disrupt the motorcar repair business by connecting drivers needing repairs with mechanics looking for work (Foy, 2014).

Even Lego, the highly profitable (and privately owned) Danish toy manufacturer, famous worldwide for its colored bricks, is not immune from digital developments. The company's traditional business model is simple, transforming plastic that costs $1 a kilo into Lego box sets that sell for $75 a kilo. However, children increasingly play games on iPads and smartphones, and Lego's sales growth slowed after 2010. How can Lego compete in the evolving digital world?

Lego's first experiment with an online game, *Lego Universe*, was not successful. They then developed a partnership with a Swedish company, Mojang, which designed *Minecraft*, a popular computer game based on virtual landscapes resembling Lego building blocks (https://minecraft.net). Lego now sells sets based on the game. Another partnership involved TT Games, to develop video games based on Lego ranges such as *Star Wars* and *Legends of Chima*. *The Lego Movie*, made in collaboration with Warner Bros, generated $500 million when it was released in 2014. In partnership with Google, *The Lego Movie* was accompanied by a video game, new construction sets (the giant Sea Cow pirate ship and the hero Emmett), and a website (http://www.buildwithchrome .com). The movie sequel is scheduled for 2017. Another innovation was *Lego Fusion*. Items built with Lego bricks are captured using a smartphone or tablet, which imports them into a 3-D digital online world where users can play using their own designs. Lego was one of the most-watched brands on YouTube. Emphasizing the continuing importance of the physical brick, and physical play, Lego's chief executive, Jørgen Vig Knudstorp, explained, "I see digital as an extra experience layer" (Milne, 2014). With record sales and earnings, Lego became the world's most popular and most profitable toymaker in 2015; the company estimates that, on average, every person on earth owns 102 Lego bricks (Milne, 2015).

A global survey by McKinsey of 850 senior executives found that most companies were planning to increase spending on digital initiatives, either to strengthen competitive advantage in an existing business, or to create new business models and revenue streams (Gottlieb and Willmott, 2014). Growth was expected to come mainly from digital customer engagement and digital innovation, including new products, operating models, and business models. In terms of digital priorities, automation ranked lowest. However, organizational hurdles were preventing faster development:

- problems finding staff with digital skills;
- organization structures unsuitable for developing digital businesses;

- inflexible business processes, designed to handle conventional initiatives;
- lack of good quality information to inform decisions;
- "inability to adopt an experimentation mindset" (Gottlieb and Willmott, 2014, p. 6).

The most pressing needs for skilled staff were in areas such as analytics, online development, project management, cloud computing, joint business enterprise, and cybersecurity. To remain competitive, therefore, many organizations may be compelled to adopt a version of Lego's pattern of rapid experimentation and innovation. The change management challenge will be to develop that approach, implementing appropriate changes to structures, processes, and information systems, and developing "experimentation" organizational cultures. Investment in training and development may be required to fill the skills gap. Further change management challenges will involve identifying opportunities, moving quickly to explore benefits, and dropping unsuccessful experiments. It may be difficult to maintain this pace without generating the stress and burnout of "initiative fatigue."

Applications of Social Media

With the development of "Web 2.0," or "the social web," the Internet moved into a new phase in the twenty-first century. Web 2.0 technologies include Internet-based information systems such as social networking (or social media), blogs, collaborative databases, and YouTube and other file-sharing sites. These applications allow a much higher degree of participation and interaction, between systems and users, and between users, than conventional Web 1.0 "flat" websites. More people now use tablets and smartphones, which are mobile devices, as well as personal computers and smart televisions, to access social networking sites. Social media are thus radically changing the ways in which we interact with each other, develop our relationships, share experiences, and form opinions. These networking tools have also changed the ways in which organizations interact with and gather information about their customers. The amount of time that we devote to the Internet is increasing. In the United States, time spent on personal computers and smartphones rose by over 20 percent between 2011 and 2012, and the use of apps doubled over that period as smartphone ownership grew and more apps became available (Bannon, 2012). Social media have three valuable properties:

1. They provide "multidirectional" flows of information between friends, colleagues, organizations, and management, compared with the static "one-way" communication from conventional web pages.
2. They allow users to develop new connections, encouraging collaboration across boundaries such as organizational silos.
3. These are "low friction" tools; they are attractive, pervasive, easy to use, and no specialized equipment is required (Gifford, 2014, p. 11).

The number of social media websites is growing. Facebook and Twitter are joined by LinkedIn and Pinterest, Blogger and Wordpress—among others. Marketing and customer services have already been affected. Social media allow consumers to share opinions of brands to a wider audience than word of mouth can reach. Facebook claims over 1 billion users; LinkedIn has 300 million; over 250 million people use Twitter; Pinterest has over

Oscar de la Renta and Instagram

As a leading fashion brand, it was normal practice for Oscar de la Renta to debut its new designs on the pages of *Vogue* or *Elle*. However, in summer 2013, it released its fall advertising campaign on Instagram. Erika Bearman, Oscar de la Renta's senior vice president of communications, had 345,000 Instagram followers, and in the caption of each image placed on Instagram, Bearman invited her followers to preorder the collection on Oscardelarenta.com.

Source: Hempel (2014).

70 million users. This list of social media outlets and their user numbers will be out of date before this book is printed. Consumers are therefore "hyper-informed" when making purchasing decisions. Customer service is also being transformed, with half of U.S. customers using social media to raise complaints or ask questions; a third of social media users say that they prefer this channel to the phone when dealing with customer service issues (Bannon, 2012). Organizations must be sensitive to these trends and respond accordingly.

Employees may be more enthusiastic about using social media than employers. Most corporate applications have an external focus and appear to have had limited impact on employee relations. A survey of the Fortune Global 100 organizations in 2012 by the public relations company Burson-Marsteller found that 70 percent had YouTube channels and 75 percent had Facebook accounts. Some had several accounts on each platform, so that they could target specific audiences and locations with regard to particular issues. The survey also found that each of those Global 100 organizations had an average of almost 56,000 mentions a month on Twitter (Stanford, 2013, p. 214).

A UK survey of 2,000 employees and 600 human resource managers in 2013 also found that while the personal use of social media was widespread, few used these tools for work. The main reasons for using social media included keeping up to date with news, building one's professional network, keeping in touch with others, sharing knowledge, learning more about areas of interest, and building reputation. Over half of senior leaders, and 40 percent of 18- to 24-year-olds, said that they used social media for work. Only one quarter of organizations surveyed had an internal social media platform, and those were used mainly for staff, human resource, and operational updates. And only one quarter allowed staff to connect personal smartphones and tablets to the organization's IT network. Internal organizational uses are not inhibited by lack of access but more by perceived lack of relevance and loss of control over information (Gifford, 2013). Many organizations do not support bring-your-own-device (BYOD) practices. A survey of 1,765 UK employers found that 80 percent had disciplined staff for using social networking sites at work, and many had banned their use (Martin et al., 2008).

There appear to be many organizational uses for social media, which promise to transform internal communications and staff engagement, recruitment, and learning. Social media could be central in encouraging more open, communicative, egalitarian, collaborative, and responsive organizational cultures. However, ease of communications can also generate information overload.

We will explore in chapter 7 how organizations are using these Web 2.0 applications, particularly to improve internal and external communications and to strengthen employee engagement.

Birkinshaw and Pass (2008, p. 15) argue that Web 2.0 could radically alter the nature of work, tapping knowledge from across the organization, encouraging informal coordination, and making the workplace more engaging. A study of corporate applications in the United Kingdom in 2013–2014 found that many organizations were advanced in using social media externally but that few had developed effective internal uses (Gifford, 2014). One exception was Adnams, an independent brewer and distiller, which encourages staff to use social media to engage with customers and develop their own online "personas" at the company through social media platforms and blogs. Another was Santa Fe Group, a global relocation service, which has developed an enterprise social learning network called "The Academy Online" to help build a common corporate culture across the group. One explanation for the slow progress with internal corporate uses of social media concerns the lack of clear return on the investment. Another factor is job and organization design not suited to the good use of social networking tools. That study concluded that social media would not alone transform organizational culture, but should be seen as a tool or a platform for change.

There appear to be three major change management challenges in these technology developments.

- The first challenge concerns finding ways to exploit digitization and social media applications effectively to achieve organizational goals. Those goals may include external relationships and reputation, and internal culture change to improve engagement, information sharing, collaboration, and the organization's ability to respond rapidly to trends and new ideas. Some applications may be sustaining, and some may be disruptive. As we have seen, these technologies can be a useful platform for organizational culture change.

- The second challenge concerns finding the best "fit" between new digital technologies and online tools, and the social system of the organization, including the needs, interests, and preferences of employees. Sociotechnical system design has become more important in this context, and given the pace of technology development, perhaps more difficult.

- A third challenge will thus be to design and redesign effective sociotechnical systems when, as noted earlier, the technologies involved are moving targets. The number and nature of digital tools and social networking sites are constantly changing and evolving. Individuals and organizations are still developing an understanding of how they can be used effectively for personal and corporate benefit.

Addressing these challenges in a context of rapid development involves experimentation, and some experiments will be unsuccessful. From a change management perspective, therefore, organizations need to be more fault tolerant. This involves welcoming the lessons from unsuccessful experiments, rather than blaming and punishing the guilty when things go wrong (Edmondson, 2011).

EXERCISE 5.1

The Nampak Story

LO 5.4

This is a story of successful organizational culture change. How can we explain this success? As you read this story, consider the following questions:

1. Which dimensions of the 7-S framework, described in chapter 4, did Eric Collins and his senior management colleagues focus on in order to change Nampak's culture? Reminder: The "hard" dimensions are strategy, structure, and systems. The "soft" dimensions include staff, skills, style, and shared values, or superordinate goals.

2. Which dimensions of the 7-S framework were not affected?

3. Where does this culture change initiative belong on the "depth" scale in figure 5.1, between shallow and deep change? In your judgement, would a different emphasis across the seven factors of that framework have produced deeper change, with better results, and how?

Context

Nampak was a South African–owned bottle and plastics manufacturer with 600 factory workers and 80 managers in the United Kingdom. A typical manufacturing company, it focused on costs, investing in machinery and processes rather than people. Labor costs were low, and the company had been very successful. In 2007, the newly appointed managing director Eric Collins realized that the company had driven efficiencies as far as it could using traditional approaches. He decided to add value through people.

Problem

Although the company was successful, the organizational culture was poor. People were treated badly and morale was low. The blame culture spread to customers. Complaints at one site reached 25 a month, which was damaging for a company that relied on three key customers. Apart from hiring, firing, and discipline, Nampak had no established human resource management policies and practices. In a staff satisfaction survey in 2007, 80 percent said that they would not recommend Nampak to friends and family as a place to work. Looking at the survey results, the new HR director, Cathie Wright-Smith, concluded, "There was everything wrong with this business that you can think of." There were also problems with the executive board, who were status-conscious and accustomed to having a high degree of control, with only a dozen people making all the key decisions.

Solution

Collins met customers to get their critical feedback on the company. But when he met his own employees in "Challenge Collins" sessions, to hear their grievances in person, he was shocked. The level of dissatisfaction was high, and the anger was directed at him. However, Collins wanted to give staff the opportunity to vent their frustrations, and to show that they had a leader who was listening.

Wright-Smith ran focus groups, asking staff what would make Nampak a better place to work. Three themes emerged. The first was communication; people did not know what was going on, and they were not involved. Second, staff did not feel that they had training and development opportunities, or a career with the company. Third, line managers rarely provided feedback on their performance. This led to the design of a new

(Continued)

performance management system, based on what employees said that they wanted: personal development, and not objectives with tick boxes. Some line managers had never had conversations like this with their staff before, and they now did this monthly. Line managers were seen as "dogsbodies," although they were key to shaping the company's culture. To emphasize their importance, they were offered the first training and development opportunities, a "leadership excellence" course, exploring influence, motivation, and team development methods. This was so successful that it generated demand from other managers for similar training.

New initiatives developed rapidly. Half the workforce were trained in a range of subjects, assessment centers replaced the traditional selection process, and induction and buddy schemes were introduced. The company launched a senior leaders program, a fast-track route for high-potential staff, undergraduate and graduate placement schemes, and a suggestions scheme offering financial rewards. A corporate social responsibility program linked with local schools, inviting pupils into the factory and sending staff to schools to talk about recycling. Shop floor staff worked with the schools attended by their children, and some staff came back on their days off to show people around the factory, with pride. Wright-Smith ran sessions for directors on leadership and emotional intelligence.

Outcomes

Collins said, "We've had a paradigm shift in culture." In the 2010 staff survey, 80 percent said that they would recommend Nampak to friends and family as a place to work, reversing the 2007 position. In addition, 90 percent said that they were satisfied with their jobs, and 98 percent said that their managers listened to them. Overhead costs per million bottles made improved by 7 percent. No closures or layoffs were needed to make savings. Customer complaints fell to zero. Collins said, "We're just a more collaborative, committed organization with pride in our work." The main costs, according to Collins, concerned the commitment of time and focus (Smedley, 2011).

EXERCISE 5.2

Organizational Culture Assessment

LO 5.4

1. What words would you use to describe the positive and negative dimensions of your organization's culture, or an organization with which you are familiar?

2. How can you explain the negative aspects of that organizational culture? Why have those dimensions developed in that way? What factors are causing, supporting, or reinforcing those dimensions?

3. What are the consequences of the negative dimensions of this organizational culture? In what ways are they harmful to the organization, its employees, suppliers, and customers?

4. What actions can you take to change the dysfunctional aspects of the culture? The 7-S framework (chapter 4) is a good place to start. What changes need to be made to the "hard" factors: strategy, structure, systems? What changes need to be made to the "soft" factors: style, staff, skills, shared values? How does senior leadership behavior have to change?

5. What would those actions cost?

EXERCISE 5.3

How Will the Digital Revolution Affect Your Organization?

LO 5.5

Briefing (1)

- You have decided to leave your organization tomorrow, to set up your own business in competition with your large, out-of-date, slow-moving, bureaucratic former employer.

- You have identified your organization's main weaknesses and vulnerabilities. Critically, you have worked out how a combination of digitization technologies and social networking tools could be used to undermine your organization's traditional business model. Or, customers may have "after-market" needs that your organization is not fulfilling.

- Describe your new business model. What digital tools and social media technologies will you use to attract customers or clients from your previous employer to your business—and perhaps from other organizations in the sector? How quickly can you set up this business? What will it cost you to set up this business?

Briefing (2)

- OK, you are not leaving the organization after all. That briefing was designed to make you think about potential threats to your organization from agile and innovative "out of sector" competitors. Let us assume that the new business model that you have just described is real, and that somebody else has already thought about it—and may already be setting it up. How can your organization respond to that threat? Better still, how can your organization counter that threat before it emerges?

- Draw up an internal action plan for transforming the organization's current business model, or for creating a separate unit or division to develop your new business model alongside the existing one.

Additional Reading

Brynjolfsson, E., and McAfee, A. 2014. *The second machine age: Work, progress, and prosperity in a time of brilliant technologies.* New York and London: W. W. Norton & Company. An optimistic analysis of the pervasiveness of digital technologies and their dramatic impact on individuals, organizations, society, and the economy.

Gratton, L. 2011. *The shift: The future of work is already here.* London: Collins. Explores how trends in globalization, society, demography, technology, and use of natural resources are reshaping work, and offers advice on how to "future-proof" your career.

Perlow, L. A. 2012. *Sleeping with your smartphone: How to break the 24/7 habit and change the way you work.* Boston: Harvard Business Review Press. Explores individual and organizational benefits and problems of "hyperconnectivity" and how to retain work-life balance and improve performance by collectively "disconnecting."

Schein, E. H. 2010. *Organizational culture and leadership.* 4th ed. San Francisco: Jossey-Bass. Classic and recently revised text exploring the nature and significance of organizational culture and the crucial role of leaders as "architects" of culture.

Roundup In answer to the question "what changes?" this chapter has introduced terms for describing different types of change, based on the metaphor of depth; some changes are shallow, others are deep. We then focused on three areas of organizational change: innovation, culture, and technology. These are not the only dimensions of organizational change, of course, but they are issues that most if not all organizations will continue to face for some time. Why have these particular themes acquired such a high priority? A failure to innovate can lead to organizational decline. Dysfunctional organizational cultures can have disastrous consequences. Digitization and social media have the potential to create new and potentially disruptive business models, making many established business models obsolete. The "controlling" images of change management—director, navigator, caretaker—may be less useful in this context. Dealing with a rapidly developing, uncertain, and unpredictable climate, the "shaping" images of change management may be more appropriate—coach, interpreter, navigator.

Here is a short summary of the key points that we would like you to take from this chapter, in relation to each of the learning outcomes:

LO 5.1   *Explain several different ways of categorizing different types of change.*
Organizational changes are typically varied and multifaceted. Change one aspect of an organization and the interdependencies lead to "knock-on" or "ripple" effects that lead to further change elsewhere. We introduced a number of different ways of describing and classifying change, and these are summarized in table 5.3. The concepts of transformational change and disruptive innovation have become fashionable. Given the rapid pace of technology development, and of change driven by other socioeconomic, cultural, and legislative pressures, transformation and disruption appear to be attractive

Reflections for the Practicing Change Manager

- In what kinds of change initiatives are you currently involved—shallow, deep, mixed? If your current involvement concerns mostly shallow initiatives, how will that affect your ability to answer questions about your change management experience at the next job/promotion interview? Do you need to "reposition" your profile to include deeper changes?

- Does your personal comfort zone favor involvement in major, transformational, deep changes? Why? Or are you more comfortable implementing lower-risk, shallow changes—which can of course still be highly effective? In your judgement, what are the personal and organizational implications of your preferences?

- In your judgement, does your organization need disruptive innovation, in which areas, and why? Or would those changes be too "disruptive" and less effective than continuing to implement sustaining innovations?

- You are a social media user, accessing your favorite websites from at least one mobile device—your smartphone or tablet. You also use those sites through your smart Internet-connected television. How do you feel about your organization using social media to communicate with you? Does this open up new sources of information and fresh communication channels with management and staff? Or will this open you to 24/7 availability and give you information overload? How do employees in general in your organization feel about this?

options. However, we have to recognize that less profound, shallow, simple changes can often be valuable in context. Small changes can also underpin and trigger major initiatives. The potential organizational value of shallow change should therefore not be underestimated.

TABLE 5.3
Different Types of Change

Type of Change	Description
Planned	Implemented in anticipation of, or in response to, known developments
Emergent	Just happens, or has to happen, in response to unforeseen events
Incremental	Gradual, small scale
Transformational	Radical, groundbreaking, disruptive
First-order	Solves a problem using methods based on current assumptions
Second-order	Transforms the organization with creative thinking and new business models
Third-order	Habitual overturning of assumptions, continual adaptation and self-renewal
Shallow	Another label for incremental, small-scale change, fine-tuning
Deep	Another label for transformational, disruptive change, mold-breaking

LO 5.2   *Identify practical implications of different types of change for the change manager.*
One practical implication of our change classification system concerns, as just mentioned, the potential of small changes to deliver benefit in their own right and to contribute to deeper initiatives. A second implication for the change manager is that shallow changes are likely to be more straightforward to implement: less cost, less risk, less disruption, less resistance. Organizational transformations present a different order of change management challenge. A third implication, however, is that a change manager's involvement in deep change is more likely to contribute to experience, reputation, and career than managing small initiatives. This leads to the suspicion that some deep changes could be designed to address personal interests rather than corporate needs.

At any given time, especially in larger organizations, there are likely to be many change initiatives under way, across the spectrum of figure 5.1, from shallow, to mid-range, to deep. The problem of coordinating such a pattern of change has led to the establishment of program management offices (PMOs) in many organizations. PMOs can thus support change and help to avoid the duplication of effort and cost. Where they are seen as "change police," their contributions may be curtailed.

LO 5.3   *Understand the difference between sustaining and disruptive innovation, and explain the practical implications of this distinction for change management.*
Sustaining innovations improve current practice, while disruptive innovations introduce wholly new ways of doing things. From a change management perspective,

it is usually easier to persuade others of the value of sustaining innovations; disruptive innovations are more difficult to explain, and because they make current practice obsolete, they may be seen as more risky. Most organizations do not have established procedures or routines for handling disruptive innovations—which are thus often implemented by small start-up companies rather than large established organizations.

The change manager can become a "disruptive innovator" by adopting five habits: associating, questioning, observing, experimenting, and networking. These are habits that anyone can develop, with practice.

LO 5.4 *Assess the significance of organizational culture with regard to organizational performance and reputation, and the role of leaders as culture architects.*

Organization culture is regarded by some commentators as an abstract concept with limited organizational use. Defining culture as "the way we do things," however, it seems that some organizations have dysfunctional cultures, which can lead to highly undesirable consequences. We saw how dysfunctional cultures at Barclays bank, NASA, and BP contributed to financial crisis, loss of life and serious injury, widespread economic and environmental damage, damage to the reputations and careers of senior management, loss of public trust and confidence in the organization, and massive fines for misconduct. Culture change, where necessary, becomes a priority in the face of such evidence, and culture change programs have consequently become popular.

LO 5.5 *Assess the potential impact of new digital technologies in general, and the potential organizational benefits of applications of social media in particular.*

A "moving target," digitization offers three sets of strategic opportunities: enhanced interaction with stakeholders, improved management decisions, and new business models. Many organizations have seen their successful business models undermined by digital start-ups. Social media also seem to have many applications with regard to communications, staff engagement, recruitment, and learning. These tools could thus offer platforms for developing more open, communicative, egalitarian, collaborative, and responsive cultures. However, organizations have been slow to respond to these opportunities, and we may be in an "experiment and learn" phase. As mentioned earlier, this context puts a premium on the coach, interpreter, and navigator images of change management.

References

Aldrick, P. 2013. How it all went wrong at Barclay's. *The Telegraph*, April 3, http://www.telegraph.co.uk/finance/newsbysector/banksandfinance/9969642/How-it-all-went-wrong-at-Barclays.html.

Arnold, M., and Sharman, A. 2014. Barclays moves to cut 7,000 jobs in retreat from investment banking. *Financial Times*, May 8, http://www.ft.com/cms/s/0/af9ed69a-d675-11e3-907c-00144feabdc0.html#slide0.

Bannon, D. 2012. *State of the media: The social media report.* New York: Nielsen.

Barabba, V. 2011. *The decision loom: A design for interactive decision-making in organizations*. Axminster, Devon: Triarchy Press.

Bate, P. 1994. *Strategies for cultural change*. Oxford: Butterworth-Heinemann.

Beeson, J. 2009. Why you didn't get that promotion: Decoding the unwritten rules of corporate advancement. *Harvard Business Review* 87(6):101–5.

Birkinshaw, J., and Pass, S. 2008. *Innovation in the workplace: How are organizations responding to Generation Y and Web 2.0 technologies?* London: Chartered Institute of Personnel and Development.

Brynjolfsson, E., and McAfee, A. 2014. *The second machine age: Work, progress, and prosperity in a time of brilliant technologies*. New York and London: W. W. Norton & Company.

Christensen, C. M. 2000. *The innovator's dilemma: When new technologies cause great firms to fail*. New York: HarperCollins.

Christensen, C. M., and Overdorf, M. 2000. Meeting the challenge of disruptive change. *Harvard Business Review* 78(2):66–76.

CIPD. 2013. *Employee outlook: Focus on rebuilding trust in the city*. London: Chartered Institute of Personnel and Development.

Coghlan, D., and Rashford, N. S. 2006. *Organizational change and strategy: An interlevel dynamics approach*. Abingdon, Oxon: Routledge.

Columbia Accident Investigation Board. 2003. *Columbia accident investigation board report, volume I*. Washington, DC: National Aeronautics and Space Administration and the Government Printing Office.

Colvin, G. 2013. Great job! *Fortune*, August 12:62–65.

Costello, M., and Leroux, M. 2014. Bob's house demolished brick by brick. *The Times*, May 9:45.

Cunliffe, A. L. 2008. *Organization theory*. London: Sage Publications.

Dyer, J., Gregersen, H., and Christensen, C. M. 2011. *The innovator's DNA: Mastering the five skills of disruptive innovators*. Boston: Harvard Business School Press.

The Economist. 2012. The last Kodak moment? January 14:25.

The Economist. 2014. Second wind. June 14:76.

Edmondson, A. 2011. Strategies for learning from failure. *Harvard Business Review* 89(4):48–55.

Emery, R. E., and Trist, E. L. 1960. Socio-technical systems. In *Management science, models and techniques*, ed. C. W. Churchman and M. Verhulst (83–97). London: Pergamon Press.

Foy, H. 2014. Website drives a revolution in car repairs. *Financial Times*, July 12:17.

Gifford, J. 2013. *Social technology, social business?* London: Chartered Institute of Personnel and Development.

Gifford, J. 2014. *Putting social media to work.* London: Chartered Institute of Personnel and Development.

Goff, S. 2014. Ipad generation drives banking shake-up. *Financial Times*, July 12:3.

Gordon, G. G., and DiTomaso, N. 1992. Predicting corporate performance from organizational culture. *Journal of Management Studies* 29(6):783–98.

Gottlieb, J., and Willmott, P. 2014. *McKinsey Global Survey results: The digital tipping point.* New Jersey and London: McKinsey & Company.

Graban, M. 2009. *Lean hospitals: Improving quality, patient safety, and employee satisfaction.* Boca Raton: CRC Press.

Gratton, L. 2011. *The shift: The future of work is already here.* London: Collins.

Hammer, M. 2004. Deep change: How operational innovation can transform your company. *Harvard Business Review* 82(4):84–93.

Hempel, J. 2014. Instagram is ready to take its shot. *Fortune*, July 7:73–78.

Hirt, M., and Willmott, P. 2014. *Strategic principles for competing in the digital age.* Taipei and London: McKinsey & Company.

Hwang, J., and Christensen, C. M. 2008. Disruptive innovation in health care delivery: A framework for business-model innovation. *Health Affairs* 27(5):1329–35.

Lawson, E., and Price, C. 2010. The psychology of change management. *The McKinsey Quarterly*, (special edition: the value in organization):31–41.

Mahler, J. G., and Casamayou, M. H. 2009. *Organizational learning at NASA: The Challenger and Columbia accidents.* Washington, DC: Georgetown University Press.

Martin, G., Reddington, M., and Kneafsey, M. B. 2008. *Web 2.0 and HR: A discussion paper.* London: Chartered Institute of Personnel and Development.

Milne, R. 2014. Lego: King of the castle. *Financial Times*, July 10:13.

Milne, R. 2015. Lego shores up title of most profitable toymaker. *Financial Times*, February 26:18.

National Commission on the BP Deepwater Horizon Oil Spill and Offshore Drilling. 2011. *Deep Water: The Gulf oil disaster and the future of offshore drilling.* Washington, DC: National Commission.

Perlow, L. A. 2012. *Sleeping with your smartphone: How to break the 24/7 habit and change the way you work.* Boston: Harvard Business Review Press.

Peters, T. 2014. Beyond the matrix organization. *McKinsey Quarterly*, September:1–16 (first published 1979).

Project Management Institute. 2012. *The project management office: In sync with strategy*. Philadelphia: PMI Inc.

Rogers, E. 1995. *The diffusion of innovation*. 4th ed. New York: Free Press.

Romanelli, E., and Tushman, M. L. 1994. Organizational transformation as punctuated equilibrium: An empirical test. *Academy of Management Journal* 37(5):1141–66.

Salz, A. 2013. *Salz review: An independent review of Barclay's business practices*. London: Barclays PLC.

Schein, E. H. 2010. *Organizational culture and leadership*. 4th ed. San Francisco: Jossey-Bass.

Smedley, T. 2011. A lot of bottle. *People Management*, April:38–41.

Stanford, N. 2013. *Organization design: Engaging with change*. London: Routledge.

Treanor, J. 2014. Barclays to set up business academy for training. *The Guardian*, July 3:25.

Ward, J., and Daniel, E. 2013. The role of project management offices (PMOs) in IS project success and management satisfaction. *Journal of Enterprise Information Management* 26(3):316–36.

Weick, K. E. 2000. Emergent change as a universal in organizations. In *Breaking the code of change*, ed. M. Beer and N. Nohria (223–41). Boston: Harvard Business School Press.

Yuanqing, Y. 2014. I came back because the company needed me. *Harvard Business Review* 92(7/8):104–8.

Chapter 6

Vision and the Direction of Change

Learning objectives

By the end of this chapter you should be able to:

LO 6.1 Explain the arguments for and against the concept of vision, and how approaches to this issue depend on the image held of managing organizational change.

LO 6.2 Identify the characteristics of effective visions.

LO 6.3 Assess how the context in which a vision is developed affects its meaning.

LO 6.4 Apply different methods and processes for developing vision.

LO 6.5 Explain why some visions fail.

LO 6.6 Explain the arguments concerning the relationship of vision to organizational change.

www.CartoonStock.com

The Coca-Cola Company Vision

Our vision serves as the framework for our Roadmap and guides every aspect of our business by describing what we need to accomplish in order to continue achieving sustainable, quality growth.

People: Be a great place to work where people are inspired to be the best they can be.

Portfolio: Bring to the world a portfolio of quality beverage brands that anticipate and satisfy people's desires and needs.

Partners: Nurture a winning network of customers and suppliers, together we create mutual, enduring value.

Planet: Be a responsible citizen that makes a difference by helping build and support sustainable communities.

Profit: Maximize long-term return to shareowners while being mindful of our overall responsibilities.

Productivity: Be a highly effective, lean and fast-moving organization.

Source: From http://www.coca-colacompany.com/our-company/mission-vision-values (accessed November 3, 2014).

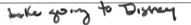
like going to Disney

LO 6.1 Vision: Fundamental or Fad?

> Mission: *This relates to goals, and refers to the overriding purpose of the organization. It is sometimes described in terms of the apparently simple but challenging question: "what business are we in?" The mission statement helps keep managers focused on what is central to their strategy.*
>
> Vision: *This too relates to goals, and refers to the desired future state of the organization. It is an aspiration which can help mobilize the energy and passion of organizational members. The vision statement, therefore, should answer the question: "what do we want to achieve?"*
>
> (Johnson et al., 2011, p. 8)

There is understandable confusion between the terms "mission" and "vision." Mission emphasizes purpose and outcomes. Vision, in contrast, focuses on future aspirations and can thus be a key driver of organizational change. This helps to explain why most of the change management perspectives explained in chapter 10 emphasize the importance of a clear and meaningful vision, without which direction and motivation will be weak or absent. There is, however, debate over whether vision is truly fundamental to change and effectiveness, or whether this is just a management consultancy fad.

Highlighting the importance of vision and direction, Paul Victor and Anton Franckeiss (2002, p. 41) argue, "It is imperative that change is aligned with a clear vision and business strategy and that subsequent activities and interventions are coordinated and consistent." Hans Hinterhuber and Wolfgang Popp (1992, p. 106) argue that vision underpins successful entrepreneurial activities and corporate change programs, defining vision as "an orientation point that guides a company's movement in a specific direction. If the vision is realistic and appeals both to the emotions and the intelligence of employees, it can integrate and direct a company." Effective visions, they add, can be expressed clearly—and are thus easily communicated—in just a few words (e.g., "Our vision is to achieve price leadership and good design at the same time").

Visions are thus linked to strategy and competitive advantage, enhancing organizational performance and sustaining growth. Clear visions enable boards to determine how well organizational leaders are performing and to identify gaps in current practices. Visions help staff identify with the organization, and inspire the motivation to achieve personal and corporate objectives. Organizations preparing for transformational change often undertake "revisioning" exercises to guide them into the future. The visioning process itself can enhance the self-esteem of those who are involved, because they can see the outcomes of their efforts. Jeffrey Pfeffer (2010, p. 92) argues that vision is a source of influence: "Make the vision compelling. It's easier to exercise power when you are aligned with a compelling, socially valuable objective." Opponents will struggle to challenge such an agenda.

A lack of vision, on the other hand, is associated with organizational decline and failure. Graham Beaver (2000, p. 205) argues, "Unless companies have clear vision about how they are going to be distinctly different and unique in adding and satisfying their customers, then they are likely to be the corporate failure statistics of tomorrow." The absence of a clear and compelling vision may explain why some companies fail to exploit their core competencies despite having access to adequate resources. Business strategies lacking in visionary substance may fail to identify when organizational change is required. Lack of an adequate process for translating shared vision into collective action may be associated with the failure to produce transformational organizational change.

The concept of vision is powerful. However, it remains controversial, and invites cynicism when every organization expresses a bland vision that includes "excellence," "corporate responsibility," "empowered employees," and "delighted customers." However, there has been little research in this area, and there is disagreement on how to define and measure the term. As with change management in general, there is a lot of advice on how to develop a vision, with little or no consensus on effective approaches. Some commentators have argued that the preoccupation with vision has meant that the term has been overused and trivialized (Beaver, 2000) and is thus in danger of losing any value.

Debates around appropriate definition and substance do not necessarily invalidate the value of vision in clarifying an organization's purpose and direction. The challenge for the organization in general, and the change manager in particular, is to avoid an abstract statement of vision accompanied with platitudes and grandiose statements that provide little detail about what the future should look like. On the other hand, a vision that is too specific, focusing on short-term targets and goals, and encouraging only incremental improvement is also of limited value. Visions become useful when they are midway between these two extremes, setting out an engaging picture of the future, with sufficient meaningful detail to which those involved can relate (Belgard and Rayner, 2004).

These arguments reflect a deeper question. The link between vision and organizational change depends on the image of change management in use. Table 6.1 illustrates how each of the six different images expresses a different understanding of this link. We invite the reader to use this table to identify how different images focus attention on some issues and approaches, and not others.

We begin by showing that the development of a meaningful vision depends on three features. The first concerns the content or attributes of the vision: what it is and says. The

TABLE 6.1
Change Management Image and Vision: Links and Focus

Image	Vision-Change Link	Focusing Attention On
Director	Vision is essential to successful change, and must be articulated at an early stage by leaders	Need for clear vision to drive change linked to strategy and goals Analytical and benchmarking processes used How context affects the impact of the vision Top-down responsibility to tell/sell the vision
Navigator	Vision is important, but can be compromised by competing visions of different stakeholders	Vision is the product of debate The change manager has to handle "vision collision" when competing groups disagree
Caretaker	External forces shape the change process, and vision rarely has a major influence	Visionary or charismatic leaders have limited impact when vision is not related to the events driven by those external forces
Coach	Vision emerges through the leader's facilitation skills, shaping agendas and desired futures	Vision emerges through consultation and co-creation Vision will fail without participation
Interpreter	Vision articulates the core values and ideology that underpin the organization's identity	Visions are developed intuitively through imagery and imagination, using framing, scripting, and staging techniques Vision is the "inner voice," the "system core" Vision emerges through change
Nurturer	Visions are always temporary, emerging from the clash of shifting and unpredictable forces for change	Visionary change leaders cannot predict accurately the outcome of systemic forces Vision is an organizational property, not an individual product, and can survive chaos

second concerns the context in which the vision is used: where it is used and by whom. The third concerns the process by which the vision is developed: how it emerges and who has contributed.

Following this we identify why visions can fail to produce their intended effects. Finally, we focus on three contentious issues relating to the role of vision in organizational change: whether vision initiates and drives change, or rather emerges as change unfolds; whether vision helps or hinders change; and whether vision is best understood as an attribute of heroic leaders, or of heroic organizations.

LO 6.2 The Characteristics of Effective Visions

John Kotter (2006) argues that visions must be focused yet flexible. While this may sound relatively straightforward, the attributes that make visions "visionary" and useful have provoked debate. Some commentators focus on the content of vision statements, while others explore the context in which visions are used. The roles of leaders in articulating visions and the process by which visions are developed have also attracted attention. Here, we will consider the content of visions, including their style and other

What Makes an Effective Vision?

How do you build a vision? Many people assume that vision-building should resemble long-term planning: design, organize, implement. But defining a vision of the future does not happen according to a timetable or flowchart. It is more emotional than rational. It demands a tolerance for messiness, ambiguity, and setbacks. The half-step back usually accompanies every step forward. Day-to-day demands pull people in different directions. Having a shared vision does not eliminate tension, but it does help people make trade-offs. The alternative is to bog down in I-win, you-lose fights. Leaders must convey a vision of the future that is clear, appealing to stakeholders, ambitious yet attainable. Effective visions are focused enough to guide decision-making yet are flexible enough to accommodate individual initiative and changing circumstances. (Kotter, 2006, p. 14)

attributes, and also explain how the concept of vision is distinguished from the related concepts of organizational mission and values.

Vision Attributes

Table 6.2 shows several definitions of organizational vision. Most refer to a future or to an ideal to which organizational change should be directed. The vision itself is presented as a picture or image that serves as a guide to that future ideal. Visions can thus be inspiring, motivational, emotional, or analytical, depending on whose definition we are using.

Definitions do not necessarily help to determine the actual content of visions. Observing that "little is known about what the essential properties of a vision are," Kimberly Boal and Robert Hooijberg (2001, p. 527) argue that visions have two components:

- a *cognitive* (intellectual) component, which is based on information and expresses outcomes and how these will be achieved;
- an *affective* (emotional) component that appeals to values and beliefs, and thus underpins the motivation and commitment that are key to implementation.

Table 6.3 summarizes the views of a number of commentators on the components of a good vision. As this table shows, most commentators point to similar attributes: they mostly suggest that visions should be aspirational, clear, desirable, distinctive, easy to communicate, feasible, flexible, future-focused, inspiring, meaningful, memorable, motivating, and should recognize the problems facing the organization. This sounds like a long list of attributes to incorporate in a brief statement that can be quickly communicated and easily remembered. Some commentators, therefore, have sought to distill the essence of these guidelines. For example, Paul Nutt and Robert Backoff (1997) identify four generic attributes of visions that are likely to enhance organizational performance:

1. *Possibility*: Points to innovative possibilities for dramatic improvements
2. *Desirability*: Based on shared values and norms about the way things should be done
3. *Actionability*: Indicates the roles and contributions of those who will make the vision a reality
4. *Articulation*: Communicates the future clearly through powerful imagery

TABLE 6.2
Vision Definitions

Definitions	Sources
A statement of purpose determined by management based on the organization's core values and beliefs that defines the organization's identity and combines an ideal manifestation of its direction together with a tangible prescription for realizing its goals	Landau et al., 2006a, p. 147
Image of an "ideal future." It is aspirational and idealistic, a guiding star with dreamlike qualities	Haines et al., 2005, p. 139
A picture of the future of our organization	Auster et al., 2005, p. 50
A detailed description of a desired future that provides clarity as to how the organization will need to operate differently in order to meet the changing conditions of its markets, customers, and overall business environment	Belgard and Rayner, 2004, p. 116
An ideal that represents or reflects the shared values to which the organization should aspire	Kirkpatrick et al., 2002, p. 139
An ambition about the future, articulated today; it is a process of managing the present from a stretching view of the future	Stace and Dunphy, 2001, p. 78
Articulates where the organization is headed and what it is trying to accomplish	Deetz et al., 2000, p. 54

John Pendlebury et al. (1998) specify three components of visions key to change management:

1. *Why the change is needed*: The problem that validates the need for change
2. *The aim of the change*: The solution, which must be credible, meaningful, and feasible
3. *The change actions that will be taken*: The means, how actions will be mobilized and delivered

We can thus identify the desirable features of vision statements. However, this does not reveal the criteria on which those features should be assessed. This suggests that the affective or "feel good" content of vision is important; we know it when we see it, but this is difficult to define or to measure. Consider the sample of vision statements taken from leading (Fortune 100) global companies. Which of these vision statements have the characteristics that we have identified so far? Which do not have these characteristics? Based on these vision statements, for which of these companies would you find it attractive to work? Whose vision statements would turn you away? Why? How do you explain your preferences and dislikes with regard to these visions?

Ira Levin (2000, p. 92) argues that some vision statements have a "bumper sticker" style, based on jargon and fashionable terms. Their similarities thus mean that they could be used by several different companies, and they are not inspirational. Hugh Davidson (2004) calls these "me-too" statements that lack distinctiveness, such as Ericsson's vision in the 1990s, "to be the leading company in tomorrow's converged data and telecommunications market." Levin (2000) advocates instead the development of "vision stories" that

TABLE 6.3
The Characteristics of Effective Visions

Characteristics	Advocates
imaginable: conveys a picture of the future desirable: appeals to stakeholder interests feasible: embodies realistic, attainable goals focused: guides decision making flexible: enables initiative and response to changing environments communicable: can be explained in five minutes	Kotter (2012a)
provides a sense of direction sets the context for making decisions reflects the organization's values and culture recognizes and responds to pressing needs identifies current actions to create a strong future	Deetz et al. (2000)
aspiration: how the new organization will look inspiration: getting people excited about where they are headed perspiration: highlights the work required to achieve the vision	Scott-Morgan et al. (2001)
clear direction conveys ambition and excitement memorable motivating relevant, to staff and customers can be translated into measurable strategies	Davidson (2004)
future focused: what will our business look like in 5 to 10 years' time directional: describes where the organization is going clear and easily understood: guides decisions and independent action relevant: reflects the past as well as current challenges purpose-driven: connecting to a meaningful sense of purpose values-based: shared beliefs that influence behavior and attitudes challenging: stretch goals that set a high standard unique: reflects what makes the organization different vivid: provides a striking mental image of the future inspiring: captures the heart, and engages people to commit to a cause	Ambler (2013)

portray the future in a manner to which people can relate. Table 6.4 outlines the process for producing vision stories. Levin cites Arthur Martinez, chief executive of Sears, as someone adept at using vision stories. Martinez required his senior managers to write stories about the businesses that they managed and how customers related to those businesses (Domm, 2001).

Vision Statements from Fortune 100 Companies

Exxon Mobil: Exxon Mobil is committed to being the world's premier petroleum and petrochemical company. To that end, we must continuously achieve superior financial and operating results while adhering to the highest standard of business conduct. These unwavering expectations provide the foundation for our commitments to those with whom we interact.

Wal-Mart Stores: To become the worldwide leader in retailing.

Chevron: To be the global energy company most admired for its people, partnership, and performance.

Sinopec: To become the largest chemical fertilizer manufacturer and most effective resources processing enterprise in the chemical industry in China, which is also geared up for competing in the international market.

Toyota Motor: Toyota aims to achieve long-term, stable growth in harmony with the environment, the local communities it serves, and its stakeholders.

HSBC Holdings: We aspire to be one of the world's great specialist banking groups, driven by our commitment to our core philosophies and values.

Gazprom: To establish itself as a leader among global energy companies by entering new markets, diversifying its activities, and ensuring reliable supplies.

Carrefour: The Carrefour Group has one simple ambition: making Carrefour the preferred retailer wherever it operates.

AT&T: To design and create in this decade the new global network, processes, and service platforms that maximize automation, allowing for a reallocation of human resources to more complex and productive work.

Nestlé: To bring consumers foods that are safe, of high quality, and provide optimal nutrition to meet physiological needs. In addition to nutrition, health, and wellness, Nestlé products bring consumers the vital ingredients of taste and pleasure.

Industrial and Commercial Bank of China: ICBC adheres to the concept of scientific development for obtaining new driving force for growth, striving to ameliorate its operational structure, and strengthening the internal management and promoting innovative development.

Home Depot: To create a company that would keep alive the values that were important to us. Values like respect among all people, excellent customer service, and giving back to communities and society.

U.S. Postal Service: The U.S. Postal Service is committed to actions that promote sustainability—meeting the needs of the present without compromising the future. We are working to create a culture of conservation among our 663,000 employees in our more than 34,000 facilities.

BMW: To be the most successful premium manufacturer in the industry.

Source: From Kolk (2010). Organizations update their vision statements from time to time, and this list may not be current. The aim is to offer typical illustrations for the purposes of assessment.

Offering a subtly different answer to the question, "What are the characteristics of effective visions?" Levin (2000, pp. 105–6) concludes: "A well-conceived and articulated vision offers the promise of serving as both a springboard and a frame of reference for fuelling such aligned action. Yet, the traditional vision statement with its abstract, lofty, and generic language fails to fulfil this promise. The vision story, on the other hand, with its rich imagery and vivid description, is more effective in fulfilling this promise. The

TABLE 6.4
Vision as
Storytelling—
How to
Develop the
Narrative

Source: Based on
Levin (2000),
pp. 99–105.

Step	Actions for the Senior Team
1. Become informed	*Leadership team articulate their vision for the future—five to fifteen years ahead—of the organization, taking into account:*
	External impacts and future business challenges? Economic, social, political, and technological trends and developments? What are other organizations doing to prepare for the future? Core values and beliefs?
2. Visit the future	*Imagine it is five years into the future, and the organization has been so successful that business magazines want to report the story, covering:*
	What is the organization's reputation and what do competitors envy? What is the customers' experience? What contributions have been made to the community? What do employees tell friends and family about working here? What new business ventures have been developed?
3. Create the story	*Write the vision story as a narrative (1,500 to 2,000 words):*
	Describe the actors, events, actions, and consequences What are the key messages and themes? What's happening in the marketplace? How are staff providing services and interacting with customers? What is the mood—what are people experiencing and feeling?
4. Deploy the vision	*Develop the story for further discussion across the organization:*
	Explain the business case for change and the desired outcomes Explain what is not negotiable—values, operating principles Collect responses—what needs clarification, elaboration, explanation? Finalize the vision story—translate into strategies, targets, goals

vision story provides people with a lifelike glimpse into the future of possibilities and directly answers the fundamental question: What will this future mean for me?"

Vision, Mission, and Goals

Visions are often confused with other terms such as mission statements, goals, and organizational values. Visions and missions can be particularly difficult to disentangle. Most commentators adopt the position set out at the beginning of this chapter, from Johnson et al. (2011). *Mission* concerns what an organization is and does. *Vision* describes a future scenario, where the mission is advanced, and where goals and strategy are being effectively achieved. Nutt and Backoff (1997) treat visions as being similar to missions and goals, in providing direction and identifying necessary changes. However, although goals may identify desired results, such as improved morale, lower costs, or bigger market share, they do not necessarily articulate the actions necessary to produce those outcomes. Nor do they usually address the role of organizational values in achieving the result. Visions, in contrast, usually paint a picture of the future and are inspirational. Mission statements tend to be more purposive and instrumental in outlining what needs to be done.

Vision and Market Strategy

Some commentators argue that, to create competitive advantage, an organization's vision and strategy must be unconventional, perhaps even counterintuitive, and must also be distinct from those of other companies. Michael Hay and Peter Williamson (1997), for example, note that visions have an external and an internal dimension. The external dimension concerns a shared view of the outside world: how markets work, what drives customers, competitors, industry dynamics, macroeconomic trends, the impact of geopolitical events. Most car tire manufacturers, they note, such as Goodyear, Michelin, and Bridgestone/Firestone, have a market vision that sees the large car manufacturing companies as their main customers, where large market share and high volumes are the way to drive down costs. In contrast, the comparatively unknown Cooper Tire and Rubber Company had a different market vision. They decided that, as Americans were holding onto their cars for longer, the independent replacement tire outlets were their main market.

Hay and Williamson (1997) argue that having a well-specified external vision helps to identify how the company will grow and compete. Only then can an internal vision be developed, pointing to the capabilities that need to be acquired to compete, and also to what the organization seeks to become. External and internal dimensions of the vision thus have to be aligned.

LO 6.3 How Context Affects Vision

What is the relationship between vision and the organizational context in which it is articulated and used? Context, for the purposes of this discussion, includes organization culture.

Nutt and Backoff (1997, pp. 316–17) assess four organizational contexts in terms of their abilities to produce visionary strategic change. These abilities are assessed in relation to the degree of acceptance of the need for change (change susceptibility) and the extent to which resources for strategic change are available (resource availability).

- *Rigid organizations* have limited available resources and lack acceptance of the need for change. Such organizations tend to be hierarchical and inflexible (such as Eastern and Pan Am before their collapse).
- *Bold organizations* have limited resources, but acceptance of the need for change is high. They tend to be more organic and less rule-bound. Visionary leadership is more likely to emerge in this context, although this entails freeing up resources and ensuring that key stakeholders are carefully cultivated in the process of developing the vision.
- *Overmanaged organizations* have high resource availability but little acceptance of the need for change. They tend to be limited in their ability to accept the need for a new

vision, due to a comparatively stable environment dominated by past practices that are seen to have worked well and which remain relevant.

- *Liberated organizations* have a context in which visionary processes are likely to be most successful. Hewlett-Packard and Intel, for example, have been regarded as having high acceptance of the need for change and high availability of resources that can be allocated to the strategic change process.

When does a vision "take"? This context analysis suggests the need for a "trigger" that alerts organization members to the need for a new vision, thus strengthening acceptance of change. The power of the vision, remember, lies with the way in which it can give meaning to the current situation and promise to solve the organization's problems. Triggers can include external turbulence and uncertainty, crises demanding new strategies or ways of working, poor organizational performance, or transitions such as entrepreneurial start-up to growth. In addition, change leaders can use their influence and storytelling capabilities to frame interpretations of the current situation so as to heighten dissatisfaction with the status quo (Lewin, 1951), thus enhancing the desire for change. In other words, change leaders can generate a crisis situation through their visionary and rhetorical skills, rather than waiting for one to appear (Denning, 2004 and 2005).

The national and cultural contexts in which an organization is embedded are also factors contributing to whether or not visions "take." For example, Jerry Wind and Jeremy Main (1999) note that Donald Burr's vision for the airline *People Express* was "to become the leading institution for constructive change in the world." That, they observe, was vague and preposterous. In Japan, on the other hand, a past chairman of Canon, Ryuzaburo Kaku, referred to himself as an evangelist, saying that the organization was guided by "living and working together for the common good." While similar in intent to Burr's vision, Wind and Main argue that Kaku's vision "worked" in Japan, where organizations are more closely aligned with national and social interests than they are in the United States. Consider again the vision statements in table 6.4, and in particular those that you assessed as less attractive. Did those come from companies based in another country and culture?

LO 6.4   How Visions Are Developed

How are visions developed? We will consider three answers to this question, exploring approaches to "crafting" a vision, the kinds of questions that can help to develop a vision, and connecting the vision to the organization's "inner voice."

Crafting the Vision

Lawrence Holpp and Michael Kelly (1988, p. 48) argue that crafting a vision is "a little like dancing with a 500-pound gorilla. It takes a little while to get the steps down, but once the dance is over, you know you've really accomplished something." There are different approaches (or dances) to crafting or creating a vision, and some of these are outlined in table 6.5 (based on a concept similar to the "leadership styles continuum," discussed in chapter 10, table 10.7).

For some commentators, crafting a vision is a senior management responsibility, typically discharged by having a small team analyze needs, identify choices, and develop

TABLE 6.5
Approaches to
Vision-Crafting

Approach	What It Means	Used When
Tell	Chief executive creates the vision and gives it to staff	Involvement is not seen as important
Sell	Chief executive has a vision that he or she wants staff to accept	Chief executive is attracted to the vision and wants others to adopt it
Test	Chief executive seeks feedback on ideas about a vision	Chief executive wants to see which aspects of the vision find support
Consult	Chief executive seeks the creative input of staff, within set parameters	Chief executive needs help to develop the vision
Co-create	Shared vision is created by chief executive and staff	Chief executive wants to identify shared visions throughout the organization

recommendations (Pendlebury et al., 1998). But some see this as a collaborative effort, involving both the top team and those who will be affected by the vision. Lynda Gratton (1996), for example, describes how seven European companies engaged in a democratic vision process, drawing on a range of cross-functional groups instead of imposing a top-down approach. Allowing the vision to emerge from debates among those multifunctional groups, she argues, can potentially lead to more creative visions and subsequent actions. This democratic approach also ensures that the need for change (which may be urgent) is transmitted across the organization, and it provides executives with a better understanding of the risks and trade-offs involved in implementing the vision.

Adopting a similar approach, Nutt and Backoff (1997) suggest three vision-crafting processes.

1. *Leader-dominated approach.* The CEO provides the strategic vision for the organization. This is similar to the "tell" and "sell" approaches in table 6.5. This approach is not consistent with the concept of empowerment, which argues that people across an organization should be involved in the processes and decisions that affect them.

2. *Pump-priming approach.* The CEO provides visionary ideas and gets selected individuals and groups to further develop these ideas within some broad parameters. This adapting and shaping process is similar to the "test" and "consult" approaches in table 6.5.

3. *Facilitation approach.* Similar to the "co-create" approach in table 6.5, this draws directly on a participative management perspective by involving a significant number of people in the process of developing and articulating the vision. The CEO acts as facilitator, orchestrating the crafting process. Nutt and Backoff (1997) argue that this approach is likely to produce better visions and more successful organizational change because those who have contributed will be more committed to making the vision work.

Three sets of structured guidelines or "routines" for producing a vision are summarized in table 6.6. While similar in style, they provide different levels of detail with regard to the nature of the process and the steps that should be involved. There is no "one best way" to do this.

TABLE 6.6
Guidelines for Structuring the Vision Process

Core Steps in Creating a New Vision		
1 Use a qualified facilitator	Develop trial vision statements	Leadership team defines the timeline
2 Assess where you have been and where you are	Discuss these with staff and customers	Conduct an environmental scan of threats and opportunities
3 Think about a new direction	Revise the vision	Develop appropriate interview questions
4 Co-construct a statement about the organization's future direction	Rediscuss the vision	Use questions to interview leadership team to obtain their ideal vision of the future
5 Identify roadblocks	Repeat the process until an agreed vision is produced	Draft a vision of the future
6 Take action quickly to capitalize on enthusiasm; develop a strategic plan to integrate vision throughout organizational practices		Get feedback from across the organization
7 Develop a system for monitoring and adjusting the vision, such as performance review workshops		Develop a second draft
8		Share vision with leadership team to gain commitment: develop a catch-phrase that captures its essence, and a communication plan
9		Assess implications and develop specific action plans
Deetz et al. (2000)	Davidson (2004)	Belgard and Rayner (2004)

Questions That Help to Develop a Vision

The approaches that we have discussed so far distinguish between different degrees of involvement in the development of an organization's vision. However, they do not directly address the question of how to develop the substance of the vision itself.

Holpp and Kelly (1988) identify three different approaches and sets of questions through which vision may be developed. They label these approaches *intuitive, analytical,* and *benchmarking.*

The *intuitive* approach relies on the use of imagination and imagery to encourage staff to participate in vision development. Managers are asked to imagine doing their jobs in such a way that they really achieve what they want from themselves and from the other people with whom they work:

First, they are asked to list up to ten things that they want to achieve personally and professionally, and then to prioritize these, focusing on the top two or three.

Second, they focus on their current situation as a way to identify the tension between their current lived experiences and their desired image.

Third, they are provided with support to help identify and implement structured action plans to work toward achieving their vision.

The *analytical* approach sees visions as defined in relation to organizational or departmental missions and roles. Vision is thus related to purpose and focuses on the following questions:

- Who is served by the organization?
- What does the organization do?
- Where does the organization place most of its efforts?
- Why does the organization focus on particular work and goals?
- How does the organization operationalize these efforts?

The aim of these questions is to guide the organization as a whole, and individual departments, from the current situation to a desired future state.

The *benchmarking* approach bases the vision on the actions and standards of the organization's toughest competitors. This involves asking:

- What do our competitors do well?
- How can we surpass this?
- What quantitative and qualitative measures would indicate that we had achieved this?
- What will it be like, and how will it feel, when those standards have been achieved?

The benchmarking approach is more externally focused, compared with the intuitive and analytical approaches, which have an internal focus. Here are some of the problems with these approaches:

- The intuitive approach, which follows an organization development perspective, may produce personal visions that are not connected to the core business of the organization and to current or anticipated industry trends.
- The analytical approach serves more to align the vision to the mission of the organization, but pays less attention to the values and guiding logics of the organization. By aligning too tightly with mission, the analytical approach may neglect the inspirational element of visions.
- The benchmarking approach assumes that the organization's future will be linked to current competitors. However, it may be more valuable to identify who will be the new competitors in the future, especially where an organization and sector are facing transformational change.

Connecting to the Organization's "Inner Voice"

Robert Quinn (1996, p. 197) makes an interesting contribution to the process of identifying change visions. He points out that, in many organizations, people want to know what the vision is and look to the chief executive to provide it. Paradoxically, however, where vision statements are available, such as on corporate business cards, these are likely to be rejected as being in name only; they are not what people are "willing to die for." He argues that developing a vision to guide organizational actions has to go beyond superficial statements and "confront the lack of integrity that exists in the system," an exercise for which few managers are well equipped.

To illustrate this view, he tells the story of a speech given by Mahatma Gandhi at a political convention in India. When he rose to speak, many in the audience also rose, left their seats, and paid little attention to him. However, as he spoke about what Indians really cared about—not politics, but bread and salt—the audience sat down again and listened. His message was unusual: "This small, unassuming man had journeyed through their heartland and captured the essence of India. He was vocalizing it in a way they could feel and understand. Such articulation is often at the heart of radical, deep change" (Quinn, 1996, p. 199). For Quinn, it is this ability to find the organization's "bread and salt" that makes a vision appealing, passionate, and beyond the superficial. This search for the "inner voice" of the organization is necessary in order to develop visions that resonate and narrow the gap between "talk and walk." Such "bread-and-salt" visions are achieved in a circular manner involving a bottom-up and top-down dialogue to reach the "inner voice" of the organization.

Adopting a similar position, Chris Rogers (2007, p. 229) maintains that "vision is as much about insight as far sight." Visions need to connect with people's desires, feelings, and ambitions, as well as with the organization's intentions. Resonating with the *interpreter* image of change management, this implies that visions are important in encouraging the members of an organization to develop and explore "new ways of seeing," to gain fresh insights, make new connections, and to be better prepared to work with the challenges that a new vision is likely to bring.

Purpose beyond Profit

A focus on purpose goes beyond asking questions about whether a business is operating profitably or whether an action is legal—it engages a soul-searching focus on questions at a core level, such as: What is a business's sense of purpose (shared identity and goals)? How and why did a particular business begin (imprinting effects of founding philosophies)? Who founded the enterprise and what did they want to achieve (entrepreneurial values, mission, and vision)? How does a sense of purpose relate to all the stakeholders in the organization and to the context in which it operates (stewardship and governance)? How does a business understand itself relative to society, and what is it doing to create a shared sense of purpose (institutional norms and logics)?

Source: From Hollensbe et al. (2014), p. 1228.

Table 6.7 provides examples of "bad" and "good" purpose statements (Craig and Snook, 2014, p. 109). Many organizations express their vision in vague and general terms: "Help others excel," "Ensure success," "Empower my people." These statements do not include a plan for translating purpose into action. Some organizations try to cover every

Purpose-Driven Leadership

Nick Craig and Scott Snook (2014) explore the concept of "purpose-driven leadership," arguing that the leader's sense of purpose contributes to a clear statement of the organization's vision and mission:

Doctors have even found that people with purpose in their lives are less prone to disease.

Purpose is increasingly being touted as the key to navigating the complex, volatile, ambiguous world we face today, where strategy is ever changing and few decisions are obviously right or wrong. (p. 106)

TABLE 6.7
From Bad to Good Purpose Statements

From Bad ...	To Good ...
Be a driver in the infrastructure business that allows each person to achieve their needed outcomes while also mastering the new drivers of our business as I balance my family and work demands	Bring water and power to the 2 billion people who do not have it
Continually and consistently develop and facilitate the growth and development of myself and others, leading to great performance	With tenacity, create brilliance

possibility with jargon: "Empower my team to achieve exceptional business results while delighting customers" (p. 108). Now consider these two visions:

Google: "To organize the world's information and make it universally accessible and useful"

Charles Schwab: "A relentless ally for the individual investor"

In order to develop a sense of purpose that has an impact, leaders must clarify their own purpose based on experience, preferences, and ambitions. Craig and Snook also argue that leaders have to imagine the impact that "living the purpose" will have on their world. While actions matter more than words, the language in which purpose statements are expressed is important, as table 6.8 suggests.

Leaders must therefore clarify their own unique sense of purpose, and put that to work.

TABLE 6.8
The Language of Purpose-to-Impact Planning

Traditional Development Planning	Purpose-to-Impact Planning
Uses standard business language	Uses meaningful, purpose-infused language
Focuses on weaknesses to address performance	Focuses on strengths to realize career aspirations
States a business- or career-driven goal	A statement of purpose explaining how you lead
Measures success with metrics tied to the firm's mission and goals	Sets incremental goals related to living your leadership purpose
Focuses on the present, working forward	Focuses on the future, working backward
Generic; addresses the job or role	Unique to you, addresses who you are as a leader
Ignores responsibilities outside the office	Takes a holistic view of work and family

LO 6.5 Why Visions Fail

Visions can fail for a number of reasons. For example, this can happen when a vision is:

- too specific; fails to appreciate the inability to control change, and the degree of uncertainty often associated with outcomes
- too complex; difficult to understand
- too vague; fails to act as a landmark toward which change actions are directed
- inadequate; only partially addresses the presenting problem
- irrelevant; clear picture, not firmly attached to the business
- blurred; no clear picture of the future
- unrealistic; perceived as not achievable
- a rearview mirror; pictures the past, extrapolated into the future

Be Specific *Alan Lafley at P&G*

The chief executive of Procter & Gamble (P&G), Alan Lafley, is reflecting on his five years of leading change inside the company. One of his key comments is that he found it important to provide more than just a briefly stated vision, because people responded better to specifics:

So if I'd stopped at "We're going to refocus on the company's core businesses," that wouldn't have been good enough. The core businesses are one, two, three, four. Fabric care, baby care, feminine care, and hair care. And then you get questions: "Well, I'm in home care. Is that a core business?" "No." "What does it have to do to become a core business?" "It has to be a global leader in its industry. It has to

have the best structural economics in its industry. It has to be able to grow consistently at a certain rate. It has to be able to deliver a certain cash flow return on investment." So then business leaders understand what it takes to become a core business.

Why did this extra level of detail help? According to Lafley, there were two factors. One was the size and diversity of the P&G workforce—100,000 people from over 100 cultures. The second was that, for managers with so much going on in their businesses, the provision of more detail on the implications of the vision helped them to focus on what was needed to implement it (Rajat Gupta and Jim Wendler, 2005, p. 3).

Todd Jick (2001, p. 36) adds that a vision is likely to fail when leaders spend 90 percent of their time articulating it (but not necessarily in clearly understood terms), and only 10 percent of their time implementing it. Table 6.9 suggests other reasons why visions fail. The sidebar "A Lack of Shared Vision?" tells a short story about the absence of a shared vision. We will now consider two further reasons for vision failure; inability to adapt over time, and the presence of competing visions.

TABLE 6.9
**Visions Fail
When ...**

Source: Based on
Lipton (1996),
pp. 89–91.

Visions Fail When ...	Because ...
The walk is different from the talk	When managers do not match their words with actions, the vision is treated by staff as an empty slogan
They are treated as the "holy grail"	The expectations will be unrealistic, and visions are not magic solutions
They are not connected to the present	Visions need to recognize current obstacles if they are to be believable and seen as achievable
They are too abstract, or too concrete	Visions must be idealistic, realistic, and tangible
Development does not involve a creative process	It is often the process as well as the final vision that helps to secure the organization's future
Participation is limited	Consensus must be built around the vision, which has to be diffused throughout the organization
People are complacent	Visions that are projected too far into the future are not seen as urgent

A Lack of Shared Vision?

John Symons (2006) tells the following humorous story:

The man in the hot air balloon was lost. Descending sufficiently he shouted to a walker on the ground asking where he was. "You are 30 feet up in the air," was her immediate response before she walked away.

Asked subsequently by a companion to explain this unhelpful behavior she said: "He was a typical manager. He didn't know where he was, or how to get to where he wanted to go without the help of those underneath him." Somewhat mischievously she added, "Why should I do more than necessary to help someone who got to where he was by hot air and did not tell me where he was planning to go?"

As John Symons comments:

She obviously did not know or share the balloonist's vision. The lesson for managers is clear. As well as enthusing those underneath, the leader needs to communicate where he or she is in relation to achieving the vision.

Failure to Adapt

Some visions stand the test of time and remain applicable and adaptable to new situations and environments. Others, however, need to be overhauled in order to remain relevant. This situation is illustrated by the investigation by Lloyd Harris and Emmanuel Ogbonna (1999) into two medium-sized UK retail companies and the impact of the founders' visions on strategic change. In both cases, the vision was established well over 100 years ago by the company founder and there was evidence of an escalation of commitment to the vision by subsequent management. In one company, the vision was paternalistic (commitment toward staff) and focused on prudent growth. This led to a strong focus on sales and profitability in each new store location. These characteristics were still present in the current management of the company. The vision itself was seen as flexible and responsive to the prevailing environmental conditions facing the company. The researchers label the founder's vision in this case as providing a "strategic dividend" for subsequent management.

By contrast, in the other company, the founder's vision was to have a store in every town in a particular region. A second aspect of this vision concerned family control of the company. The researchers argue that this original vision continued to drive senior management. However, in contrast to the first company, this vision served as a "strategic hangover." The closed nature of the vision led successive management teams to make decisions that were out of step with changes in the environmental conditions facing the sector, such as the movement of large retail stores into the region, and a shift in focus of such stores from price to quality and service. As a result, the company almost faced financial ruin on two separate occasions. In relation to subsequent strategic change actions taken by management in these two companies, the authors argue that "whether the original vision of the founder results in a legacy or a hangover is clearly dependent on the original flexibility of the strategy and the later environmental appropriateness" (Harris and Ogbonna, 1999, p. 340).

Presence of Competing Visions

Visions may also fail due to what Rosabeth Moss Kanter et al. (1992) call "vision collisions," involving the presence of multiple and conflicting visions. This can happen, for example, when the vision is crafted by organization strategists who are convinced of the need for change, but where this sense of urgency is not shared by those who will implement or be affected by the change (who may still be trying to embed previous changes). Vision collisions can also occur where there is a gap between the visions of management and stakeholders. In the mid-1980s, the vision of Nike, the sportswear company, was to make athletic footwear. However, the company found that a different market segment was buying their shoes: not athletes, but people who were wearing Nike trainers instead of casual shoes. Nike responded by introducing its own brand of casual shoes. This strategy failed because Nike had not understood that customers were buying expensive "overengineered sneakers" because they appealed to their image. In other words, the company's vision was out of step with its customers' vision of Nike. Multiple and conflicting visions can also arise with company mergers. Colin Mitchell (2002), for example, cites the failure in 2000 of the merger between Deutsche Bank and Dresdner Bank. In this merger, there was a "failure of management to persuade Deutsche's investment bankers of the vision for how the newly merged company would compete. Many key employees left, and the threat of mass walkout forced Deutsche to abandon the deal after considerable damage to the share price of both companies" (p. 104).

We need to close this discussion with a note of caution. There is limited research into the concept and process of vision failure. As Davidson (2004) argues, while there are many tales of failed visions, there are also many corporate insiders who have a vested interest in declaring success.

LO 6.6   Linking Vision to Change: Three Debates

In this section, we explore three debates concerning the links between vision and organizational change. First, we ask if vision is a driver of change, or if vision emerges through the change process. Second, we ask whether vision helps or hinders change. Third, we assess whether vision is better attributed to heroic, charismatic leaders, or is better understood as an organizational attribute.

Debate One—Vision: Driving Change, or Emerging During Change?

Vision drives change: The change management approaches and frameworks described in chapter 10 give vision a prominent role in underpinning and implementing organizational change.

- For Kanter et al. (1992), establishing a vision is the first step toward change. Without a vision, changes may seem arbitrary and unnecessary. Vision provides clarity about the goals of change, avoiding the perception that this is just another cost-cutting exercise. The vision can motivate staff to embrace change, engaging in what may seem to be daunting or risky actions.
- For Pendlebury et al. (1998), vision determines the scope, depth, and time frame of change, and the areas that will be affected. Having a vision at the start of change is needed for both transformational change (outlining the broader strategic intent to which all actions are directed) as well as incremental or adaptive change (where the vision can be more specific in terms of specifying change objectives and procedures).

The need for vision at the start of change is also embedded in the strategy literature, where the term *strategic intent* is often used to represent vision. It is most usually associated with the work of Gary Hamel and C. K. Prahalad (1989, p. 4), who argue that "strategic intent envisions a desired leadership position and establishes the criterion the organization will use to chart its progress." They point to Komatsu's "Encircle Caterpillar," and Canon's "Beat Xerox" as visionary statements that capture strategic intent. The strategic intent behind such statements was long term and encompassed a number of different change programs and actions over the short and medium term that were designed to work toward the longer-term vision. The strategic intent expressed the desired end result without specifying or prescribing the necessary steps for achieving it.

Vision emerges during change: Although important, it may not be possible to articulate a clear vision at an early stage during transformational or discontinuous change. Robert Shaw (1995) argues that organization structures and management processes may require fundamental change. It may not be possible to develop a vision until after the process has begun to unfold, because the relevant information may not be available in the current configuration (customer expectations, competition). In other words, discontinuous change has to be under way in order to make that information available to inform the development of vision. Those who are leading the change are surrounded by the presenting problems and are able to make real-time adjustments in the context of the results of their ongoing efforts. Robert Quinn (1996, p. 83) describes this as "building the bridge as you walk it."

Other commentators have adopted an even stronger position, arguing that "the vision thing" is overrated in terms of driving change. For Frederick Hilmer and Lex Donaldson (1996), business planning, not vision or visionary leaders, produces successful change. Analyzing corporate change at GE, they observe that "there was no clear vision to guide the transformation" (p. 126) and that the actions of Jack Welch were pragmatic and "based on the application of conventional business ideas about the need for productivity improvement and high market share" (p. 127). Many visions were produced over the period of Welch's tenure, and a clear vision did not emerge until most of the transformational changes had been implemented. Hilmer and Donaldson (1996) argue that "vision rhetoric" was used simply to make management decisions appear to be more acceptable.

Debate Two—Vision: Help Change or Hinder Change?

Vision helps change: Lipton (1996) identifies five tangible benefits that skillful visions can bring to an organization:

- *Enhance performance*: The studies by James Collins and Jerry Porras (1991, 1996, 2005) found that companies labelled as visionary were likely, over time, to deliver a greater dividend to shareholders compared to others.
- *Facilitate change*: Visions provide road maps that assist the transition process.
- *Enable sound strategic planning*: Plans that have embedded within them imagery of the future are more likely to inspire people to action.
- *Recruit talent*: This applies particularly to the Generation Xers who want to maximize their incomes while feeling that they are engaging in challenges greater than simply making a profit.
- *Focus on decision making*: Vision helps to develop the distinctive competencies that characterize an organization.

Emmanuel Metais (2000) supports this position, arguing that "strategic vision" helps to produce stretch in an organization by creating a sense of incompetence resulting from the gap between the future and the current reality. This perceived incompetence encourages creativity and the search for new ways of acquiring and using resources. At the same time, vision can also help to leverage these resources by stimulating innovative ways of using them. Stretch and leverage combined, Metais argues, can be used to identify new strategies for achieving the vision, including actions such as:

flanking: exploiting a weakness in a dominant competitor

encircling competitors: gaining greater control of the market

destabilizing the market: changing the competitive rules

Paul Schoemaker (1992) also links strategic vision with helping to decide the products that an organization should make and the markets in which it should operate. Performance appraisals and incentive systems can then be managed so that they align with the vision.

Vision hinders change: Vision can impede the process of organizational change when visionary or charismatic leaders use emotional appeal as the basis for engagement and neglect the operational details needed to make change work. A related problem is that vision focuses on the future, diverting attention from current problems (see "Lou Gerstner on Vision," below). One example is the failure of the UK Internet company Boo.com, which raised $135 million to deliver its vision, which was to have a global presence in online clothes shopping (Lissack and Roos, 2001). It launched operations

Lou Gerstner on Vision

Louis V. Gerstner Jr., chief executive of IBM, argued in a press conference in the mid-1990s that "the last thing IBM needs right now is a vision." He later wrote that this was "the most quotable statement I ever made." This statement has often been cited as evidence that he downplayed or even dismissed the role of vision in organizational change. For example, Michael Raynor (1998, p. 368) argues that "for a good many critics Gerstner's comment was greeted with a heartfelt 'it's about time'—that is, it is about time that a senior executive had the courage to speak up and put all that rhetoric about visions and missions in its place."

Gerstner argues, however, that those who have portrayed this view of him have misinterpreted (or even misquoted) him, often failing to pay attention to the "right now" part of the statement. He maintains that IBM had a number of vision statements: it was now time to implement these, rather than engage in further visioning exercises, because by that time, "fixing IBM was all about execution."

Source: Based on Gerstner (2003).

in 17 different countries but had problems with slow software, which frustrated potential buyers:

> Boo's vision called for a broadband world of cool kids with large budgets. Boo's reality consisted of 56k modems, fussy buyers, and tight budgets. Boo was consistent with its vision but out of sync with its present landscape. (Lissack and Roos, 2001, p. 61)

Vision can thus be a drawback when the wrong vision drives the change, when leaders exaggerate perceptions of crisis, and when the vision fails to deliver its promise and followers become disillusioned and lose confidence in both the leader and the organization. Further problems will arise when there is a significant gap between the vision and the organizational capabilities that would be required to realize it.

Vision development approaches that do not involve the people who will be affected are thought to have negative consequences for producing successful organizational change. For example, Harvey Robbins and Michael Finley (1997, p. 175) point out that:

> Where organizations go wrong is in assuming that the vision is some precious grail-like object that only the organizational priests are privy to—that it appears in a dream to the executive team, who then hold it up high for the rank and file to ooh and ahh over. The problem with the priestly approach to vision-and-mission is that the resulting vision is often a lot of garbage. The outcome, instead of being a useful reminder to keep to the change track, is a paragraph held to be so sacred that no one dares change it.

Vision can further hinder change where, once developed, senior management become so committed to it that they are unwilling to reevaluate and test its ongoing utility and relevance. To do this could challenge the assumptions that the top team is truly in control, that they have better foresight than anyone else, and that they do indeed have a clear and compelling vision of the organization's future. Senior management may feel uncomfortable questioning those issues.

Visions can hinder organizations when they have been developed using sense-making processes that are linked to current or past practices. Lissack and Roos (2001) argue that this approach is flawed, because predicting the future on this basis reifies the desired outcome without enabling future changes to be built into it. Vision is based on the world in the future being stable and predictable. Outcomes are locked in and goals are set. The problem is that the vision may prevent the organization from pursuing new, unanticipated opportunities that may emerge.

For Lissack and Roos (2001), the concept of vision is limited by other assumptions. One assumption is that organizational boundaries are well defined: staff, customers, suppliers. In a world of fuzzy organizational networks, this assumption is questionable. A second assumption is that the identity of the organization is fixed, with the vision built around that identity. We think of Lego, for example, as a toy company. However, corporate identity—what the organization does—is constantly changing; as we saw in chapter 5, Lego is also now an online games company. Lissack and Roos (2001, p. 61) prefer the term "coherence" to vision. Coherence involves, "acting in a manner consistent with who you are given your present spot in the business landscape." An interesting argument, but it is unlikely that the term "coherence," emphasizing debates around boundaries and organizational identity, will replace the concept of vision, which is deeply embedded in change management thinking.

How does vision impact individual rather than organizational identity, and can this propel or impede change? This issue has generated debate. Landau et al. (2006a and b) note that staff may identify strongly with an organization's original vision, and with the underlying beliefs and assumptions. However, when an attempt is made to inject a new vision, this is likely to be resisted if it disrupts individual images and self-definitions. The new vision will therefore hinder change. This problem can be addressed if it is possible to ensure that new objectives and goals remain consistent with the values and beliefs that underpinned the original vision.

Jeffrey Ford and William Pasmore (2006) question this position for two reasons. First, it is not clear that vision does directly affect individual identity-forming processes. This is an empirical question that needs to be examined, and is likely to vary across organizations. Second, even if we accept that there is a direct relationship between individual identity and vision, the problem lies with staff who are deeply committed to an existing identity, which they are reluctant to change, despite the need for a new vision (and perhaps, therefore, a new identity)—even if the new vision is necessary to secure the organization's survival. They note, "People should be entitled to their identities, but at the same time, organizations do need people who are committed to a viable, sustainable vision to survive" (p. 176). This argument reminds us that changes in vision may challenge individual identities, thereby producing resistance to change. When developing a new vision, therefore, it is important to assess, first, whether this will enable or disable identity-forming processes, and second, whether this will encourage or discourage those affected to become involved in the change.

Debate Three—Vision: An Attribute of Heroic Leaders, or Heroic Organizations?

Vision is an attribute of heroic leaders: Some commentators argue that successful organizational change depends on effective leadership. For David Nadler and Robert Shaw (1995, p. 219), "heroic leaders" energize and support their followers and provide them with a vision that "provides a vehicle for people to develop commitment, a common goal around which people can rally, and a way for people to feel successful." As we have already noted, the vision has to be clear, compelling, challenging, and credible, but it must also be reflected in the expressions and actions of the leader who is articulating it. Nadler (1998, p. 276) points to visionary leaders such as Jamie Houghton at Corning, who painted "an engrossing picture of a culture in which Corning would be one of the most competent, profitable, and respected corporations in the entire world." He also identifies Scott McNealy of Sun Microsystems as envisioning "an information world where people would be free to choose from a range of vendors rather than held captive by a single, all-powerful mega-corporation."

Ironically, some of those who are cited as visionary leaders do not see themselves as visionary or heroic, and have challenged the significance of vision:

Robert Eaton, who managed Chrysler after Lee Iacocca, downplayed vision in favor of measurable short-term results.

Bill Gates, one of the founders of Microsoft, once declared that "being visionary is trivial" (Lipton, 1996, p. 86).

Nevertheless, those leaders are often praised for articulating clear, appealing, challenging images of the future of their organizations—the hallmarks of effective visions.

William Gardner and Bruce Avolio (1998) argue that effective charismatic, visionary leaders create "identity images" that are valued and desired by others, incorporating trustworthiness, credibility, morality, innovativeness, esteem, and power. Drawing on a dramaturgical perspective, they argue that charismatic leaders enact (or perform) their visions through four processes:

1. *Framing*: The art of managing meaning, influencing others to accept the leader's interpretation of the vision by stressing its importance and aligning it with their values;
2. *Scripting*: The process of coordinating and integrating more specific sets of ideas and actions including:

    casting of the appropriate key roles
    dialogue, using various rhetorical devices, such as metaphors and stories, to increase the appeal of the message
    providing direction, using verbal and nonverbal behavior and emotional displays
3. *Staging*: The selection of symbols, artifacts, props, and settings to reinforce the vision
4. *Performing*: Enacting the vision by personally demonstrating the behaviors required to achieve the vision

It is important to note that, although having a vision is considered by many commentators to be a prerequisite for successful change leadership, others disagree. Vision may be a necessary component of inspirational leadership, but may not be sufficient. Robert Goffee and Gareth Jones (2000) argue that, to complement energy and vision, other qualities are necessary, including:

- revealing personal weaknesses to followers in order to gain their trust
- sensing how things are in the organization and the wider environment, picking up and interpreting subtle cues and signals
- showing "tough empathy," being passionate, caring, but realistic, focusing on what others need rather than what they want
- daring to be different, signalling and maintaining their uniqueness, while maintaining social distance

It has also been argued that visionary leaders are needed at an everyday level throughout the organization, and not just at the top. Such individuals provide what Chris Rogers (2007) calls "supervision," using interactions, conversations, and role modelling to demonstrate:

perspective, concerning the challenges facing the organization

purpose, both personal and organizational

processes, to respond more effectively to customers

possibilities, by challenging current constraints

potential, concerning personal contributions

passion, to channel energies in meaningful ways

In this perspective, therefore, to maintain engagement and motivation, providing vision must be a day-to-day activity involving many leaders across the organization, and not an occasional process led by a single senior figure or a small top team.

Vision is an attribute of heroic organizations: Collins and Porras (2005) argue that visionary leaders are not necessary in order to create visionary companies, claiming that the role of charisma in setting vision has been exaggerated. A charismatic leader may even be an impediment to the creation of a visionary organization; sustained organizational effectiveness depends on embedded visions, values, and ideologies, rather than on pronouncements from one senior figure. The leader's role is to act as a catalyst, facilitating the development of, and commitment to, the vision. This is a process that can be achieved through a variety of leadership and management styles. It is more important to create an organization with a vision than to have a charismatic chief executive with a personal vision.

In this perspective, vision incorporates core ideology, which is unchanging, and defines what the organization stands for and why it exists. An envisioned future is what the organization aspires to and changes toward over time. Ideology comprises core values and core purpose. Core values are durable guiding principles: "the HP Way," Walt Disney Company's "imagination and wholesomeness," Procter & Gamble's "product excellence," Nordstrom's "customer service." Collins and Porras (2005) note that most companies have only three to five shared core values. Core purpose, on the other hand, defines the reason for the organization's existence:

3M: "solve unsolved problems innovatively"

Mary Kay Cosmetics: "give unlimited opportunity to women"

McKinsey & Company: "help leading corporations and governments be more successful"

Walmart: "give ordinary folk the chance to buy the same things as rich people"

Core purpose should be durable (designed to last a century, perhaps), and differs from goals and business strategies, which change constantly over time. The purpose may not change, but it should inspire change, development, and progress. The envisioned future, in contrast, consists of "BHAGs"—Big, Hairy, Audacious Goals, or daunting challenges with specified timelines, which can involve:

Common enemy logic: Philip Morris in the 1950s wanted to "knock off RJR as the number one tobacco company in the world"; Nike in the 1960s aimed to "crush Adidas"

Role model logic: Stanford University in the 1940s wanted to become "the Harvard of the West"; in 1996, Watkins-Johnson's goal was to "become as respected in 20 years as Hewlett-Packard"

Internal transformation logic: The goal for GE in the 1980s was to "become number one or number two in every market we serve, and revolutionize this company to have the strengths of a big company combined with the leanness and agility of a small company"; Rockwell in 1995 wanted to "transform this company from a defense contractor into the best diversified high-technology company in the world."

A further component of envisioned future, vivid descriptions, consists of vibrant, passionate, and engaging descriptions of what it will be like in the future when goals are achieved. Envisioning the future is a creative process, engaging staff across the organization.

The Complete Vision at Merck

Collins and Porras (2005) argue that complete visions have three components: a core ideology (values and purpose); an envisioned future (big, hairy, audacious goals); and vivid descriptions. They offer the following example from the pharmaceutical company Merck in the 1930s:

Core Ideology	Envisioned Future
core values: social responsibility, excellence, and science-based innovation	*BHAG*: to transform from a chemical manufacturer to a world drug company with research capacity rivalling major universities
Purpose	**Vivid Description**
to preserve and improve human life	with the tools we have supplied, science will be advanced, knowledge increased, and human life win ever greater freedom from suffering and disease

The work of Collins and Porras offers a sensitive treatment of the relationship between vision and change. Vision (which they also call "industry foresight") is broken down into component parts, some of which remain stable and some of which change over time. Many change models that refer to the need for vision to guide organizational change lack this degree of sophistication. Vision is often presented as something that guides change, handed down to the organization by the chief executive and the top management team. However, for Collins and Porras, vision (as core ideology) serves as an enduring background component, not so much guiding change as reflecting how change will be achieved (by following core values, for example). It is the envisioned future of vision that offers concrete change direction, concerning what should be changed, and how.

EXERCISE 6.1

Interviewing Change Recipients

`LO 6.1`

Your task is to interview three employees; they can be in the same or different organizations. Ask them to think back to an organizational change that they experienced, and to answer the following questions:

1. Were they presented with an organizational vision for this change, and if so:
   What was the vision?
   What effect did this have on them?
   Were they involved in developing the vision?
   To what extent did the vision motivate them to engage in the change?
   How central was the vision to implementing the change?

2. If your interviewees were not given an organizational vision for this change, ask them:
   Would a vision have helped them to understand and become involved in the change?
   How important is vision to achieving organizational change?

When you have completed your interviews, consider the responses that you have documented. What general conclusions emerge regarding the relationship between vision and organizational change? What have you learned from this exercise?

EXERCISE 6.2

Analyze Your Own Organization's Vision

`LO 6.2`

Consider your own current organization, or another with which you are familiar, which could be the institution where you are studying.

Refer back to the description, from Collins and Porras (2005), of "The Complete Vision at Merck." Identify your chosen organization's vision in those terms: core ideology (and values), envisioned future, BHAGs, and vivid descriptions.

Does your organization's vision help to drive change, or not? Why?

Is the vision just a "public relations" exercise, or is it used in practice? How can you tell?

EXERCISE 6.3

The Role of Vision at Mentor Graphics

`LO 6.5`

As you read this case, consider the following questions:

1. How would you describe the way vision was used at Mentor Graphics?
2. Did it strengthen or weaken the company? How? Why?
3. Of the reasons discussed in this chapter concerning why visions fail, which are applicable to Mentor Graphics?
4. What is your assessment of the vision content and the process through which it was introduced in the Mentor Graphics context? What lessons emerge from your assessment?
5. Based on what happened at Mentor Graphics, what are the implications for the three debates discussed in this chapter: whether vision drives change or emerges during change; whether vision helps or hinders change; and whether vision is an attribute of heroic leaders or heroic organizations?
6. Of the six change images outlined in table 6.1, which images of vision can be applied to this case study? What lessons emerge from this?

Gerard Langeler (1992), president of Mentor Graphics Corporation, described the role of vision in his company over a decade. Formed in the early 1980s, Mentor Graphics started with an unarticulated vision to "Build Something That People Will Buy." On this basis, they spent a number of months interviewing potential customers and designing a computer-aided engineering workstation product.

At the same time, a competitor, Daisy Systems, was engaged in the same task and, in the early years, outcompeted Mentor Graphics. Eventually, "Beat Daisy" became the new vision, driven by the need to survive as a business.

By 1985 Mentor's revenues were higher than Daisy's; their vision had been realized. The company continued to grow despite the recession, but it suffered from typical growth problems, including decline in product quality and problems of internal company coordination. Stock value also suffered, and a number of staff approached Langeler seeking a new vision for the company.

The new vision was developed based on "Six Boxes," which represented the six different businesses in which the company sought market leadership. The "Six Boxes" became a company mantra, but in the late 1980s, one of the businesses, computer-aided publishing, was not paying dividends. However, the fact that it constituted one of the "Six Boxes" meant that they could not shut it down, and be left with a "Five Boxes" vision. In this case, the existence of the vision disrupted the ability to make sound financial judgements. It also stopped them from moving more quickly to using Sun platforms, something they thought was too conventional for them.

A new vision was developed—the "10X Imperative"—that mirrored the push other companies were making toward quality through Six Sigma and other similar quality programs. However, customers did not really understand the new vision: it was too abstract and elusive.

In 1989 yet another vision emerged: "Changing the Way the World Designs Together." In retrospect, Langeler depicts this vision as "the final extension of vision creep that began with Six Boxes." It was very grand and had little to do with the actual businesses in which Mentor Graphics operated, including the development of its new 8.0 generation of software.

The realization, by the early 1990s, that the company's vision detracted from what the company was actually trying to achieve led to the dumping of the vision and its replacement with one that echoed the early beginning of the company: "Our current short-, medium-, and long-term vision is to build things people will buy." This was seen as a more pragmatic vision for a company that had lost its way, caught up in a cycle of visions that were increasingly irrelevant to the core business and which inhibited their ability to make sound business decisions.

Additional Reading

Hollensbe, E., Wookey, C., Hickey, L., and George, G. 2014. Organizations with purpose. *Academy of Management Journal* 57(5):1227– 34. Discusses vision and purpose in terms of the "greater good" and the organization's contribution to society. Argues that an organization's sense of purpose must recognize the interdependence of business and society.

Ibarra, H. 2015. *Act like a leader, think like a leader*. Boston: Harvard Business Review Press. Offers advice on thinking strategically and avoiding the distractions of short-term priorities. Citing George W. Bush and his dismissive comment about "the vision thing,"

Herminia Ibarra argues that "the ability to envision possibilities for the future and to share that vision with others distinguishes leaders from nonleaders" (p. 40).

Kotter, J. P. 2012b. Accelerate! *Harvard Business Review* 90(11):44–52. (Also available in a book with the same title.) Develops his work on transformational change, first published in 1995, and echoes the arguments in his 2012 book *Leading Change*. This article puts vision at the heart of designing, implementing, and accelerating the pace of change: formulate a strategic vision, communicate the vision, and accelerate movement toward the vision. Kotter describes this as a "head and heart, not just head" approach (p. 49).

Roundup   Here is a short summary of the key points that we would like you to take from this chapter, in relation to each of the learning outcomes:

LO 6.1   *Explain the arguments for and against the concept of vision, and how approaches to this issue depend on the image held of managing organizational change.*
Some commentators argue that vision is indispensable, providing direction, purpose, and inspiration, and also strengthening the motivation to accept and become involved in change. Others, however, argue that the concept of vision is abstract and vague, becoming meaningless—and attracting cynicism—when most organizations articulate similarly bland visions that typically incorporate excellence, social responsibility, empowered employees, and delighted customers.

The concept of vision varies with the image of change management that is in use. For example, the director image assumes that responsibility for framing vision lies with senior leaders. The caretaker assumes that an organization's vision is shaped primarily by external forces. The coach facilitates the consultation and co-creation process through which vision is developed by staff across the organization. The nurturer sees visions emerging from the clash of unpredictable forces, and therefore as temporary constructs.

Reflections for the Practicing Change Manager

What criteria do you use in order to decide whether a particular vision or vision statement is likely to be useful in your organization? What other criteria might you wish to take into account?

What is your preference: a short vision statement or a longer vision story? Why? How do you use vision statements or stories?

How do you distinguish vision from mission, planning, and goals? Are these important distinctions? In your organization, how aligned is vision with these other factors? Are there competing visions in your organization? How are these resolved?

What is your experience: are visions more likely to "take" in some organizations or cultural contexts compared with others? Why is this the case? What criteria can you develop to help assess when you should use vision to assist in organizational change?

What process have you used, or seen in use, to craft an effective vision? Do you have a personal preference toward an intuitive or an analytical approach to vision development? Why?

Is there an "inner voice" in your organization? What are the "bread-and-butter" issues? Are there "undiscussable" issues in your organization?

What is your judgement: When do visions fail, and when does their effectiveness fade? Can visions be revitalized? How?

What is your position: Does vision drive change? Does vision help change? Does vision need visionary leaders?

LO 6.2 *Identify the characteristics of effective visions.*
Evidence and experience suggest that, to be effective, visions should be clear, appealing, vivid, ambitious, and attainable, providing a sense of direction and guiding decision making, but also flexible enough to accommodate initiative and change. Effective visions also describe a desirable—perhaps ideal—future for the organization. A further emotional property of the effective vision, although difficult to define, is that it "feels good." Some commentators argue a vision should be expressed in a brief, memorable statement. Others, however, claim that lengthier and more detailed "vision stories" can provide a better frame of reference for change and answer the question that all those who are involved will ask: what will this future mean for me?

LO 6.3 *Assess how the context in which a vision is developed affects its meaning.*
For the purposes of this discussion, "context" includes the organization's culture as well as the external environment. We identified four stereotypical organizational contexts: rigid, bold, overmanaged, and liberated. These contexts vary in terms of degree of acceptance of the need for change, and resource availability. Rigid organizations are characterized by low acceptance and resources. Bold organizations have limited resources but high acceptance. Overmanaged organizations have high resource availability but little acceptance of the need to change. The context in which vision processes are most likely to be effective is the liberated organization, with high acceptance and high resource availability.

National cultures can also be influential. A corporate vision that would be acceptable and effective in Japan, where organizations are more closely linked to national and social interests, would be less acceptable in the United States, where organizations are more preoccupied with financial performance.

LO 6.4 *Apply different methods and processes for developing vision.*
There are many approaches to developing vision, ranging on the familiar continuum from "tell" (the chief executive determines the vision) to "co-create" (everyone participates in the development). There is no "one best way," and choice is influenced by the change management image in use. Leader-dominated methods can be rapid, and may be inspirational, but are not consistent with the concepts of employee empowerment and engagement. Most commentators suggest that co-creation methods, where the role of senior leaders is to "orchestrate" the vision-crafting process, are more likely to produce better visions and more successful change.

Other approaches to crafting vision have been described as intuitive, analytical, and benchmarking. Intuitive approaches rely on imagination and creative imagery: what are our personal and organizational priorities, and what do we need to do to work toward our desired future? An analytical approach links vision to purpose and goals, using questions such as: Who do we serve? What do we do? Where do we place most of our efforts? How do we operationalize those efforts? A benchmarking approach is more externally focused and develops vision in relation to key competitors: What do our competitors do well? How can we do better than them? How should we measure our achievement? What will it be like when those standards have been met?

LO 6.5 *Explain why some visions fail.*
Visions can fail for many reasons: too specific, too vague, too complex, fails to address known problems, detached from the business, unrealistic, or does not offer a clear view of the future. Lack of adaptation to changing circumstances can make a vision obsolete,

contributing to decisions that are not consistent with new environmental conditions and constraints. Visions also fail because of "vision collisions"—the presence of too many competing visions for an organization.

LO 6.6

Explain the arguments concerning the relationship of vision to organizational change.
We explored three key debates. First, does vision drive change, or does vision emerge from the organizational change process? Second, does vision contribute to or hinder the organizational change process? Third, are visions attributes of heroic leaders, or of heroic organizations? With compelling arguments on both sides of these debates, the answers are not clear.

The traditional view sees the vision of the heroic, charismatic leader driving and contributing positively to the organizational change process. There is evidence and argument to challenge that perspective. The importance of charisma and vision may have been exaggerated. Charismatic senior figures perhaps contribute less to sustained organizational effectiveness than embedded visions, core values, and enduring ideologies. Visions are emergent because it is difficult to articulate a clear image of the future at the start of a disruptive transformational change process. Visions can impede change by making strong emotional appeals to the future instead of focusing on current operational problems, and where organizational capabilities are inadequate to achieving the vision.

The change manager must be aware of these debates and tensions and take these considerations into account before embarking on a vision development process at a particular time in a specific context. The weight of commentary, from academic research and management consultants, appears to endorse the value of articulating clear and compelling visions. However, this perspective should not be taken for granted, and a more cautious, skeptical, critical approach is perhaps advisable. The role of and need for vision should be assessed in relation to each specific organizational change situation. What has been effective for one organization, given its history, current challenges, and future aspirations, may not be wholly appropriate for another organization with a different background, a different set of problems, and a different desired future.

References

Ambler, G. 2013. 10 characteristics of an effective vision. Online blog accessed October 14, 2014: http://www.georgeambler.com/10-characteristics-of-an-effective-vision/.

Auster, E. R., Wylie, K. K., and Valente, M. S. 2005. *Strategic organizational change: Building change capabilities in your organization.* New York: Palgrave Macmillan.

Beaver, G. 2000. The significance of strategic vision, mission and values. *Strategic Change* 9(4):205–7.

Belgard, W. P., and Rayner, S. R. 2004. *Shaping the future: A dynamic process for creating and achieving your company's strategic vision.* New York: Amacom.

Boal, K. B., and Hooijberg, R. 2001. Strategic leadership research: Moving on. *Leadership Quarterly* 11(4):515–49.

Collins, J. C., and Porras, J. I. 1991. Organizational vision and visionary organizations. *California Management Review* 34(1):30–52.

Collins, J. C., and Porras, J. I. 1996. Building your company's vision. *Harvard Business Review* 74(5):65–77.

Collins, J. C., and Porras, J. I. 2005. *Built to last: Successful habits of visionary companies*. 2nd ed. New York: HarperCollins.

Craig, N., and Snook, S. A. 2014. From purpose to impact: Figure out your passion and put it to work. *Harvard Business Review* 92(5):104–11.

Davidson, H. 2004. *The committed enterprise: How to make vision, values and branding work*. 2nd ed. London: Routledge.

Deetz, S. A., Tracy, S. J., and Simpson, J. L. 2000. *Leading organizations through transitions: Communication and cultural change*. Thousand Oaks, CA: Sage Publications.

Denning, S. 2004. Telling tales. *Harvard Business Review* 82(5):122–29.

Denning, S. 2005. *The leader's guide to storytelling: Mastering the art and discipline of business narratives*. San Francisco: Jossey-Bass.

Domm, D. R. 2001. Strategic vision: Sustaining employee commitment. *Business Strategy Review* 12(4):39–48.

Ford, J. D., and Pasmore, W. A. 2006. Vision: Friend or foe during change? *Journal of Applied Behavioral Science* 42(2):172–76.

Gardner, W. L., and Avolio, B. J. 1998. The charismatic relationship: A dramaturgical perspective. *Academy of Management Review* 23(1):32–58.

Gerstner, L. V. 2003. *Who says elephants can't dance? Inside IBM's historic turnover*. New York: Harper Business.

Goffee, R., and Jones, G. 2000. Why should anyone be led by you? *Harvard Business Review* 78(5):63–70.

Gratton, L. 1996. Implementing a strategic vision: Key factors for success. *Long Range Planning* 29(3):290–303.

Gupta, R., and Wendler, J. 2005. Leading change: An interview with the CEO of P&G. *McKinsey Quarterly*, July:1–6.

Haines, S. G., Aller-Stead, G., and McKinlay, J. 2005. *Enterprise-wide change: Superior results through systems thinking*. San Francisco: Pfeiffer.

Hamel, G., and Prahalad, C. K. 1989. Strategic intent. *Harvard Business Review* 67(3):2–14.

Harris, L. C., and Ogbonna, E. 1999. The strategic legacy of company founders. *Long Range Planning* 32(3):333–43.

Hay, M., and Williamson, P. 1997. Good strategy: The view from below. *Long Range Planning* 30(5):651–64.

Hilmer, F. G., and Donaldson, L. 1996. *Management redeemed: Debunking the fads that undermine our corporations*. New York: Free Press.

Hinterhuber, H. H., and Popp, W. 1992. Are you a strategist or just a manager? *Harvard Business Review* 70(1):105–13.

Hollensbe, E., Wookey, C., Hickey, L., and George, G. 2014. Organizations with purpose. *Academy of Management Journal* 57(5):1227–34.

Holpp, L., and Kelly, M. 1988. Realizing the possibilities. *Training and Development Journal* 42(9):48–55.

Ibarra, H. 2015. *Act like a leader, think like a leader*. Boston: Harvard Business Review Press.

Jick, T. D. 2001. Vision is 10%, implementation the rest. *Business Strategy Review* 12(4):36–38.

Johnson, G., Whittington, R., and Scholes, K. 2011. *Exploring strategy: Text and cases*. 9th ed. Harlow, Essex: Financial Times Prentice Hall.

Kanter, R. M., Stein, B. A., and Jick, T. D. 1992. *The challenge of organizational change: How companies experience it and leaders guide it*. New York: Free Press.

Kirkpatrick, S. A., Wofford, J. C., and Baum, J. R. 2002. Measuring motive imagery contained in the vision statement. *Leadership Quarterly* 13(2):139–50.

Kolk, A. 2010. Visions & missions of Fortune Global 100. http://www.slideshare.net/openinnovation/visions-missions-of-fortune-global-100, accessed October 14, 2014.

Kotter, J. P. 2006. Transformation: Master three tasks. *Leadership Excellence* 23(1):14.

Kotter, J. P. 2012a. *Leading change*. 2nd ed. Boston: Harvard University Press.

Kotter, J. P. 2012b. Accelerate! *Harvard Business Review* 90(11):44–52.

Landau, D., Drori, I., and Porras, J. 2006a. Vision change in a governmental R&D organization. *Journal of Applied Behavioral Science* 42(2):145–71.

Landau, D., Drori, I., and Porras, J. 2006b. Vision: Friend and foe during change: A rejoinder to reviewers' comments. *Journal of Applied Behavioral Science* 42(2):177–81.

Langeler, G. H. 1992. The vision trap. *Harvard Business Review* 70(2):5–12.

Levin, I. M. 2000. Vision revisited: Telling the story of the future. *Journal of Applied Behavioral Science* 36(1):91–107.

Lewin, K. (ed.). 1951. *Field theory in social science: Selected theoretical papers by Kurt Lewin*. London: Tavistock Publications. (UK edition published 1952, edited by Dorwin Cartwright.)

Lipton, M. 1996. Demystifying the development of an organizational vision. *Sloan Management Review* 37(4):83–92.

Lissack, M., and Roos, J. 2001. Be coherent, not visionary. *Long Range Planning* 54(1):53–70.

Metais, E. 2000. SEB group: Building a subversive strategy. *Business Strategy Review* 11(4):39–47.

Mitchell, C. 2002. Selling the brand inside. *Harvard Business Review* 80(1):99–105.

Nadler, D. A. 1998. *Champions of change: How CEOs and their companies are mastering the skills of radical change*. San Francisco: Jossey-Bass.

Nadler, D. A., and Shaw, R. B. 1995. Beyond the heroic leader. In *Discontinuous Change: Leading Organizational Transformation*, ed. D. A. Nadler, R. B. Shaw, and A. E. Walton (217–31). San Francisco: Jossey-Bass.

Nutt, P. C., and Backoff, R. W. 1997. Crafting vision. *Journal of Management Inquiry* 6(4):308–28.

Pendlebury, J., Grouard, B., and Meston, F. 1998. *The ten keys to successful change management*. London: John Wiley & Sons Ltd.

Pfeffer, J. 2010. Power play. *Harvard Business Review* 88(7/8):84–92.

Quinn, R. E. 1996. *Deep change: Discovering the leader within*. San Francisco: Jossey-Bass.

Raynor, M. E. 1998. That vision thing: Do we need it? *Long Range Planning* 31(3):368–76.

Robbins, H., and Finley, M. 1997. *Why change doesn't work: Why initiatives go wrong and how to try again—and succeed*. London: Orion.

Rogers, C. 2007. *Informal coalitions: Mastering the hidden dynamics of organizational change*. New York: Palgrave Macmillan.

Schoemaker, P. J. H. 1992. How to link strategic vision to core capabilities. *Sloan Management Review* 34(1):67–81.

Scott-Morgan, P., Hoving, E., Smit, H., and Van Der Slot, A. 2001. *The end of change: How your company can sustain growth and innovation while avoiding change fatigue*. New York: McGraw-Hill.

Shaw, R. B. 1995. The essence of discontinuous change: Leadership, identity and architecture. In *Discontinuous change: Leading organizational transformation*, eds. D. A. Nadler, R. B. Shaw, A. E. Walton, and Associates (66–81). San Francisco: Jossey-Bass.

Stace, D. A., and Dunphy, D. 2001. *Beyond the boundaries: Leading and re-creating the successful enterprise*. 2nd ed. Sydney: McGraw-Hill.

Symons, J. 2006. The vision thing. *E.learning Age*, April:18.

Victor, P., and Franckeiss, A. 2002. The five dimensions of change: An integrated approach to strategic organizational change management. *Strategic Change* 11(1):35–42.

Wind, J. W., and Main, J. 1999. *Driving change: How the best companies are preparing for the 21st century*. London: Kogan Page Ltd.

Chapter 7

Change Communication Strategies

Learning objectives

By the end of this chapter you should be able to:

LO 7.1 Identify key elements in the change communication process.

LO 7.2 Understand how gender, power, and emotion affect change communication processes.

LO 7.3 Understand the power of language in influencing responses to change.

LO 7.4 Explain and assess appropriate strategies for communicating change.

LO 7.5 Understand how successful communication processes vary with the type and stage of organizational change.

LO 7.6 Assess the utility of a range of different change communication channels, including applications of social media.

"Let's work on your communication style."

123RF.com/Andrew Grossman

LO 7.1 The Change Communication Process

The ways in which changes are presented and discussed are critical to success. All of the approaches to change management explored in chapters 9 and 10 give communication a central role in the process. Understanding and commitment depend largely on how change proposals are communicated. From their review of the literature on change processes, Karen Whelan-Berry and Karen Somerville (2010) note that communication is one of the most frequently identified change drivers, by explaining the need for change and how change will be achieved. Poor communication is a leading explanation for change failure. The evidence also suggests that change communication should be two-way—telling and listening. Communication is thus important throughout the change process, and not just at the beginning—and it should be resourced accordingly, addressing resistance, encouraging individual adoption and support, highlighting key issues, and sustaining momentum.

Whelan-Berry and Somerville (2010, p. 181) define change-related communication as "Regular two-way communication specifically about the change initiative, its implementation, related successes, challenges and their resolution." With regard to taking the corporate vision to groups and individuals, communication "facilitates employee understanding and engagement" and "addresses employees' questions and concerns through two-way communication, which allows individuals to remain committed to the change. It also ensures that any obstacles are properly identified and removed" (p. 181). To sustain momentum, communication "signals the organization's commitment to the change initiative, communicates successes and challenges, and ongoing change implementation" (p. 181).

Lars Christensen and Joep Cornelissen (2011) offer a novel, counterintuitive perspective on the significance of change communication. They first note that communication has attracted increasing attention due to a number of factors: the nature and consequences of stakeholder communications; the emergence of ideas such as corporate social responsibility, sustainability, and corporate citizenship; and the growing numbers of corporate communication professionals, procedures, and systems. They see communication as "an important force of organizing" and as "the building block of organizations" (p. 398) because the act of communicating constructs or defines the change in the understanding of those who are going to be involved. In other words, change communication is a key part of the process of collective sense-making (see chapter 9).

Change communication, they note, aims to influence the opinions of many different audiences, inside and external to the organization. This suggests that clarity and consistency are important. However, Christensen and Cornelissen (2011, pp. 402–3) argue that organizations have to work with many voices, with different views and ideas (technical term, "polyphony"). In other words, it may often be desirable for change communications to be ambiguous and inconsistent, for the following reason:

> [V]ague and equivocal language allows organizations to talk about themselves in ways that integrate a variety of members and stakeholders without alienating anyone. Too much clarity and consistency in the formulation of "shared values" may actually prevent managers from establishing accord with some corporate audiences. Although writings in corporate communication and branding call for organizations to eliminate ambiguity, ambiguity is

essential in promoting "unified diversity," the ability for differences to coexist within the unity of the organization. Ambiguity and polyphony may even be a conscious management strategy designed to foster identification and reduce tension by allowing different audiences to apply different interpretations to what is seen as one corporate message.

The process of communicating change—what is going to happen and why—can therefore be more complex than it first appears. In this chapter, we explore the communication process and then discuss different communication strategies, before considering the evolving role of social media in corporate communication. First, however, we will consider how images of change management influence communication strategies, and the implications for change managers.

Communication Is Not a "Soft" Function

The American consulting company Towers Watson (2013) argues that communication is key to organizational performance. From a global survey of 650 organizations, they found that those with effective communication practices were three times more likely to show superior financial performance, compared with those that did not use those practices. The best practices were:

1. Helping employees to understand the business
2. Educating employees about organization culture and values
3. Providing information on financial objectives and organizational performance
4. Integrating new employees
5. Communicating how employee actions affect customers
6. Providing information about the value of individuals' total compensation package
7. Asking for rapid feedback from employees about their opinions of the company

Borrowing from consumer marketing, Towers Watson also argue that effective organizations categorize employees into groups based on the value of their skills and on personal characteristics. This approach to employee "segmentation" means that communication strategy can be tailored to focus on behaviors that are critical to performance. The most effective companies pay close attention to employees when they are planning change, evaluating culture, and assessing employee readiness and

the impact that change will have. Middle and front-line managers need to be good at articulating what employees need to do differently to be successful, communicating what change means to individual employees, and creating a sense of ownership about change initiatives.

Three factors in particular now put a premium on "communication effectiveness":

- **Workforce:** Increasingly diverse workforce, with rising expectations of the employment deal
- **The stakes:** The competitive advantage to be gained from "discretionary effort"—the willingness of employees to "go the extra mile" to improve company performance
- **Shorter timelines:** The need to communicate rapidly, driven by developments in technology and globalization, tighter resources, and increased concerns for security

They conclude:

Today, top-performing organizations are building community—fostering the sense that employees at all levels are in it together. These organizations create the opportunity for social interaction using the latest new media technologies, display the appetite and courage to hear from employees, and establish ongoing forums conducive to collaboration rather than top-down communication. Those that do this well typically see better financial performance. (Towers Watson, 2013, p. 9)

Dianne Gayeski and Jennifer Majka (1996) argue that one of the challenges for communicators concerns the expectation of what can be achieved. They argue that an outdated "director" image has dominated our understanding, linking corporate communication with control and manageability. They claim that communication is better understood in terms of chaos and complexity (a "nurturer" image). The nurturer image may decrease the frustration of not being able to control events in the way that a director image assumes. Change managers may be able to shape but not always control the communication of change. More generally, each of the six images of change outlined in chapter 2 is associated with a different strategy for communicating change; see table 7.1.

We will first outline a classic model of the communication process, indicating how language, power, gender, and emotions are central to an understanding of how this operates. We will then consider how this model applies to change communication, and explore the dilemmas facing the manager designing a change communication strategy. Is it possible

TABLE 7.1
Change Images and Communication Purpose

Image	Purpose of Communication
Director	Ensure that people understand what is going to happen and what is required of them. Answer the why, what, who, how, and when questions. Present the "value proposition" of the change. Modify leadership style and information to "fit" the type of change and organizational levels affected. Avoid "spray and pray" methods, which lead to message overload. Do not distort the message.
Navigator	Outline the nature of the change, paying attention to the range of interests affected, power relationships, and actions that could disrupt the change. Problems identified can thus be addressed, and the change "replotted" if necessary to generate the best outcomes in the situation. To win staff over, "tell and sell" communication methods are appropriate.
Caretaker	Let people know the "why" of the changes, their inevitability, and how best to cope and survive. This involves the use of reactive communication methods, recognizing employee concerns and responding accordingly ("identify and reply").
Coach	Ensure that people share similar values, and understand what actions are appropriate to those values. Model consistency in actions and words. The director "gets the word out"; the coach "gets buy-in" to change by drawing on values and positive emotions. Team-based communications are effective (not top-down led by chief executive). Key messages are emphasized to check understanding and encourage two-way dialogue ("underscore and explore").
Interpreter	Give employees a sense of "what is going on" through storytelling and metaphors. Recognize the multiple sense-making that occurs in different groups with regard to change. Present a persuasive account of the change to ensure that as many people as possible will have a common understanding. Recognize that not everyone will accept the change story. Aim to provide the dominant account using "rich" personal and interactive communications (media richness is discussed below).
Nurturer	Reinforce the view that change processes cannot always be predicted, and that creative and innovative outcomes can be achieved, even though few in the organization could have anticipated these.

to communicate too much? How can communication strategy be tailored to the type of change, and to the phases of the change process? Should the aim be to "get the word out" or the "get buy-in," or both? Where should responsibility for communicating change lie? The different images in table 7.1 are likely to offer different answers to these questions. Finally, as explained earlier, we will then assess the use of different media for communicating change, including the evolving use of different forms of social networking technologies.

Modelling the Communication Process

Interpersonal communication typically involves much more than the simple transmission of information. Pay close attention to the next person who asks you what time it is. You will often be able to tell how they are feeling, and about why they need to know—if they are in a hurry, perhaps, or if they are anxious or nervous, or bored with waiting. In other words, their question has a purpose or a meaning. Although it is not always stated directly, we can often infer that meaning from the context and from their behavior. The same considerations apply to your response. Your reply suggests, at least, a willingness to be helpful, may imply friendship, and may also indicate that you share the same concern as the person asking the question ("We are going to be late"; "When does the film start?"). However, your reply can also indicate frustration and annoyance: "Five minutes since the last time you asked me!" Communication thus involves the transmission of both information and meaning.

This process of exchange is illustrated in figure 7.1, which illustrates the main components of interpersonal communication. This model is based on the work of Claude Shannon and Warren Weaver (1949), who were concerned with signal processing in electronic systems, rather than with organizational communication.

At the heart of this model, we have a *transmitter* sending a *message* through an appropriate *channel* to a *receiver*. We will consider the range of change communication channels later. It is helpful to think of the way in which the transmitter phrases and expresses the message as a *coding* process. The success of communication depends on

FIGURE 7.1
Exchanging Meaning: A Model of the Communication Process

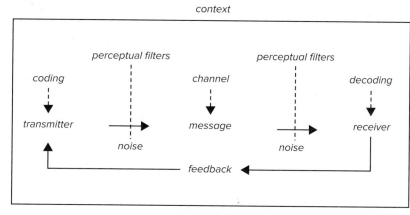

the accuracy of the receiver's *decoding*; did the receiver understand the language used, and also tone and implications of the message. *Feedback* is therefore critical, to check understanding. Communication often fails where transmitters and receivers have different frames of reference and do not share experience and understanding, even if they share a common language. We make judgements—which may or may not be accurate—about the honesty, integrity, trustworthiness, and credibility of others, and decode their messages and act on them accordingly. When communicating details of a major change initiative, therefore, it cannot be assumed that all of the recipients of the message will have the same understanding as each other, and as the transmitter.

Perceptual filters also play a role here, particularly affecting our decoding. This can involve, for example, a readiness or predisposition to hear, or not to hear, particular kinds of information. Preoccupations that are diverting our attention can also filter information. Past experience affects the way in which we see things today, and can influence what we transmit and how, and what we receive. In an organizational setting, people may have time to reflect, or they may be under time pressure, or experience "communication overload," which again means that some content may be filtered out.

The physical, social, and cultural *context* in which change communication takes place is also significant. In organizations where staff are widely dispersed across a number of locations, the ability to share and compare views is more difficult than when everyone is in the one place. The logistics of communicating with a large number of dispersed staff can be complex and costly. The casual remark by a colleague across a café table ("We could all be laid off by the end of the year") could be dismissed with a laugh. The same remark made by a manager in a formal planning meeting could be a source of alarm. If an organization's culture emphasizes openness and transparency, staff may become suspicious if communication is less informative than expected. However, staff may also become suspicious if management (without a good explanation) suddenly start to share large amounts of information openly in a culture that has in the past been less transparent.

Context is particularly important when considering change communication, as this can influence how receivers will decode a message. One aspect of an organization's context that is critical in this respect is past history. Change communication is more likely to be welcome in an organization with a track record of successful changes than in one where past changes have been seen as ineffective or damaging. Current circumstances are also a key feature of the communication context. Is change a positive response to business growth and development, or a defensive approach to problems that will lead to budget and staffing cuts? If staff feel that they have been misled by management in the past concerning the goals and consequences of change, that perception is likely to have an influence on the decoding of further communication concerning change proposals.

When designing a communication strategy, it is therefore important to assess how aspects of the context could affect the coding and decoding of the message, and to design the message content and channels accordingly. Terry Nelson and Helene Coxhead (1997) highlight three particular problems to consider when designing change communications:

Message overload: More new information is provided more quickly than recipients can process.

Message distortion: Intentional or unintentional misinterpretation when transmitting or receiving the message.

Message ambiguity: As noted earlier, ambiguity allows different interpretations, but this should not exceed recipients' ability to tolerate ambiguity (which can be reduced by anxiety).

These problems can be avoided by adopting a common language with regard to the change, and where top management consistently model the desired behaviors. Enhancing employee involvement and self-esteem, and using specialist staff to monitor the change process, can also help to reduce communication errors.

Anything that interferes with a communication signal is called *noise* by electronics experts, and this applies to interpersonal and organizational communication, too. This does not just refer to the sound of equipment, or other people talking. Noise includes coding and decoding problems and errors, perceptual filters, and any other distractions that damage the integrity of the communication channel, including issues arising from the context. Relationships can introduce noise, affecting the style and content of conversation (formal or informal) and what we are prepared to share. Status differences can introduce noise; we do not reveal to the boss what we discuss with colleagues. Motives, emotions, and health can also constitute noise; coding and decoding are affected by anxiety, pressure, stress, and also by levels of enthusiasm and excitement. This last point is particularly significant, as change communication itself can, of course, generate anxiety and stress, or stimulate excitement.

LO 7.2 Gender, Power, and Emotion

The basic communication model that we have discussed can help to explain why communication sometimes breaks down. However, we also need to understand the impact of gender, power, and emotion on communication in general, and on change communication in particular.

Gender

Gender differences also affect the communication process. Here are two examples:

Confidence and boasting. Women tend to emphasize their doubts and uncertainty, but men tend to express greater confidence and play down their doubts.

Asking questions. Women are more likely to ask questions than men; the downside is that male managers may interpret women as knowing less than their male peers.

An assessment by a male manager of how well a woman is coping with change, compared with male colleagues, may thus conclude: "She seems very uncertain since she is always asking questions." However, this assessment may have more to do with gender differences related to a willingness to question (about the change) than to real differences in attitude toward the change itself.

Deborah Tannen (1995, p. 141) also observes that even the apparently simple choice of which pronoun to use can influence who gets the credit:

> In my research in the workplace, I heard men say "I" in situations where I heard women say "We." For example, one publishing company executive said, "I'm hiring a new manager. I'm going to put him in charge of my marketing division," as if he owned the corporation. In stark contrast, I recorded women saying "we" when referring to work that they alone had done. One woman explained that it would sound too self-promoting to claim credit in an obvious way by saying, "I did this." Yet she expected—sometimes vainly—that others would know it was her work and would give her the credit she did not claim for herself.

Other gender differences relate to how feedback is given and received, how compliments are exchanged, and whether the communication is direct or indirect. Kate Ludeman and Eddie Erlandson (2004) argue that many senior managers are "alpha" males: fast thinkers who have opinions on every topic, who are analytical, data-driven, impatient, and think that they are smarter than most other people. As a result, their communication style can intimidate those around them. Alpha males are not good listeners, they miss subtleties, and they put others under extreme pressure to perform.

The alpha male communication style can be softened with coaching (see exercise 7.2), but this is not an easy transformation. When a male manager changes to a communication style that is not direct, competitive, confrontational, and authoritative, they can be seen as "going soft," becoming "touchy-feely," and "losing their grip" (Linstead et al., 2005, p. 543). The change manager may therefore need to find a balance between maintaining credibility with colleagues while adopting a communication style that is appropriate to the change context and to those who are involved.

Power

The use of language can also reflect underlying power and gender relationships—factors that can also interfere with the change communication process (as with communications in general). For example, the manner in which change managers seek staff comments on proposals can reinforce power differentials. Telling staff to provide input may result in responses different from those obtained when the request conveys respect for their opinions. Power differences are normally a barrier to communication. Those who are more powerful may not wish to disclose information that could make them appear to be less powerful or that could weaken their power base. Those who are less powerful may not wish to disclose information that could potentially be used against them.

The term "power tells" describes the various signs and clues that indicate how powerful someone is—or how powerful they want to be (Collett, 2004). The power tells of dominant individuals include:

- sitting and standing with legs far apart (men);
- appropriating the territory around them by placing their hands on their hips;
- using open postures;

- using invasive hand gestures;
- smiling less, because a smile is an appeasement gesture;
- establishing visual dominance by looking away from the other person while speaking, implying that they do not need to be attentive;
- speaking first, and dominating the conversation thereafter;
- using a lower vocal register, and speaking more slowly;
- being more likely to interrupt others, more likely to resist interruption by others.

The power tells of submissive individuals include:

- modifying speech style to sound more like the person they are talking to;
- more frequently hesitating, using lots of "ums" and "ers";
- adopting closed postures;
- clasping hands, touching face and hair (self-comfort gestures);
- blushing, coughing, dry mouth, heavy breathing, heavy swallowing, increased heart rate, lip biting, rapid blinking, and sweating are "leakage tells" which reveal stress and anxiety.

We can thus "read" the power signals of others. More importantly, however, change managers may need to control their own "tells" in order to appear less dominant and less powerful, particularly when communicating change in a manner that will encourage staff feedback, engagement, and support.

Emotion

Communication models have been criticized for ignoring the role of emotions in organizational change, focusing instead on the rational and cognitive dimensions of communication. Nevertheless, change managers need to be aware of, to understand, and where appropriate to respond to emotional responses to change. Emotions can interfere with the communication process, but emotions can also be a positive resource, contributing to staff willingness, commitment, and support for change.

Shaul Fox and Yair Amichai-Hamburger (2001) emphasize the need for congruence between cognitive understanding of change and emotional perceptions. Emotional appeals communicate vision and urgency and can aid the formation of powerful change coalitions. Table 7.2 summarizes the range of practical steps that can help establish the "positive emotions" that generate "excitement and anticipation" around a change program. Michele Williams (2007) suggests that the anticipation that change will be personally threatening or harmful can generate negative emotions and a loss of trust in management, thus making cooperation and engagement difficult to achieve. Change managers can avoid this situation by:

Perspective taking: Thinking about how others are likely to think and feel about a change.
Threat-reducing behavior: Engaging in intentional, interpersonal interactions with staff to minimize their perceptions that changes are likely to lead to harm for them.
Reflection: Self-evaluation to reduce the emergence of negative emotions and to identify corrective actions where necessary.

TABLE 7.2
How to Get Emotional Commitment to Change

Address These Issues	How This Is Done
The Core Message	
Emotional arguments	Positive words signal future success; negative terms indicate what will happen if change fails
Metaphors	The use of familiar metaphors can help staff to picture the future and make it appear less strange or unusual
Packaging the Message	
Emotional mode	Capture attention with music, color, slogans, pictures—but avoid excessive use of any one mode
Humor	Humor can reduce the gap, and tension, between manager and staff
Display emotion	Use feelings, tone of voice, body language, and facial expressions to generate warmth and confidence
Change leader characteristics	Messages are perceived as more credible and attractive when they are consistent with leader behavior
Change Manager Behavior	
Fairness and justice	Decisions should be seen to be fair and follow legitimate, recognized procedures, with opportunities to raise issues
Setting	
Group dynamics	Use groups and teams to strengthen commitment to change
Ceremonies	Stimulate emotions and reinforce the benefits of change with celebrations that also signal departure from the past
Atmosphere	Speak in warm, informal terms, to produce positive feelings toward the change (not formal and cold)

Source: Based on Fox and Amichai-Hamburger (2001, pp. 87–92).

Understanding the emotional side of change is important. However, whether change managers can produce positive emotional responses to change is open to question for four reasons. First, there is an underlying assumption that emotions are produced and contained within the organization. The impact of external factors (how friends and family talk about a change, how change is presented in the media) can be overlooked. Second, an underlying assumption is that all people respond in the same way to the same emotional appeals. This view overlooks differences in work motivation, and how these influence perceptions of change. With increasing workforce diversity, we also have to be aware of cultural differences in modes of emotional expression and response. Third, not all change managers have the skills or the credibility to manage the emotional responses of staff to change, and to achieve positive emotional responses. Finally, it may be easier to achieve positive emotional responses to some (exciting, developmental, progressive) changes and not others (routine, tedious, defensive).

Table 7.3 summarizes the main barriers to successful organizational change communication.

TABLE 7.3
Barriers to Effective Organizational Change Communication

Language	Choice of words and tone of message can lead to misunderstandings and misinterpretations
Gender differences	Men and women use different communication styles, which can lead to misunderstanding; men tend to talk more; women tend to listen, and ask more questions
Power differences	Research shows that employees distort upward communication, and that superiors often have a limited understanding of subordinates' roles, experiences, and problems
Context	Organization culture and history, as well as physical setting, can color the way in which change communications are transmitted and interpreted
Cultural diversity	Different cultures have different expectations concerning formal and informal communication; lack of awareness of those norms creates misunderstanding
Emotion	Emotional arousal interferes with message transmission and receipt, and emotional responses to change communication can be negative (anxiety, anger) or positive (exciting, stimulating)

The communication process appears to be simple, but it is prone to errors arising on both sides of the exchange. We cannot confidently assume that receivers will always decode our messages in a way that gives them the meaning that we intended to transmit. Communication is central to organizational change, but this claim has practical implications. It seems that organizations function better where:

- communications are open,
- relationships are based on mutual understanding and trust,
- interactions are based on cooperation rather than competition,
- people work together in teams, and
- decisions are reached in a participative way.

These features are not universal, and are not present in all countries, cultures—or organizations.

LO 7.3   Language Matters: The Power of Conversation

As we discussed at the beginning of this chapter, communication does not just involve a transfer of information or ideas. The language that we use to describe reality also helps to create—or to constitute—that reality for others; communication thus involves the creation and exchange of *meaning*. For example, Deborah Tannen (1995) points out that language reflects and reinforces underlying social relationships. She offers

There's Nothing Like a Good Story

As chief executive at Hewlett-Packard (HP), Mark Hurd wanted the company to develop a more sales-oriented culture. To reinforce this message, he told the story about how, in his first week as a newcomer at NCR, he made a successful sale to a San Antonio tractor maker for some printing equipment. However, he failed to fill in the order form correctly and the person in the NCR billing department refused to process the order because of a minor mistake that he had made in the paperwork. When Hurd informed his manager about the situation, his manager phoned the guy in billing:

"Hey, did my man just come down here with an order?" asked the manager as Hurd listened. "The next time he does, I want you to get your ass out from behind your desk, and I want you to shake his hand. And I want you to thank him for keeping your ass employed. If there's anything wrong with the order, I want you to fix it so that he can get about the job of continuing to keep you employed." (Lachinsky, 2006, p. 93)

the following illustrative statements, which each require the same response but signal different information about the relationship between those involved:

> *"Sit down!"* This signals higher status of the person uttering the statement, perhaps indicating anger, and informal conversation is not appropriate.
> *"I would be pleased if you would sit down."* This signals respect, or possibly sarcasm, depending on the tone of voice and the situation.
> *"You must be so tired. Why don't you sit down?"* This signals either a concern and closeness for the person, or condescension.

Language is particularly important in organizational change contexts due to the sensitivity of the issues ("Will I lose my job?") and the possibility for confusion ("That is not what management said last week"). The choice of language that the change manager uses can therefore affect whether proposals will be seen as exciting or routine, as clear or muddled, as progressive or mundane, as threatening or developmental. These meanings can be shared in documentation and through formal meetings. However, for the change manager, the understanding of change is typically shared in a range of formal and informal meetings and conversations. Even brief, unplanned, casual conversations can be powerful channels for exchanges of ideas and understanding between the change manager and those who are involved in the proposals. Silence during a conversation also sends signals.

Managing change also involves different conversations at different stages of the change process. Conversations across those stages, however, must have "linguistic coherence," and managers should try to align their use of language with the type of change that is being implemented. It is also important to create a shared language of change among the stakeholders who are involved.

Talking in Stages

Jeffrey and Laurie Ford (1995) do not see communication simply as a tool for producing intentional change; rather, it is through communication that change happens. In other words, "the management of change can be understood to be the management of conversations" (p. 566). Drawing on "speech act theory," they argue that change takes place through four types of conversation.

Initiative conversations draw attention to the need for change, whether reactive or proactive, and can take the form of:

> assertion "We have to bring the finances under control."
> request "Can you restructure your division to achieve greater operating efficiencies?"
> declaration "We are going to increase market share."

Conversations for understanding help others to appreciate the change issues and the problems that need to be addressed, through three main elements:

> specifying the "conditions of satisfaction" that will make the change successful: "We need to make sure that there are no more than two customer complaints per thousand units produced"
> enabling the involvement of those affected by the change
> confirming interpretations and enabling shared meaning and understanding

Conversations for performance focus on producing the change, and involve the action stage when:

> promises are made
> obligations are entered into
> accountabilities are established
> deadlines are set

Conversations for closure signal the completion of the change, and facilitate the movement of people into new projects and initiatives. These conversations involve:

> acknowledgements
> celebrations
> rewards

Breakdowns in change and conversations occur when:

- Initiative conversations are held with people who are not in a position to proceed with the change.
- There is a lack of shared understandings about the intended changes and the expectations for the "conditions of satisfaction."
- There is shared understanding, but performance conversations do not take place, so people do not know who is accountable for specific actions.
- Requests for action and performance are not rigorous and fail to specify intentions regarding results and deadlines.
- Closure conversations do not take place, and people feel that they are still involved with the change, while being asked to move on to new initiatives.

Ford and Ford (1995) emphasize that change managers need skills in handling change conversations, while recognizing that not all change conversations take place in a linear manner; some stages may be skipped during the process. The practicing change manager thus needs to consider the following:

- Where managers are engaged in multiple change processes, there will be issues relating to how smoothly they are able to transition themselves among the different conversations.
- The stages of the conversations may be open to multiple interpretations among participants. Where managers assume that some conversations are complete and that it is appropriate to move on to another stage in the change conversations, others may have differing views.
- It is not clear that all managers are able to be trained or are able to exhibit all of these conversation skills successfully. For example, some managers may have more affinity with initiative conversations rather than performance conversations, and so on.
- Change managers need to confront the notion of power. The willingness of participants to be involved meaningfully in each of the four change conversations may be affected by significant power imbalances. Some understandings may thus need to be enforced rather than shared.

Talking Coherently

John Sillince (1999) also emphasizes the role of language in change conversations, focusing on the coherence of change conversations. Drawing on linguistic and political science theories, he outlines four dominant language forms that are found in organizational change conversations:

ideals	which express preferences
appeals	which seek support
rules	which seek to direct the behavior of others
deals	which serve as a form of bargaining and exchange

An overreliance on one of these language forms can lead to problems. For example, a focus on deals rather than ideals may encourage an individualist culture. Sillince (1999, p. 492) argues that "motivating change during the early stage of organizational change requires the communication of appeals for support and statements of goals or ideals, and that the later stage requires the communication of rules and the negotiation of deals." He illustrates this with the restructuring at AT&T in the 1970s and 1980s. Sillince (1999, p. 499) concludes that, despite the absence of a planned communication process, a logical sequence of language forms can be detected:

> moving from attacking current ideals in 1973 (corresponding to the "unfreezing" stage in Lewin, 1951), to supporting new ideals in 1973–1978, to attacking current rules or the lack of rules in 1979–1980, and increasingly supporting new ideals and new rules after 1981 (the "change" stage in Lewin, 1951). The few deals referred to occur after 1981. Appeals tend to be promises and warning before change takes place and requests for support and exhortations to action during and after change.

In comparing successful changes at AT&T with less successful changes at Chrysler, Sillince notes that the former had a linguistic coherence that was lacking at Chrysler. He

IBM's Script for Offshoring Jobs

Internal IBM documents reported in *The Wall Street Journal* in January 2004 suggested that IBM was planning to move high-cost programming jobs offshore to countries such as Brazil, India, and China, where labor costs were lower (Bulkeley, 2004). Rather than pay $56 per hour in the United States, the documents indicated that a comparable programming job would cost only $12.50 per hour in China. The documents also revealed that IBM was aware that this "offshoring" process was a sensitive issue and provided managers with a draft "script" for presenting information to affected staff.

One memo instructed managers to ensure that any written communication to employees should first be "sanitized" by communications and human resource staff ("Do not be transparent regarding the purpose/intent"), and also directed that managers should not use terms such as "onshore" and "offshore." Part of the "suggested script" for informing staff that their jobs were being moved offshore was to say, "This is not a resource action" (an IBM euphemism for being laid off), and that the company would try to find them jobs elsewhere. This script also proposed that the news should be conveyed to staff by saying, "This action is a statement about the rate and pace of change in this demanding industry. It is in no way a comment on the excellent work you have done over the years." And, "For people whose jobs are affected by this consolidation, I understand this is difficult news."

concludes that linguistic coherence in the use of different forms of language at different stages is a hallmark of successful change. (See box, "IBM's Script for Offshoring Jobs.") Sillince gives us a macro-level analysis, in which different change phases unfold over lengthy periods of time. It is therefore interesting that he sees these phases as underpinned by Lewin's (1951) model of unfreezing, moving, and refreezing. As we have discussed in previous chapters, however, change is rarely a tidy, orderly, sequential process, and it may be difficult to maintain coherence across different chaotic and nonsequential stages. Nevertheless, this perspective alerts the change manager to the different linguistic modes that are available when communicating change, and highlights the option of switching from one linguistic mode to another if appropriate when, for example, one approach is not having the desired effect.

Aligning Language with the Change

Robert Marshak (1993) argues that change fails when the imagery and metaphors used by managers are not aligned with the type of change being implemented. This lack of alignment confuses those who are involved in the change. He describes a situation where a large corporation had to reposition fundamentally its business due to a decline in the government contracts that had been a mainstay of the company. Unfortunately, when communicating the need for this change to middle management, the chief executive's explanation was based on the need to build on the company's past success, as a way of developing into the future. Instead of shifting the company in radically new directions, middle managers continued to develop past practices. The imagery of "developing" was not aligned with the "transformational" change that was necessary.

To avoid such problems, Marshak advises managers to align their language closely with the planned change. He identifies four different images of change and the language appropriate to each:

Machine imagery	Based on a "fix and maintain" view, portraying the organization as "broken," and the change as a "fix." The change manager is the repairperson; terms such as *repair*, *adjust*, and *correct* are aligned to this type of change.
Developmental imagery	Based on a "build and develop" view, in which the organization has to improve performance by building on past and current practices. The change manager is trainer or coach; terms such as *nurturing*, *growing*, and *getting better* are aligned to this type of change.
Transitional imagery	Based on a "move and relocate" view, in which change is designed to alter how the organization operates, for example by introducing online sales and services. The change manager is guide or planner; terms such as *moving forward* and *leaving the past behind* are aligned to this type of change.
Transformational imagery	Based on a "liberate and re-create" view, where change involves reinvention, or radical change to the nature of the business or market in which the organization trades. The change manager is visionary, helping to discover new possibilities; terms such as *reinvention*, *re-creation*, and *adopting a new paradigm* are aligned to this change.

These insights concerning the need to align language and change highlight how change managers can easily communicate mixed signals with regard to what is required. Change managers are thus advised to reflect on how their metaphors for describing and communicating about their organizations and changes may be trapped and influenced by dominant or root metaphors. New insights, actions, and unanticipated directions can be generated by adopting new language and new metaphors (see "The NASCAR Model"). We must also recognize that managers may not always be able to introduce metaphors that will necessarily resonate with staff throughout an organization. New metaphors often compete with dominant

The NASCAR Model

Apparelizm (pseudonym) is a Fortune 500 retailer, with over 1,000 stores nationwide, which began a major organizational change effort resulting from a review of its strategy. As part of the effort to build support, the change team drew from a NASCAR analogy, NASCAR being a sport well understood and liked by many of the staff. The change team argued that store staff were like a NASCAR race crew. Past store practice was likened to a race crew member driving the car, pumping the gas, and changing the tires during the race. A "pit crew" would do the ordering and receiving of goods and put them on the shelves after they arrived. The "drivers" would be responsible for helping customers as they moved around the store. The "racetrack manager" would monitor the traffic flow in the store, removing the "multicar pileups" that happened when sales associates/"drivers" congregated together (rather than servicing customers). The metaphor was further extended to a parallel between the need for NASCAR racing teams "to be fast, responsive, and knowledgeable" if they were to be successful. A similar point was made with regard to the need for excellent communication between the "drivers," "pit crew," and so on.

The metaphor worked well. Staff understood and accepted the analogy and saw how the changes would help them to work more like an effective racing team (based on Roberto and Levesque, 2005).

logics, embedded ways of operating, ingrained ways of perceiving the organizational world, and formal policies and procedures. Change managers need to focus on redesigning policies, systems, and processes that conflict with the language of the change. For example, if change concerns "leaving the past behind," then transformational metaphors may be weakened if, say, compensation and performance appraisal systems remain based on past practice.

Creating a Common Change Language

Managers are not alone in using—or misusing—terms and phrases in ways that cause amusement and confusion. It is important to check the assumption that different individuals and groups involved in change have a shared view of the terms—the language—being used. (See "Misused Terminology?")

Choice of terms has a significant impact on the way in which an issue such as organizational change is understood by others. Problems will thus arise when those who are responsible for managing a change cannot among themselves adopt a "common language." Checking the shared meanings of concepts in use is thus important in order to avoid confusion and conflict. For example, Loizos Heracleous and Michael Barrett (2001) attribute the failed implementation of an electronic risk management system in the London insurance market to the lack of shared language and meaning among the parties that were involved. Over a period of five years, they studied the language of the main stakeholders, including market leaders, brokers, and underwriters, and also observed how the language of those stakeholders changed over time.

Misused Terminology?

Term	Meaning?
Emergent strategy	Justifies a lack of strategic thinking; if a strategy does emerge, we do not have to do anything
Learning organization	We were right to neglect training; all we have to do is tell employees that we like them to learn for themselves
Empowerment	A magic word which, if we repeat it often enough, will make a downsized and delayered structure work without any further effort from us
Culture	Culture is what we say we will change when we cannot think of anything else to do

Source: Based on Hussey (1998).

Heracleous and Barrett distinguish between "surface-level" communication and the underpinning "deep discursive structures." Deep structures include interpretive schemes, central themes, root metaphors, and rhetorical strategies. A focus on the different discursive structures explains the resistance of brokers and underwriters to the new system, and the failure of the project:

> [W]e saw stakeholder groups talking past each other, rather than to each other, because of their almost diametrically opposed discourses, at both the deeper structure levels and communicative action levels, and their lack of common ground on which to base a dialogue. (Heracleous and Barrett, 2001, p. 774)

Culture, Language, and Change in General Motors Poland

General Motors (GM) began to develop its Opel Polska car plant on a greenfield site in Poland in 1996. One of the key tasks for management was to develop working practices consistent with a car plant that could be competitive in the twenty-first century. Although part of the challenge was due to the lack of exposure to competition during decades as part of the Soviet bloc, there seemed to be a more fundamental issue rooted in hundreds of years of Polish culture. A high value was placed on *fantazja* (imaginativeness), which was directly opposed to the idea of being systematic or well organized—the latter being equated with boring and unnecessary. Fantazja was also associated with independence and freedom from subjugation—the opposite to following standard operating procedures.

The practices designed for the new plant clearly required a high level of discipline and coordination. Managers were concerned that while fantazja could contribute to the continuous improvement processes that were to be part of the plant's operating

model, the cultural tolerance for disorder could be damaging. There was no shortage of Polish workers: 46,000 applied for 1,800 positions in the new plant, which meant that the company was in a very powerful position (but threats of job loss for noncompliance were not to be used). The European managers met with their new employees (along with translators). Although cultural values and linguistics appeared to lie at the heart of employee resistance to GM's working practices, the solution was also found in the same roots. As in English, the term "development" in Polish can mean "to start something" and also "to progress." In turn, "to progress" is the opposite of stagnation. For the Poles, stagnation is something that lacks fantazja. Through discussion, "disciplined organization" was positively reframed using concepts and values that were already part of Polish culture. By 2000, the plant had the best quality and performance figures of all GM plants worldwide (based on Dobosz-Bourne and Jankowicz, 2006).

Change managers thus need to understand the deep discursive structures that underpin the surface communication of different stakeholders, in order to support major organizational and technology changes. Surface agreement may be artificial and tenuous where there is a lack of understanding of those deeper structures that may explain inertia or resistance. Although they acknowledge that understanding the interpretive schemes of different stakeholders will not guarantee success, Heracleous and Barrett (2001, p. 774) conclude that "Uncovering and appreciating other stakeholders' deep structures, however, can be of help in avoiding dead ends and self-defeating compromises in change implementation."

LO 7.4 Change Communication Strategies

The Importance of High-Quality Communication

Researchers have focused on the importance of effective communication with employees during change. Empirical research has demonstrated that high-quality change communication increases acceptance, openness, and commitment to change. Furthermore, the failure

to provide sufficient information or providing poor-quality information can result in a number of problems, including cynicism about change and widespread rumors, which often exaggerate the negative aspects of change (Rafferty et al., 2013, p. 122).

In this section, we will focus on the communication strategy questions facing the change manager: Can you communicate too much, how to get "buy-in," when to use communication strategies other than "spray and pray," and who will take responsibility for communicating the change? We will also explore two contingency approaches to communication strategy, one based on the type of change and the other related to different phases of the change process.

In spite of its importance, change communication is an issue that many organizations overlook. A survey of 100 UK employers (Wolff, 2010) found that only 40 percent had formal communication strategies. However, companies with formal strategies were four times more likely to agree that this contributed to their success. The main goals of internal communications were keeping staff informed of changes and strategies, staff engagement, and providing information about policies and procedures. The most popular communication methods were department meetings, one-on-one meetings with line managers, team meetings, letters and memos, and email. Social media were unpopular: online video, instant messaging, internal blogging, wikis, Skype, and podcasts were used by very few organizations. There was no one best communication method. Face-to-face was seen as more effective than print or computer-based methods. Intranet sites were only used for information on policies, procedures, and legal requirements. Top management briefings were considered best in terms of employee engagement, opinion surveys the best way to encourage feedback, and meetings with line managers the best way to improve individual performance. What are the best ways to communicate change?

Can You Communicate Too Much?

The claim that "we need more communication around here" is common. Many commentators argue that it is not possible to overcommunicate, but this view is not shared by all change managers and researchers. Geigle and Bailey (2001) describe a reengineering project that affected 400 employees in a federal agency. The change team was committed to open, organization-wide communication regarding the project, to a degree that was unprecedented in the organization's history. The outcome of this strategy was change recipient anxiety and cynicism about the change, for two reasons.

First, staff suffered information overload, one saying, "It's almost like they know with all this information, we won't read it." Information overload can be problematic in organizations where employees are already in receipt of a high volume of other information. Second, the agency's communication strategy did not involve real participation. The change team had no strategy for incorporating feedback into the change program: "I feel like they may be informing me of everything that's going on, but I have absolutely zero say in what goes on." Geigle and Bailey (2001) conclude that there may be symbolic importance in pursuing an open communication strategy, but that this is not sufficient for success. They argue that a change team is at its best when acting not as reporters, but as sense-makers, facilitating understanding for change recipients and helping them to identify (filter and distill) what is important. This distinction is instructive: from her research, Laurie Lewis (1999) argues that change managers act more often as reporters, disseminating information, than as sense-makers, seeking and processing feedback during planned change processes. For a more detailed exploration of the perspective that sense-making brings to organizational change, see chapter 9.

Getting the Word Out, or Getting Buy-In?

The federal agency example illustrates the difference between "getting the word out" (providing information about a change) as opposed to "getting staff buy-in" (support and involvement). Both are important (Guaspari, 1996). We cannot always assume that management alone has all the good ideas concerning what is required to make a change successful. We do know, however, that those who are going to be affected by change need to be informed about what is happening, and that when frontline staff are allowed to take the initiative to drive change, the success rate is higher (Keller et al., 2010).

Communication designed to generate "buy-in" involves capturing from staff information that will be useful in delivering the change, identifying what is important to them, and discovering what they see as the costs and benefits. It is therefore important to identify a clear "value proposition" that addresses the interests and motives of individual staff. Examples include (Guaspari, 1996, p. 35):

> "As a result of the new skills you'll learn in order to perform your job in the newly reengineered organization, you will have significantly increased your value internally and your marketability externally."
>
> "The work will be backbreaking. The pace will be relentless. You stand to make a ton of money."
>
> "We are making these changes to enable us to rewrite the rules in our industry, to improve by orders of magnitude the value we can create for our customers."

Getting "buy-in" depends on what people are being asked to purchase. Do they see this as having personal value? Have the changes been adequately justified? The evidence indicates that explaining and justifying the need for change relates positively to perceived fairness with regard to both the change process and the outcomes. From his study of 183 employees in companies that had relocated to Chicago, Joseph Daly (1995) found that management's justification was particularly important when the move was viewed unfavorably by staff. However, that justification was not as important where the move was welcomed. Daly (1995, p. 426) concludes that some managers may thus be tempted to avoid explaining change decisions to employees if they think that the change outcomes will be welcome anyway. However, that may not apply to staff judgements about the change process.

> [E]mployees are likely to expect an explanation for a change decision regardless of whether the outcomes are positive or negative. If those employees are not given an explanation, they are likely to feel that the procedures used to make and implement the decision were unfair, leading in many cases to resentment against the decision process and the decision makers.

Daly's (1995) findings are consistent with other research, which has found that managers are more likely to be trusted by staff when they:

- provide accurate information and feedback;
- adequately explain the basis for their decisions;
- use open communication, enabling an exchange of ideas.

Thirteen Points for an Effective Communication Strategy

1. Convince top management that communication is important.
2. Build alliances across the organization to support initiatives.
3. Recognize that no one method will be effective.
4. Use a mix of approaches and use all available channels where relevant.
5. Target communication to the audience; different methods for shop floor and managers.
6. Respect cultural diversity and vary approaches accordingly.
7. Make sure that messages are consistent, over time and between audiences.
8. Ensure clarity of message and keep things simple.
9. Train managers in communication skills.
10. Develop and sustain two-way communication, dialogue, and feedback.
11. Ensure that employees feel that they can say what they think without discomfort.
12. Ensure that communication is built into the planning stages of all activities.
13. Review communication initiatives to check what has worked, what hasn't, and why

Source: Cannell (2010), pp. 2–3.

Beyond "Spray and Pray"

Phillip Clampitt and colleagues (2000) locate communication strategies on the continuum shown in figure 7.2. At one end of this continuum is "spray and pray," transmitting lots of information, to little effect. At the other extreme, "withhold and uphold" offers little information, and is also ineffective. All five strategies on this continuum are summarized in table 7.4. The authors argue that "underscore and explore," which involves dialogue, is more likely to succeed, by allowing staff concerns to be combined with management initiatives. They note that some organizations mix these strategies. For example, in one organization, "spray and pray" (also known as the "communication clutter" approach) was used to "bombard" staff with information on organizational performance. However, when faced with downsizing and operational

FIGURE 7.2
The Communication Strategy Continuum

Source: Clampett, The Communication Strategy Continuum, *Academy of Management Journal*, p. 48, 2000.

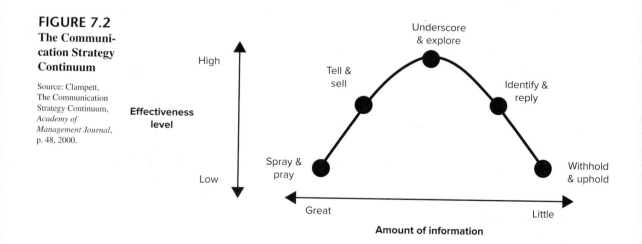

TABLE 7.4
Communication Strategies

Strategy	Actions
Spray and pray	Shower employees with a range of information; more is better. Managers pray that staff will see what needs to be done. *Benefit*: Staff are exposed to company information. *Downside*: Staff overloaded with information, may not be able to identify what is more important, and may be able to understand what is happening, but not why.
Tell and sell	Limit the information provided to core issues. Management tells staff about the changes and "sells" them on why these are necessary. *Benefit*: Can be done rapidly. *Downside*: Staff are passive recipients, and lack of dialogue opens potential for staff skepticism and cynicism.
Underscore and explore	Focus on fundamentals, but engage employees in dialogue to identify obstacles and misunderstandings that need to be addressed. *Benefit*: Staff engagement solves problems, strengthens support for change and can generate useful ideas. *Downside*: Takes time.
Identify and reply	Defensive approach to identifying and responding to rumors and innuendo, and to reduce staff confusion about changes. *Benefit*: Can resolve problems at an early stage. *Downside*: Reactive approach that assumes (sometimes incorrectly) that staff understand the organizational problems that the changes need to address.
Withhold and uphold	Withhold information until it is absolutely necessary to communicate. Management publicly defend the change strategy. Information is not disclosed openly. *Benefit*: Management retain a high degree of control. *Downside*: Staff bitterness and resentment.

Source: Based on Clampitt et al. (2000).

A Dozen Tips from the Experts

Rebecca Saunders (1999) has collected the following suggestions for communicating change:

1. Specify the nature of the change.
2. Explain why.
3. Let staff know the scope of the change, including the good and the bad news.
4. Continually repeat the purpose of the change and how it will occur.
5. Use graphics.
6. Make the communication two-way.
7. Target supervisors.
8. Support change with new learning.
9. Point to progress emanating from the change.
10. Don't limit communications to meetings and print.
11. Institutionalize information flow about the change.
12. Model the changes yourself.

changes, a "withhold and uphold" strategy was used, in order to avoid exposing staff to promises about the future that they were not able to meet. This dual approach led to discontent and mistrust, as staff saw management providing them with significant amounts of information, but avoiding the issues about which they cared the most.

This argument supports the use of "underscore and explore" change communication strategies, the benefits of which arise from dialogue and engagement. This approach, however, takes time to organize. This may not be appropriate—and could cause damaging delays—if rapid organizational change action is necessary. The best strategy may thus depend on the situation.

Who Should Be Responsible for Communicating the Change?

A common view is that chief executives should be personally involved in the communication of change in order to demonstrate their commitment. It could be damaging to delegate this responsibility to others, signalling a lack of top management support. However, other commentators argue that first-line supervisors are more appropriate change communicators, because they are opinion leaders, who are more likely to be known to and trusted by staff. This is the view adopted by T. J. and Sandar Larkin (1996). First-line supervisors are in regular personal contact with staff, in small groups (rather than in large formal assemblies), and are thus better able to communicate about change. They propose the two-stage supervisory briefing strategy summarized in table 7.5.

Jeanie Duck (1993, p. 110) argues that the key to change communication lies with "managing the conversation between the people leading the change effort and those who are expected to implement the strategies." This does not necessarily give priority to the role of either the chief executive or supervisors. She maintains that managers often fail to realize that they are sending out messages even when they are not formally communicating. For example, a change task force may meet to discuss how to accomplish a change, feeling that there is no need to communicate more widely at that time. Duck (1993, p. 110) points out that this

TABLE 7.5
Two-Stage Supervisory Briefing Strategy

Round One: Seek Opinions and Recommendations		Round Two: Report Back to Supervisors	
What to Do	**Why**	**What to Do**	**Why**
One senior manager meets with 8 to 10 supervisors for a maximum of 90 minutes	Makes clear that all ideas and opinions are welcome; relatively short meeting maintains focus	The same manager meets with the same group of supervisors	Makes clear that they are dealing with a management representative
Single sheet of paper with two columns: "not willing to change" (what management want to retain) and "willing to change" (for supervisors' recommendations)	Clarifies the ground rules—what is not going to change—and gives an opportunity for supervisors to make suggestions to take back to the senior change management team	Single sheet of paper with supervisors' recommendations and senior management responses; answer questions without argument and defensiveness	Convey what has happened with regard to their recommendations, not attempting to convince supervisors of the merits of what has happened
Ensure that supervisors understand that final decisions rest with the senior change management team	Clarifies that opinions are being sought, and not their permission	Distribute a booklet outlining the change and draw attention to major features	Help supervisors in the face-to-face conversations that they will have with their staff

Source: Based on Larkin and Larkin (1996, pp. 102–3).

"virtually guarantees that the change effort will fail," because people will be aware that the task force is meeting, rumors will circulate, and people will avoid buy-in to the final outcome. Instead, she suggests setting up a "transition management team," which is a group of senior staff who work full time on the change initiative and who report to the chief executive. The role of the transition management team is to stimulate conversation and allow information to be shared across (potentially obsolete) internal organizational boundaries. The concept of managing conversations is also reflected in the use of "tag teams" (see box).

Communicating Change through Tag Teams

USAA is a financial services company that employs 25,800 people, has over 10 million members, and is based in San Antonio, Texas. In moving through an organizational change, USAA used "tag teams" to ensure that change occurred in different units at the same time, minimizing disruption to existing operations. A core team worked on a particular change but was joined by "tag teams" comprised of volunteers from different parts of the organization who attended core team meetings. They were charged with asking questions about how change initiatives would affect customer services and with conveying the concerns and fears of their colleagues in relation to the change. After the core team meetings, they returned to their jobs and acted as informal conduits, taking information back to their colleagues and work groups (based on Olofson, 1999).

LO 7.5 Contingency Approaches to Change Communication

We explore contingency approaches to change implementation in chapter 8. Contingency perspectives have also been applied to the design of change communication strategies. Two main contingencies—or dependencies—concern the type of change and the stage of change.

Communication Strategy and Type of Change

Doug Stace and Dexter Dunphy (2001) argue that a communication strategy must reflect the type of organizational change that is being proposed:

- *Developmental or incremental transitions* aim for widespread involvement, emphasizing face-to-face communication and the use of change teams to identify initiatives and broaden commitment.
- *Task-focused transitions* seek to align employee behavior with management initiatives, so these are primarily top-down in nature, using formal communication channels such as email broadcasts and memos.
- *Charismatic transformations* need to stimulate emotional commitment to new ways of working, and thus require more personalized top-down forms of communication, ideally combined with at least symbolic two-way communication.
- *Turnarounds* tend to follow from organizational crises, and draw on formal, top-down modes of communication that attempt to force compliance with the new direction.

Stace and Dunphy outline how these approaches vary in terms of communicating goals, who is to be involved, the kinds of issues that will be addressed, the communication channels and directions (top-down, lateral, one-way/two-way) that will be used, and the balance of power that will need to be managed among relevant parties.

Each of these change communication strategies makes different demands on the capabilities of the change manager. Developmental transitions demand sophisticated social and interpersonal skills. Task-focused transformations rely on carefully crafted formal messages. Charismatic transformations need to be underpinned by visionary and inspiring messages. In the interests of speed and effectiveness, post-crisis turnarounds may require a directive, autocratic style, with which many experienced change managers may be uncomfortable, especially if they are accustomed to more participative, engaging modes of change communication and implementation.

Open the Files

Think back to a recent change in your organization, and consider the following questions:

1. Did your organization have a strategy for initially announcing the change?

2. What strategy was used to communicate information during the change process? Was one or more of the strategies from figure 7.2 used? Was this strategy adopted consistently, and for all members across the organization?

3. On a scale from 1 (ineffective) to 5 (very effective), how would you rate the communication strategy overall?

4. With hindsight, what changes would you have made to improve the effectiveness of the change communication strategy?

5. To what extent will those recommendations apply to future changes in this organization? To what extent will that depend on the further changes that are proposed?

Bill Quirke (2008, p. 236) also argues that communication strategy should be determined by the degree of change that is going to be implemented. The more significant the change, the more employees need to be involved. He uses "the communication escalator" (figure 7.3) as a guide to designing communications strategy. Degrees of involvement thus range from awareness, understanding, support, and involvement, to commitment.

FIGURE 7.3
The Communication Escalator

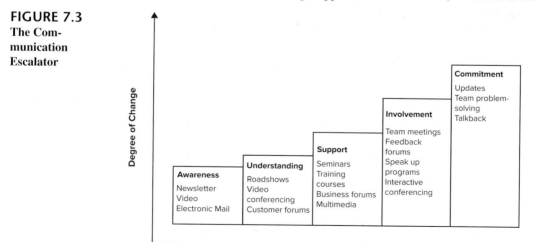

Communication in a Crisis What Can We Learn from BP's Mistakes?

Communication in a crisis is critical, affecting the organization's reputation and performance. Aikaterini Valvi and Konstantinos Fragkos (2013) assess BP's communication after the explosion on the Deepwater Horizon oil drilling rig in the Gulf of Mexico in April 2010. The incident killed 11 of the 126 crew members, and injured 17 others. Oil poured from the wellhead on the seabed and drifted toward the Louisiana coast, threatening wildlife and the local fishing and tourism industries. Spilling 5 million barrels of crude oil into the Gulf, this was the biggest environmental disaster in the United States since the *Exxon Valdez* spilled 750,000 barrels in Prince William Sound in 1989. With financial penalties and reputational damage, BP struggled to restore profitability.

Crises are expected to trigger significant organizational change to prevent a recurrence. Many stakeholders are involved—employees, shareholders, local businesses, the public, regulatory agencies, government. Tony Hayward, BP's chief executive, took personal responsibility for providing information following the Deepwater incident. He was slow to respond to the crisis, and made five other mistakes in his communication with the media, government, and public:

1 *The fake images*: Fake photographs were given to the press, with the claim that these related to blank spots on the video; original images were quickly supplied, but this damaged BP's credibility.

2 *"I want my life back"*: Under pressure from various sources, Hayward in a television interview in May said, "I want my life back." As the Deepwater incident had caused 11 deaths, this damaged his credibility and reputation.

3 *The incident with the yacht*: With oil still spilling into the Gulf, Hayward took time off to watch his yacht, *Bob*, compete in the UK Isle of Wight island race.

4 *We were not prepared*: Speaking to the *Financial Times* in Texas, Hayward said, "We did not have

the tools you would want in your toolkit"—not a reassuring statement.

5 *Self-interest*: During a hearing with the U.S. Cabinet, Hayward appeared to show an overriding concern with his own position, which he believed was not under threat, saying that he was ignoring press and television accounts of the disaster so as not to "cloud his judgement."

U.S. president Barack Obama criticized BP for spending $50 million on radio, television, and online advertising during the crisis, suggesting that it would have been better to spend that money on dealing with the oil spill. The company made this worse by issuing a statement claiming that "not a cent" had been diverted from their response to the oil spill to pay for advertising. BP's communication with its own employees was ineffective. When staff involved in the oil cleanup operation were hospitalized with dizziness, headaches, and respiratory problems, Hayward blamed food poisoning, showing lack of concern for their well-being. Strategies for communicating with shareholders were more effective, reminding them of BP's past record, blaming other companies for the disaster, and promising to meet long-term dividend obligations. Nevertheless, Hayward was replaced in October 2010.

What advice can other organizations take from this experience? Develop a crisis communication plan. Appoint experienced staff to work from a designated public relations office. Communications with the media must be direct and sincere. Use press conferences, a crisis web page, and social network accounts. Monitor media reports closely, and respond immediately to clarify issues when appropriate. Do not run advertising campaigns to promote your image during a crisis. Concentrate on restoring trust. Finally, make it clear from the start that "things will change."

(Other aspects of this incident are discussed in chapter 5.)

The escalator indicates the communications methods appropriate to each degree of involvement (suggestions—these are not comprehensive). For commitment, the organization should consider using all of those types of communication methods, and any others that are available. At the awareness level, the focus is simply on providing information. However, for involvement and commitment, communication also needs to concentrate on improving the quality of interactions and relationships.

Communication Strategy and Stage of Change

Adopting a differing contingency focus, Kathleen and Kevin Reardon (1999) suggest that the most appropriate communication strategy depends on the stage of the change process. First, they identify four leadership styles, each of which uses different communication processes and strategies:

Commanding style: Leaders are performance- and results-oriented, and their communication style is directive.

Logical style: Leaders explore the available strategic options through analysis and reasoning, and their communication style involves explaining their intentions and their plans.

Inspirational style: Leaders develop a vision of the future around which they seek to encourage cohesion, and their communication style involves creating trust and mobilizing people around the change program.

Supportive style: Leaders are concerned with creating an open and consensual environment, and their communication style is based on involvement.

Reardon and Reardon (1999) argue that different modes of communicating should be used at different stages of the change process. Using a five-stage process, their argument is summarized in table 7.6.

TABLE 7.6
Stages of Change and Leadership Style

Stage	Leadership Style
Planning	Focus on identifying what needs to change requires a combination of logical and inspirational leadership styles
Enabling	As people are selected and trained in relation to the change process, a combination of logical, inspirational, and supportive styles are needed
Launching	As change unfolds, combine logical and commanding styles
Catalyzing	Use inspirational and supportive leadership styles to motivate and engage
Maintaining	To encourage staff to continue with a change effort, perhaps in the face of obstacles, inspirational and supportive leadership styles are helpful

This framework recognizes that no one individual is likely to have all the change management skills required at different stages of a change process. More than one style—or more than one image of change management—may be necessary. As discussed in the following chapter, however, change management can often be more of a team effort than a solo performance. Team members may thus have different strengths—or styles—which they can use to compensate for each other.

This framework has some drawbacks. First, change rarely unfolds in the logical manner shown in table 7.6 (see chapter 10). Second, there may be several changes unfolding at once, but each at a different pace in an organization, raising questions about the management styles of those involved in more than one initiative. Third, it can be difficult to identify when one stage has ended and another has begun, as these can overlap significantly. Fourth, the model offers clear advice, but without supporting evidence. Finally, to apply this framework, change managers are required to have a good self-understanding of their leadership and communication preferences and styles. As with many such frameworks, this is useful as long as it is treated as a guide and not as a rigid set of rules.

LO 7.6 Communication Channels and the Role of Social Media

Getting the (Change) News *What Works Best for You?*

You are an employee of a large organization about to go through a major restructuring.

1. What do you think you need to know about the restructuring?

2. From whom would you like to get this information? Why?

3. Would you prefer to receive this information in person or in a group setting?

4. What for you would be the best channel (e.g., management briefing, email, video) for receiving this information? Why?

5. As a change manager, how will you use your answers to these questions to help design a communication strategy?

At the heart of our model of communication (figure 7.1) sits a key issue that we have not directly discussed: the channel, or the medium through which the message will be transmitted. This is not a mere technical issue. As Marshall McLuhan (1964) argued, "the medium is the message," suggesting that the properties of a chosen medium can influence the meaning of a message and its interpretation. The change manager selecting an inappropriate medium with which to transmit important information to key groups affected by a change proposal may not be taken seriously, may be seen as insensitive, or may strengthen disaffection. In the final section of this chapter, therefore, we will consider the characteristics of different media, and how these can affect change communication. We then explore the impact on change communication of developments in social media and mobile technology.

Media Richness

One of the main characteristics on which communication media vary is "information richness," a concept developed by Robert Lengel and Richard Daft (1988). Richness concerns the amount and the kind of information that can be transmitted. The three characteristics of a communication medium that affect richness are (1) the ability to handle many items of information at the same time, (2) the availability of rapid feedback, and (3) the ability to establish a personal focus. Based on these characteristics, they classify media on the "hierarchy of richness" shown in figure 7.4.

FIGURE 7.4
Media
Richness
Hierarchy

Source: Lengel and
Daft, Media Richness
Heirarchy, *Academy of
Management Execu-
tive*, p. 226, 1988.

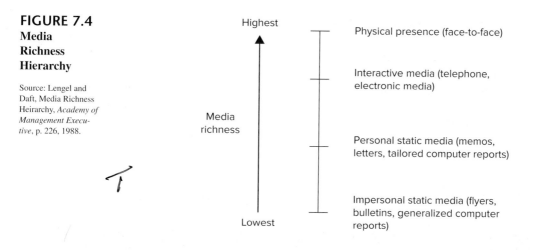

Highest

Media
richness

Lowest

Physical presence (face-to-face)

Interactive media (telephone,
electronic media)

Personal static media (memos,
letters, tailored computer reports)

Impersonal static media (flyers,
bulletins, generalized computer
reports)

Face-to-face communication is the richest because it meets all three criteria: multiple information cues, immediate feedback, and personal focus. Moving down the hierarchy, telephone allows quick feedback, but the information cues that are available from nonverbal behavior in face-to-face communication are absent; body language such as eye contact, posture, gesture, and head movements. Written communications can be directed at individuals, but carry limited information, and feedback is likely to be delayed. At the bottom of the hierarchy, impersonal bulletins and computer reports are limited on all three criteria and are therefore "information poor" or "lean."

This is not an argument in favor of rich communications. On the contrary, the degree of richness that is appropriate depends on the nature and content of what is being communicated, and in particular on where the issue lies on a continuum from routine to nonroutine. Routine issues are commonplace, simple, rational, straightforward, and contain no surprises. Nonroutine issues, in contrast, concern novel, complex, unexpected events and are often characterized by time pressure, ambiguity, and surprise. The potential for misunderstanding is thus greater with nonroutine issues, and a richer exchange of information is therefore necessary in order to establish a common frame of reference. Lengel and Daft (1988, pp. 229–31) suggest six rules for "matching" media richness to the message:

Rule 1:   Send nonroutine, difficult communications through a rich medium—preferably face-to-face.

Rule 2:   Send routine, simple communications through a lean medium.

Rule 3:   Use rich media to extend your personal presence throughout the organization.

Rule 4:   Use rich media for implementing company strategy.

Rule 5:   Don't let the media in use "censor" information about critical issues; formal written reports simplify multidimensional issues and mask the nonroutine.

Rule 6:   Evaluate new communication technology as a single channel in the media spectrum.

For the change manager, these rules indicate that incremental changes that simply build on current practice may be comparatively routine, and they should be communicated as such, using lean media. This is more suited, for example, to the transmission of factual or technical information. On the other hand, information-rich media should be used when changes are novel, more complex, and widespread in their implications. Information richness may be more difficult to achieve in a large organization, and the change manager may need to consider a wider range of options, including the use of the social technologies discussed shortly. In most instances of nonroutine change, it is likely that a portfolio of communication strategies will be desirable, tailored to the particular circumstances.

Adopting a different contingency approach, Bill Quirke (2008) suggests that different change communication media are better suited to some audiences than to others. With regard to change communication he suggests that there are four types of target audience, whose needs differ:

Waking up	They will be affected by the change, but have not noticed, yet
Engaging	They know that they will be affected, and are interested and concerned
Educating	They will affected marginally, and only need to be told about what is happening
Reassuring	They will also be marginally affected, but are concerned nevertheless

Media-rich face-to-face communication needs to be directed toward those who will be most impacted by change—those who need waking up, and those who need to be engaged. Leaner forms of communication can be used with those who only need education or reassurance.

A New Range of Communication Tools—the Potential Uses of Social Media

The social networking service Facebook was launched in 2004. This is now one of many Internet-mediated tools that allow people to create, share, and exchange information, ideas, pictures, and videos. Unlike previous "flat" Internet applications, these social media tools allow *two-way*, *real-time* communication, interaction, collaboration, and co-creation. To use social media, one needs some form of Internet access, which used to mean a computer. The development of mobile technology has made social media independent of traditional computing; we are now more likely to access the Internet with a laptop, smart television, tablet, ebook reader, or smartphone. Social media and mobile technologies are also "low friction" tools: they are ubiquitous, easy to use, flexible, and do not require specialized equipment. Another feature is their rapid development; this section of this chapter will be out of date before this book is published.

A study by McKinsey Global Institute concluded that social media could increase the productivity of knowledge workers by 20 to 25 percent, as people would spend much less time looking for information (Chui et al., 2012). In January 2015 Facebook launched a corporate version of its social networking platform, called Facebook at Work. A number of corporate "partners" were asked to experiment with its possibilities, to discover if this could increase employee productivity by sharing ideas through posts, groups, and messages. This development was triggered by the observation that Facebook's own staff were using the network instead of email for internal communication. This new platform sought to address organizational concerns over data security, intellectual property, and privacy. Unlike "personal" Facebook, information shared on Facebook at Work belonged to the employer, and employees who leave will not have access to their corporate account (Kuchler, 2015).

Social media are therefore "information rich," close to the top of the hierarchy in figure 7.4, and they are in widespread use, especially by younger employees. In 2015, Facebook, with a market value of $209 billion, had over 1.35 billion monthly active users; Twitter had 250 million. These technologies could thus make significant contributions to organizational communication in general, and to change communication in particular. Jonny Gifford (2013) argues that the main applications include:

Efficient communication:	Increase efficiency of communication and knowledge transfer, getting the right information to the right people.
Employee voice:	Seek employee views, giving employees a platform.
Networking and collaboration:	Create meaningful connections with people we would otherwise not know, and facilitating collaboration.
Learning and development:	Use social media to support e-learning and development and to encourage self-directed learning.
Recruitment and job hunting:	Social networking sites are now widely used for recruitment; employers and job seekers use social media to check each other to inform their choices.

Can social media help organizations to become more innovative and responsive to change? Applications in marketing and recruitment are straightforward. The use of social media in relation to employee engagement, productivity, innovation, and communication, however, is more diffuse. The applications listed above have the potential to transform change communication by tailoring information to individuals and groups, with the ability to communicate simultaneously with large numbers regardless of location, creating dialogue concerning change proposals, encouraging networks and collaboration, and providing flexible change-specific training. Social networking sites can also reveal (to potential employers) information concerning candidates' openness to change, and also reveal (to potential employees) an organization's receptiveness to change and innovation.

Social Media Drivers

A survey of executives found that the main drivers of social media adoption were (Matthews, 2015):

1. Responding faster to changing needs
2. Optimizing business processes
3. Increasing revenue and profits
4. Attracting the best talent in a competitive market
5. Better-engaged employees

Change managers thus have a set of new and powerful tools to help with two-way communication, staff participation, and change implementation.

How are these media being applied in practice? In 2011, the consulting company McKinsey held a contest to find companies using social media tools and technologies in innovative ways, to improve management methods and engage frontline employees

(McKinsey & Company, 2011). Demonstrating the uses and benefits of these tools, here are some of the winners:

The Dutch Civil Service

Dutch government employees faced bureaucratic hurdles, such as having to book meeting rooms in their own buildings through an external agency, which was time-consuming and costly. Following a frustrated tweet from one staff member, a group formed, and they used open-source software to develop their own reservation system. This now covers over 50 offices and over 550 workplaces in government buildings across the country.

Essilor International

Essilor is a global manufacturer of ophthalmic lenses and has a training program that uses personal and social media methods to share best practices across 102 sites in 40 countries. It now takes one year to reach the level of skill that once took three years, and social networking allows coaching across different locations. A lens-processing center in Thailand developed a game to teach new employees how to understand the shape of a particular type of lens, and this game is now also used in Brazil.

Best Buy

Best Buy is a consumer electronics retailer with 1,500 locations and 100,000 employees. To ensure that top management understood what frontline staff learned from customers, the company created an online feedback system that allowed everyone to see the customer information gathered in all the stores. This influenced a range of company practices, from improving shop signs to complex decisions about implementing a national promotion. This was a fast, flexible, and inexpensive way of responding to "the voice of the customer."

Cemex

Cemex is a large Mexico-based cement company, which developed an approach to employee collaboration called Shift. This helped to reduce the time taken to introduce new products and process improvements. Shift uses wikis, blogs, discussion boards, and web-conferencing to help employees around the world collaborate with each other. For example, 400 employees working on ready-mix products helped to identify which worked well, and which were obsolete, slimming the product line and updating the global catalogue. Now, with over 500 active communities, Shift is used to solve local problems, using global resources, as well as storing and sharing the knowledge that is generated.

These organizations may be relatively rare examples. A survey of 2,100 UK employees and 590 human resource management staff suggests that development of novel uses of social media has been slow (Gifford, 2013). Applications have been mainly driven by personal access, rather than by organization strategy; employees are probably more sophisticated in the use of social media tools in their private lives than are employers with regard to organizational applications. Where organizations were using these technologies, they were more likely to be targeting external (customers, other stakeholders) rather than internal audiences. Applications of "employee voice" were superficial, with management seeking employee views, but not necessarily being more responsive or open to influence as a result. The technology is in place, but most employees tend to use their laptops, smartphones, and tablets for personal purposes. There seems to be limited corporate support for BYOD (bring-your-own-device) practices, and some organizations ban the use of social media at work.

A study in 2013 examined how chief executives in American organizations used four social networks: Twitter, LinkedIn, Facebook, and Google Plus. Around 30 percent were LinkedIn members, but participation in other networks was "dismal." Faced with those findings, Linda Pophal (2014, p. 23) asks, "Is it any wonder that so many of us are stymied in our ability to sell the C-suite on the value of social media? It appears that few CEOs and other senior executives are familiar with, or convinced of, the benefits of communicating via social media." Access to social networking and mobile technology is not a barrier; a perceived lack of organizational relevance is.

The development of *enterprise-specific* social networks may help to realize the potential of these technologies. Employees can be involved in two-way discussions using a secure "gated" corporate networking platform for incubating ideas and feeding these to senior management. This can also be used to facilitate ad hoc communication and collaboration. Social networking can be a more engaging medium than traditional communication tools, to send corporate messages, quickly capture employee reactions, check that messages have been understood, and for information-sharing in general. A corporate social network could strengthen the sense of shared purpose by celebrating achievements, reinforcing mission and values, and strengthening identification with the organization.

Antisocial Media

Lloyds Bank has a company intranet, which provides opportunities for staff to give feedback to senior management. In January 2015, during a major reorganization that involved cutting costs and the closure of 150 branches with job losses, the human resources director Rupert McNeill decided to assess staff morale. He posted an intranet article that praised employees, describing them as "a fantastic team" and an "agile workforce." Staff were asked to leave comments, and hundreds responded. Most of the feedback expressed resentment and complaints (Donellan, 2015):

"If you want promotion do every extracurricular task that you can. Don't worry about the quality of the work as it is irrelevant."

"Either execs are lying, or somewhere down the line people are misrepresenting what is being communicated from above."

"Why should we trust you after what you did on pensions?"

Most complaints concerned the decision to close the generous final salary pension scheme. This happened at the same time as the chief executive was awarded a £586,000 pension contribution as part of his £7.8 million annual package, and was seen as "a disgraceful display of double standards." Staff were also critical of excessive bureaucracy and a lack of top management support. The corporate intranet makes it easy for management to capture staff feedback. That feedback, however, may be unfavorable, particularly when management actions are seen as being inconsistent or unfair.

From a study of seven organizations with internal networks, Gifford (2014) offers this advice:

- Enterprise networks need a clear rationale or purpose if they are to be used and become embedded. They need to support day-to-day activities.
- The process of identifying uses is better developed bottom-up, coming from staff themselves. But effective uses need to be identified and replicated if they are to spread and be sustained.

- It helps if there is a key individual, or a team of "community champions," guiding and encouraging the use of social media until this reaches critical mass.

- Enterprise social networks are time-efficient ways for senior leaders to engage with large numbers of staff and to increase their visibility. However, the effects will be negative if senior management challenge or criticize comments with which they disagree.

- Social networks should be self-managed and not censored; policies should be "light touch" (with an expectation that posts will be "respectful"); negative comments should be dealt with frankly and openly; employees should be informed if comments have caused offense.

Social media offer the change manager a novel range of powerful, flexible, "information-rich" communication channels, which appear to have valuable uses. Organizations that have experimented with these technologies have achieved significant benefits. Most of the tools are public and require little skill to use. In order to develop beneficial applications, it also seems that creativity, innovation, and experimentation will be necessary in order to tailor these new methods to local conditions and organizational goals.

When they were developing their theory of media richness, Robert Lengel and Richard Daft (1988) may not have foreseen the development of social media and mobile technologies in the twenty-first century. However, their conclusions with regard to computing technology in general speak to the change manager today. They observed that "electronic media" were just one potential channel in the media spectrum. All the other channels have their uses and advantages. They also concluded that "there is no electronic substitute for face-to-face discussions when issues are nonroutine" (Lengel and Daft, 1988, p. 231). Social media can therefore be misused. They should not, for example, be used to provide an excuse to avoid difficult interpersonal conversations—about forthcoming organizational changes, perhaps, or other controversial or sensitive issues.

EXERCISE 7.1 *Listen to Who's Talking* LO 7.2 LO 7.3	Deborah Tannen (1995) argues that the way we communicate reinforces power and gender differences. This can affect our interpretations of what we think is happening in a particular situation. 1. Observe a work meeting, preferably with up to 10 people. 2. Listen to the language being used. What different types of languages in use can you observe, such as commanding, respectful, demonstrating concern, displaying condescension? 3. Do individuals tend to use one type of language in their interactions? 4. Who does most of the talking? Who asks most of the questions? 5. To what extent does the talk convey information about power and gender differences? For example, who takes credit, who exudes confidence, who asks more questions? 6. What conclusions can you draw from your analysis about the way language constructs and reinforces differences within the organization? 7. As a change manager, how will your awareness of these differences influence your future interactions with staff?

EXERCISE 7.2

How Defensive Are You?

LO 7.2

Many alphas think that looking interested when someone speaks to them demonstrates a high degree of openness when, in fact, that's just the bare minimum one must do not to be labeled defensive. Alphas can use this tool to chart their progress toward a more constructive state of mind and to see how their behavior appears to others.

Are you open, or defensive? What are your normal behaviors? Where are your preferences? What do you need to change? How would this improve your relationships and personal effectiveness?

Highly Open

+10 Plan the change, engage others, set milestones, and implement.
+9 Communicate genuine enthusiasm about making a change.
+8 Think out loud, making new associations about the problem.
+7 Take full responsibility for the problem and its ramifications.
+6 Request information and examples about the problem.
+5 Openly wonder about your role in creating the problem.
+4 Express genuine curiosity about the issue and how to resolve it.
+3 Express appreciation for the messenger, regardless of delivery.
+2 Summarize key points without interjecting your own thoughts.
+1 Look interested, breathe, demonstrate an open posture.

Breakthrough: choosing curiosity over being right

−1 Show polite interest while inwardly preparing your rebuttal.
−2 Provide a detailed explanation of your point of view.
−3 Justify actions with compelling logic and an interpretation of events.
−4 Interrupt to give your perspective.
−5 Interpret comments as attacks and feel misunderstood.
−6 Convince them that you're right and they're wrong.
−7 Make snippy replies and show your irritation nonverbally.
−8 Blame or complain about someone who's not present.
−9 Intimidate or attack the messenger.
−10 Appear to comply, with no intention of doing what you say you'll do.

Highly Defensive

EXERCISE 7.3

Social Media at the Museum

"In the past, institutional mission and strategic vision were reviewed every four years; now, they are reviewed every time someone posts to Facebook, comments on a blog, or opens a new Twitter account."

—Dana Allen-Greil and colleagues

Social media could themselves trigger dramatic organizational changes, as well as creating new channels of communication with regard to other changes. For example, social media are changing the ways in which museums interact with the public, and also how museum staff communicate and work with each other. Dana Allen-Greil and colleagues (2011) argue that, used effectively, social media can further the mission of the organization and foster more agile and collaborative organization cultures. There are many wider cultural, political, and social pressures encouraging openness and collaboration. Social media offer a new set of tools with which organizations can respond to those pressures.

Allen-Greil and colleagues studied three museums: the Smithsonian's National Museum of American History (NMAH); Monticello, a historic house and research institution; and the J. Paul Getty Trust (the Getty). These museums have adopted different approaches to the use of social media.

At NMAH, social media contribute to *public programming*, focusing on education and visitor services, complementing the existing email newsletter, website, and other online communications. At Monticello, the focus lies with *relationships building*, and in particular on increasing the organization's "social media outreach." This means using social media to increase the number of "online visitors." In contrast, the Getty is using social media to *"get off the hill."* The Getty has a reputation for being inaccessible, as it is located on a hill above the 405 freeway, and visitors have to take a quarter-mile tram ride to get up there. Social media thus allow the Getty to "take the collections and programs into the community" and to promote their educational and research work.

Sometimes the Best Thing Managers Can Do Is Get Out of the Way

Staff who have collaborated on social media projects in these museums have created new channels of communication and new ways of thinking and working with each other. The leadership of these initiatives was mainly "bottom-up," and did not rely on senior management experts. Allen-Greil and colleagues note that "effective collaboration means staff members need to cross lines traditionally drawn between different working groups, and probably across lines drawn between hierarchical levels within the institution." Social media may thus lead to flatter hierarchies and "horizontal working." The study also found that an increased level of online engagement with the public led to an increase in face-to-face conversations among staff. Why? Social media project staff had to meet with colleagues across the organization: human resources, legal department, registrars, publishers, educators. The authors argue: "Social media are pushing us together in a very personal way. New conversations between staff members who have never had any reason to talk before are establishing new relationships and new lines of engagement."

A Perpetually Beta State of Mind

Senior managers need to encourage staff to experiment with social media to develop more efficient and effective processes. However, at the Getty, the use of different social media platforms by different groups of staff meant that initiatives were often uncoordinated, and some even competed with each other: "In a large, hierarchical institution, this kind of testing, rapid prototyping, and risk-taking is pushing the boundaries of the usual, highly-controlled content development processes." Although exciting for staff, spontaneous experimentation may not be sustainable. However, Allen-Greil and colleagues ask us to consider: "What would it *really* be like if we could work in a *perpetually beta* state of mind? If we could try, fail, and try again? We are closer than you think because it's already happening at every museum that uses social media."

Now that you have read this case, consider the following questions:

1. In what ways could social media applications contribute to the mission of your organization?

2. How could social media change or strengthen the culture of your organization, with regard to widening collaboration and becoming more agile and responsive?

3. To what extent will your current organization silos and hierarchies inhibit the communication and collaboration opportunities opened up by social media? Or, will social media help you to break down those silos and hierarchies, and encourage more "horizontal working"?

4. How should your organization balance the need for management control with the desire to open up conversations more widely across the organization in order to encourage experimentation with social media?

5. In your assessment, would your organization benefit or suffer from working in a "perpetually beta" state of mind, constantly experimenting, learning—and improving—from the mistakes?

Additional Reading

Chui, M., Manyika, J., Bughin, J., Dobbs, R., Roxburgh, C., Sarrazin, H., Sands, G., and Westergren, M. 2012. *The social economy: Unlocking value and productivity through social technologies.* New York and London: McKinsey & Company/McKinsey Global Institute. Analyzes the economic impact and business potential of social technologies, considering current applications and future possibilities. Argues that the use of social technologies to improve collaboration within and across organizations has reached only a fraction of its potential. Improvements in value creation and productivity will depend on finding innovative ways to exploit these technologies, while protecting individual and corporate rights.

Keller, S., Meaney, M., and Pung, C. 2010. *What successful transformations share.* Chicago and London: McKinsey & Company. Identifies the tactics that lead to successful change. Emphasizes the power of widespread employee engagement, collaboration, co-creation, sense of ownership, and in particular the importance of ongoing communication and involvement.

Rafferty, A. E., Jimmieson, N. L., and Armenakis, A. A. 2013. Change readiness: A multilevel review. *Journal of Management* 39(1):110–35. Stresses the role of communication to influence cognitive and emotional responses to increase change readiness. Argues that, to influence emotions, the use of pictures (see following recommendation), color, music, and atmosphere are helpful. Concludes that high-quality change communication can increase readiness, and that poor communication can damage the change process.

Sibbet, D. 2013. *Visual leaders: New tools for visioning, management, and organizational change*. Hoboken, NJ: John Wiley & Sons Inc. Introduces an innovative range of visual tools for improving corporate communications and visual IQ. Demonstrates how visualization can engage, inspire, and contribute to thinking. Argues that these tools are particularly useful in driving organizational change. Describes with case studies (the GM Saturn project; the quality improvement program at HealthEast) a "storymapping" approach for anticipating, managing, and communicating the stages of the change process.

Roundup

Here is a short summary of the key points that we would like you to take from this chapter, in relation to each of the learning outcomes:

LO 7.1

Identify key elements in the change communication process.
We emphasized the argument that communication is not a "soft" topic, but one that has a direct impact on organizational effectiveness and financial performance. We introduced a well-known model of the change communication process—a process for exchanging meaning as well as transmitting information. A transmitter codes a message, which is transmitted through a chosen channel to a receiver, who then decodes that message and, depending on the channel, provides feedback. A number of factors can interfere with this apparently simple process: perceptual filters, noise, and the wider organizational context in which communication takes place. The organization's past history of change is important, as this can influence responses to current change proposals.

Reflections for the Practicing Change Manager

1. In what ways does your personal use of language reinforce power and gender differences in your organization? What effect do you think this has in terms of how your change messages are received? What modifications to your approach would help you to communicate change more effectively?

2. Do you see yourself as a reporter of change information? Or are you a sense-maker, helping staff to understand change actions, and seeking input from them?

3. To what extent do you focus on getting the word out, rather than seeking staff buy-in? Do you tend to use the same communication methods, or do you adopt different approaches depending upon the type of change? Do you "spray and pray" information or "underscore and explore"?

4. Are you more comfortable using "rich" communication media (face-to-face), or "leaner" media (email)? Do you adopt different forms of communication depending on the type or stage of change? With which communication media have you had the most success, and why?

5. Does your organization have a strategy for using social media? If so, how would you assess the effectiveness of this approach, and what recommendations would you make in order to strengthen the benefits of using social media tools? If not, how would you advise your organization in developing a social media strategy, balancing the benefits and risks?

LO 7.2   *Understand how language, gender, power, and emotion can affect the change communication process.*

The use of language, gender and power differences, and emotional responses can all have an effect on the success of the communication process. Men and women can communicate in different ways. Women emphasize doubts and uncertainties, and men display confidence and minimize concerns. Women ask more questions, which men can mistakenly interpret as a comparative lack of knowledge. Power differences are also a barrier to effective communication, as the powerful may not wish to disclose information that could weaken their power, and the less powerful may not disclose information that could be damaging to them. Change managers must be alert to the significance of emotional responses to change proposals, and we identified a number of strategies for strengthening emotional commitment to change.

LO 7.3   *Understand the power of language in influencing responses to change proposals.*

We explored the proposition that the management of change involves the management of conversations. For the change manager, even informal conversations are powerful tools for exchanging meaning and influencing perceptions of change proposals, as well as ways of assessing responses. Choice of language in such conversations is therefore critical. That language may need to reflect the stage of the change process; we discussed different conversations for initiating, understanding, performing, and finally closing change initiatives. There is clearly a need for coherence and for shared understanding in order to avoid confusion. It is also appropriate, we argued, to align choice of language and imagery with the type of change that is proposed, once again in the interests of avoiding "mixed signals."

LO 7.4   *Explain and assess appropriate strategies for communicating change.*

We addressed a number of key practical questions.

Is it possible to communicate too much? Probably not, as long as information overload is avoided, and the communication process is two-way, capturing and exploring concerns and ideas as well as transmitting information.

Is it more important to get the word out, or to get buy-in? Both are important; but without buy-in, the chances of change failure are increased.

Which strategies are more effective than others? A communication strategy of "underscore and explore," which involves a genuine dialogue with those involved, is the most effective approach. Two strategies in particular, "spray and pray" and "withhold and uphold," are likely to be less effective because the communication is one-way, and the staff who are going to be affected have no opportunity to comment or discuss.

Who should be responsible for communicating the change? The "obvious" answer, the chief executive, may not always be the correct answer. This indeed may not be the right question, which is concerned with how to manage the conversation between those who lead the change and those who will have to implement it. The role of opinion leaders in the organization may be key, whether these are senior staff or first-line supervisors, or dedicated transition teams.

LO 7.5 *Understand how successful communication processes vary with the type and stage of organizational change.*

Communication should be tailored to the *type* of change. Widespread face-to-face communication is effective with developmental changes. However, task-focused transitions and post-crisis turnarounds may need to be driven with formal top-down communication. Charismatic transformations also require top-down communication, but with a more personalized approach, allowing dialogue. The "communication escalator" also suggests that the degree of employee involvement, and the range of communication media used, should reflect the degree of change: significant change calls for a wider range of communication and a high degree of staff involvement.

Communication and leadership style should also be tailored to the *stage* of the change process: at the planning stage, a combination of logical and inspirational styles; at the enabling stage, a combination of logical, inspirational, and supportive styles; at the launch stage, a combination of logical and commanding styles; at the catalyzing stage, inspirational and supportive styles; at the maintenance stage, inspirational and supportive styles. One change manager may not have all of the skills and the behavioral flexibility required, reinforcing the importance of building a capable change team.

LO 7.6 *Assess the utility of a range of different change communication channels, including applications of social media.*

Communication media vary in terms of "information richness," which involves handling many items of information simultaneously, rapid feedback, and personal focus. Face-to-face communications are information rich; reports and flyers are lean. Information-rich media are more appropriate when dealing with complex nonroutine issues. Lean media are more appropriate for simple routine matters. Social media based on mobile technologies are information rich, allowing two-way communication and encouraging information sharing, networking, and collaboration. Social media thus have the potential to transform organizational change communication. However, most organizations have been slow to exploit these technologies for internal communication; most applications address external audiences. Employees may be more sophisticated in their use of these new technologies in their private lives than employers with regard to organizational applications. The development of enterprise-specific networks may help to realize the potential of these technologies.

References

Allen-Greil, D., Edwards, S., Ludden, J., and Johnson, E. 2011. Social media and organizational change. Paper presented at Museums and the Web 2011 Conference, Philadelphia, April 6–9, http://museumsandtheweb.com/mw2011/papers/social_media_and_organizational_change, accessed February 5, 2015.

Bulkeley, W. M. 2004. IBM documents give rare look at sensitive plans on "offshoring." *The Wall Street Journal*, January 19. http://www.wsj.com/articles/SB107438649533319800 (accessed March 9, 2015).

Cannell, M. 2010. *Employee communication factsheet*. London: Chartered Institute of Personnel and Development.

Christensen, L. T., and Cornelissen, J. 2011. Bridging corporate and organizational communication: Review, development, and a look to the future. *Management Communication Quarterly* 25(3):383–414.

Chui, M., Manyika, J., Bughin, J., Dobbs, R., Roxburgh, C., Sarrazin, H., Sands, G., and Westergren, M. 2012. *The social economy: Unlocking value and productivity through social technologies.* New York and London: McKinsey & Company/McKinsey Global Institute.

Clampitt, P. G., DeKoch, R. J., and Cushman, T. 2000. A strategy for communicating about uncertainty. *Academy of Management Executive* 14(4):41–57.

Collett, P. 2004. Show and tell. *People Management* 10(8):34–35.

Daly, J. P. 1995. Explaining changes to employees: The influence of justifications and change outcomes on employees' fairness judgments. *Journal of Applied Behavioral Science* 31(4):415–28.

Dobosz-Bourne, D., and Jankowicz, A. D. 2006. Reframing resistance to change: Experience from General Motors Poland. *International Journal of Human Resource Management* 17(12):2021–34.

Donellan, A. 2015. Lloyds bosses lambasted as staff survey goes awry. *The Sunday Times* (Business), February 15:2.

Duck, J. D. 1993. Managing change: The art of balancing. *Harvard Business Review* 71(6):109–18.

Ford, J. D., and Ford, L. W. 1995. The role of conversations in producing intentional change in organizations. *Academy of Management Review* 20(3):541–70.

Fox, S., and Amichai-Hamburger, Y. 2001. The power of emotional appeals in promoting organizational change programs. *Academy of Management Executive* 15(4):84–95.

Gayeski, D. M., and Majka, J. 1996. Untangling communication chaos: A communicator's conundrum for coping with change in the coming century. *Communication World* (Special Supplement), 13(7):22–26.

Geigle, S. L., and Bailey, M. R. 2001. When communication fails: An analysis of the influence of communication practices during change. Paper presented at Western Academy of Management Conference, Sun Valley, Idaho, April 5–7.

Gifford, J. 2013. *Social technology, social business?* London: Chartered Institute of Personnel and Development.

Gifford, J. 2014. *Putting social media to work: Lessons from employers.* London: Chartered Institute of Personnel and Development.

Guaspari, J. 1996. If you want your people to buy-in to change, you have to sell them— yes, sell them. *Across the Board* 33(5):32–36.

Heracleous, L., and Barrett, M. 2001. Organizational change as discourse: Communicative actions and deep structures in the context of information technology implementation. *Academy of Management Journal* 44(4):755–78.

Hussey, D. E. 1998. Words, sentences and self delusion. *Strategic Change* 7(8):435–36.

Keller, S., Meaney, M., and Pung, C. 2010. *What successful transformations share.* Chicago and London: McKinsey & Company.

Kuchler, H. 2015. Facebook at Work opens to trial partners. *The Financial Times,* January 14:8.

Lachinsky, A. 2006. The Hurd way. *Fortune* 153(7):92–102.

Larkin, T. J., and Larkin, S. 1996. Reaching and changing frontline employees. *Harvard Business Review* 74(3):95–104.

Lengel, R. H., and Daft, R. L. 1988. The selection of communication media as an executive skill. *Academy of Management Executive* 2(3):225–32.

Lewin, K. (ed.). 1951. *Field theory in social science: Selected theoretical papers by Kurt Lewin.* London: Tavistock Publications. (UK edition published 1952, edited by Dorwin Cartwright.)

Lewis, L. K. 1999. Disseminating information and soliciting input during planned organizational change: Implementers' targets, sources, and channels for communicating. *Management Communication Quarterly* 13(1):43–75.

Linstead, S., Brewis, J., and Linstead, A. 2005. Gender in change: Gendering change. *Journal of Organizational Change Management* 18(6):542–60.

Ludeman, K., and Erlandson, E. 2004. Coaching the alpha male. *Harvard Business Review* 82(5):58–67.

Marshak, R. J. 1993. Managing the metaphors of change. *Organizational Dynamics* 22(1):44–56.

Matthews, D. 2015. Digital transformation in the workplace. *The Times Raconteur Supplement,* April 9:4–6.

McKinsey & Company. 2011. Social technologies on the front line: The Management 2.0 M-Prize winners. *The McKinsey Quarterly,* September:1–4.

McLuhan, M. 1964. *Understanding media: The extensions of man.* New York: McGraw-Hill.

Nelson, T., and Coxhead, H. 1997. Increasing the probability of re-engineering/culture change success through effective internal communication. *Strategic Change* 6(1):29–48.

Olofson, C. 1999. Make change, minimize distractions: What's your problem? *Fast Company* 42(21):42.

Pophal, L. 2014. How to sell social media to the C-suite. *Communication World* 31(2):22–25.

Quirke, B. 2008. *Making the connections: Using internal communication to turn strategy into action.* 2nd ed. Aldershot, UK: Gower Publishing.

Rafferty, A. E., Jimmieson, N. L., and Armenakis, A. A. 2013. Change readiness: A multilevel review. *Journal of Management* 39(1):110–35.

Reardon, K. K., and Reardon, K. J. 1999. All that we can be: Leading the U.S. Army's gender integration effort. *Management Communication Quarterly* 12(4):600–17.

Roberto, M. A., and Levesque, L. C. 2005. The art of making change initiatives stick. *MIT Sloan Management Review* 46(4):53–60.

Saunders, R. M. 1999. Communicating change: A dozen tips from the experts. *Harvard Management Communication Letter* 2(8):2–3.

Shannon, C. E., and Weaver, W. 1949. *The mathematical theory of communication.* Urbana: University of Illinois Press.

Sibbet, D. 2013. *Visual leaders: New tools for visioning, management, and organizational change.* Hoboken, NJ: John Wiley & Sons Inc.

Sillince, J. A. A. 1999. The role of political language forms and language coherence in the organizational change process. *Organization Studies* 20(3):485–518.

Stace, D. A., and Dunphy, D. 2001. *Beyond the boundaries: Leading and re-creating the successful enterprise.* 2nd ed. Sydney: McGraw-Hill.

Tannen, D. 1995. The power of talk: Who gets heard and why. *Harvard Business Review* 73(5):138–48.

Towers Watson. 2013. *How the fundamentals have evolved and the best adapt: Change and communication report 2013–2014.* New York: Towers Watson.

Valvi, A. C., and Fragkos, K. C. 2013. Crisis communication strategies: A case of British Petroleum. *Industrial and Commercial Training* 45(7):383–91.

Whelan-Berry, K. S., and Somerville, K. A. 2010. Linking change drivers and the organizational change process: A review and synthesis. *Journal of Change Management* 10(2):175–93.

Williams, M. 2007. Building genuine trust through interpersonal emotion management: A threat regulation model of trust and collaboration across boundaries. *Academy of Management Review* 32(2):595–621.

Wolff, C. 2010. IRS internal communications survey 2010: Employer practice. *IRS Employment Review*, June.

Chapter 8

Resistance to Change

Learning objectives

On completion of this chapter you should be able to:

LO 8.1 Explain the benefits of resistance to change, as well as the disadvantages.

LO 8.2 Understand the causes of resistance to change.

LO 8.3 Identify the symptoms of resistance to change.

LO 8.4 Recognize and diagnose middle management resistance to change, which could be a blockage, or could be highly beneficial.

LO 8.5 Understand and apply different approaches to managing resistance.

www.simonkneebone.com

WIIFM, WAMI, and the Dimensions of Resistance

WIIFM stands for "What's In It For Me?" (sometimes WIIFT: "What's In It For Them?"). WAMI stands for "What's Against My Interests?" If "it" is an organizational change, and if there is nothing in it for me but frustration and grief, then I will resist. If it is not in my interests, then I will resist. Convince me of the benefits, and persuade me that it is in my interests, and then you have my support. Managing resistance to change can be seen as no more complex than that. Is it really so simple?

Resistance offers a plausible explanation for the apparently high failure rate of organizational change. Many commentators see resistance to change as a problem to be solved, a barrier to overcome, an enemy to defeat. Resistance stimulates strong emotions and strong language. Foote (2001) describes resistance as "one of the nastiest, most debilitating workplace cancers," claiming that "there isn't a more potent, paradoxical or equal-opportunity killer of progress and good intentions." Geisler (2001) refers to "bottom-feeders" who complain about and resist change because of its potential to remove the "waste" that they need to survive: infighting, bureaucracy, autocratic posturing. Maurer (2010, p. 23) observes, "The mere mention of the word unleashes a torrent of negative thoughts—fear, opposition, conflict, hassles, pain, annoyance, anger, suspicion." This kind of language encourages an adversarial approach to resistance, which can make the problem worse. However, research and experience show that resistance takes many forms, and it can be constructive as well as damaging.

Change can fail for many other reasons, even when widely supported. Attributing problems to resistance can obscure the ways in which management practices contribute to change implementation problems. We thus have to explore the various dimensions of what is commonly termed resistance, and ask whether this term, with its negative connotations, is still a helpful one.

Following this introduction, the chapter has five sections. First, we explore the argument that resistance to change, when seen and managed as a resource rather than as a problem, can often be helpful and beneficial. Second, we will explore the causes of resistance. Causes can include resistance to the substance or *content* of change, and resistance to the way in which changes are implemented, or the change *process*. Third, we then consider the signs or symptoms of resistance, some of which are public and easily recognizable, and some of which are covert and harder to detect. Fourth, we examine the stereotype of middle managers as "change blockers." The evidence suggests that this popular view is often wrong. Middle managers can subvert changes proposed by senior executives when they believe that those proposals are ill advised, and will not be effective.

Finally, as resistance can be a difficulty in some circumstances, we consider strategies for avoiding and if necessary managing resistance to change. The concepts of individual readiness for change and stakeholder management are relevant to this discussion, but as those topics were covered in chapter 4, they will not be revisited in detail in this chapter. Table 8.1 provides a brief reminder.

TABLE 8.1
Individual
Readiness and
Stakeholder
Analysis—a
Reminder

Five Components of Individual Readiness	Five Components of Stakeholder Management
Belief that change is necessary	Identify all stakeholders
Belief that change is an appropriate response	Establish what they expect to gain or lose
Perceived individual capability to implement	Check their "track record" on response to change
Belief that resources will be provided	Use planned benefits to strengthen support
Personal evaluation of costs and benefits	Address concerns by reducing losses

LO 8.1 Benefits

> *We come now to a most important point. Resistance to change is not only normal but in some ways even desirable. An organization totally devoid of resistance to change would fly apart at the seams. It must be ambivalent about radical technical innovation. It must both seek it out and resist it. Because of commitments to existing technology and to forms of social organization associated with it, management must act against the eager acceptance of new technical ideas, even good ones. Otherwise, the organization would be perpetually and fruitlessly shifting gears.*

(Schön, 1963, p. 82)

Is resistance to change a "natural" human response? If that were true, then we would never become bored with our jobs or look for promotion and more challenging work. If that were true, then manufacturers, from Apple to Ford, would have problems bringing new products to market. Does resistance to change strengthen with age? If that were true, then we would not see retirees set up new businesses, build "portfolio" or "encore" careers, and develop other new skills and interests. Florian Kunze et al. (2013) present evidence showing that resistance to change *decreases* with age. Resistance is a topic shrouded in myths. Another of these myths is that resistance is a problem.

Resistance is not inevitable. As noted earlier, change is unlikely to be challenged if those who are going to be affected believe that they will benefit in some way—if "WIIFT" is clear and positive. Outcomes that can encourage support for change thus include (Kirkpatrick, 2001):

Security	Increased demand for particular skills; stronger organizational competitive position and improved job security
Money	Higher remuneration
Authority	Promotion, power, more discretion in decision making
Status	Prestige assignments with matching job titles, a bigger office
Responsibility	Increased job scope, visibility
Better conditions	Improved physical environment, new equipment
Self-satisfaction	Greater sense of challenge and achievement
Personal contacts	More chances to meet and work with influential people
Less time and effort	Operational efficiencies

Resistance, when it does occur, is not necessarily damaging. Donald Schön (1963) argued that resistance was not just desirable, but necessary, in order to prevent the implementation of weak ideas and ineffective proposals. Unity and consensus are often viewed as desirable, while conflict and disagreement are bad. However, in some settings, a divergence of opinions can be constructive if this exposes the dimensions of an argument or the full range of consequences—positive and negative—of a change proposal. Several other commentators have thus argued for the need to recognize the utility of resistance (Waddell and Sohal, 1998; Mabin, 2001; Atkinson, 2005). Maurer (2010, p. 23) says, "Sometimes we need to hear the resistance in order to know that our plans are doomed to failure."

Jeffrey and Laurie Ford (2009) argue that resistance to change provides valuable feedback on what is being proposed. Resistance is a resource, even if it sounds like complaints and arguments. They suggest that there is no point in blaming resisters. Treated as a threat, they become defensive and uncommunicative, and the resource is no longer available. On the contrary, it is important to understand resistance, which can often be well founded. Resistance is not always irrational or self-serving. Ford and Ford (2009, p. 100) argue, "Even difficult people can provide valuable input when you treat their communication with respect and are willing to reconsider some aspects of the change you're initiating." What to you as the change manager is an annoying complaint may be a genuine expression of concern from the person who raised it. Resisters believe that they are being helpful and constructive, while you believe that they are being negative and disruptive.

Furthermore, different people interpret change, and therefore respond to change, in different ways, at different times, depending on their current role and past experience (Ford et al., 2002). We may resist your current proposals because your previous initiative did not work. We may find some parts of your proposals exciting and welcome, while being horrified by some of your other change ideas.

Ford and Ford (2009) identify five ways in which resistance can be used productively:

1. *Encourage dialogue*	Keep the conversation alive—even with complaints—to increase awareness of the change ideas and allow those affected to think through the implications.
2. *Clarify the purpose*	Those affected need to understand why their roles have to change.
3. *Consider new possibilities*	Assess and if appropriate accept the ideas of those who are resisting; the most outspoken are often closest to the operations affected and care about getting it right.
4. *Listen to the voices*	Encourage participation and engagement; people want to be heard, and noting concerns can generate novel and valuable options.
5. *Deal with the past*	Current responses to change can be based on previous failures in which today's managers were not involved; it may be necessary to resolve any "leftover" issues before going ahead with new plans.

For some change managers, adopting a "welcoming" approach to resistance to change may sound unrealistic, and personally challenging. However, Todd Jick and Maury Peiperl (2010) suggest that change managers should "rethink" the concept of resistance, recognizing this as a natural part of the process of adapting to change and thus as a potential source of energy and feedback. Rick Maurer (2010) also argues that the power of resistance can be used to build support for change. Treating resisters with respect strengthens relationships and improves the chances of success. He also advises the change manager to relax, to resist the temptation to "push back" when attacked, to learn from the resistance, to look for common ground. Although advocating this perspective, Maurer (2010) also accepts that there are situations where focusing attention on dissent can be counterproductive. This can occur, for example, where challenges to the change proposals are not well informed, or where change is necessary for organizational survival.

For the benefits to be gained, resistance must be active. But resistance can sometimes be passive, and involve silence, and withholding cooperation and information. Encouraging complaints and challenges may sound perverse, but by encouraging the dialogue, active resistance can be stimulated, and the feedback and ideas can then be used constructively.

This section has focused on the positive dimensions of resistance. We also have to recognize the damage that resistance can cause, to an organization, its members, and sometimes even to those who are resisting. Job security, for example, may be jeopardized by a failure to introduce new systems, procedures, practices, and technology. It is important, therefore, to adopt a balanced perspective on this topic, recognizing the negative as well as the positive implications.

LO 8.2 Causes *appropriateness is not a cause listed here*

> *The American composer, John Cage, once said: "I can't understand why people are frightened of new ideas. I'm frightened of the old ones"*
>
> (http://www.quotationspage.com)

Resistance can have seriously damaging organizational and individual consequences, leading to reduced performance and competitiveness, failure to acquire new capabilities, and job loss. Why then do people resist change? There are probably as many answers to that question as there are members of organizations faced with change. Broadly, the reasons fall into three categories concerning the *content* or substance of the change, the *process* through which change is implemented, and the *uncertainty* that change can generate (Hughes, 2010). We will explore in this section the common causes of resistance. Be aware that this is not an exhaustive list. It is important, however, for the change manager to diagnose the cause—or causes—of resistance before taking action.

Innate Dislike of Change

Some of us just do not like change. It is common to hear the complaint that the main impediment that managers face in introducing change is that people dislike change and will resist it. We have already argued, however, that this view is oversimplified and does not explain why people sometimes welcome and even seek change. It is not wise to assume that a dislike of change is necessarily an innate human characteristic that we all share. As individuals, we vary in our approach or "disposition" to change. Some of us prefer routine, become tense and anxious when confronted with change, do not like to change our plans, and are more rigid in our thinking. Those who have high dispositional resistance toward change are therefore less likely to accept change in general and are more likely to resist when change is imposed. But some of us dislike routine, are animated by new ideas and plans, and are comfortable with changing our minds when presented with fresh information.

While our individual disposition toward change may be a relatively stable personality trait, context is also important. Shaul Oreg (2003; 2006), for example, argues that trust in management and having the right amount of information can positively influence dispositions toward change. Information overload, however, can reinforce negative perceptions and strengthen resistance. Another significant feature of the context concerns the substance or content of the changes. You may find some ideas attractive even if you have high dispositional resistance to change in general. We therefore cannot automatically predict your reaction to the next change based on your response to current proposals.

For most of us, therefore, our responses are more likely to depend on the organizational context and the characteristics of the proposed changes than on our personality. If correct, this conclusion has profound practical implications for the change manager. We cannot manage your personality. We can, however, change our proposals, and we can manage or adjust aspects of the organizational context. The change manager has to accept, however, that some individuals, in some contexts, may have extremely high dispositional resistance to change that cannot easily be altered.

Low Tolerance of Uncertainty

Do you enjoy being taken by surprise? You look forward to the "mystery tour," destination unknown. Or do you need to know precisely what will happen next? You want to know all the journey details in advance. There are individual differences in our tolerance of uncertainty and ambiguity. If you are not confident that you have the skills and capabilities that the proposed changes will demand, then the uncertainty will be magnified. Uncertainty can of course be reduced, and support strengthened, by making clear the strategic intent of the change, and the actions that are expected of those involved. The key point here is that lack of support for change may not be due to overt resistance, or apathy, but to uncertainty and ambiguity, based on lack of information—a lack that can be remedied.

This Is Not in My Interests

We noted earlier that resistance can be based on the perception that change will work against the interests of those who will be affected. The term "interests" can cover a range of factors: authority, status, rewards (including remuneration), opportunities to apply expertise, membership of friendship networks, autonomy, security. People find it easier to support changes when their interests are not threatened, and they may resist when they perceive that their interests will be damaged.

The key term here is "perception." Seen from a different standpoint (long-term job security, for example), proposed changes may support the interests of those involved, whose focus on short-term implications (loss of currently valued skills, for example) may take priority. It is the perceptions of those who are involved that determine their responses to change, and not the perceptions of others. Perceptions are difficult to manage and to change, but the quality and volume of available information, and the roles of opinion leaders and networks, can be significant in this regard.

Fear That YouTube Will Change

Managers need to consider the way in which a proposed change—or even just the belief that a change is about to be made—can produce a reaction from stakeholders outside the organization. Managing the expectations of the external constituency, such as customers, can be as important as handling the concerns of those inside the organization.

In 2014, when Google appointed Susan Wojcicki as its senior vice president in charge of YouTube, she received a lot of correspondence from passionate fans who were worried that she would make changes that would weaken the YouTube experience that they currently enjoyed. One user expressed her concern very succinctly: "So please, I'm begging you, please, please, please, don't f*** it up" (La Porte, 2014, p. 60).

Attachment to Organization Culture and Identity

The "image" of the organization as a cultural system is a popular one. A cultural system includes values, artifacts, and beliefs concerning "the way we do things around here." Resistance to change can thus be influenced by the degree of attachment to the existing culture. Rhonda Reger and colleagues (1994, p. 33–34) argue that members of an organization interpret change proposals through their existing mental models:

> A particularly powerful mental model is the set of beliefs members hold about the organization's identity. Identity beliefs are critical to consider when implementing fundamental change because organizational identity is what individuals believe is central, distinctive, and enduring about their organization. These beliefs are especially resistant to change because they are embedded within members' most basic assumptions about the organization's character.

Reger et al. (1994) also argue that two mental barriers can undermine the acceptance of change initiatives that are seen as inconsistent with the current organizational identity. First, passive resistance (apathy, anxiety) can occur when the meaning and purpose of the change have not been made clear. Second, active resistance can be triggered when change is seen to be in direct conflict with key aspects of the organization's identity. Change managers cannot assume that other members of the organization share their mental models concerning the need for change. Strong resistance may therefore be triggered by change proposals that are perceived as threatening basic assumptions. One strategy for the change manager, therefore, is to avoid changes that carry such threats. A second approach concerns presenting proposals in a way that minimizes challenges to the current order. Third, it may be necessary to develop an overwhelmingly compelling case for fundamental culture change, if threats to current assumptions cannot be minimized or avoided.

Perceived Breach of Psychological Contract

Our understanding of the nature of the reciprocal relationship that we have with an employer has been called the "psychological contract" (Rousseau, 1995; Coyle-Shapiro and Shore, 2007). A breach or violation of this contract occurs when employees believe that the employer is no longer honoring their side of the deal. As the label suggests, the psychological contract is in part defined by a formal written agreement (job description, terms and conditions, performance appraisal), and also in part by informal social and psychological dimensions. The informal aspects are not expressed in writing. These concern expectations regarding organizational values, trust, loyalty, and recognition—features that can have just as significant an effect on employee perceptions as formal written terms. Perceived breaches of the psychological contract can thus lower performance and reduce adaptability to change (McDermott, Conway, et al., 2013).

Research has explored relationships between psychological contract and responses to change. From their study in a textiles company in Scotland, Judy Pate and colleagues (2000) found a link between perceived breaches of psychological contracts and resistance to strategic and organizational change. They conclude, "When organizations fail to respect employee interests, the low-trust relationships and levels of cynicism that invariably result severely constrain the potential for effective strategic change" (p. 481). Sjoerd van den Heuvel and René Schalk (2009, p. 283), in a study of Dutch organizations, conclude, "The more the organization had fulfilled its promises in the employee's perception, the less the employee resisted organizational change. By maintaining good psychological contracts with employees, organizations can build trust, which could prevent resistance to change."

Lack of Conviction That Change Is Necessary

The work of the change manager is more straightforward if there is widespread belief across the organization that change is needed. However, what seems obvious to some ("We have to change") is not necessarily viewed in the same way by others ("What's the problem?"). There are many reasons for complacency: a past track record of success, the absence of a visible crisis, inconsistent top management comments. We react negatively to change when we feel that there is no need for it.

Lack of Clarity as to What Is Expected

Sometimes proposed changes, and particularly strategic changes, are not accompanied by clear information about the implications for those who will be affected. How will my role change? What new knowledge, skills, and behaviors will be required? Where questions such as those are not answered, there is a heightened probability of resistance and lack of support from those who feel that they have not been adequately informed. In other words, "A brilliant business strategy is of little use unless people understand it well enough to apply it" (Gadiesh and Gilbert, 2001, p. 74). For the change manager, the key point is that resistance may not be due to opposition to the changes that have been proposed. The absence of support may instead be due to a lack of clear understanding of what will be involved for those who are going to be affected.

Belief That the Proposed Changes Are Inappropriate

Those affected by a proposed change are likely to form a view that it is either an appropriate response to current issues ("We need to do this") or a bad idea ("Whose crazy plan is this?"; "It's a fad"). This view is likely to influence readiness for change. As change advocate and manager, it is easy to see those who support the change as astute and to criticize those who do not as blinkered. The latter are then categorized as "resistant to change." However, this is not necessarily an accurate label, because resistance to *this* change does not necessarily mean resistance to *all* change. We should also consider that, in some cases, the resisters may be right; the changes may have been poorly thought through and inadequately planned. Here is another situation where resistance is valuable.

Change can also be seen as inappropriate due to fundamental differences in "vision," which is achieved through the organization's strategy. Change, as a key component in the enactment of strategy, can thus expose widely divergent views of how to achieve that vision.

Perception That the Timing Is Wrong

The change may be welcome, but the timing may be seen as wrong; "yes, but not now." This may be due to change fatigue (see next heading). Or it may be that, if the change were to be implemented now, it would have a negative impact on, say, customers or suppliers or employees or joint venture partners. Change the timing, and those undesirable outcomes would be avoided.

Excessive Change: The Consequences

In their study of "excessive change," Inger Stensaker et al. (2002) identified three common consequences: "musical chairs," "orchestrating without a conductor," and "shaky foundations."

Musical chairs (a reference to the children's game) occurs when managers move frequently between a declining number of positions in a regularly changing structure. Unless carefully managed, this can have detrimental effects. For example, the most capable managers are the most likely to leave because they will be seen as attractive to other organizations. In addition, the "churn" in positions leaves fewer managers with a strategic grasp of the purpose behind all those change initiatives.

Orchestrating without a conductor refers to the related situation where lower-level employees feel that they have been abandoned, as middle managers seem incapable of handling the change process. Middle managers may be unable to translate change proposals in a way that makes sense to the staff who will be affected. Why? Because due to the constant management restructuring, those middle managers are not sufficiently familiar with the work of those employees.

Shaky foundations refers to the resulting sense of chaos. Staff find themselves in an uncomfortable limbo between partly abandoned past practices and partly introduced new practices. Where waves of change are involved, the new practices are in various stages of implementation, from just introduced to nearly complete.

Too Much Change

Too much change can of course induce "initiative fatigue," "initiative overload," and burnout, especially when new initiatives are launched before the last changes have been fully embedded. Those suffering from initiative fatigue are likely to feel overworked and under pressure and are unlikely to welcome further change, regardless of how desirable it may seem.

Heike Bruch and Joche Menges (2010) argue that intense market pressures have increased the number and pace of change initiatives, which becomes "the new normal." This can lead an organization, they claim, into "the acceleration trap"; the pressure is unrelenting, staff are demotivated, focus is scattered, and customers become confused. They identify three damaging patterns. *Overloading*: Staff are asked to do too much and have neither the time nor the resources to do it. *Multiloading*: Staff are asked to cover too many different kinds of activities, reducing the focus on what they do best. *Perpetual loading*: The organization is operating close to capacity, denying staff any chance to escape or to "recharge"; "When is the economizing going to come to an end?" Organizations caught in this acceleration trap are thus likely to encounter more resistance to further change than organizations that have avoided or escaped from this trap. Escape strategies include halting the less important work, clarifying strategy, and having a system for prioritizing projects. At one company, the chief executive cut the number of top-priority goals that managers set from 10 down to a maximum of 3 "must-win battles," to focus attention and energy.

Yong-Yeon Ji et al. (2014) support this argument. From their study of 4,900 U.S. organizations in 18 industries, they conclude that the disruption of employment instability reduces organizational performance. However, they also found that very low instability could damage competitiveness; stable organizations are rigid and inflexible. They advise a "slow and steady" response to external conditions, rather than acting too quickly and aggressively.

The Cumulative Effects of Other Life Changes

Readiness for change at work is affected by what else is going on in an individual's life. Measures of stress, for example, typically include elements from a range of aspects of one's life, and not just those associated with employment. As a result, people may

---

Does Your Organization Have an Acceleration Culture?

Answer "yes" to five or more of these questions and you may be caught in the acceleration trap:

Are activities started too quickly?

Is it hard to get the most important things done because too many other activities diffuse focus?

Is ending activities considered a sign of weakness?

Are projects carried out pro forma because people fear ending them publicly?

Is there a tendency to continually drive the organization to the limits of its capacity?

Is it impossible for employees to see the light at the end of the tunnel?

Does the company value attendance at work and meetings more than goal achievement?

Does it value visibly hard effort over tangible results?

Are employees made to feel guilty if they leave work early?

Do employees talk a lot about how big their workload is?

Is "busyness" valued?

Are mangers expected to act as role models by being involved in multiple projects?

Is "no" a taboo word, even for people who have already taken on too many projects?

Is there an expectation in the organization that people must respond to emails within minutes?

Do countless people routinely get copied on emails because employees are trying to protect themselves?

In their free time, do employees keep their cell phones or messaging devices on because they feel they always need to be reachable?

resist organizational change in the belief that the change will add to the burden of pressures that they are already experiencing.

Perceived Ethical Conflict

Sandy Piderit (2000) argues that resistance is multidimensional and can often be motivated by a desire to act ethically. Resistance to change may thus be based on positive intentions, designed to protect the interests of the organization and its employees. The belief that some individual or groups will be disadvantaged or unreasonably pressured by proposed changes could lead to resistance. Piderit (2000) also notes, however, that resistance in these situations is likely to be covert, if perceived threats to job security and promotion discourage open expressions of concern.

The Legacy of Past Changes

Past experience is one predictor of responses to current change proposals. As our experiences shape expectations of the future, resistance may be grounded in previous bad experiences of change, while support may be strengthened by past successes. From a sense-making perspective (see chapter 9), we learn "how change works in this organization," and use that understanding as a lens through which further change initiatives are assessed (Gioia and Chitipeddi, 1991). The change manager can thus be the fortunate beneficiary, or the unfortunate victim, of sense-making experiences in which they played no part, and of which they may be unaware. The impact on responses to current change proposals may be more intense where the same organization, managers, and staff are involved. Sense-making based on personal past experience is more credible, and more powerful, than the reassurances of today's change managers.

Where past experience of change has been bad, cynicism and resistance may be default responses to fresh initiatives. Stensaker et al. (2002, p. 304) note that BOHICA (Bend Over, Here It Comes Again) is a response based on learning from experience. Cynicism can be particularly difficult to deal with because it is usually accompanied by strong emotions such as anger, resentment, and disillusionment.

Managing Change, Managing Memories

1. Begin change initiatives with a systematic inquiry into organizational members' memories of past changes.

2. Do not tell people to leave their past behind. That is not going to happen. The power and credibility of past experiences cannot be erased to order. Attempts to suppress those experiences may mean that they "go underground," but they will remain influential.

3. If past experiences are impediments to change, their influence will only be challenged if those involved are directly and fully engaged with current proposals, in ways that enable them to learn that the change experience this time can be different—and positive.

Source: Based on Geigle, 1998.

Disagreement with How the Change Is Managed

The idea that resistance to change—that is, to the *substance* of change—is a natural human response, diverts attention away from the quality of the change management *process*. "Overcoming natural resistance to change," in some situations, may actually involve "overcoming natural resistance to poor management," or "highlighting change management mistakes" (Dent and Goldberg, 1999a and b). Kahn (1982, p. 416) thus advised:

> In considering obstacles to change, we must keep in mind the deceptive nature of our concepts. When we want change, we speak of those who do not as presenting obstacles and resistance. When we want stability, we speak of perseverance and commitment among those who share our views. Behavior of people in the two situations might be identical; it is their stance relative to our own that dictates the choice of language.

In other words, labelling behavior as "resistance to change" may be an example of the fundamental attribution error—blaming individuals while overlooking the context (Ross, 1977). If those who are managing change can attribute unsatisfactory outcomes to the behavior (resistance) of others, the spotlight may not then fall on inadequate change management practices. This "blame game" can also work in the opposite direction, with organization members attributing change failures to management faults, rather than to their own behavior (Piderit, 2000).

It is therefore easy to understand how a change manager can be attracted to the proposition that the lack of success of a change program was due to resistance to change. This explanation shifts attention away from management capabilities and practices and onto the change recipients. The popular notion that people have a natural resistance to change also makes this a plausible explanation. As we argued earlier, resistance may be a natural response to change that has not been adequately considered and planned. If such resistance prompts a review, then it will have been valuable. Mark Hughes (2010) argues that the term *resistance* has negative connotations, and is thus misleading and inappropriate. He suggests that it should now be "retired" in favor of "employee responses" to change, recognizing the broad spectrum of potential reactions—positive, neutral, and negative—to organizational change initiatives.

LO 8.3 Symptoms

Despite assertions to the contrary, people aren't against change—they are against royal edicts.

(Hamel and Zanini, 2014, p. 2)

How can resistance to change be detected? The answer to this question is not as straightforward as it might seem, because the symptoms—the signs and clues—can be difficult to detect, and to interpret. For example, resistance can be overt and visible, but it can also be covert and hidden. Open criticism and heated debate are of course easier to detect than whispered private conversations. Given the potential benefits of challenges to change proposals, overt resistance may be of more value to the organization, to the change manager, and ultimately to the change process. Resistance is also three-dimensional, with emotional, cognitive, and behavioral components (Oreg, 2003). In short, the change manager has to be sensitive to how people *feel* about change, how they *think* about it, and what they intend to *do* about it (see the sidebar "Merger in Adland").

TABLE 8.2
Active and Passive Resistance

Symptoms of Active Resistance	Symptoms of Passive Resistance
Being critical, finding fault, ridiculing, arguing	Agreeing in person but not following through
Appealing to fear, starting rumors	Failing to implement change
Using facts selectively, distorting facts	Procrastinating, dragging one's feet
Blaming, accusing, intimidating, threatening	Feigning ignorance
Manipulating, sabotaging	Withholding information, suggestions, support
Blocking, undermining	Standing by and allowing change to fail

Source: Based on Hultman, 1995.

Kenneth Hultman (1995) draws a useful distinction between active and passive resistance. Table 8.2 identifies typical active and passive resistance behaviors. This illustrates the distinction, but these lists are not comprehensive, and the various symptoms are not necessarily mutually exclusive (ridiculing, and being critical, for example). Nevertheless, the change manager must be alert to the various ways in which resistance to change can be demonstrated. Hultman also reminds us that identifying the symptoms does not explain why people are resisting change, and that it is important to be clear about symptoms and causes (as in this chapter) and not to confuse one with the other.

Merger in Adland: Symptoms of Resistance?

When the Australian advertising agencies Mojo and MDA merged, they decided to locate all staff in the same building. However, as an interim step, all the creative staff (copywriters, art directors, production) moved into the Mojo offices and management ("the suits") went to the MDA offices.

One of the Mojo people required to move was the finance director, Mike Thorley. Mike was one of the original Mojo employees and had come to think of himself more as a partner in the business than as an employee. However, he was quickly disabused of this notion when, with all the other Mojo employees, he was given no warning of the merger. He reacted with shock and anger. To add insult to injury, he had to move to the MDA offices—which felt like banishment—where he would report to MDA's finance director, who was now in charge of finance for the merged organization.

The Mojo culture was much less formal than that of MDA. Mojo staff would often have a few drinks together after work, sitting around an old white bench in the office. In an attempt to make Thorley and his Mojo colleagues feel at home, a modern black laminate bar was installed in the MDA offices. One morning, Mike Thorley arrived at work with a chainsaw and cut the bar in two.

Source: Based on Coombs, 1990.

LO 8.4 Managers as Resisters

Most discussions of resistance present managers as advocates of change and cast employees in the role of resisters. However, resistance is not monopolized by "the managed." Managers can also resist change, for all the reasons identified earlier, and are therefore not always passionate advocates. Managers can be considered collectively, as a group, but sometimes differences within management can be significant. Changes proposed by one department or division may be opposed by another. Changes directed by top management may not be welcomed by middle managers. In other words managers, at least as much as any other category of employee, are likely to have within their ranks a range of opinions concerning proposed changes. Even where there is no question as to the dedication of managers to the long-term interests of the organization, it is normal to find different views as to which initiatives or changes are most appropriate.

The stance of middle managers in particular can have a critical effect on the outcome of change initiatives because they are often responsible for implementation. It is not unusual for this role to involve tensions for middle managers, who are likely to be both recipients of change initiatives from senior management, as well as implementers.

Middle managers have long been stereotyped as change blockers. However, research has consistently painted a different picture. The positive contributions of middle management to innovation and change are now widely recognized, partly due to the work of Bill Wooldridge and Steven Floyd (1990; Wooldridge et al., 2008). They argue that middle management involvement in shaping strategy leads to better decisions, higher degrees of consensus, improved implementation, and better organizational performance. They also emphasize the coordinating, mediating, interpreting, and negotiating roles of middle managers, arguing that it is the pattern of influence of middle managers that affects performance. The mediating role, combining access to top management with knowledge of frontline operational capabilities, gives middle management a valuable perspective, where appropriate acting as a counter to the strategic view of the top executive team.

With regard to blocking change, Inger Boyett and Graeme Currie (2004) report how middle managers in an Irish telecommunications firm subverted the intent of senior management by designing an alternative strategy that was more profitable. Julia Balogun (2008) argues that, even when middle managers are "change recipients," the way in which directives are interpreted and implemented may differ from—and significantly

Resistance to Change at Bloomberg

Earlier in this chapter, a range of beliefs, perceptions, and attitudes were identified as having the potential to be the underlying causes of resistance to change. Even the most senior of managers in an organization are not exempt from holding such beliefs, which may manifest as resistance.

By 2012, Bloomberg had become the world's largest financial data provider. However, after three decades of growth, it was now facing a flattening growth rate, leading to what business journalists Peter Elkind and Marty Jones (2013, p. 130) called "a traumatic identity crisis."

Bloomberg's success had been built so much on one product—the service that provided customers with financial data and which generated 85 percent of its revenue—that significant resistance arose within the ranks of senior management whenever a new direction was suggested. One such instance occurred when CEO Dan Doctoroff attempted to "diversify the business and impose professional order on a chaotic enterprise where screaming and infighting have long passed for management" (Elkind and Jones, 2013, p. 131). Founder Michael Bloomberg, due to return in January 2014 after being mayor of New York City from 2002 to 2013, would be returning to a situation of "an internal war raging between old and new factions" (Elkind and Jones, 2013, p. 130).

improve upon—senior management intentions. From their study of change in the Irish health service, Edel Conway and Kathy Monks (2011) describe how ambivalent middle managers who resisted top-down directives played a vital role by championing and implementing their own initiatives. Those initiatives assisted in dismantling outdated structures and processes, and provided solutions to the problems that those directives had identified in the first place. Aoife McDermott et al. (2013) show how middle managers and other change recipients often tailor, add to, and adapt top-down change directives so that they will work in particular local contexts.

The negative middle management stereotype thus has to be adjusted in two respects. First, middle managers are likely to attempt to block or undermine senior management directives if they believe that those proposals will not work well. This is a reasonable "self-defense" position because, were those senior management plans to be put in place and then fail, middle management would probably be blamed for mishandling the implementation. Second, where middle managers have better ideas and plans of their own, they are likely to attempt to implement those instead of senior management proposals. Employee resistance is more likely to arise at the point of implementation, by which stage it may be too late. Management resistance, however, is more likely to occur at the conceptualization and planning stage, when options still remain open. We are thus faced with yet more examples of "positive resistance," where middle management "change blocking" is not as disruptive as the label implies, but can lead to improved organizational outcomes.

LO 8.5   Managing Resistance

How widespread is the problem of resistance to change? In 2010, the consulting company McKinsey surveyed 1,890 executives who had recent experience of organizational redesign. One third of those who replied said that "employees actively resisted change or became demoralized," and a quarter said that "leaders resisted, undermined, or changed the plans for reorganization" (Ghislanzoni et al., 2010, p. 6). The problem most frequently cited as harmful in those organizations where redesign had been successful concerned senior managers undermining the change. One explanation is that "redesign that fundamentally changes the way the organization works frequently upsets those who rose to the top in the old system" (Ghislanzoni et al., 2010, p. 7).

Does it matter if some people resist a particular change? Not necessarily. Peter Senge (1990) argues that dispositions toward change vary on a continuum from commitment, through varying degrees of compliance, to noncompliance, and apathy (table 8.3). From a change management perspective, it is useful to understand the dispositions of those who are going to be affected. It is also important to be aware that dispositions can change, as understanding of the implications develops.

It may be reassuring to have everyone fully committed to an organizational change. Senge argues, however, that this is not necessary. Rather than attempt to persuade everyone to "commit," it can be more useful to analyze the level of support required from each of those individuals and groups who are involved, and to direct change management attention and energies to winning that support. With a critical mass of support in place, the noncompliance or apathy of others may have little or no impact.

TABLE 8.3
The Commitment-Compliance Continuum

Disposition	Response to Change
Commitment	Want change to happen and will work to make it happen Willing to create whatever structures, systems, and frameworks are necessary for it to work
Enrollment	Want the change to happen and will devote time and energy to making it happen within given frameworks Act within the spirit of the framework
Genuine compliance	See the virtue in what is proposed, do what is asked of them, and think proactively about what is needed Act within the letter of the framework
Formal compliance	Can describe the benefits of what is proposed and are not hostile to them—they do what they are asked and no more Stick to the letter of the framework
Grudging compliance	Do not accept that there are benefits to what is proposed and do not go along with it, but do enough of what is asked of them not to jeopardize their position Interpret the letter of the framework
Noncompliance	Do not accept that there are benefits and have nothing to lose by opposing the proposition, so will not do what is asked of them Work outside the framework
Apathy	Neither support nor oppose the proposal, just serving time Don't care about the framework

Source: Based on Senge, 1990, pp. 204–5.

Despite what we have said regarding the benefits, and the misleading nature of the label, resistance to change can be self-interested, deliberately disruptive, badly informed—and a problem for the change manager. How can such resistance be managed effectively? Given what we know about the many possible causes of resistance, there is no "one best way" to handle this situation. We will therefore explore three approaches to this task, suggesting that these should be seen as complementary rather than as competing. The first concerns allowing those who will be affected by change to recognize and to adjust to the implications in their own time; in short, "let nature take its course." The second concerns developing "attraction strategies," which seek to overcome or avoid resistance before it develops. The third involves a "contingency approach" to managing resistance, choosing and using methods that are appropriate to the context.

Let Nature Take Its Course

Individual reactions to change typically involve working through a series of natural psychological stages. This progression is known as the coping cycle, and models of this process are often based on the work of Elizabeth Kübler-Ross (1969), who studied human responses to traumatic events such as the death of a close relative. The application of her work to change management is based on the assumption that, for at least some people, major organizational and career changes can also be very traumatic. Under those conditions, resistance to change is predictable. Cynthia Scott and Dennis Jaffe (2006), for example, describe a coping cycle with four stages:

Denial	This involves a refusal to recognize the situation; "this can't be happening," "it will all blow over." The person is not receptive to new information and refuses to believe that he or she needs to behave differently, or is prepared to make only minor adjustments.
Resistance	This stage begins with the recognition that the situation is real; the past is mourned, and stress may increase; active and passive forms of resistance may be demonstrated. This can be seen as a positive stage, as the individual lets go of the past and becomes more confident in his or her ability to deal with the future.
Exploration	This involves reenergizing and a preparedness to explore the possibilities of the new situation.
Commitment	The individual finally focuses attention on new courses of action.

This is an "ideal" picture of the coping cycle. There are individual differences in how this cycle is experienced. Different people work through these stages at different paces, with some moving more quickly while others become "stuck." The organizational context may also affect progress, through sharing experience with others (or not) and encountering fresh information.

If individual responses conform broadly to this pattern, then one approach to managing resistance is to step back, to monitor what is happening, and to let nature take its natural and necessary course. However, if key individuals do become "stuck," say at the resistance stage, then doing nothing may be unwise, and some form of intervention may be helpful. Table 8.4, "Individual Resistance and Management Responses," offers a guide to dealing with different expressions of resistance.

TABLE 8.4
Individual Resistance and Management Responses

The Person Says ...	Comment	Your Response ...
I don't want to ("the block")	An authentic response, unambiguous, and easy to handle	Why? What's your concern?
Tell me exactly what you want me to do ("the rollover")	Ambiguous—may be a genuine request for information, or a form of passive resistance (if you don't tell me, I won't be responsible for the outcomes)	Tell me what you need to know.
I'll get on it first thing next week ("the stall")	May reflect lack of awareness of urgency, or indicate a desire to avoid complying	Is there anything serious that would prevent you from starting tomorrow?
Wow, what a great deal! ("the reverse")	May be genuine, but resisters will say this to keep you happy with no intention of supporting	I am pleased that you feel this way. What exactly can I count on you to deliver, and when?
I think it would be better if this were implemented first in X division ("the sidestep")	Could be correct, but resisters use this to shift the pressure to change onto somebody else	I understand your concern, but we have other plans for X. What I specifically want you to do is this.

(Continues)

TABLE 8.4 *(Continued)*

X isn't going to like this ("the projected threat")	Implies the threat that someone important will not be happy (could be true)	X has been part of this process and is fully supportive. OR I'll be speaking to X about this, but at the moment I'm more interested in your views.
You owe me one ("the press")	Involves asking to be exempt as reciprocity for a past favor	I haven't forgotten that, but I need your support right now.
See what you're making me do ("the guilt trip")	An attempt to deflect attention by focusing on the change manager's actions	I am sorry that you have a problem, and we can discuss how to help, but it is important for this change to go ahead.
But we've always done it the other way ("the tradition")	Traditions should only be maintained if they still work; but old ways often feel safer, less threatening	The other way has served us well for a long time, but things have changed. What could we do to incorporate the best of our traditional approach?

Source: Based on Karp (1996).

Attraction Strategies

From their work with healthcare professionals in U.S. hospitals, Paul Plsek and Charles Kilo (1999, p. 40) conclude, "Change is not so much about resistance, as it is about creating attraction." What is often described as "resistance," they note, is actually "attraction" to aspects of the current system. The change manager's task is to find new attractors or to use effectively those that already exist.

Strong attractors?

Find the Attractor

Physician leader Roger Resar, MD, tells of an office assistant who was resistant to a proposed change that would offer same-day appointments to patients and dramatically reduce the booking of future appointments. The assistant was attracted to the comfort of the existing scheduling system, chaotic though it was, because she understood it so well.

"Rather than simply labelling her a 'resister,' Resar engaged her in a friendly conversation about the most appealing and unappealing aspects of her job. One prominent dislike was having to call 30 or more patients to reschedule appointments when the doctor needed to be away. When Resar pointed out that the open access system would virtually eliminate the need for this activity, the assistant became actively attracted to the new idea—the same idea

that she was seen as resisting just moments before. The proposed change was now associated with the comfort attractor and the resistance vanished" (Plsek and Kilo, 1999, p. 41). Martin Lippert, chief executive of the Danish telecommunications company TDC, describes how middle management resistance to the introduction of "lean management" was addressed:

"It was a big change for them. Before, middle managers spent only about 10 or 15 percent of their time on real leadership—performance management, coaching, finding out what's going on in their organization. Instead, almost all of their time was consumed by projects, mostly to fix problems. That's a very inefficient way of working. We needed to reverse those numbers so that managers could spend 80 percent of their time being managers and leaders. Some of the managers were truly unable or unwilling to make the change. But eventually most of them saw that what we were providing was a set of techniques that they could adapt as they needed. In working together with the front line and senior leadership to design the transformation in their teams, the managers gradually came to recognize how the whole system of lean management could help them accomplish more. It took time, of course, but once they did, we saw more involvement from them than ever before" (McKinsey & Company, 2014, p. 157).

To identify appropriate attractors, change managers must have a good understanding of the issues and concerns that are important to those whose behavior they want to change—and those issues may differ from those of the change manager. Close relationships are therefore important: "Attractors are easier to create when working together in cooperative, positive relationships of trust" (Plsek and Kilo, 1999, p. 42). The focus should lie with system changes and improvements, rather than with changing the behavior of individuals in an existing system (see sidebar, "Find the Attractor"). Questions that can be helpful in identifying the attractors in a particular situation include:

- How will this change benefit individual staff, the team, customers/clients?
- How will current problems and frustrations be addressed?
- How does this relate to the interests and priorities of staff?
- How will those involved gain recognition for their efforts?
- How will performance be improved?
- How could efficiency gains be used to make further improvements?

W. Chan Kim and Renée Mauborgne (2003, p. 62) also claim that "once the beliefs and energies of a critical mass of people are engaged, conversion to a new idea will spread like an epidemic, bringing about fundamental change very quickly." In other words, that critical mass forms a "tipping point," beyond which change can be straightforward and rapid. They further note that:

> The theory suggests that such a movement can be unleashed only by agents who make unforgettable and unarguable calls for change, who concentrate their resources on what really matters, who mobilize the commitment of the organization's key players, and who succeed in silencing the most vocal naysayers.

Kim and Mauborgne (2003) illustrate their theory using the experience of Bill Bratton, an American police chief well known for his achievements in "turning around" failing or problem forces, such as in Boston and New York. One of the main hurdles to overcome, they argue, is motivational. This concerns establishing the desire to implement change, as well as making clear the need. One of the most powerful strategies that Bratton used to motivate change involved targeting the small number of key influencers in the organization. In the New York Police Department, that meant the city's 76 precinct commanders, who were each responsible for up to 400 staff. The key influencers are people with power, based on extensive networks inside and outside the organization, and on their influencing skills. Once the key influencers become attracted to the change program, they complete the task of persuading and motivating others, freeing the change manager to focus on other issues.

Attraction strategies suggest, therefore, that resistance can be avoided if the change manager is able to design and present proposals in ways that are appealing and compelling to those who will be involved. We will meet this argument again, in a different form, in chapter 10. One way in which to ensure that change is attractive is to involve those who will be directly affected in deciding what and how to change in the first place.

Contingency Approaches

There is no "one best way" to manage resistance. As suggested in the last section, action to deal with resistance should be based on a diagnosis of the cause or causes; people may resist change for more than one reason. Those resisting a particular change may do so for different reasons; different stakeholders thus have to be managed differently. Allies and supporters need to be kept on your side. Opponents need to be converted or neutralized. These observations point to the need for a contingency approach, with actions tailored to the circumstances and the context.

One of the most widely cited contingency approaches to managing resistance was developed by John Kotter and Leo Schlesinger (2008). Their approach has two dimensions, concerning pace and management strategies. With regard to pace, they advise the change manager to decide the optimal speed of the change; how quickly or how slowly should this happen? They suggest moving quickly if there is a crisis affecting performance or survival. They suggest moving slowly where:

- information and commitment from others will be needed to design and implement;
- the change manager has less organizational power than those who will resist;
- resistance will be intense and extensive.

They then identify the six strategies for managing resistance summarized in table 8.5: education, participation, facilitation, negotiation, manipulation, and coercion. Those strategies each have advantages and drawbacks. Education is time-consuming—a disadvantage. Coercion can be quick—a key advantage in some contexts. Personal values and social norms suggest that the first three of those strategies will be more common. But in practice, there are times when negotiation, manipulation, and coercion should be considered. The conditions in which each strategy is appropriate are also identified in table 8.5 ("Use When ..."), and these strategies can be used in combination, if appropriate.

Building Commitment to Change *Make the Process Attractive*

Attraction strategies to overcome resistance can focus on the change process as well as the substance of the changes. Rosabeth Moss Kanter (1985, p. 55) suggests how to do this:

- Allow room for participation in the planning of the change.

- Leave choices within the overall decision to change.

- Provide a clear picture of the change, a "vision" with details about the new state.

- Share information about change plans to the fullest extent possible.

- Divide a big change into manageable and familiar steps; let people take a small step first.

- Minimize surprises; give people advance warning about new requirements.

- Allow for digestion of change requests—a chance to become accustomed to the idea of change before making a commitment.

- Repeatedly demonstrate your own commitment to the change.

- Make standards and requirements clear—tell exactly what is expected of people in the change.

- Offer positive reinforcement for competence; let people know they can do it.

- Look for and reward pioneers, innovators, and early successes to serve as models.

- Help people find or feel compensated for the extra time and energy change requires.

- Avoid creating obvious "losers" from the change. (But if there are some, be honest with them—early on.)

- Allow expressions of nostalgia and grief for the past—then create excitement about the future.

TABLE 8.5
Strategies for Dealing with Resistance to Change

Strategies	Advantages	Disadvantages	Use When Resistance Is Caused By
Education and communication	increases commitment, reconciles opposing views	takes time	misunderstanding and lack of information
Participation and involvement	reduces fear, uses individual skills	takes time	fear of the unknown
Facilitation and support	increases awareness and understanding	takes time and can be expensive	anxiety over personal impact
Negotiation and agreement	helps to reduce strong resistance	can be expensive and encourage others to strike deals	powerful stakeholders whose interests are threatened
Manipulation and co-optation	quick and inexpensive	future problems from those who feel they were manipulated	powerful stakeholders who are difficult to manage
Explicit and implicit coercion	quick and overpowers resistance	change agent must have power; risky if people are angered	deep disagreements and little chance of consensus

Clayton Christensen et al. (2006) also advocate a contingency approach to managing resistance. They argue that the organizational context of change varies on two main dimensions. The first concerns the extent to which people agree on the outcomes or goals of change. The second concerns agreement on the means, on how to get there. Low agreement and high agreement contexts need to be managed in different ways. Where there is low agreement concerning both goals and means, they argue—along with Kotter and Schlesinger—that coercion, threats, fiat, and negotiation become necessary.

When dealing with resistance, the change manager thus has a range of tools and approaches. Give those affected time to come to terms with what is required and the implications. Find ways to avoid resistance by identifying the features that will make change attractive to those who will be involved. Select an appropriate strategy or strategies depending on the cause or causes of the resistance. These three broad sets of approaches are not mutually exclusive, and it may be appropriate to deploy a number of approaches, at the same time, with the same or different individuals and groups.

EXERCISE 8.1 *Diagnosing and Acting* LO 8.2	Consider a change in which you were involved and that was seriously affected by resistance. 1. When did you first become aware of resistance? 2. What form did the resistance take? 3. What were your first thoughts (anger, betrayal, confusion, relief)? 4. What made you decide that you had to do something? 5. What actions did you take? 6. What was the impact in (a) the short term and (b) the long term? 7. If you could "rewind the tape," what would you do differently?

EXERCISE 8.2 *Jack's Dilemma* LO 8.5	Jack White is the newly appointed general manager of the pet food division of Strickland Corporation. He has completed a strategic review that has convinced him that the division needs to undergo rapid and substantial change in a number of areas, given the recent strategic moves of key competitors. Although Jack is new, he is familiar enough with the company to know that there will be significant resistance to the changes from a number of quarters. He also suspects that some of this resistance will come from people with the capacity to act in ways that could seriously impede successful change. Jack reflects on the situation. He believes that it is important to introduce the proposed changes soon, but he also recognizes that if he acts too quickly, he'll have virtually no time to have a dialogue with staff about the proposed changes, much less involve them in any significant way. One option is to act speedily and to make it clear that "consequences" will follow for anyone not cooperating. He certainly has the power to act on such a threat. The risk, Jack knows, is that even if no one shows outright resistance, there's a big difference between not cooperating and acting in a manner that reflects commitment. He knows that he needs the cooperation of key groups of staff, and that sometimes "minimum-level compliance" can be as unhelpful as resistance when it comes to implementing change. "But maybe I'm exaggerating this problem," he thinks to himself. "Maybe I should just go ahead with the change. If people don't like it, they can leave. If they stay, they'll come around." But Jack is not sure. He considers another option. Maybe he should spend more time on building up support at least among key groups of managers and staff, if not more broadly across the organization. "Maybe," he reflects, "the need to change is not quite as immediate as I think. I just know that I'd feel a whole lot better if this consultation could happen quickly." **Your Task** Jack respects your opinion on business matters and has asked you for your views on his situation. What would be your recommendation? What factors should Jack take into account in deciding what course of action to take?

use AAA model

EXERCISE 8.3

Moneyball

LO 8.2, 8.3, 8.5

The *New York Times* best seller *Moneyball* (Lewis, 2003) is a book about baseball. It describes how Billy Beane, the general manager of the Oakland Athletics, revolutionized Major League Baseball (MLB) by introducing a new approach (sabermetrics) to assessing the value of a player to a team (see Wolfe et al., 2006). The established approach to assessing player talent favored future potential, but sabermetrics focused on past performance. Also, the established approach focused on the statistics of batting average (BA) and earned run average (ERA). The new approach was based on the argument that different statistics such as on-base percentage and slugging percentage (OSP) were better predictors of a player's performance. Beane introduced sabermetrics, but the underlying concept was not his. The writer Bill James had argued (and been ignored) for three decades that research attested to its superiority as a basis for determining a player's true value to a team.

Beane's application of the new approach was successful, and the Oakland Athletics moved close to the top of the league despite being outspent by most of their competitors. As a result, the team had approaches from many interested businesses and sporting bodies, including teams from the NFL and MLB, Fortune 500 companies, and Wall Street firms.

However, other MLB teams continued to show a lack of interest in the new approach, and some were openly hostile to it. Why? The MLB was bound in tradition and characterized by deep respect for convention and precedent. Sabermetrics challenged treasured orthodoxies for two reasons. First, it questioned the value of established predictors of performance. Second, sabermetrics based decisions on statistics, and thus reduced the importance of professional judgement. In other words, sabermetrics sidelined the field managers who had previously enjoyed significant control over talent selection and in-game tactics. Sabermetrics thus threatened the job security of many who had been appointed on the strength of their knowledge of individual characteristics and aspects of the game that were no longer considered to be important.

We can explore how the introduction of sabermetrics affected team management and players in the movie *Moneyball* (2011, director Bennett Miller). Brad Pitt plays Oakland's manager, Billy Beane, who is losing his star players to wealthier clubs. The Athletics' owner Stephen Schott (Bobby Kotick) will not provide more money. How can he build a competitive team with a limited budget? Beane hires an economics graduate, Peter Brand (Jonah Hill). Brand introduces him to James' statistics-based approach to picking talent, looking at the complementary skills of the players in the team as well as focusing on individual capabilities. Using this method, Beane puts together a team of previously unknown players. However, Beane's senior manager Art Howe (Philip Seymour Hoffman) will not allow Beane to use these recruits, and refuses to discuss the matter. The team's talent scouts do not like the new method either. As you watch this movie, consider the following questions:

1. Who is resisting this change and why?

2. What behaviors are used to demonstrate that resistance?

3. What role do emotions play, on both sides of this argument?

4. What tactics and behaviors do Billy Beane and Peter Brand use to overcome resistance to their new approach?

5. What lessons can you take from this experience concerning the nature of resistance and methods for overcoming resistance to change?

Additional Reading

Battilana, J., and Casciaro, T. 2013. The network secrets of great change agents. *Harvard Business Review* 91(7/8):62–68. Explores the importance of the change agent's networks in dealing with resisters and fence-sitters, as well as with those who support the change.

Ford, J. D., and Ford, L. W. 2009. Decoding resistance to change. *Harvard Business Review* 87(4):99–103. Argues that vigorous resistance can be valuable and suggests practical ways to use resistance productively.

Harvey, T. R., and Broyles, E. A. 2010. *Resistance to change: A guide to harnessing its positive power.* Lanham, MD: R&L Education. Develops the view that resistance is natural, positive, and necessary, rather than destructive, offering practical guidance with illustrations.

Maurer, R. 2010. *Beyond the walls of resistance.* 2nd ed. Austin, TX: Bard Books. An easy-to-read, "no nonsense" practical guide to resistance, its benefits, its causes, and its management.

Roundup

Resistance is a multifaceted topic. The negative label suggests damage, but we have seen how resistance can be constructive, and we have argued that the term itself is thus potentially misleading. Resistance can have a number of different causes, takes several different forms, and reveals itself in a range of symptoms. However, there are several approaches or strategies available for managing resistance effectively, where that becomes necessary, and depending on a diagnosis of the situation. In sum, resistance is not the change manager's worst nightmare, as some commentary has suggested.

Reflections for the Practicing Change Manager

- What symptoms of resistance to change have you observed? Have you observed both active and passive forms? Have you as a recipient resisted change? Have you experienced resistance while responsible for initiating and managing a change?

- Which of the various causes of resistance to change do you believe to be the most common? What are the "top three" causes in your experience?

- As a change manager, which of the various reasons for resisting change do you believe to be the most difficult to deal with? What are your "top three" in this regard?

- When senior managers resist change at the strategic level, they are in a position to cause more damage than employees resisting changes at an operational level. Have you worked in an organization where you believe that there was management resistance to change? As a manager, what action would you take to prevent this?

- Which particular approaches to the management of resistance attract you? Why do you make this choice? Do you think those approaches are more effective, or do your choices relate to your views about how people should be managed?

- From your experience as a change manager, what are the three main pieces of advice that you would give to someone new in this role concerning diagnosing and managing resistance?

Here is a short summary of the key points that we would like you to take from this chapter, in relation to each of the learning outcomes:

LO 8.1   *Explain the benefits and disadvantages of resistance to change.*
Resistance can threaten organizational performance, competitiveness, and survival, and lead to job loss in some cases. Resistance can also mean a failure to learn new skills and abilities, with long-term implications for individual employability. However, those who resist are those who are going to be affected directly by change, and who therefore have a good understanding of how it might work. Their feedback can be particularly valuable in identifying whether or not change has been adequately considered and planned. Resistance can therefore be seen not as damaging, but as constructive feedback. This may not happen in every instance; there can be many reasons behind displays of resistance. However, the change manager who views resistance positively, and who listens with genuine interest to the concerns and challenges that are raised, is more likely to implement an effective change, while improving relationships with those involved.

LO 8.2   *Understand the causes of resistance to change.*
There are many potential causes for resistance, and we have only explored a number of the most common in this chapter. Diagnosing cause in a given situation is a key task for the change manager. In making that diagnosis, the change manager must be aware of two issues. First, resistance may be underpinned by several causes, not just one (although there may be one main concern). The management response thus has to take this into consideration. Second, the cause or causes of resistance can change over time, as an initiative develops, as other parallel initiatives are introduced, and as new information is uncovered. The task of diagnosing resistance is thus an ongoing one.

LO 8.3   *Identify the symptoms of resistance to change.*
Once again, there are many potential symptoms of resistance, which can be active or passive. The passive resistance may be more difficult to detect. Paradoxically, active resisters—those who shout and complain the loudest—may be more valuable. At least the change manager knows what they are thinking and can address that, and they may have genuine concerns that could inform and improve change design, planning, and implementation.

LO 8.4   *Recognize and diagnose middle management resistance to change, which could be a blockage, or could be highly beneficial.*
We know that managers at all levels can sometimes resist change and that such behavior is not restricted to frontline or operational staff. However, the stereotype of the middle manager as change blocker is not consistent with the evidence. Middle managers often subvert or block top leadership directives, but only to put in place something more effective.

LO 8.5   *Understand and apply different approaches to managing resistance.*
We explored a range of resistance management strategies: allow people naturally to adjust, develop "attractors" to avoid or minimize resistance in the first place, and develop a contingency approach depending on the cause or causes of the resistance. As in most management contexts, there is no "one best way," and action has to be based on a diagnosis of the problem.

We have seen how resistance to change can be viewed from a number of different perspectives. How in turn is this phenomenon interpreted by different images of the change manager? The different images' perspectives are summarized in table 8.6. Which of these perspectives most closely fits your own view of organizational change, resistance, and change management?

TABLE 8.6
Images of Change Management and Perspectives on Resistance

Image	Perspective on Resistance
Director	Resistance is a sign that not everybody is on board in terms of making the change. Resistance can and must be overcome in order to move change forward. Change managers need specific skills to ensure that they can deal with resistance.
Navigator	Resistance is expected. It is not necessarily a sign of people being outside their comfort zone but that there are different interests in the organization and some of these may be undermined by the change. We cannot always overcome resistance, but this should be achieved where possible.
Caretaker	Resistance is possible but likely to be short-lived and ultimately futile. This is because changes will occur in spite of attempts to halt them. At best, resistance might temporarily delay change rather than halt its inevitable impact.
Coach	Resistance needs to be recognized and expected as change takes people out of their comfort zones. Change managers need to work with resistance to show how these actions are not consistent with good teamwork.
Interpreter	Resistance is likely where people do not fully understand what is happening, where the change is taking the organization, and the impact it will have on those involved. Making sense of the change, helping to clarify what it means, and linking individual identity with the process and the expected outcomes of the change will help to address the underlying problems that led to the resistance.
Nurturer	Resistance is irrelevant to whether or not change happens. Changes will occur but not always in predictable ways. Therefore, resisting change will be a matter of guesswork by the resister, as change often emerges from a clash of chaotic forces and it is usually not possible to identify, predict, or control the direction of change.

References Atkinson, P. 2005. Managing resistance to change. *Management Services*, Spring:14–19.

Balogun, J. 2008. *When organizations change: A middle management perspective on getting it right.* London: Advanced Institute of Management Research.

Battilana, J., and Casciaro, T. 2013. The network secrets of great change agents. *Harvard Business Review* 91(7/8):62–68.

Boyett, I., and Currie, G. 2004. Middle managers moulding international strategy: An Irish start-up in Jamaican telecoms. *Long Range Planning* 37(1):51–66.

Bruch, H., and Menges, J. I. 2010. The acceleration trap. *Harvard Business Review* 88(4):80–86.

Christensen, C. M., Marx, M., and Stevenson, H. H. 2006. The tools of cooperation and change. *Harvard Business Review* 84(10):73–80.

Conway, E., and Monks, K. 2011. Change from below: The role of middle managers in mediating paradoxical change. *Human Resource Management Journal* 21(2):190–202.

Coombs, A. 1990. *Adland: A true story of corporate drama.* Melbourne: Heinemann.

Coyle-Shapiro, J. A-M., and Shore, L. 2007. The employee-organization relationship: Where do we go from here? *Human Resource Management Review* 17(2):166–79.

Dent, E. B., and Goldberg, S. G. 1999a. Challenging "resistance to change." *Journal of Applied Behavioral Science* 35:25–41.

Dent, E. B., and Goldberg, S. G. 1999b. "Resistance to change": A limiting perspective. *Journal of Applied Behavioral Science* 35:45–47.

Elkind, P., and Jones, M. 2013. The trouble at Bloomberg. *Fortune,* December 23:130–44.

Foote, D. 2001. The futility of resistance (to change). *Computerworld,* January 15. http://www.computerworld.com/s/article/56246/The_Futility_of_Resistance_to_Change_.

Ford, J. D., and Ford, L. W. 2009. Decoding resistance to change. *Harvard Business Review* 87(4):99–103.

Ford, J. D., Ford, L. W., and McNamara, R. T. 2002. Resistance and the background conversations of change. *Journal of Organizational Change Management* 15(2):105–21.

Gadiesh, O., and Gilbert, J. L. 2001. Transforming corner-office strategy into frontline action. *Harvard Business Review* 79(5):72–79.

Geigle, S. 1998. Organizational memory and scripts: Resistance to change or lessons from the past. Paper presented to the Annual Conference of the Academy of Human Resource Development, Chicago, March.

Geisler, D. 2001. Bottom-feeders: People who resist change. *Executive Excellence* 18(12):19.

Ghislanzoni, G., Heidari-Robinson, S., and Jermiin, M. 2010. *Taking organizational redesign from plan to practice.* London: McKinsey & Company.

Gioia, D. G., and Chitipeddi, K. C. 1991. Sensemaking and sensegiving in strategic change initiation. *Strategic Management Journal* 12(6):433–88.

Hamel, G. and Zanini, M. 2014. *Build a Change Platform, Not a Change Program.* London: McKinsey & Company.

Harvey, T. R., and Broyles, E. A. 2010. *Resistance to change: A guide to harnessing its positive power.* Lanham, MD: R&L Education.

Hughes, M. 2010. *Managing change: A critical perspective.* London: Chartered Institute of Personnel and Development.

Hultman, K. E. 1995. Scaling the wall of resistance. *Training and Development* 49(10):15–18.

Ji, Y.-Y., Gutherie, J. P., and Messersmith, J. G. 2014. The tortoise and the hare: The impact of employee instability on firm performance. *Human Resource Management Journal* 24(4):355–73.

Jick, T. J., and Peiperl, M. 2010. *Managing change: Cases and concepts*. 3rd ed. New York: McGraw-Hill.

Kahn, E. F. 1982. Conclusion: Critical themes in the study of change. In *Change in organizations*, ed. P. S. Goodman and Associates (407–29). San Francisco: Jossey-Bass.

Kanter, R. M. 1985. Managing the human side of change. *Management Review* 74(April):52–56.

Karp, H. B. 1996. *The change leader*. San Francisco: Pfeiffer.

Kim, W. C., and Mauborgne, R. 2003. Tipping point leadership. *Harvard Business Review* 81(4):60–69.

Kirkpatrick, D. L. 2001. *Managing change effectively*. Boston: Butterworth-Heinemann.

Kotter, J. P., and Schlesinger, L. A. 2008. Choosing strategies for change. *Harvard Business Review* 86(7/8):130–39 (first published 1979).

Kübler-Ross, E. 1969. *On death and dying*. Toronto: Macmillan.

Kunze, F., Boehm, S., and Bruch, H. 2013. Age, resistance to change, and job performance. *Journal of Managerial Psychology* 28(7/8):741–60.

La Porte, N. 2014. Rebooting YouTube. *Fast Company*, September:58–64.

Lewis, M. 2003. *Moneyball: The art of winning an unfair game*. New York: W. W. Norton & Company.

Mabin, V. J., Forgeson, S., and Green, L. 2001. Harnessing resistance: Using the theory of constraints to assist change management. *Journal of European Industrial Training* 25(2):168–91.

Maurer, R. 2010. *Beyond the walls of resistance*. 2nd ed. Austin, TX: Bard Books.

McDermott, A. M., Conway, E., Rousseau, D., and Flood, P. C. 2013. Promoting effective psychological contracts through leadership: The missing link between HR strategy and performance. *Human Resource Management* 52(2):289–310.

McDermott, A. M., Fitzgerald, L., and Buchanan, D. A. 2013. Beyond acceptance and resistance: Entrepreneurial change agency responses in policy implementation. *British Journal of Management* 24(S1):93–225.

McKinsey & Company. 2014. *The lean management enterprise: A system for daily progress, meaningful purpose, and lasting value*. New York: McKinsey Practice Publications.

Oreg, S. 2003. Resistance to change: Developing an individual differences measure. *Journal of Applied Psychology* 88(4):680–93.

Oreg, S. 2006. Personality, context, and resistance to organizational change. *European Journal of Work and Organizational Psychology* 15(1):73–101.

Pate, J., Martin, G., and Staines, H. 2000. Exploring the relationship between psychological contracts and organizational change: A process model and case study evidence. *Strategic Change* 9(8):481–93.

Piderit, S. K. 2000. Rethinking resistance and recognizing ambivalence: A multi-dimensional view of attitudes towards an organizational change. *Academy of Management Review* 25(4):783–94.

Plsek, P. E., and Kilo, C. M. 1999. From resistance to attraction: A different approach to change. *Physician Executive* 25(6):40–42.

Reger, R. K., Mullane, J. V., Loren T., Gustafson, L. T., and DeMarie, S. M. 1994. Creating earthquakes to change organizational mindsets. *Academy of Management Executive* 8(4):31–43.

Ross, L. 1977. The intuitive psychologist and his shortcomings: Distortions in the attribution process. In *Advances in Experimental Social Psychology*, ed. L. Berkowitz (173–220). New York: Academic Press.

Rousseau, D. M. 1995. *Psychological contracts in organizations: Understanding written and unwritten agreements*. Thousand Oaks, CA: Sage Publications.

Scott, C. D., and Jaffe, D. T. 2006. *Change management: Leading people through organizational transitions*. 3rd ed. Cincinnati, OH: Thomson Learning.

Schön, D. A. 1963. Champions for radical new inventions. *Harvard Business Review* 41(2):77–86.

Senge, P. 1990. *The fifth discipline: The art and practice of the learning organization*. New York: Doubleday Currency.

Stensaker, I., Meyer, C. B., Falkenberg, J., and Haueng, A. C. 2002. Excessive change: Coping mechanisms and consequences. *Organizational Dynamics* 31(3):296–312.

van den Heuvel, S., and Schalk, R. 2009. The relationship between fulfilment of the psychological contract and resistance to change during organizational transformations. *Social Science Information* 48(2):283–313.

Waddell, D., and Sohal, A. S. 1998. Resistance: A constructive tool for change management. *Management Decision* 36(8):543–48.

Wolfe, R., Wright, P. M., and Smart, D. L. 2006. Radical HRM innovation and competitive advantage: The Moneyball story. *Human Resource Management* 45(1):111–26.

Wooldridge, B. J., and Floyd, S. W. 1990. The strategy process, middle management involvement, and organizational performance. *Strategic Management Journal* 11(3):231–41.

Wooldridge, B., Schmid, T., and Floyd, S. W. 2008. The middle management perspective on strategy process: Contributions, synthesis, and future research. *Journal of Management* 34(6):1190–221.

Chapter 9

Organization Development and Sense-Making Approaches

Learning objectives

By the end of this chapter you should be able to:

LO 9.1   Appreciate more clearly the organizational change approaches underpinning the coach and interpreter images of managing change.

LO 9.2   Understand the organization development (OD) approach to change.

LO 9.3   Be aware of extensions of the OD approach such as appreciative inquiry, positive organizational scholarship, and dialogic OD.

LO 9.4   Understand the sense-making approach to change.

NOISE TO SIGNAL   RobCottingham.com @robcottingham

We're brainstorming here, and there are no dumb ideas. But if we *weren't* brainstorming, that would have been a really, *really* dumb idea.

Cartoon by Rob Cottingham – www.RobCottingham.com

LO 9.1 Alternative Approaches to Managing Change

Of the six images of managing change, the *caretaker* and *nurturer* images have their foundations in the field of organization theory; the other four images—*director, coach, navigator,* and *interpreter*—have stronger foundations in the organizational change field. This chapter and the next delve further into the foundations of the four images that are rooted in the organizational change field and explore their implications for how to manage organizational change. They are also the four images that, in various ways, assume that the change manager has an important influence on the way change occurs in organizations. In contrast, the first two images, *caretaker* and *nurturer*, have in common an assumption that change managers *receive rather than initiate* change. This chapter, and the one that follows, therefore explore the four images that assume that change managers have an active role in the initiation, support, and outcomes of organizational change. This chapter considers the foundational approaches associated with the *coach* and *interpreter* images; the following chapter considers the foundational approaches associated with the *director* and *navigator* images.

Underpinned by the *coach* image, the organization development (OD) approach is one where its adherents present their developmental prescriptions for achieving change as being based, at least traditionally, upon a core set of values, values that emphasize that change should benefit not just organizations but the people who staff them.

OD has played a central role in the organizational change field for over half a century. In their 2012 review of OD, Burnes and Cooke (p. 1396) argue that it "has been, and arguably, still is, the major approach to organizational change across the Western world, and increasingly globally." However, as this chapter and the next illustrate, different images of change management are associated with different ideas about what sort of approaches (and techniques) should be used to try to bring about change within organizations. It is not surprising, therefore, that OD's long history has been accompanied, from time to time, by expressions of concern as to its continuing relevance, leading some writers to raise the question of whether OD is "in crisis"; both the *Journal of Applied Behavioral Science* (vol. 40, no. 4, 2004) and *OD Practitioner* (vol. 46, no. 4, 2014) have had special issues focused on the question of OD's ongoing relevance. A long-standing criticism of OD has been the claim that it has been sidelined from the concerns of the business community because of its preoccupation with humanistic values rather than with other issues such as business strategy (Hornstein, 2001; Beer, 2014).

Approaches to managing change other than OD have emerged. For example, underpinned by the *interpreter* image, the sense-making approach maintains that change emerges over time and consists of a series of interpretive activities that help to create in people new meanings about their organizations and about the ways in which they can operate differently in the future.

We begin by considering the approaches underpinned by the *coach* image and then move on to the *interpreter* image. Further approaches to managing change are addressed in chapter 10.

LO 9.2 Organization Development (OD)

In this section, we consider the underlying tenets of the OD approach to managing change, along with the role of the OD practitioner. We then review a number of challenges that have been directed at OD, including the continuing relevance of the values underlying the OD approach, the universal applicability of these values, and the relevance of OD to large-scale change.

Traditional OD Approach: Fundamental Values

As set out in table 9.1, OD as a change intervention technique has developed over time, being influenced by a number of different trajectories. As such there is no single, underlying theory that unifies the field as a whole. Rather, it is informed by a variety of differing perspectives, including theorists such as Herzberg, Maslow, Argyris, and Lewin (Bazigos and Burke, 1997). In drawing together the common threads of these perspectives, Beckhard (1969) depicts the classic OD approach as one that has the following characteristics:

- *It is planned* and involves a systematic diagnosis of the whole organizational system, a plan for its improvement, and provision of adequate resources.
- *The top of the organization* is committed to the change process.
- *It aims at improving the effectiveness* of the organization in order to help it achieve its mission.

TABLE 9.1

The Evolution of Organization Development (1940s–1980s)

Period	Background	Developers	Focus
1940s/1950s+	National Training Laboratories (NTL) and T-groups	Kurt Lewin, Douglas McGregor, Robert Blake, Richard Beckhard	Interpersonal relations, leadership and group dynamics; use of team building to facilitate personal and task achievement
1940s/1950s+	Action research and survey feedback	Kurt Lewin, John Collier, William Whyte, Rensis Likert	Involvement of organizational members in researching themselves to help create new knowledge and guide change actions
1950s/1960s+	Participative management	Likert	Assumption that a human relations approach, with its emphasis on participation, is the best way to manage an organization
1950s/1960s+	Productivity and quality of work-life	Eric Trist and Tavistock Institute, W. Edward Deming, and Joseph Juran	Better integration of people and technology through joint participation of unions and management, quality circles, self-managing workgroups; creation of more challenging jobs; total quality management
1970s/1980s+	Strategic change	Richard Beckhard, Christopher Worley	Need for change to be strategic, aligning organization with technical, political, cultural, and environmental influences

Source: Developed from Cummings and Worley (2015).

- *It is long term*, typically taking two or three years to achieve effective change.
- *It is action-oriented.*
- *Changing attitudes and behavior* is a focus of the change effort.
- *Experiential-based learning* is important as it helps to identify current behaviors and modifications that are needed.
- *Groups and teams* form the key focus for change.

Though it is commonly presented as being aimed at incremental, developmental, first-order change, other writers claim that what unifies the OD field, at least traditionally, is an emphasis on a core set of values. These values build upon humanistic psychology and emphasize the importance of developing people in work organizations and helping them to achieve satisfaction (Nicholl, 1998a). Three value sets are involved:

- *Humanistic values* relate to openness, honesty, and integrity.
- *Democratic values* relate to social justice, freedom of choice, and involvement.
- *Developmental values* relate to authenticity, growth, and self-realization (Nicholl, 1998c).

Human development, fairness, openness, choice, and the balance between autonomy and constraint are fundamental to these values (Burke, 1997). It is said that these values were radical and "a gutsy set of beliefs" in relation to the time in which they were developed; that is, in the 1940s and 1950s when organizational hierarchy was dominant, emphasizing authority, rationality, and efficiency rather than humanism and individuality (Nicholl, 1998b). In this sense, the traditional practice of OD has as its focus people and is not necessarily meant to be solely focused on the interests of management or the profitability of the firm (Nicholl, 1998a).

The OD Practitioner

Central to the traditional OD approach is the role of the "OD practitioner," who may be either internal or external to the organization. A typical OD practitioner helps to "structure activities to help the organization members solve their own problems and learn to do that better" (French and Bell, 1995, p. 4). Where this is based upon action research, it involves a variety of steps, such as (Cummings and Worley, 2015):

1. *Problem identification.* Someone in the organization becomes aware of what that person thinks is a problem that needs to be addressed.
2. *Consultation with an OD practitioner.* The client and the practitioner come together, with the latter endeavoring to create a collaborative dialogue.
3. *Data gathering and problem diagnosis.* Interviews, observations, surveys, and analysis of performance data occur to assist in problem diagnosis. Each of these techniques is recognized as an intervention in itself in the sense that it involves an interaction with people.
4. *Feedback.* The consultant provides the client with relevant data, at the same time protecting the identity of people from whom information was obtained.
5. *Joint problem diagnosis.* As part of the action research process, people are involved in consideration of information and discuss what it means in terms of required changes.
6. *Joint action planning.* The specific actions that need to be taken are identified.
7. *Change actions.* The introduction of and transition to new techniques and behaviors occur.

8. *Further data gathering.* Outcomes of change are determined and further actions identified.

In coaching people through such change processes, Cummings and Worley (2015) argue that OD practitioners need a variety of skills, including:

1. *Intrapersonal skills*: having a well-developed set of values and personal integrity including the ability to retain their own health in high-stress organizational situations.

2. *Interpersonal skills*: which are needed in order to work with groups, gain their trust, and "provide them with counseling and coaching."

3. *General consultation skills*: including knowledge about intervention techniques (such as those discussed in chapter 4) to assist them in diagnosing problems and designing change interventions.

4. *Organization development theory*: to ensure that they have a current understanding of the specialist field of which they are a part.

Underpinning these OD practitioner interventions is the classic change process model developed by Kurt Lewin (1947). He developed a three-stage model of how change occurs: *unfreezing* how the organization operates, *changing* the organization in specific ways, and then *refreezing* the changes into the operations of the organization. How Lewin's model of change relates to the actions of the OD practitioner is set out in table 9.2.

TABLE 9.2
Classic OD Change Intervention Processes

Lewin's Change Process	OD Action Research Change Process
Unfreezing: establishing the need for change	• Identification of problems • Consultation with OD practitioner • Gathering of data and initial diagnosis
Movement: to new behavior through cognitive restructuring	• Client group feedback • Joint problem diagnosis • Joint planning of change actions • Engagement in change actions
Refreezing: integration of new behaviors into social and organizational relationships	• Post-action data gathering and evaluation

Sources: Adapted from French and Bell (1995), Cummings and Worley (2015).

Criticisms of OD

As application of OD as an approach to managing change became more widespread, so did attention to its limitations. Even advocates of the OD approach began to acknowledge that there are problems in the field. For example, French and Bell (1995) identified six of these:

1. *OD definitions and concepts.* OD may consist of single or multiple interventions over different periods of time, so establishing the relationship between "OD" and its ability to enhance "organizational effectiveness" is difficult, especially given that the latter term itself also lacks precise definitions.

OD and the Challenge of Managing Covert Processes

Bob Marshak is a very experienced and highly regarded OD consultant. For Marshak, one of the great OD challenges is dealing with what he describes as "covert processes," those "powerful processes that impact organizations but remain unseen, unspoken, or unacknowledged [and which] include hidden agendas, blind spots, organizational politics, the elephant in the room, secret hopes and wishes, tacit assumptions, and unconscious dynamics" (Marshak, 2006, p. xi).

To reduce the likelihood that covert processes thwart an attempt to bring about organizational change, Marshak (2006) identifies five "keys" to dealing with covert processes in the context of an OD intervention:

1. **Create a (psychologically) safe environment**
   Do whatever you can to create a climate of trust and respect where people feel safe to reveal their thoughts and beliefs

2. **Seek movement, not exposure**
   Focus on moving the situation forward, not being judgmental about matter revealed (i.e., progress, not punishment).

3. **Assume that people are trying their best**
   Put the focus on inquiry rather than judgement.

4. **Look in the mirror**
   Be self-aware so that your behavior as the consultant is driven by the situaion of the people you are working with and not your own covert norms and beliefs.

5. **Act consistently with expectations**
   Stay within the scope of your brief as explained to participants at the outset unless you explicitly renegotiate expectations with them.

2. *Internal validity problems.* This relates to whether the change that occurred was caused by the change intervention or a range of other factors.

3. *External validity problems.* This is the generalizability question and relates to whether OD and its techniques are appropriate to all organizational settings.

4. *Lack of theory.* There is no comprehensive theory of change to assist researchers in knowing what to look for in what they study.

5. *Problems with measuring attitude changes.* Using pre-change and then post-change surveys to measure attitudinal changes is problematic, as people may view the scale differently when they answer it a second time.

6. *Problems with normal science approaches to research.* The ability to use these techniques (hypothesis testing, assessing cause–effect relationships, etc.) is questioned in relation to OD being a process based on action research.

French and Bell (1995, p. 334) adopted an optimistic view of this situation, arguing that "these do not appear to be insurmountable problems at this time, although they continue to plague research efforts." However, other writers were critical of such optimism, pointing out that the approach is largely descriptive and prescriptive, often failing to adequately consider the inherent limitations and underlying assumptions of its own techniques (Oswick and Grant, 1996). OD has been presented with a range of other criticisms relating to the extent to which it deals adequately with issues such as leadership, strategic change, power, and reward systems (Cummings and Worley, 2015). Three further criticisms relate to the current relevance of OD's traditional values, the universality of those values, and the ability of OD to engage in large-scale change. Each of these issues is addressed next.

Current Relevance of OD's Traditional Values

Despite its longevity, or perhaps because of it, the issue of the ongoing relevance of the values underlying OD continues to be a matter of debate, the topic still featuring heavily in 2014 in the pages of the journal *OD Practitioner* (vol. 46, no. 1). Going back 20 years, prominent OD thought leader Warner Burke (1997, p. 7) argued that, for many experienced OD practitioners, "the profession has lost its way—that its values are no longer sufficiently honored, much less practiced, and that the unrelenting emphasis on the bottom line has taken over." This sentiment was a reaction to the growing role of some OD practitioners as advisers on corporate restructurings, mergers and takeovers, and so on, despite the lack of evidence of the values core to OD being central to such changes.

As a result, a view formed that "OD has lost some of its power, its presence, and perhaps its perspective" (Burke, 1997, p. 7). An editor of *OD Practitioner* at the time, Dave Nicholl, agreed with Burke's general assessment, pointing to how many of the values of OD are confrontational to many of the values held in our organizations, leading to "stark contrasts" between being relevant and value-neutral or being value-laden and marginal (Nicholl, 1998c). Nicholl argued that OD practitioners need to remind themselves of the dilemma they face, of assisting both individual development and organizational performance—which he characterizes as "contradictory elements." By delving back into OD's heritage, Nicholl (1999) suggested that they regain their humility and present to clients not certainty but educated conjecture. Finally, he proposed the need for a paradigm shift in how the corporation is viewed and rebuilt, allowing space to recognize that corporations are not necessarily just institutions for profit but social institutions.

Other OD writers have challenged managers to make their organizations more inclusive (multiple levels of involvement in decision making), to create mutual accountability

---

OD Values *An Anachronism or Something Worth Preserving?*

The valuing of inclusion, open communication, collaboration, and empowerment has caused OD to struggle in recent decades in the face of a perception that these are values from a "gentler" time and inconsistent with fiercely competitive markets where only rapid change, driven by top-down edict, can give hope of survival. However, Burnes and Cooke (2012) query this characterization of OD. Instead they ask, are we in a time when the issue of values has never been more important? They suggest that many countries are struggling with the impact of organizations exhibiting unethical, and financially or environmentally unsustainable, practices. If this is so, they (2012, p. 1417) argue, OD "with its humanist, democratic and ethical values, wide range of participative tools and techniques, and experience in promoting behavior changes, is ideally placed ... to play a leading role in the movement to a more ethical and sustainable future."

Similarly, a widely experienced professor and consultant, Harvard Business School's Mike Beer (2014, p. 61), argues:

> With the corporate scandals of the past decade, clear evidence that we are doing damage to our planet, and the great recession of 2008, higher ambition CEOs are reframing the purpose of their firm from increasing shareholder value to contributing to all stakeholders. This trend is opening up new opportunities for the field of OD to help these higher ambition leaders to create a better world. Higher ambition companies integrate head, heart, and hands.

(linking performance remuneration to adherence to core values, stakeholders, and corporate sustainability), to reinforce interdependence (between individuals, organizations, and the wider society), to expand notions of time and space (such as considering the impact of decisions for future generations), to ensure the wise use of natural resources (such as consideration of renewable and nonrenewable resources), and to redefine the purpose of the organization in terms of multiple stakeholders (including customers, stockholders, community, planet, descendants, organizational leaders, employees, and directors) (Gelinas and James, 1999).

Are OD Values Universal?

One challenge leveled at OD is whether the approach and the values underpinning it are relevant outside of the United States, where it was predominantly developed. As with the issue of the continuing relevance of OD values over time (as discussed above), debate over the global appropriateness of OD values continues (see, e.g., Sorenson and Yaeger, 2014).

Some advocates portray OD change values as being universal, with cultural differences serving as "a veneer which covers common fundamental human existence" (Blake et al., 2000, p. 60). For example, Blake et al. (2000) claim that the classic *Managerial (or Leadership) Grid* framework developed by Robert Blake and Jane Mouton in the 1960s has been applied successfully in many different countries. For Blake et al. (2000, p. 54), this framework was "probably the first systematic, comprehensive approach to organizational change" and had played a central role in the development of OD. They argue that the grid sustains and extends core OD values in seeking greater candor, openness, and trust in organizations. The grid maps seven leadership styles that vary in terms of their emphasis on people versus results: controlling, accommodating, status quo, indifferent, paternalist, opportunist, and sound—the latter style being preferred insofar as it portrays a leadership style that is concerned for both results and people (Blake et al., 2000).

The grid has been used as the basis for change leadership seminars, helping to establish both individual awareness and skills. In response to the question of the grid's applicability outside of the United States, they claim that it has been used extensively in a variety of countries (including within Asia), in part because of "its ability to effectively employ a universal model of effective management and organizational development within diverse cultures" (Blake et al., 2000, p. 59).

Similarly, for Sorenson and Yaeger (2014, p. 58) the evidence from years of application of OD in diverse countries is that national cultural values are more akin to "a veneer that covers more fundamental and universal needs, needs which are reflected in the fundamental values of OD."

However, other OD advocates are more circumspect about how far the OD approach is relevant across cultural boundaries. For example, Marshak (1993) contends that there are fundamentally different assumptions underlying Eastern (Confucian/Taoist) and Western (Lewinian/OD) views of organizational change. These differences are outlined in table 9.3. Marshak's (1993) view is that OD practitioners need to view with care any assumptions they may hold that OD practices have universal applicability, while Mirvis (2006) recommends that OD become more open to a pluralism of ideas by drawing from both Eastern and Western styles of thought. Similarly, Fagenson-Eland et al. (2004,

TABLE 9.3 Is OD Change Culture-Bound?	**Lewinian/OD Assumptions**	**Confucian/Taoist Assumptions**
	• Linear (movement from past to present to future) • Progressive (new state more desirable) • Goal oriented (specific end state in mind) • Based on creating disequilibrium (by altering current field of forces) • Planned and managed by people separate from change itself (application of techniques to achieve desired ends) • Unusual (assumption of static or semi-static state outside of a change process)	• Cyclical (constant ebb and flow) • Processional (harmonious movement from one state to another) • Journey oriented (cyclical change, therefore no end state) • Based on maintaining equilibrium (achieve natural harmony) • Observed and followed by involved people (who constantly seek harmony with their universe) • Usual (assumption of constant change, as in the yin-yang philosophy, each new order contains its own negation)

Source: Adapted from Marshak (1993).

p. 461), based on the findings of a seven-nation study, conclude that "OD practitioners should carefully consider dimensions of national culture when recommending specific OD interventions."

Engaging in Large-Scale Change

One of the biggest challenges to the traditional OD field was the criticism that it was ill suited to handle large-scale organizational change. Traditional OD techniques focused on working with individuals and group dynamics through processes such as survey feedback and team building. Such methods came under attack as being insufficient to deal with the large-scale changes needed by organizations to cope with the hypercompetitive business world that confronts them (Manning and Binzagr, 1996, p. 269). OD was seen as "too slow, too incremental and too participative" to be the way to manage change at a time when organizations often faced the need to make major change and to do so with speed (Burnes and Cooke, 2012, p. 1397).

As a result of such criticisms, many OD practitioners began to move their focus from micro-organizational issues to macro, large-system issues, including aligning change to the strategic needs of the organization (Worley et al., 1996). This has led to the development of a range of techniques designed to get the whole organizational system, or at least representatives of different stakeholders of the whole system, into a room at the same time.

Whole system techniques take a variety of forms and names, including search conference (see table 9.4), future search, real-time strategic change, World Café (see box), town hall meetings, simu-real, whole-system design, open-space technology, ICA strategic planning process, participative design, fast-cycle full participation, large-scale interactive process, and appreciative future search (Axelrod, 1992; Bunker and Alban, 1992, 1997; Dannemiller and Jacobs, 1992; Emery and Purser, 1996; Fuller et al., 2000; Holman et al., 2007; Klein, 1992; Levine and Mohr, 1998; Manning and Binzagr, 1996). Such techniques are typically designed to work with up to thousands of people at a time.

TABLE 9.4
An Example of a Search Conference Format

Phase 1	Identifying relevant world trends = shared understanding of global environment	
Phase 2	Identifying how trends affect specific issue, organization, institution = how global trends impact on operations of the system	
Phase 3	Evolution of issue, organization, institution = creation of its history including its chronology (timeline)	
Phase 4	Future design of issue, organization, institution = use of small-group creativity and innovation to design a consensus scenario for the way forward	
Phase 5	Strategy formulation = generation of agreed action plans	

Source: Adapted from Baburoglu and Garr (1992).

The various techniques do entail differences. Some techniques assume that organizational participants can shape and enact both their organization and its surrounding environment; others are based on the assumption that the environment is given (although its defining characteristics may need to be actively agreed upon) and that organizations and their participants join together democratically to identify appropriate adaptation processes. Other differences relate to the extent to which the technique includes a majority of organizational members and stakeholders. Some techniques are highly structured and use a consultant who manages the process, whereas others utilize a more flexible self-design approach (Manning and Binzagr, 1996).

World Café

World Café is a large-scale OD intervention technique developed by Juanita Brown and David Isaacs (2005). It has been described by Jorgenson and Steier (2013, p. 393) as "one of a new generation of methods that attempt to achieve collective change by bringing all members or stakeholders of a system together in one place, using a highly structured process of movement to create flexible and coevolving networks of conversations."

Typically, the event is held away from the normal workplace and uses small face-to-face groupings seated at a collection of small café-like tables as the basis for rounds of conversations. Convened by one or more facilitators, the World Café involves a series of issues/questions being addressed by participants. Table membership changes between various rounds (of questions), although one person usually remains as the "table host." Each table usually "reports back" (orally) to the group as a whole between rounds, and the meeting ends with the whole group discussing what has occurred.

Jorgenson and Steier (2013, p. 393) note:

> The event is densely symbolic. Tables are often covered with red and white checked tablecloths reminiscent of an Italian restaurant as well as bud vases with flowers. Sheets of butcher block paper laid on each table along with colored markers or crayons are intended to evoke an atmosphere of play and allow participants, if they desire, to capture emerging ideas with sketches or notes.

Source: Adapted from Jorgenson and Steier (2013).

What unites these techniques is an underlying assumption that "the few are no longer left in the position of deciding for the many" as a result of the inclusion of "new and different voices" in the change process (Axelrod, 2001, p. 22). These techniques are designed to assist organizations in being responsive to their current business conditions by providing the means "for getting the message to the total system by enhancing everyone's understanding of the organization's situation and its context. This reframing leads to a common recognition of the changes required and becomes the impetus for concerted actions" (Bunker and Alban, 1992). An example of this technique in a large setting, involving over 4,000 people who came together to identify how the World Trade Center 9/11 site should be developed, is outlined below.

Large-Scale Interventions *"Listening to the City": Town Hall Meeting on Rebuilding the World Trade Center after 9/11*

In New York City on July 20, 2002, over 4,300 New York citizens came together for what has been billed as the largest town hall meeting ever held. The meeting was organized by *AmericaSpeaks*, a nonprofit organization headed by Carolyn Lukensmeyer that uses twenty-first-century town meetings to design and facilitate large-scale dialogues on public issues. Up to 5,000 people are grouped into one room and profiled in such a way that they represent the various interests and stakeholders associated with the issues for discussion and debate. They are arranged into small groups of around a dozen people, each having a facilitator. Each group has a networked computer that records the ideas of participants and a wireless network within the room transfers these data to a central computer. This enables a "theme team" to read the data from each group, identify key themes in real time, distill them, and present them back to the whole room via large overhead video screens. Each participant in the room has a wireless keypad that he or she can then use to vote in relation to the distilled themes. This provides instant feedback to the entire group, which, at the conclusion of the day, receives a summary of the major issues and outcomes. Involving key decision makers in the meeting is an important way of trying to ensure that the outcomes of the day have a meaningful input into public policy.

In the case of the World Trade Center, the town hall meeting was held after five months of organizing, sponsored in part by the Lower Manhattan Development Corporation (LMDC) and the Port Authorities of New York and New Jersey. During this period, a representative sample of New Yorkers was identified and invited to the July 20 meeting, which was titled "Listening to the City." The room contained 500 tables, each with a facilitator. Theme team members provided feedback throughout the day, and issue experts were on hand to answer specific questions from participants. Representatives from various federal, state, and city agencies also were present. A key outcome of the meeting was an expression of dissatisfaction with the six memorial site options being considered and a demand for one having more open space; the meeting also made recommendations regarding expansion of the transit service and more affordable housing. The outcome was that the LMDC began a new planning process for the World Trade Center and the Port Authority agreed to reduce the amount of commercial development planned for the site in order to enable more space for hotel and retail. As reported by the *New York Daily News* (July 21, 2002), "the process was an exercise in democracy."

Sources: Lukensmeyer and Brigham, 2002; *New York Daily News*, http://www.nydailynews.com, July 21, 2002.

World Café on a Small Scale—the Museum of Science and Industry

The Museum of Science and Industry (MOSI) is in Tampa, Florida, and has used a World Café format for various purposes, including meetings that involved staff and members of the local community in the discussion of planning and design matters. Having had World Café experience, a decision was made to try this format for a meeting of its 30-member executive board that was scheduled to explore possible futures—and identify "actionable ideas"—for MOSI. World Café was seen as an approach that would signal to members that this was intended to be a very different sort of meeting from the highly structured ones which were the executive board norm in its usual setting (a traditional boardroom with members seated around the one large elliptical table).

Participants sat at small round tables (seating four). The purpose of the event and the World Café process was explained, and the first round began with them being asked to discuss their own experiences of really good conversations and what it was about those conversations that made them "really

good." Future rounds included asking respondents to discuss questions such as "What could MOSI be like in five years?" and "We're now five years in the future and MOSI has attained these goals. What did we do to get here?" (Jorgenson and Steier, 2013, p. 396).

Postscript: Reactions to this use of World Café differed between participants. While several of the board members agree with one colleague's enthusiastic response that "this was the first time in a long time that we really talked to each other" and that "maybe this is what a board meeting *could* be like," another responded rather ambiguously, "Yes, this has been great but now let's get down to business" (Jorgenson and Steier, 2013, p. 396). For some people, an experience like World Café opens up a new set of possibilities as to how they could work with each other in the future; for others, it is dismissed as a (possibly interesting) diversion before they return to "business as usual."

Source: Jorgenson and Steier (2013).

Although designed, as the name suggests, for application in large-scale system-wide situations such as that represented in the World Trade Center example, these methods have also been applied in smaller-scale situations such as that described below involving the Museum of Science and Technology.

Proponents of large-scale intervention approaches are glowing, sometimes almost evangelical, in expounding their benefits. Weisbord (1992, pp. 9–10) claims that future search conference outcomes "can be quite startling" and produce restructured bureaucratic hierarchies in which "people previously in opposition often act together across historic barriers in less than 48 hours." Results emerge "with greater speed and increased commitment and greatly reduced resistance by the rest of the organization" (Axelrod, 1992, p. 507), enhancing "innovation, adaptation, and learning" (Axelrod, 2001, p. 22).

However, alongside testaments to the success of these techniques are disagreements regarding both the origin of large-scale, whole-system change techniques and their likely effectiveness in highly volatile environments. Some writers disagree with the version of "OD history" that depicts the field as having moved over time from a micro to a macro focus. They maintain that large-scale techniques have always been part of the OD approach and that "ODers have a strong tendency to neglect their past" (Golembiewski, 1999, p. 5). Others, such as Herman (2000), maintain that because of the need for more rapid responses, system-wide culture change programs are less relevant today than more specific, situational interventions such as virtual team building and management of merger processes.

Aligned with this critique is the issue of the feasibility of system-wide changes in an era when "[t]he old model of the organization as the center of its universe, with its customers, share-owners, suppliers, etc. rotating around it, is no longer applicable in 'new-era' organizations" (Herman, 2000, p. 110). As one OD practitioner argues, "I'm not sure that 'system wide' change is really possible, since the real system often include[s] a number of strategic partners who may never buy into changes that fit one company but not another" (cited in Herman, 2000, p. 109).

However, others disagree. For OD consultant Susan Hoberecht and her colleagues (2011), the increasing centrality of interorganizational alliances and networks in the business world provides an opportunity for change methods with a system-wide focus, because in such an environment a greater than ever premium is placed on the effective operating of interdependencies. In such an environment, Hoberecht et al. (2011) argue, large-scale interventions have particular relevance.

For an empirically based assessment of various aspects of the effectiveness of large-scale interventions, see Worley, Mohrman, and Nevitt (2011).

LO 9.3 Appreciative Inquiry (AI)

Techniques of "inclusion" appropriate to large-scale or large-group interventions led to them being labelled as part of a new "engagement paradigm" (Axelrod, 2001, p. 25), a "new type of social innovation" (Bunker and Alban, 1992, p. 473), a "paradigm shift" (Dannemiller and Jacobs, 1992, p. 497), and "an evolution in human thought, vision and values uniquely suited to our awesome 21st Century technical, economic, and social dilemmas" (Weisbord, 1992, p. 6). They represented a shift from the emphasis on problem-solving and conflict management, common to earlier OD programs, to a focus on joint envisioning of the future. For example, Fuller and colleagues (2000, p. 31) maintain that with a problem-solving approach comes the assumption that "organizing is a problem to be solved," one that entails steps such as problem identification, analysis of causes and solutions, and the development of action plans.

Contrary to this logic, Fuller et al. (2000) point to the assumptions underlying the appreciative inquiry approach to change, which seeks to identify what is currently working best and to build on this knowledge to help develop and design what might be achieved in the future. They outline the technique as involving four steps:

- *Discovery* or appreciating the best of what is currently practiced.
- *Building* on this knowledge to help envision (or dream) about what the future could be.
- *Designing* or co-constructing (through collective dialogue) what should be.
- *Sustaining* the organization's destiny or future.

The technique is also depicted diagrammatically in figure 9.1. An illustrative sample of questions for this four-step process is provided in table 9.5.

In these techniques the act of participation or inclusion of a wide variety of voices itself constitutes a change in the organization: the "what" to change and the "how" to change cannot be easily separated.

FIGURE 9.1
Appreciative Inquiry 4-D Cycle

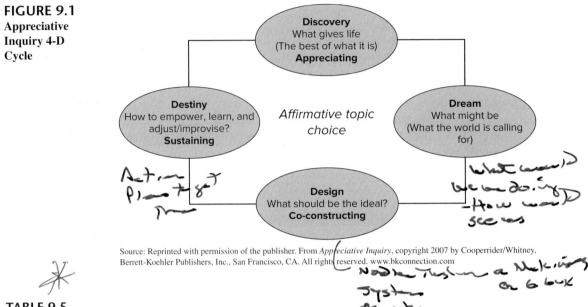

Source: Reprinted with permission of the publisher. From *Appreciative Inquiry*, copyright 2007 by Cooperrider/Whitney, Berrett-Koehler Publishers, Inc., San Francisco, CA. All rights reserved. www.bkconnection.com

TABLE 9.5
An Illustrative Sample of Appreciative Inquiry Questions
The following questions were part of an AI-based OD engagement that consultant Meghana Rao (2014, p. 81) carried out in a U.S. social services agency.

Stage	Questions
Discovery	"Describe a time when you were most proud to be a member of your organization. What was the situation? Who was involved? What made it a proud moment?"
Dream	"Imagine yourself and your organization have been fast-forwarded by five years. What do you see around you? What does the structure look like? How have clients been created, retained, and expanded?"
Design	"What will your ideal organizational structure look like?—people, systems? . . . What structures need to be in place for the organization to sustain and for employees to flourish?"
Destiny	"What are the action items that we need to cover to create the organization of the future? What additional resources will be needed?"

In their outline of the benefits of appreciative inquiry, Fuller et al. (2000, p. 31) claim that it "releases an outpouring of new constructive conversations," "unleashes a self-sustaining learning capacity within the organization," "creates the conditions necessary for self-organizing to flourish," and "provides a reservoir of strength for positive change." These are not minor claims. Certainly, the techniques have been reportedly used successfully in a variety of organizational settings (Weisbord, 1992). However, whether these approaches are successful in achieving their outcomes is difficult to establish, being based most often on the assertions of their proponents rather than on rigorous research evidence.

Appreciative Inquiry at Roadway Express

Roadway Express, a North American industrial and commercial transportation company, adopted an appreciative inquiry approach in order to change its culture and management. Working with Case Western Reserve University, the company embarked on a major leadership training program in order to develop skills and capabilities for sustained economic performance. In what was called the Break-through Leadership Program, 150 Roadway Express leaders went through personal discovery exercises involving developing personal vision statements, identifying personal strengths and weaknesses, developing personal learning plans, and experimenting with these back in the work setting. Executive coaches served to facilitate these processes.

In the next phase, David Cooperrider, who co-founded appreciative inquiry, worked with them in convening summits (large group meetings), each held over two days and consisting of a cross section of stakeholders (customers, staff, suppliers, dock workers, and others). The aim of these summits was to identify what the "ideal" was for the organization in relation to a variety of business issues. Each summit went through the four AI stages (discovery, dream, design, and destiny) in order to facilitate cooperation and collaboration throughout the organization. From 2000 to 2004, 8,000 Roadway people experienced this process, with over 70 summits being held in this time. At the end of each summit, in what was referred to as the "open microphone" segment, participants "publicly pledged their commitment to each other to see the changes embodied in the action plans through to completion" (Van Oosten, 2006, p. 712).

Source: Van Oosten (2006).

LO 9.3 Positive Organizational Scholarship (POS)

Dubbed as a "new movement in organizational science," positive organizational scholarship (POS) is an umbrella term that emerged in the early 2000s to encompass approaches such as appreciative inquiry and others, including positive psychology and community psychology (Cameron and Caza, 2004, p. 731). POS developed out of a view that for most of the history of OD, attention had mainly been paid to identifying instances of "negatively motivated change" (or problems) in organizations and designing change programs to eliminate them (Cameron and McNaughton, 2014). Following this line of argument, thinking about the positive aspects of organizational life—and building change programs to spread these aspects elsewhere in organizations—has been relatively neglected.

To take a POS perspective involves what one of its founders, Kim Cameron, describes as "four connotations" (Cameron and McNaughton, 2014, p. 447):

   (i) "adopting a positive lens," which means that whether one is dealing with celebrations/successes or adversity/problems, the focus is on "life-giving elements";

  (ii) "focusing on positively deviant performance," which means investigating outcomes that are well in excess of any normally expected performance, that is, outcomes that are spectacular, surprising, or extraordinary;

 (iii) "assuming an affirmative bias" involves holding the view that positivity generates in individuals, groups, and organizations the capacity for greater achievements; and

 (iv) "examining virtuousness" involves assuming that all "human systems" are inclined toward "the highest aspirations of mankind."

In line with the coaching metaphor, POS can be depicted as coaching organizations to identify their "best plays," to understand the behaviors and dynamics underlying them, and then to work out how to spread them to other parts of their "game" (the organization).

POS has had its critics. Fineman (2006, pp. 270–73) raises four issues that question whether POS can really live up to its "positive" aims. First, he questions whether we can really agree on which behaviors are "positive." What passes for being positive will vary in different environments. For example, in reviewing a number of research studies, he points out how "'courageous,' 'principled' corporate whistle-blowers are also readily regarded as traitors, renegading on the unspoken corporate code ('virtue') to never wash one's dirty linen in public."

Second, he (2006, pp. 274–75) questions whether the positive can be separated from the negative or whether they are really "two sides of the same coin, inextricably welded and mutually reinforcing." For example: "Happiness may trigger anxiety ('will my happiness last?'). Love can be mixed with bitterness and jealousy. Anger can feel energizing and exciting." By focusing on positive experiences, he maintains, approaches such as appreciative inquiry fail "to value the opportunities for positive change that are possible from negative experiences, such as embarrassing events, periods of anger, anxiety, fear, or shame."

Third, he (2006, p. 276) points to how what are regarded as positive behaviors and emotions differ, not just in different organizational environments but across different cultural environments. Drawing on the work of writers on culture, he points out how "[e]ffusive hope, an energizing emotion in the West, is not a sentiment or term prevalent in cultures and sub-cultures influenced by Confucianism and Buddhism."

Fourth, he (2006, p. 281) suggests that there is "an unarticulated dark side to positiveness." This occurs where there is a lack of recognition that there are different interests in organizations and that not all people respond well to so-called positive programs like empowerment and emotional intelligence or practices that impose a "culture of fun" in the workplace. These programs "have a mixed or uncertain record, and some can produce the very opposite of the self-actualization and liberation they seek" (Fineman, 2006, p. 281).

In response to these criticisms, defenders of POS argue that their perspective complements and expands rather than replaces the perspective of those who "only wrestle with the question of what's wrong in organizations" (Roberts, 2006, p. 294). Indeed, those whose focus is on the latter question "may inadvertently ignore the areas of human flourishing that enliven and contribute value to organizations, even in the face of significant human and structural challenges" (Roberts, 2006, p. 295). POS is presented as "concerned with understanding the integration of positive and negative conditions, not merely with an absence of the negative" (Cameron and Caza, 2004, p. 732). Rather than assume that there are no universally positive virtues, the task of POS is to "discover the extent to which virtues and goodness are culturally influenced" (Roberts, 2006, p. 298). Roberts (2006) suggests that criticism of POS may be due to a combination of the critics not wanting to step outside of their comfort zone—an approach to managing change that is focused on identifying problems—and lack of consideration for the relative infancy of POS as an area of practice.

Where does this leave the manager of change? On the one side, proponents of POS wish to change organizations with "an implicit desire to enhance the quality of life for individuals who work within and are affected by organizations" (Roberts, 2006, p. 294). On the other side are critical scholars who do not lay out an alternative call to action for agents of change so much as caution them if they assume that they will be successful in their "positive" ventures. Instead, the critics of POS urge POS advocates to recognize how underlying power relationships and interests in organizations (and beyond) will limit their actions; they also are urged to recognize that what passes as being positive will vary in different contexts and may not be shared by all. However, such critical reflections do not seem to have dented, in any significant way, the increasing momentum that the POS movement has gained, at least in North America. Whether it achieves the same momentum outside of the United States remains to be seen.

Cameron and McNaughtan (2014, p. 456) revisit the findings of a decade of application of POS ideas to organizational change covering such variables as virtuous practices (e.g., compassion), humanistic values, the meaningfulness of work, high-quality interpersonal communication, hope, energy, and self-efficacy. They summarize the results as "provid[ing] support for the benefits of positive change practices in real-world work settings." However, adding a note of caution, they (2014, p. 456) state that the relative newness of the approach means that not enough is yet known to be able to be sure of "what, how or when" it is most successful.

LO 9.3   Dialogic Organizational Development

As OD developed through its various manifestations such as large group interventions and appreciative inquiry, it was moving more and more away from the classic, diagnosis-driven approach to OD (as described in the initial sections of this chapter). Gervase Bushe and Bob Marshak (2009) characterized this change by contrasting the traditional "diagnostic OD" with what they described as "dialogic OD."

Bushe and Marshak (2009) contrast the characteristics of diagnostic and dialogic OD. Whereas traditional/diagnostic OD emphasizes that any problem requiring change could be addressed by first applying an objective diagnosis of the circumstances of the situation,

From the Originators of Dialogic OD   *Gervase Bushe and Bob Marshak*

By 2005 each of us had separately concluded that various OD change methods were being practiced that didn't follow the basic orthodoxies found in OD textbooks. Although we didn't really know each other at that time, we decided to collaborate on defining the premises and practices we believed underlay approaches as disparate as Open Space Technology, Appreciative Inquiry, and the Art of Hosting, to name a few. In a 2009 article we originated the name and concept of "Dialogic OD," based on the principle that change comes from changing everyday conversations, and contrasted it with the foundational form of OD we named "Diagnostic OD."

Later we articulated key ideas derived from the interpretive and complexity sciences that lead to a Dialogic OD Mindset and the "secret sauce" of ingredients that in combination produce transformational change. Those ingredients, occurring in no specific order, include: disruption of ongoing patterns of social agreement such that the emergence of new patterns of organizing become possible; introduction of a "generative image," for example *sustainable development*, that stimulates new thinking and possibilities not previously considered; and development of new narratives that become part of the day-to-day conversations that guide how organizational actors think about and respond to situations.

(Continued)

We believe Dialogic OD is especially effective in a VUCA [volatility, uncertainty, complexity, ambiguity] world of continual change. Given those conditions, instead of trying to control the uncontrollable, Dialogic OD asks leaders to enrich stakeholder networks, promote open-ended inquiry, and support groups that self-generate small experiments that challenge conventional wisdom and may lead to new outcomes not previously considered.

Leaders stay involved by amplifying and embedding new ideas and practices that work. In brief, leaders become sponsors and framers of dialogic processes that stimulate innovation and invention, rather than trying to maintain illusory control as directors or managers of planned change.

Source: Private correspondence from Bob Marshak to the authors, March 11, 2015.

dialogic OD treats reality as subjective so that the priority in intervening in an organization was to identify and acknowledge different stakeholders' interpretations of what for them was "reality." In parallel with this, the role of the OD consultant moved from being the provider of data for fact-driven decision making to being the facilitator of processes that encouraged "conversations" around change issues (Marshak, 2013).

Central to the dialogic OD approach is the view that "real change" only occurs when mindsets are altered and that this is more likely to occur through "generative conversations" than persuasion by "facts." Altered mindsets are represented by changes at the level of language and associated changes at the level of actions taken by organization members. This changed approach is also associated with moves away from (i) seeing change as a relatively manageable, plannable, linear process to one that could be unpredictable, with far from predictable moves from diagnosis to outcomes, and (ii) "the shift from fixing a problem to cultivating a system capable of addressing its own challenges" (Holman, 2013, p. 20) (see table 9.6).

For more detail on dialogic OD, see Gervase Bushe and Robert Marshak, *Dialogic Organization Development: The Theory and Practice of Transformational Change* (Oakland, CA: Berrett-Koehler, 2015), or the earlier *OD Practitioner* (vol. 45, no. 1, 2013) special issue on this topic.

TABLE 9.6
How Dialogic OD and Diagnostic OD Are Different—Base Assumptions

	Dialogic OD	Diagnostic OD
How the OD practitioner influences the organization	Working with people in a way that creates new awareness, knowledge, and possibilities	Carrying out diagnosis of the organizational situation before intervening
What makes change happen?	Engaging with stakeholders in ways that disrupt and shift existing patterns of norms, beliefs, and behaviors, leading to the emergence of new possibilities and associated commitments	Applying known expertise to identify, plan, and manage the change in a systematic unfreeze-change-refreeze sequence
The consultant's orientation	As an involved facilitator who becomes part of the situation being changed	As a neutral facilitator who retains a separateness/distance from those being affected

Source: Adapted from Marshak (2015), table 1, p. 48.

As OD continues to evolve, it remains a major "school of thought" as to how organizational change should be managed. However, not all OD practitioners are sure that a move from [diagnostic] OD to dialogic OD is sufficient to position OD optimally for being able to have an influence on how change in organizations is managed. For example, both Worley (2014) and Bartunek and Woodman (2015) argue that the diagnostic-dialogic dichotomy is unhelpful and that "we should be talking about whether a comprehensive and systematic diagnostic OD can be integrated with a really good dialogic OD to create a powerful change process" (Worley, 2014, p. 70). For Worley (2014, p. 70), the dialogic-diagnostic focus places too much attention on "OD as process"; he argues that for OD "to capture its full potential," practitioners must complement their process skills with skills and knowledge "related to the principles and frameworks of strategy and organization design."

Michael Beer on What OD Must Do to Be Influential

Michael Beer is Professor Emeritus at Harvard Business School, and cofounder and Chairman of management consulting firm TruePoint Partners. Reflecting on 50 years of involvement in the field of OD (Beer, 2014, pp. 60–61), he argues that OD is "at a crossroads" in terms of its capacity to be influential. According to Beer, even if the specific nature of their engagement directly involves just one of the following processes, the OD practitioner must consider how what they are doing will enhance all three of:

(i) Performance alignment – high performance that flows from the organization's design, processes, and capabilities being aligned with its strategy.

(ii) Psychological alignment – the commitment of people that follows from alignment between the organization's culture and humanistic values.

(iii) Capacity for learning and change – the organization supporting, on an ongoing basis, honest conversations on any matters that inhibit (i) and (ii).

OD in Different Settings

1. **The United States Army**
   Kohnke, A., and Gonda, T. 2013. Creating a collaborative virtual command center among four separate organizations in the United States Army: An exploratory case study. *Organization Development Journal*, Winter:75–92.

2. **Nonprofit organization**
   Fox, H. L. 2013. The promise of organizational development in nonprofit human services organizations. *Organization Development Journal*, Summer: 72–80.

3. **Military hospital**
   Regan, A.-M. C., and Hobbs, L. M. 2012. Walter Reed Bethesda—much more than changing names. *OD Practitioner* 44(3):31–36.

4. **Private company**
   Blesoff, D. E. 2011. Making sustainability sustainable: Lessons from Radio Flyer. *OD Practitioner* 43(4):17–22.

5. **Media organization**
   Birmingham, C. 2012. How OD principles of change still matter in an impossible situation. *OD Practitioner* 44(4):61–64.

6. **Mergers and acquisitions**
   Marks, M. L., and Mirvis, P. H. 2012. Applying OD to make mergers and acquisitions work. *OD Practitioner* 44(3):5–12.

7. **Big data**
   Church, A. H., and Dutta, S. 2013. The promise of big data for OD. *OD Practitioner* 45(4):23–31.

LO 9.4 Sense-Making

As discussed in chapter 2, the *interpreter* image emphasizes the role of the change manager as a "manager of meaning," that is, it emphasizes that a core skill of a change manager is the capacity to frame meaning for those involved. Times of change can be confusing to those affected, and a key element of what change managers do through their various actions and communications is convey a sense of "what's going on." Organizational change is a process which is "problematic" in terms of its outcomes "because it undermines and challenges [people's] existing schemata, which serve as the interpretive frames of reference through which to make sense of the world" (Lockett et al., 2014).

Change often means that the leaders of an organization are seeking to take it in a significantly new direction and/or to have the organization function in a significantly different manner. In order to do so, the sense-making process is likely to involve a sequence that Mantere and colleagues (2012) describe as beginning with "sense-breaking" (as the leaders challenge the appropriateness of the status quo), followed by "sense-giving" (their attempts to reshape people's understandings of the direction they should be heading).

Managers lacking self-awareness will often convey a message that is other than they would intend. People in organizations interpret managers' actions symbolically and, particularly where formal communications leave ambiguity, such interpretations will fill the "meaning gap." Good change managers are likely to have a high level of self-awareness and recognize that their capacity to provide a narrative along the lines of "what's going on and why?"—that is, acting as an interpreter—can meet a need.

Drawing on the *interpreter* image of managing organizational change, Karl Weick's (2000; Weick et al., 2005) sense-making model provides an alternative approach to the OD school. Weick's (2000) point of departure is to argue against three common change assumptions.

The first is the *assumption of inertia*. Under this assumption, planned, intended change is necessary in order to disrupt the forces that contribute to a lack of change in an organization so that there is a lag between environmental change and organizational adaptation. He suggests that the central role given to inertia is misplaced and results from a focus on structure rather than a focus on the structuring flows and processes through which organizational work occurs. Adopting the latter perspective leads one to see organizations as being in an ongoing state of accomplishment and re-accomplishment, with organizational routines constantly undergoing adjustments to better fit changing circumstances.

The second *assumption is that a standardized change program is needed*. However, Weick (2000) says that this assumption is of limited value since it fails to activate what he regards as the four drivers of organizational change. As outlined in chapter 2, these drivers are:

- *Animation* (whereby people remain in motion and may experiment, e.g., with job descriptions).
- *Direction* (including being able to implement, in novel ways, directed strategies).
- *Paying attention and updating* (such as updating knowledge of the environment and reviewing and rewriting organizational requirements).
- *Respectful, candid interaction* (which occurs when people are encouraged to speak out and engage in dialogue, particularly when things are not working well).

These drivers emerge from a sense-making perspective that assumes "that change engages efforts to make sense of events that don't fit together" (Weick, 2000, p. 232).

For Weick, most programmed or intentional changes fail to activate one or more of these sense-making forces that assist individuals in managing ambiguity.

The third *assumption is that of unfreezing*, most often associated with Kurt Lewin's unfreezing–changing–refreezing change formula. Unfreezing is based on the view that organizations suffer from inertia and need to be "unfrozen." However, "if change is continuous and emergent, then the system is already unfrozen. Further efforts at unfreezing could disrupt what is essentially a complex adaptive system that is already working" (Weick, 2000, p. 235). If there is deemed to be ineffectiveness in the system, then his position is that the best change sequence is as follows: *take orgayz), and self.e*

- *Freeze* (to show what is occurring in the way things are currently adapting).
- *Rebalance* (to remove blockages in the adaptive processes).
- *Unfreeze* (in order to enable further emergent and improvisational changes to occur).

In this view of organizational change, change agents are those who are best able to identify how adaptive emergent changes are currently occurring, many of which often are dismissed as noise in the system.

As noted in chapter 2, from a sense-making perspective, it is up to managers of change "to author interpretations and labels that capture the patterns in those adaptive choices [and] within the framework of sense-making, management sees what the front line says and tells the world what it means" (Weick, 2000, p. 238). Sense-making is "a social process of meaning construction and reconstruction through which managers understand, interpret, and create sense for themselves and others of their changing organizational context and surroundings" (Rouleau and Balogun, 2010, p. 955).

More Than Noise in the System? *Change as Ongoing Patching*

An alternative to large-scale structural change is what Eisenhardt and Brown (1999) term "patching." They argue that this is a strategic process of small-scale changes that enable constant realignment of organizational processes to external changes. Patchers have distinct mindsets that involve making many small organizational changes in relation to target markets, including additions, splits, exits, transfers, and combinations. Change managers with patching mindsets create organizational routines to support the process:

For instance, Cisco's pattern for adding businesses includes routines for selecting acquisition targets (the preference is for new companies about to launch their first product), for mobilizing special integration teams, for handling stock options, and for tracking employee retention rates. The routines also cover mundane details like when and how to change the contents of the vending machines at the acquired company. (Eisenhardt and Brown, 1999, p. 76)

Similar patching processes are also found, Eisenhardt and Brown argue, in high-performance companies such as Hewlett-Packard, 3M, and Johnson & Johnson. They suggest that patching decisions should be made quickly, the direction of the patching should emerge from consideration of three or four alternative ways of proceeding, in some cases part of the organization should experiment with it to reduce major errors and problems, and scripts need to be developed to help with the ongoing coordination of tasks, work, and people as the new patch is applied. The authors argue that patching helps organizations "to stay poised on the edge of chaos" and underpins shareholder value by helping to drive business growth (Eisenhardt and Brown, 1999, pp. 77–80).

Source: Eisenhardt and Brown (1999). Selections reproduced with permission of Harvard Business School Publishing.

In a landmark study in using and extending the sense-making framework to the management of organizational change, Jean Helms Mills (2003) investigated organizational change within Nova Scotia Power, a large electrical utility company based on the eastern shore of Canada. From 1982 to 2002, Nova Scotia Power went through a variety of major organizational changes, including:

- The introduction of a cultural change program.
- Privatization.
- Downsizing.
- Business process reengineering.
- Strategic business units.
- Balanced scorecard accounting.

Helms Mills (2003) found that there were a variety of interpretations within the organization about these change programs. Drawing on the work of Weick (2000), she argues that these differing sense-making activities across the organization are indicative of the importance of understanding change as the accomplishment of ongoing processes for making sense of organizational events. She uses Weick's (2000) eight features of a sense-making framework to show how they impacted on understandings of organizational changes in the company. She draws out from each feature its implications for change managers (see table 9.7).

TABLE 9.7
Eight Features of a Sense-Making Framework

Sense-Making Framework Feature	Definition	Implications for Change Managers
Sense-making and identity construction	The different ways in which people make sense of the same organizational change events and how it is related to their understanding of the way their identities are constructed within organizations (Helms Mills, 2003, p. 126).	The "top-down initiatives requiring dramatic changes of self (i.e., from humanist to efficiency focused) are highly problematic and need either to be avoided or handled with great skill" (Helms Mills, 2003, p. 145).
Social sense-making	The need that people have to make sense of their situations not just as individuals but as social individuals is connected to a variety of influences on them such as supervisors, management, trade unions, and so forth.	An understanding of social sense-making highlights the need for managers to identify the social factors that influence sense-making in their organizational contexts.
Extracted cues of sense-making	The need for managers of change to be aware of the way people draw on a variety of "cues" or ideas and actions, perhaps taken from the external environment, in order to make sense of various decisions.	Change managers need to identify appropriate cues and match them to intended change programs. The way in which these cues are interpreted, however, may inadvertently create problems for staff in accepting the legitimacy of the change program and its intended purposes.

Ongoing sense-making	Sense-making changes over time as new cues are experienced and events addressed.	Change managers need to understand "that on-going sense-making stabilizes a situation and how change acts as a shock, generating emotional response and new acts of sense-making" (Helms Mills, 2003, p. 164).
Retrospection	Reference to Karl Weick's argument that people make sense of their actions retrospectively.	Change managers need to understand that different groups will apply their own retrospective sense-making in order to understand emerging organizational events.
Plausibility	The way that change management programs need to be sold so that the "story" about the change is plausible rather than necessarily accurate.	Change managers need to understand the way the context and power relations impact on their ability to provide plausible stories that gain widespread acceptance of the need for change.
Enactment	Whereas the above aspects of sense-making act as influences on sense-making, "enactment is about imposing that sense on action" (Helms Mills, 2003, pp. 173–74).	Enactment alerts change managers to the need to connect sense-making to actions.
Projective sense-making	The ability of a powerful actor to project sense-making onto a situation, shaping the interpretations of others.	The implication of this is that using legitimate power to impose sense-making on parts of the organization may be an important aspect of understanding the implementation of change.

Source: Based on Helms Mills (2003).

Similarly, in a study of downsizing in Telenor, Norway's main telecom organization, Bean and Hamilton (2006) point to the way its corporate leaders used sense-making to frame changes to the company in terms of making it an innovative, flexible, learning organization. After the downsizing, while some staff accepted the corporate "alignment" frame, others adopted an "alienated" frame, feeling marginalized and fearing for their job security. The researchers suggest that framing of change is fragile, with employees' interpretations of senior management pronouncements varying from *frame-validating* (accepting) to *frame-breaking* (challenging). That is, when the change manager acts as interpreter, there is no guarantee that the manager's interpretations will not be contested.

As noted in chapter 8 on the topic of resistance to change, people in organizations can hold very strong views about an organization including what it "stands for" and how it should operate, and these views ("mental models") can make people resistant to change that they see as inconsistent with these views. Another way of expressing this same point is that people in organizations can be disinclined to accept the change manager's construction of events (i.e., his/her interpretation). As noted in chapter 7 on change communication strategies, the communicated message is not necessarily the message as understood by the

Contested Interpretations in Metropolitan Police Department

Metropolitan (a pseudonym) Police Department began a change process that involved an organizational restructuring in which an increased share of resources was allocated to proactive policing (intelligence gathering) and to a mode of organizing that prioritized having the capacity to rapidly deploy police when and where they were needed. The change managers' narrative emphasized the importance of the need to make these specific changes so that the police could be more "flexible" and by so doing deal more effectively with organized crime, which was demonstrating a capacity to speedily form and/or disband criminal teams to meet current needs.

However, the framing of the need for change as a matter of needed "flexibility" was not viewed that way by many of the police because the change was experienced by them as involving regular turnover in squad membership. The significance of this experience was that consistency and longevity of squad membership were seen by many police as vital elements in producing both deep knowledge about specific areas of crime (e.g., armed robbery) and deep relations of trust (between squad members), which they saw as central to effective policing.

Source: Based on Dunford et al. (2013).

receiver. In regard to the construction of events as provided by the change manager, it is not just that there may be some misunderstanding of the "story" the manager is seeking to communicate; the story may be well and truly understood, but not accepted as "the facts of the situation."

The sense-making approach alerts change managers to the different facets that influence interpretations of events. At the same time, it is clear that these influences are often deeply embedded and less tangible than a clear set of steps that can be followed. Intangible does not mean less important or helpful, but they do require change managers to be what Bolman and Deal (2003, p. 19) call more "artistic" than "rational." Managing change as artistry "is neither exact not precise. Artists interpret experience and express it in forms that can be felt, understood, and appreciated by others."

Change managers who are comfortable with these concepts are likely to find the sense-making framework of assistance to them in exploring the "tangled underbrush" of organizational change (Bolman and Deal, 2003, p. 13). At the same time, they need to be mindful of organizational limitations on their sense-making abilities. This point is made by Balogun and Johnson (2004, p. 545) in their study of sense-making by middle managers when they "question the extent to which leaders can manage the development of change recipients' schemata, particularly in the larger, geographically dispersed, modularized organizations we are increasingly seeing."

In reviewing the sense-making framework, it is clear that it provides less a set of prescriptions for managers of change and more a set of understandings about how to proceed. It acknowledges the messiness of change and accepts that competing voices mean that not all intended outcomes are likely to be achieved. However, critical to engaging these competing voices is the ability to shape and influence how they make sense of organizational events.

Can Sense-Making Success Become a Problem?

"The Office" is a Nordic organization that began a change process as a result of an announced forthcoming merger with another organization. As part of the change process, the top management of the Office put a lot of effort into convincing staff that the current organization was substantially underperforming due to being overly bureaucratic and as a result failing to be the innovative organization that it was intended to be. The strategy of the Office was presented by top management to staff as outdated and inappropriate.

The discrediting of the current arrangements at the Office—as described above—provided the basis for "sense-breaking." "Sense-giving" occurred through top management framing the merger as a way in which the staff of the Office would become part of a new and much higher-performing entity, capable of operating with a quality, flexibility, and level of customer service that the Office could not deliver in its present form. This "sense-giving"

succeeded, and the staff of the Office bought into the message being "sold."

Unfortunately, complications then arose in the interorganizational negotiations, and the merger was abruptly cancelled less than a week before the planned merger date. The Office's top management presented the failed merger as a good outcome and announced the reintroduction of a strategy almost identical to the one they had been following for 10 years. The reaction from the Office staff: "a sullen lack of enthusiasm" (Mantere et al., 2012, p. 186), even a sense of betrayal.

The top management had done such a good job of sense-breaking and sense-giving that the pre-merger version of the Office had been reframed by staff as no longer appropriate or acceptable, and this situation/interpretation was not changed just because the merger had not proceeded.

Source: Based on Mantere et al. (2012).

While (as noted earlier in this chapter) OD has been subject to critique as it has evolved, this is much less the case for sense-making. For an exception, see Sandberg and Tsoukas (2015).

Managing Change from a Sense-Making Perspective *Some Basic Advice*

1. Change managers should try to provide a clear narrative that articulates the what, why, and how of a proposed change. ~~looking for cues~~

2. Humans are creatures who abhor a "meaning vacuum"; in the absence of clear communication they will draw conclusions, that is, attribute meaning to fill the void. This is something that an organization should try to avoid at a time of change, as all sorts of misconstructions might take hold and make change more difficult to achieve.

3. There is no guarantee that change managers' attempts at sense-giving will be successful, as organizational members live in a world of multiple narratives and, regardless of authority structures, the interpretation being presented by a

change manager need not have greater credibility than other narratives. For example, some organizations are characterized by a very strong sense of identity, which can give the "what we stand for, how we do things, what we value" an almost moral quality that can make organizational members very disinclined to "switch narratives."

4. Managers (including those in change management roles) are "creators of meaning" whether they like it or not. They cannot choose to opt out of this role. Their only choice is how consciously/explicitly to play it. Managers' actions have symbolic meaning and will be interpreted (by other organizational members) in this way. In this regard, see exercise 9.4. ~~role models~~

~~As Scheme models~~

EXERCISE 9.1 *Reports from the Front Line* LO 9.2	This exercise requires you to interview two organization development practitioners about how they go about doing their work. Compare and contrast them in terms of the following issues: • Their background. • The values they espouse. • The steps that they say they use in approaching a consulting assignment. • The tensions they identify in working as an OD practitioner. • Their perceptions of the way the OD field has changed and likely will change into the future. What general conclusions do you draw about the practice of OD?
EXERCISE 9.2 *Designing a Large-Scale Change Intervention* LO 9.2	Choose a current issue in your local neighborhood. The aim of this exercise is to design a large-scale change intervention program in relation to this issue. Consider the following: • How many people would it make sense to involve? • Where and when would you hold it? • How would you ensure that you have a representative cross sample of relevant people in the room at the same time? What data sources would you need to achieve this? • Who are the key decision makers in relation to this issue? What arguments will you use to get them to attend the meeting? • How will you structure the agenda of the meeting? What would be the best way of doing this so that people who attend on that day have appropriate buy-in to it? • How would you run the actual meeting? • What technology would you need to make it work well? • What would people take away from the meeting? • What follow-up actions would you plan to ensure that actions and decisions flowed from it? • What possible funding sources might you draw on to finance the meeting? • As a result of considering such questions, what new issues emerge for you, as a large-scale change intervention agent, to consider? What specific skills would you need to make such an event work well? Which of these skills would you need to develop more?
EXERCISE 9.3 *Making Sense of Sense-Making* LO 9.4	Identify a current change in an organization with which you are familiar. Alternatively, identify a current public issue about which "something must be done." Consider what sense-making changes might need to be enacted and how you would go about doing this. Assess this in terms of the eight elements of the sense-making framework suggested by Helms Mills as set out in table 9.7: identity construction rospection social sense-making plausibility extracted cues enactment ongoing sense-making projection Which did you feel you might have the most/least control over? Why? What implications does this have for adopting a sense-making approach to organizational change?

EXERCISE 9.4

Interpreting the Interpreter: Change at Target

LO 9.4

Target is the U.S. third-largest retailer after Walmart and Costco, but in the last decade it has seen its earnings drop from $3.2 billion to $1.5 billion (in 2014) with net income as a percentage of sales similarly dropping from 4.6 percent to 2 percent during this period. These were key elements of the context into which Brian Cornell arrived in August 2014 as Target's new CEO. Since arriving, some of the actions that Brian has taken include:

1. He made an impromptu and incognito visit to a Target store in Dallas to talk to customers. Unrecognized by store employees or customers, he sought candid opinions from shoppers. This was a surprise to Target executives because it was a significant departure from normal practice. Prior to Cornell's arrival, store visits did occur—supposedly as intelligence-gathering exercises—but they were "meticulously planned affairs, only less formal than, say, a presidential visit," with the store managers notified in advance and "the 'regular shoppers' handpicked and vetted" (Wahba, 2015, p. 86).

2. When he first arrived at Target's headquarters (in Minneapolis) he was allocated the newly refurbished CEO's suite, but he insisted that he be moved to a smaller office close to Target's global data nerve center. The 10 staff in this center monitor live feeds from social media—including Pinterest, Facebook, and Twitter—and TV stations for stories/information on product launches, customer comments, and so on. The nerve center staff watch these media on large screens and use software to aggregate data for later analysis.

3. With the intention of putting pressure on Amazon and Walmart, he changed Target policy to one offering free shipping for online orders during the holidays, a "decision that was made in a matter of days rather than the months it would have taken in the past" (Wahba, 2015, p. 88).

4. It is not unusual for him ask colleagues about their "work-life" balance and especially their workout habits. He encourages colleagues to take time for fitness activities and "isn't the type who exalts the machismo of outlandish hours" (Wahba, 2015, p. 88). Cornell relaxed the company's dress code and eats in the company café, where he mixes with staff. He has moved the company's recruitment policy to change the situation where Target was "long populated by lifers" to one making more effort to "recruit outsiders with fresh ideas" (Wahba, 2015, p. 94).

Consider the proposition that managers' actions have symbolic meaning and will be interpreted (by other organizational members) in this way:

1. What do you see as the symbolism associated with Target CEO Brian Cornell's actions?

2. If you were a Target employee, what might you conclude about the nature of the change happening in Target?

Source: Wahba (2015).

As we walked through the manufacturing areas of DuPont, the plant manager, Tom Harris, greeted each worker by name. The plant was on a site that stretched over 10 acres beside the South River on the edge of town, and it was the major employer in the community.

The plant seemed to be a permanent fixture, or at least more permanent than most things. There had been changes, big ones, but the plant was still the plant. The Orlon manufacturing operation had been shut down, the equipment dismantled and sent to China. As far as I could find out early in my work there, these changes, despite their magnitude, were seen as doing the regular business of the enterprise. No one framed the changes as needing unusual attention, so there was no change management design. The projects—getting rid of one operation and installing another—were planned and executed just like any project. Change management was not a rubric used to either accomplish or explain what was going on. More changes were coming, whether there was any formal practice of change management or not. The plant would soon enough look very different from what I saw on that first tour with Tom.

I first met Tom when he came to the University of Virginia seeking to make contact with the academic community in order to bring some of the latest thinking in business to his operation. His interest lay in introducing his managers to new ideas and in applying those ideas to improving the plant. He was not, he said, looking for solutions to specific problems, but rather to improve overall organization effectiveness. This was important because he was under increasing pressure to do more with less.

In February this general bulletin was sent to all employees, and I began the fieldwork from which a portrayal of the work culture would be built.

> Gib Akin, a professor from the University of Virginia, will be spending time at the plant. He has been asked to give us some new perspectives on our work and our organization that we might use to help us develop people and continually improve. Most importantly, he is here to help us appreciate and develop what goes right, assist us in building on our strengths, to make the plant work better for everybody. His presence is not due to any particular problem, but is a result of our desire to continuously improve.

Over the next six months I conducted interviews with workers and managers, spending time in the workplace, learning about everyday life there. This yielded a thick description of the shared stock of knowledge that organizational members used to interpret events and generate behavior. What we made explicit with this process was the local, widely used, everyday, commonsense model of work performance unique to this scene. In a sense, this was the local organization theory that people used for getting along at work.

Of course, this theory was more important than any imported academic theory of organization, because it had to work well or the users would not be successful in their work. This was the practical theory in use every day and by everyone. Such culturally embedded theory also tends to create what it is intended to explain, thus making it even more powerful and generative. For example, in this plant, the local model of teamwork was organized around a Southern stock car racing metaphor, which was not only used to explain teamwork but was also the pattern for accomplishing it. And since everyone knew the metaphor, and used it, it became so.

Tom and the other managers were surprised to learn of the NASCAR (the premier stock car racing organization) metaphor, but it explained why they had not recognized existing teamwork in the workplace (they had a different metaphor for teamwork) and gave them a language in which to introduce change for improvement. Similarly, illumination of the local meaning of effective supervision, high performance, and what constituted a good day at work gave those with leadership roles constructs to work with for making improvements, and the language for introducing change.

Managers, and particularly first-line supervisors, were asked to use this new understanding gained from the findings of the study. Their new understanding could be used to interpret the local meaning of effective work to capitalize on strengths to expand and develop existing good practices in order to swamp problems, that is, to render problems less troublesome even if unsolved.

The findings of the study also could be used as the basis for experiments. Members of the so-called Leadership Core Team were instructed to introduce change as an experiment—something to be tried and watched closely, and after a designated time, if it is not working as hoped, it can be stopped. Framing changes as experiments requires thinking through what is expected and how and when to measure the results. And by interpreting the possible results before they happen, all outcomes can be positive. Even if things don't go as hoped, what does happen can yield learning. All experiments are successes at one level or another.

Tom embraced the framing of change as experiment, and it was probably his most pervasive concept regarding change. "A notion I use all the time is that everything is an experiment. If you describe every change as an experiment, the ability of people to digest it goes up an order of magnitude. And that goes for officers as well as people on the shop floor. As a matter of fact, nothing is forever anyway."

Questions

1. To what extent are the following approaches to change embedded in the DuPont story (justify your answer, providing specific examples)?
   a. OD
   b. Appreciative inquiry
   c. Sense-making

2. In your opinion, how compatible are these three approaches? Why? What evidence is there in the DuPont story for your answer? As a change manager, to what extent could you utilize insights from each approach?

3. Imagine you are an OD practitioner brought into DuPont at the time of the Orlon manufacturing operation closure. Describe the steps you would take to help manage this change based upon action research.

4. As a class, decide on a fictional large-scale change that could affect DuPont. Divide the class into three groups (and role-play the situation in two acts). In Act 1, one group will take a problem-solving approach and introduce the change with the second group (DuPont staff affected by the change). In Act 2, a third group (the appreciative inquiry group) will introduce the change with the second group (DuPont staff affected by the change). After the exercise, compare and contrast the steps taken in each approach. From the point of view of group two (DuPont staff), which approach seemed to work better? Why? From the point of view of groups one and three, how easy/difficult was it adopting this approach? What broad conclusions can be drawn?

Additional Reading

Bunker, B. B., and Alban, B. T. 2006. *The handbook of large group methods: Creating systemic change in organizations and communities.* San Francisco: Jossey-Bass. Provides details on methods used in large group interventions and multiple cases studies illustrating the successful use of large group methods in a range of industries and countries.

Burnes, B., and Cooke, B. 2012. The past, present and future of organization development: Taking the long view. *Human Relations* 65(11):1395–1429. Provides a concise treatment of the history of OD and some speculation about its future.

Bushe, G. R., and Marshak, R. J. (eds.). 2015. *Dialogic organizational development: The theory and practice of transformational change.* Oakland, CA: Berrett-Koehler. A comprehensive introduction to the evolving field of dialogic OD from the originators of this approach to managing organizational change.

Cameron, K., and McNaughtan, J. 2014. Positive organizational change. *Journal of Applied Behavioral Science* 50(4):445–62. Provides a concise summary of positive organizational change and its roots within POS.

Cooperrider, D. L., Whitney, D., and Stavros, J. M. 2008. *The appreciative inquiry handbook: For leaders of change.* 2nd ed. San Francisco: Berrett-Koehler. A detailed guide to the application of AI, including rationale and examples, from originators of the concept.

Cummings, T. G., and Worley, C. G. 2015. *Organization development and change.* 10th ed. Stamford, CT: Cengage Learning. A comprehensive and classic textbook on "diagnostic" OD.

Lewis, S. 2011. *Positive psychology at work: How positive leadership and appreciative inquiry create inspiring organizations.* West Essex, UK: Wiley-Blackwell. Written by a consultant for a manager/practitioner audience, this book links research within the POS tradition to management interventions/practices designed to address various management challenges.

Maitlis, S., and Christianson, M. 2014. Sense-making in organizations: Taking stock and moving forward. *Academy of Management Annals* 8(1):57–125. Provides a comprehensive review of the sense-making in organizations literature that goes well beyond just sense-making and organizational change.

Roundup

Here is a short summary of the key points that we would like you to take from this chapter, in relation to each of the learning outcomes:

LO 9.1

Appreciate more clearly the organizational change approaches underpinning the coach and interpreter images of managing change.

While two of the change images—*caretaker* and *nurturer*—present change managers as receiving rather than initiating change, the other four images—*director, coach, navigator,* and *interpreter*—present the change manager as having an active, as opposed to reactive, role in how change occurs in organizations. The image of the change manager as *coach* is particularly strong in the approach to change that has developed with what is known as organizational development (OD) and its derivatives including appreciative

Reflections for the Practicing Change Manager

- Do you model the change behavior you desire?
- Whose interests do you serve when you engage in change?
- Is your approach value-laden or value-neutral? If value-laden, can you articulate what these values are? Are you comfortable with them?
- What do you mean when you talk about a change being successful? What criteria do you use? Do they relate to organizational performance? How can you determine this?
- Are there other people, inside or outside your organization, who have differing perspectives on such questions? What would you say are the criteria they use to evaluate change? Is

your organization open to having conversations around this issue?

- If you manage across different countries, to what extent have you observed the necessity for different ways of engaging in organizational change in those countries? Why is this the case?
- Can you identify different sense-making activities going on during organizational change? What ability do you have to influence these? Do you exercise power in your attempts to influence the interpretations others have of change situations? With what success? What are the implications of this?

inquiry (AI), change as viewed from within the perspective of positive organizational scholarship (POS), and dialogic OD. The coach link is that each of these approaches involves encouraging a willingness to change and the developing of change capabilities in people, rather than seeking to bring about change by top-down edict. The image of the change manager as *interpreter* links closely to a sense-making view of the role of the change manager.

LO 9.2   *Understand the organization development (OD) approach to change.*
Underpinned by the *coach* image, the organization development (OD) approach is one where its adherents present their developmental prescriptions for achieving change as being based, at least traditionally, upon a core set of values, values that emphasize that change should benefit not just organizations but the people who staff them. The valuing of inclusion, open communication, collaboration, and empowerment and an association with incremental change has meant that there is an active debate as to whether OD represents the essence of how to successfully bring about change in organizations or an approach inconsistent with the demands of rapidly changing, highly competitive environments.

LO 9.3   *Be aware of extensions of the OD approach such as appreciative inquiry, positive organizational scholarship, and dialogic OD.*
OD incorporates a diverse and still evolving range of approaches. Appreciative inquiry uses a four-stage framework—discovery, dream, design, and destiny—which begins with a focus on (appreciation of) the best of the current organization rather than the traditional problem-based point of entry. In a similar vein, positive organizational scholarship looks for the positive in human behavior (even in adverse circumstances) and assumes that a focus on the positive is the way to inspire people to greater performance. While some developments within OD move it more in the direction of delivering tangible, measurable outputs, POS explicitly asserts the importance of organizational interventions that improve the "human condition" in ways that are not reducible to

"traditionally pursued organizational outcomes" such as profitability (Cameron and McNaughtan, 2014). Dialogic OD takes the view that real change only occurs when mindsets are altered and that this is more likely to occur through "generative conversations" than persuasion by "facts." The dialogic approach is associated with moves away from seeing change as a relatively manageable, plannable, linear process to one that could be unpredictable, with far from predictable moves.

LO 9.4 *Understand the sense-making approach to change.*

As Helms Mills' study of Nova Scotia Power showed, there are a number of different levels on which the change manager as *interpreter* operates, each of which requires attention. At the same time, this approach does not imply that mastering each of these levels will always enable intended outcomes to be achieved. Wider forces, both inside and outside the organization, will ensure that there will always be competing forces vying for a privileged place in providing for organizational members an interpretation of "what's going on here" as well as "what needs to go on here." The interpreter image therefore points out to change agents the need to have a realistic view of what can be achieved in undergoing organizational change. While managers of change may find the sense-making approach to be more difficult given that it is less tangible in terms of "what needs to be done," it is also likely to give other managers comfort in reaffirming their experience of the messiness of change and identification of new ways of approaching it.

References

Axelrod, D. 1992. Getting everyone involved: How one organization involved its employees, supervisors, and managers in redesigning the organization. *Journal of Applied Behavioral Science* 28(4):499–509.

Axelrod, R. H. 2001. Terms of engagement: Changing the way we change organizations. *Journal for Quality & Participation*, Spring:22–27.

Baburoglu, O. N., and Garr, M. A. 1992. Search conference methodologies for practitioners: An introduction. In *Discovering common ground*, ed. M. R. Weisbord (72–81). San Francisco: Berrett-Koehler.

Balogun, J., and Johnson, G. 2004. Organizational restructuring and middle manager sense-making. *Academy of Management Journal* 47(4):523–49.

Bartunek, J. M., and Woodman, R. W. 2015. Beyond Lewin: Toward temporal approximation of organization development and change. *Annual Review of Organizational Psychology and Organizational Behavior* 2:157–82.

Bazigos, M. N., and Burke, W. W. 1997. Theory orientations of organization development (OD) practitioners. *Group & Organization Management* 22(3):384–408.

Bean, C. J., and Hamilton, F. E. 2006. Leader framing and follower sense-making: Response to downsizing in the brave new workplace. *Human Relations* 59(3):321–49.

Beckhard, R. 1969. *Organization development: Strategies and models.* Reading, MA: Addison-Wesley.

Beer, M. 2014. Organization development at a crossroads. *OD Practitioner* 46(4):60–61.

Blake, R., Carlson, B., McKee, R., Sorenson, P., and Yaeger, T. F. 2000. Contemporary issues of grid international: Sustaining and extending the core values of OD. *Organizational Development Journal* 18(2):54–61.

Bolman, L. G., and Deal, T. E. 2003. *Reframing organizations: Artistry, choice, and leadership.* San Francisco: Jossey-Bass.

Brown, J., and Isaacs, D. 2005. *The World Café.* San Francisco: Berrett-Koehler.

Bunker, B. B., and Alban, B. T. 1992. Editors' introduction: The large group intervention—a new social innovation? *Journal of Applied Behavioral Science* 28(4):473–579.

Bunker, B. B., and Alban, B. T. 1997. *Large group interventions: Engaging the whole system for rapid change.* San Francisco: Jossey-Bass.

Bunker, B. B., and Alban, B. T. 2006. *The handbook of large group methods: Creating systemic change in organizations and communities.* San Francisco: Jossey-Bass.

Burke, W. W. 1997. The new agenda for organization development. *Organizational Dynamics* 26(1):7–20.

Burnes, B., and Cooke, B. 2012. Review article: The past, present and future of organization development: Taking the long view. *Human Relations* 65(11):1395–1429.

Bushe, G. R., and Marshak, R. J. 2009. Revisioning organizational development: Diagnostic and dialogic premises and patterns of practice. *Journal of Applied Behavioral Science* 45(3):348–68.

Bushe, G. R., and Marshak, R. J. (eds.). 2015. *Dialogic organizational development: The theory and practice of transformational change.* Oakland, CA: Berrett-Koehler.

Cameron, K. S., and Caza, A. 2004. Contributions to the discipline of positive organizational scholarship. *American Behavioral Scientist* 47(6):731–39.

Cameron, K., and McNaughtan, J. 2014. Positive organizational change. *Journal of Applied Behavioral Science* 50(4):445–62.

Cooperrider, D. L., and Whitney, D. 2005. *Appreciative inquiry: A positive revolution in change.* San Francisco: Berrett-Koehler.

Cooperrider, D. L., Whitney, D., and Stavros, J. M. 2008. *The appreciative inquiry handbook: For leaders of change.* 2nd ed. San Francisco: Berrett-Koehler.

Cummings, T. G., and Worley, C. G. 2015. *Organization development and change.* 10th ed. Stamford, CT: Cengage Learning.

Dannemiller, K. D., and Jacobs, R. W. 1992. Changing the way organizations change: A revolution of common sense. *Journal of Applied Behavioral Science* 28(4):480–98.

Dunford, R., Cuganesan, S., Grant, D., Palmer, I., Beaumont, R., and Steele, C. 2013. "Flexibility" as the rationale for organizational change: A discourse perspective. *Journal of Organizational Change Management* 26(1):83–97.

Eisenhardt, K. M., and Brown, S. L. 1999. Patching: Re-stitching business portfolios in dynamic markets. *Harvard Business Review* 77(3):72–82.

Emery, M., and Purser, R. E. 1996. *The search conference.* San Francisco: Jossey-Bass.

Fagenson-Eland, E., Ensher, E. A., and Burke, W. W. 2004. Organization development and change interventions: A seven-nation comparison. *Journal of Applied Behavioral Science* 40(4):432–64.

Fineman, S. 2006. On being positive: Concerns and counterpoints. *Academy of Management Review* 31(2):270–91.

French, W. L., and Bell, C. H. 1995. *Organization development: Behavioral science interventions for organization improvement.* Englewood Cliffs, NJ: Prentice Hall.

Fuller, C., Griffin, T., and Ludema, J. D. 2000. Appreciative future search: Involving the whole system in positive organization change. *Organization Development Journal* 18(2):29–41.

Gelinas, M. V., and James, R. G. 1999. Organizational purpose: Foundation for the future. *OD Practitioner* 31(2):10–22.

Golembiewski, R. 1999. Process observer: Large-system interventions, II: Two sources of evidence that ODers have been there, been doing that. *Organization Development Journal* 17(3):5–8.

Helms Mills, J. 2003. *Making sense of organizational change.* London: Routledge.

Herman, S. 2000. Counterpoints: Notes on OD for the 21st century, Part 1. *Organization Development Journal* 18(2):108–10.

Hoberecht, S., Joseph, B., Spencer, J., and Southern, N. 2011. *OD Practitioner* 43(4): 23–27.

Holman, P. 2013. A call to engage. *OD Practitioner* 45(1):18–24.

Holman, P., Devane, T., and Cody, S. (eds.). 2007. *The change handbook: Group methods for shaping the future.* 2nd ed. San Francisco: Berrett-Koehler.

Hornstein, H. 2001. Organizational development and change management: Don't throw the baby out with the bath water. *Journal of Applied Behavioral Science* 37(2):223–26.

Jorgenson, J., and Steier, F. 2013. Frames, framing, and designing conversational processes: Lessons from the World Café. *Journal of Applied Behavioral Science* 49(3):388–405.

Klein, D. C. 1992. Simu-real: A simulation approach to organizational change. *Journal of Applied Behavioral Science* 28(4):566–78.

Levine, L., and Mohr, B. J. 1998. Whole system design (WSD): The shifting focus of attention and the threshold challenge. *Journal of Applied Behavioral Science* 34(3): 305–26.

Lewin, K. 1947. Frontiers in group dynamics. *Human Relations* 1:5–41.

Lewis, S. 2011. *Positive psychology at work: How positive leadership and appreciative inquiry create inspiring organizations.* West Essex, UK: Wiley-Blackwell.

Lockett, A., Currie, G., Finn, R., Martin, G., and Waring, J. 2014. The influence of social position on sense-making about organizational change. *Academy of Management Journal* 57(4):1102–29.

Lukensmeyer, C. J., and Brigham, S. 2002. Taking democracy to scale: Creating a town hall meeting for the twenty-first century. *National Civic Review* 91(4):351–66.

Maitlis, S., and Christianson, M. 2014. Sense-making in organizations: Taking stock and moving forward. *Academy of Management Annals* 8(1):57–125.

Manning, M. R., and Binzagr, G. F. 1996. Methods, values, and assumptions underlying large group interventions intended to change whole systems. *International Journal of Organizational Analysis* 4(3):268–84.

Mantere, S., Schildt, H. A., and Sillince, J. A. 2012. Reversal of strategic change. *Academy of Management Journal* 55(1):172–96.

Marshak, R. J. 1993. Lewin meets Confucius: A re-view of the OD model of change. *Journal of Applied Behavioral Science* 29(4):393–415.

Marshak, R. J. 2006. *Covert processes at work.* San Francisco: Berrett-Koehler.

Marshak, R. J. 2013. The controversy over diagnosis in contemporary organization development. *OD Practitioner* 45(1):54–59.

Marshak, R. J. 2015. My journey into dialogic organization development. *OD Practitioner* 47(2):47–52.

Mirvis, P. 2006. Revolutions in OD: The new and the new, new things. In *Organization development: A Jossey-Bass reader*, ed. J. V. Gallos (39–88). San Francisco: Jossey-Bass.

Nicholl, D. 1998a. From the editor: Is OD meant to be relevant? Part I. *OD Practitioner* 30(2):3–6.

Nicholl, D. 1998b. From the editor: Is OD meant to be relevant? Part II. *OD Practitioner* 30(3):3–6.

Nicholl, D. 1998c. From the editor: Is OD meant to be relevant? Part III. *OD Practitioner* 30(4):3–6.

Nicholl, D. 1999. From the editor: A new profession for the next millennium. *OD Practitioner* 31(4).

Oswick, C., and Grant, D. 1996. Organization development and metaphor—mapping the territory. In *Organization development: Metaphorical exploration*, ed. C. Oswick and D. Grant (1–3). London: Pitman.

Rao, M. 2014. Cultivating openness to change in multicultural organizations: Assessing the value of appreciative discourse. *Organizational Development Journal*, Fall:75–88.

Roberts, L. M. 2006. Shifting the lens on organizational life: The added value of positive scholarship. *Academy of Management Review* 31(2):292–305.

Rouleau, L., and Balogun, J. 2010. Middle managers: Strategic sense-making, and discursive competence. *Journal of Management Studies* 48(5):953–83.

Sandberg, J., and Tsoukas, H. 2015. Making sense of the sense-making perspective: Its constituents, limitations, and opportunities for further development. *Journal of Organizational Behavior* 36:S6–S32.

Sorenson, P. F., and Yaeger, T. F. 2014. The global world of OD. *OD Practitioner* 46(4):56–59.

Van Oosten, E. B. 2006. Intentional change theory at the organizational level: A case study. *Journal of Management Development* 25(7):707–17.

Wahba, P. 2015. Back on Target. *Fortune*, March:86–94.

Weick, K. E. 2000. Emergent change as a universal in organizations. In *Breaking the code of change*, ed. M. Beer and N. Nohria (223–41). Boston: Harvard Business School Press.

Weick, K. E., Sutcliffe, K. M., and Obstfeld, D. 2005. Organizing and the process of sense-making. *Organizational Science* 16(4):409–22.

Weisbord, M. R. 1992. Applied common sense. In *Discovering common ground*, ed. M. R. Weisbord (3–17). San Francisco: Berrett-Koehler.

Worley, C. G. 2014. OD values and pitches in the dirt. *OD Practitioner* 46(4):68–71.

Worley, C. G., Hitchin, D. E., and Ross, W. L. 1996. *Integrated strategic change: How OD can create a competitive advantage.* Reading, MA: Addison-Wesley.

Worley, C. G., Mohrman, S. A., and Nevitt, J. A. 2011. Large group interventions: An empirical field study of their composition, process, and outcomes. *Journal of Applied Behavioral Science* 47(4):404–31.

Chapter 10

Change Management, Processual, and Contingency Approaches

Learning objectives

By the end of this chapter you should be able to:

 LO 10.1   Understand and identify the factors that can cause change to fail.

LO 10.2   Assess the strengths and limitations of checklists for managing change effectively.

 LO 10.3   Evaluate the advantages of stage models of change management.

LO 10.4   Assess the theoretical and practical value of processual perspectives on change.

LO 10.5   Understand and apply contingency approaches to change management.

"IMPLEMENTING THESE CHANGES WON'T BE EASY. WE'RE PRETTY SET IN DOING THINGS THE WRONG WAY."

www.CartoonStock.com

Alternative Approaches to Managing Change

The checklists, models, perspectives, and frameworks discussed in this chapter offer "technical" advice on managing change. These approaches make no mention of, or concessions to, the personal styles and preferences of different individual change managers. Let us fill this gap before we proceed.

The Director and Navigator Images of Change Management

Two of our six images of change management are particularly relevant to the approaches explored in this chapter. The *director* image underpins the change management approaches associated with the work of large consulting companies, and also of academics who work as change consultants in this field. Those who adopt such approaches take a strategic view, adopting a pragmatic, managerialist approach to achieving lasting organizational change. The checklists and stage models that we explore fall into this category: they suggest that change can be managed and controlled in a predictable manner as long as the correct steps are taken, in more or less the correct sequence. However, given the number of different sets of recipes and frameworks that are available, it is not always clear which to adopt, or the criteria on which the choice should be made.

Contingency frameworks can also be seen as consistent with the *director* image. Rather than claiming to have discovered "the one best approach," however, these frameworks argue that "it depends" on a number of context factors, such as the scale and urgency of the proposed changes. But one of these contingency frameworks, the change kaleidoscope (Hope Hailey and Balogun, 2002), does not offer prescriptive advice on how to implement change in particular contexts. That framework instead highlights for the change manager the contextual issues to consider when reaching an informed judgement with regard to change implementation design options. This approach is consistent to some extent with the *navigator* image of change management: change can be controlled in part, but external factors (contextual enablers and constraints, competing interests) can generate emergent and unintended outcomes over which the change manager has little or no influence.

The idea of establishing the correct "fit" between implementation and organizational context is not consistent with a processual view of change. As discussed in chapter 2, process theories see change unfolding over time in a messy and iterative way and thus rely more heavily on the image of change manager as *navigator*. Here, the change outcomes are shaped by a combination of factors, including the past, present, and future *context* in which the organization functions; the *substance* of the change; the implementation *process*; *political behavior*, inside and outside the organization; and the interactions between these factors. The role of the change manager is not to direct, but to identify options, accumulate resources, monitor progress, and to *navigate* a path through the complexity.

It is therefore important for change managers to be fully aware of, and perhaps on many occasions to put to one side, their preferred image of change management. It is also important that managers are comfortable with their actions, with regard to both personal capability and how actions are perceived to fit with the context. However, implementation design decisions should ideally be more heavily influenced by the context factors that we explore in this chapter than by personal considerations.

LO 10.1 Why Change Fails

"Anyone who has never made a mistake has never tried anything new."

—Albert Einstein

"Trying is the first step towards failure."

—Homer Simpson

In this chapter, we explore approaches to implementing organizational change effectively, drawing on a range of change management, processual, and contingency perspectives. First, however, we will explore why change fails. If we understand the common mistakes, perhaps we can avoid them.

Ask a group of managers to reflect on their experience and to identify what to do in order to make organizational change fail. Their response usually comes in two stages. First, they laugh. Second, they generate without difficulty a list of practical actions to guarantee that an initiative will not be successful. Table 10.1 shows the typical results of such a discussion, produced by a small group of Australian managers in 2013. This invites two conclusions. First, ensuring that change fails—should one wish to do that—is not difficult. There are many tools at one's disposal, involving a combination of actions and inactions. Second, if we have such a good understanding of what can go wrong, then getting it right should not be difficult. Just turn the negatives around: clear vision, commitment and leadership support, honest communication, simplicity, break down the silos, highlight successes and positives, and so on. Sadly, while this approach is helpful, "getting it right" is not quite this easy.

TABLE 10.1
How to Make Change Fail

Choose the most expensive way to do it	Commitment without leadership support
Demotivate the group	Do not recognize the power of the team
Distort the vision	Divert attention and resources
Don't buy into the process	Don't follow the process
Highlight past failures	Highlight the negatives
Lack of honesty	No communication
Political games	Set up silos
Team up with others	Too many policies and procedures

From his research into over 100 companies (most, but not all, American), John Kotter (2007) argues that transformational changes often fail because of the mistakes that are identified in table 10.2. The fourth of those mistakes involves "undercommunicating the vision by a factor of ten" (Kotter, 2007, p. 100). In his book on the subject, Kotter (2012a) sets out the following argument:

Assume that an employee receives 2,300,000 words or numbers in corporate communications over a three-month period. A typical vision statement for an organizational change might consist of one 30-minute speech, one hour-long meeting, one 600-word article, one 2000 word memo. That adds up to around 13,400 words or numbers over three months. Do the math:

$$13,400 \div 2,300,000 = 0.0058$$

Based on this calculation, information about your change initiative constitutes about half of one percent of an employee's total quarterly exposure to corporate communications. This does not take into account the quality of the communication, the inspirational nature of the message, the enthusiasm with which it is delivered, or the motivation of staff to pay attention. Kotter thus asks, what impact is your "half percent sound bite" likely to have on the response to change?

TABLE 10.2
Why Transformation Efforts Fail

Mistakes	Nature and Remedy
No urgency	If employees don't see the need, then they will not be motivated to change; management must create a sense of urgency
No coalition	One or two people acting on their own can't drive big change; management must create a coalition with the expertise and the power to make it happen
No vision	Without a picture of the future that is easy to explain and understand, a change program becomes confusing; change needs a clear vision
Poor communication	Giving people an important message once is not enough; the vision must be communicated repeatedly by management, in words and actions
Obstacles not removed	Structures, design of jobs, reward and appraisal systems, and key individuals can get in the way; the obstacles must be confronted and removed
No wins	Change takes time, and momentum can be lost without interim achievements to celebrate; management should create and reward short-term wins
Premature victory	The job is not done when improvements appear; it is a mistake to "declare victory" too soon, before the changes are embedded
No anchoring	Change that is not seen to be beneficial will decay, and the next generation of managers may not continue the work; the change must be seen to have worked, and successors must champion the changes of their predecessors

Source: Based on Kotter (2007 and 2012a).

We will meet this work again, in our section on "Stage Models of Change Management," as Kotter turns these mistakes into a model of successful transformation. That involves careful planning, working through these issues more or less in sequence, and not missing or rushing any of them—which takes time. However, given the rapid pace of contemporary change, many organizations perhaps try to take too many shortcuts, in an attempt to put change in place quickly, and get it wrong as a result.

While it may be an oversimplification to claim that successful change just means avoiding these mistakes, they should be avoided nevertheless. It is also important to recognize that there are many of these mistakes, and that in any particular setting, several of those factors may be combining to ensure that the change program fails. Success or failure can rarely be explained with reference to only a single factor. What are the costs involved in avoiding these mistakes? Almost all of the remedies are cost-neutral, involving changes in leadership and management style, and in organizational policies and procedures. In short, while ensuring that change will fail involves little or no cost, most of the actions required to "get it right" are also free.

They All Say the Same Thing

Considering the findings of research into IT project failure, Richard Bacon and Christopher Hope (2014, p. 2) conclude that:

They all say roughly the same thing: if what you want keeps changing; or you can't commit the required money; or you keep changing the person in charge; or the person at the top doesn't care about the project or you have an unrealistic timetable; or you fail to test the system properly; or if you don't provide enough training; or you don't have a Plan B; or you don't realize that the bigger the project the greater the chance of its being overtaken by events or new technology; or you don't realize that the suppliers are quite capable of telling you that they can deliver when they can't; then don't be surprised if you end up with a mess that damages your organization, costs much more than it is supposed to, and doesn't work.

LO 10.2 Change by Checklist

> "There is a certain relief in change even though it be from bad to worse; as I have found travelling in a stage-coach, it is often a comfort to shift one's position and be bruised in new places."
>
> —Washington Irving

The landscape of practical advice for the change manager is dominated by simple checklists. These have also been described as "*n*-step recipes," where "*n*" is the number of items on the list. This approach is open to the criticism that it oversimplifies a complex process. However simplified, it is probably accurate to claim that, in most cases, if the change manager does not follow most of the advice in these checklists, then the change program could run into trouble.

Checklist approaches to change management assume that the process is logical and linear, and can therefore be controlled by planning and then following the correct set of steps. This "rational linear'" model of change has been widely criticized (e.g., Graetz and Smith, 2010), but it remains popular with professional bodies and management consultancies. This is probably because these checklists or recipes codify what is usually a messy and iterative process, and thus offer the busy change manager straightforward advice on what to do in order to improve the chances of success. In this section, we will consider some of these checklists, and assess the strengths and limitations of this approach.

For example, from their review of the research evidence, and recognizing the messy nature of change, Jeffrey Pfeffer and Robert Sutton (2006) advise change managers to focus on four issues to ensure that, once the decision to go ahead has been taken, change happens fast and is effective:

1. Create Dissatisfaction

If people are happy with the way things are, they will be more reluctant to change. A key change management task, therefore, is to make people unhappy with the status quo.

2. Give Direction

People need to know what they are expected to do, and why. The change manager must therefore be relentless in communicating the message (as Kotter, 2012a, also advises), over and over again.

3. Have Faith

The change manager must make it clear that the benefits will be worth the time, money, and effort, balanced with discussion of the uncertainties and problems, taking new information into account.

4. Embrace the Mess

Change is an untidy business. Despite careful planning, there will always be mistakes and setbacks. This is normal. Management must learn from and fix the problems, and not focus on who is to blame.

Reducing the task to four dimensions provides reassurance that, in spite of the uncertainties and untidiness, change can be controlled and managed effectively in a more or less logical and predictable manner. Also, having to handle such a small number of issues appears to lessen the scale of the challenge that the change manager has to face. Success appears to be pretty much guaranteed.

The UK Chartered Institute of Personnel and Development (CIPD, 2014) offers another example of a simple checklist, with what they call "the seven Cs of change," which are:

1. *Choosing* a team: Identify key roles and responsibilities, perhaps with different people making different contributions as the change process unfolds.
2. *Crafting* the vision and path: Establish a flexible "road map" or process framework to guide the development of change, from vision, through planning, to implementation.
3. *Connecting* organization-wide change: Establish processes to recognize linkages to other initiatives, and to areas (e.g., roles, policies, facilities) that will be affected.
4. *Consulting* stakeholders: Anticipate the reactions, positive and negative, of the different stakeholders in the change, and plan how they will be managed.
5. *Communicating*: Establish regular, consistent, and targeted communications to internal and external stakeholders, making creative use of a range of existing and new channels.
6. *Coping with change*: Change is stressful, subjecting those involved to an emotional roller coaster, which differs in timing and significance from one person to another.
7. *Capturing learning*: Given the pace and scale of changes, develop the organizational capability to reorganize effectively on a regular basis.

These "seven Cs" offer more detailed advice than Pfeffer and Sutton (2006), but some of these guidelines overlap: give direction/communicating; have faith/coping with change; embrace the mess/capturing learning. This overlap is a common feature of change management checklists.

Management consulting companies often develop their own recipes, often with a memorable acronym. The DICE model developed by the Boston Consulting Group, for example, identifies four factors that determine whether a change program will "fly or die": duration, integrity, commitment, and effort. These four factors are outlined in table 10.3 (Harold Sirkin et al., 2005).

DICE Factor	Meaning
Duration	The duration of time until the program is completed if it has a short life span; if not short, the amount of time between reviews or milestones
Integrity	The project team's performance integrity; its ability to complete the initiative on time, which depends on members' skills relative to the project's requirements
Commitment	The commitment displayed by top management and employees who are affected
Effort	The effort required that is over and above the usual demands on employees

TABLE 10.3 DICE—Will Your Change Program Fly or Die?

Change managers are advised to calculate scores for each of the DICE factors. For example, duration scores highly if the overall project timescale is short with frequent reviews, but scores badly if reviews are more than eight months apart. Integrity scores well if a skilled and motivated project team has a capable and respected leader, and scores badly if those features are absent. Are those who will be affected by the change enthusiastic and supportive (high commitment score), or are they concerned and obstructive (low score)? Does the project require a small amount of additional work (high effort score) or a lot of extra effort on top of an already heavy load (low score)? The combined scores reveal whether a project is in the *win zone*, the *worry zone*, or the *woe zone*. Knowing where the weaknesses are, management can develop an action plan to move the change into the *win zone*.

The ADKAR change model was developed by the consulting company Prosci (Jeff Hiatt, 2004 and 2006). Here, the acronym is based on five elements: awareness, desire, knowledge, ability, and reinforcement. Many commentators have observed that organizations change by changing one person at a time (e.g., McFarland and Goldsworthy, 2013). Following that premise, the focus of the ADKAR model lies with the *individuals* who will be involved in and affected by change. In other words, the change manager is advised to concentrate on individual awareness, individual desire, individual knowledge, individual ability, and the extent to which reinforcement is meaningful and relevant to the individual. The ADKAR elements are described in table 10.4.

As with DICE, the change manager can use ADKAR as a diagnostic and planning tool, to identify areas of potential resistance, to develop communication and staff development strategies, and to strengthen change implementation by addressing gaps and problems. Paying close attention to individual perceptions, strengths, and weaknesses is a strength of the ADKAR approach, particularly with regard to generating enthusiasm, overcoming resistance, and developing new skills. In addition, this is one of the few models that explicitly addresses the issue of sustaining change (which we will explore in chapter 11). However, ADKAR pays less attention to the nature and implications of the wider organizational context and the process of change—factors that are emphasized in other models.

Our final example of a change checklist was developed by the consulting company McKinsey, and it offers a sharp contrast to the individual focus of the ADKAR approach. From a global survey of 2,500 executives, Scott Keller and colleagues (2010) identify the tactics that make transformational change successful. They define transformational change as "any large-scale change, such as going from good to great performance, cutting costs, or turning around a crisis" (p. 1). The executives who were surveyed identified four sets of tactics that had contributed to the success of their changes: goals, structures, involvement, and leadership (table 10.5). Individual perceptions, motivations, and capabilities are only

TABLE 10.4
ADKAR—Five Elements Influencing Change Success

ADKAR Elements	Factors Influencing Change Success
Awareness of the need for change	Individual views of the current state and problems Credibility of those sending the awareness messages Circulation of rumors or misinformation Contestability of the reasons for change
Desire to support and participate in change	The nature and impacts of the change Perception of the context or environment for change Each individual's personal situation Intrinsic motivators
Knowledge of how to change	The individual's knowledge base Personal capability to absorb new knowledge Education and training resources available Access to the required information
Ability to apply new skills and behaviors	Psychological blocks and physical capabilities Intellectual capability Time available to develop the required skills Availability of resources to support skills development
Reinforcement to sustain the change	Meaningful and specific to the person affected Link with demonstrable progress No negative consequences Accountability system to continually reinforce the change

Source: Based on Hiatt, 2006, p.45.

TABLE 10.5
The McKinsey Checklist for Successful Transformational Change

Tactics	Explanation
Goals	Go for growth and progressive, developmental change, with "stretch" targets Avoid defensive transformations that are reactive and focus on cost cutting Focus on strengths and achievements, not just problems Set unambiguous measures of success and monitor progress
Structures	Logical program design Break processes down into clearly defined initiatives Allow those involved to co-create the program Clear roles, responsibilities, and accountabilities
Involvement	High levels of engagement and collaboration Frontline ownership of events Initiative to drive change also comes from the front line High levels of communication and involvement at all stages
Leadership	Personal commitment and visible involvement of the chief executive Leaders "role model" the desired changes and "mindset" Develop capacity and capability for continuous improvement Culture becomes more receptive to further innovation

implicit in this model, which lays the emphasis instead on leadership and management behaviors, and on organizational characteristics and processes.

Goals: Progressive Change with "Stretch" Targets

One of the main themes from this study concerned the need to focus on strengths and achievements, and not just on problems. It was also important to have unambiguous measures of success, using "stretch targets," with milestones and information systems to ensure that progress was constantly monitored and problems could be addressed quickly. Interestingly, they also found that *progressive transformations* (going for growth, improved performance, expansion) succeeded 50 percent more often than *defensive transformations* (reactive, cutting costs).

Structures: Logical Program

Success was linked to breaking the change process down into specific, clearly defined initiatives, with a logical program, which those who were involved were allowed to shape or to "co-create." Almost a quarter of the successful change initiatives had used planning groups of 50 or more, compared with only 6 percent of unsuccessful change programs. Clear roles and responsibilities, so that staff felt accountable for producing results, were also important success factors.

Involvement: Ownership and Engagement

Success was also associated with high levels of employee engagement and collaboration. Changes were more likely to be successful when frontline staff felt a sense of ownership of what was happening and took the initiative to drive the changes. This meant high levels of communication and involvement at all stages of the transformation process.

Exercising Strong Leadership

Leadership capabilities are important, along with the personal commitment and visible involvement of the chief executive. Leaders should "role model" the desired changes, focusing on organization culture and developing capacity for continuous improvement. Staff gain new capabilities through the transformation process, and organization cultures become more receptive to further innovation.

Goals, structures, engagement, leadership—these are common themes in change management advice. They appear in similar ways in the other checklists that we have explored in this section, and we will meet them again when considering stage and contingency models of change. However, Keller and colleagues also found that these four sets of tactics were more powerful when they were combined. Of the organizations that used all of these tactics, 80 percent met their aims, compared with only 10 percent of those organizations that had used none of these approaches. Even with defensive transformations, the chance of success using all of these tactics was 64 percent. A survey carried out by McKinsey in 2014 found that companies adopting this comprehensive transformation approach reported a 79 percent success rate, which was three times the average (Jacquemont et al., 2015).

Checking the Checklist

How should the change manager choose between the checklists and recipes that are on offer? The length of these checklists varies; some are much longer than those we have discussed here. While the contents of these checklists are often similar, they can also highlight different aspects of the change management process. Pfeffer and Sutton (2006) emphasize change management behaviors. The CIPD (2014) identifies implementation factors. DICE (Sirkin et al., 2005) advises the change manager to calculate scores for the change timing, team, commitment, and demands on staff. ADKAR (Hiatt, 2006) focuses on individual perceptions, motivations, and capabilities. The McKinsey model (Keller et al., 2010) indicates that success lies with leadership, management, and organizational properties.

Will Heinz Swallow the 3G Capital Recipe?

What do you think would be the elements in a checklist if one was used to introduce change in Heinz?

What in your assessment are the strengths and limitations of the 3G change checklist?

In 2013, Heinz, the iconic food company with an annual revenue of $11.6 billion, was bought for $29 billion by Warren Buffett's Berkshire Hathaway and the Brazilian private equity firm 3G Capital.

The new owners wasted no time making changes. Eleven of the twelve most senior executives were replaced, 600 staff were laid off, the corporate planes were sold, individual offices were dispensed with, executives when travelling were to stay at a Holiday Inn hotel and not at the Ritz-Carlton, and much longer working hours were expected. Micromanagement limited each member of staff to 200 copies a month; printer usage was tracked. Executives were allowed only 100 business cards per year.

Many of the Heinz employees referred to "an insular management style in which only a small inner circle knows what is really going on." One commented, "It's a bit like God—you feel there's a grand plan, but you aren't sure what it is" (Reingold and Roberts, 2013, p. 189). On the other hand, 3G had a young team of mostly Brazilian executives, who moved as directed from company to company across countries and industries, loyal first and foremost to 3G, not Heinz, and driven to work hard in order to receive bonuses or stock options.

The driving force behind these changes was "the 3G way"—a philosophy that 3G had used to bring about change in previous acquisitions, such as Burger King. Efficiency was key, everything was measured, "nonstrategic costs" were slashed. In this perspective, "leanest and meanest" wins, and human capital was not seen as a key component of corporate success. Employees were assumed to be motivated by the economic returns that came from owning company shares rather than by any sense of purpose or mission.

Those likely to be affected by a 3G deal often saw a "how to" guide written by consultant Bob Fifer as a "must read," because it had been popular with the partners at 3G (as it had been with Jack Welsh, the iconic chief executive at GE). The guide was titled "Double Your Profits: 78 Ways to Cut Costs, Increase Sales, and Dramatically Improve Your Bottom Line in 6 Months or Less." Chapter titles included "Cut Costs First, Ask Questions Later" and "Don't Be Afraid to Use a Shotgun."

However, in the minds of many food industry experts, while some of 3G's previous acquisitions would have been prime candidates for a regime of cost cutting, Heinz was not the most obvious candidate to "hack and slash." The company had already been through several years of efficiency improvements ("slimming and trimming"), and it was already a relatively lean and efficient operation.

Summing up the situation, business journalists Jennifer Reingold and Daniel Roberts (2013, p. 186) speculated that "the experiment now under way will determine whether Heinz will become a newly invigorated embodiment of efficiency—or whether 3G will take the cult of cost cutting so far that it chokes off Heinz's ability to innovate and make the products that have made it a market leader for almost a century and a half." In March 2015, Heinz and the food industry giant Kraft announced a merger that would create an entity with annual revenue of $28 billion, the third largest food company in the United States and the fifth largest in the world. Annual cost savings of $1.5 billion were expected.

Sources: Reingold, J., and Roberts, D. 2013. Squeezing Heinz. *Fortune*, October 28:184–92.
http://fortune.com/2013/10/10/squeezing-heinz/

One answer to "how to choose?" may simply be—does it matter? As long as advice in this form is used as a structured starting point, then the details and issues that are relevant to a specific change in a particular organization should emerge in the discussion and the planning. Another answer concerns "fit"; some models and approaches will be more appropriate than others to a particular context. This will depend on the size of the organization, the nature, scale, and urgency of the change, the problems to be solved, numbers affected, the organization's history of change, and so on. The third answer, of course, is why choose? Why not work through several of these approaches and assess their value in application? Two or more approaches applied to the same change program may suggest similar—or widely different—implications for practice. The similarities can be reassuring. The differences may trigger further insights and investigation, and contribute to better implementation planning.

These recipes are "high-level" guides, not detailed "best practice" road maps. They can be useful in practice as long as they are used in that way (although academics complain that they are atheoretical). Unlike the recipes in your kitchen cookbook, these guidelines list the ingredients without explaining how to cook the dish. You have to "fill in the blanks" and work that out for yourself. This can be a source of frustration for change managers seeking concrete advice on "what works and what doesn't." Checklists just identify factors that need to be addressed; the challenge is to construct a change implementation process that fits the organizational context (Rod et al., 2009). That is the hard part. Change from this perspective is to some extent a technical exercise, understanding the issues to consider, but also requires a blend of local knowledge, informed judgement, and creative flair.

LO 10.3 Stage Models of Change Management

> *Kanter's Law: "Welcome to the miserable middles of change. Everything looks like a failure in the middle. Everyone loves inspiring beginnings and happy endings; it is just the middles that involve hard work."*
>
> (Rosabeth Moss Kanter, 2009)

Change can be viewed, not just as a checklist of "to dos," but as a series of stages unfolding over time, from initiation, through implementation, to conclusion. This stage approach does not necessarily disqualify the checklists and recipes. However, stage models suggest that the actions that the change manager is advised to take will vary over the implementation cycle. The steps that are necessary to initiate change are thus to be different from those that are required during the implementation stage, and different actions again are necessary to conclude and sustain the change. Stage models can thus complement the checklist approach by introducing this temporal dimension.

Probably the most famous model of this kind was developed by Kurt Lewin (1951), who argued that change has three main stages, each requiring different actions from the change agent:

Unfreezing	Changing attitudes by making people feel uncomfortable about the way things are because they could be improved, and so establishing the motive to change
Moving	Implementing the change to move to the desired new state

Refreezing	Embedding or institutionalizing the new behaviors, to prevent people from drifting back to previous ways of doing things

It is not difficult to see how each of these three stages makes different demands on the change manager: first, convincing those involved of the need to change; second, putting the change in place; third, redesigning roles, systems, and procedures to prevent a return to past practice. With regard to "unfreezing," Pfeffer and Sutton (2006) were referring to Lewin's model when they argued that, if people are happy with the way things are, they will be more reluctant to change. The change manager's first task in this perspective, therefore, is to make people unhappy. But this is a "positive dissatisfaction," which encourages people to believe that "we can do better."

Lewin's second stage can invoke "Kanter's Law" (from Rosabeth Moss Kanter, quoted earlier), which says that change often looks like a failure in the middle. This "law" was captured by David Schneider and Charles Goldwasser (1998), who plotted "the classic change curve" (figure 10.1). In the middle of the curve sits the "valley of despair." Those who are affected start to realize that this could mean loss and pain for them. Schneider and Goldwasser (1998, p. 42) argue that this is probably inevitable, but that it is useful to be aware of this and to weaken the impact if possible:

> A leader of change must anticipate employees' reactions, another key factor in the process. As shown [figure], these reactions occur along a "change curve." The solid line represents what is, unfortunately, typical. Unrealistically high expectations at the outset of a program lead to a relatively deep "valley of despair" when change doesn't come as quickly or easily

FIGURE 10.1
The Classic Change Curve

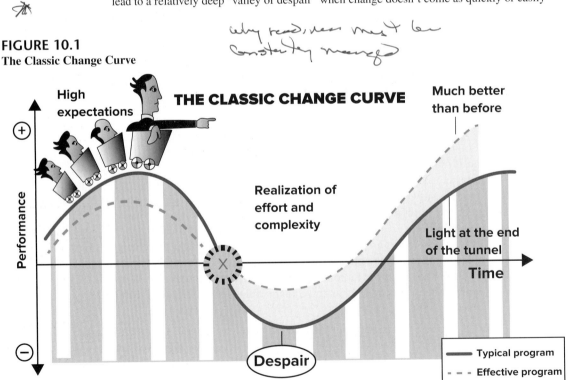

as anticipated. Over time, employees do see a "light at the end of the tunnel" and the change eventually produces some positive results. The dashed line illustrates what is possible with effective change management: a less traumatic visit to the valley and greater results as the program reaches completion. Can you avoid the "valley of despair" altogether? Probably not. All change programs involve some loss. The best approach is to acknowledge that employees will mourn the loss of business as usual, much as people experience stages of grieving when trauma invades their personal lives.

Most contemporary stage models of change have followed Lewin's approach, offering more detail and using some different terms. For example, the U.S. Institute for Healthcare Improvement (IHI) advocates a five-stage implementation framework for large-scale change (figure 10.2), starting with "make the status quo uncomfortable," followed by "execute change," and closing with "sustain improved levels of performance" (Reinertsen et al., 2008, p. 4). Does the terminology sound familiar?

FIGURE 10.2
The Institute for Healthcare Improvement Large-Scale Change Framework

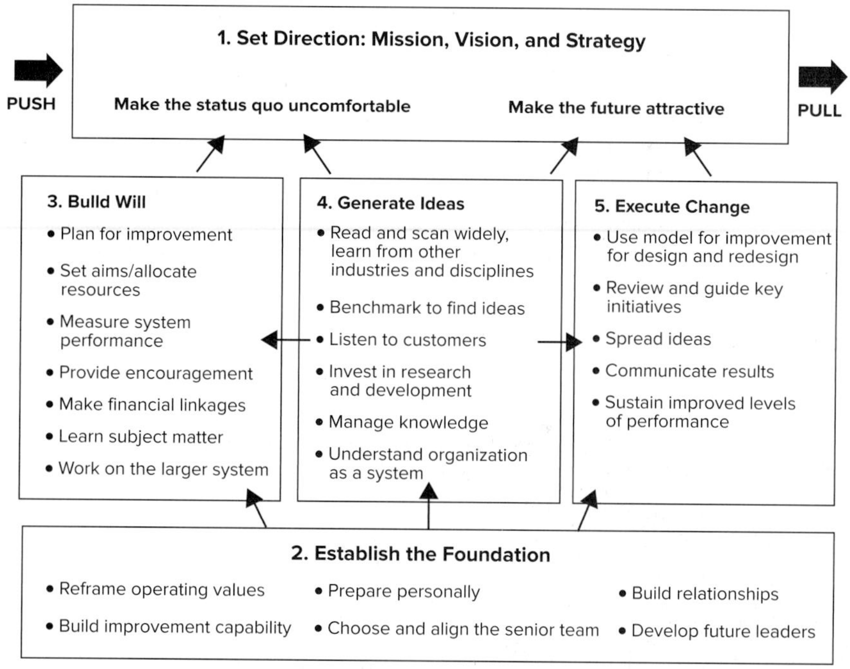

The IHI framework details the stages more comprehensively than did Lewin, with detailed advice (checklists) for "building will," "generating ideas," and "executing and sustaining the change." This framework also highlights the importance of "establishing the foundation," which involves personal preparation, building relationships and organizational change capability, getting top team commitment, and developing future leaders. The healthcare sector in all developed economies faces a range of pressures—social, demographic, medical, economic, technological, political—and is therefore not sheltered from the need for large-scale transformational change.

Probably the most widely cited and widely applied stage model of change is the one developed by John Kotter (2007 and 2012a), mentioned earlier in this chapter. Kotter's model is summarized in table 10.6. This is sometimes presented as another checklist, but

TABLE 10.6
Kotter's Eight-Stage Model of Transformational Change

Stage	What Is Involved
1. Establish a sense of urgency	Examine market and competitive realities Identify and discuss crises and opportunities
2. Form a powerful guiding coalition	Assemble a group with power to lead the change Encourage this group to work together as a team
3. Create a vision	Create a vision to direct the change effort Develop strategies to achieve that vision
4. Communicate the vision	Communicate thoroughly the vision and strategies Have the guiding coalition model the new behaviors
5. Empower others to act on the vision	Remove obstacles to change Change systems or structures that undermine the vision Encourage risk taking and unconventional thinking
6. Plan for and create short-term wins	Plan for visible performance improvements Reward employees involved in improvements
7. Consolidate gains, produce more change	Change systems, structures, and policies that don't fit the vision Hire and develop staff who can implement the vision Maintain momentum with new themes, projects, and change agents
8. Institutionalize new approaches	Link the new behaviors clearly with corporate success Ensure leadership development and succession

this is a misrepresentation. Note how his eight-stage approach to transformational change opens with "create a sense of urgency" (unfreeze), passes through "empower others to act" (move), and ends with "institutionalize new approaches" (refreeze). Lewin's echo can be heard in this model, too.

Kotter advises the change manager to work through those eight stages more or less in sequence. To rush or to miss out on any of the stages increases the chance of failure. However, Kotter also recognizes that this is an "ideal" perspective, as change is often untidy and iterative. As with the checklists, this model codifies the stages of change in a clear and easily understood manner. However, the change manager still has to combine local knowledge with creative thinking in order to translate this advice into practical actions that are appropriate to the organizational context and to the nature of the changes that are being proposed. There are many ways, for example, in which to "create a sense of urgency" or to "communicate the vision" or to "institutionalize new approaches." As with checklists, these stage models are also "high-level" guides, rather than detailed "best practice" frameworks.

Steven Appelbaum and colleagues (2012) have reviewed the evidence relating to the effectiveness of Kotter's transformational change model. They found support for most of the individual steps in the model. However, despite Kotter's argument about integrating the eight stages, no studies had evaluated the framework as a whole. On the other hand, there was no evidence to challenge the practical value of the approach, which remains popular. The authors argue that "Kotter's change management model appears to derive its popularity more from its direct and usable format than from any scientific consensus on the results" (Appelbaum et al., 2012, p. 764). They conclude, therefore, that Kotter's model is useful in change implementation planning but should be complemented by other tools in order to adapt the change process to local conditions.

Kotter (2012b, p. 52) subsequently revised his framework, arguing that the components identified in table 10.6 should be seen as "change accelerators," to speed up change. The new argument has three aspects. First, Kotter argues that the accelerators must operate concurrently, rather than in sequence. Second, change must not rely on a small powerful core group, but on many change agents from across the organization. Third, traditional hierarchy must be complemented by flexible and agile networks. Kotter is not alone in advocating the use of multiple levers to pursue goals, adopting a "distributed" approach to change leadership, and strengthening organizational flexibility.

Stage models thus complement a checklist approach by highlighting the manner in which change unfolds over time, developing through different phases. As we have noted, change is likely to make different demands on the change manager—and on those who are affected by change—at each of those different stages. Although the manner in which change unfolds is rarely tidy, knowing in advance the probable sequence of events, and how that sequence may be disrupted, allows the change manager to anticipate and to prepare for potential difficulties.

Stage models are open to three critical observations. First, despite the emphasis on events unfolding over time, these models rarely refer to what has gone before the current intervention. What has happened in the past, however, with regard to previous change attempts, will influence responses to current change proposals. Consider, for example, the change management actions that may be required in order to "create a sense of urgency" in an organization that has seen many unsuccessful changes that senior management drove with a "sense of urgency," and where top team credibility is now low. Contrast this with the organization where the opportunity or threat is clear to all staff, who, on the basis of recent experience of change, place a high degree of trust in the top team. It may thus often be helpful to extend the timeline backwards, and to identify (and if necessary to compensate for) previous events and outcomes that may influence today's action plans.

Second, it may also be helpful to extend the timeline forwards, beyond "consolidate" and "institutionalize." Even changes that are successful will eventually decay without appropriate maintenance. Paradoxically, successful changes can also inhibit the implementation of further innovation, which may be seen as novel, risky, and a threat to currently effective operations. The issues that arise in managing the sustainability of change are explored in chapter 11.

Finally, as with change checklists, stage models offer further "high-level" guidance, leaving change management to determine how in practice to apply that advice in a given context. There is no clear, unambiguous statement of "this is what to do." The contingency approaches to change management explored in the section below, however, seek to advise the change manager how to adjust implementation strategy effectively to different contexts and conditions.

Benefits Management at Nottingham University Hospitals Trust UK

Stage models tend to focus on implementation and do not always address in any detail the issues of achieving the outcomes, meeting the goals, and realizing the benefits of change. Faced with multiple pressures, Nottingham University Hospitals Trust in England (14,500 staff, £825 million revenue) launched an ambitious transformation program, based on a five-step change process. They designed this process themselves, for use by staff to implement their own project ideas within the overall program (Guyler et al., 2014). Benefits management was a key component, evolving through the different stages of the project:

Project Stage	Involves	Benefits	
1. Setup and plan	Engage key stakeholders and establish scope; identify potential benefits; set up team and hub	Define project objectives; identify potential outcomes and associated benefits	Sighted
2. Discovery	Detailed analysis to establish areas requiring change; value or process mapping of current and future state; identify issues and problems to be solved	Benefits dependency map; benefits measures	Ranged
3. Design and trial	Test future state in a real environment; assess whether trials deliver anticipated benefits	Construct benefit profiles; produce benefits realization plan	Targeted
4. Implementation and rollout	Controlled implementation and/or rollout of future state and realization of benefits identified	Refine benefits and measures	Implemented
5. Embed and sustain	Ensure changes are sustainable; handover to operational environment	Monitor and deliver benefits	Realized

Management did not want to stifle staff enthusiasm and commitment by insisting that the benefits of a change should be specified in detail at the start. When implementing something new, the potential benefits are often unclear, which is why the model only asks that they be "sighted" then "ranged" and so on as the work develops, and the outcomes crystallize. They chose the term "trial" instead of "pilot" because the latter usually means a carefully designed project that will be made to work before being "rolled out" across other units or divisions. A "trial," on the other hand, can be a rapidly developed, small-scale initiative, which can be abandoned, with little or no cost, and no reputational damage, if it does not work out as anticipated. This transformation program and five-stage process saved the hospital £40 million over four years and improved staff engagement and quality of care.

LO 10.4 Process Perspectives on Change

Change is a process, and not an event. This is a straightforward observation and is reflected in the stage models of change management discussed in the previous section. Process perspectives, however, highlight other significant aspects of organizational change and draw the attention of the change manager to issues not covered by either checklists or stage models. While potentially making change appear to be more complex, process thinking encourages the change manager to adopt a more comprehensive approach to designing, planning, implementing, and reviewing change activities.

One of the original architects of the processual perspective, Andrew Pettigrew (1985, 1987), cautioned against looking for single causes and for simple explanations for change. Instead, he pointed to the many related factors—individual, group, organizational, social, political—that can affect the nature and outcomes of change. Pettigrew observed that change was indeed a complex and "untidy cocktail" that included rational decisions mixed with competing individual perceptions, often stimulated by visionary leadership and spiced with "power plays" to recruit support and to build coalitions behind particular ideas.

In this view, the unit of analysis is not "the change": a new organization structure. The unit of analysis is "the process of change in context": how a new structure will be implemented and developed in this particular organizational setting. This subtle shift in perspective has two related implications. First, this means paying attention to the flow of events and not thinking of change as either static or as neatly time-bounded with defined beginning and end points. Second, this also means paying attention to the wider context in which change is taking place and not thinking in terms of a particular location in time and geography (this new machine in this factory bay). In short, process perspectives argue that, to understand organizational change, one has to understand how the substance, context, and process interact over time to produce the outcomes.

This processual perspective has been developed further by Patrick Dawson (2003; Dawson and Andriopoulos, 2014). Dawson also makes it clear that, to understand change, we need to consider:

1. The past, present, and future *context* in which the organization functions, including external and internal factors.
2. The *substance* of the change itself, which could be new technology, process redesign, a new payment system, or changes to organization structure and culture.
3. The transition *process*, tasks, activities, decisions, timing, sequencing.
4. *Political* activity, both within and external to the organization.
5. The *interactions* between these factors.

This argument is summarized in figure 10.3 (Dawson and Andriopoulos, 2014, p. 213), which emphasizes the role of the politics of change. This is a feature that the checklists and stage models that we have examined so far either do not mention, or deal with briefly (form a powerful coalition, for example). As organizations are political systems, and as change is inevitably a politicized process, Pettigrew and Dawson both argue that the change manager must be willing to intervene in the politics of the organization. In this respect, the key task is to legitimize change proposals in the face of competing ideas. The

**FIGURE
10.3**
**Determinants
of Organiza-
tional Change**

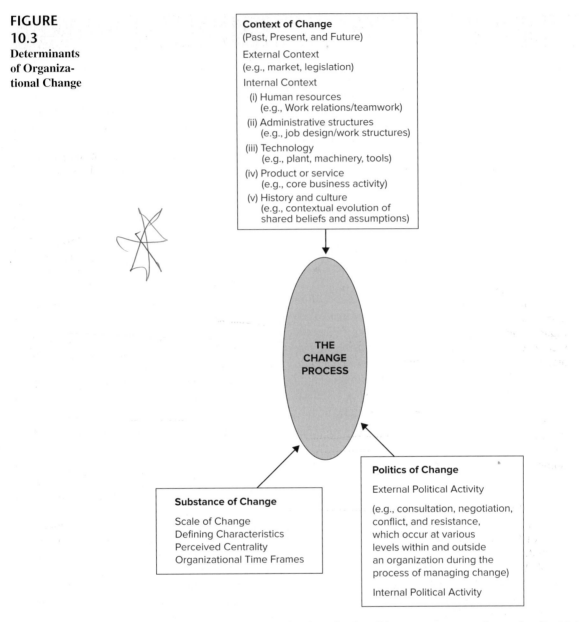

Context of Change
(Past, Present, and Future)

External Context
(e.g., market, legislation)

Internal Context

  (i) Human resources
    (e.g., Work relations/teamwork)

  (ii) Administrative structures
    (e.g., job design/work structures)

  (iii) Technology
    (e.g., plant, machinery, tools)

  (iv) Product or service
    (e.g., core business activity)

  (v) History and culture
    (e.g., contextual evolution of
    shared beliefs and assumptions)

**THE
CHANGE
PROCESS**

Substance of Change

Scale of Change
Defining Characteristics
Perceived Centrality
Organizational Time Frames

Politics of Change

External Political Activity

(e.g., consultation, negotiation,
conflict, and resistance,
which occur at various
levels within and outside
an organization during the
process of managing change)

Internal Political Activity

management of change can thus be described as "the management of meaning," which involves symbolic attempts to establish the credibility of particular definitions of problems and solutions, and to gain consent and compliance from other organization members. Part of this task, therefore, is to do with "the way you tell it," or more accurately with "the way you *sell* it" to others.

Dawson identifies five aspects of the internal context: human resources, administrative structures, technology, product or service, and the organization's history and culture. The organization's history is critical. As noted earlier, it is easy to forget how past events can

From Hot Breakfasts to Strategic Change *How Did That Happen?*

Process theory argues that the outcomes of change are produced by the interactions of several factors over time in a given context. What does this look like in practice? Donde Plowman and colleagues (2007) give a fascinating narrative of what they call "radical change accidentally." They studied the turnaround of *Mission Church*, a failing organization in a large Southwestern U.S. city.

The organizational context was unstable. The church was faced with a potentially terminal problem. Seen as a traditional "silk stockings" church, the organization was asset rich but cash poor. Attendance and membership were declining. There were ongoing conflicts involving a KKK plaque, the playing of jazz in the church, and whether gays and lesbians should be accepted as members. The purpose and identity of the church created further tensions, particularly with regard to including the homeless and others who were excluded. With several previous changes in leadership, there had been two pastors in three years, resulting in the controversial appointment of two co-pastors.

How did change begin? A group of youngsters who did not like the traditional church school program had the idea of providing hot breakfasts for homeless people on Sunday mornings. Some of those youngsters were not even church members; they were soon serving 500 people every Sunday. The hot breakfasts idea was never intended to produce radical change. However, Plowman and colleagues argue that small actions such as this were "amplified" by the unstable context.

What were the outcomes? Church membership recovered, involving a wider range of the local population including the homeless and minorities. Homeless individuals joined the church, sang in the choir, and served as ushers. The style of worship, formality of dress, and music changed, as did the profile of the congregation; this was no longer a "silk stockings" church. The church got city funding to provide a day center, which offered shelter to several thousand homeless and was soon serving over 20,000 meals a year. In addition to breakfasts and clinics, the church provided legal assistance, job training, laundry services, and shower facilities. The church motto changed to include "justice into action."

Why did this happen? The "contextual configuration" that encouraged ongoing change included:

* the dissatisfied youngsters who came up with the hot breakfasts idea

* a doctor working as a volunteer offered to treat medical problems instead, and soon recruited others, leading to full-scale medical, dental, and eye clinics as part of the Sunday activity

* the removal of the KKK plaque—a major symbolic act

* leaders acting as "sense-givers," providing meaning rather than directing changes, and choosing the language labels; "purging," "recovering," "reaching out to the marginalized"

* affluent members left as the church focused increasingly on the homeless, and new (less affluent) members were attracted by the message of inclusivity

The features of the organizational context encouraged a series of small changes to emerge, and amplified these into an unplanned, radical, and successful change process. There was no top-down transformation designed by senior leaders. This is a good example of a processual account of change unfolding over time, illustrating how factors at different levels of analysis interact to produce the outcomes. Plowman et al. offer the following advice for the change manager. First, be sensitive to context. Second, be prepared to be surprised; the emergence of small changes is not an orderly process. Third, view those small changes opportunistically, in terms of how they might be developed.

shape current responses. He also identifies four key features of the substance of change: the scale, its "defining characteristics," its perceived centrality, and the time frame of change initiatives. The substance of change affects the scale of disruption to existing structures and jobs. The transition process may be incremental and slow, or rapid. In addition, managers can draw upon evidence from the context and substance of change to marshal support and to legitimate their own proposals through political action. It is the *interaction* between context, substance, and political forces that shape the process of change.

From their processual perspective, Dawson and Andriopoulos (2014) identify eight "general lessons" concerning change management practice.

1. There are no universal prescriptions or simple recipes for how best to manage change.
2. Change is a political process, and change leaders need be politically sensitive and astute.
3. Time, planning, and flexibility are essential in changing attitudes and behaviors and in gaining commitment for change.
4. They advocate "critical reflection," challenging taken-for-granted assumptions—for example with regard to resistance, which may be desirable if it subverts a weak initiative.
5. It is important to learn from both positive and negative experiences.
6. Education, training, and development should be aligned with new operating procedures.
7. Communication is fundamentally important in steering processes in desired directions.
8. "Contradictions provide health food for critical reflection": change requires constant adaptation to contextual circumstances.

Most of this advice echoes the guidance from checklists and stage models. However, where the checklists say, "do this," process accounts advise, "be aware of this," noting that there are no universal "best practice" recipes for change. Process perspectives differ in the emphasis placed on the role of politics in shaping change outcomes. One implication of this emphasis is that the change manager must be politically skilled, and be both willing and able to use those skills. The capabilities of the change manager are explored in chapter 12, where this theme will be developed further.

Processual perspectives on change thus appear to have three strengths.

1. They recognize the complexity of change, drawing attention to the interaction between many factors at different levels, shaping the nature, direction, and consequences of change.
2. They recognize change as a process with a past, a present, and a future, rather than as a static or time-bounded event or discrete series of events.
3. They highlight the political nature of organizations and change, emphasizing the importance of political skill to the change manager.

A processual/contextual perspective has three limitations:

1. Change in this perspective is in danger of being presented as overly complex and overwhelmingly confusing, and thus as unmanageable.
2. Those who are involved in the change process are sometimes portrayed as minor characters in a broad sequence of events, relegated to the role of sense-givers and interpreters controlled by social and contextual forces, rather than as proactive "movers and shakers."

3. It does not lend itself readily to the identification of specific guidelines, focusing on awareness rather than prescription. Advice is thus limited to those issues to which change management should be sensitive: complexity, process, context, political influences, opportunity.

LO 10.5   Contingency Approaches to Change Management

Dawson and Andriopoulos (2014) are not alone in noting that there are no universal prescriptions for how best to manage change. This has led to the development of contingency approaches, which argue that the best way to manage change depends on contextual and other factors. In this section, we will explore four contingency approaches: *where to start?*, *the change leadership styles continuum*, *the Stace-Dunphy contingency matrix*, and *the Hope Hailey-Balogun change kaleidoscope*.

Where to Start?

The problem has been diagnosed, and appropriate organizational changes have been agreed. What to do next? Where to begin? Veronica Hope Hailey and Julia Balogun (2002, p. 158) discuss this briefly in their contingency model (explained in the following pages), arguing, "Change can start from top-down, bottom-up, or some combination of the two, or as another alternative, be developed from pockets of good practice. Should change be implemented throughout the organization simultaneously, or can it be delivered gradually through pilot sites?" The change manager is thus faced with a range of options.

Adopting a novel approach to the question of where to start, Marco Gardini et al. (2011) argue that change should begin with those staff whose contributions will have the most significant impact on the aspects of performance that need to change. Identifying those "pivotal roles" is vital, but this is not always obvious. They reached this "pivotal roles" conclusion from experience with a large European retail bank. This bank, with 6,000 branches, faced increasing competition from more "customer-friendly" local banks. To deal with this threat, management developed a new organizational model, which reduced central supervision and control and gave branch managers more autonomy to tailor their marketing, promotions, and offering to their local areas. The new model was communicated quickly to all staff, and the way in which the new roles would work was explained. Top management did this through road shows, memos, intranet articles, and by publishing the new organization charts. Everyone received the same information, and the changes were all to happen at the same time.

Reviewing progress a few months later, however, most staff had not changed their working practices. In particular, the branch managers were still using the previous structure and procedures because they were afraid of making mistakes or annoying more senior staff. The regional supervisors were meant to act as coaches to the branch managers, but many did not have coaching skills, and many branch managers did not have the skills to run their own branches and make their own decisions. Realizing that they had tried to change too much at the same time, top management decided to focus on those who could deliver the change the fastest. The regional managers, perhaps, or the branch supervisors? Neither of those groups qualified; they had no impact on daily branch activities, could therefore not affect results, and had little credibility with frontline staff. The branch managers themselves had the greatest influence on the outcomes of the planned changes because:

- their work had direct and significant impact on the revenue stream;
- they were connected with many other groups across the organization;
- they could decide how people got things done.

In other words, the branch managers combined managerial impact with local control, but they lacked the skills and attitudes to drive change quickly. The change implementation plan was redesigned, now focusing initially on the 6,000 branch managers. The training designed specially for them began with their role in the new organizational model, and it covered commercial skills, credit and asset management capabilities, quality and customer satisfaction principles, and other skills such as managing people, communications, and conflict resolution. Only when the branch managers were ready—six months later—did the bank start to work with other staff and supervisors, with different programs designed for different roles. This time the results were much better. Eighteen months later:

- the number of products sold per branch rose by 15 percent;
- the time spent making credit decisions fell by 25 percent;
- branch relationship managers were spending 30 percent more time with customers due to the streamlined process;
- customer responses to marketing campaigns doubled, with a national survey showing a 20 percent improvement in customer satisfaction;
- knowledge sharing and mutual support increased, and the bank became more receptive to ideas from frontline staff.

Gardini et al. (2011) conclude that change is more likely to be successful if implementation has two key components. First, start with the "pivotal people," whose work is closest to the activities that need to be improved. Second, design a comprehensive program with clear and meaningful goals, linking those in pivotal roles with the changes that the rest of the organization has to make. This question of "where to start?" is not addressed explicitly by the checklist, stage model, or processual approaches. This of course is not the only contingency affecting the appropriate mode of change implementation.

The Change Leadership Styles Continuum

One of the oldest contingency approaches addresses the question of change management style, which can range over a continuum from autocratic to democratic (Tannenbaum and Schmidt, 1958, p. 96). The cultures—or, at least, the management textbooks—of developed Western economies have endorsed more participative approaches to change management, for which evidence has long established the benefits (e.g., Coch and French, 1948). Those who are involved in the design and implementation of change are more likely to contribute to its success than those on whom change has been imposed. However, the change manager should be aware of the range of choice available with regard to style, and of the disadvantages and advantages of these (table 10.7). For example, "telling" people without participation is quick and decisive (but may cause resentment, and does not capture staff ideas). On the other hand, "inviting participation" increases commitment and access to useful information

TABLE 10.7
Change Management Styles—Disadvantages and Advantages

Style	Disadvantages	Advantages
Tell	May cause resentment Does not use staff experience and ideas	Quick, decisive, unambiguous Management in full control
Tell and sell	May be seen as cosmetic, especially if consequences for staff are negative and serious	Selling can be fairly quick Management remains in control
Consult	Time-consuming Resentment if staff views are then ignored	More information, better decisions Staff commitment higher if views have influenced decisions
Invite participation	Time-consuming Logistics can be problematic Conflicts with concept of management accountability Management lose some control over outcomes	Uses all available information Should lead to better decisions Higher commitment from staff who share ownership of the decision-making process

(but is time-consuming and involves a loss of management control). In a crisis where a rapid response is required, "inviting participation" can be damaging. In an organization that values the knowledge and commitment of its staff, the resentment caused by "telling" them about planned changes can also be damaging. Choice of change management style thus needs to reflect the context.

The Stace-Dunphy Contingency Matrix

However, participative approaches to change management have also been challenged by the work of two Australian researchers, Doug Stace and Dexter Dunphy (Stace and Dunphy, 2001). Their approach begins by establishing a scale of change, from "fine-tuning" to "corporate transformation" (table 10.8; see also our "Assessing Depth of Change" model, chapter 1, figure 1.1). They then identify four styles of change (table 10.9; see also table 10.7).

Plotting scale of change against style of change produces the matrix in figure 10.4. This identifies four strategies: participative evolution, charismatic transformation, forced evolution, and dictatorial transformation. Figure 10.4 also advocates the use of different change management styles depending on the attributes of the context. Stace and Dunphy

TABLE 10.8
Scale of Change

Fine-tuning	Refining methods, policies, and procedures, typically at the level of the division or department
Incremental adjustment	Distinct modifications to strategies, structures, and management processes, but not radical enough to be described as strategic
Modular transformation	Restructuring departments and divisions, potentially radical, but at the level of parts of the organization and not the whole
Corporate transformation	Strategic change throughout the organization, to structures, systems, procedures, mission, values, and power distribution

TABLE 10.9
Styles of
Change

Collaborative	Widespread employee participation in key decisions
Consultative	Limited involvement in setting goals relevant to areas of responsibility
Directive	The use of authority in reaching decisions about change and the future
Coercive	Senior management impose change on the organization

(2001) thus argue that participative strategies are time-consuming as they expose conflicting views that are difficult to reconcile. Where organizational survival depends on rapid and strategic change, dictatorial transformation is appropriate:

> Perhaps the toughest organizational change program in Australia in recent years has been the restructure of the New South Wales Police Force. The person leading that restructure and playing a classic Commander role is Police Commissioner Peter Ryan. Ryan was appointed from the United Kingdom to stamp out corruption in the force and modernize it. In his own words, he initially adopted a management style that was "firm, hard and autocratic, and it had to be that because that is what the organization understood." (Stace and Dunphy, 2001, p. 185)

Once again, we have a contingency perspective that argues that, while collaborative-consultative modes will work well under some conditions, there are circumstances where directive-coercive modes of change management are likely to be more appropriate

FIGURE 10.4
The Stace-
Dunphy Contin-
gency Approach
to Change
Implementation

Scale of change:	Incremental change strategies	Transformative change strategies
Style of change:	*Participative evolution*	*Charismatic transformation*
Collaborative—consultative modes	Use when the organization needs minor adjustment to meet environmental conditions, where time is available, and where key interest groups favor change	Use when the organization needs major adjustments to meet environmental conditions, where there is little time for participation, and where there is support for radical change
	Forced evolution	*Dictatorial transformation*
Directive—coercive modes	Use when minor adjustments are required, where time is available, but where key interest groups oppose change	Use when major adjustments are necessary, where there is no time for participation, where there is no internal support for strategic change, but where this is necessary for survival

and effective. In particular, where major changes are necessary for survival, where time is short, and where those affected cannot agree on the changes, then dictatorial transformation may be the necessary choice of style. Inviting participation under those conditions would take time and would be unlikely to produce any agreement.

The Hope Hailey-Balogun Change Kaleidoscope

Veronica Hope Hailey and Julia Balogun (2002; Balogun, 2006) also advocate a context-sensitive approach to the design and implementation of change. Their framework identifies the characteristics of the organizational context that should be taken into consideration when making change implementation design choices. They describe this framework as "the change kaleidoscope," shown in figure 10.5 (based on Hope Hailey and Balogun, 2002, p. 156).

FIGURE 10.5
The Change Kaleidoscope

Organizational change	
Context factors: **enablers and constraints**	**Implementation options**
Timing Scope Need for continuity Diversity of attitudes Capability of those involved Capacity of the organization Readiness for change Power of the change manager	What type of change is required? Where should we start? What implementation style will we use? What targets are we aiming for? What intervention strategies will be appropriate? What change implementation roles are needed?

The argument that change implementation should reflect the organizational context is not a novel one, but Hope Hailey and Balogun argue that other contingency models focus on too narrow a range of factors such as type of change, time frame, the power of the change manager, and the degree of organizational support for change. The eight context factors in the change kaleidoscope are:

Time   Depending on urgency, what is the necessary speed of the change?

Scope   How narrow or broad is the scope of the change agenda?

Preservation Is there a need to maintain a degree of continuity on some dimensions, in some areas?

Diversity   Are the attitudes and values of those affected similar, or are there diverse subcultures?

Capability	Do the individuals involved have the necessary skills and knowledge?	
Capacity	Does the organization have the resources to implement more change?	
Readiness	What is the degree of acceptance of or resistance to change?	
Power	What is the power of the change manager relative to other stakeholders?	

These eight context factors can be either constraints (e.g., shortage of time, low capability) or enablers (e.g., broad agreement on need for change, powerful change manager). The point is that the design of the change implementation process should be influenced by the nature of those context factors. Hope Hailey and Balogun (2002, p. 161) identify the six design options summarized in table 10.10.

TABLE 10.10
Change Kaleidoscope Implementation Options

Design Options	Meaning
Type	The scope and speed of the proposed change
Start point	Top-down, bottom-up, a combination, or pilot sites and pockets of good practice
Style	From coercive to collaborative, varied by staff group and phase of change
Target	Focus on changing outputs, behaviors, attitudes, and values
Interventions	Levers and mechanisms: technical, political, cultural, education, communication
Roles	Responsibility for implementing: leadership, change teams, external facilitation

As well as offering a diagnostic approach to understanding context, and identifying the range of options, Hope Hailey and Balogun (2002, p. 154) also argue that the kaleidoscope "encourages an awareness of one's own preferences about change and how this limits the options considered." In other words, the change manager who adopts a *director* image may use the kaleidoscope in a manner quite different from the manager adopting the *navigator* image.

The aim of this framework, therefore, is to trigger a questioning approach to the context and an informed approach to choosing design options. There is no mechanistic way to "read" a particular configuration of design choices from the results of an analysis of the context. As with all of the approaches in this chapter, the change manager's local knowledge and informed judgement are key to choosing the contextually appropriate change design from the wide range of options available, as Hope Hailey and Balogun (2002, p. 163) explain:

> Understanding the contextual constraints and enablers is key to understanding the type of change an organization is *able* to undertake as opposed to the type of change it *needs* to undertake, and therefore what sort of change path is required. Similarly, understanding the contextual constraints and enablers is central to making choices about startpoint and style. More participative change approaches require greater skills in facilitation, a greater readiness

for change from those participating, more time, and therefore, often, more funds. Choices about the change target and interventions may obviously be affected by the scope of change, but also by, for example, capacity. Management development interventions can be expensive and may not be accessible to organizations with limited funds. In reality choosing the right options is about asking the right questions and exercising change judgement.

The argument that "the best approach" depends on context is an appealing one. Contingency approaches, however, are not beyond criticism. First, the idea of "fitting" change implementation to a particular type of change in a given context may be easier to explain in theory than to put into practice. As the change kaleidoscope implies, the change manager needs considerable depth and breadth of understanding of the change context in order to make informed judgements. Second, contingency approaches are more ambiguous and difficult to explain than the simpler "off the shelf" competition from checklists and stage models. Third, contingency approaches require a degree of behavioral flexibility, especially with regard to style, with which some senior managers may be uncomfortable if they lack the necessary capabilities. Fourth, if managers adopt different approaches at different times and in different conditions, will this weaken their credibility with staff? Finally, is everything contingent? Are there no "universals" when it comes to organizational change?

EXERCISE 10.1 *Develop Your Own Change Model* LO 10.1–10.5	In this chapter, we have explored five change checklists, four stage models of implementation, the processual approach to change, and four contingency frameworks. These approaches are similar in some respects and different in others. Can they be combined? Try the following experiment: 1. Bring the advice from these different models into a single list, omitting the overlaps. 2. Reflecting on your own experience and knowledge of organizational change, consider what issues and steps are missing from these guidelines; add these to your master list. Now create your own composite change management model; if possible, do this as a group activity. 3. Can you prioritize this advice? What items are more important, and which are less important? Taking a contingency approach, in which organizational contexts do particular items become more or less significant? 4. Can you identify a preferred sequence of change implementation steps? And can you explain and justify this recommendation? 5. Looking at your composite change management model, identify three management skills associated with each of the elements. Use this as the basis of a personal assessment; what are your strongest and your weakest change management skills? 6. Looking at the elements in your composite change management model, and reflecting on your own experience of organizational change, which elements are usually handled well, and which are often handled badly? Why do you think this is this the case?

As you read this case, consider the following questions:

1. With reference to John Kotter's eight-stage model of change, what mistakes did BA make in this instance, and what aspects of the change management process did they handle well?

2. How can the union's response to the introduction of swipe cards for check-in staff be explained from a processual perspective? If those who were managing this change had adopted a processual perspective, what particular issues would have appeared to be more important, and how would they have addressed those issues?

3. Choose one of the contingency frameworks that was introduced in this chapter and carry out a similar assessment. Which aspects of the organizational context of this change were addressed in an appropriate and effective manner? Which context factors were overlooked?

4. In your judgement, is there any one change management approach, or combination of approaches, that provides the best understanding of the swipe card debacle? Why?

5. You are a change management consultant hired to advise BA top management on how to avoid a situation like this happening in the future. What advice will you offer, and on which change implementation perspectives will your advice be based?

The Strike

On Friday, July 18, 2003, British Airways (BA) staff in Terminals 1 and 4 at London's busy Heathrow Airport held a 24-hour wildcat strike. The strike was not officially sanctioned by the trade unions but was a spontaneous action by over 250 check-in staff who walked out at 4 pm. The strike occurred at the start of a peak holiday season weekend, which led to chaotic scenes at Heathrow. Around 60 departing flights were grounded, and over 10,000 passengers were left stranded. The situation was heralded as the worst industrial situation BA had faced since 1997 when a strike was called by its cabin crew. BA's response was to cancel its services from both terminals, apologize for the disruption, and ask those who were due to fly not to go to the airport as they would be unable to service them. BA also set up a tent outside Heathrow to provide refreshments, and police were called in to manage the crowd. BA was criticized by many American visitors, who were trying to fly back to the United States, for not providing them with sufficient information about what was going on. Staff returned to work on Saturday evening, but the effects of the strike flowed on through the weekend. On Monday, July 21, BA reported that Heathrow was still extremely busy. Their news release said: "There is still a large backlog of more than 1,000 passengers from services cancelled over the weekend. We are doing everything we can to get these passengers away in the next couple of days."

As a result of the strike, BA lost around £40 million and its reputation was severely dented. The strike also came at a time when BA was still recovering from other environmental jolts such as 9/11, the Iraq war, the SARS outbreak, and attacks on its markets from budget airlines. Afterwards, BA revealed that it lost over 100,000 customers as a result of the dispute.

The Swipe Cards

BA staff were protesting about the introduction of a system for electronic clocking-in that would record when they started and finished work for the day. Staff were concerned that the system would enable managers to manipulate their working patterns and shift hours.

The clocking-in system was one small part of a broader restructuring called the *Future Size and Shape* recovery program. Over the previous two years, this had led to approximately 13,000 (almost one in four) jobs being cut within the airline. As *The Economist* (2003) noted, the side effects of these cuts were emerging, with delayed departures resulting from a shortage of ground staff at Gatwick and "a high rate of sickness causing the airline to hire in aircraft and crew to fill gaps. Rising absenteeism is a sure sign of stress in an organization that is contracting."

For BA management, introduction of the swipe card system was a way of modernizing BA and "improving the efficient use of staff and resources." As one BA official said, "We needed to simplify things and bring in the best system to manage people" (Tran, 2003). Staff, however, saw this as a way to radically change their working hours, cut their pay, and demand that they work split shifts. One check-in worker said, "This used to be a job which we loved but we are now at the end of our tether. What comes next? They will probably force us to swap shifts without agreement and all this for less money than working at Tesco" [a supermarket] (Jones, 2003).

One commentator argued that "the heart of the issue is that the workforce wants respect"; it was not until the strike that CEO Rod Eddington was aware that "there was a respect deficit to be plugged." Specifically, staff were concerned that "BA will try to turn them into automata, leaving Heathrow at quiet times of the day only to be brought back at the busiest moments, while not paying any extra for the disturbance. Women, in particular, want to preserve their carefully constructed capacity to balance the demands of work and home" (Hutton, 2003). Although BA denied that the system would be used to make staff change their hours without notice, staff did not accept this promise—wondering why the system was being introduced if that was not the intended use. A union official said, "We know that BA breaks its agreements" (Webster, 2003). Another worker said that the strike was meant to be a "short, sharp shock" for BA: "They would then be able to bring us in any time they wanted, which is just not on, especially for those of us with families" (McGreevy and Johnston, 2003).

The Change Process

Unions argued that the walkout was triggered when BA senior management abandoned talks over the introduction of swipe cards and announced that they would be imposed with five days' notice. This unilateral decision by BA, and the lack of consultation with affected staff, were cited as the key reasons for the strike. Even BA's pilots, who did not oppose a check-in system, were said to be sympathetic with the check-in staff, as they also felt that the implementation of the swipe cards had been mishandled by the airline. One commentator described the change process as a "commercial disaster," which served as "an important warning about the dangers of management by diktat, certainly, but, more profoundly, about an incipient revolt against the close control and monitoring of our lives and movements that modern information technology enables" (Hutton, 2003).

The Economist newspaper argued that it was a mistake to introduce new working practices at the beginning of the summer quarter—when the airline generates most of its revenue. Similarly, *The Times* (2003) also said that this was a major management blunder: "To pick July, the start of the peak holiday season, to launch an unpopular new clock-in system, is asking for trouble. To push through a scheme without realizing the extent of the resistance by those involved suggests a management aloof from the mood of its employees. And to allow managers to give contradictory statements on the use of the new cards seems guaranteed to foment mistrust."

(Continued)

As Hutton (2003) argued, with 20,000 other BA workers using the swipe card system, "Imposing them after months of inconclusive talks must have seemed—especially given the pressure to contain costs, with the airline set to report its worst ever quarterly loss of £60 million this week—a risk worth taking. It was a massive miscalculation of the workforce's mood." This miscalculation was related to staff cynicism and bitterness about the redundancy program that had been conducted, staff fears of a lack of consultation, poor pay rates, and dissatisfaction with management, who would have considerable knowledge on which to act in the future. The *Guardian* (2003) echoed this viewpoint, noting that "the trigger was undoubtedly the back-handed way BA management at Heathrow tried to force the introduction of swipe cards at exactly the wrong time, when the peak of the summer boom was approaching. They should have known how important it was to approach any potential changes in the working patterns of women juggling with childcare schedules in a very sensitive way."

Rod Eddington, chief executive of BA, acknowledged that it was wrong of senior management to introduce the new clock-in system in the way they did. On BBC Radio, presented with the claim that BA was guilty of "bad management" and "crass stupidity" for not predicting the level of anger to the swipe card, he replied, "With the gift of hindsight, it's difficult to disagree with you" (Clark, 2003).

The Resolution

As a result of the walkout, BA's news release on Tuesday, July 22, said that it would hold talks with representatives from three unions: Amicus MSF, Transport and General Workers Union, and GMB. The introduction of the swipe cards would be delayed until Wednesday, July 23. Following further talks, BA finally announced on July 30 that they had reached agreement with the unions to delay making the swipe card system operational until September 1. They also agreed to a 3 percent pay rise for administrative staff for 2003, not on the basis of introducing the swipe card system, but based on being "confident that the remaining *Future Size and Shape* cost efficiencies will be delivered."

As one person observed: "You have to ask, how important was this scheme to the future operation of BA in the first place? How much money was it going to save and wouldn't it be better to wait a few months for discussion to reassure the staff they are not going to get turned over?" (Behar, 2003).

EXERCISE 10.3

The Italian Job

LO 10.5

As you read this case account, consider the following questions:

1. Refer to the change kaleidoscope, and identify the contextual constraints and enablers affecting the changes that Erick Thohir and his management team want to implement.

2. Based on your analysis of the context, what advice can you give to Erick Thohir and his team about the change implementation design options that they should consider?

3. Also based on your context analysis, what major mistakes would you advise them to avoid when implementing their proposed changes?

The Background

The Indonesian business tycoon Erick Thohir acquired a 70 percent share in the famous Italian football club Inter Milan in 2013. The previous owner of Inter Milan, Massimo Moratti, retained the remaining share. Thohir thus became the first Indonesian businessman to buy a leading European team, and only the second foreign owner of a top Italian club. A sports fan, Thohir had previously set up the Indonesian basketball association, but then he became interested in U.S. sports, which are much more business-oriented. He invested in the Philadelphia 76ers basketball team in 2011, and in the Washington major league soccer team, D.C. United, in 2012.

The Problem

In 2013, Inter Milan had an estimated enterprise value of around €375 million but was heavily in debt. Inter Milan had won five Italian championships between 2006 and 2010, and also won the Champions' League in 2010. Since then, however, the team's performance had been poor, finishing only fifth in Italy's premier league (known as Serie A) between 2011 and 2013. The team's fans were disappointed. The club culture was heavily "Italo-centric," using Italian players and management. Italy's "hardcore" football fans—the "ultras"—had a reputation for xenophobia, racism, and violence.

In 2013, with €169 million in revenues, the club dropped to fifteenth in the Football Money League produced by the accounting group Deloitte. The Serie A league had a reputation for being corrupt and inward-looking, and it was only now opening up to overseas investment. Few clubs made significant profits, and ageing stadiums were not suitable for families and corporate hospitality. Inter Milan was one of six teams under investigation by the governing body, the Union of European Football Associations (UEFA), for breaching "financial fair play" rules.

The Solution

As the new owner, Thohir wanted to develop a different approach to running the club:

> Football is changing. I want to use the US model, where sport is like the media business, with income from advertising and content, mixed with the consumer goods industry, selling jerseys and licensed products.

Thohir's goal was to turn Inter Milan into one of the world's 10 biggest revenue-generating clubs. However, he had to change the club's organization culture, as well as fixing the finances. He decided to recruit British and American executives with experience in media as well as sport. Michael Bolingbroke, previously chief operating officer at Manchester United (one of the most profitable football clubs in the world), was appointed as chief executive. Thohir recruited a marketing director from Apple iTunes, a head of global partnership from the U.S. sports and entertainment group AEG, and a chief financial officer from D.C. United.

Inter Milan had 280 million fans around the world, 60 percent of whom were in Asia, with 18 million in Indonesia alone. Thohir and his new management team, therefore, wanted to focus on Asia, where Inter Milan was not as popular with middle-class football fans as Manchester United, Liverpool, and Real Madrid. Thohir saw growing opportunities in Asia to develop the Inter Milan brand, increase merchandise sales, sign country-based sponsorship deals, and generate more revenue from close-season tours. When he recruited Nemanja Vidić from Manchester United in 2014, Inter Milan fans asked what this ageing defender could do for their club. The answer was that Vidić was "a good brand for the Asian market." The management team asked, "Will this player help us compete on the field, and what about on the marketing side?" Considering the pressure from fans and the Italian sporting media, Thohir commented, "When you're standing on top of the hill, the wind blows hard."

Sources: Bland, B. 2014. The Italian job: Erick Thohir, Inter Milan. *The Financial Times*, October 5. http://www.ft.com/cms/s/0/6e2769c0-4970-11e4-9d7e-00144feab7de.html#axzz3FRxv4AFC.
This case was written in mid-2014, as this edition of our book was being developed. Check the further success of Thohir's change strategy on Inter Milan's website: http://www.inter.it/en/hp.

Additional Reading

Dawson, P., and Andriopoulos, C. 2014. *Managing change, creativity and innovation.* London: Sage Publications. Comprehensive and clearly explained account of a processual perspective on change and innovation, theoretical and practical.

Hamel, G., and Zanini, M. 2014. *Build a change platform, not a change program.* London: McKinsey & Company. Argue that the leader's role is not to design a change program, but to build a change platform, by allowing anyone in the organization to set priorities, diagnose barriers, suggest solutions, recruit support, and initiate change. The executive role is less change agent and more "change enabler in chief," creating the environment in which deep change addressing pressing issues can happen anywhere, at any time.

Ji, Y.-Y., Gutherie, J. P., and Messersmith, J. G. 2014. The tortoise and the hare: The impact of employee instability on firm performance. *Human Resource Management Journal* 24(4):355–73. Studied 4,900 U.S. organizations in 18 industries. Some organizations ("hares") respond rapidly to changing conditions. Others ("tortoises") focus on consistency and make smaller adjustments. Found that employment instability was disruptive, and lowered performance. But also found that while very high instability was damaging, so was very low instability; highly stable organizations can be too rigid and inflexible. Advise a "slow and steady" approach, changing in response to external conditions, retaining talented employees. Organizations that react too quickly damage their competitiveness.

Kotter, J. P. 2012b. Accelerate! *Harvard Business Review* 90(11):44–52. Explains how to drive strategic, transformational change without disrupting daily operations. This is a development of Kotter's original eight-stage model of transformational change.

Pustkowski, R., Scott, J., and Tesvic, J. 2014. *Why implementation matters.* Sydney: McKinsey & Company. Identifies seven core change implementation capabilities from an executive survey: organization-wide ownership, focus on priorities, clear accountability, program management, early planning for sustainability, continuous improvement, and sufficient resources. Describes implementation as an individual discipline that can be developed.

Roundup

Here is a short summary of the key points that we would like you to take from this chapter, in relation to each of the learning outcomes:

LO 10.1

Understand and identify the factors that can cause change to fail.
Making change fail is relatively easy; there are many things that one can do, and not do, to achieve that result. John Kotter identifies eight main failure factors: lack of urgency, no supportive coalition, no vision, poor communication, obstacles to change not removed, no "wins" or achievements to celebrate, declaring victory too soon, and not anchoring or embedding the changes. Lack of communication is a particularly significant cause of change failure.

LO 10.2

Assess the strengths and limitations of checklists for managing change effectively.
We introduced five checklists or "recipes" for managing change:

• The big four	(Pfeffer and Sutton, 2006)
• The seven Cs of change	(CIPD, 2014)
• DICE	(Sirkin et al., 2005)

Reflections for the Practicing Change Manager

- Do you work with a "one size fits all" approach to change management? To what extent do you adapt your approach to the scale and timing of the change, staff readiness, your own relative power, and other context features identified in this chapter?
- How capable are you in adopting more than one change image? Are you more comfortable with a top-down or a bottom-up approach—or somewhere in between? Do you need to develop any particular skills to achieve greater flexibility (assuming you believe that flexibility will give you an advantage)?

- Is there a dominant change approach in your organization? If so, how appropriate is it? What would you need to do in order to modify or replace that dominant approach?
- How do you handle the many different change initiatives that are unfolding in your organization or business unit at a given time—when these are all at different stages? Is this a problem? If not, why not? If it is, what is your preferred solution? If possible, share and discuss your responses to this question and the others in this "reflection" with colleagues.

- ADKAR   (Hiatt, 2006)
- Successful transformational change   (Keller et al., 2010)

One strength of these approaches is that they provide clarity and simplicity in an area that can be complex and untidy. Another strength is that different checklists tend to offer much the same advice, which is reassuring. One limitation is that these checklists tend to lack any theoretical underpinning, relying often on an argument that sounds like, "This worked for us, so it should work for you." From a practitioner perspective, another limitation is that these are generic "high-level guides," and not detailed "best practice" road maps. The change manager is left with the often challenging task of translating this general guidance into a detailed change implementation plan that will fit the organizational circumstances. These checklists do not substitute for local knowledge, informed judgement, and creativity.

We discussed the question concerning when to use each of these checklists. As they tend to offer broadly similar advice, it may not matter. However, some of these checklists appear to apply to relatively straightforward, well-bounded changes, while the McKinsey model applies to large-scale transformational changes. The more appropriate question, we argued, is *how* to use these checklists. They should be seen as high-level guides and not detailed road maps, and will be helpful as long as they are not used in a tightly prescriptive manner, but to trigger discussion, diagnosis, and planning. These comments concerning when and how to use change management guidelines apply to all of the models and frameworks in this chapter.

LO 10.3   *Evaluate the advantages of stage models of change management.*
We introduced four stage models of change management:

- Unfreeze, move, refreeze   (Lewin, 1951)
- The IHI large-scale change framework   (Reinertsen et al., 2008)
- Kotter's eight-stage model   (Kotter, 2012a)
- Nottingham Hospitals' five-step process   (Guyler et al., 2014)

Stage models complement a checklist approach by emphasizing how change unfolds and develops over time, making changing demands on the change manager, and on those who are affected, at each stage. Although change rarely develops in a neat and tidy manner, approaching the process in this way encourages the change manager to anticipate and to prepare for possible future problems. It may also be helpful to consider a more extended timeline, considering how past events could influence current proposals, and how changes will be sustained, and eventually decay, into the future.

LO 10.4   *Assess the theoretical and practical value of processual perspectives on change.*
A process perspective argues that the outcomes of change are shaped by the combination and interaction of a number of factors over time in a given context. Those factors include the context and substance of the change, the implementation process, and also the internal and external organizational politics. One strength of the process perspective is that it recognizes and emphasizes the role of organizational politics, which is often overlooked or regarded as marginal by other approaches. The practical advice flowing from this perspective is broadly similar to that provided by checklists and stage models: plan, train, communicate, learn from mistakes, adapt to circumstances. However, where some practical change management advice recommends "do this," the process perspective advocates "be aware of this," leaving the change manager with the task of reaching informed judgements with regard to appropriate action.

Process perspectives highlight the complexity and politicized nature of change, and view change as a process with a past, present, and future, rather than as a static or time-bounded event. However, there are dangers in this perspective, in presenting change as overly complex and unmanageable, in placing the focus on context at the expense of individual and team contributions, and in the focus on awareness rather than clear direction.

LO 10.5   *Understand and apply contingency approaches to change management.*
We presented four contingency approaches:

• Where to start?	(Gardini et al., 2011)
• The change leadership styles continuum	(Tannenbaum and Schmidt, 1958)
• The Stace-Dunphy contingency matrix	(Stace and Dunphy, 2001)
• The change kaleidoscope	(Hope Hailey and Balogun, 2002)

Contingency approaches argue that change implementation should take into account the attributes of the organizational context concerned. However, these approaches differ with regard to the contingencies—the key factors—that the change manager needs to consider. For example, "where to start?" argues that change should begin with the "pivotal roles," where changes will have the biggest impact on the behavior and performance that is of concern. Those "pivotal roles" will vary from one change initiative to another. The styles continuum suggests choosing a change leadership style based on considerations of available time, use of available expertise, and staff commitment. A dictatorial approach to management in general, and to change management in particular, probably runs counter to most management beliefs. However, the Stace-Dunphy contingency framework suggests that, where change is vital, time is short, and consensus is unlikely, a dictatorial approach is more likely to be effective. The most elaborate of these models, the change kaleidoscope, identifies eight sets of organizational context factors and six sets of change implementation design options. The design options, this approach argues, need to reflect the context diagnosis.

It may seem obvious to argue that "the best approach" depends on the context. However, this idea of "fitting" change to the setting is easier to explain in theory than to put into practice. A detailed diagnosis of the context takes time and requires considerable local knowledge and insight. A contingency approach also demands flexibility in style from change leaders and managers, who may in some instances be required to move out of their "comfort zones," and inconsistent behavior may weaken management credibility. Our two final questions are: is everything contingent in this area, and are there no universals in organizational change?

References

Appelbaum, S. H., Habashy, S., Malo, J.-L., and Shafiq, H. 2012. Back to the future: Revisiting Kotter's 1996 change model. *Journal of Management Development* 31(8): 764–82.

Bacon, R., and Hope, C. 2014. The billions we have spent on IT that doesn't work. *The Times*, August 20:2–3.

Balogun, J. 2006. Managing change: Steering a course between intended strategies and unanticipated outcomes. *Long Range Planning* 39(1):29–49.

Behar, D. 2003. BA to back down in Heathrow strike. *Daily Mail*, July 30:32.

Bland, B. 2014. The Italian job: Erick Thohir, Inter Milan. *The Financial Times*, October 5. http://www.ft.com/cms/s/0/6e2769c0-4970-11e4-9d7e-00144feab7de.html#axzz3FRxv4AFC.

Chartered Institute of Personnel and Development. 2014. *Change management factsheet.* London: Chartered Institute of Personnel and Development.

Clark, A. 2003. BA bosses share the blame. *Guardian*, August 1.

Coch, L., and French, J. R. P. 1948. Overcoming resistance to change. *Human Relations* 1:512–32.

Dawson, P. 2003. *Reshaping change: A processual approach.* London: Routledge.

Dawson, P., and Andriopoulos, C. 2014. *Managing change, creativity and innovation.* London: Sage Publications.

The Economist. 2003. Britain: Terminal; British Airways. July 26:31.

Gardini, M., Giuliani, G., and Marricchi, M. 2011. *Finding the right place to start change.* Rome and Milan: McKinsey & Company.

Graetz, F., and Smith, A. C. T. 2010. Managing organizational change: A philosophies of change approach. *Journal of Change Management* 10(2):135–54.

Guardian. 2003. Back from the brink: Both sides can learn from the BA dispute. August 1:25.

Guyler, T., Ward, P., and Buchanan, D. 2014. From the front line up: Lessons from a whole hospital transformation. *Health Service Journal*, September 23:27–29.

Hamel, G., and Zanini, M. 2014. *Build a change platform, not a change program*. London: McKinsey & Company.

Hiatt, J. M. 2004. *Employee's survival guide to change*. Loveland, CO: Prosci Research.

Hiatt, J. M. 2006. *ADKAR: A model for change in business, government, and our community*. Loveland, CO: Prosci.

Hope Hailey, V., and Balogun, J. 2002. Devising context sensitive approaches to change: The example of Glaxo Wellcome. *Long Range Planning* 35(2):153–78.

Hutton, W. 2003. How BA clipped its own wings. *Observer*, July 27. http://www.theguardian.com/politics/2003/jul/27/theairlineindustry.britishairwaysbusiness.

Jacquemont, D., Maor, D., and Reich, A. 2015. *How to beat the transformation odds*. New York: McKinsey & Company.

Ji, Y.-Y., Gutherie, J. P., and Messersmith, J. G. 2014. The tortoise and the hare: The impact of employee instability on firm performance. *Human Resource Management Journal* 24(4):355–73.

Jones, A. 2003. BA "swipe card" dispute talks continue. *PA News*, July 24.

Kanter, R. M. 2009. Change is hardest in the middle. *Harvard Business Review* Blog Network, August 12. http://blogs.hbr.org/2009/08/change-is-hardest-in-the-middl/.

Keller, S., Meaney, M., and Pung, C. 2010. *What successful transformations share*. Chicago and London: McKinsey & Company.

Kotter, J. P. 2007. Leading change: Why transformation efforts fail. *Harvard Business Review* 85(1):96–103 (first published 1995).

Kotter, J. P. 2012a. *Leading change*. 2nd ed. Boston: Harvard University Press.

Kotter, J. P. 2012b. Accelerate! *Harvard Business Review* 90(11):44–52.

Lewin, K. (ed.). 1951. *Field theory in social science: Selected theoretical papers by Kurt Lewin*. London: Tavistock Publications. (UK edition published 1952, edited by Dorwin Cartwright.)

McFarland, W., and Goldsworthy, S. 2013. *Choosing change: How leaders and organizations drive results one person at a time*. New York: McGraw-Hill Professional.

McGreevy, R., and Johnston, C. 2003. Thousands stranded by Heathrow walkout. *The Times*, July 19:2.

Pettigrew, A. M. 1985. *The awakening giant: Continuity and change in ICI*. Oxford: Basil Blackwell.

Pettigrew, A. M. 1987. Context and action in the transformation of the firm. *Journal of Management Studies* 24(6):649–70.

Pfeffer, J., and Sutton, R. I. 2006. *Hard facts, dangerous half-truths, and total nonsense: Profiting from evidence-based management.* Boston: Harvard Business School Press.

Plowman, D. A., Baker, L. T., Beck, T. E., Kulkarni, M., Solansky, S. T., and Travis, D. V. T. 2007. Radical change accidentally: The emergence and amplification of small change. *Academy of Management Journal* 50(3):515–43.

Pustkowski, R., Scott, J., and Tesvic, J. 2014. *Why implementation matters.* Sydney: McKinsey & Company.

Reinertsen, J. L., Bisognano, M., and Pugh, M. D. 2008. *Seven leadership leverage points for organization-level improvement in health care.* 2nd ed. Cambridge, MA: Institute for Healthcare Improvement.

Reingold, J., and Roberts, D. 2013. Squeezing Heinz. *Fortune*, October 28:184–92.

Rod, M., Ashill, N., and Saunders, S. 2009. Considering implementing major strategic change? Lessons from joint venture in the UK health technology sector. *International Journal of Pharmaceutical and Healthcare Marketing* 3(3):258–78.

Schneider, D. M., and Goldwasser, C. 1998. Be a model leader of change. *Management Review* 87(3):41–45.

Sirkin, H. J., Keenan, P., and Jackson, A. 2005. The hard side of change management. *Harvard Business Review* 83(10):108–18.

Stace, D. A., and Dunphy, D. 2001. *Beyond the boundaries: Leading and re-creating the successful enterprise.* 2nd ed. Sydney: McGraw-Hill.

Tannenbaum, R., and Schmidt, W. H. 1958. How to choose a leadership pattern. *Harvard Business Review* 37:95–102.

The Times. 2003. Air pocket—British Airways has run into rough weather. July 29:17.

Tran, M. 2003. BA staff take a swipe at new security system. *The Guardian*, July 22:14. http://www.theguardian.com/business/2003/jul/22/theairlineindustry.britishairways.

Webster, B. 2003. Staff sign in, but do not sign out. *The Times*, July 28:2.

3

Running Threads: Sustainability, and the Effective Change Manager

Part 3 focuses on two themes which are distinct from, but which run through, the first two parts of this book. The first of these "running threads" concerns the sustainability of organizational change. We know that even successful changes can "decay," and the benefits be lost. What actions are necessary to ensure, or at least to improve, the sustainability of change? In many of the implementation models that we explored in part 2, sustainability is treated as the final step in the change process. Chapter 11 argues that sustainability has to be considered from the start, built into the implementation process. In most cases, it will be too late to treat sustainability as an issue to be managed after implementation has been completed. The second running thread, the core theme that this text as a whole addresses, concerns what it takes to be an effective change manager. We consider who the change managers are in an organization, and if they are necessarily senior leaders. The role of middle managers—traditionally seen as change blockers—turns out to be key in initiating and implementing change. Finally, we set out a six-step approach to developing personal change management capabilities.

Chapter 11

Sustaining Change versus Initiative Decay

Learning objectives

By the end of this chapter you should be able to:

LO 11.1 Understand the causes of initiative decay—threats to the sustainability of change.

LO 11.2 Distinguish between change initiatives that are "blameworthy," and should not be sustained, and those that are "praiseworthy."

LO 11.3 Identify and apply actions that can contribute to the sustainability of change.

LO 11.4 Understand the pitfalls that can arise when seeking to sustain change.

"We're ready to begin the next phase of keeping things exactly the way they are."

Peter C. Vey The New Yorker Collection/The Cartoon Bank

LO 11.1 Initiative Decay and Improvement Evaporation

Your reorganization was implemented successfully. Significant benefits were achieved. Revisiting the initiative some months later, however, you find that the new working practices and increased performance levels appear not to have been maintained. Things have gone back to where they were before you started. How did this happen? Unfortunately, this is a common story. Even successful initiatives can decay, leading to "the improvement evaporation effect" as the gains are lost.

For many organizations, it is a strategic imperative to embed, to have "stickability," to maintain changes and their contribution to performance. This chapter focuses on the problems of sustaining change and on the practical steps that can be taken to increase the probability that changes once implemented will endure, that they will become institutionalized and regarded as normal practice. This is not a new problem, having been famously identified by Kurt Lewin (1951) as the need to "refreeze" behavior once change has taken place. The attention of practicing managers and academic researchers has focused on the first two stages of his model, "unfreezing" and "moving." The problems of refreezing, or sustaining change, are less well understood. There may be a widespread assumption that, if changes have been successful, they will automatically be sustained. That assumption, however, appears often to be incorrect. Paradoxically, for the change manager, sustaining changes may in some instances present a more difficult challenge than implementing them in the first place.

Sustainability implies that new working methods and performance levels are maintained for an appropriate period, or that new practices and processes are routinized until they become obsolete. What are the causes of initiative decay? What steps can be taken to increase the probability that changes will be sustained and become embedded in the organization as routine practice? As we have explored in other chapters, what is considered to be achievable with regard to sustaining change depends on how managing change is understood. The views of sustainability from each image of change management are summarized in table 11.1.

TABLE 11.1
Images of Managing and Sustaining Change

Image	View of Sustainability
Director	It is the responsibility of the change manager to design the change process and direct others to comply, to ensure that planned objectives are achieved.
Navigator	The change manager designs the change process to fit the context, recognizing that modifications will be required and that the outcome may not be as intended.
Caretaker	Change outcomes will be determined primarily by contextual factors, and not by management intervention.
Coach	The change manager's main role is to help others to develop the capabilities necessary to achieve the intended outcomes of the change.
Interpreter	The change manager develops understanding of the meaning and significance of the changes and what will count as successful outcomes.
Nurturer	Change outcomes are in constant flux, and are largely beyond management control.

Momentum Busters

Robert Reisner (2002) examines the U.S. Postal Service, which, during the 1990s, "transformed itself from the butt of sitcom jokes into a profitable and efficient enterprise" (p. 45). By 2001, however, morale and performance were low, and losses were predicted. Why was the transformation not sustained? Reisner (vice president for strategic planning) blames three "momentum busters": the indifference of senior managers, who regarded some aspects of strategy as a "distraction"; resistance from trade unions, whose role and voice had been marginalized; and inability to steer funding through a budget process that favored traditional initiatives over innovations. Innovation was also stifled by governance constraints. What one competitor, UPS, achieved, the Postal Service could not have initiated without a prior hearing process before the Postal Rate Commission, and major structural changes would have required congressional sanction. The situation was exacerbated by a weak economy, problems with e-commerce, and terrorist assaults on the American postal service.

Reisner's (2002, p. 52) conclusion is optimistic: "Despite the limits to any transformation effort, accomplishing meaningful change in even the largest, most complex, and tradition-bound of organizations is achievable." However, the leadership, organizational, and contextual causes of initiative decay need to be addressed in order to sustain these changes (Buchanan et al., 2005).

initiative decay

We have to recognize that management may have no direct control over many of the factors that can jeopardize the sustainability of change. That does not mean, however, that it is not possible to anticipate and to counter those factors in some manner.

For changes to "stick," they must "seep into the bloodstream," become "the new norm," "baked into the organization" or, as Kotter (2007, p. 103) observes, accepted as "the way we do things around here." That is, it must become an integral part of the organizational culture, or what has also been described as the "mind-set" of the organization's members (Lawson and Price, 2003). This means that new structures, processes, and working practices are no longer seen as "change," with all the emotional, political, and operational connotations that accompany that term. Unless this happens, change may prove to be just a passing diversion, a temporary disruption. However, as we explored in chapter 5, culture change is not a straightforward process. As Lou Gerstner (2002, pp. 182 and 187) once said, referring to his leadership of the successful transformation of IBM:

> I came to see, in my time at IBM, that culture isn't just one aspect of the game—it is the game. Vision, strategy, marketing, financial management—any management system, in fact—can set you on the right path and can carry you for a while. But no enterprise—whether in business, government, education, health care, or any area of human endeavor—will succeed over the long haul if those elements aren't part of the DNA. . . .
>
> What you can do is create the conditions for transformation. You can provide incentives. You can define the marketplace realities and goals. But then you have to trust. In fact, in the end, management doesn't change culture. Management invites the workforce itself to change the culture.

Not a coerced change but change by living

What are the main threats to the sustainability of change? David Buchanan et al. (2007) identify the "top ten" factors that can lead to initiative decay:

The new values within the new context

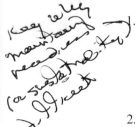

1. *The initiators and drivers move on.* Managers who have been successful at implementing change may be more interested in moving on to the next change challenge than in staying around for a period of relative stability. In addition, experienced and successful change agents may be sought by other divisions or organizations, which have other novel change agendas to progress. It can be difficult to turn down promotion opportunities such as these.

2. *Accountability for development has become diffuse.* The responsibility for driving change is normally (but not always) clear, with formal change or project management roles, often accompanied by steering groups, task forces, and implementation teams. Once the changes are in place and operational, those individuals and groups return to their normal roles. There are change managers, but organizations tend not to appoint "sustainability managers." Just who is accountable for ensuring that the changes are now embedded, that they become the new norm, is often unclear.

3. *Knowledge and experience with new practice are lost through staff turnover.* Change initiatives that involve new skills and knowledge are usually supported by staff training and development programs. Everyone who is going to be affected will be invited to attend these programs, creating a "critical mass" of participants for training sessions. However, as individuals subsequently leave and are replaced, it may be difficult to repeat those development sessions for small numbers of participants. The knowledge that is lost when staff leave is therefore not replaced.

4. *Old habits are imported with recruits from less dynamic organizations.* Linked to factor 3, new recruits bring with them habits and working practices from previous employers. Once again, they are unlikely to be offered retraining, but instead expected to learn new practices "on the job," by observation. The likelihood of initiative decay thus increases with the numbers of new recruits.

5. *The issues and pressures that triggered the initiative are no longer visible.* As we discussed in chapter 3, organizations usually change in response to a combination of internal problems, external environmental challenges, and new opportunities. Those triggers, however, may not be durable; the problems are solved, the challenges are addressed, the opportunities are developed. The rationale for change can thus fade with the triggers, and again lead to initiative decay.

6. *New managers want to drive their own agendas.* For personal satisfaction, visibility, and reputation, newly appointed managers often want to appear to be innovative and energetic, and to "make a mark" on their new organization. This means enhancing their careers by designing and implementing their own change initiatives. Continuing with work that was started by others is less interesting and satisfying, and could limit one's promotion prospects.

7. *Powerful stakeholders are using counter-implementation tactics to block progress.* Successful implementation does not always silence the powerbrokers. They may remain in post, and if they did not welcome the changes, they may wait for opportunities to undermine the changes. This becomes easier if factor 1 applies; the initiators are no longer there to protect their changes.

8. *The pump-priming funding runs out.* Many changes are allocated additional funding in order to support the implementation costs. This can include the temporary appointment of specialist staff or external consultants, and the cost of training programs to provide new skills and knowledge. As those resources are consumed, and the

temporary appointments and the training come to an end, support for the changes is weakened, and initiative decay becomes more likely.

9. *Other priorities come on stream, diverting attention and resources.* Most organizations today do not suffer a shortage of internal and external pressures for change. As other urgent problems and opportunities arise, the focus inevitably shifts away from past pressures and the changes that those prompted. If those past problems have indeed been addressed, then it may be appropriate for attention and resources to move to more urgent issues. However, this will generate problems if the shift in focus to new priorities simply recreates the situation that past changes were implemented to address.

10. *Staff at all levels suffer initiative fatigue, enthusiasm for change falters.* The experience, or the perception, of "too much change," successful or not, can threaten sustainability by generating a desire to "get back to normal." Initiative decay can result when management do not pay attention to the pace and timing of the changes that staff are expected to deal with, and generate burnout and initiative fatigue by attempting to drive too many changes too rapidly (Abrahamson, 2004).

Initiative decay can be caused by many factors, at different levels of analysis. Several of those factors may be operating in a given context at any one time. In the absence of proactive management steps to address those factors, initiative decay, and not sustained change, may be the norm.

LO 11.2 Praiseworthy and Blameworthy Failures

The failure of an intended change is not always a problem that needs to be solved. A change can fail because it was inappropriate for some reason. Mitchell Marks and Robert Shaw (1995) argue that "productive failure" is valuable, if an organization has the capacity to add the learning from such experiences to its store of knowledge rather than to conduct a witch hunt to find who to blame. A learning organization treats occasional failure as natural and as an opportunity to develop better understanding and to improve future performance. Marks and Shaw also argue that an organization may gain more in the long term from a productive failure than from an "unproductive success"—a change that has gone well, but nobody quite knows why: "We must be doing something right."

Some changes, if they do not meet their intended goals, must therefore be allowed to decay. Most organizations, however, do treat such "failures" harshly. Those who were responsible may even be punished in some manner, and perhaps find that their career opportunities have become more limited. In chapter 3, we discussed the work of Amy Edmondson (2011, p. 50), who describes a spectrum of reasons for failure (table 11.2), from blameworthy at one extreme, to praiseworthy at the other. Not all of these failure modes concern change, but those that do are more likely to be praiseworthy.

Most managers, Edmondson argues, do not distinguish blameworthy from praiseworthy failures, treating them all equally. This is not helpful, and is potentially wasteful:

> When I ask executives to consider this spectrum and then to estimate how many of the failures in their organization are truly blameworthy, their answers are usually in single digits—perhaps 2% to 5%. But when I ask how many are *treated* as blameworthy, they say (after a pause or a laugh) 70% to 90%. The unfortunate consequence is that many failures go unreported and their lessons are lost. (Edmondson, 2011, p. 50)

Productive Failure at McDonald's

In 2001, McDonald's opened two four-star Golden Arch hotels in Switzerland. They were distinctive, with a 24-hour McDonald's restaurant attached, and rooms with a patented curved wall, arch-shaped headboards, and a cylindrical, see-through shower (that was partially in the bedroom). The idea had been proposed by the McDonald's Switzerland chairman, Urs Hammer, in response to a push from the parent company for diversification and new ideas.

The hotels were not a financial success. There were problems with the interior design (lack of privacy in the shower) and the phrase "golden arches" is not associated with McDonald's in German-speaking countries (it also didn't help that "arch," when pronounced by German speakers, sounded like a vulgar German word for posterior). Also, and more importantly, although the restaurant venture made use of many of the company's core competencies in areas such as franchising and real

estate management, the McDonald's brand simply didn't work when applied to a four-star hotel.

However, international marketing professor Stefan Michel (2007) argues that the decision by McDonald's to pilot this initiative was not as bizarre as it seemed. For example: (1) diversifying into hotels gave McDonald's a chance to test the multibillion-dollar restaurant industry; (2) it required what was a relatively small investment for McDonald's; (3) the damage to the McDonald's brand was limited through the use of the name Golden Arches, and restricting the experiment to Switzerland; and (4) the losses on real estate and operations were insignificant in relation to the overall McDonald's business. Most significantly, the venture was a statement of support for entrepreneurial ideas within the company, and the outcome was treated as an important, and relatively inexpensive, learning experience (based on Michel, 2007).

TABLE 11.2
A Spectrum of Reasons for Failure

Reason	Description	
Deviance	An individual chooses to violate a prescribed process or practice.	*blameworthy* ↑
Inattention	An individual inadvertently deviates from specifications.	
Lack of ability	An individual doesn't have the skills, conditions, or training to execute a job.	
Process inadequacy	A competent individual adheres to a prescribed but faulty or incomplete process.	
Task challenge	An individual faces a task too difficult to be executed reliably every time.	
Process complexity	A process composed of many elements breaks down when it encounters novel interactions.	
Uncertainty	A lack of clarity about future events causes people to take seemingly reasonable actions that produce undesired results.	
Hypothesis testing	An experiment conducted to prove that an idea or a design will succeed fails.	*praiseworthy* ↓
Exploratory testing	An experiment conducted to expand knowledge and investigate a possibility leads to an undesired result.	

Changes that fail can therefore be valuable, discouraging further experiments of that kind and revealing what adjustments may be necessary in order to make the next attempt successful. To build such a learning culture, experimentation should be encouraged, and failures (including near misses) need to be detected and subjected to an analysis that looks beyond the obvious. It is also necessary to avoid making the "fundamental attribution error," which means blaming individuals and ignoring the context in which they were working (Ross, 1977).

Based on experience at a children's hospital in Minnesota, Edmondson (2011, pp. 52–53) describes five practices for building a "psychologically safe environment" in which to learn from failures:

1. *Frame the work accurately.* People need a shared understanding of the kinds of failures that can be expected to occur in a given work context (routine production, complex operations, or innovation) and why openness and collaboration are important for surfacing and learning from them. Accurate framing detoxifies failure.

2. *Embrace messengers.* Those who come forward with bad news, questions, concerns, or mistakes should be rewarded rather than shot. Celebrate the value of the news first and then figure out how to fix the failure and learn from it.

3. *Acknowledge limits.* Being open about what you don't know, mistakes you've made, and what you can't get done alone will encourage others to do the same.

4. *Invite participation.* Ask for observations and ideas and create opportunities for people to detect and analyze failures and promote intelligent experiments. Inviting participation helps defuse resistance and defensiveness.

5. *Set boundaries and hold people accountable.* Paradoxically, people feel psychologically safer when leaders are clear about what acts are blameworthy. And there must be consequences. But if someone is punished or fired, tell those directly and indirectly affected what happened and why it warranted blame.

Will adopting such a "soft" and "understanding" management approach to failures make staff more careless, and encourage more mistakes? Edmondson (2011, p. 55) argues

⌐ AAA strategies

Sustaining Successful Change Means Permanently Changing Mindsets

Emily Lawson and Colin Price (2003) argue that the success and sustainability of change relies on people thinking differently about their jobs, and not just on persuading them to change the way they work. This is particularly the case with fundamental changes to organization culture, for example, from reactive to proactive, from hierarchical to collegial, from introspective to externally focused. There are four conditions for the necessary change in mindsets.

First, those who are affected by a change need to understand the purpose, and agree with it. There is no point in management telling people that things must be done differently: "Anyone leading a major change program must take time to think through its 'story'—what makes it worth undertaking—and

to explain that story to all of the people involved in making change happen, so that their contributions make sense to them as individuals" (p. 33).

Second, reward and recognition systems need to be consistent with the new behaviors. Third, staff must have the necessary skills, and be given time to absorb new information, to link that to existing knowledge and to apply it effectively in practice.

And finally, "they must see people they respect modelling it actively" (p. 32). We all tend to model our behavior on "significant others" and especially those in influential positions. Management at all levels thus become role models, and must "walk the walk" if mindsets are to change (p. 35).

that a failure to encourage experimentation, combined with a failure to learn from the inevitable mistakes, poses greater risks to organizational change and effectiveness. Change initiatives that do not work cannot be sustained. However, if management want to sustain the generation of further new ideas for change, then those who develop praiseworthy failures should be recognized and rewarded, and not blamed and punished.

LO 11.3 Actions to Sustain Change

What actions will increase the probability that change will be sustained? No specific set of steps can guarantee success, but awareness of the threats to sustainability can lead to timely and effective responses. Action to secure sustainability is often identified as the final point in the "change recipes" that we discussed in chapter 10. For example, "institutionalize new approaches" is step 8 in John Kotter's (2007) eight-step model of transformational change. However, sustainability depends not just on what happens after implementation, but also on the cumulative effects of decisions and actions during the change process. In other words, it is more effective to plan for sustainability from the beginning than to regard this as an issue that can be left until a later stage.

Here are eight sets of actions that should be considered when designing a change initiative, in order to build sustainability into the process from the beginning, or at least from an early stage.

Busting the Momentum Busters

Reflecting on his experience of the "momentum busters" that derailed transformational change in the U.S. Postal Service, Robert Reisner (2002, pp. 51–52) identifies "four hard lessons" for organizations undertaking a major change initiative in a turbulent economic environment:

1. *Don't miss your moment*
   We missed numerous market opportunities that competitors such as UPS seized. Furthermore, we let pass at least two chances to capitalize on high morale and momentum within the Postal Service, moments that provided the best opportunity to overcome organizational resistance to change

2. *Connect change initiatives to your core business*
   Most of the innovative programs we launched to boost revenue existed at the fringes of our business. And we never established a path for them to migrate to the heart of our operations.

3. *Don't mistake incremental improvements for strategic transformation*

[O]ur tremendous success in improving delivery times, which we enthusiastically celebrated, blinded us to the need for strategic change. For a time, we slipped into complacency, ignoring our competition and challenges and declaring ourselves the winner in a race with ourselves.

4. *Be realistic about your limits and the pace of change*
   [I]n a change initiative, it is important to identify which obstacles are in your control and which aren't. Some of what we wanted to do may simply not have been possible, at least at the time. . . . While some of our constraints—our regulatory framework, if not our very size and complexity—are specific to us, every organization has limits of one kind or another. It may seem heretical to say so in the can-do environment of American business, but sometimes you need to accept those limits. A failure to acknowledge that you sometimes *can't* do certain things can breed discouragement and cynicism, ultimately undermining those change initiatives that are achievable.

Redesign Roles

Organizational change, particularly where new structures, processes, and technologies are involved, often leads to the redesign of existing roles and to the creation of new ones. However, these role changes may be a critical dimension of the process, and not just a product of change. Michael Beer et al. (1990) argue that most change programs do not work because they focus on attempts to change attitudes and beliefs by introducing new perspectives. The assumption that underpins this approach, that changes in behavior will follow changes in attitudes, is in their view fundamentally flawed. The causal arrow, they suggest, runs in the opposite direction. Behavior is influenced by the context in which people find themselves—by their responsibilities, relationships, and roles. In short, first redesign roles, which require new behaviors, and attitude change will then follow. It is difficult to revert to past behavior with a new formal role definition, which is one of a network of similarly redesigned roles. Sustainability is not guaranteed by this approach, but it is significantly encouraged.

Redesign Reward Systems

Beer and Nohria (2000, p. 267) also observe, "There are virtually no fundamental changes in organizations that do not also involve some changes in the reward system." This is one consequence of redesigning roles and responsibilities. Anne Fisher (1995, p. 122) cites the example of Integra Financial, a $14 billion (in assets) bank holding company that was formed through a merger. In order to reinforce the company's commitment to a teamwork initiative, management implemented a carefully designed evaluation and reward system, "to discourage hot-dogging, grandstanding, filibustering, and other ego games" and to ensure that "the best team players get the goodies." Fisher (1995, p. 122) also notes, "One thing that you can count on: Whatever gets rewarded will get done." This also means that whatever is not rewarded (such as pre-change working practices) will not get done. Changing the reward system can thus contribute significantly to sustainability by removing the financial motivation to return to old behaviors.

Rewards should also include public recognition of behaviors that are consistent with the desired change: this both reinforces individual behavior and sends strong signals to others. The opposite also applies: management failure to respond to behavior that is in direct opposition to the change undermines the credibility of the program. Lack of action in this respect can increase rapidly the rate of initiative decay. The organization's pay system can thus support or derail a change initiative.

Link Selection to Change Objectives

Staff selection, and promotion processes, can be subtle but powerful ways in which to embed and sustain assumptions and values—to change and to maintain the organization's culture. As with the rewards system, appointments and promotions, particularly to key and influential roles, have symbolic significance in signalling whether top management really support a change, or not. A single inappropriate senior appointment during the change process can quickly derail all the implementation work that has already been undertaken.

To support organizational changes with selection, a number of organizations have adopted "values-based recruitment" systems, which seek to select staff whose motives, attitudes, and values support what the organization is trying to achieve. For example,

Jonathan Rapping (2009) describes a values-based recruitment, training, and mentoring program for selecting and developing public defenders to represent poor clients in criminal cases in Georgia. Poor defendants often have problems finding lawyers, who then refuse to visit them in jail. To change this traditional culture, recruitment and selection changed to emphasize values relating to enthusiastic and loyal representation, advocating the client's cause, studying and preparing the case, and communicating with the client.

Triggered by failures in quality of social care in the United Kingdom, Jacqui Goode (2014) describes a values-based recruitment toolkit to help employers to find people with values appropriate to working in this sector. This toolkit includes sample job advertisements, an online personality profiling questionnaire, and suggested values-based interview questions such as: "What excites you about working in adult social care?" and "Can you give an example of where your understanding of what another person may be going through has helped you to develop your compassion for that person?" and "Tell me about a time when you have 'gone the extra mile' at work." The answers to these kinds of questions reveal candidates' behavior and their values with regard to care and compassion.

Walk the Talk

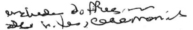

This is a well-known cliché. However, senior management can seriously jeopardize the sustainability of change if their words and actions are interpreted by employees as signalling, "We don't really mean it." In other words, if the top team does not support this change, why should we? Little is more damaging to the credibility of a change program than a lack of consistency between the statements and behaviors of the change advocates. Even if management did not mean to send negative signals, "unintentional hypocrisy" can be equally damaging (Fisher, 1995).

One indicator of consistency concerns changes in management practices that are clearly aligned with the goals of the change. For example, who is praised and promoted and why? Is management enthusiastically advocating teamwork while still rewarding individual performance? Where are resources—finance, staffing, expertise—being allocated? The commitment of resources to an initiative in such a way that to withdraw would be extremely costly conveys unambiguous management support (as Alan Lafley did—see box). All of these management decisions and actions have symbolic as well as tangible effects. Edgar Schein (2010) argues that managers signal what is important by what they systematically pay attention to. "Communication" is not confined to conversations, meetings, presentations, and emails, but includes all management actions—and omissions—that send signals concerning goals and priorities (and we have also to recognize that those signals may or may not be interpreted in the manner that management intended).

Alan Lafley's Moment of Truth

Early in his time as chief executive at Procter & Gamble, Alan Lafley had to decide whether to approve a major marketing effort to launch several new products. This would require significant commitment of funds, and P&G had just missed earnings targets two quarters in a row. But Lafley had been working hard communicating the message that innovation was P&G's lifeblood. Lafley describes his response: "So we locked arms and we went ahead. I had to make choices like these to convince P&G managers we were going to go for winning" (Gupta and Wendler, 2005, p. 4).

Encourage Voluntary Acts of Initiative

John Kotter (2012) emphasizes the value of having many change agents in an organization, and not just the usual small elite team, arguing that vision and strategy should be communicated in a manner that creates buy-in and attracts a growing "volunteer army" (p. 52). From their four-year study of organizational change in six corporations, Michael Beer et al. (1990) conclude that in encouraging change, the most effective senior managers specified the general direction in which they wanted the company to move and left the details of specific changes to be decided "closer to the action," lower down the organization. They found that change was more likely to become embedded if those at the operational level were supported when they developed for themselves the specific changes that they believed appropriate for their local circumstance.

Measure Progress

A focus on measurement is important for two reasons. First, metrics and milestones are fundamental to tracking the progress of change, highlighting the need for any corrective action. Second, what gets measured can significantly affect how people act, because measurement signals the importance of that aspect of performance. Less attention is paid to dimensions of performance that are not measured. From a survey of the change experiences of over 2,000 executives, Giancarlo Ghislanzoni et al. (2010, p. 8) found that two of the top five procedures used by organizations whose changes had been successful were "defining detailed metrics for reorganization's effect on short- and long-term performance and assessing progress against them" and "using detailed plans, split into workstreams with milestones for delivery and someone accountable for reaching each." Progress measurement is thus important both for implementation and for sustainability.

It is important to choose appropriate metrics (see "Change Metrics: The Continental Airlines Experience"). David Nadler (1997) argues that organizations should carry out a comprehensive progress check on major change initiatives within six months after they have begun, and then annually thereafter. These checks should use a combination of quantitative performance measures, attitude surveys, focus groups, and interviews with individuals. Kanter et al. (1992) suggest that two kinds of measures are particularly helpful. First, *results measures*: How will we know that we have achieved our objectives? Second, *process measures*: How will we know that we are doing what is necessary to achieve those objectives, and how plans may need to be adjusted? The Price Waterhouse Change Integration Team (1995) argue that a balanced set of performance measures should include:

- *Leading measures*, which reveal the immediate results of a new initiative, such as changes in processing time, or time-to-market for new products
- *Lagging measures*, such as financial performance, and corporate image, that can take time to become apparent
- *Internal measures*, focusing on intra-organizational processes and efficiencies
- *External measures*, such as the perspectives of stakeholders, customers, and suppliers, and how the organization compares with benchmark competitors
- *Cost-based measures*, that are directly financial
- *Non-cost measures*, such as market share and brand image

Exercise 11.1 asks you to apply these measures to a current change in your own organization, or one with which you are familiar. Do all of these measures apply? If not, why not?

Celebrate en Route

Months or years can pass before the outcomes of a change initiative are fully realized. Most of those who are involved expect to see convincing evidence that their efforts are being rewarded. A lack of clear evidence of success strengthens the views of those who initially resisted the change. Skepticism concerning the value of the change may thus be increased by delays in demonstrating the benefits. However, it is often the case that some tangible benefits can be identified at an early stage in the process. John Kotter (2012, p. 52) thus argues that one of the "accelerators" of change is to celebrate significant short-term wins. Celebrating the early benefits, even if they are relatively small in scale, recognizes and rewards those who are involved, strengthens the credibility of the program, and helps to weaken the skepticism.

Celebrating Success at Sandvik

Sandvik Materials Technology produces advanced alloys and ceramic materials, and employs over 8,000 people in 50 production and 30 sales units across the world. When a change program focusing on business processes was introduced, some of Sandvik's units soon achieved very significant improvements. People from these units then visited other units, in particular those where there was skepticism about the change. These visits spread knowledge of successes and helped people in other units see what improvements could be achieved through the change initiative. Later, when a key financial target was reached, this was acknowledged by having a photograph taken of the Sandvik management team standing on top of a pile of gravel. However, according to Sandvik president Peter Gossas, "When we looked at the photo we thought, 'Yes, success should be celebrated but hey, this is the wrong message.' So we added five bigger piles to symbolize mountains we have yet to climb" (Ahlberg and Nauclér, 2007, p. 3).

In addition, the links between changed systems and working practices and organizational performance should be made clear. Staff who have to work out those links for themselves may not make accurate assumptions. And successes, if they are effectively publicized and widely understood, can act as catalysts for further changes (see "Celebrating Success at Sandvik"). A further implication of the focus on celebrating "en route" concerns the allocation of resources to priority areas; those areas that need the most urgent attention may provide the best opportunities to demonstrate clear and immediate benefits, which can then be celebrated as short-term wins. Failure to establish those priorities at an early stage in the change process may be a direct cause of change failure.

Change Metrics *The Continental Airlines Experience*

When Gordon Bethune became chief executive of Continental Airlines in 1994, it had been losing money for most of the previous decade, had a debt-to-equity ratio of 50 to 1, and had served some time in Chapter 11 of the federal bankruptcy code. During this period, Continental had emphasized competing on the basis of cheaper fares than its major competitors. However, although it achieved the lowest cost per available seat mile (of the major airlines), it also had the lowest revenue per available seat mile and a loss overall. Bethune reflects on this situation:

I firmly believe that what you measure is what you get. This is an example of a company that said that it couldn't compete with the big boys unless it was able to have cheaper fares. That set the culture and mind-set. So, we had a culture that said, "Cost is everything." That's the Holy Grail. We even had pilots turning down the air-conditioning and slowing down airplanes to save the cost of fuel. They made passengers hot, mad and late. That's a dysfunctional measure, a measure some accountant dreamed up who does not understand our business.

Bethune responded by investigating what factors most influenced passengers' level of satisfaction with airlines. This revealed that on-time performance was the most significant factor. Unfortunately, at the time of Bethune's arrival, Continental ranked 10th of the 10 largest U.S. carriers on this criterion. Nonetheless, Bethune changed the core metric used inside Continental to on-time performance:

> We use that measure for two reasons. One because it is the single most vital sign of a functioning airline, and two, it's ranked by our Government and we can't screw the metrics.

To reinforce the centrality of this factor, a new system of rewards was established in which bonuses were paid to all staff each month that Continental was ranked in the top 5 of the 10 largest U.S. carriers for on-time performance. The cost of the bonus payments was more than covered by the reduction in the amount—that had risen to $6 million per month—that Continental had been paying to put passengers on other airlines, put them up in hotels, bus them across town, and so forth.

The next month, March 1995, we wound up in first place. We had never been in first place in 60 years. I mean, Continental, the worst company in America for the last 20 years, is first place in "on time" which is a metric everyone kind of understands.

By 1996 (and again in 1997), Continental had won the J. D. Power & Associates award for customer satisfaction as the best airline for flights of 500 miles or more and was in the top three in terms of fewest customer complaints and lost baggage. From 1995 to 1998, Continental's market capitalization rose from $230 million to $3 billion.

Fine-Tuning

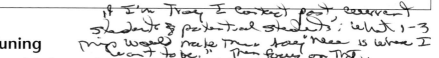

Despite careful advance planning, most change initiatives do not unfold as anticipated. The need for corrective action is to be expected. Making timely modifications in the light of experience will normally be more effective than attempting not to deviate from plan. Problems arise for two main reasons. First, by definition, the implementation of change always involves doing something new, something that has never been done before. A particular type of change program may of course have been implemented in another division, or another organization—but that change will always be new here, in this organization, in this division, at this time, for these reasons, with those resources, affecting our staff. In other words, change management always involves "building the plane as you fly," and it is not surprising if parts fall off. Second, organizational changes are multifaceted, affecting many different factors that are themselves inter-linked. It is therefore difficult to anticipate all of the "knock on" effects or "ripples" that a change in one area will have elsewhere.

For the change manager, this means adjusting and refining aspects of the implementation process without this being seen as an admission of failure. This can be difficult in practice, because "we have learned from experience" can also be described as "you made mistakes in the planning." This can be addressed by communicating the fine-tuning in terms of consistency with the original goals. As we have noted elsewhere, part of the change management responsibility is to help others to make sense of what is happening, to shape and to retell the story, and to explain that the core principles that lie behind the change remain intact.

Fine-Tuning at Ford

In 1995, Ford Motor Company introduced a series of changes to the way the company designed and manufactured its cars and trucks. This involved changing from an existing functional structure, consolidating activities into five vehicle centers, and using a reduced number of platforms for its vehicle range. After a year and a half, senior management decided to make modifications in light of the initial experience. However, the changes had been viewed with some skepticism by some groups and individuals both inside the company and in the financial community. As a result, when the time came to announce the modifications (e.g., consolidating further from five to three vehicle centers), the company paid a lot of attention to making sure that the further changes were presented as a refinement, that is, a logical adjustment completely in keeping with the spirit and intent of the original change (Nadler, 1997).

In this section, we have discussed eight sets of actions to consider when designing a change initiative, in order to build sustainability into the process from the beginning, or at least from an early stage. These include redesign roles, redesign reward systems, link selection to organizational objectives, walk the talk, encourage voluntary acts of initiative, measure progress, celebrate en route, and fine-tuning. Finally, based on a study by David Buchanan et al. (2007) of the UK National Health Service, one of the largest employing organizations in the world, table 11.3 summarizes key sustainability "actions and cautions." This research emphasizes that sustainability relies on local management judgement and on two main forms of action: preventive maintenance and developmental maintenance. *Preventive maintenance* involves action to sustain the status quo, to keep new working

TABLE 11.3
Managing the Improvement Evaporation Effect

Sustainability Actions	Sustainability Cautions
Define what "sustainability" means in your context: a static or a dynamic perspective, and what timescale?	Do not defer sustainability planning, as some modes of development and change implementation will damage sustainability
Identify the factors (contextual, temporal, organizational, political) that affect the sustainability of new methods in your context	Do not expect changes to survive because they are now working; staff leave, resources are reallocated, novel ideas become familiar
Determine what combination of factors can you control and adjust in order to increase the probability of sustaining change	Do not ignore the risk factors: if you are unable to sustain successful changes, that will reduce the probability of other sites adapting the approach and will jeopardize future changes
Monitor the support conditions and implement an appropriate mix of preventive and developmental maintenance	Do not allow efforts to sustain change to block the development of other good ideas
Allow or encourage changes to decay when they no longer fit the context or when better methods become available	Do not withdraw preventive and developmental maintenance as long as you wish the approach to be sustained

Source: Based on Buchanan et al. (2007).

practices operating as intended, to meet predetermined targets and objectives. *Developmental maintenance* involves continuing to adapt the changes to local circumstances in order to sustain an improvement trajectory, to exceed expectation, to meet higher targets. Preventive maintenance sustains the changes; developmental maintenance both sustains and builds on the benefits.

LO 11.4 Words of Warning

It can be difficult to manage sustainability after a change has been successfully implemented; by then, it may be too late. Building sustainability into a change initiative from the beginning provides no secure guarantees, but it is more likely to be an effective approach. However, there are a number of further factors about which the change manager needs to be aware.

Expect the Unanticipated

Most change initiatives will generate unanticipated consequences, unless the links between the changes and outcomes are controllable and predictable (which is rare). Unanticipated consequences may be positive and support the change process. For example, staff may demonstrate greater levels of enthusiasm and commitment to making the changes work than was initially anticipated; cost savings may be higher than planned; processing times may be cut more dramatically. On the other hand, support may be more limited than expected, causing disruption and delay; cost savings may not materialize; time savings may be minimal. Unanticipated outcomes are not necessarily a sign of management failure; in complex change processes, the unexpected is to be expected. No amount of careful preplanning is likely to overcome this.

The change management challenge is to respond in timely and appropriate ways to the unexpected, which, on some occasions, may be early warnings of more serious problems, requiring a combination of resilience and improvisation.

Unanticipated Consequences at FedEx

Federal Express (FedEx) introduced a new aircraft routing system with the intention of increasing the productivity of its pilots. More powerful computers and developments in scheduling algorithms made this seem feasible, the estimated savings in the hundreds of millions of dollars made it attractive, and the pilots had a record of supporting measures intended to improve competitive efficiencies.

However, things didn't work out as planned. The new system produced flight plans that required pilots to cross the time zones of two hemispheres, undertake back-to-back trans-Pacific and trans-Atlantic flights, and spend hours travelling by land to change aircraft. Efforts by FedEx to improve the working of the new system failed to produce any improvement, but the company persisted with the new system. In response, the pilots' union, despite having a reputation for compliance with management requirements, threatened a work stoppage if the system was not abandoned. Then, having taken this stance, their demands extended to a substantial wage increase, fewer flying hours, and improved retirement benefits.

Faced with the prospect of a strike by the pilots—which would have been the first pilot strike in the company's history—FedEx management relented, and the new scheduling system was abandoned (from Pascale et al., 2000).

Beware the Limitations of Measurement

The benefits derived from new ways of doing things (online customer satisfaction, brand image, and reputation) may not immediately be reflected in traditional measures (sales per square foot, stock turnover, market share). The credibility of a new idea may be threatened if it does not succeed on established criteria. However, in some circumstances, a change may be regarded as successful even where the intended aims have not been met—such as a major process redesign initiative that achieved few of the intended goals but which increased the organization's receptiveness to and capacity for further changes. Assessing the effectiveness of change is therefore complex and challenging.

"Premature measurement" can also create problems. As discussed earlier, celebrating short-term wins can be valuable, but measuring the overall success of a change initiative should be related to the timescale over which benefits are expected to be delivered. A focus on short-term gains and quick fixes can weaken the persistence that is often required in order to achieve gains that develop over a longer period. In addition, organizational change rarely flows in a linear fashion, and the outcomes tend to be shaped by the combination and interaction of multiple factors. At times, change may appear to be progressing rapidly, while at other times, it may appear to have stalled. In some instances, performance may deteriorate before it improves, as people learn how to adjust to and work with new structures, systems, procedures, and practices. This initial dip followed by an uptick in performance is known as the "J-curve" (figure 11.1). This is also known as (Rosabeth Moss) "Kanter's Law," which states that "Everything can look like a failure in the middle" (Kanter, 2009).

FIGURE 11.1
The J-curve

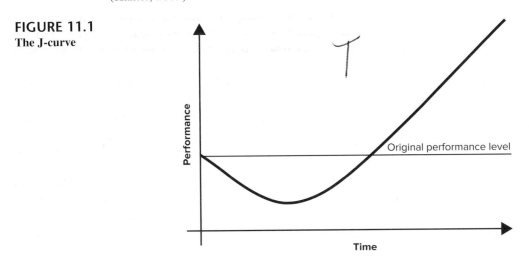

The shape of the J-curve, and the timescale over which it operates, will of course vary from one setting to another (performance may not dip in some cases, and may never recover in others). Assessment of how well a change is progressing must consider not only which metrics to apply, but also the timing of those measurements. The J-curve can be helpful in managing the expectations of others, with regard to justifying a deterioration in performance, and also explaining the rate at which the benefits of the change are likely to become apparent.

Beware Premature Declaration of Victory

Embedding and sustaining organization culture change can take a considerable amount of time—years in some cases. For any transformational change, John Kotter (2012, p. 52) advises the change manager to "never let up; keep learning from experience; and don't declare victory too soon." In other words, celebrate the wins, but do not declare overall victory. Until a change is firmly embedded, the possibility of a return to previous working practices will remain possible. There may be significant numbers of people who are hoping that the change will not succeed, and that "things will return to normal." Those who feel this way may not make their views known. Anne Fisher uses the term "vicious compliance" to describe those who display support in public ("they will nod and smile and agree with everything that you say") but are resentful of the change and are waiting for the opportunity to return to the "old ways" of working to which they remain committed.

Beware the Escalation of Commitment

It is important to recognize that not all proposed changes are going to be beneficial. If a change is not producing the desired outcome, then this may be a "praiseworthy failure," which it would be wise to discontinue. However, it is also wise to guard against the understandable tendency of the advocates of this change to argue that failure to deliver is due to insufficient funding and that more time is needed to demonstrate the benefits. If those arguments are accepted, then further resources will be allocated to the initiative, creating an "escalation of commitment." Barry Staw and Jerry Ross (2004) identify four factors that can lead to escalation:

1. *Project determinants.* Commitment is likely to increase where the lack of progress is considered to be due to a temporary problem, or where additional funding is considered likely to be effective, or where the relative payoff to come from additional investment is considered to be large.

2. *Psychological determinants.* "Sunk costs are not sunk psychologically." Escalation can result from self-justification biases in which having been personally responsible for a decision can lead to continued commitment in order to try to avoid being associated with losses.

3. *Social determinants.* Escalation may occur as those most closely identified with a project commit more resources in an attempt to revive it and thereby save face by not being associated with a failure. This response is encouraged by the existence of "the hero effect," or the "special praise and adoration for managers who 'stick to their guns' in the face of opposition and seemingly bleak odds" (Staw and Ross, 2004, p. 209).

4. *Organizational determinants.* Organizational units are likely to resist the abandonment of a project that is seen as central to their identity. Staw and Ross cite the example of Lockheed's L1011 Tri-Star Jet program, arguing that the company persisted with this project for more than a decade, despite huge losses—and predictions that it was unlikely to earn a profit—because to abandon it would have meant admitting that they were simply a defense contractor and not, as they preferred to believe, a pioneer in commercial aircraft.

How can escalation of commitment be avoided? Mark Keil and Ramiro Montealegre (2000) identify the following advice:

- Don't ignore negative feedback or external pressure.
- Hire an external assessor to provide an independent view on progress.
- Don't be afraid to withhold further resources/funding; as well as limiting losses, it has symbolic value in that it is a fairly emphatic signal that there is concern with progress.
- Look for opportunities to redefine the problem and thereby generate ideas for courses of action other than the one being abandoned.
- Manage impressions. Frame the "de-escalation" in a way that saves face.
- Prepare your stakeholders, because, if they shared the initial belief in the rationale for the change, their reaction to an announcement of the abandonment of the change may be to resist.
- Look for opportunities to deinstitutionalize the project; that is, to make clear that the project is not a central defining feature of the organization, so that "stepping back" does not imply any weakening of commitment to the central mission of the organization.

Dipankar Ghosh (1997) suggests three further steps that can help to reduce the escalation of commitment. First, *unambiguous feedback* on progress reduces escalation. Where feedback is ambiguous, the tendency to filter information selectively can lead to escalation by those who are already committed to the change. Second, *regular progress reports*, including explanations for deviations from budget. If progress reports are not a requirement, then they will not necessarily be requested before further resources are committed.

Sustainable Organizations

Jeffrey Pfeffer (2010) argues that, in order to build sustainable organizations, we need to treat human sustainability as seriously as we do environmental and ecological concerns. Organization policies and management practices influence the human and social environment and affect employee well-being in various ways: provision of health insurance, effects of layoffs, working hours and work-life balance, job design and stress, income inequalities, organization culture, and emotional climate:

> Companies that do not provide health insurance, lay people off, pay inadequate wages, and have work arrangements that stress and overwork their employees also impose externalities that others pay for even as they save on their own costs. (p. 42)

However, "green management," which is concerned with environmental awareness, energy efficiency, and carbon emissions, has not been matched by a parallel focus on employee welfare, "even though that might be an interesting and informative

indicator of what companies are doing about the sustainability of their people" (p. 36). Actions affecting the physical environment are more visible:

> You can see the icebergs melting, polar bears stranded, forests cut down, and mountaintops reshaped by mining, and experience firsthand the dirty air and water that can come from company economic activities that impose externalities. Reduced life expectancy and poorer physical and mental health status are more hidden from view. Even the occasional and well-publicized act of employee or ex-employee violence has multiple causes and is often seen as aberrant behavior outside of the control and responsibility of the employer. (p. 41)

Pfeffer proposes a research agenda to explore the implications of "human sustainability" policies on both employee welfare and organizational effectiveness. What steps is your organization taking to address human and social sustainability? What further action would be desirable, and why?

Third, *information on future benefits*. In the absence of these data, decisions will be too heavily influenced by historical costs.

Awareness of the phenomenon of escalation of commitment is the starting point for identifying solutions. However, this can be a challenging problem to manage, as the line between optimistic "can-do-ism" and overcommitment can be difficult to establish.

EXERCISE 11.1

A Balanced Set of Measures

LO 11.3

It is helpful to consider appropriate measures of success for a change initiative. Thinking of a change initiative that is currently under way in your organization (or a change that is taking place in an organization with which you are familiar), identify the measures that you think should be applied, and list them in the following table. By ticking the appropriate column √), note which type of measures you have identified. It may be possible to classify any one measure in more than one category; brand image, for example, may be lagging, external, and non-cost.

If the measures that you are proposing do not include all six types of measures, you need to explain why the "missing" types are not included. If you cannot give a good explanation, you may need to propose additional measures.

		Type of Measure				
Measure	**Leading**	**Lagging**	**Internal**	**External**	**Cost**	**Non-cost**
1.						
2.						
3.						
4.						
5.						

EXERCISE 11.2

Treating Initiative Decay

LO 11.3

Earlier in this chapter, we identified "the top ten" causes of initiative decay. Which of these factors apply to the recent changes in your organization? What additional factors, not mentioned here, could cause initiative decay in your organization? Considering each cause in turn, what treatment would you prescribe in order to avoid or to reduce the decay?

Cause	Prescribed Treatment
1. Initiators move on	
2. Accountability becomes diffuse	
3. Knowledge lost through staff turnover	
4. Old habits imported with new recruits	
5. Change triggers no longer visible	
6. New managers with their own agendas	
7. Powerbrokers blocking progress	
8. Pump-priming funds have run out	
9. Other priorities diverting attention	
10. Initiative fatigue, lack of enthusiasm	
11. Other	

EXERCISE 11.3

The Challenger *and* Columbia *Shuttle Disasters*

`LO 11.3,11.4`

We discussed the 2003 *Columbia* shuttle disaster in chapter 3. There, we explored reasons why organizations (in this case NASA) often fail to change following accidents such as this one, having previously lost the shuttle *Challenger* in 1986. We also explored the organization culture at NASA in chapter 5, emphasizing that, while the blame for both shuttle losses was linked to technical problems, the more significant contributory factors lay with leadership, management, and organization culture issues. This is a familiar pattern, seen in many major catastrophes. Here is a fuller account of both disasters, which contain lessons concerning organizational change in general and the sustainability of change in particular. The space exploration program is unique in many respects, but from a change management perspective, the lessons from these experiences are generic.

As you read this case account, consider the following questions:

1. What aspects of NASA practice revealed following the *Columbia* disaster suggest that the changes that were recommended following the *Challenger* disaster were not sustained?

2. This chapter has discussed actions that can be taken to sustain change. In your judgement, which of the following would have been most useful to NASA after the *Challenger* disaster?

   - Redesign roles
   - Redesign reward systems
   - Link selection to organizational objectives
   - Walk the talk
   - Encourage voluntary acts of initiative
   - Measure progress
   - Celebrate en route
   - Fine-tuning

3. This chapter has explained "words of warning" in terms of what to be alert to in regard to sustaining change. Which of the following do you see as most applicable to NASA?

   - Recognize productive, praiseworthy failures
   - Expect the unanticipated
   - Beware the limitations of measurement
   - Beware premature declaration of victory
   - Beware the escalation of commitment

The *Challenger* Disaster

On January 28, 1986, the space shuttle *Challenger* rose into the sky, its seven crew strapped into their padded seats while the 2,000-ton vehicle vibrated as it gained speed and altitude. The launch was going perfectly. Seventy seconds had passed since liftoff and the shuttle was already 50,000 feet above the earth. From NASA Mission Control at Houston's Johnson Space Center, Spacecraft Communicator Richard Covey instructed, "Challenger, go at throttle up." "Roger, go at throttle up," replied *Challenger* commander Dick Scobee.

In the next few seconds, however, *Challenger* experienced some increasingly violent maneuvers. The pilot, Mike Smith, expressed his sudden apprehension: "Uh-oh." In Mission Control, the pulsing digits on the screen abruptly stopped. Mission Control spokesman Steve Nesbitt sat above the four console tiers. For a long moment he stared around the silent, softly lit room. The red ascent trajectory line was stationary on the display screen. Finally he spoke: "Flight controllers here looking very carefully at the situation. Obviously a major malfunction."

Headed by former secretary of state William Rogers, the Presidential Commission that was set up to investigate the cause of the *Challenger* disaster had little trouble identifying the physical cause. One of the joints on a booster rocket failed to seal. The "culprit" was one of the synthetic rubber O-rings that were designed to keep the rockets' superheated gasses from escaping from the joints between the booster's four main segments. When one of the O-rings failed, the resulting flames burned through the shuttle's external fuel tank. Liquid hydrogen and liquid oxygen then mixed and ignited, causing the explosion that destroyed *Challenger*.

However, the Rogers Commission investigations also revealed a great deal about the internal workings of NASA. It was a geographically dispersed matrix organization. Headquarters were in Washington, DC, where its most senior managers, including its head, NASA administrator James Begg, were mainly involved in lobbying activity, reflecting the dependence on federal funds (and its vulnerability to fluctuations in funding). Mission Control was located at the Johnson Space Center in Houston, Texas. All propulsion aspects—main engines, rocket boosters, fuel tanks—were the responsibility of the Marshall Space Center in Huntsville, Alabama. Assembly and launch took place at the Kennedy Space Center, Cape Canaveral, Florida.

These various centers existed in an uneasy alliance of cooperation and competition. The Marshall Center in particular was known for its independent stance based on its proud tradition going right back through the Apollo program to the early days of rocketry with Werner von Braun. One manifestation of this pride, reinforced by its autocratic leader William Lucas, was that loyalty to Marshall came before all. Any problems that were identified were to be kept strictly "in-house," which at Marshall meant within Marshall. Those who failed to abide by this expectation—perhaps by speaking too freely to other parts of NASA—could expect to receive a very public admonishment. Marshall was also at the center of a "can-do" attitude within NASA, supporting the idea that great objectives are achievable if only the will is there. Born of the Apollo success, this took form in Marshall as pride in the achievement of objectives and strongly held views that if a flight was to be delayed for any reason, it would never be because of something caused by Marshall.

The Commission also concluded that NASA was working with an unrealistic flight schedule. The formal schedule demanded twelve flights in 1984, fourteen in 1985, seventeen in 1986 and again in 1987, and twenty-four in 1988. In practice, NASA had managed five launches in 1984 and eight in 1985. Congressional critics had begun to question the appropriateness of continuing the current (high) level of program funding when NASA was falling so far short in meeting its own goals. However, rather than revise its schedules, these were retained and senior NASA managers increased the pressure on staff and contractors to meet the schedules.

Most of the design and construction work in the shuttle program was contracted out. One of the contractors was Morton Thiokol, a Brigham City, Utah-based company that had won the contract to produce the solid rocket boosters. At the time of the *Challenger* launch, Thiokol and NASA were in the middle of contract renewal negotiations.

(Continued)

The Commission revealed that there had been doubts about the reliability of the O-rings for some time. Since 1982, they had been labelled a "criticality 1" item, a label reserved for components whose failure would have a catastrophic result. However, despite evidence of O-ring erosion on many flights, and requests from O-ring experts both from NASA and Thiokol that flights be suspended until the problem was resolved, no action had been taken. There was no reliable backup to the O-rings. This violated a long-standing NASA principle, but each time a flight was scheduled, this principle was formally waived.

A cold front hit Cape Canaveral the day before the scheduled launch. Temperatures as low as 18°F were forecast for that night. Engineers from Thiokol expressed their serious reservations about the wisdom of launching in such conditions because the unusually cold conditions at the launch site would affect the O-rings' ability to seal. As a result, a teleconference was called for that evening.

At the teleconference, Roger Boisjoly, Thiokol's O-ring expert, argued that temperature was a factor in the performance of the rings, and Robert Lund, Thiokol's vice president for engineering, stated that unless the temperature reached at least 53°F, he did not want the launch to proceed. This position led to a strong reaction from NASA, and from Lawrence Mulloy, Marshall's chief of the solid rocket booster program, and George Hardy, Marshall's deputy director of science and engineering. Hardy said that he was "appalled" at the reasoning behind Thiokol's recommendation to delay the launch, and Mulloy argued that Thiokol had not proven the link between temperature and erosion of the O-rings, adding, "My God, Thiokol, when do you want me to launch, next April?" A view expressed at the Commission was that the Thiokol engineers had been put in a position where, in order for a delay to be approved, they were being required to prove that the O-rings would fail, rather than to prove that they would be safe at the low temperatures before a go-ahead was approved.

The teleconference took a break, to allow the Thiokol management team to consider their position. The Thiokol engineers were still unanimously opposed to a launch. Jerald Mason, Thiokol's senior vice president, asked Robert Lund to "take off his engineering hat and put on his management hat." Polling just the senior Thiokol managers present, and not any of the engineers, Mason managed to get agreement to launch. The teleconference was then reconvened. The Thiokol approval was conveyed, no NASA managers expressed any reservations, and the OK to launch was given.

Post-*Challenger* Changes at NASA

The Commission's recommendations included that NASA restructure its management to tighten control, set up a group dedicated to finding and tracking hazards with regard to shuttle safety, and review its critical items as well as submitting its redesign of the booster joint to a National Academy of Sciences group for verification. The official line within NASA was that the necessary changes had been successfully implemented. A NASA news release on January 22, 1988, stated that:

> In response to various reviews of NASA safety and quality programs conducted in the aftermath of the Challenger accident and associated recommendations for improvements, NASA has acted to elevate agency emphasis on safety and implement organizational changes to strengthen SRM&QA [Safety, Reliability, Management & Quality Assurance] programs. There has been a 30 percent increase in NASA personnel assigned to SRM&QA functions since January 1986.

The *Columbia* Disaster

On February 1, 2003, the space shuttle *Columbia*'s braking rockets were fired as the shuttle headed toward a landing at Kennedy Space Center. As it passed over the United States, observers spotted glowing pieces of debris falling from the shuttle. At 8:59:32 am EST, commander Rick Husband replied to a call from Mission Control, but his acknowledgment ceased mid-transmission. About a minute later, *Columbia* broke up, killing its seven astronauts.

The Columbia Accident Investigation Board (CAIB or Board) was formed to identify what had happened. In its August 2003 final report, it identified the physical cause of the accident. A 1.67-pound slab of insulating foam fell off the external fuel tank 81.7 seconds after *Columbia* was launched (on January 16), hit the left wing, and caused a breach in the tiles designed to protect the aluminum wing from the heat of reentry. On reentry, the breach allowed superheated gas into the wing, which, as a result, melted in critical areas.

But the Board also addressed the nonphysical factors that contributed to the disaster. Because of no improvement in the level of NASA funding, NASA administrator Daniel Goldin pushed a "Faster, Better, Cheaper" (FBC) initiative that impacted on the shuttle program.

The premium placed on maintaining an operational schedule, combined with ever-decreasing resources, gradually led shuttle managers and engineers to miss signals of potential danger. Foam strikes on the orbiter's thermal protection system (TPS), no matter what the size of the debris, were "normalized" and accepted as not being a "safety-of-flight risk."

The shuttle workforce was downsized, and various program responsibilities (including safety oversight) had been outsourced. Success was being measured through cost reduction and the meeting of schedules, and the shuttle was still being mischaracterized as operational rather than developmental technology.

The Board particularly identified NASA's organization culture as being as much to blame as the physical causes. According to the Board:

> Though NASA underwent many management reforms in the wake of the *Challenger* accident, the agency's powerful human space flight culture remained intact, as did many practices such as inadequate concern over deviations from expected performance, a silent safety program, and schedule pressure.
>
> Cultural traits and organization practices detrimental to safety and reliability were allowed to develop, including: reliance on past success as a substitute for sound engineering practices (such as testing to understand why systems were not performing in accordance with requirements/specifications); organizational barriers which prevented effective communication of critical safety information and stifled professional differences of opinion; lack of integrated management across program elements, and the evolution of an informal chain of command and decision-making processes that operated outside the organization's rules.

According to the Board: "NASA's blind spot is that it believes it has a strong safety culture [when in fact it] has become reactive, complacent, and dominated by unjustified optimism." The Board found that while NASA managers said that staff were encouraged to identify safety issues and bring these to the attention of management, there was evidence to the contrary, including insufficient deference to engineers and other technical experts. Also, while NASA's safety policy specified oversight at headquarters combined

(Continued)

with decentralized execution of safety programs at the program and project levels, the Board found that NASA had not been willing to give the project teams the independent status for this to actually work.

The external tank of the shuttle was designed with a layer of insulation tiles that were designed to stick to the tank, not to be shed. Similarly, the shuttle's heat shield was not designed to be damaged; the tiles were fragile, such that the shuttle wasn't allowed to fly in rain or stay outside in hail.

However, the experience of previous launches was that foam sometimes did fall off and tiles sometimes were damaged. But this was occurring without any noticeable negative effect on the functioning of the shuttle. Of 112 flights prior to the fatal *Columbia* flight, foam had been shed 70 times, and tiles had come back damaged every time. Over time, NASA managers got used to the idea that such damage would occur and convinced themselves there was no safety-of-flight issue. The Board reported that "program management made erroneous assumptions about the robustness of a system based on prior success rather than on dependable engineering data and rigorous testing."

The report cites eight separate "missed opportunities" by NASA during the 16-day flight to respond to expressions of concern or offers that could have assisted. For example, engineer Rodney Rocha's email four days into the mission, asking Johnson Space Center if the crew had been directed to inspect *Columbia*'s left wing for damage, had been left unanswered. Also, NASA had failed to accept the U.S. Defense Department's offer to obtain spy satellite imagery of the damaged shuttle.

The CAIB faulted NASA managers for assuming that there would be nothing that could be done if the foam strike had indeed caused serious damage to the TPS. After the accident, NASA engineers, working on the request of the CAIB, concluded that it might have been possible either to repair the wing using materials on board *Columbia* or to rescue the crew through a sped-up launch of the shuttle *Atlantis*. The Board also criticized NASA managers for not taking steps to ensure that minority and dissenting voices were heard, commenting:

> All voices must be heard, which can be difficult when facing a hierarchy. An employee's location in the hierarchy can encourage silence. Organizations interested in safety must take steps to guarantee that all relevant information is presented to decision makers. This did not happen in the meetings during the *Columbia* mission. Program managers created huge barriers against dissenting opinions by stating preconceived conclusions based on subjective knowledge and experience, rather than on solid data.

The NASA Intercenter Photo Working Group had recommended that the loss of foam be classified as an in-flight anomaly—a much more critical designation than it currently had—but this was not approved by the program requirements control board. The engineers were placed in the situation of having to prove that a safety-of-flight issue existed before the shuttle program management would take action to get images of the left wing. The Board found that this was just one example of a more general situation where those concerned with safety found themselves having to prove that a situation was unsafe, whereas it might be reasonably expected that the emphasis would be on proving instead that a high level of safety existed. The Board also concluded that there was an unofficial hierarchy among NASA programs and directorates that hindered the flow of communications:

Management decisions made during *Columbia's* final flight reflect missed opportunities, blocked or ineffective communication channels, flawed analysis, and ineffective leadership. Perhaps most striking is the fact that management displayed no interest in understanding a problem and its implications. Because managers failed to avail themselves of the wide range of expertise and opinion necessary to achieve the best answer to the debris strike question—"was this a safety-of-flight concern?"—some space shuttle program managers failed to fulfill the implicit contract to do whatever is possible to ensure the safety of the crew. In fact, their management techniques unknowingly imposed barriers that kept at bay both engineering concerns and dissenting views, and ultimately helped create "blind spots" that prevented them from seeing the danger the foam strike posed.

The Board concluded that the post-*Challenger* changes "were undone over time by management actions" and that "the pre-*Challenger* layers of processes, boards and panels that had produced a false sense of confidence in the system and its level of safety returned in full force prior to *Columbia*."

Sources:

Berger, B. 2003. Columbia report faults NASA culture, government oversight. Space.com, August 26. http://www.space
.com/19476-space-shuttle-columbia-disaster-oversight.html.

Columbia Accident Investigation Board. 2003. *Columbia Accident Investigation Board report, volumes I to VI*. Washington, DC:
National Aeronautics and Space Administration and the Government Printing Office.

Covault, C. 2003. Failure an option? NASA's shallow safety program put Columbia and her crew on same path as Challenger.
Aviation Week & Space Technology 159(9):27–30.

Magnusson, E. 1986. A serious deficiency. *Time*, March 10:34–36.

McConnell, M. 1987. *Challenger: A serious malfunction*. London: Simon & Schuster.

Morring, F., Jr. 2003. Culture shock. *Aviation Week & Space Technology* 159(9):31–34.

Additional Reading

Buchanan, D. A., Fitzgerald, L., and Ketley, D. (eds.). 2007. *The sustainability and spread of organizational change: Modernizing healthcare*. London: Routledge. Reports a study of the problems of diffusing and sustaining new working practices in the UK National Health Service. Based on case studies of sustainability practice in different areas of healthcare, offers practical advice on the dissemination of new ideas and the steps necessary to sustain those once implemented. The organization and management issues—and implications for practice—apply to other organizations and sectors and are not confined to healthcare.

Mahler, J. G., and Casamayou, M. H. 2009. *Organizational learning at NASA: The Challenger and Columbia accidents*. Washington, DC: Georgetown University Press. Offers a fresh analysis of the two NASA shuttle disasters, in terms of organizational learning. What did NASA learn from the *Challenger* disaster? How much of that learning was symbolic, and not substantive? What did NASA not learn? And what did NASA learn and then forget—thus contributing to the loss of the shuttle *Columbia*? External political and budgetary pressures were often to blame for the non-learning and forgetting, and these are factors that also jeopardize the sustainability of the kinds of organizational changes that NASA was advised to make.

Pfeffer, J. 2010. Building sustainable organizations: The human factor. *Academy of Management Perspectives* 24(1):34–45. Argues that environmental sustainability has attracted most of the attention and that human and social sustainability are equally important. Suggests that, while "green management" can benefit an organization financially and in terms of reputation, a similar focus on human sustainability should also generate returns. Proposes a research agenda to explore links between human and social sustainability practices and organizational effectiveness.

Sull, D., Homkes, R., and Sull, C. 2015. Why strategy execution unravels—and what to do about it. *Harvard Business Review* 93(3):58–66. Strategy execution seems to be more problematic than developing strategy, because execution is misunderstood. The problem is not alignment, but coordination; research shows that people in other units (internal and external) are not reliable. Execution does not mean "sticking to the plan" where changing conditions demand flexibility. Communications from top management may be frequent, but they are often inconsistent; only half of middle managers can name any of their organization's top priorities. Does execution require a "performance culture"? Perhaps, but agility, teamwork, and ambition should also be rewarded. The idea that execution should be driven from the top is a myth; execution "lives and dies with managers in the middle— but they are hamstrung by the poor communication from above" (p. 66). Concludes that fostering coordination and building agility are key to strategy execution: the same guidelines apply to change implementation.

Roundup   Here is a short summary of the key points that we would like you to take from this chapter, in relation to each of the learning outcomes:

LO 11.1   *Understand the causes of initiative decay—threats to the sustainability of change.*
This chapter has emphasized that even changes that have been implemented successfully are liable to decay. Sustainability cannot be taken for granted. The "improvement

Reflections for the Practicing Change Manager

- If you have been involved previously as a manager of change, how would you rate yourself in terms of your handling of the need to take actions that sustain change? What have you done well? What not so well?

- When you have been on the receiving end of the change initiatives of others, how well have they handled the need to take actions that sustain change? What have they done well? What not so well?

- Of the cases presented in this chapter, which one resonates best with you? What is it about this case that you can relate to? Are

there any implications for how you would act in the future?

- How good are you at handling unanticipated outcomes? How could you improve in this area?

- If there was one main idea that you took away from this chapter that you believe can be of most use to you as a change manager, what would it be?

- If you were to add an idea, suggestion, or practice to the treatment of sustaining change that is provided in this chapter, what would be your contribution?

evaporation effect," as the benefits from change are lost, is common. The change manager may have little direct control over the factors that lead to initiative decay, but measures can be put in place to counter those factors and to increase the probability that change will be sustained. Initiative decay can be caused by many factors, and we identified 10: initiators move on, accountability becomes diffuse, knowledge is lost with staff turnover, old habits are imported with new recruits, the change triggers are no longer visible, new managers have their own agendas, powerbrokers block progress, start-up funding runs out, other priorities emerge, staff suffer initiative fatigue—and enthusiasm for change drops. The change manager thus has to remain vigilant with regard to potential threats to sustainability such as these. Many of the change models and frameworks discussed in chapter 10 identify sustainability as a final step in the process. Managing sustainability as an afterthought, however, can be problematic. It is more appropriate to design sustainability into a change initiative from the start.

LO 11.2 *Distinguish between change initiatives that are "blameworthy," and should not be sustained, and those that are "praiseworthy".*
We also emphasized that, when a change does not work out as planned, this is not necessarily a problem. Failures are not always bad. We discussed the distinction between blameworthy and praiseworthy failures. The former include deliberate or inadvertent deviations from prescribed practice. Experiments designed to improve performance, and reasonable actions that have undesirable but unpredictable outcomes, are praiseworthy—because they offer opportunities from which to learn. Many organizations, however, treat most failures as blameworthy. This is wasteful, because the lessons are lost, and those who are inappropriately punished are likely to be demotivated. The change management challenge is to establish a psychologically safe environment that welcomes experimentation, recognizes and rewards praiseworthy failures, and enables learning.

LO 11.3 *Identify and apply actions that can contribute to the sustainability of change.*
Although some of the threats to sustainability are beyond direct management control, awareness of those threats and their impact can generate timely and appropriate responses. We discussed eight sets of possible actions to strengthen the sustainability of a given change: redesign roles, redesign reward systems, link staff selection to change objectives, "walk the talk," encourage voluntary acts of initiative, measure progress, celebrate "smaller wins" en route, and fine-tune the approach when the process (as almost always happens) does not unfold as anticipated. We also distinguished between sustaining the substance of change (new working practices, for example) and an improvement trajectory (further reductions in time to market, for example). Preventive maintenance involves action to sustain the former, to keep those practices operating as intended. Developmental maintenance, on the other hand, involves adapting to circumstances to gain increasing benefits.

LO 11.4 *Understand the pitfalls that can arise when seeking to sustain change.*
We closed the chapter with a number of words of warning for the change manager. First, expect the unexpected and manage the (positive and negative) unintended consequences. Second, beware the limitations of measurement, and recognize the

implications of the J-curve and Kanter's Law, which states that "Everything looks like a failure in the middle." Third, beware the premature declaration of victory, which may divert energy and attention from the change process, but continue to celebrate the "small wins" as appropriate. Finally, beware the escalation of commitment to struggling change initiatives, by accepting the requests of advocates for further resources, when it is becoming clear that the initiative is not going to deliver the planned outcomes (but may be a praiseworthy failure).

References

Abrahamson, E. 2004. *Change without pain: How managers can overcome initiative overload, organizational chaos, and employee burnout.* Boston: Harvard Business School Press.

Ahlberg, J., and Nauclér, T. 2007. Leading change: An interview with Sandvik's Peter Gossas. *McKinsey Quarterly*, January:1–3.

Beer, M., Eisenstat, R. A., and Spector, B. 1990. Why change programs don't produce change. *Harvard Business Review* 68(6):158–66.

Beer, M., and Nohria, N. (eds.). 2000. *Breaking the code of change.* Boston: Harvard Business School Press.

Buchanan, D. A., Fitzgerald, L., and Ketley, D. (eds.). 2007. *The sustainability and spread of organizational change: Modernizing healthcare.* London: Routledge.

Buchanan, D. A., Ketley, D., Gollop, R., Jones, J. L., Lamont, S. S., Neath, A., and Whitby, E. 2005. No going back: A review of the literature on sustaining organizational change. *International Journal of Management Reviews* 7(3):189–205.

Edmondson, A. 2011. Strategies for learning from failure. *Harvard Business Review* 89(4):48–55.

Fisher, A. B. 1995. Making change stick. *Fortune* 131(7):121–24.

Gerstner, L. V. 2002. *Who says elephants can't dance? Inside IBM's historic turnaround.* New York: Harper Business.

Ghislanzoni, G., Heidari-Robinson, S. and Jermiin, M. 2010. *Taking organizational redesign from plan to practice.* London: McKinsey & Company.

Ghosh, D. 1997. De-escalation strategies: Some experimental evidence. *Behavioral Research in Accounting* 9:88–112.

Goode, J. 2014. *Value based recruitment toolkit: Evaluation of 12 month pilot final report.* London: The National Skills Academy for Social Care.

Gupta, R., and Wendler, J. 2005. Leading change: An interview with the CEO of P&G. *McKinsey Quarterly*, July:1–6.

Kanter, R. M. 2009. Change is hardest in the middle. *Harvard Business Review* webinar, August 12. https://hbr.org/2009/08/change-is-hardest-in-the-middl/ (accessed February 21, 2015).

Kanter, R. M., Stein, B. A., and Jick, T. D. 1992. *The challenge of organizational change.* New York: Free Press.

Keil, M., and Montealegre, R. 2000. Cutting your losses: Extricating your organization when a big project goes awry. *Sloan Management Review* 41(3):55–68.

Kotter, J. P. 2007; first published 1995. Leading change: Why transformation efforts fail. *Harvard Business Review* 85(1):96–103.

Kotter, J. P. 2012. Accelerate! *Harvard Business Review* 90(11):44–52.

Kurtzman, J. 1998. Paying attention to what really counts. *Art of Taking Charge* 3(1): 1–12.

Lawson, E., and Price, C. 2003. The psychology of change management. *The McKinsey Quarterly*, (special edition: the value in organization):31–41.

Lewin, K. (ed.). 1951. *Field theory in social science: Selected theoretical papers by Kurt Lewin.* London: Tavistock Publications. (UK edition published 1952, edited by Dorwin Cartwright.)

Mahler, J. G., and Casamayou, M. H. 2009. *Organizational learning at NASA: The Challenger and Columbia accidents.* Washington, DC: Georgetown University Press.

Marks, M. L., and Shaw, R. B. 1995. Sustaining change: Creating the resilient organization. In *Discontinuous change: Leading organizational transformation*, ed. D. A. Nadler, R. B. Shaw, and A. E. Walton (97–117). San Francisco: Jossey-Bass.

Michel, S. 2007. The upside of falling flat. *Harvard Business Review* 85(4):21–22.

Nadler, D. A. 1997. *Champions of change: How CEOs and their companies are mastering the skills of radical change.* 2nd ed. San Francisco: Jossey-Bass.

Pascale, R., Millemann, M., and Gioja, L. 2000. Surfing the edge of chaos: The laws of nature and the new laws of business. New York: Crown Business.

Pfeffer, J. 2010. Building sustainable organizations: The human factor. *Academy of Management Perspectives* 24(1):34–45.

Price Waterhouse Change Integration Team. 1995. *The paradox principles: How high-performance companies manage chaos, complexity, and contradiction to achieve superior results.* New York: McGraw-Hill.

Rapping, J. 2009. You can't build on shaky ground: Laying the foundation for indigent defense reform through values-based recruitment, training, and mentoring. *Harvard Law & Policy* 3(Spring):161–84.

Reisner, R. A. F. 2002. When a turnaround stalls. *Harvard Business Review* 80(2):45–52.

Ross, L. 1977. The intuitive psychologist and his shortcomings: Distortions in the attribution process. In *Advances in experimental social psychology*, ed. L. Berkowitz (173–220). New York: Academic Press.

Schein, E. H. 2010. *Organizational culture and leadership*. 4th ed. San Francisco: Jossey-Bass.

Staw, B. M., and Ross, J. 2004. Understanding behavior in escalation situations. In *Psychological dimensions of organizational behavior*, ed. B. M. Staw (206–14). Upper Saddle River, NJ: Pearson Prentice Hall.

Sull, D., Homkes, R., and Sull, C. 2015. Why strategy execution unravels—and what to do about it. *Harvard Business Review* 93(3):58–66.

Chapter 12

The Effective Change Manager: What Does It Take?

Learning objectives

By the end of this chapter you should be able to:

LO 12.1 Recognize the nature and significance of the contributions of change managers at all levels of an organization, regardless of their formal roles or responsibilities.

LO 12.2 Appreciate the challenges and rewards that accompany performing a change management role.

LO 12.3 Identify the competencies in terms of the skills, knowledge, and other attributes that are ideally required in order to be an effective change manager.

LO 12.4 Understand the significance of political skill to the role and effectiveness of change managers.

LO 12.5 Develop an action plan for improving your own change management capabilities.

Sidney Harris The New Yorker Collection/The Cartoon Bank

It's all right to do your regular work, Sanders, but haven't you caught on yet?
The big money is in breakthroughs.

LO 12.1 Change Managers: Who Are They?

This chapter explores the personal competencies—skills, knowledge, and other attributes—that are ideally required in order to design and implement organizational change. First, we need to identify those who carry out these responsibilities, as this can involve significant numbers of people. Change is rarely a solo performance. Typically, many members of an organization, from across all levels, can be involved in encouraging, catalyzing, facilitating, supporting, driving, and otherwise contributing to the implementation of change. That involvement is not always associated with a formal leadership or management job title. There may even be circumstances in which a formal title could be a barrier to generating participation and support, stimulating suspicion and distrust instead. Having identified who an organization's change managers are likely to be, we then consider what kind of role this is, in terms of the challenges and rewards. We will then explore the competency requirements.

Given the numbers of people involved, and the range of contributions which they can make, many commentators use the general term "change agent" to cover all those engaged in implementing change (we discussed this terminology issue at the start of chapter 2). To be consistent with the rest of this book, however, we will continue to use the term *change manager*.

Champions, Deviants, and Souls-of-Fire

A number of other terms have been used to describe change managers, often indicating the nature of the role, and the kinds of people and capabilities involved. Donald Schön (1963, p. 85) studied *product champions*, senior managers with "considerable power and prestige." Tom Peters and Bob Waterman (1983, p. 40) describe those who "damn the bureaucracy and take it on themselves to maneuver their projects through the system" as *change champions*. Modesto Maidique (1980) distinguishes the role of *technological entrepreneur* from those of *sponsor* (senior manager) and *executive champion* (power broker). Richard Ottaway (1983) identifies three categories of change manager: *change generators*, *change implementers*, and *change adopters*. Patrick Connor and Linda Lake (1988) identify four roles: the *catalyst*, who encourages dissatisfaction with the status quo; the *solution giver*, who offers suggestions for improvement; the *process helper*, who assists others; and the *resource linker*, who brings together people, funding, and knowledge. Carol Beatty and John Gordon (1991) distinguish senior management *patriarchs*, who originate ideas, from *evangelists*, who implement them. Torbjörn Stjernberg and Åke Philips (1993) argue that change relies on a small number of committed individuals whom they call *souls-of-fire*, from the Swedish "eldsjälar," meaning "driven by burning enthusiasm." Michel Syrett and Jean Lammiman (2002) identify five roles in innovation and change: *sparks*, *sponsors*, *shapers*, *sounding boards*, and *specialists*, noting that those who generate ideas can come from any level in an organization. Discussing "your company's secret change managers," Richard Pascale and Jerry Sternin (2005) advise a bottom-up approach that encourages the *positive deviants* in the organization. These are people who are already doing things differently and better. They also argue that "the key is to engage the members of the community you want to change in the process of discovery, making

TABLE 12.1

The Other Names That Change Managers Have Been Called (Alphabetic Order)

Catalyst	Product champion
Change adopter	Resource linker
Change champion	Shaper
Change generator	Solution giver
Change implementer	Souls-of-fire
Evangelist	Sounding board
Executive champion	Spark
Patriarch	Specialist
Positive deviant	Sponsor
Process helper	Technological entrepreneur

them the evangelists of their own conversion experience" (Pascale and Sternin, 2005, p. 74). Arguing for the importance of networking skills, Julie Battilana and Tiziana Casciaro (2013) stay with the conventional term "change agent."

These labels are summarized in table 12.1. Some of these terms offer clues concerning those who become change managers: catalysts, champions, deviants, evangelists, generators, shapers, sparks, souls-of-fire. Motivation and commitment thus appear to matter as much as technical and professional capabilities. This discussion also suggests that change relies on the complementary contributions, advice, and support of a number of change managers, rather than on small select groups of senior staff. Change management responsibilities can be widely dispersed across all levels of the organization hierarchy.

Changing from the Middle

Research has consistently demonstrated the key role that middle managers play in organizational change. We discussed this issue briefly in chapter 8, challenging the stereotype of middle managers as change blockers. This challenge is not new. Joseph Bower (1970) was one of the first to recognize the importance of middle managers as change managers, exerting upward influence on strategy based on their knowledge of the frontline operational context and by nurturing, testing, and championing initiatives. Rosabeth Moss Kanter (1982, p. 95) argues that "a company's productivity depends to a great degree on how innovative its middle managers are," adding that loosely defined roles and assignments encourage managers to develop and promote their own ideas.

Bill Wooldridge and Steven Floyd (1990; Wooldridge et al., 2008) develop a typology of four kinds of middle management contributions to organizational innovation, change, and strategy:

1. Gathering and synthesizing information
2. Justifying and championing alternatives
3. Facilitating adaptability by relaxing rules and "buying time"
4. Translating goals into action and selling initiatives to staff

They also emphasize the coordinating, mediating, interpreting, and negotiating roles of middle managers, arguing that it is difficult to isolate an individual's contribution, because it is the pattern of influence of middle managers that affects organizational change and outcomes.

Leading Change from the Middle *How to Win Support for New Ideas*

Susan Ashford and James Detert (2015, p.73) argue that "organizations don't prosper unless managers in the middle ranks identify and promote the need for change." However, when it comes to sharing those ideas, middle managers are often discouraged by the top leadership style ("if an idea was any good, we would have already thought of it"), and valuable opportunities are missed. Ashford and Detert asked middle managers to describe their experiences of selling three kinds of ideas: new products, processes, or markets; improvements to existing products and processes; and better ways to meet employees' needs. This helped them to identify seven influence tactics that middle managers use to attract senior executive attention and resources:

[handwritten annotation: Difficult to sell change laterally - almost impossible to sell upwards.]

Tactic	Base Your Approach on These Questions
Tailor your pitch	Where does my audience stand on this issue? What does my audience find most convincing or compelling?
Frame the issue	How can I connect my issue to organizational priorities? How can I best describe its benefits? How can I link it to other issues receiving attention? How can I highlight an opportunity for the organization?
Manage emotions	How can I use my emotions to generate positive rather than negative responses? How can I manage my audience's emotional responses?
Get the timing right	What is the best moment to be heard? Can I "catch the wave" of a trend, or tap into what's going on in the outside world? What is the right time in the decision-making process to raise my issue?
Involve others	Which allies from my network can help me sell my issue? Who are my potential blockers, and how can I persuade them to support me? Who are my fence-sitters, and how can I convince them that my issue matters?
Adhere to norms	Should I use a formal public approach, an informal casual one, or a combination?
Suggest solutions	Am I suggesting a viable solution? If not, am I proposing a way to discover one, instead of just highlighting the problem?

Ashford and Detert offer three other pieces of advice to middle managers. First, choose your audience; your immediate boss may not be the best place to start to promote your idea. Second, use several of these tactics rather than just one or two; they are more powerful in combination. Finally, choose your battles; some ideas can just be too difficult to sell.

One example, discussed in chapter 8, concerns a study of change in the Irish health service, which showed how middle managers who resisted top-down directives played a vital role in change by championing and implementing their own initiatives, and mediating between different parts of the organization (Conway and Monks, 2011). The changes championed by those middle managers helped to dismantle outdated structures and processes, while also solving the problems that the top team had initially identified. The middle management role is thus not necessarily confined to implementing changes directed by others. Aoife McDermott et al. (2013) also show how middle managers and other "change recipients" become change managers, by tailoring, adding to, and adapting top-down directives so that they work more effectively in particular local contexts.

Middle managers may not always be free to exercise those organizational change roles. Donald Kuratko and Michael Goldsby (2004) identify the conditions that can discourage what they describe as *the entrepreneurial middle manager* from taking risks and innovating:

- systems and policies that encourage consistent, safe, conservative behavior;
- complex approval cycles with elaborate documentation;
- controls that encourage micromanagement;
- top-down management and lack of delegated authority.

Middle managers can thus be key to change implementation. Their understanding of frontline operations and issues is usually much better than that of senior management. They are therefore able to mediate between front line and top team. However, the organizational context has to enable them to make these contributions. Otherwise, they may be a misunderstood and underutilized resource.

Stealth and Hustle below the Radar

Do we really need transformational leaders to bring about transformational change? Some commentators argue that transformational leaders can damage an organization's performance. For example, Rakesh Khurana (2002) argues that charismatic, transformational leaders are a curse because they can destabilize organizations in dangerous

Kaiser Permanente's Innovation Consultancy

Lew McCreary (2010) describes how Kaiser Permanente, a managed care consortium based in Oakland, California, has developed a novel approach to innovation and improvement. The company set up its own internal Innovation Consultancy unit. This unit employs change experts to observe people, ask them how they feel about their work, take notes and photographs, make drawings, and identify better ways of doing things. This involves, McCreary (p. 92) suggests, "a combination of anthropology, journalism, and empathy," exploring how staff and patients live, work, think, and feel before trying to solve a problem.

A key part of the approach involves "uncovering the untold story"—finding out "what is really going on here?" For example, to prevent nurses being interrupted during medication rounds, and thus to reduce errors, a "deep dive" event was held, including nurses, doctors, pharmacists, and patients. The event generated around 400 ideas, some straightforward and some "outlandish." This led to the design of a smock that said "leave me alone" on it (known as "no-interruption wear") and a five-step process for ensuring the correct dispensing of medication.

Another example concerned the exchange of patient information between nursing shifts. This used to take 45 minutes, and delayed the next shift's contact with patients. In addition, nurses would compile and exchange information in idiosyncratic ways, potentially missing important details. The revised Nurse Knowledge Exchange is faster and more reliable, with new software and with information presented in standard formats.

Members of the Information Consultancy unit do not dictate the changes that are to be made, but work with staff as "codesigners" on change projects. This approach allows Kaiser Permanente to achieve the aim of implementing innovation and change quickly and economically.

ways. As we have already noted, research has demonstrated that change management can be found at all levels of an organization, and that major changes that are not driven from the top can be just as effective. Debra Meyerson (2001a and b) stresses the importance of the modest and less visibly heroic change that takes place behind the scenes, or "below the radar." The quiet change managers or *tempered radicals* that she describes do not belong to the top management group, and they may not have middle management roles either. They are, however, instrumental in challenging the prevailing culture, initiating and driving change by leveraging "small wins" and engaging others. Using those approaches, they can bring about transformational change by incremental means. Joseph Badaracco (2001 and 2002) makes a similar argument for "a quiet approach to leadership" that is neither glamorous nor heroic, and that focuses instead on "small things, careful moves, controlled and measured efforts" (Badaracco, 2001, p. 126). Badaracco's *quiet leaders* drive change and improvement effectively by being patient, buying themselves time, managing their political capital, and bending the rules.

Paddy Miller and Thomas Wedell-Wedellsborg (2013) advise innovative change managers not to take their new ideas directly to senior management for approval. This puts an untested idea in the "corporate spotlight," and it may never go ahead if the idea is turned down. If the idea does get backing, however, the initiator comes under pressure to demonstrate results. Instead, they suggest "going into stealth mode" and "innovating under the radar." This is especially appropriate where there are many "gatekeepers" to navigate, when bureaucratic processes will slow things down, where the risks of failure are low, and when the reputational damage from being discovered will be minimal.

The first challenge for the *stealth innovator* is to find sponsors and allies. These are likely to be colleagues at the same level in the organization, or one or two grades higher. They may not have top executive power, but they are more numerous and are easier to access, they are more likely to understand the context for the idea, and they can help to get the project started. A second challenge is to generate "proof of concept"—evidence that the idea works and will generate real benefits. This involves conducting small-scale experiments, building a prototype, demonstrating viability, and making it work. The stealth innovator must have access to funding and other resources to keep the project running; beg, borrow, barter, and scavenge is the advice here. Finally, the stealth innovator needs "stealth branding," or a "cover story," in order to work on the project without attracting attention. This means giving credible answers when asked about how their time is being spent, and being careful with the choice of language (avoiding the word "project," for example). A final piece of advice for the stealth innovator is this (Miller and Wedell-Wedellsborg, 2013, p. 97):

> [M]eet regularly with your advisers, providing them with frequent updates, and solicit their feedback. Informal sponsors within the organization are not just a means to getting your ideas off the ground; they serve as a trusted, level-headed sounding board that can give you perspective on your own actions. Use your advisers, and use them constantly. With the right backing and some hustle and ingenuity, young breakthrough ideas can be nurtured into successful corporate initiatives.

We have introduced more new labels: *tempered radicals*, *quiet leaders*, and *stealth innovators*. These take us far from the stereotype of change managers as senior figures, working on their own, often from outside the organization, using conventional change management methods. These labels, and the roles that they describe, highlight the importance of creativity, ingenuity, networks, interpersonal relationships, communication skills, risk-taking, and the political skills involved in working quietly, stealthily, below the corporate radar. In sum, an organization's most valuable change managers may not be visible, and may not be those who have been formally appointed to change roles.

Spotting Your Souls-of-Fire

If some (or all) of the key change managers in an organization are champions, entrepreneurial middle managers, quiet leaders, and stealth innovators who operate below the radar, how can they be recognized? One answer comes from the work of Fiona Patterson (1999), who identified four sets of behaviors (summarized in table 12.2) that can reveal the innovative thinker and change manager.

TABLE 12.2
The Profile of the Innovative Change Manager

Behavioral Area	Indicators
Motivation to change: *high*	Bored easily, thrives on change
Challenging behaviors: *high*	Assertive, nonconforming, doesn't ask for permission
Adaptation: *low*	Thinks of imaginative ways to solve problems
Consistency of work style: *low*	Undisciplined, doesn't follow procedures or instructions

These indicators may help us to identify the souls-of-fire, but they also highlight the management problems. How many organizations want to employ people who are easily bored, act without permission, are not adaptable, and do not follow instructions? It is important to recognize that:

- change managers can be difficult nonconformists, mavericks who take risks and who do not always present themselves well in an employee selection context;
- change managers are often regarded as troublemakers who break rules, and they may be blamed when things go wrong;
- an organization needs a balance of personalities—too many radical innovators can be just as ineffective as having too many conformists who do what they are told.

Adopting a similar perspective to seeking out the key change managers, Thomas Davenport et al. (2003) studied the *ideas practitioners* who bring new management ideas into an organization. Consistent with the findings of other research, they found this to be a diverse and scattered group, but with common ways of working. Ideas practitioners seem to work in four stages:

Scouting	They read a lot, attend conferences, explore interdisciplinary perspectives, and look to other fields for ideas
Packaging	They translate and tailor their ideas for a wider audience, and express ideas in terms of key issues—innovation, efficiency, effectiveness—that interest senior management
Advocating	They sell, run marketing campaigns, find early adopters, persuade other managers
Implementing	They make things happen, manage change, roll it out from boardroom to front line

In terms of personality, ideas practitioners tend to be intelligent, optimistic, passionate about ideas, intellectually restless, mild-mannered (not fanatical), and self-confident. They also tend to be boundary spanners with extensive personal networks. Davenport et al. (2003) argue that if ideas practitioners are not recognized and supported, they will leave. They must be allowed to pursue ideas, and they need to be rewarded with recognition and intellectual stimulation as well as money.

Who Are Your Most Capable Strategic Change Leaders?

Research by the consulting company Pricewater-houseCoopers (PwC) has found that only 8 percent of senior managers have the strategic leadership capabilities required to drive organizational change (Lewis, 2015). From a survey of 6,000 managers in Europe, the highest proportion of strategic leaders were women over the age of 55—a group that has traditionally been overlooked in the search for change agent skills.

PwC defines a strategic leader as someone who has "wider experience of settings, people, and also of failure, which engenders humility or perspective and resilience, so that they know what to do when things don't work" (Lewis, 2015, n.p.). Women over 55 were more likely to:

- see situations from multiple perspectives;
- think and work outside the existing system;
- identify what needs to change;
- be able to persuade or inspire others to follow them;
- use positive language;
- be open to frank and honest feedback;
- exercise power courageously.

One consultant (female) at PwC said, "Historically women over the age of 55 would not have been an area of focus, but as the research suggests, this pool of talent might hold the key to transformation and in some cases, business survival" (Lewis, 2015).

Patterson (1999) and Davenport et al. (2003) suggest that change managers (innovative thinkers, ideas practitioners) have particular characteristics, personalities, and capabilities. They are "special people," who can be identified if we know what attributes to look for. In contrast, from their work on those whom they call *disruptive innovators*, Jeff Dyer et al. (2011) argue that anyone can be innovative, by learning the five habits that we discussed in chapter 5 (table 5.2): *associating* (making connections), *questioning* (challenging assumptions), *observing* (watching for new ways of doing things), *experimenting* (testing new ideas), and *networking* (attending conferences and social events).

Some of us are more creative and innovative than others, and disruptive innovators can be identified by observing their behavior. But Dyer et al. (2011) suggest that we can all become more innovative if we learn those five habits and collaborate with "delivery-driven" colleagues. They also argue that organization policies can reinforce these habits, by encouraging staff to connect ideas, challenge accepted practices, observe what others are doing, take risks, experiment, and get out of the organization to meet others. As well as attempting to identify the organization's change managers, therefore, here is an approach to creating more of them.

From their study of change in Britain's National Health Service (one of the 10 largest employing organizations in the world), Julie Battilana and Tiziana Casciaro (2013, p. 64) also found that the success of change managers depended on their informal networks. They identify different types of networks. In *cohesive networks*, the members know each other, and their actions are easier to coordinate. The members of *divergent networks* are connected indirectly by their link to the change manager, and these networks can be a source of new ideas and information. Change managers were more successful where:

- they held central positions in the organization's informal network, regardless of their roles in the formal hierarchy;
- the nature of their network matched the type of change that they were pursuing;
- they also had good relationships with "fence-sitters" who were ambivalent about the changes.

The organization chart is not a good guide to finding the champions, the ideas practitioners, the souls-of-fire, the change managers. Lili Duan et al. (2014) argue that managers need to find these "hidden influencers." They claim, however, that managers asked to identify the influencers in their organizations are almost always wrong. Informal influencers are those to whom other staff turn for advice, and they can have a major impact on attitudes to change. Retail cashiers, for example, can have considerable influence because they are well connected with many others. Spotting the change managers thus involves understanding the informal organizational networks, and how these function.

Case Study *Boosting Factory Yields*

Aaron De Smet et al. (2012, p. 4) describe the following example of a change manager faced with a particularly difficult challenge. How would you assess his approach? Is this a style that you would be prepared to use in your own organization? Or would you consider this style to be too risky?

Conor, as we'll call one European plant manager, needed to boost yields using the company's new production system. In the past, the industrial giant would have assigned engineers steeped in lean production or Six Sigma to observe the shop floor, gather data, and present a series of improvements. Conor would then have told plant employees to implement the changes, while he gauged the results—a method consistent with his own instinctive command-and-control approach to leadership. But Conor and his superiors quickly realized that the old way wouldn't succeed: only employees who actually did the work could identify the full range of efficiency improvements necessary to meet the operational targets, and no attempt to get them to do so would be taken seriously unless Conor and his line leaders were more collaborative.

Workers were skeptical: a survey taken at about this time (in 2009) showed that plant workers saw Conor and his team as distant and untrustworthy. Moreover, the company couldn't use salary increases or overtime to boost morale, because of the ongoing global economic crisis.

Conor's leadership training gave him an opportunity to reflect on the situation and provided simple steps he could take to improve it. He began by getting out of his office, visiting the shop floor, and really listening to the workers talk about their day-to-day experiences, their workflows, how their machines functioned, and where things went wrong. They'd kept all this information from him before. He made a point of starting meetings by inviting those present to speak, in part to encourage the group to find collective solutions to its problems.

Conor explained: "As I shared what I thought and felt more openly, I started to notice things I had not been aware of, as other people became more open. We'd had the lean tools and good technology for a long time. Transparency and openness were the real breakthrough." As the new atmosphere took hold, workers began pointing out minor problems and additional areas for improvement specific to their corners of the plant; within just a few months its yields increased to 91 percent, from 87 percent. Today, yields run at 93 percent.

LO 12.2 Change Managers: What Kind of Role Is This?

Forget Nice

Do managers have to be assholes? Do they have to be tough, ruthless bastards who drive through change at any cost?

Management surely is about taking difficult decisions either in the interests of shareholders or (if one prefers) in the interests of the company more broadly. That means often having to pass over, demote or fire perfectly decent human beings, some of whom you may quite like. It means having to grow a thick skin and care little whether other people like you.

Nice people mind if they hurt other people's feelings. They are self-effacing, generous, patient and sometimes have bouts of self-doubt. You would willingly offer them a seat at your breakfast table—but we should continue to insist that they never get anywhere near a seat on the board.

Source: From Kellaway (2000), pp.116–17.

Before exploring the specific competencies of the change manager, it is useful to consider the nature of the role, and in particular the challenges and potential rewards that it can bring. From the previous discussion concerning who becomes a change manager, it is clear that this is not necessarily a formal appointment, that the most effective change managers do not always occupy senior positions on the organization chart. In addition, much of the work may be done behind the scenes, below the radar.

The evidence shows that the experience of many change managers has two main, and perhaps opposing, dimensions. First, this can be a challenging, stressful, high-pressure, fast-paced, high-risk role. Senior management expect rapid results. There may be open and covert resistance from those who are affected. Any concerns, complaints, and sometimes anger may be directed at the change manager in person. Change managers thus have to be comfortable with and able to handle conflict. Those who need to be liked by others and who do not like to lose friends will be uncomfortable in a change management role.

The Change Manager's Experience

- The change manager's job is demanding; it can be lonely and risky. This is not a job for everyone.
- It involves big highs and lows—rewarding when it's going well and awful when it's not.
- It involves pursuing goals that are often intangible, and the outcomes are not always under your control, but it offers rare opportunities to make a difference.
- You acquire new skills and discover new opportunities, so this is an opportunity for personal and career development.
- The main rewards are not necessarily financial, and recognition may be lacking.
- You need to believe in it to do it well.
- The job is never finished.

Source: Based on Hutton (1994, pp. 252–58).

One study of an organization redesign program (Buchanan, 2003) found that change managers not only had to cope with personal stress but also had to deal, at the same time, with the stress experienced by those involved in the change, who were described as "scarred" and as "hurt and bruised people." Those who help others to cope with the stress of change have themselves been described as "toxic handlers," with skills in listening and problem-solving (Frost and Robinson, 1999). Finally, when change goes wrong, regardless of why, the change manager will be blamed.

Given the pressure, pace, stress, risks, and vulnerability of the role, change managers ideally need to be resilient. Resilience can be defined as "the successful adaptation to life tasks in the face of social disadvantage or highly adverse conditions" (CIPD, 2011, p. 2). Conditions for change managers are not always "highly adverse" but are rarely problem-free. Other terms that describe resilience include adaptability, equanimity, perseverance, self-reliance, mental toughness, and bouncebackability. These are capabilities that we all benefit from on occasion. Change managers in particular, however, need to be able to "bounce back" when plans go wrong, and to persevere in spite of difficulties. Some of us are more resilient than others, but resilience is an attribute that can be developed. Exercise 12.2 at the end of this chapter provides a diagnostic, "How Resilient Are You?" This diagnostic invites you to assess your level of resilience and to consider actions to develop your resilience if necessary.

Confessions of a Change Manager

If the change manager's role is so demanding, why would anyone accept the responsibility? We met a Finnish woman who was working with a large utility company in South Australia. She described her change manager's role as risky, pressured, and stressful, just as we have discussed here. So we asked, "Why did you take this job?" This was her answer:

> I wanted a job to look forward to in the morning, and not want to leave in the evening. I saw it as a great opportunity to learn. I get charged up with more learning. I need that. I needed to get my hands dirty. It gave me a chance to show my capabilities. It is a very tiring and frustrating job. On the other hand, it gives you a great opportunity to excel.
>
> I am a risk taker. I need some excitement and power play while at work. It gave me an opportunity to work with some highly motivated and committed individuals. Together we were able to make it happen. I believe that the only way to meet the challenges of the external business environment is to offer the customer what they really want.
>
> I have thick skin. I realized that I was going to make some enemies during the change process—as well as some very influential and powerful friends. I was able to accept the challenge due to the stage of my personal lifestyle (boyfriend overseas, dog at home). I sacrificed my spare time for the company—and for the financial and nonfinancial rewards.
>
> Even though I was an inexperienced change manager, I was confident that I had skills, knowledge, and attributes to make it happen. Or that I could find an expert (internal or external) to assist me to make it happen. If I would fail, I could still work with [this organization]—or elsewhere, because I am tolerant of ambiguity.

This account reveals the second and more positive dimension of the change manager's experience. Especially with "deep" changes (figure 1.1), the change manager is exposed to a wider range of internal and external corporate and strategic issues than is the case in most general or operational management positions, which tend to be more narrowly defined. As a consequence, the role of change manager can be challenging in an exciting, stimulating, and energizing way. Here is an opportunity to demonstrate one's capabilities, to pick up new knowledge, to develop new skills, and to add powerful and influential colleagues to one's network. Successful experience as a change manager has "resumé value."

Our Finnish change manager made several comments that reveal aspects of her personality: "I get charged up with learning"; "I need to get my hands dirty"; "I am a risk taker"; "I need excitement and power play"; "I have thick skin"; "I realized that I was going to make enemies"; "I was confident that I would be able to make it happen"; "I am tolerant of ambiguity." These attributes appear to be appropriate for someone working in such a challenging role. Personality is only one factor contributing to personal effectiveness; capability and context are also important. However, the need for action, learning, excitement, and power play, along with tolerance of ambiguity, risk, and conflict, all appear to be useful personal attributes for a change manager to possess, or to develop.

On the one hand, the role of the change manager is stressful and the position is a vulnerable one. On the other hand, the role can offer substantial opportunities for personal development and for career progression. As we mentioned in chapter 1, when interviewed for the next promotion, stories about the success and impact of the changes (preferably deep changes) for which one has been responsible are typically more likely to impress than stories about shallow initiatives—or no stories at all. John Beeson (2009, p. 103) identifies

Look In

Nate Boaz and Erica Fox (2014, p. 1) argue that changes often fail because the leaders overlook the need to make basic changes in themselves. Two common mistakes, they claim, concern focusing on business outcomes and on developing skills. These "outward-looking" preoccupations ignore the changes in "mindset" that have to be made, to translate new behaviors into better performance.

Change leaders also need to "look in," to engage in self-discovery and self-development. This involves developing "state awareness" and "profile awareness." State awareness concerns "what's driving you at the moment": mindset, beliefs, hopes and fears, desires and defenses, impulses to act. Those impulses may need to be controlled, so that actions are appropriate to the context. Profile awareness concerns habits, emotions, and hopes. Change leaders need to understand their profile and how this can affect others. Profile awareness concerns managing "the big four" of your "inner team":

Inner Negotiator	Focus of Attention	Power Source
Chief executive officer: *inspirational*	What I want, what I don't want	Intuition
Chief financial officer: *analytical*	My opinion, my ideas	Reason
Chief people officer: *emotional*	How we both feel, our level of trust	Emotion
Chief operating officer: *practical*	What task to do, what line to draw	Willpower

This inner team governs how change leaders function. Which inner executive are you going to call on in this situation, at this time, for this purpose? Can you use each of the "big four" consciously and effectively to deal with different issues? Boaz and Fox argue that the success of long-term, high-impact change relies on a combination of "looking out and looking in."

the "core selection factors" for senior executive appointments. Most of these do not relate to business knowledge or technical ability but to "soft" skills. Here are four of those core selection factors, all related to demonstrable change implementation capabilities:

- Setting direction and thinking strategically; spotting marketplace trends and developing a winning strategy that differentiates the company.
- Managing implementation without getting involved at too low a level of detail; defining a set of roles, processes, and measures to ensure that things get done reliably.
- Building the capacity for innovation and change; knowing when new ways of doing business are required; having the courage, tolerance for risk, and change management skills to bring new ideas to fruition.
- Getting things done across internal boundaries (lateral management); demonstrating organizational savvy; influencing and persuading colleagues; dealing with conflict.

Change managers thus enjoy several intrinsic rewards: challenge, excitement, personal development, and job satisfaction. The extrinsic rewards in terms of career progression can also be substantial.

LO 12.3   Change Management Competencies

What competencies—skills, knowledge, and other attributes—do change managers ideally require? This question is significant for at least three reasons. First, change that is badly managed can cause serious damage to the organization and units involved, to those who are directly affected by the change, and to other stakeholders. Second, although this work is often carried out by full-time change managers and external consultants, many general and functional managers combine change responsibilities with their regular duties. Third, as discussed earlier in this chapter, responsibility for change management has become increasingly distributed, involving staff at all organizational levels. In other words, the demand for change management competencies is also now widely distributed.

When discussing this topic, it is difficult to escape from competency frameworks, which each itemize the various skill and knowledge requirements. These lists can make tedious reading, especially when one framework says much the same as the next, with only subtle variations in content and emphasis. One variation concerns simply the number of items in the framework. We can choose between "the nine habits of successful change leaders" (Wooldridge and Wallace, 2002) and "the ten commitments of a change leader" (Kouzes and Posner, 1995). These frameworks tend to agree, however, on two fundamental issues. First, the change manager's role is a multifaceted one. Second, change management roles make considerable demands on those who perform them—as we have already seen.

We will describe three competency frameworks, two from the 1990s and one more recent. We will then explain a controversial approach to encouraging change, based on intimidation. This choice illustrates the similarities and contrasts between frameworks. We also need to note that these models should be seen not as rigid prescriptions, but as guides that have to be tailored to fit specific contexts.

TABLE 12.3
The McBer Competency Model for the "Top-Notch Change Manager"

Interpersonal Skills

- Ability to express empathy
- Positive expectations of people
- Genuineness

Diagnostic Skills

- Knowledge of the principles of individual and organization development
- Ability to collect meaningful data through interviews, surveys, and observations
- Ability to draw conclusions from complex data and make accurate diagnoses

Initiation Skills

- Ability to influence others and market your skills, to persuade internal customers to use your services
- Ability to make presentations in a concise, interesting, and informative manner
- Ability to manage groups and group dynamics
- Problem-solving and planning skills, making recommendations and helping customers with problem-solving, goal setting, and planning to improve organizational performance

Organizational Skills

- Ability to design adult learning curricula and organization development exercises
- Ability to administer resources such as personnel, materials, schedules, and training sites

First, from a management consultancy rather than an academic research source, the McBer competency model, described by Edward Cripe (1993), has been widely cited and applied. The competencies of the "top-notch" change manager are listed in table 12.3, which identifies a combination of interpersonal, diagnostic, initiation, and organizational skills. This model relates to formally appointed change managers who have to "market their skills to internal customers" in order to initiate changes and stimulate performance improvements. Such roles are common, in central corporate organization development and change management support units, and in program management offices. However, those four sets of skills would perhaps also be valuable to quiet leaders, stealth innovators, ideas practitioners, and other "below the radar" change managers.

Our second (research-based) model was developed by David Buchanan and David Boddy (1992), who asked middle and senior managers who were in charge of information technology projects to keep a diary of their change management experiences. The resulting model is shown in table 12.4, which identifies 15 competencies in five areas: goals, roles, communication, negotiation, and managing up.

Neither of these frameworks (McB and BB) claims to be fully comprehensive. Cripe (1993) suggests that organizations should customize this model, omitting less relevant competencies and adding others. The frameworks are similar. The McB "interpersonal skills" can be found under the BB "communication" heading. The McB "diagnostic skills" are listed under "goals" in the BB model. "Initiation skills" in McB are covered by BB under the "goals," "roles," and "negotiation" headings.

TABLE 12.4
The Buchanan-Boddy Change Manager Competency Model

Goals

1. *Sensitivity* to changes in key personnel, top management perceptions, and market conditions, and to the way in which these impact the goals of the project in hand.
2. *Clarity* in specifying goals, in defining the achievable.
3. *Flexibility* in responding to changes outside the control of the change manager, perhaps requiring major shifts in project goals and management style—and risk taking.

Roles

4. *Team building* capability, to bring together key stakeholders and establish effective working groups, and clearly to define and delegate respective responsibilities.
5. *Networking* skills, in establishing and maintaining appropriate contacts, within and outside the organization.
6. *Tolerance of ambiguity*, to be able to function comfortably, patiently, and effectively in an uncertain and unpredictable environment.

Communication

7. *Communication skills*, to transmit effectively to colleagues and subordinates the need for changes in project goals and in individual tasks and responsibilities.
8. *Interpersonal skills* across the range, including selection, listening, collecting appropriate information, identifying the concerns of individuals, and managing meetings.
9. *Personal enthusiasm* in expressing plans and ideas.
10. *Stimulating motivation and commitment* in those involved in the change process.

Negotiation

11. *Selling* plans and ideas to others by creating a desirable vision of the future.
12. *Negotiating* with key players for resources, or for changes in procedures, and resolving conflict.

Managing Up

13. *Political awareness*, in identifying potential coalitions, and in balancing conflicting goals and perceptions.
14. *Influencing skills*, to gain commitment to change ideas and initiatives from potential skeptics and subversives.
15. *Helicopter perspective*, to stand back from the immediate project and take a broader view of priorities.

There are, however, two main differences. First, the McB framework identifies "organization" skills (designing learning and "administering resources"), which BB does not mention. Second, the BB model identifies a set of competencies under the heading "managing up": political awareness, influencing skills, and helicopter perspective. The McB model does cite "persuading others" as a competence, but does not mention political skills. Many of the competency frameworks in this area overlook the political dimension of organizational change, and the need for change managers to have political skill—which we explore in the following section.

TABLE 12.5
The CMI Change Manager Master Level—Competency Model

Skill Area	Demonstrates Understanding of/Capabilities In
Facilitating change	Principles of change; the environment Business focus; change readiness; culture awareness
Strategic thinking	Vision; assess readiness Strategic view; sustainable outcomes
Thinking and judgement	Analytical thinking; holistic perspective; decision making
Influencing others	Customer/stakeholder focus; professional presence Networking; interpersonal skills (selling ideas; use of power)
Coaching for change	Adult learning principles; change management Needs analysis; organizational capability to manage change Role model; champion new skills
Project management	Plan development; monitor and manage progress Cost management; risk and opportunity management; vendor management; review project outcomes
Communication	Relationships building; empathy; oral and written communication Measures effectiveness of communication
Self-management	Personal responsibility; prioritization and time management Resilience; flexibility; emotional intelligence
Facilitation—meetings and workshops	Design; participatory environment Structure (agenda, physical environment) Process (facilitation tools, inclusion, timing)
Professional development	Updates knowledge and develops skills Promotion of change management
Specialist expertise (1) Learning and development	Needs identification; training plan Solution delivery; evaluation
Specialist expertise (2) Communication	Needs identification; plan; solution design and development; Solution delivery; evaluation

Table 12.5 summarizes a third "change manager master level—competency model," developed by the Change Management Institute (CMI), a global not-for-profit organization headquartered in Australia (Leys, 2012). This model identifies twelve skill areas, with up to six capabilities under each heading (over 50 capabilities in total). This model again relates to the full-time professional change manager, heading up or working in a specialist corporate unit, or hired as an external adviser or consultant. We have already seen most of the capabilities identified here in the other two models: understanding the change process, interpersonal and communication skills, influence and persuasion, self-management. The CMI model also emphasizes a more strategic perspective, expecting the "master" change manager to have environmental knowledge, stakeholder focus, and sustainable outcomes. Based on the CMI model, table 12.6 identifies the two or three key competencies that are particularly relevant to each of our six images of change management. For the director,

TABLE 12.6
Images of Change and Key Competencies

Image	Sound Bite	Approach to Change	Key Competencies
Director	"This is what is going to happen"	Management choice, command and control	Strategic thinking Facilitating change
Navigator	"I will tell you what I'd like to happen"	Plan with care, but expect the unexpected	Facilitating change Project management
Caretaker	"Let us explore what might be possible"	Accept the force of external context and adapt as necessary	Thinking and judgement Influencing others
Coach	"How can we develop capability to deal with change?"	Shape systemic capabilities—values, skills, drills—to respond effectively to change	Coaching for change Influencing others
Interpreter	"We need to think differently about this"	Managing meaning through interpretations that explain and convey understanding	Learning and development Communication
Nurturer	"This is everybody's problem—how will we fix it?"	Develop resilience, encourage involvement, continuous learning, and self-organizing	Facilitation Learning and development Communication

strategic thinking and facilitating change are critical. For the nurturer, facilitation, learning and development, and communication are more important. Self-management and professional development apply to all six images.

The Great Intimidators

Echoing the quote at the beginning of the section on the nature of the change management role, Roderick Kramer (2006) challenges the view that change managers must be nice and not tough, and should be humble and self-effacing rather than intimidating. Kramer argues that intimidation is an appropriate style when an organization has become rigid or unruly, stagnant or drifting, and faces inertia or resistance to change. Abrasive leadership, he argues, gets people moving. Intimidators are not bullies, but they can use bullying tactics when time is short and the stakes are high. Kramer (2006, p. 90) makes his positive view of intimidators clear when he argues, "They are not averse to causing a ruckus, nor are they above using a few public whippings and ceremonial hangings to get attention. They're rough, loud, and in your face."

Intimidators have what Kramer calls "political intelligence." Socially intelligent managers focus on leveraging the strengths of others, using empathy and soft power. Politically intelligent managers focus on weaknesses and insecurities, using coercion, fear, and anxiety. However, working for an intimidating leader can be a positive experience. Their sense of purpose can be inspirational, their forcefulness is a role model, and intimidators challenge others to think clearly about their objectives. Kramer (2006, p. 92) quotes a journalist who said, "Don't have a reputation for being a nice guy—that won't do you any good." Intimidation tactics include:

Get up close and personal: Intimidators work through direct confrontation, invading your personal space, using taunts and slurs to provoke and throw you off balance.

Get angry: Called "porcupine power," this involves the "calculated loss of temper" (use it, don't lose it), using rage and anger to help the intimidator prevail.

Keep them guessing: Intimidators preserve an air of mystery by maintaining deliberate distance. Transparency and trust are fashionable, but intimidators keep others guessing, which makes it easier to change direction without loss of credibility.

Know it all: "Informational intimidators" who appear to have mastery of the facts can be very intimidating indeed. It doesn't matter whether "the facts" are correct, as long as they are presented with complete confidence at the right time.

This is a style that will not work well in all situations. Kramer is careful to suggest, however, that this approach may be appropriate—even necessary—in order to overcome either apathy or resistance to change. As a change manager, do you feel that intimidation is appropriate in some circumstances? Are you comfortable using the four intimidation tactics that Kramer identifies?

A Great Intimidator at Work

The Devil Wears Prada (2006, director David Frankel) is based on the novel by Lauren Weisberger. The movie tells the story of a naive, young aspiring journalist, Andrea Sachs (played by Anne Hathaway) who gets a job as assistant to the famous editor in chief of the New York fashion magazine *Runway*. The magazine's powerful and ruthless editor, Miranda Priestly (Meryl Streep) is a legend in the industry. At the beginning of the movie, we see Andrea arriving for her job interview as "second assistant" with Miranda's "first assistant" Emily Charlton (Emily Blunt), but Miranda decides to conduct the interview herself. Start watching as Andrea comes out of the lift and heads for the *Runway* reception desk. Stop when Emily runs after Andrea and calls her back into the office.

1. How would you describe Miranda Priestly's management style?
2. What impact does Miranda's style have on the performance of those around her?
3. Good boss or bad boss: what is your assessment of this management style?
4. Given her style, why do so many people desperately want to work for Miranda?
5. Why do you think Miranda Priestly gave Andrea Sachs the job?

Kramer (2006) defines "political intelligence" in a narrow way. In the following section, we will explore organization politics and use a wider definition of the concept of "political skill."

Case Study   *Closing a Plant*

Aaron De Smet et al. (2012, pp. 4–5) describe the following example of a change manager faced with a particularly difficult challenge. What is your assessment of his approach? Could you use this open and "authentic" style in your own organization? Or would you consider this to be difficult and risky?

Pierre, as we'll call him, was managing a plant in France during the darkest days of the global financial crisis. His plant was soon to close as demand from several of its core customers went into a massive and seemingly irreversible tailspin. The company was in a tricky spot: it needed the know-how of its French workers to help transfer operations to a new production location in another country, and despite its customers' problems it still had €20 million worth of orders to fulfill before the plant closed. Meanwhile, tensions were running high in France: other companies' plant closures had sparked protests that in some cases led to violent reactions from employees. Given the charged situation, most companies were not telling workers about plant closures until the last minute.

Pierre was understandably nervous as he went through leadership training, where he focused intently on topics such as finding the courage to use honesty when having difficult conversations, as well as the value of empathic engagement. After a lengthy debate among company executives, Pierre decided to approach the situation with those values in mind. He announced the plant closing nine months before it would take place and was open with employees about his own fears. Pierre's authenticity struck a chord by giving voice to everyone's thoughts and feelings. Moreover, throughout the process of closing the plant, Pierre recounts, he spent some 60 percent of his time on personal issues, most notably working with his subordinates to assist the displaced workers in finding new jobs and providing them with individual support and mentoring (something other companies weren't doing). He spent only about 40 percent on business issues related to the closure.

This honest engagement worked: over the next nine months, the plant stayed open and fulfilled its orders, even as its workers ensured that their replacements in the new plant had the information they needed to carry on. It was the only plant in the industry to avoid violence and lockouts.

LO 12.4   Political Skill and the Change Manager

Political awareness and political intelligence appeared in the previous discussion as capabilities relevant to the change manager. Organizations are political systems, and change is almost always a politicized process. Why? Individuals, groups, and divisions have to compete with each other for resources of different kinds (people, money, space), and political tactics are tools that can be used in that competition. Change can often upset the established allocation of resources among stakeholders, thus triggering even more intense conflict. The change manager must be aware of the organization politics, but must also be prepared to engage with the politics—to "play the game." Political skill is particularly important in addressing resistance to change (see chapter 8). David Buchanan and Richard Badham (2008) argue that the change manager who is not politically skilled will fail. It is rarely possible for the change manager to escape from this dimension of the role.

Age and Treachery *The Inescapable Reality of the Politics of Change*

Bill Bratton is an American police chief known for his achievements in "turning around" failing or problem forces.

"In 1980, at age 34 one of the youngest lieutenants in Boston's police department, he had proudly put up a plaque in his office that said: *Youth and skill will win out every time over age and treachery.* Within just a few months, having been shunted into a dead-end position due to a mixture of office politics and his own brashness, Bratton took the sign down. He never again forgot the importance of understanding the plotting, intrigue, and politics involved in pushing through change." The advice is: know who the key players are, understand how they play the politics game, and know their attitudes and positions in relation to change proposals (Kim and Mauborgne, 2003, p. 68).

Organization politics is a topic that is generally regarded as unsavory and damaging, associated with backstabbing and dirty tricks. "Machiavellian" is an insult, not a compliment. Henry Mintzberg's (1983, p. 172) definition is a popular one, and has been widely cited:

> **Politics**: "individual or group behavior that is informal, ostensibly parochial, typically divisive, and above all, in the technical sense, illegitimate—sanctioned neither by formal authority, accepted ideology, nor certified expertise."

This is one source of the enduring negative perception of politics—parochial, divisive, illegitimate. How could managers in general, and change managers in particular, be advised to develop capabilities such as these? However, research has revealed the positive, constructive uses of political tactics. This involves the use of political skill. Ferris et al. (2000, p. 30) provide this definition:

> **Political skill**: "an interpersonal style construct that combines social astuteness with the ability to relate well, and otherwise demonstrate situationally appropriate behavior in a disarmingly charming and engaging manner that inspires confidence, trust, sincerity, and genuineness."

Ferris and colleagues call this "savvy and street smarts," and they argue that political skill has four key dimensions. *Social astuteness* concerns the ability to observe and to understand the behavior and motives of others. *Interpersonal influence* concerns the ability to engage and influence others in a compelling way. *Networking ability* involves building a variety of relationships across and outside the organization. *Apparent sincerity* means being seen as forthright, open, honest, and genuine. This model is summarized in table 12.7 (Ferris et al., 2005a and 2007; Brouer et al., 2006). They have also developed an assessment inventory, to measure individual skills in those four areas. Studies using university staff and students as participants produced the following conclusions:

- political skill correlates with measures of self-monitoring and emotional intelligence;
- those who score high on political skill display less anxiety and are less likely to perceive stressful events as threatening;
- political skill is not correlated with general intelligence;
- political skill predicts job performance and subordinate evaluations of leadership ability;
- the dimension of political skill related most strongly to performance rating is social astuteness.

TABLE 12.7
Dimensions of Political Skill

Dimension	Definition	Sample Inventory Items
Social astuteness	Attuned observers, good interpreters of behavior, self-aware, sensitive to others, clever	I understand people very well. I pay close attention to people's facial expressions.
Interpersonal influence	Subtle and convincing style, calibrate actions to the situation, to the "target," be flexible	I am able to make most people feel comfortable and at ease around me. I am good at getting people to like me.
Networking ability	Adept at using networks, develop friendships and build alliances easily, skilled in negotiation and conflict resolution	I spend a lot of time and effort at work networking with others. At work, I know a lot of important people and am well connected.
Apparent sincerity	Appear honest and open, and to have integrity, authenticity, sincerity, genuineness, no ulterior motives	It is important that people believe I am sincere in what I say and do. I try to show a genuine interest in other people.

To what extent do the statements in the "sample inventory items" column describe you? Are these not characteristics that all managers should perhaps have? Describing those with a high degree of political skill, Ferris et al. (2005a, p. 128) observe that:

> Politically skilled individuals convey a sense of personal security and calm self-confidence that attracts others and gives them a feeling of comfort. This self-confidence never goes too far so as to be perceived as arrogance but is always properly measured to be a positive attribute. Therefore, although self-confident, those high in political skill are not self-absorbed (although they are self-aware) because their focus is outward toward others, not inward and self-centered. . . . We suggest that people high in political skill not only know precisely what to do in different social situations at work but how to do it in a manner that disguises any ulterior, self-serving motives and appears to be sincere.

Political skill is only one factor affecting the personal effectiveness of change managers, managers, and leaders. Used effectively, however, political skill can be a powerful way to influence others and to motivate action to change, while strengthening the change manager's reputation. How does political skill work in practice? David Buchanan and Richard Badham (2008) identify the following categories of political tactics, from relatively harmless image building, to disreputable "dirty tricks":

Image building	We all know people who didn't get the job because they didn't look the part—appearance is a credibility issue
Information games	Withholding information to make others look foolish, bending the truth, white lies, massaging information, timed release
Structure games	Creating new roles, teams, and departments, abolishing old ones, in order to promote supporters and sideline adversaries, and to signal new priorities

Scapegoating	This is the fault of another department, external factors, my predecessor, trading conditions, a particular individual
Alliances	Doing secret deals with influential others to form a critical mass, a cabal, to win support for and to progress your proposals
Networking	Lunches, coffees, dinners, sporting events, to get initiatives onto management agendas, improve visibility, gather information
Compromise	All right, you win this time, I won't put up a fight and embarrass you in public—and perhaps you will back me next time
Rule games	I'm sorry, but you have used the wrong form, at the wrong time, with the wrong arguments; we can't set inconsistent precedents
Positioning	Switching and choosing roles where one is successful and visible; avoiding failing projects; position in the building, in the room, at the table
Issue-selling	Packaging, presenting, and promoting plans and ideas in ways that make them more appealing to the target audience
Dirty tricks	Keeping dirt files for blackmail, spying on others, discrediting and undermining, spreading false rumors, corridor whispers

If you are a practicing manager and/or change manager, you are probably using some of these kinds of tactics already. Choice of tactics is of course dependent on your goals, the context, and those whom you are seeking to influence. Is image building really harmless? This is also called "impression management," and it involves appearing and behaving in a manner that presents the public image or "persona" that you want others to see. Dress and act differently, and others will see a different persona. Image building can thus be a good way to manipulate the perceptions, beliefs, and behavior of others. At the other end of that list of political tactics, can you imagine any circumstances in which those "dirty tricks" could be seen as useful, ethical, appropriate, professional management actions?

Take a Moment and Think about a Leader

Take a moment and think about a leader in your organization whom you would consider to be political. How would you describe that leader? Some common descriptions that may immediately come to mind are self-serving, manipulative, phony, or untrustworthy. You may conjure up images of secret pacts made behind closed doors or on the golf course. Or, perhaps, you came up with descriptions such as influential, well-connected, trustworthy, or concerned for others. Often, the idea of a leader being political is associated with negative perceptions and behaviors. In reality, though, political skill is a necessity and can be a positive skill for leaders to possess when used appropriately. Indeed, when we view political skill through this lens, it is difficult to envision any leader being effective without it (Braddy and Campbell, 2014, p. 1).

One of the political tactics that we have just mentioned is "issue-selling." This is not captured by Ferris' model of political skill but, for obvious reasons, is particularly relevant to the change manager. Novel ideas for improvement, development, and change in an organization are always competing with other good ideas; and as we know, good ideas do not always sell themselves. Most organizations find it difficult to resource all of the good ideas that are circulating at any one point in time, so those ideas are competing with each other. How can you, as a change manager, increase the probability that your ideas are implemented, and not the plans of others? Jane Dutton et al. (2001) identify three sets of issue-selling tactics, which they call "behind-the-scenes moves to promote ideas for change."

Packaging moves concern the ways in which ideas are "wrapped" to make them more appealing, urgent, and acceptable. This means linking the proposals to "the bottom line" and other issues such as profitability or market share, repeatedly raising the idea to prepare the audience for the full proposal, and where appropriate "chunking" big ideas into component parts to make them more acceptable.

Involvement moves concern the ways in which relationships can be exploited to build support for ideas. For the change manager, this means knowing who to involve and when, clearing ideas with a senior sponsor, involving other departments and outside consultants, and where appropriate using formal committees and task forces to legitimize the ideas.

Process moves concern the groundwork that may need to be done in advance of selling the issues. There are choices regarding preparation, timing, and degree of formality. The change manager needs to consider the amount of background information to collect in order to persuade others to back the idea. Another choice concerns knowing when to move, when to hold back, and when to persist, depending on the level of support for the idea. Finally, there will be situations where an informal approach (to assess top team support, for example) may be advisable, and times when formality may be appropriate (to finalize agreement on funding, for example).

Skills of the Change Architect   *How to Block Interference*

We discussed the management of resistance to change in chapter 8. Looking at resistance through the lens of organization politics, Rosabeth Moss Kanter (1983, p. 231) identifies the following eight tactics for blocking interference to a change initiative. As we mentioned previously, those who are blocking may not be displaying open resistance. They may, however, be using political tactics themselves, to "run interference" on a change initiative. Political tactics such as these may therefore be useful in countering that behavior:

Wait them out	They should eventually go away
Wear them down	Keep pushing and arguing, be persistent

Appeal to higher authority	You had better agree because they do
Invite them in	Ask them to join the party
Send emissaries	Have friends in whom they trust talk to them
Display support	Have "your" people present and active at key meetings
Reduce the stakes	Make concessions in areas that are especially damaging to them
Warn them off	Let them know that senior management will notice their dissent

The Gang of Four: *Middle versus Senior Management*

Ole Hope (2010) examines how middle managers "redefined" senior management plans for change in the claims handling division of a Nordic insurance company. The claims handling process was time-consuming and costly, and it was difficult for customers to use. Middle management, however, did not agree with senior management plans, and a back office management team, who called themselves "The Gang of Four," decided to implement their own proposals instead. The "micro practices" that they used in order to influence the change outcomes included:

- Disobeying management decisions about project representation
- Handpicking loyal and skilled people to fill project roles

- Taking control over the subproject staffing
- Controlling information gathering by deciding what questions were to be asked
- Producing a memo supporting their own position and aims
- Holding back information, and distributing information selectively
- Questioning the expertise of the external consultants
- Taking advantage of the new division head and his lack of direct local experience
- Rejecting unfavorable decisions and insisting on a "replay" to reach different outcomes

Middle management were thus able to implement their more effective proposals.

The popular perception of politics as damaging is only partly correct. Political tactics can benefit the individuals involved and the organization as a whole. The nature of change puts a premium on political skill for those who manage the process. The change manager who is not comfortable playing politics will find the role challenging. Some managers argue that playing politics is a time-wasting diversion from the real work. For the change manager, however, managing the organization politics *is* the real work. Dealing with political issues can take time, but that investment early in the change process often means that events move more quickly at later stages, because barriers have been addressed and support has been won. In addition, skilled organization politicians experience less anxiety and stress. Some change managers even enjoy the political dimension of the role.

How can the change manager develop political skill? This requires a combination of self-awareness, careful observation of the motives and behaviors of others, modelling the approaches and actions of politically skilled colleagues, and practice. This also involves finding and nurturing your inner Machiavelli. Playing politics involves taking informed risks, and one also has to be prepared to make mistakes—and to learn from those. Phillip Braddy and Michael Campbell (2014, p. 15) have developed the short self-assessment in table 12.8. This is based on the four dimensions of the political skills model introduced earlier. More checks on the right indicate that you are already effectively using political skill. More checks on the left indicate room for improvement.

If necessary, how will you develop your profile? To develop *social awareness*, for example, focus on understanding the language and body language, feelings, motives, and agendas of others, and on how your proposals can help them to meet their goals. To develop *interpersonal influence*, ask more questions, listen actively, use self-disclosure, play down power differences, learn about others' professional and personal interests, and sell your ideas instead of imposing them. *Networking ability* can be developed by monitoring who you approach for advice, giving them something in return, building a more

TABLE 12.8
Political Skills Assessment
Which statements describe you? For each pair of statements, place a check mark by the statement that best describes your behavior:

Do I behave like this?	Or do I behave like this?
Social Awareness	
Focus primarily on my own agenda and myself	Try to understand other people's motives
Struggle with knowing how to present myself	Consistently make positive impressions on others
Have difficulty making small talk or carrying on conversations	Naturally know the right things to say to influence others in most situations
Interpersonal Influence	
Find it difficult to establish rapport with others	Put people at ease
Struggle to communicate with others	Interact easily and effectively with colleagues
Have difficulty getting to know others	Have a knack for getting others to like me
Networking	
Stay to myself and spend virtually all my time at work completing job-related tasks	Deliberately spend time networking with others at work
Primarily spend time with a close group of coworkers and friends with whom I feel comfortable	Invest in building relationships with diverse and influential people
Almost exclusively rely on formal processes for securing resources and getting things done	Often leverage my networks and relationships to secure valuable resources and get things done
Sincerity	
Only show interest in others when I need something from them	Take time to regularly show genuine interest in people at work
Come across as being manipulative because I say and do what is needed to get what I want	Act sincerely around others
Have a tendency to be very secretive and to keep people on a strict "need to know" basis	Communicate openly and transparently with others

Machiavelli's Memorandum

"So if, in the coming months, you find that your enemies call you Machiavellian, do not be disheartened. It means you are doing something right" (*The Economist*, 2013).

diverse network through new relationships outside your team or department, and taking time to maintain those relationships. To strengthen *apparent sincerity*, follow through on your commitments, ensure that others see you as authentic, do not appear to be withholding information, be prepared to reveal your emotions and vulnerabilities, and "Don't rush trust; it takes a long time to build and only a short time to lose" (Braddy and Campbell, 2014, p. 19).

LO 12.5 Developing Change Management Expertise

We explored the development of political skill in the previous section. Finally, we will consider, using a six-step approach, the development of this and other change management capabilities.

1. Career Moves

First, is this the right role for you at this point in your career? You know what being a change manager involves, and you understand the capabilities that are required in order to be effective. But do you still want the job? David Hutton (1994) argues that this is not a job for everyone, because it can be demanding, tiring, lonely, and risky, as well as satisfying. Hutton also describes the desirable and undesirable characteristics of change managers, and these are summarized in table 12.9. The question is, which of these profiles fits you? If you have more of the undesirable characteristics, then it may be advisable to consider other career choices, or to change your behavior where appropriate. Become more persistent and enthusiastic, more flexible and approachable. Become less impatient, less arrogant, less risk averse, less adversarial.

TABLE 12.9
Desirable and Undesirable Characteristics of the Change Manager

Desirable	Undesirable
Believes that this is the right thing to do	Sees this job as a stepping stone in career
Patient, persistent	Impatient, lacking persistence
Honest, trustworthy, reliable	Devious, unreliable, untrustworthy
Positive and enthusiastic	Unable to convey enthusiasm
Confident but not arrogant	Has high need for praise and recognition
Good observer and listener	Poor listener, insensitive to others' feelings
Flexible and resourceful	Inflexible, arrogant, cold, unapproachable
Not easily intimidated	Moral putty, changes view to fit context
Good sense of humor	Status-conscious
Willing to accept risks and challenges	Risk averse, protective of image and career
Recognizes and deals with office politics	Political and manipulative
Prefers an inclusive, cooperative style	Prefers a secretive, adversarial style

2. Repositioning

Second, refer back to figure 1.1, "Assessing Depth of Change." Where does your past and present change management experience sit in that framework? Mostly shallow, mainly deep, or a mix? Although all experience can be useful, deep change is more challenging and risky, because there is a higher chance that things could go wrong. However, deep change offers much greater potential for personal development, and it also increases the visibility and reputation of the change managers responsible, as long as things go well. Interview panels and promotion boards are likely to be more impressed by involvement in successful deep change than in shallow change. Given this assessment and your recent and current roles, do you need to consider "repositioning" yourself with regard to current and forthcoming change initiatives in your organization? Do you need to become associated more closely with the deeper, high-impact changes, as long as you are confident that these are likely to succeed? Where possible, of course, avoid association with initiatives that are likely to fail.

3. The Politics

Third, are you comfortable with the political dimension of change management? As we have seen, some managers see this as unethical and time-wasting. However, this is an aspect of the change management role from which it is difficult to escape, and political skill is a prerequisite for success in most if not all general management and leadership positions. Given the contested nature of much organizational change, political skill is at a premium for the change manager. Political skill can be developed, as we explored in the previous section, but if you are not comfortable with these behaviors, these "games," then developing and using political skill will be difficult.

4. Strengths

Fourth, refer back to table 12.5 and the "CMI Change Manager Competency Model," and add intimidation and political skills to the model's list of competencies. Most of these competencies apply to most general management positions. As an experienced manager, you will probably find that you are already well-equipped to handle the challenges of change, if you have not already done so. However, it may still be useful to confirm—what skills, knowledge, and other attributes do you already possess that are relevant to a change management role? The question here is, how do you plan to maintain and to build on those capabilities and strengths? Will this involve further training and development, careful "repositioning" with regard to future experience (step 2 above), or internal and external job moves to consolidate, diversify, and improve those existing skills?

5. Gaps

Fifth, looking again at table 12.5 and the other competencies identified in this chapter, where do you see personal gaps? Realistically, is it going to be possible for you to fill these gaps? Remember that this may not be necessary, as other colleagues are likely to have different and overlapping skill sets. Decide which areas of competence you feel that you must develop as a matter of priority, which areas are less important for you, and which you feel that it would be acceptable to avoid.

6. Action

Finally, prepare a personal action plan that covers these three issues:

1. *Building strengths*: How will I maintain and build on the strengths that I currently have as a change manager?
2. *Allowable weaknesses*: Which of my weaknesses will I not try to develop, as this would be unnecessary, or time-consuming, or particularly difficult for some reason?
3. *Filling gaps*: Which skills, knowledge, and attributes do I need to strengthen as a matter of urgency? What are my options for building those capabilities: taking on further change responsibilities, partnering with others in change management teams, secondments, networking, mentoring, specialist training and development, guided reading, other?

The actions required to develop change management capabilities are not necessarily costly. Most of the possibilities are free, because they are experience-based, but they do involve a significant time commitment. In terms of personal and career development, however, that investment can generate returns in terms of personal skills development and career progression.

EXERCISE 12.1

Networking— How Good Are You?

LO 12.3

Networking is a core change manager capability. Use the following diagnostic to assess your own networking skills and to determine what action you may need to take to improve.

Tick whether you agree, or disagree, with each of the following statements.

	Agree	Disagree	
I enjoy finding out what other people do.	❑	❑	1
I feel embarrassed asking people for favors.	❑	❑	2
I send Christmas cards to ex-colleagues and business contacts.	❑	❑	3
I usually call or email former colleagues and contacts when I am struggling with a particularly difficult problem.	❑	❑	4
I do not like to waste time going to conferences.	❑	❑	5
I cannot remember the names and family details of all my team members.	❑	❑	6
I cut out articles from the press that I think might interest colleagues.	❑	❑	7
I prefer to write emails or letters to picking up the phone.	❑	❑	8
I am quick to return phone calls.	❑	❑	9
I pursue opportunities to work on committees, task forces, and projects.	❑	❑	10
I like to solve problems on my own.	❑	❑	11
I am happy to ask people for their business cards.	❑	❑	12
I go to social events with people outside my team.	❑	❑	13
I have lost touch with my ex-bosses.	❑	❑	14
I use the Internet to make contact with people in my field.	❑	❑	15
I do not mix work and social life.	❑	❑	16

Networking: How Did You Score?

Give yourself one point each if you *agreed* with these items, scoring up to 9:

1	3	4	7	9	10	12	13	15

Give yourself one point each if you *disagreed* with these items, scoring up to 7:

2	5	6	8	11	14	16

Add these two scores to produce your final total score out of 16:

Score:	Implications:
0 to 5	You do not appear to do much networking, and you may need to be careful that you are not overlooked for promotion. What can you do to lift your profile, to make yourself more visible?
6 to 9	You network a little, but you could do more to develop relationships that would improve your career opportunities. Where are the gaps in your networking efforts, and how can you fill them?
10 to 13	You are a competent networker, but you could improve. What areas are you not covering? Do you need to do more external networking?
14 to 16	It looks like you are a natural networker. However, you may need to be careful not to overplay this aspect of your profile building, as there is a danger that this can annoy some people.

Based on Yeung (2003).

EXERCISE 12.2

How Resilient Are You?

LO 12.2

Rate your agreement with each of these 25 statements, and put your score in the right-hand column.

		Disagree					Agree		Score
1	When I make plans I follow through with them	1	2	3	4	5	6	7	
2	I usually manage one way or another	1	2	3	4	5	6	7	
3	I am able to depend on myself more than anyone else	1	2	3	4	5	6	7	
4	Keeping interested in things is important to me	1	2	3	4	5	6	7	
5	I can be on my own if I have to	1	2	3	4	5	6	7	

(Continued)

		Disagree						Agree		Score
6	I feel proud that I have accomplished things in my life	1	2	3	4	5	6	7		
7	I usually take things in my stride	1	2	3	4	5	6	7		
8	I am friends with myself	1	2	3	4	5	6	7		
9	I feel that I can handle many things at a time	1	2	3	4	5	6	7		
10	I am determined	1	2	3	4	5	6	7		
11	I seldom wonder what the point of it all is	1	2	3	4	5	6	7		
12	I take things one day at a time	1	2	3	4	5	6	7		
13	I can get through difficult times because I've experienced difficulty before	1	2	3	4	5	6	7		
14	I have self-discipline	1	2	3	4	5	6	7		
15	I keep interested in things	1	2	3	4	5	6	7		
16	I can usually find something to laugh about	1	2	3	4	5	6	7		
17	My belief in myself gets me through hard times	1	2	3	4	5	6	7		
18	In an emergency, I'm someone people generally can rely on	1	2	3	4	5	6	7		
19	I can usually look at a situation in a number of ways	1	2	3	4	5	6	7		
20	Sometimes I make myself do things whether I want to or not	1	2	3	4	5	6	7		
21	My life has meaning	1	2	3	4	5	6	7		
22	I do not dwell on things that I can't do anything about	1	2	3	4	5	6	7		
23	When I'm in a difficult situation, I can usually find my way out of it	1	2	3	4	5	6	7		
24	I have enough energy to do what I have to do	1	2	3	4	5	6	7		
25	It's okay if there are people who don't like me	1	2	3	4	5	6	7		
									Your Total:	

Resilience Scoring

Add the scores that you have given to each of the 25 items.
> Your resilience score total will lie between 25 and 175. Higher scores reflect higher resilience.
> The scores of adults on this test normally lie between 90 and 175, with a mean of 140.
> A resilience score of 150 or above is considered to be high.

- If you have a low resilience score, say below 140, what steps do you think you could take to improve your resilience?
- How would you advise a colleague with a low resilience score?

Source: This diagnostic is based on Wagnild and Young (1993).

EXERCISE 12.3

How Political Is Your Organization?

LO 12.4

To what extent do the following statements describe your organization? Tick the appropriate box on the right:

	Disagree	Maybe	Agree
1: Who you know around here matters a lot more than what you know.	❑	❑	❑
2: The most competent people in the business don't always get promoted.	❑	❑	❑
3: Decisions are often taken outside formal meetings or behind closed doors.	❑	❑	❑
4: Resource allocations between departments are a source of argument and conflict.	❑	❑	❑
5: You have to be prepared to socialize to build effective networks and alliances.	❑	❑	❑
6: Information is jealously guarded and not shared openly between groups and departments.	❑	❑	❑
7: People suspect that there are "hidden agendas" behind management decisions.	❑	❑	❑
8: Some individuals always seem to be better informed than everyone else.	❑	❑	❑
9: Individuals are having their reputations damaged by "whispers in the corridors."	❑	❑	❑
10: Those who take the credit are not always those who made the biggest contribution.	❑	❑	❑
11: You have to know how to "play the rules"—breaking and bending them—to get things done.	❑	❑	❑
12: When mistakes are made, people are quick to start putting the blame on others.	❑	❑	❑
13: Most people recognize that you're not going very far here unless you have the support of the key players.	❑	❑	❑
14: Being open and honest all the time can seriously damage your career.	❑	❑	❑
15: People will criticize others' ideas merely to help win support for their own proposals.	❑	❑	❑

Scoring instructions on next page →

How Political Is Your Organization? Scoring

Give yourself:

- 1 point for each item where you ticked "disagree"
- 3 points for each item where you ticked "maybe"
- 5 points for each item where you ticked "agree"

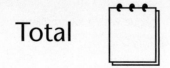

Total

This will give you a score between 15 and 75

The politics-free zone: if you score around 25 or lower. We are all coming to work with you. Your organization has a relatively low level of political behavior. Either that, or you are just not aware of the degree of politics going on behind your back. In such a *politics-free zone*, are you concerned that:

- There is not enough discussion and debate before key decisions are made?
- There is not enough constructive conflict and debate to stimulate creativity?

The free-fire zone: if you score around 65 or above. There is a high level of political behavior in your organization. Either that, or you are reading too much into routine decisions and actions. In such a *free-fire zone*, are you concerned that:

- Too much time and energy is going into the politics game, and not enough into strategic thinking and performance improvement?
- The discussions and debates are motivated more by personal goals and are less related to the organization's strategies and goals?

The average behavior zone: score between approximately 30 and 60. Your organization is typical, middle of the road in terms of the degree of political behavior that you can expect to witness. In such an *average behavior zone*, are you concerned that:

- There is still too much political behavior to stimulate the quality of discussion and debate around key issues and decisions?

    On the basis of your scoring, what advice applies to you and to other change managers with regard to dealing with the politics in your organization?

Source: This diagnostic is from Buchanan, D.A. and Badham, R. (2008). *Power, Politics, and Organizational Change: Winning the Turf Game*. London: Sage Publications, Second Edition.

Additional Reading

Battilana, J., and Casciaro, T. 2013. The network secrets of great change managers. *Harvard Business Review* 91(7/8):62–68. Describes the nature and functions of two different kinds of networks—cohesive and divergent. The power and influence of change managers depends not on formal title or seniority but on position in the organization's informal networks. Offers practical advice to change managers on developing and leveraging these networks effectively.

Buchanan, D. A., and Badham, R. 2008. *Power, politics, and organizational change: Winning the turf game*. 2nd ed. London: Sage Publications. Comprehensive discussion of the nature, tactics, and ethics of organization politics. Describes the constructive use of political tactics to maintain personal reputation and further organizational objectives. Offers guidance on the use of political tactics and advice on the development of political skill or expertise.

Dutton, J. E., Ashford, S. J., O'Neill, R. M., and Lawrence, K. A. 2001. Moves that matter: Issue selling and organizational change. *Academy of Management Journal* 44(4):716–36. Describes the academic research that developed the "issue-selling" tactics described in this chapter—tactics for "successfully shaping change from below by directing the attention of top management" (p. 716).

Pfeffer, J. 2010. Power play. *Harvard Business Review* 88(7/8):84–92. Argues that power and influence are prerequisites for management success and offers advice on leveraging power. Concludes: "So, welcome to the real world. It may not be the world we want, but it's the world we have. You won't get far, and neither will your strategic plans, if you can't build and use power. Some of the people competing for advancement or standing in the way of your organization's agenda will bend the rules of fair play or ignore them entirely. Don't bother complaining about this or wishing things were different. Part of your job is to know how to prevail in the political battles you will face" (p. 92).

Roundup

Reflections for the Practicing Change Manager

1. How would you describe your role as a change manager using the terms introduced in this chapter: champion, soul-of-fire, quiet leader, positive deviant, disruptive innovator? How is this reflected in your behavior? Would you become more or less effective as a change manager if you "dropped below the radar"?

2. How effectively do you use your informal networks to drive change in your organization? How could you develop and make better use of those networks?

3. Do you feel that you have the resilience required to operate effectively as a change manager? If necessary, what steps can you take to maintain and to strengthen your resilience?

4. As a practicing manager, you probably already have most of the required capabilities of the change manager. But how do you feel about using intimidation to motivate others to change? Are there circumstances when this would be appropriate in your organization?

5. Are you politically skilled? Do you use political skills to advance your change agenda? Who are the other "politicians" in your organization? Are you able to manage their support, and to block their attempts to interfere with your change agenda?

Here is a short summary of the key points that we would like you to take from this chapter, in relation to each of the learning outcomes:

LO 12.1   *Recognize the nature and significance of the contributions of change managers at all levels of an organization, regardless of their formal roles or responsibilities.*
Change managers can be found at all levels of an organization. Given the pace and scale of change in most organizations, the shared leadership of change has become a necessity. Contrary to the popular stereotype, middle managers are often among the most important change managers in an organization. The power and influence of many

change managers come not from a formal, senior position, but from their position in the informal networks in an organization. Those with more informal connections can be more influential, and the organization chart is not a good guide to identifying them. The terminology that commentators have used to describe this variety of change manager offers insights into the nature of the role, and of those who take on these responsibilities: champions, evangelists, positive deviants, souls-of-fire, tempered radicals, quiet leaders, stealth innovators, ideas practitioners, disruptive innovators. Those innovators and "souls-of-fire" are highly motivated and assertive, but they are also nonconformists and do not follow instructions, and they can thus be difficult to manage.

LO 12.2 *Appreciate the challenges and rewards that accompany a change management role.*
The role of the change manager is often a demanding one: challenging, lonely, stressful, fast-paced, and risky. Dealing simultaneously with senior management expectations and different modes of resistance from those who are going to be affected can make the role particularly pressured. However, the opportunities for personal development and career progression can be significant, and the role is especially satisfying and rewarding when the change process is successful. Given the pressures, a high degree of resilience is often required. Resilience can be developed, and exercise 12.2 offers a personal diagnostic.

LO 12.3 *Identify the competencies in terms of the skills, knowledge, and other attributes that are ideally required in order to be an effective change manager.*
We considered three competency frameworks. The most comprehensive of these was developed by the Change Management Institute. Their model identifies over 50 capabilities under 12 skills headings: facilitation, strategic change, judgement, influencing, coaching, project management, interpersonal and corporate communications, self-management, facilitation, professional development, learning and development. While this appears to be a daunting specification, most of those capabilities are relevant to most general management positions. We also discussed the value of "intimidation" as a change management style. While many managers may feel uncomfortable with this approach, it can be appropriate in certain circumstances, particularly when an organization has become rigid, apathetic, stagnant, and change-resistant. We also discussed a small number of intimidation tactics: confrontation, the "calculated loss of temper," maintaining an air of mystery, and "informational intimidation," which involves the appearance of having mastered the facts.

LO 12.4 *Understand the significance of political skill to the role and effectiveness of change managers.*
Organizations are political systems, and change is a politicized process. Politics is often seen in negative terms, as damaging and unnecessary. However, effective leaders and change managers need political skill in order to exert influence over others. Change managers must be aware of the perceptions and agendas of other stakeholders, and be able to engage them in consultation where their views are valuable, and also when necessary to counter attempts to subvert or resist change with political tactics. We identified several types of political tactics: image building, information games, structure games, scapegoating, alliances, networks, compromise, rule games, positioning, issue-selling, and "dirty tricks." One model of political skill identifies four key

dimensions: social astuteness, interpersonal influence, networking ability, and apparent sincerity. We offered a self-assessment covering those four skill dimensions, and suggested ways in which political skill can be developed.

LO 12.5   *Develop an action plan for improving your own change management capabilities.*
We set out a six-step approach to personal development. First, do you still want this job, knowing how challenging and stressful it is, and what kinds of attributes contribute to success? Second, do you need to consider your personal positioning with regard to the depth of the change initiatives for which you are responsible, or with which you are associated? Deeper changes can be more risky, but they offer greater opportunities for personal development. Third, make sure that you are comfortable with the political dimension of the role, and follow the guidelines for developing political skill—if you feel this is relevant with regard to your current and future change management roles. Fourth, identify your strengths as a change manager, and determine how to maintain those capabilities. Fifth, identify gaps in your capability profile, and decide whether or not it is possible and desirable to address those—or to delegate those aspects of your change management role to other team members. Finally, develop a practical action plan to build on your strengths, recognize and manage allowable weaknesses, and address the gaps in your profile with further development.

References

Ashford, S. J., and Detert, J. 2015. Get the boss to buy in. *Harvard Business Review* 93(1/2):72–79.

Badaracco, J. L. 2001. We don't need another hero. *Harvard Business Review* 79(8): 121–26.

Badaracco, J. L. 2002. *Leading quietly: An unorthodox guide to doing the right thing.* Boston: Harvard Business School Press.

Battilana, J., and Casciaro, T. 2013. The network secrets of great change managers. *Harvard Business Review* 91(7/8):62–68.

Beatty, C. A., and Gordon, J. R. M. 1991. Preaching the gospel: The evangelists of new technology. *California Management Review* 33(3):73–94.

Beeson, J. 2009. Why you didn't get that promotion: Decoding the unwritten rules of corporate advancement. *Harvard Business Review* 87(6):101–5.

Boaz, N., and Fox, E. A. 2014. Change leader, change thyself. *McKinsey Quarterly*, March:1–11.

Bower, J. L. 1970. *Managing the resource allocation process.* Boston: Graduate School of Business Administration, Harvard University.

Braddy, P., and Campbell, M. 2014. *Using political skill to maximize and leverage work relationships.* Greensboro, NC: Center for Creative Leadership.

Brouer, R. L., Ferris, G. R., Hochwarter, W. A., Laird, M. D., and Gilmore, D. C. 2006. The strain-related reactions to perceptions of organizational politics as a workplace stressor: Political skill as a neutralizer. In *Handbook of organizational politics*, ed. Eran Vigoda and Amos Drory (187–206). Thousand Oaks, CA: Sage Publications.

Buchanan, D. A. 2003. Demands, instabilities, manipulations, careers: The lived experience of driving change. *Human Relations* 56(6):663–84.

Buchanan, D. A., and Badham, R. 2008. *Power, politics, and organizational change: Winning the turf game*. 2nd ed. London: Sage Publications.

Buchanan, D. A., and Boddy, D. 1992. *The expertise of the change manager: Public performance and backstage activity*. Hemel Hempstead, UK: Prentice Hall.

Chartered Institute of Personnel and Development. 2011. *Developing resilience: An evidence-based guide for practitioners*. London: CIPD.

Connor, P. E., and Lake, L. K. 1988. *Managing organizational change*. New York: Praeger.

Conway, E., and Monks, K. 2011. Change from below: The role of middle managers in mediating paradoxical change. *Human Resource Management Journal* 21(2):190–202.

Cripe, E. J. 1993. How to get top notch agents of change. *Training and Development* 47(12):52–57.

Davenport, T. H., Prusak, L., and Wilson, H. J. 2003. Who's bringing you hot ideas and how are you responding? *Harvard Business Review* 81(2):58–64.

De Smet, A., Lavoie, J., and Hioe, E. S. 2012. Developing better change leaders. *McKinsey Quarterly*, April:1–6.

Duan, L., Sheeren, E., and Weiss, L. 2014. Tapping the power of hidden influencers. *McKinsey Quarterly*, March:1–4.

Dutton, J. E., Ashford, S. J., O'Neill, R. M., and Lawrence, K. A. 2001. Moves that matter: Issue selling and organizational change. *Academy of Management Journal* 44(4):716–36.

Dyer, J., Gregersen, H., and Christensen, C. M. 2011. *The innovator's DNA: Mastering the five skills of disruptive innovators*. Boston: Harvard Business School Press.

The Economist. 2013. Machiavelli's memorandum. September 28:53.

Ferris, G. R., Perrewé, P. L., Anthony, W. P., and Gilmore, D. C. 2000. Political skill at work. *Organizational Dynamics* 28(4):25–37.

Ferris, G. R., Davidson, S. L., and Perrewé, P. L. 2005a. *Political skill at work: Impact on work effectiveness*. Mountain View, CA: Davies-Black Publishing.

Ferris, G. R., Treadway, D. C., Kolodinsky, R. W., Hochwarter, W. A., Kacmar, C. J., Douglas, C., and Frink, D. D. 2005b. Development and validation of the political skill inventory. *Journal of Management* 31(1):126–52.

Ferris, G. R., Treadway, D. C., Perrewé, P. L., Brouer, R. L., Douglas, C., and Lux, S. 2007. Political skill in organizations. *Journal of Management* 33(3):290–320.

Frost, P., and Robinson, S. 1999. The toxic handler: Organizational hero—and casualty. *Harvard Business Review* 77(4):96–106.

Hope, O. 2010. The politics of middle management sensemaking and sensegiving. *Journal of Change Management* 10(2):195–215.

Hutton, D. W. 1994. *The change manager's handbook: A survival guide for quality improvement champions.* Milwaukee, WI: ASQC Quality Press.

Kanter, R. M. 1982. The middle manager as innovator. *Harvard Business Review* 60(4):95–105.

Kanter, R. M. 1983. *The change masters: Corporate entrepreneurs at work.* London: George Allen & Unwin.

Kellaway, L. 2000. *Sense and nonsense in the office.* Harlow, Essex: Financial Times Prentice Hall.

Khurana, R. 2002. The curse of the superstar CEO. *Harvard Business Review* 80(9): 60–66.

Kim, W. C., and Mauborgne, R. 2003. Tipping point leadership. *Harvard Business Review* 81(4):60–69.

Kouzes, J. M., and Posner, B. Z. 1995. *The leadership challenge.* Englewood Cliffs, NJ: Prentice Hall.

Kramer, R. M. 2006. The great intimidators. *Harvard Business Review* 84(2):88–96.

Kuratko, D. F., and Goldsby, M. G. 2004. Corporate entrepreneurs or rogue middle managers? A framework for ethical corporate entrepreneurship. *Journal of Business Ethics* 55(1):13–30.

Lewis, G. 2015. Women over 55 best suited to lead transformational change, finds PwC. *People Management*, May 18. http://www.cipd.co.uk/pm/peoplemanagement/b/weblog /archive/2015/05/18/women-over-55-best-suited-to-lead-transformational-change-finds -pwc.aspx (accessed June 5, 2015).

Leys, F. 2012. *Change manager master level—competency model.* Sydney, Australia: Change Management Institute.

Maidique, M. A. 1980. Entrepreneurs, champions and technological innovation. *Sloan Management Review* 21(2):59–76.

McCreary, L. 2010. Kaiser Permanente's innovation on the front lines. *Harvard Business Review* 88(9):92–97.

McDermott, A. M., Fitzgerald, L., and Buchanan, D. A. 2013. Beyond acceptance and resistance: Entrepreneurial change agency responses in policy implementation. *British Journal of Management* 24(S1):93–225.

Meyerson, D. E. 2001a. Radical change, the quiet way. *Harvard Business Review* 79(9):92–100.

Meyerson, D. E. 2001b. *Tempered radicals: How people use difference to inspire change at work*. Boston: Harvard Business School Press.

Miller, P., and Wedell-Wedellsborg, T. 2013. The case for stealth innovation. *Harvard Business Review* 91(3):90–97.

Mintzberg, H. 1983. *Power in and around organizations*. Upper Saddle River, NJ: Prentice Hall.

Ottaway, R. N. 1983. The change agent: A taxonomy in relation to the change process. *Human Relations* 36(4):361–92.

Pascale, R. T., and Sternin, J. 2005. Your company's secret change managers. *Harvard Business Review* 83(5):72–81.

Patterson, F. 1999. *The Innovation Potential Indicator: Test manual and user's guide*. Oxford: Oxford Psychologists Press.

Peters, T. J., and Waterman, R. H. 1983. Corporate chariots of fire. *Across the Board* 20(5):40–47.

Pfeffer, J. 2010. Power play. *Harvard Business Review* 88(7/8):84–92.

Schön, D. A. 1963. Champions for radical new inventions. *Harvard Business Review* 41(2):77–86.

Stjernberg, T., and Philips, A. 1993. Organizational innovations in a long-term perspective: Legitimacy and souls-of-fire as critical factors of change and viability. *Human Relations* 46(10):1193–221.

Syrett, M., and Lammiman, J. 2002. *Successful innovation: How to encourage and shape profitable ideas*. London: The Economist/Profile Books.

Wagnild, G. M., and Young, H. M. 1993. Development and psychometric evaluation of the resilience scale. *Journal of Nursing Measurement* 1(2):165–78.

Wooldridge, B. J., and Floyd, S. W. 1990. The strategy process, middle management involvement, and organizational performance. *Strategic Management Journal* 11(3): 231–41.

Wooldridge, B., Schmid, T., and Floyd, S. W. 2008. The middle management perspective on strategy process: Contributions, synthesis, and future research. *Journal of Management* 34(6):1190–221.

Wooldridge, E., and Wallace, L. 2002. Modern times: Public sector modernization. *People Management* 8(7):28–30.

Yeung, R. 2003. *The ultimate career success workbook*. London: Kogan Page.

Name Index

Waters, J. A., 37
Weaver, W., 209, 247
Webster, B., 343, 351
Wedell-Wedellsborg, T., 131, 135, 390, 422
Weick, K. E., 42, 43, 60, 142, 169, 298, 299, 300, 314
Weisbord, M. R., 41, 60, 103, 104, 136, 290, 291, 292, 314
Wendler, J., 187, 202, 364, 382
Westergren, M., 234, 241, 245
Wheat, A., 78, 98
Whelan-Berry, K. S., 206, 247
White, M. C., 40, 60
Whitney, D., 292, 308, 311
Whittington, R., 116, 135, 172, 179, 203
Wiggins, J., 72, 100
Wilkinson, A., 131, 136
Williams, M., 213, 247
Williamson, P., 180, 202
Willmott, P., 157–158, 168
Wind, J. W., 181, 204
Wofford, J. C., 176, 203
Wolfe, R., 271, 277

Wolff, C., 223, 247
Woodcock, M., 128, 136
Woodman, R. W., 57, 59, 297, 310
Wookey, C., 185, 198, 203
Wooldridge, B. J., 262, 277, 387, 397, 422
Worley, C. G., 124–127, 136, 281, 282, 283, 284, 287, 291, 297, 308, 311, 314
Wylie, K. K., 176, 201

Y

Yaeger, T. F., 286, 311, 314
Yeung, R., 413, 422
Young, H. M., 415, 422
Yuanqing, Y., 151, 169

Z

Zahra, S. A., 118, 136
Zanini, M., 125, 135, 260, 275, 346, 350
Zellner, W., 64, 98

Subject Index